What's New in This Edition

One of the highlights of this edition is the inclusion of Acadia Software's Infuse, a JavaScript development tool, on the CD-ROM. Richard Wagner shows you how to use Infuse to create JavaScript scripts in step-by-step examples in an all-new chapter. Netscape's new dynamic HTML technologies, layers and JavaScript style sheets, are also explored in depth. You can use JavaScript with these new features to add a dynamic look and feel to your Web page. This edition also explores other new JavaScript 1.2 capabilities that are supported in Netscape Communicator 1.0.

One of the most frustrating issues developers face when working with JavaScript is determining whether a particular language element is supported in a certain browser or a particular release. This edition contains an easy-to-decipher list to help you resolve compatibility issues. You'll also see examples of how to write relatively global scripts.

Throughout this edition, we've also highlighted new objects, methods, and properties of the language, as well as new tools, such as Microsoft's Script Debugger. Many of the important version differences appear in note boxes to help you find them as you read.

JavaScript™
Second Edition

Richard Wagner, et al.

sams
net

201 West 103rd Street
Indianapolis, IN 46290

UNLEASHED

Publisher and President	*Richard K. Swadley*
Publishing Manager	*Rosemarie Graham*
Director of Editorial Services	*Cindy Morrow*
Managing Editor	*Brice P. Gosnell*
Director of Marketing	*Kelli S. Spencer*
Product Marketing Manager	*Wendy Gilbride*
Assistant Marketing Manager	*Rachel Wolfe*

Acquisitions Editor
Corrine Wire

Development Editor
Marla Reece

Software Development Specialist
John Warriner

Production Editor
Gayle L. Johnson

Copy Editors
Margaret Berson
Chuck Hutchinson

Indexer
Chris Wilcox

Technical Reviewer
Blake Hall

Editorial Coordinator
Katie Wise

Technical Edit Coordinator
Lorraine Schaffer

Resource Coordinator
Deborah Frisby

Editorial Assistants
Carol Ackerman
Andi Richter
Rhonda Tinch-Mize

Cover Designer
Jason Grisham

Book Designer
Gary Adair

Copy Writer
David Reichwein

Production Team Supervisors
Brad Chinn
Charlotte Clapp

Production
Georgiana Briggs
Cyndi Davis
Ian A. Smith
Mary Ellen Stephenson

Contents

Part III JavaScript Objects

Part V   Programming Techniques

19   Site Navigation with JavaScript   485

20   Forms and Data Validation   507

Part IX Appendixes

Acknowledgments

I would like to express my deepest thanks to each of the following people, who in some way contributed to this book:

- Acadia Software, for its strong support throughout this project.
- Gary Griffin, Kim Daniels, and Bill Chosiad, for their interest in working on this book from the get-go.
- Corrine Wire, for her assistance in keeping me on schedule, as well as for her courteous and ever-cheerful attitude.
- Gayle Johnson, Marla Reece, Margaret Berson, and Chuck Hutchinson, for their excellent editing assistance.
- Chris Van Buren at Waterside Productions, for getting me involved in this project in the first place.
- Finally, Kimberly and the Js, for your tenacity and patience to see yet another book project through to the end.

—Richard Wagner

About the Authors

Richard Wagner is Vice President of Product Development for Acadia Software and is chief architect of Acadia Infuse, a visual editor for JavaScript. In addition to being an experienced author in the computer industry, he has considerable development experience in both Web and client/server applications. Wagner is a contributing editor for *Delphi Informant,* in which he has a monthly column called *File\New,* which focuses on trends in software development. Wagner wrote *Inside Paradox for Windows* (three editions), *CompuServe Internet Tour Guide,* and *Inside CompuServe* (three editions). He cowrote *Ultimate Windows 3.1, Inside Windows NT, Inside Microsoft Access, Inside dBASE for Windows,* and *Integrating Windows Applications.* He has a BA in Political Science from Taylor University and pursued a graduate degree at American University. He welcomes your comments at rwagner@acadians.com.

Kim Daniels is Director of Software Development for Acadia Software. She specializes in client/server database application development using Delphi, as well as various Internet development tools in conjunction with JavaScript. She received a BS in Management Information Systems from Rensselaer Polytechnic Institute in Troy, New York. She welcomes your comments at kdaniels@acadians.com.

Gary Griffin develops Internet applications for Acadia Software. He specializes in JavaScript, C++, and Java, and he is pursuing a degree in Computer Science at the University of Massachusetts. Please forward any comments or suggestions to ggriffin@acadians.com.

Christopher D. Haddad (chaddad@rockcreek.com) is Senior Vice President and a cofounder of Rock Creek Technologies, an Internet software development and consulting firm. His responsibilities include expanding the company's technical infrastructure and capabilities, monitoring Internet technology, developing strategic alliances, and overseeing software development. Haddad is currently developing Internet applications and tools for corporations in the Washington, DC area. An expert with extensive C++, Java, JavaScript, and Web server programming experience, he has hands-on familiarity with the subjects contained in this book. He has also been a contributing author for several other Sams.net books.

Jimmy Nasr is an Internet Architect at IBM Global Services, based in Atlanta, Georgia. He designs and builds large Internet (especially eCommerce) and intranet solutions for mostly Fortune 500 companies. He is a founder of MJN Computer Consulting, located in Newington, Connecticut, which specializes in Web design and security. He earned a BS in Computer Science from Coventry University in England and an MBA from the University of Connecticut. He can be reached at jnasr@mjn.com.

First Edition Authors

Arman Danesh (armand@bwc.org) is the author of *Teach Yourself JavaScript in a Week* and a coauthor of *JavaScript Developer's Guide*. He is the World Wide Web specialist for a large public information Web site, he is fluent in several programming languages, and he has experience managing large-scale production systems. Danesh is also a technology reporter and columnist for several publications in the Far East. He can be reached at armand@juxta.com.

Rick Darnell began his career at a small weekly newspaper after graduating from Kansas State University with a degree in broadcasting. While spending time as a freelance journalist and writer, he has seen the full gamut of personal computers since starting out with a Radio Shack Model I in the late 1970s. He is a coauthor of *FrontPage Unleashed*. He may be reached at darnell@montana.com.

Heather Downs is a software consultant specializing in compilers and various Internet technologies. She holds a degree in math from the Massachusetts Institute of Technology. In her spare time, she enjoys maintaining her Web site, http://www.bungalow.com/, and writing obfuscated C programs. She can be reached via e-mail at heather@bungalow.com.

Michael Kmiec is an Applications Developer with PFN Incorporated in Cambridge, Massachusetts. With a background in C, C++, and philosophy, he uses JavaScript to fuel some of the functionality of a network publishing system.

Stephen Le Hunte is an independent software developer and freelance technical author who specializes in HTML, WinHelp, Visual Basic, and C++. He is currently trying to finish his PhD at the University of Wales, Swansea.

Michael Moncur is the owner of Starling Technologies, a consulting firm specializing in networking and the Internet. He is also a freelance Webmaster and author; he has worked with the Internet since 1989. He is the author of *Laura Lemay's Web Workshop: JavaScript*.

Claudia Piemont is a German freelance author and computer science journalist. She earned a BS in Computer Science from FH Darmstadt in Germany. She has a broad knowledge of both software development and consulting, gained through practical experience in a major German corporation. Her special interests include object-oriented technology, the Internet, and multimedia.

Robert L. Platt (http://www.realtime.net/~rlp) has worked for AT&T Bell Laboratories and Tandem Computers as a software developer and as a project manager. He has worked on a variety of projects, including advanced graphical user interfaces and speech recognition. His areas of interest include the Internet, graphical user interfaces, object-oriented programming, and financial analysis. He can be reached at rlp@acm.org.

Ed Smith is an Internet Consultant and Web Site Developer in York County, Pennsylvania. His company, E.T. Smith Associates, develops, establishes, and maintains Internet sites for businesses and organizations specializing in highly interactive sites. A former armored cavalry officer, he worked in the electric utility industry as an engineer for 11 years before leaving to start his own Internet business.

Tell Us What You Think

As a reader, you are the most important critic of and commentator on our books. We value your opinion and want to know what we're doing right, what we could do better, what areas you'd like to see us publish in, and any other words of wisdom you're willing to pass our way. You can help us make strong books that meet your needs and give you the computer guidance you require.

If you have access to CompuServe or the World Wide Web, check out our CompuServe forum by typing GO SAMS at any prompt. If you prefer the World Wide Web, check out our site at http://www.mcp.com.

> **NOTE**
>
> If you have a technical question about this book, call the technical support line at (317) 581-3833.

As the Publishing Manager of the group that created this book, I welcome your comments. You can fax, e-mail, or write me directly to let me know what you did or didn't like about this book—as well as what we can do to make our books stronger. Here's the information:

Fax: (317) 581-4669
E-mail: enterprise_mgr@sams.mcp.com
Mail: Rosemarie Graham
         Sams.net Publishing
         201 W. 103rd Street
         Indianapolis, IN 46290

Introduction

JavaScript is quickly emerging as a significant tool for Web development, whether for simple enhancements to HTML pages or full-fledged Web-based applications. But because its *raison d'être* is not as glamorous, JavaScript will perhaps never be as popular as Java, ActiveX, or even HTML. Having said that, JavaScript does something none of the others can do: It makes divergent technologies work together seamlessly. Indeed, the jack-of-all-trades nature of JavaScript is perhaps what gives this language its staying power.

Most people probably see JavaScript as a client-side language. That it is—and much of this book focuses on how to embed JavaScript into HTML to run under a Netscape or Microsoft browser. However, JavaScript is also emerging as a server-side scripting language. Netscape's LiveWire is one of the first of many products that will use JavaScript as its Web scripting language. This book takes an in-depth look at Netscape's LiveWire.

JavaScript has strong vendor support. The following software companies have announced that they will use JavaScript as part of a forthcoming product: Acadia Software, America Online, Apple Computer, Architext Software, AT&T, Borland International, Brio Technology, Computer Associates, Digital, Hewlett-Packard, Iconovex Corporation, Illustra, Informix, Intuit, Macromedia, Metrowerks, Microsoft, Novell, Oracle, Paper Software, Precept Software, RAD Technologies, The Santa Cruz Operation, Silicon Graphics, Spider Technologies, Sybase, and Verity.

I am a developer by trade, and the more I use JavaScript, the more I see its wide-ranging applicability in the applications my company develops. It is my hope that JavaScript's ability to handle a wide variety of tasks will become evident as you read this book. Here are a few of the many questions this book will answer:

- What is the relationship between JavaScript and HTML?
- What is the difference between JavaScript and JScript?
- Are there any compatibility issues surrounding the many versions of JavaScript and JScript?
- How can you create special effects with JavaScript?
- How can you create smart frames with JavaScript?
- What is the JavaScript object model?
- How does JavaScript integrate with ActiveX controls, Netscape plug-ins, and Java applets?
- How does JavaScript handle state maintenance?
- How can I use JavaScript on my Web server?
- How does JavaScript compare to Java?
- How can I connect to my SQL database using JavaScript?

Who Should Read This Book?

Because of its status as the primary Web scripting language, JavaScript is used by all sorts of people for all sorts of tasks. These people include

- Webmasters
- HTML authors and designers
- Java developers
- Database application developers
- Power users

I believe that readers in each of these categories will appreciate this book. I assume that you have basic Web and HTML knowledge. You don't need JavaScript experience, but you should have some programming experience in a scripting or full language. If you've never programmed before, this doesn't mean that this book isn't for you. But this book doesn't offer much instruction in beginner programming issues that aren't germane to JavaScript. In the advanced server- and database-related chapters, some server and database experience is required.

System Requirements

In order to use JavaScript, you need a capable computer that has access to the Web. The authors of this book primarily used Windows 95 and Windows NT, but the same JavaScript code will work on Netscape Navigator versions for Macintosh and UNIX.

How This Book Is Organized

JavaScript Unleashed, Second Edition provides a whole-hog look at JavaScript and related technologies. It's divided into nine parts, each of which is summarized in the following sections.

Part I: Getting Started with JavaScript

Part I is a complete introduction to JavaScript and JavaScript tools. Chapter 1 takes a unique look at JavaScript, focusing on how and where it fits into the Web application development framework. You will also see how it relates to other Web technologies, on both the client side and the server side. In Chapter 2, you will learn about the relationship between JavaScript and HTML and how the browser interprets your code at runtime. Chapter 3 looks at the software tools you need to develop in JavaScript, and Chapter 4 focuses on one such tool—Acadia Infuse, the first JavaScript editor available on the market.

Part II: The JavaScript Language

Part II presents a thorough look at the JavaScript language. In Chapters 5 through 8, you will learn about language basics, operators, control structures, and functions.

Part III: JavaScript Objects

Part III dives into the heart of JavaScript: objects. After an introduction to object-oriented concepts and the JavaScript object model in Chapter 9, Chapter 10 looks at how you can handle user and system events. Chapters 11 through 14 explore each of the built-in JavaScript objects in depth. Chapter 15 rounds out the discussion on objects by focusing on how you can create your own. It includes many innovative ideas related to custom object development within JavaScript.

Part IV: Visual Programming Techniques

Part IV focuses on some of the "cool" things people are doing with JavaScript on the Web. Chapter 16 looks at how you can create animations, banners, and other special effects in JavaScript—without using any Java applets. Chapter 17 concentrates on the new layers technology introduced in Netscape Composer, and Chapter 18 discusses how to program dynamic style sheets using JavaScript.

Part V: Programming Techniques

Part V builds on much of what you have learned by looking at specific areas of interest to JavaScript developers. Chapter 19 discusses how you can use JavaScript to make your Web site easier to navigate, and Chapter 20 explores how you can enhance HTML forms with JavaScript, such as by providing client-side data validation. Chapter 21 introduces the notion of maintaining lookup tables on the client side to lessen the need to access the server. Chapter 22 dives into error-handling and debugging JavaScript applications.

Part VI: Advanced JavaScript

Part VI explores three advanced subjects, each of which is emerging as a key topic as JavaScript matures. Chapter 23 looks at one of the most critical issues for JavaScript developers: compatibility between JavaScript and JScript and the various versions of the language. Chapter 24 looks at a more conceptual topic: JavaScript security. This chapter not only looks at the key issues surrounding this subject but also provides some helpful advice as you consider using JavaScript for your Web site. Chapter 25 looks at cookies and other techniques for handling and maintaining state in the Web's stateless environment.

Part VII: JavaScript Connectivity

JavaScript is an important tool to connect HTML with other client-side technologies. Part VII looks at how you can use JavaScript to work with these controls. Chapters 26 through 28 cover the hot topic of integrating JavaScript with Java applets, ActiveX controls, and Netscape plug-ins. Chapter 29 looks at integrating JavaScript with multimedia and LiveAudio.

Part VIII: Server-Side JavaScript

Parts I through VII focus on client-side JavaScript, and Part VIII focuses on its server-side counterpart. Within Netscape's LiveWire, you can use JavaScript as a server-side scripting language. In doing so, you are removed from writing CGI scripts and dealing with languages such as Perl. Part VIII also deals with using JavaScript to connect to databases. Many corporations use the Web to access their data. As a result, how JavaScript can access data will be an increasingly important topic as the technology matures.

Part IX: Appendixes

Part IX provides some extra information. Appendixes A and B provide basic references for JavaScript and HTML. Appendix C compares VBScript and JavaScript. Appendix D lists online JavaScript resources. Appendix E provides an overview of Java from a JavaScripter's perspective.

Conventions Used in This Book

This book uses certain conventions to help make the book more readable and helpful:

- JavaScript code listings, JavaScript method names, and screen messages or displays appear in a special `monospace` font.
- Placeholders (words that stand for what you actually type) appear in `monospace italic`.
- Terms that are introduced or defined appear in *italic*.
- Menu selections are separated with a vertical bar. For example, "Select File | Open" means that you pull down the File menu and choose the Open option.
- Sometimes a line of JavaScript code is unable to fit on a single line of this book. When this happens, the line is broken and continued on the next line, preceded by a ➥ character.

In addition, this book uses special sidebars that are set apart from the rest of the text. These sidebars include Notes, Tips, Cautions, Warnings, and Resources.

I

PART

Getting Started with JavaScript

JavaScript and the World Wide Web

CHAPTER 1

The popular adage of the day is that an Internet year is equal to three calendar months. With that in mind, I recommend fastening your seat belt and jumping into JavaScript head-first. Before diving into the nuts and bolts of creating JavaScript code, it's important to look at the purpose of JavaScript within the context of the Web application framework. Just like other Web technologies, such as browser software, HTML, Java, CGI, and Netscape plug-ins, JavaScript by itself is rather limited in scope. JavaScript emerges as a powerful tool as you begin using it with other technologies to provide effective and deliberate solutions.

In this chapter, I provide an overview of JavaScript and then look at JavaScript within the context of the Web application framework. After that, I'll look at the major uses of JavaScript today and then close with a look at current browsers' support for JavaScript.

Introducing JavaScript

Like everything else connected to the Web, JavaScript is a new technology—even newer than Java itself. JavaScript was initially developed by Netscape under the name of LiveScript. This scripting language was intended to extend the capabilities of basic HTML and provide an alternative to using CGI scripts. After Netscape saw Java, however, it began to work with Sun to provide a scripting language even more closely linked to Java itself—hence the name change to JavaScript.

One of the motivations behind JavaScript was the recognition for logic to exist on the client, not simply on the server. With all logic on the server side, all processing is forced to go to the server, even for simple tasks such as data validation. In fact, with no logic on the front end, the Web environment falls into the outdated terminal-to-host architecture that was replaced with the PC revolution in the 1980s. Providing logic within the browser can empower the client and make the relationship a true client/server arrangement.

Java is a step in this direction, but it's implemented as an adjunct to HTML itself and not intended to be integrated from a language standpoint. Also, as a strongly typed language, Java isn't optimal for gluing together divergent applets. Furthermore, Java requires low-level programming skills, something that most HTML developers would rather not exercise just to provide some logic behind HTML form elements. A higher-level, client-side scripting language seemed like a natural missing piece in the Web development tool arena.

Since its rollout in December 1995, JavaScript has drawn support from the major industry vendors, including Apple, Borland, Sybase, Informix, Oracle, Digital, HP, and IBM.

The plot thickened, however, when Microsoft entered the equation. Realizing the importance of Web scripting, Microsoft wanted to provide support for JavaScript as well. However, when Netscape was slow to provide technology to Microsoft, Redmond reverse-engineered JavaScript to create its own iteration, JScript, which is supported in Microsoft Internet Explorer versions 3.0 and higher. JScript 1.0 is roughly compatible with JavaScript 1.0, which is supported in Netscape Navigator 2.0 and higher. However, the myriad of JavaScript versions and various platform-specific quirks have left Web developers with headaches when they try to deploy

JavaScript-enabled Web sites. (See Chapter 23, "JavaScript Compatibility Issues," for more information on working with the various JavaScript versions.)

Fortunately, help is on the way for frustrated JavaScripters. Netscape, Microsoft, and other vendors agreed to turn over the language to an international standards body, named ECMA. ECMA is now responsible for finalizing a language specification that all vendors will agree on. Although this ECMA standard will help, it's extremely likely that both Netscape and Microsoft will both continue to extend JavaScript beyond the language standard, making complete language uniformity unachievable.

In addition to JScript, Microsoft has its own competitor to JavaScript called VBScript, which is essentially a subset of the Visual Basic language for the World Wide Web. Because Netscape isn't supporting VBScript, its primary uses are for developers already familiar with Visual Basic, and intranets (or internet sites) that will have a high concentration of Microsoft Internet Explorer users.

Even considering VBScript, JavaScript is emerging as the standard Web scripting language. As vendors produce Web development tools that require a scripting language, it is expected that JavaScript will often be used for that purpose. Netscape uses JavaScript as a server-side scripting language in its LiveWire environment, something you will dive into later in Chapter 30, "Server-Side JavaScript Extensions Using LiveWire."

Another example from Borland International is IntraBuilder. It is a Web database development tool that uses JavaScript as its native language. However, IntraBuilder extends the JavaScript language for its own uses within the product. If other vendors continue to do the same, JavaScript will become ubiquitous for scripting on the World Wide Web.

RESOURCE

Visit Borland's home page at `http://www.borland.com` for the latest information and downloads on IntraBuilder.

Ten JavaScript Facts Every Scripter Should Know

Trying to learn a new tool such as JavaScript can be challenging, because it can be difficult to understand how it's used and how it fits into the general picture. I have boiled down the basics of JavaScript to 10 facts that will help you as you begin to work with it. Study them before you continue.

JavaScript Is Embedded into HTML

Perhaps the most important JavaScript fact is its marriage with HTML. If you deal with JavaScript, there is hardly any separation of the two. JavaScript code is usually housed within

HTML documents and executed within them. Additionally, by itself, JavaScript has no user interface; it relies on HTML to provide its means of interaction with the user. Along this line, most of the JavaScript objects have HTML tags that they represent. If you have little background in HTML, you will discover that to be an effective JavaScript developer, you also need to learn the ins and outs of HTML.

JavaScript uses HTML as a means of jumping into the Web application framework. It also extends the normal capabilities of HTML by providing events to HTML tags and allowing event-driven code to execute within it.

Although I'll wait for future chapters to explain JavaScript, Listing 1.1 provides an example of how JavaScript code is embedded in HTML source code. The text in bold represents the JavaScript-specific code in the document. Everything else is plain HTML.

Listing 1.1. JavaScript embedded in an HTML file.

```
<html>
<head>
<title>Status Bar</title>
<SCRIPT LANGUAGE="JavaScript">
<!--
    window.defaultStatus = "Welcome to the large URL page."

    function changeStatus() {
        window.status = "Click me to go to the Acadia Software
          home page."
    }

    function changeDefaultStatus() {
        window.defaultStatus = window.document.statusForm.messageList.
          options[window.document.statusForm.messageList.
          selectedIndex].text
    }
//-->
</SCRIPT>
</head>

<body>
<p> </p>
<p> </p>
<p align=center>
<font color="#008040">
<font size=7>
<strong>http://www.acadians.com</strong></font></font></p>
<p align=center>
<a href="http://www.acadians.com" onMouseOver="changeStatus()
    ;return true">Go...</a></p>

<form name="statusForm" method="POST">
<p><br>
<br>
<br>
<br>
</p>
<p align=center>
```

```
<font size=1>To change the default status bar message, select
a message from the list below and click the Change button. </font></p>
<p align=center><select
    name="messageList"
    size=1>
    <option selected>Welcome to the large URL page.</option>
    <option>On route to Acadia Software</option>
    <option>This page intentionally left (nearly) blank.</option>
    <option>An exciting example of changing status bar text.</option>
    </select>
<input
    type=button
    name="Change"
    value="Change"
    onClick="changeDefaultStatus()"></p>
</form>
</body>
</html>
```

JavaScript Is Browser-Dependent

JavaScript is but a scripting language, not a tool in and of itself. The software that actually runs the JavaScript code you write is the Web browser—whether it's Netscape Navigator, Microsoft Internet Explorer, or whatever. JavaScript depends on the Web browser to support it, as shown in Figure 1.1. If the browser doesn't support it, your code will be ignored. Even worse, if you don't account for unsupporting browsers, the JavaScript code itself is displayed as text on your page, as shown in Figure 1.2. (See Chapter 2, "How JavaScript and HTML Work Together," for details on how to prevent your code from being displayed.)

FIGURE 1.1.

Microsoft Internet Explorer 3.0 supports JavaScript.

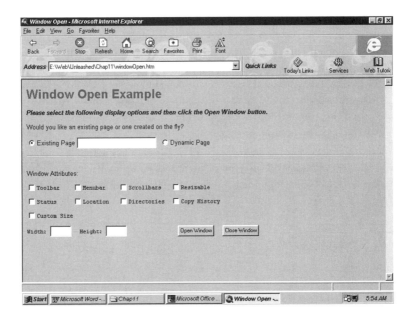

FIGURE 1.2.

Spry Mosaic doesn't support JavaScript.

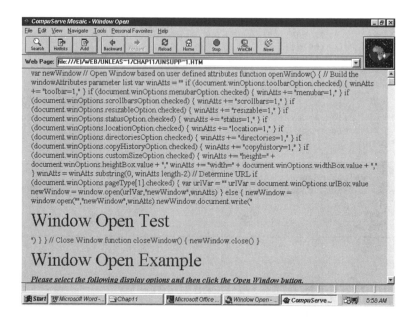

FIGURE 1.2.

Spry Mosaic doesn't support JavaScript.

It's critical to remember this dependence as you decide when and where to use JavaScript in your application solution. Will you require a browser that supports JavaScript? If so, how should you notify users who use an unsupporting browser? Will you create a non-JavaScript solution as well? You need to answer all these questions as you develop your JavaScript applications.

> **NOTE**
>
> When they were first released, frames were an innovative solution but could be viewed only if you had Netscape Navigator 2.0. HTML authors had to decide when to use frames and what to do when a browser didn't support them. With the continued popularity of Netscape, and Microsoft's support for them in Internet Explorer 3.0, frames are becoming ubiquitous. In fact, the unspoken assumption of many is that if you're "with it," you already have a browser that supports frames.
>
> Fortunately for JavaScript developers, it's likely that the same will hold true for JavaScript support. Netscape Navigator 2.x and above and Microsoft Internet Explorer 3.0—the browsers with some 90 percent of the market—do provide JavaScript support. If these trends continue, browser dependence will become less of an issue.

JavaScript Is an Interpreted Language

As with most scripting languages, JavaScript is interpreted at runtime by the browser before it's executed. JavaScript isn't compiled into an actual program—like an .EXE file—but remains part of the HTML document to which it is attached. The disadvantage of an interpreted language is that it takes longer for the code to execute because the browser compiles the instructions at runtime just before executing them. However, the advantage is that it's much easier to update your source code. You don't have to worry about old versions of a JavaScript script hanging around, because if you change it in your source HTML file, the new code is executed the next time the user accesses the document.

JavaScript Is a Loosely Typed Language

JavaScript is far different from strongly typed languages such as Java or C++, in which you must declare all variables of a certain type before using them. In contrast, JavaScript is much more flexible. You can declare variables of a specific type, but you don't need to. You can also work with a variable when you might not know the specific type before runtime. A short code snippet can demonstrate this. Suppose you want to declare a variable called myVal, assign a string value to it, and then display it in a message box. You could use the following code:

```
function flexible() {
    var myVal     // declare variable myVal
    mVal = "Pi"   // assign value to myVal
    alert(myVal)  // use it
}
```

Although it's generally a good practice to declare your variables explicitly, you aren't required to do so. The following code, perfectly valid in JavaScript, would be unthinkable in a strongly typed language:

```
function flexible() {
    mVal = "Pi"   // assign value to an undeclared variable myVal
    alert(myVal)  // use it
}
```

To further illustrate JavaScript's flexibility, you can change the type of value the variable represents as well. For example, the myVal variable changes from a string to a number value during the course of the function's execution:

```
function flexible() {
    var myVal = "Pi"
    alert(myVal)
    myVal = 3.14159
    alert(myVal)
}
```

JavaScript Is an Object-Based Language

You might see JavaScript referred to as an object-oriented programming (OOP) language by Netscape and others, but this is actually a stretch of the true meaning of OOP. As you will learn in Chapter 9, "The JavaScript Object Model," JavaScript is really an *object-based* language.

You do work with objects that encapsulate data (properties) and behavior (methods). (If you've used dot notation—whether in Visual Basic, Java, or Delphi—you will find JavaScript quick to pick up.) However, although you can work with objects, you can't subclass them. The JavaScript object model is instance-based, not inheritance-based.

JavaScript Is Event-Driven

Much of the JavaScript code you write will be in response to events generated by the user or the system. The JavaScript language itself is equipped to handle events. HTML objects, such as buttons or text fields, are enhanced to support event handlers. If you're coming from a Java or Visual Basic background, this event-driven environment is second nature. If you come from a procedural, top-down language environment, the event-driven nature of JavaScript might require some study. Chapter 10, "Handling Events," provides a complete look at JavaScript events.

JavaScript Is Not Java

As you surf the Web, you may run into a phrase on some JavaScript-related Web sites: *JavaScript is not Java*. As discussed previously, Java and JavaScript were created by two different companies, and the primary reason for the name similarity is purely for marketing purposes. I'll save the in-depth comparison between JavaScript and Java for Appendix E, "Java from a JavaScripter's Perspective," but it might be helpful to briefly mention some of the differences (and similarities) that exist between them in this context as well.

First, although JavaScript is tightly integrated into HTML, a Java applet is simply connected to an HTML document through the <APPLET> tag. The applet itself is stored in another file, which is downloaded from the server.

Second, with strong typing, true object-orientation, and a compiler, Java is a more robust and complete language. Keep in mind, Java is for applets or complete applications; JavaScript is primarily for scripts.

If you look at the language itself, JavaScript's syntax does resemble Java. If you get used to the JavaScript control structures, you could use that as a head start to learning Java itself.

NOTE

For anecdotal evidence on the confusion between JavaScript and Java, I offer my own story. I recently gave an interview about Acadia Infuse, a visual editor for JavaScript, with a popular Web magazine. After spending 30 minutes with the magazine's senior editor, explaining what JavaScript is and how it differs from Java, the editor continued to call JavaScript "Java," even at the end of the interview.

JavaScript Is Multifunctional

JavaScript is multifaceted and can be used in a variety of contexts to provide a solution to a Web-based problem. Later in this chapter in the section "JavaScript's Role in Application Development," I'll discuss the variety of uses for JavaScript. Some of the primary purposes include the following:

- Enhance and liven static HTML pages, through special effects, animations, and banners.
- Validate data without passing everything to the server.
- Serve as a building block for client/server Web applications.
- Develop client-side applications.
- Serve as client-side glue between HTML objects, Java applets, ActiveX controls, and Netscape Plug-ins.
- Serve as an extension to a Web server.
- Provide database connectivity without using CGI.

JavaScript Is Evolving

Earlier in this chapter, I discussed how new JavaScript is as a technology. If you add that fact to the rapid rate of change on the Web, it's easy to recognize that JavaScript itself continues to evolve as a language. As you develop JavaScript applications, not only do you need to consider whether the browser supports JavaScript, but also which iteration of JavaScript (or JScript) it supports. With three JavaScript versions (1.0, 1.1, and 1.2) and two JScript versions (1.0 and 2.0), it can become maddening trying to deal with the variations.

RESOURCE

Visit Netscape's home page at http://home.netscape.com for information on future enhancements to JavaScript. For JScript enhancements, visit Microsoft at http://www.microsoft.com.

The JavaScript Language Spans Contexts

To repeat something mentioned earlier in this chapter: JavaScript is a language, not a tool. As a Web scripting language, it can be useful in a variety of contexts. Much of the focus on JavaScript by Web developers (and this book) is for client-side scripting. However, you can also use it on the server side in the Netscape Enterprise Server and LiveWire environment and Microsoft's ActiveX Server framework. It is also used as the native language for Web development tools, such as Borland's IntraBuilder, mentioned earlier in the chapter. When you think of JavaScript, don't think of it exclusively as a client-side scripting language. Moreover, recent reports indicate that future versions of Microsoft Windows will support JavaScript on the desktop.

The Four Phases of the World Wide Web

The revolutionary changes in Web technology over the past six years make the Web a constantly moving target. Before I discuss Web applications, it will be helpful to review the evolution of the Web from its humble beginnings as an extension of the Internet into a culture that is changing technology today. You can view this transformation as four distinct phases of the Web.

Phase I: Character-Based Hypertext

The Web was a text-based hypertext system when it started in 1989. This limitation was primarily because the computers that accessed the Web had no good way of displaying graphics. In the Web's early days, users were forced to type in a number representing the page they wanted to access. In time, you could select highlighted text and then move to the associated page. For the Web's scientific and academic uses, the hypertext nature of the Web was revolutionary.

Phase II: Graphical-Based Static HTML Documents

The second phase of the Web began in 1993 with the release of the first graphical Web browser called NCSA Mosaic. Mosaic was developed by undergraduate student Marc Andreessen for the National Center for Supercomputing Applications (NCSA). Although the concept of the Web was already proving useful for the scientific and academic communities, a graphical browser suddenly harnessed the raw power of the Internet and made it easy to navigate. At the same time, graphical environments were becoming more popular than character-based systems on the desktop. Microsoft was winning the desktop war with Windows 3.1.

Adding a graphical browser on top of the graphical desktop environment proved to be the "killer" application that the media looked for. In just a matter of months, a frenzy of activity emerged from the media, computer companies, and corporations racing to provide content or services on the Web.

The Web itself remained static, as shown in Figure 1.3. Its content consisted of text or graphic documents and little else. Perhaps a page contained a sound or video file, but you would typically download the file and then play it using an external application.

FIGURE 1.3.
A static HTML page.

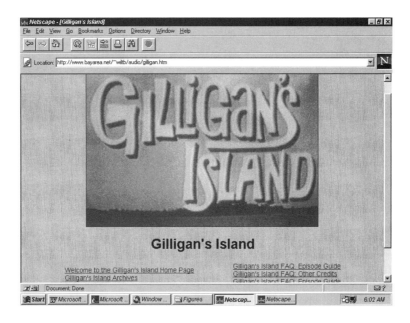

Phase III: Dynamic HTML Documents

During Phases I and II, Web pages were created using an HTML text editor and placed on a Web server. Once they were placed on the server, most pages remained static until the author modified them. Static pages are satisfactory for some Web uses but not for others. To meet the need for dynamically generated HTML documents, Web developers started using Common Gateway Interface (CGI) scripts on the Web server to generate HTML documents on-the-fly. This provided the first level of interaction with the user on the Web. With this enhancement, the Web could be the platform for hypertext documents but also serve as a distinct application environment. The FedEx Web site, shown in Figure 1.4, proved to be one of the first Web applications that demonstrated the power of the Web.

Phase IV: Active HTML Documents

The fourth phase of the Web began slowly in 1995 with the use of plug-ins in Netscape Navigator but rose to prominence with the release of Java later that year. The major focus of this phase has been to empower the client and not rely exclusively on the server to either run the application or process information entered by the user.

The hype surrounding Java is due primarily to the fact that the Web is no longer simply a collection of HTML documents but can be a true client/server environment in which the client has some independence from the server. This is where JavaScript fits in. With JavaScript, Java, ActiveX, and other client extensions, the browser can become a powerful operating environment in which to run Web applications.

FIGURE 1.4.

FedEx offered one of the first compelling Web applications.

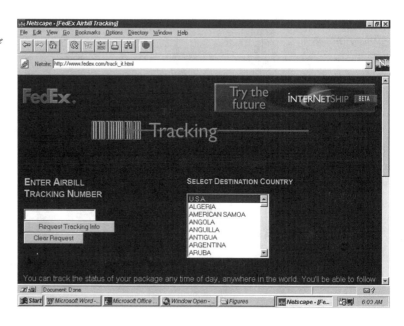

The Web Application Framework

Using the Web as a development environment is a relatively new phenomenon. With the advent of Java, JavaScript, ActiveX, and other technologies, the idea of developing Web-centric applications has many attractive qualities.

The Web as a development environment can seem rather confusing. Because of the distributed nature of the Web, a Web application can be composed of many parts, using a variety of technologies. In a typical LAN-based client/server architecture, you might have a client-based application attached to a database server on the network. You would often develop the client application using a single tool such as Delphi or Visual Basic. The server side of the application is typically developed and maintained using a SQL server's administrative tools.

In contrast, a Web application can have many parts. Figure 1.5 shows the various parts that make up the application framework. The next sections examine each of these parts.

The Web development framework is truly an example of the sum being greater than the parts. By themselves, each of these technologies are limited and rather narrow in scope. When combined into cohesive applications, they provide a convincing means of developing Internet and intranet solutions.

FIGURE 1.5.
A Web application framework.

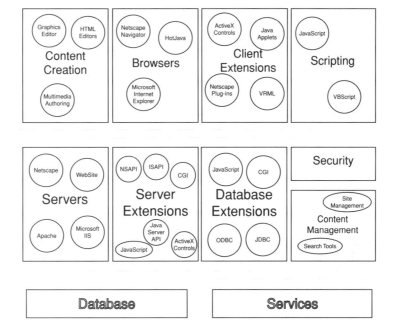

Client Side

The client side of the Web application framework consists of four building blocks:

- Web browser
- HTML (Hypertext Markup Language)
- Client-side extensions (Java applets, ActiveX controls, and Netscape plug-ins)
- Scripting languages (JavaScript and VBScript)

This section examines each of these technologies and how they work together. Figure 1.6 shows their interrelationships.

Browsers

Undoubtedly the most important component of a Web application is the browser itself. The browser alone is the window to the Web for the user and serves as the user interface for your application. Browser technology is relatively simple (reading HTML and displaying it appropriately on-screen), but the advent of nonstandard enhancements, such as Netscape frames and JavaScript, has made the selection of your browser software a critical one as you determine a Web development platform.

FIGURE 1.6.

A client-side frame-work.

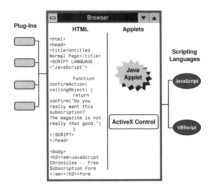

If you're creating an intranet application, you can probably ensure that all users are using a standard Web browser. You can then make certain assumptions when you develop your application. However, if you're creating an Internet application that the world will use, your application design decisions become more complicated, continuously weighing features against compatibility.

Table 1.1 highlights the two major browsers today and notes the versions that support the specified client-side technologies.

Table 1.1. Browser support of client-side technologies.

	Netscape Navigator	*Microsoft Internet Explorer*
JavaScript support	2.0 and above	None
JScript support	None	3.0 and above
VBScript support	None	3.0 and above
Java support	2.0 and above	3.0 and above
ActiveX support	3.0 (plug-in)	3.0 and above
Netscape plug-ins	2.0 and above	3.0 and above

HTML

HTML is obviously one of the primary technologies upon which the Web is built. HTML is a markup language that is used to provide structure and formatting to a plain text file. As a "technology," it's rather mundane—some would say outdated. Nonetheless, the commonness of the language gives it its power.

Although the browser provides the window for displaying Web-based content to the user, the content itself comes in the form of HTML text. It doesn't matter if you're presenting static documents, returning a query result, providing a feedback form, or displaying a JavaScript-based application. Regardless of the means of obtaining this data, it is ultimately converted into HTML tags for presentation.

Client Extensions

As the need for active Web pages increased, simply beefing up Web browsers wasn't considered the best solution. Some extensions are mere third-party add-ons to the browser software to make it more powerful. However, there was also the need to work with "executable content" within the browser. Although the browser needs to support the technology, it need not be tied to the browser to run. What is emerging today are three separate client-side extensions. They all have similarities, but they also have their distinct identity.

Java Applets

If you've never heard of the Java programming language, one could call you Rip Van Winkle. After all, Java has been hyped like no other programming language before. I want to back up and discuss it within the context of the Web application framework.

RESOURCE

For information on Java, go to the main Java site at Sun at http://java.sun.com/.

Java is a multiplatform programming language developed by Sun Microsystems. The reason for all the hype is the capability to create executable content—called a Java applet—that can be executed on a multitude of platforms.

The applet is linked via an <APPLET> tag in the HTML document and can be downloaded onto the client computer. The applet comes to the browser in *bytecodes*. If a browser supports Java, it interprets these bytecodes and executes them on the client machine. The Java applet reference is ignored in browsers that aren't Java-enabled.

Java applets have several uses, and as the language itself matures, the uses grow more convincing as well. Figures 1.7 and 1.8 provide two examples of uses of Java.

ActiveX Controls

Formerly known as OCXs, ActiveX controls are Microsoft's answer to Java applets. They are similar to Java applets in that you can use ActiveX controls as a means of providing executable content across the Web, as shown in Figure 1.9. Unlike Java, ActiveX controls are limited to the Microsoft Windows operating environments.

FIGURE 1.7.

A Java applet moves the plane across the screen.

FIGURE 1.8.

An interactive Java map.

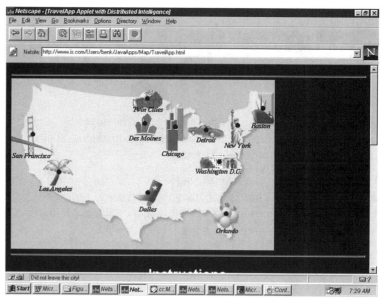

FIGURE 1.9.

Is it a Java applet or an ActiveX control?

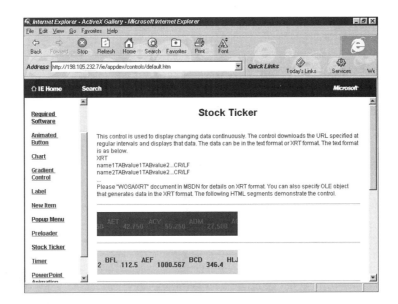

Although ActiveX controls are limited to running on a single operating environment, they aren't necessarily limited to Web applications. For example, you can use the same ActiveX control in a Web application with an ActiveX-enabled browser, as shown in Figure 1.10, and with a Windows programming tool such as Delphi or Visual Basic, as shown in Figure 1.11.

FIGURE 1.10.

An ActiveX control embedded in an HTML document.

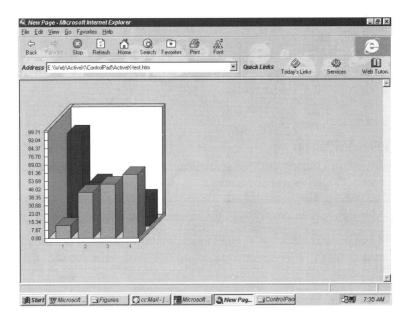

FIGURE 1.11.

The same ActiveX control used in a Delphi application.

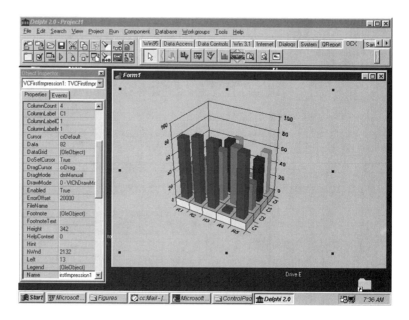

The jury is still out on whether Java or ActiveX will become the applet standard as the Web development environment matures. Both have strengths and weaknesses. Fortunately for you as a JavaScript developer, your programs can interact with both of these applet technologies. Chapter 27, "ActiveX Scripting," discusses how JavaScript and ActiveX controls work together.

RESOURCE

For information on ActiveX, go to Microsoft's Internet Center at `http://www.microsoft.com/internet/`.

Netscape Plug-Ins

Plug-ins are a slightly different technology, but they're still a client-side extension of the Web browser. Plug-ins essentially extend the normal capabilities of the Netscape Navigator browser to provide support for additional data types and other features. Specifically, you use a plug-in to display a specific MIME (Multipart Internet Mail Extension) type file.

When you start Netscape, it looks in its `program\plugins` folder for any plug-ins to register. Netscape then calls a plug-in on an "as-needed" basis when it comes across a matching MIME file type.

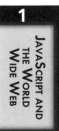

Plug-ins become added modules onto the browser and don't require any user interaction to start once installed. They are proving especially useful for multimedia data, such as sound, video, and graphics. Figure 1.12 demonstrates the use of a plug-in that lets you view Adobe Acrobat files within Netscape.

FIGURE 1.12.
Viewing a .PDF file using a plug-in.

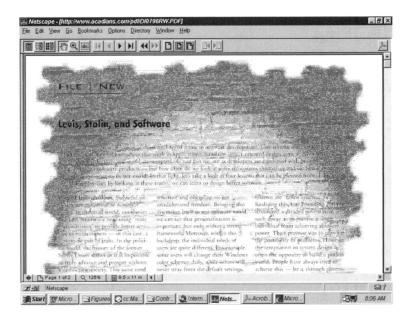

You can use JavaScript to communicate with plug-ins. Chapter 28, "Working with Netscape Plug-Ins," explores this subject in detail.

Client Scripting Languages

The final pieces of the puzzle on the client side are the client scripting languages. JavaScript is the leading scripting language today, but Microsoft is now promoting VBScript as an alternative. Because of the millions of Visual Basic developers, it's likely that VBScript will also prove popular for this community. Appendix C, "Comparing JavaScript with VBScript," compares and contrasts JavaScript and VBScript.

Server Side

The server side of the Web application framework consists of the Web server itself along with extensions to the server software. As you will learn, these extensions can take various forms and be employed using a variety of technologies. Figure 1.13 shows the interrelationships of the server-side framework.

FIGURE 1.13.
A server-side framework.

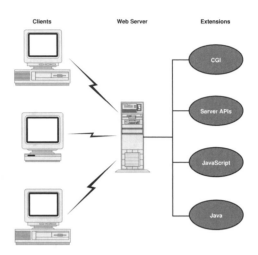

Servers

The Web server is charged with handling requests for HTML documents from the client and returning them for viewing. The server software is an application that runs on a TCP/IP-enabled machine. Popular servers today include Netscape Commerce Server, Microsoft Internet Information Server (IIS), Apache, and WebSite.

Server Extensions

By itself, the Web server provides static HTML pages to the client when requested and performs a variety of other functions. However, several extensions to servers are being developed to provide capabilities that the server itself doesn't support. These include CGI, server APIs, JavaScript, and Java.

CGI

CGI (Common Gateway Interface) is the *de facto* standard means of interfacing external programs with Web servers. Using CGI, you can execute CGI programs or scripts on the server to generate dynamically created content for displaying to the user. A typical scenario is that a request is generated from an HTML form and sent to the server. The request runs the CGI program or script, which is located in a special directory on the server. The CGI program processes the request and then returns an HTML document with the result.

You can write a CGI program using any programming language—such as Delphi, C++, Visual Basic, or FORTRAN—as long as it can be executed on the Web server. Common in the UNIX world is writing CGI scripts in scripting languages such as Perl or a UNIX shell.

Server APIs

Another means of integration with the server is through its native application programming interface (API). Two of the most commonly used Web server APIs are the Netscape Server API (NSAPI) and the Microsoft Internet Server API (ISAPI). Using the APIs provides tighter integration with the server. For example, in the Windows world, you would create a DLL that is accessed by the server, not a separate EXE.

The advantage to using these server APIs is that the processes are much more efficient than CGI programs. CGI requires that a separate instance of the program is executed for each client request or submittal. Not only is this more expensive, but it also limits the amount of data sharing that can be performed.

The disadvantage to using a proprietary server API is that your solution is specific to that single server. Your ISAPI DLL won't work with a Netscape server. If you're working primarily with one of these servers, then the negative aspect of this limitation is minimized.

Server-Side JavaScript

Much of the attention given to JavaScript to date has been because of its capabilities on the client side. However, you can use JavaScript as a server-side scripting tool as well. The first such environment out the door is, as you would expect, Netscape.

Netscape's LiveWire environment allows you to use JavaScript scripts to extend the capabilities of a Netscape server. LiveWire has several server-side extensions to the JavaScript language that provide the additional capabilities of generating dynamic HTML, communicating with the client, accessing external files on the server, and connecting to SQL databases. LiveWire also lets you compile JavaScript scripts for greater server-side performance. Netscape is working to more closely integrate server-side JavaScript/LiveWire technology into its Web servers themselves, making it part of Enterprise Server 3.0.

Additionally, Microsoft is supporting JScript in its Active Server framework as a server-side scripting language.

Java

As the technology matures, Java will also be used as a programming tool to develop server-side programs to extend the Web server.

What Can You Do with JavaScript?

Now that you have surveyed the technologies that make up Web applications, you can look at the role that client-side JavaScript can play in developing Web applications.

Client-Side Applications

You can use JavaScript to develop entire client-side applications. Although JavaScript isn't an all-encompassing language like Java, it does provide rather substantial capabilities when it comes to working with HTML tags and associated objects. One of the best known JavaScript applications is hIdaho Design's ColorCenter (`http://www.hidaho.com/c3/`), shown in Figure 1.14. You can use this JavaScript application to select browser-related colors and preview them in a separate frame. Trying to design such an application using Java would be much more complex because of the interaction that is required with HTML. For certain cases, JavaScript provides the ideal programming backbone on which to develop the application.

FIGURE 1.14.

hIdaho Design's ColorCenter.

> **NOTE**
>
> I have seen JavaScript applications referred to by some as "Weblications." I hope that the term will die a quick death and not catch on.

"Smart Frame" Support

Multiframe windows are proving to be a powerful means of presentation for Web developers. Displaying multiple frames within the browser provides you much more control over the user interface of the application. When dealing with multiframe windows, JavaScript proves its worth as providing a powerful means for control. Netscape's home page, shown in Figure 1.15, shows an example of using JavaScript with smart frames.

Figure 1.15.
Netscape's home page employs JavaScript.

Data Validation

JavaScript gives you, as a Web developer, a basic means of validating data from the user without hitting the server. Within your JavaScript code, you can determine whether values entered by the user are valid or fit the correct format, as shown in Figure 1.16. JavaScript becomes a much more efficient validation method than throwing unqualified values to a server process. Not only is the process more efficient for the user entering the data, but it's better for the server as well. By the time data is transferred to the server for processing, you can be assured the data has been qualified in a proper state for submission.

Creating Interactive Forms

Another common use of JavaScript is livening up HTML forms. Part of this task might include validating data, which is discussed in the last section. It can also include additional features that are unavailable with straight HTML, such as providing information to the user on the status bar, opening a second browser window for help information, and so on. Figure 1.17 shows an example of a JavaScript-enabled form.

FIGURE 1.16.

Using JavaScript to validate data.

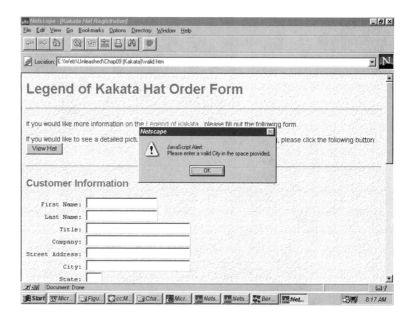

FIGURE 1.17.

An interactive HTML form.

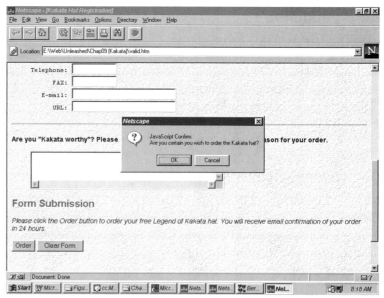

Client-Side Lookup Tables

Besides including data validation, another means of minimizing the need to access the server is to employ JavaScript to generate and maintain client-side lookup tables. The data must be embedded in the HTML document itself, however, so you will want to limit your use of lookup tables to small, read-only databases of information.

State Maintenance

In the stateless environment of the Web, you can use JavaScript to help maintain state between exchanges between the client and the server. The most use of state maintenance is with cookies (information stored by the browser on the client's PC). JavaScript provides a means for you to store and retrieve cookies on the client's PC. Figure 1.18 shows an example of using a cookie to display information specific to the current user. See Chapter 25, "Cookies and State Maintenance," for more information on working with cookies in JavaScript.

FIGURE 1.18.

Using cookies in JavaScript.

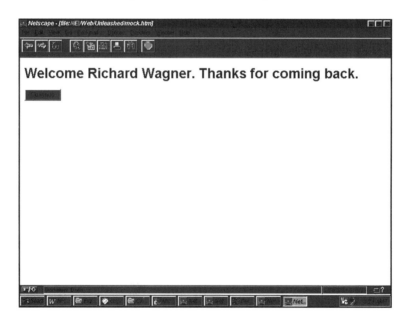

Working with Java Applets, ActiveX Controls, and Plug-Ins

As the JavaScript language is enhanced, it continues to have increased capabilities in working with client-side extensions, including Java applets, ActiveX controls, and Netscape plug-ins. You can access a Java or ActiveX object's properties and execute its methods. You can also determine whether a plug-in is installed. As this capability is enhanced, JavaScript will be considered an essential glue that holds together HTML, applets, and client-side extensions.

Browser Support for JavaScript

Compared to other applications you use, browsers are relatively simple pieces of software, but they are evolving into more powerful applications as Web technology matures. A browser is your window into the Web; therefore, no matter what JavaScript's potential is, it does no good if a browser doesn't support it. This section examines the browsers available today and their support for JavaScript.

Because JavaScript is an interpreted language and embedded in HTML documents, it's entirely dependent on the browser software to work. If you use an old browser, it won't know what to do with the code and will ignore it.

Netscape Navigator

During the mid-1990s, Netscape became perhaps the single most important player in the Web industry. Not only was it the first to market many important technological breakthroughs, but it also teamed up with other industry leaders—such as Sun—to push the "technology envelope" on many fronts on the Web.

Although the emergence of Microsoft as a Web powerhouse could change the scene, it's likely that Netscape will continue to dominate the browser market for some time.

Obviously, because Netscape developed JavaScript, you would expect its phenomenally successful Navigator browser to support the scripting language. Navigator 2.0 was the first browser to support JavaScript. Later versions provide important enhancements to the language itself. Figure 1.19 shows the Netscape Navigator 3.0 window.

FIGURE 1.19.

Netscape Navigator 3.0.

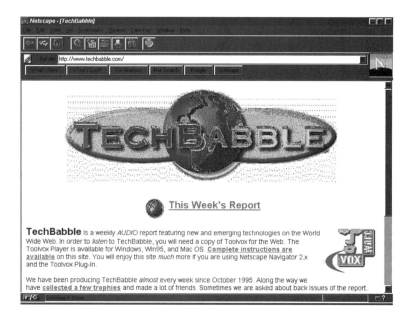

Microsoft Internet Explorer

Microsoft Internet Explorer 3.0, shown in Figure 1.20, is the first non-Netscape browser to support JavaScript/JScript. Older versions of Internet Explorer (that is, versions 1.0 and 2.0) don't support JScript.

FIGURE 1.20.
Microsoft Internet Explorer 3.0.

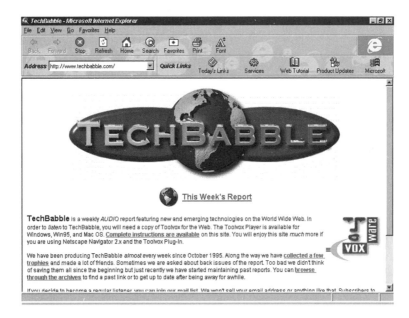

Other Browsers

At the time this chapter was written, no other browsers provided support for JavaScript. Sun's HotJava browser is expected to provide support in the future.

> **NOTE**
>
> Most ActiveX control browsers don't provide JavaScript support. Microsoft's WebBrowser ActiveX control, however, does provide JScript support.

Summary

This chapter looked at the Web application framework, and how each of the pieces of Web technology fit together. JavaScript is an important tool in a Web developer's toolkit. As you learned in this chapter, JavaScript serves many important functions within the Web application framework, and it's becoming more of a standard in the Web development marketplace.

Because JavaScript is a language and not a tool itself, it's dependent on browser software in order to execute. Although Netscape Navigator and Microsoft Internet Explorer are the only browsers that currently provide JavaScript support, these two browsers own the lion's share of the marketplace, making JavaScript support fairly dependable.

Now that we have a solid foundation on which to look at JavaScript, we can begin to look in the next chapter at the details of how JavaScript interacts with HTML.

How JavaScript and HTML Work Together

CHAPTER 2

HTML gives you the ability to create remarkable static Web pages. Although these documents can be creative, interesting, and by all means useful, JavaScript gives you the ability to make these static pages interactive and more responsive to user actions and input. Extending your HTML pages with JavaScript gives your page more power and gives you more flexibility with what your HTML can do. JavaScript, an interpreted language that is processed by the browser when the page loads, can't stand alone; it's always tied to your HTML page and the browser.

JavaScript lets the Web developer create more dynamic pages by embedding a scripting language in the existing HTML structure. You can now put processes behind buttons, run calculations on form-entered data, or perform actions when the user moves the mouse cursor over an HTML object. In general, you get more bang for your HTML buck.

JavaScript offers advantages over client-based interactive documents such as CGI, because JavaScript-based documents are less dependent on client-side processing, so they are quicker to respond to user interactions and requests.

Embedding JavaScript in Your HTML

JavaScript scripts are integrated into HTML using the HTML <SCRIPT> and </SCRIPT> tags. An HTML document may contain multiple <SCRIPT> pairs, and each pair may enclose more than one set of JavaScript statements. Both the start and end tags are required for <SCRIPT>, and the LANGUAGE attribute and the SOURCE attribute are the only attributes currently available. LANGUAGE is used to specify the scripting language in which the script is written, and the SOURCE attribute (SRC) is used to specify the filename of the JavaScript statements, if they are stored in a separate file.

Language

The following tag specifies JavaScript version 1.0 (JavaScript for Navigator 2.0):

```
<SCRIPT LANGUAGE="JavaScript">
```

The following tag specifies JavaScript version 1.1 (JavaScript for Navigator 3.0):

```
<SCRIPT LANGUAGE="JavaScript1.1">
```

Finally, the following tag specifies JavaScript version 1.2 (JavaScript for Navigator 4.0):

```
<SCRIPT LANGUAGE="JavaScript1.2">
```

TIP

If the LANGUAGE attribute isn't defined, Navigator 2.0 will assume JavaScript 1.0, Navigator 3.0 will assume JavaScript 1.1, and Navigator 4.0 will assume JavaScript 1.2. If you don't specify the correct LANGUAGE attribute, the browser might make incorrect assumptions and not interpret your JavaScript code as you intended.

By defining multiple sets of JavaScript functions, browsers that support JavaScript 1.1 can take advantage of newer functions, and they can be hidden from older version of JavaScript. The simplest method to take advantage of these options is shown in Listing 2.1.

Listing 2.1. Using multiple versions of JavaScript.

```
<SCRIPT LANGUAGE="JavaScript">
//Define JavaScript1.0 functions in this section
</SCRIPT>
</HEAD>
<SCRIPT LANGUAGE="JavaScript1.1">
//Redefine JavaScript1.0 functions
//and add in new functions for JavaScript1.1
</SCRIPT>
<SCRIPT LANGUAGE="JavaScript1.2">
//Redefine JavaScript1.0 and JavaScript1.1 functions
//and add in new functions for JavaScript1.2
</SCRIPT>
</HEAD>
```

Another method for accomplishing this would be to replace the current HTML page with a JavaScript 1.1 and a JavaScript 1.2 version of the same page if the browser supports JavaScript 1.1 or 1.2. You would use the same processes as defined in Listing 2.1, except that instead of redefining the functions, you would replace the current page with a new page.

> **WARNING**
>
> Once future language extensions are available, JavaScript will no longer be the "assumed" language. It is advisable to specifically define your language as JavaScript so that it won't conflict with future versions of browsers and HTML.

Source

You have two options when integrating JavaScript statements into your HTML document. The method that you choose depends on your requirements when viewing and modifying code. The first option lets you view all your codes simultaneously and involves writing JavaScript statements directly into your HTML document. All your statements are embedded in your HTML page between the <SCRIPT> tags. The other option, available only in Netscape 3.0 and higher, is to write your JavaScript code into a separate file and save the file with an extension of .js. You can then call this file from your HTML on the first <SCRIPT> tag line.

Here is the first option for embedding JavaScript in your HTML:

```
<SCRIPT LANGUAGE="JavaScript">
function options() {
document.write("embedding the code")
```

```
}
</SCRIPT>
```

Here is the other option:

```
<SCRIPT SRC="myscript.js">
</SCRIPT>
```

In the second option, you will create a file called `myscript.js`, which will have one line of code:

```
document.write("calling from a separate file")
```

Using this second option, you should include a single statement between the <SCRIPT> tags to give feedback to user if the `.js` file is incorrect or not available; otherwise, the user might see incorrect page behavior and not know why.

When you load the script from another file, the Language attribute is not necessary as long as you use the `.js` extension. Using this methodology, you can modify your JavaScript code without ever opening and risking unwanted changes to your HTML pages. Thus, your code is more modular and portable for use without HTML documents. The downside to this method is that you might have to modify two sets of code, depending on your JavaScript changes. For example, if you change the name of a function in your JavaScript code, you will also have to remember to change the name in the function call in the HTML code. Another downside is that external JavaScript files can't contain HTML tags; they can only contain JavaScript-specific statements.

> **NOTE**
>
> The option of defining and using external JavaScript source code with the SRC attribute is available in Netscape 3.0 and later.

Viewing JavaScript Code

Because you can write JavaScript code inline with your HTML code, you can easily view and edit it. You can view JavaScript code with any HTML editor as well as from your Web browser. You should be familiar with the Document Source menu option that is available in your browser (in Netscape, it's on the View menu) to view the source of an HTML page. When you view the source of the document, you can also view the JavaScript code that is included in the document, as shown in Figure 2.1. (This is obviously not the case when your JavaScript statements are called from the `.js` file instead of written into the document. All you will see is the call to the `.js` file in the script tag.) JavaScript doesn't need a special viewer, and because it is just interpreted code and not compiled, it appears in your document source by default.

FIGURE 2.1.
Viewing JavaScript code.

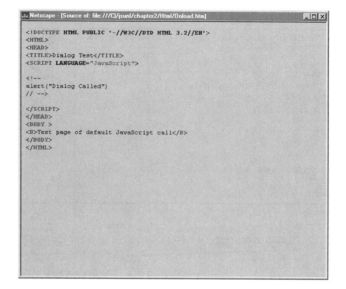

Executing Scripts

JavaScript execution begins after the HTML document loads into the browser but before the user can interact with the document. The browser reads in all JavaScript statements, as it does HTML statements, and then begins interpreting the JavaScript code.

If your JavaScript scripts are stored in a separate file, they are also evaluated when the page loads and before any script actions take place.

All JavaScript statements that are contained within a function block are interpreted, and execution does not occur until the function is called from a JavaScript event. JavaScript statements that are not within a function block are executed after the document loads into the browser. The execution results of the latter will be apparent to the users when they first view the page.

Loading a Page

JavaScript statements that require immediate processing are executed after the page is loaded but before it is displayed in the browser. Listing 2.2 demonstrates the display of an alert dialog after the document is open. No function is called—JavaScript statements are simply processed in order after the page has loaded.

Listing 2.2. Calling to display the alert dialog directly.

```
<!DOCTYPE HTML PUBLIC "-//W3C//DTD HTML 3.2//EN">
<HTML>
<HEAD>
<TITLE>Dialog Test</TITLE>
<SCRIPT LANGUAGE="JavaScript1.2">
<!--
alert("Dialog called")
// -->
</SCRIPT>
</HEAD>
<BODY>
<B>Test page of default JavaScript call</B>
</BODY>
</HTML>
```

The onLoad function appears to be an exception to what seems to be the rule. In this case, the function onLoad is called not by a user-triggered event but by the event of the document itself loading into the browser. In this instance, the alert dialog will again display immediately upon the loading of the page, as shown in Figure 2.2, even though it isn't called directly. Listing 2.3 demonstrates the function opendoc(), called by the document itself after its Load event. You will have the same results in both of the examples that follow, but they have been achieved through two scripting methodologies.

FIGURE 2.2.

The alert dialog called directly from JavaScript.

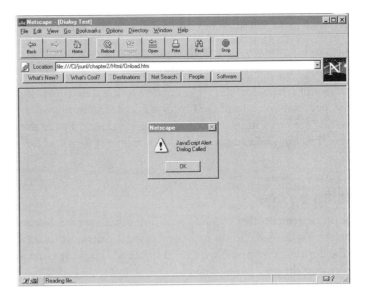

Listing 2.3. Calling to display the alert dialog onLoad.

```
<!DOCTYPE HTML PUBLIC "-//W3C//DTD HTML 3.2//EN">
<HTML>
```

```
<HEAD>
<TITLE>Dialog from onLoad</TITLE>
<SCRIPT LANGUAGE="JavaScript1.2">
<!--
function opendoc()
{
alert("Dialog called ")
}
// -->
</SCRIPT>
</HEAD>
<BODY onLoad="opendoc()">
<B>Test page of onLoad JavaScript call</B>
</BODY>
</HTML>
```

User Action

The second process by which JavaScript statements are executed is through function calls. Any statement contained within a function won't be executed until a JavaScript event calls the function. JavaScript events can be triggered in numerous ways on an HTML page, including user action and explicit event calls from within the script itself. User actions on your document might trigger JavaScript events in many instances when you're unaware that they could happen. Be sure to fully test your JavaScript statements to be sure that user interaction with your page doesn't cause unnecessary or unwanted events to occur.

Chapter 10, "Handling Events," provides a more detailed explanation of JavaScript events and how they're implemented and incorporated into your HTML.

In Listing 2.4, the dialog appears when the pushbutton is clicked.

Listing 2.4. Calling a function to display the alert dialog.

```
<!DOCTYPE HTML PUBLIC "-//W3C//DTD HTML 3.2//EN">
<HTML>
<HEAD>
<TITLE>Dialog from function call</TITLE>
<SCRIPT LANGUAGE="JavaScript1.2">
<!--
function opendoc()
{
alert("Dialog called by Push Button")
}
// -->
</SCRIPT>
</HEAD>
<BODY>
<B>Test page of function called from Push Button</B>
<FORM METHOD="POST">
<P>
```

continues

Listing 2.4. continued

```
<INPUT TYPE="Button" NAME="BUTTON1" VALUE="PUSH" onclick="opendoc()">

</P>
</FORM>
</BODY>
</HTML>
```

Figure 2.3 shows the results of the function call.

FIGURE 2.3.

The alert dialog called from the submit *event handler.*

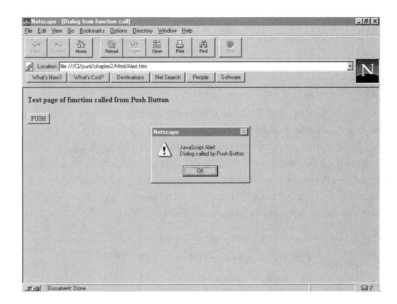

User actions or explicit event calls are the more frequent methods by which JavaScript is executed. One key advantage of JavaScript is that it can increase the amount of user interaction with your HTML document by providing you with a way to process and evaluate user input in a timely manner.

Accommodating Unsupported Browsers

The quick pace of changes in HTML and JavaScript makes it necessary to be wary of browsers that don't support the documents you're creating. Not all browsers will be current with the newest HTML enhancements, and you, as the programmer, must make your documents as user-friendly as possible for all browsers and environments.

> **TIP**
>
> Testing your HTML and JavaScript in as many browser environments as possible will give your documents better stability and usability.

Although using JavaScript can allow you to provide HTML enhancements for your users, you must always remember that many older browsers might not be able to make full use of the JavaScript code you have written. By surrounding all statements that are inside the `<SCRIPT>` and `</SCRIPT>` tags with HTML comment tags, you will allow users with older browsers to still view your page but not process the JavaScript code. They won't get the full effect of your page, but at least they won't see unwanted text in the browser. Listing 2.5 shows how to hide JavaScript code from older browsers. Note the use of the following two HTML comment statements in Listing 2.5 and how they enclose the lines of JavaScript code:

```
<!-- hide your code from older browsers
// stop JavaScript code hiding -->
```

Listing 2.5. Hiding scripts from older browsers.

```
<!DOCTYPE HTML PUBLIC "-//W3C//DTD HTML 3.2//EN">
<HTML>
<HEAD>
<TITLE>Hide From Browser</TITLE>
<SCRIPT LANGUAGE="JavaScript1.2">
<!-- hide your code from older browsers
document.write("I can view JavaScript code")
// stop JavaScript code hiding -->
</HEAD>
<BODY">
</BODY>
</HTML>
```

The use of the JavaScript comments tag, `//`, in the last HTML comment line keeps JavaScript from interpreting this statement during processing. Without these comment markers, JavaScript will attempt to process the statement, and you will receive a JavaScript error upon evaluation.

Using Netscape HTML Enhancements

The ever-changing world of the Internet always has room to improve current technology. This holds true for Netscape and HTML.

Netscape continues to improve its Web browser to keep up with the changes to HTML standards. This section provides an overview of some of the new enhancements. However, to remain completely up-to-date on the newest additions and changes to HTML and Netscape, keep an eye on the sites listed next.

Because of the increasing interest in Java, JavaScript, and the user interactivity in HTML, developers are focusing quite a bit of their enhancement efforts in these areas. As a JavaScript programmer, you should stay aware of strategic changes to keep ahead of the game.

The issues surrounding the use of JavaScript with unsupported (not JavaScript-enabled) browsers applies also, in principle, to HTML and Netscape enhancements (discussed later in this chapter), and the use of older browsers. Netscape is watching the continuing stream of technological changes and releasing new versions to stay current. Keep in mind that not all browsers will be able to handle some of the newer tags, scripting, Java, and other enhancements. If your Web pages rely heavily on some of the new technology, it is wise to also provide a simpler version. Otherwise, users viewing your pages with older browsers will probably find your HTML documents of little or no use.

NOTE

The methodology for accommodating browsers that don't support JavaScript is similar to the methodology that you've probably seen on many Web sites that use frames. The user is given the option of loading the document with or without frames. Functionality may be lost without frames, but at least the document can be viewed.

An Overview of HTML 3.2 and Netscape Enhancements

The enhancements that are outside of JavaScript are worth noting, because they will give your JavaScript development some added functionality. There are both enhancements to HTML (as defined in the current HTML 3.2 document) and ongoing enhancements to Netscape. Netscape introduced significant amounts of new functionality in Netscape 3.0 and more new features in Netscape 4.0 (Communicator).

Netscape Enhancements

A new feature of Netscape puts much more power behind JavaScript and HTML development. JavaScript evaluation allows your HTML documents to become more dynamic. You can now define the attributes of the right side of an HTML object to be JavaScript expressions or function calls. Information from one tag or a function calculation can drive the attributes of another tag.

Listing 2.6 demonstrates using JavaScript evaluation to change the width of an image based on the current time in seconds.

Listing 2.6. JavaScript evaluation.

```
<!DOCTYPE HTML PUBLIC "-//W3C//DTD HTML 3.2//EN">
<HTML>
<HEAD>
<TITLE>Javascript Evaluation Test</TITLE>
</HEAD>
<SCRIPT LANGUAGE="JavaScript1.2">
<!--
function getSeconds()
{
        var temp = new Date();
        return(temp.getSeconds());
}
//-->
</SCRIPT>
<BODY>
<IMG SRC="mypict.gif" HEIGHT="36" WIDTH="&{getSeconds() * 10};">
</BODY>
</HTML>
```

Additional non-JavaScript–specific enhancements won't directly affect your JavaScript development but will increase your overall development capabilities with Netscape. Netscape 3.0 has added the following capabilities:

- Better image control: You can change GIF and JPEG images automatically, either at specified intervals or with user input from a button.

- Enhanced image capabilities: You can select an image in an HTML document (with a right-click) and make it a Windows desktop wallpaper.

- Enhanced plug-in capabilities: You can detect plug-ins for a page and react correctly to them. If the correct plug-ins are not detected, you can make plug-in substitutions to keep the look of the page as designed.

- Increased performance of JavaScript scripts.

- Reduced JavaScript memory usage.

Netscape 4.0 adds more new HTML functionality, which will be discussed in later chapters. The two most important pieces of new functionality are these:

- Layers allow objects in an HTML document to be stacked on top of each other. These layers may be transparent or opaque, and they can be used in page animation. With the addition of JavaScript, layers become more dynamic and can be controlled with very little JavaScript code. See Chapter 17, "Controlling Layers with JavaScript," for more information.

- Style sheets give HTML authors better control over the presentation and layout of the HTML document. See Chapter 18, "JavaScript Style Sheets," for more information.

HTML Enhancements

The current standard set for HTML is HTML 3.2. The previously written set of standards for HTML 3.0 is no longer being maintained and has been replaced by the new HTML 3.2 standards. The new standard incorporates the majority of HTML 3.0 features and adds other significant features. This document will continue to evolve as features are added and modified.

The following new text-related attributes enhance text formatting on HTML pages (see Figure 2.4 for in-document examples):

`<S>` strikes out text. Netscape version 2.0 also supported strikethrough text but used the `<STRIKE>` tag. Both the `<S>` and `<STRIKE>` tags are supported in Netscape browsers.

`<U>` underlines text.

`<BIG>` displays text in a larger font than normal.

`<SMALL>` displays text in a smaller font than normal.

`<SUB>` displays text as a subscript to the other text on the page. Subscript text appears in a smaller font than normal text.

`<SUP>` displays text as a superscript to the other text and uses a smaller font than normal text.

`<P>` defines paragraph breaks in the HTML document. (This tag doesn't require the corresponding `</P>`.)

`<DIV>` defines a logical division block in the body of the text. This tag has no formatting value except to end the previous paragraph tag. Nested `<DIV>` tags can organize the document. `<DIV>` takes a few attributes. The main one is the `Class`, which specifies the type of division block. You can use division blocks to put restrictions on certain sections of an HTML page.

The HTML 3.2 standard states that all HTML documents should begin with the `<!DOCTYPE>` tag. This standard was present in previous HTML versions but is becoming increasingly critical as HTML evolves. This tag helps browsers distinguish the version of HTML in which a document was created. Currently, it specifically differentiates the HTML 3.2 version from all others. This tag isn't required, but in the future it will help distinguish which version of HTML a document was written in. Here's an example:

```
<!DOCTYPE HTML PUBLIC "-//W3C//DTD HTML 3.2//EN">
```

`<FORM>` Enhancements

The `FORM` attribute of `ACTION` specifies the URL to which the document input is submitted. In the following code, the form input—that is, the file—is sent to www.acadians.com. (See the next section for more information on the `<INPUT>` type of file.) The `FORM` attribute of `ENCTYPE` gives the specifications for the MIME content type of encryption to use when sending file information as input.

```
<FORM ACTION="http://www.acadians.com"
METHOD=POST ENCTYPE="APPLICATION/X-WWW-FORM-URLENCODED">
Send this File to me:
<INPUT NAME="KimsFile" TYPE="FILE" VALUE=" MyFile">
<HR><HR>
<INPUT TYPE="SUBMIT" VALUE="Send File">
</FORM>
```

Figure 2.5 shows the use of `"FILE"` as an input type.

FIGURE 2.4.

New text features.

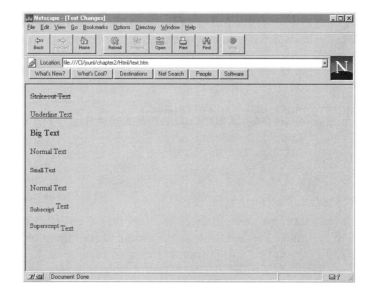

FIGURE 2.5.

Using `<ENCTYPE>` *and
an input of type*
`"FILE"`.

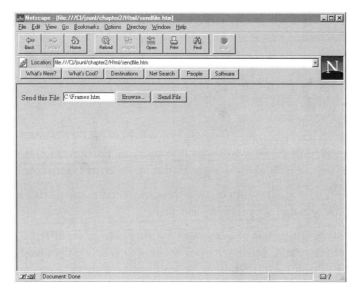

<INPUT> Type Additions and Enhancements

The new RANGE input type is displayed in the document as a slider bar. The start and end values of the slider are specified by the values defined in the MIN and MAX attributes. (RANGE is currently the only INPUT type to use MIN and MAX values.)

The SCRIBBLE input type is a graphical scratch pad. The scratch pad, or image onto which the user can scribble, is defined in the SRC attribute. This attribute is required for this input type to define the image. To accommodate browsers that don't support SCRIBBLE, be sure to put text in the VALUE attribute of the input. In browsers that don't support SCRIBBLE, HTML will display a text box with text from the VALUE attribute. (SCRIBBLE is not yet supported in Netscape 3.0.)

```
<!DOCTYPE HTML PUBLIC "-//W3C//DTD HTML 3.2//EN">
<HEAD>
<BODY>
<FORM>
<INPUT NAME="MyScribble" TYPE="SCRIBBLE"
SRC="C:\CSERVE\MOSIAC\CIM.GIF"  VALUE="no scribbling">
</FORM>
</BODY>
</HEAD>
```

The INPUT type of FILE lets the user enter a filename as Web page input. The ACCEPT attribute lets you specify file type restrictions and thus limit the file types that can be accepted.

SUBMIT and RESET have been enhanced to accept the SRC attribute in their tag definitions. SRC contains the name of an image file to use instead of the button object. The "image" button behaves the same as the "button" SUBMIT and RESET input types.

<INPUT> Attribute Enhancements

Several attributes that were added to the <INPUT> tag increase the flexibility the developers have when accepting user input.

DISABLED lets you disable the input element on the document. Enabling and disabling input fields through JavaScript opens up programming possibilities to make certain elements active only in specific instances. HTML 2.0 browsers ignore this attribute, and the element is displayed as usual.

ERROR lets you inform the user when the content of field is in error. The error "reason" is found in the VALUE of the error attribute. It's up to you, the programmer, to display the error reason to the user when an error is triggered during JavaScript execution.

The attributes of MIN and MAX define minimum and maximum values for the new RANGE input type (discussed in the preceding section).

The ALIGN attribute is now available for image object input types. These include SCRIBBLE, IMAGE, and SUBMIT, and RESET when SRC is used to define the image. This attribute allows you to align the image in relation to the surrounding text.

Frames

Frames are important development tools when you're writing JavaScript and HTML pages. Frames let you have multiple independent windows on your page that can interact with each other. JavaScript scripts can react to events in one frame and apply them in another frame. Frames expand the capabilities available to you as your HTML code and JavaScript become more complex.

As with browsers that don't support JavaScript, you must also allow for browsers that don't support frames. An important tag to remember when using frames in your JavaScript script is <NOFRAMES>. The tag pair of <NOFRAMES> and </NOFRAMES> goes inside your initial <FRAMESET> tag. You should place some descriptive text inside these tags to inform users that they won't be seeing the full effect of your Web document because their browsers don't support frames. The text inside these tags will display only if the browser doesn't support frames.

JavaScript lets you update certain "windows"—frames of your document based on input from other frames. This is possible because frames are completely independent, so the entire page doesn't have to change every time.

The following example uses a main document window, defined in Listing 2.7, and two separate frame documents, HTML pages defined in Listings 2.8 and 2.9. This is a basic example of how you can use JavaScript in conjunction with basic HTML when using frames. Clicking the Submit button in `frame2.htm` redisplays the number from the input text box in the result text box and also rebuilds the document in `frame1.htm` to include the input number.

Listing 2.7. `frames.htm`.

```
<HTML>
<HEAD>
<TITLE>Main Frame</TITLE>
<FRAMESET Rows="34%,*">
<FRAME SRC=FRAME1.HTM NAME="frame1" SCROLLING="yes">
<FRAME SRC=FRAME2.HTM NAME="frame2" SCROLLING="yes">
<NOFRAMES>
</NOFRAMES>
</FRAMESET>
</HEAD>
<BODY>
</BODY>
</HTML>
```

Listing 2.8. `frame1.htm`.

```
<HTML>
<HEAD>
<TITLE>Frame 1</TITLE>
</HEAD>
```

continues

Listing 2.8. continued

```
<BODY>
<B>This is the original text in Frame 1<B>
<P>
<B>It will be replaced on button click in frame #2 <B>
</BODY>
</HTML>
```

Listing 2.9. frame2.htm.

```
<HTML>
<HEAD>
<TITLE>Frame 3</TITLE>
<SCRIPT LANGUAGE="JavaScript1.2">
function printtoframe(form)
{
if (confirm("Do you want to update the top frame?"))
{
form.result.value = eval(form.input.value);
parent.frame1.document.open();
parent.frame1.document.open();
parent.frame1.document.write("<HTML>");
parent.frame1.document.write("<BODY>");
parent.frame1.document.write(eval(form.input.value));
parent.frame1.document.write("</BODY>");
parent.frame1.document.write("</HTML>");
parent.frame1.document.close();
}
else
alert("Please come back again")
}
</SCRIPT>
</HEAD>
<BODY>
<FORM>
Enter a number to evaluate:
<INPUT TYPE="text" NAME="input" SIZE=15>
<INPUT TYPE="submit" VALUE="pushbutton" ONCLICK="printtoframe(this.form)">
<BR>
Print it here again:
<BR>
<INPUT TYPE="text" NAME="result" SIZE=15>
<BR>
<B> And notice it has printed in frame above also <B>
</FORM>
</BODY>
</HTML>
```

Figures 2.6 and 2.7 show the changes.

FIGURE 2.6.

Before the button click.

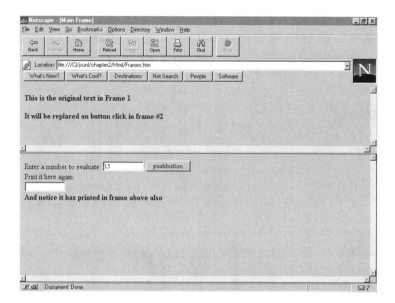

FIGURE 2.7.

After the button click.

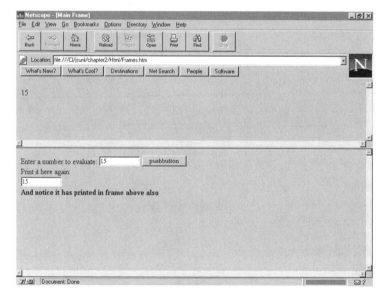

2

HOW JAVASCRIPT
AND HTML
WORK TOGETHER

Enhancements available in Netscape 3.0 (and, consequently, still available in Netscape 4.0) offer two areas of added functionality to frame design and frame navigation. Netscape improved the navigation capabilities within frames. The Netscape toolbar's Back button now functions more accurately in relation to frames. The Back button returns your document to the previous frame state, and the Forward button moves one frame state ahead. This behavior is similar to that of the Back and Forward buttons on pages, which are used to go back on page "state."

Another new feature is the addition of three attributes to both the FRAME and FRAMESET tags. These enhancements give you better control of your frame design. The FRAMEBORDER attribute lets you turn frame borders on and off, BORDER lets you specify the thickness of the border around your frames, and BORDERCOLOR lets you define the specific color of your border.

Tables

Tables are HTML objects that allow for the display of data in a table grid format. They are useful for displaying data gathered through JavaScript input or organizing sets of information. All attributes of the table tag itself are optional but can be useful in setting the size of the table. The table rows are defined separately, and, unlike the table tags, the table row (TR) and table header (TH) elements don't require end tags. Figure 2.8 displays a basic table in an HTML document.

FIGURE 2.8.

Using tables in HTML documents.

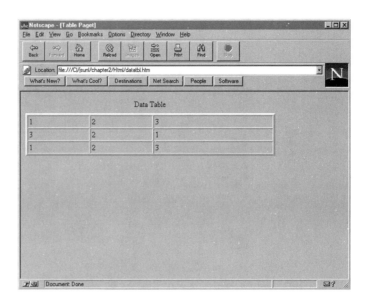

textarea

Often the simple text input type isn't sufficient for entering large amounts of text information, and using multiple text inputs isn't reasonable either. The input type textarea resolves these issues.

textarea expands on the text input field by allowing larger memo-like inputs of data on the page. textarea takes the attributes of ROWS and COLS to determine row and column size, as well as the WORDWRAP attribute to indicate whether the lines wrap.

New to HTML 3.0 were the DISABLED and ERROR attributes for textarea, which were implemented in a previous version of HTML as FORM input objects. textarea now also provides the

ALIGN attribute. Because textarea is implemented as an image, HTML 3.0 (and later) lets you use the ALIGN properties of top, middle, bottom, left, and right to align the textarea with surrounding text.

Creating a JavaScript Script

The basics behind creating JavaScript scripts are simple. Create your basic HTML page or edit an existing one using your favorite HTML authoring tool, and then insert your script tags in the <HEAD> section. Listing 2.10 shows a basic page that you can start from. Note the normal HTML tags with the script tags defined in the HEAD section of the document.

Listing 2.10. A basic JavaScript document.

```
<!DOCTYPE HTML PUBLIC "-//W3C//DTD HTML 3.2//EN">
<HTML>
<HEAD>
<TITLE>My first HTML page</TITLE>
<SCRIPT LANGUAGE="JavaScript1.2">
</SCRIPT>
</HEAD>
<BODY>
</BODY>
</HTML>
```

The beginning <SCRIPT> tag should include the LANGUAGE attribute to specify that the script enclosed in the tags is in fact JavaScript.

Writing the Script

As with any other programming language, JavaScript statements can be implemented using various methodologies. I have found that the practice of defining JavaScript functions in the <HEAD> section and then calling these functions within the HTML body is the best way to take advantage of the object-based JavaScript language.

The JavaScript language itself isn't difficult, and for developers with an object-based background, the hurdles are fewer. Once you grasp the concepts of object-based development, the creation of JavaScript functions becomes fairly straightforward. Note the following example:

```
document.write("I can view JavaScript code")
```

In plain English, this statement says, "On my document, write the following text."

> **NOTE**
>
> Although HTML statements aren't case-sensitive, JavaScript statements are.

When beginning to write your code, keep the following items in mind:

- Code reuse
- Readability
- Ease of modification

You can use JavaScript tags in either the body or the head of a document. As I mentioned earlier, placing the <SCRIPT> tag in the head rather than the body ensures that all statements will be evaluated (and executed, if necessary) before the user interacts with the document. The hazards of putting script statements in the body of the document are varied. Depending on the specific tags and the order of the document, you can never be positive that the user will interact with the script in the correct manner or will react to the page before the script has fully loaded or executed. If either of these situations occurs, the effect that you want for your page might not be seen. (After all your effort, who wants that?)

The practice of defining your JavaScript functions and then calling them from the body will ensure that all the functions are evaluated before the user can begin interacting with the page. Listing 2.11 shows an example of this practice, and Listing 2.12 shows the alternative.

Listing 2.11. Calling from a function.

```
<!DOCTYPE HTML PUBLIC "-//W3C//DTD HTML 3.2//EN">
<HTML>
<HEAD>
<TITLE>Page with Pushbutton</TITLE>
<SCRIPT LANGUAGE="JavaScript1.2">
<!--
function pushbutton() {
alert("pushed")
}
// -->
</SCRIPT>
</HEAD>
<BODY>
<FORM>
<INPUT TYPE="SUBMIT" NAME="BUTTON1" VALUE="PUSH" onclick="pushbutton">
</FORM>
</BODY>
</HTML>
```

Listing 2.12. Putting script directly in onclick.

```
<!DOCTYPE HTML PUBLIC "-//W3C//DTD HTML 3.2//EN">
<HTML>
<HEAD>
<TITLE>Page with Pushbutton</TITLE>
</HEAD>
<BODY>
<FORM>
```

```
<INPUT TYPE="SUBMIT" NAME="BUTTON1" VALUE="PUSH" onclick="alert("pushed")">
</FORM>
</BODY>
</HTML>
```

Listing 2.12 shows that it's possible to put JavaScript statements directly in your HTML tags. I can relate the drawbacks of this practice to the code-writing guidelines I mentioned earlier. Modifying and reusing the code in tags is difficult. You must search for the tag and then cut and paste the code. Only then can it be reused or redefined in a function call.

You also limit readability and ease of modification for both you and subsequent developers when you don't place your JavaScript statements in functions in the <HEAD> section. Endlessly searching for code that could have been easily segregated is tedious and unnecessary.

Styles are as important in JavaScript as they are in any programming language. Keeping your styles consistent, your variables defined, and your formatting neat will save future development time.

Creating your JavaScript scripts function by function, piece by piece, will help you build stable interactive documents that have the functionality you want. Because JavaScript is interpreted and not compiled, the debugging process is not always completely straightforward. Many issues, or bugs, won't be apparent until the document is rigorously tested. I recommend that someone other than the developer test the page to ensure that all situations are encountered when testing the document and integrated JavaScript. (You never know what checking a checkbox out of order might do to your script.)

Running the Script

As you've probably realized, JavaScript scripts are as simple to load as HTML documents. You don't have to explicitly execute any code to run your scripts. Because you place your code in the HTML document or call it explicitly in the first script line, your script will run when the page loads. Remember that not all the code will necessarily execute immediately upon loading. Code that is enclosed in a function call is evaluated only when the page loads but doesn't execute until the function is explicitly called from a JavaScript event. Code that isn't enclosed in a function call runs after the page finishes loading but before the user has a chance to interact with the page.

Summary

It is apparent that although JavaScript is a scripting language separate from HTML, the two are very closely integrated when it comes to full-scale document design, development, and implementation. JavaScript can be written directly into HTML, expanding the current capabilities of your Web documents. It is also viewable and loadable right along with the HTML.

The enhancements that are continuously arising in HTML itself, as well as Netscape- and Microsoft-specific enhancements such as frames, tables, and input options, make it possible to add more functionality to your JavaScript code. By using these features, you can expand your documents to make them more interactive and user-friendly.

Assembling Your JavaScript Toolkit

CHAPTER 3

IN THIS CHAPTER

Like any development language, JavaScript requires a development environment in which to work. Java sports Symantec's Visual Café as one example of an integrated development environment (IDE), but JavaScript doesn't have any IDEs specifically available for it. Nonetheless, with the plethora of Web tools, you can create a toolkit that works for you. In this chapter, I examine the various tools that you can add to your toolkit for client-side JavaScript development. I'll close the chapter by looking at two products that you can use for developing server-side JavaScript applications.

An Overview of Necessary Tools

To be productive as a developer, you need to assemble a group of tools that you are comfortable working with. If you're developing Windows applications in Delphi, Visual Basic, or PowerBuilder, for example, your Windows toolkit probably is relatively small, because these visual tools contain nearly everything you need out of the box. The same definitely can't be said of JavaScript. As a result, you need to work with the following principal tools to build a development environment:

- A JavaScript editor for writing JavaScript scripts
- An HTML editor for HTML page development
- A Web browser for testing your JavaScript scripts and applications

NOTE

If you're using Microsoft's JScript, you can use its Script Debugger to debug your scripts. However, the Script Debugger operates only within Microsoft Internet Explorer and, hence, only with JScript. See Chapter 22, "Error Handling and Debugging in JavaScript," for additional information on the Script Debugger.

JavaScript Editors

Choosing an editor is often a very personal choice for a software developer, much like choosing a bat is for a baseball player. Although no one can really recommend what's best for you, I'll offer some information to assist in your selection process by outlining three tool options for writing JavaScript code: text editors, HTML editors, and JavaScript-specific editors.

Text Editors

Because JavaScript code is contained within HTML pages, all you really need in order to develop with JavaScript is a text editor. In Windows, you can use WordPad, shown in Figure 3.1, or Notepad, shown in Figure 3.2. In UNIX, you can use emacs or vi. The advantage of using an ordinary text editor is that you probably already have the software installed on your computer. However, the disadvantage is that it offers no features to facilitate learning the JavaScript language or to enhance your productivity (for example, code libraries or wizards).

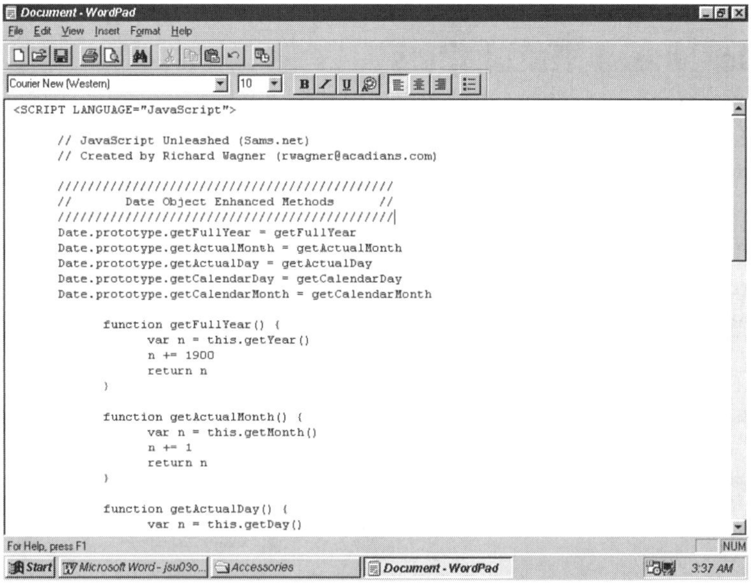

FIGURE 3.1.
You can use WordPad as a JavaScript editor.

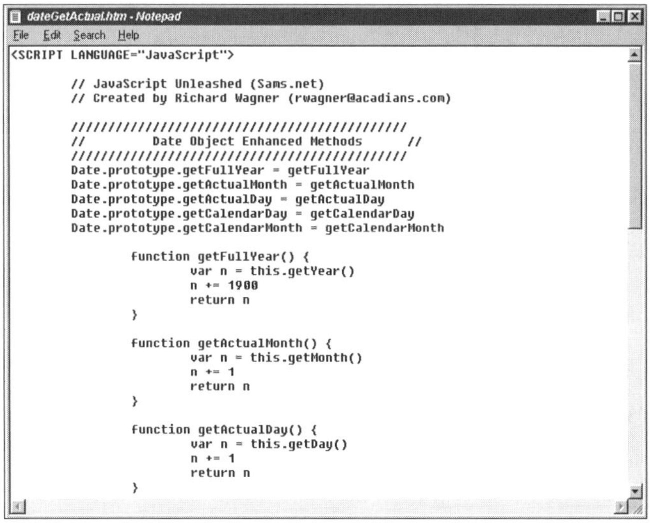

FIGURE 3.2.
Notepad is an even more rudimentary editor for JavaScript development.

3
ASSEMBLING YOUR JAVASCRIPT TOOLKIT

As you consider the various options before you decide, look at what features are available in the editor. For example, you will find search-and-replace commands critical once you start doing any serious JavaScript programming. This feature alone makes the Windows 95 WordPad a much more attractive option than Notepad.

Text-Based HTML Editors

Any text-based HTML editor also lets you develop code in its environment. Third-party HTML editors such as Allaire HomeSite are starting to provide limited support for JavaScript development.

What makes an HTML editor (see Figure 3.3) a better option than a plain-text editor is that you often work with HTML page design as you work on JavaScript programming tasks. A single environment eliminates the need to deal with multiple software packages. Additionally, many of these editors also let you integrate with a Web browser for testing—something WordPad and Notepad don't allow.

FIGURE 3.3.

Editing HTML source code in the HotDog editor.

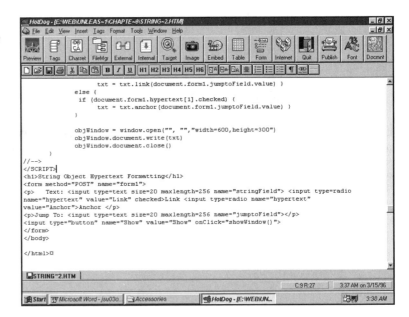

RESOURCE

You can find Allaire HomeSite at `http://www.allaire.com`. WebEdit is located at `http://www.nesbitt.com`. You can find HotDog at `http://www.sausage.com`.

JavaScript-Specific Editors

The final category of editor is one that is specifically devoted to JavaScript script development. Acadia Infuse, developed by Acadia Software, is the first visual editor on the market for JavaScript developers. Some of its features include the following:

- Drag-and-drop text editing
- Drag-and-drop HTML tags
- Drag-and-drop JavaScript object methods and properties
- Visual JavaScript object model
- Syntax highlighting for JavaScript keywords and HTML tags
- Search-and-replace functionality
- Integration with multiple browsers for testing and debugging

NOTE

A trial version of Acadia Infuse is included on the CD. You can also find it on the Acadia Software Web site at `http://www.acadians.com`.

Infuse is not necessarily intended as a replacement for an HTML text editor; it's designed to work in concert with one.

RESOURCE

The Acadia Infuse home page can be found at `http://www.acadians.com/infuse`.

Figure 3.4 shows the Infuse user interface and highlights its capabilities.

NOTE

Chapter 4 devotes an entire chapter to creating JavaScript scripts with Acadia Infuse.

FIGURE 3.4.

Editing JavaScript code using Infuse.

HTML Editors

Lest you forget the nature of the environment you're working in, a second tool you need to add to the toolkit is an HTML editor. The purpose of this tool is not so much to develop JavaScript scripts but to design the HTML pages to which you can later add your JavaScript code. The two types of HTML editors on the market are text and visual. Depending on your tastes and needs, you may use one or both.

Text-Based HTML Editors

As discussed earlier in this chapter, text-based HTML editors provide an environment that lets you work with HTML tags. As shown in Figure 3.5, a text-based HTML editor doesn't try to hide the messy details of HTML tags. Instead, it provides a suite of features supporting HTML development that make it more productive than a plain text editor.

Visual HTML Editors

A second type of HTML editor is one that hides the hypertext formatting language from the page creator by providing a visual (or WYSIWYG) environment that generates HTML code behind the scenes. Therefore, page creation is performed in a point-and-click environment, as you would expect in this graphically based computer world.

FIGURE 3.5.

HomeSite is a text-based editor.

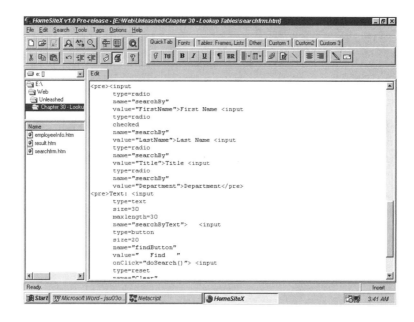

Netscape has a visual HTML editor called Composer, which is built into its Netscape Communicator product. Composer lets you easily edit HTML documents within an integrated browser environment, as shown in Figure 3.6. Although Composer's visual environment lets you work with basic HTML page layout, it doesn't provide sufficient power to visually work with multiframe windows, tables, and so forth.

FIGURE 3.6.

Netscape Composer.

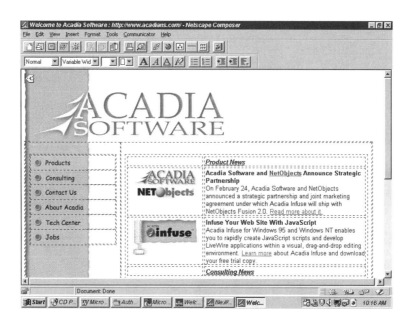

RESOURCE

Check the Netscape home page at `http://home.netscape.com` for the latest build of Netscape Composer.

Microsoft FrontPage, shown in Figure 3.7, is a more sophisticated option. It includes one of the best visual HTML editors available. Not only does the FrontPage Editor support enhanced options (such as framesets and tables), but it also includes an expanded set of templates to speed up the process of developing a Web page.

FIGURE 3.7.

Creating HTML pages visually using Microsoft FrontPage.

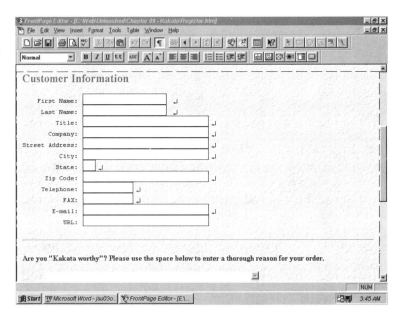

FrontPage is more than just an editor, however. The three tools included with it—FrontPage Explorer, FrontPage Editor, and To Do List—let you build and administer a Web site. It also comes with a personal Web server that lets you create a test Web site on your computer.

RESOURCE

Check the Microsoft home page at `http://www.microsoft.com` for the latest information on FrontPage.

A current disadvantage of visual HTML editors is their inability to let you go into a text-based mode and edit raw HTML. For both Composer and FrontPage, you need an external editor to do that. Additionally, both of these editors hardly know what to do with JavaScript code, so don't even think of using either of these tools as a JavaScript editing environment. Nonetheless, when used in combination with an editor such as Infuse, these tools provide a quick head start to developing sophisticated Web pages.

> **CAUTION**
>
> If you intend to use FrontPage 1.1, be sure to surround all your code with HTML comment tags (`<!--` and `-->`). (I recommend putting them just inside your `<SCRIPT>` and `</SCRIPT>` tags.) FrontPage 1.1 doesn't support the `<SCRIPT>` tag and will treat your code as if it were normal text. FrontPage 97, however, does recognize `<SCRIPT>` tags.

Web Browsers

The final component that you need to have is a Web browser that supports JavaScript, as shown in Figure 3.8. Chapter 1, "JavaScript and the World Wide Web," discussed the various Web browsers and their support for JavaScript, so I won't dive into that discussion here. However, because various versions of browsers provide different levels of JavaScript language support, you probably need to have many of these available during your testing phase.

FIGURE 3.8.
The quintessential JavaScript-enabled browser.

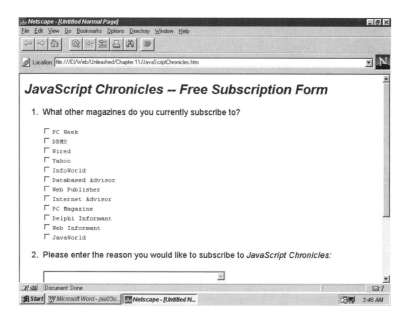

The basic rule of thumb is to test your script using all the possible types of browsers that will access the page. For intranet applications, you might have but a single browser to test, but for public Internet applications, you need to consider that the following browsers might access your JavaScript-enabled site:

- The latest Netscape Navigator (4.0 or above)
- An earlier Netscape Navigator (2.0)
- The latest Microsoft Internet Explorer (4.0 or above)
- A browser that doesn't support JavaScript

Your JavaScript application doesn't necessarily have to support all browsers. For example, you might need to use a JavaScript feature that was added in Netscape Navigator 4.0 and then require that version of the browser (or a later one). However, having previous versions available for testing can be invaluable to providing the best application environment possible.

> **TIP**
>
> Because Netscape Navigator and Microsoft Internet Explorer are emerging as the most popular Web browsers, you'll probably find it helpful to regularly test your code in both of these browser environments. Infuse allows quick access to both of these browsers within its editing environment.

The JavaScript Development Process

Once you have your toolkit elements, you need to assemble them into a workable development environment. Before you perform this process, it's helpful to understand how the JavaScript application development process is often structured. Figure 3.9 shows a typical scenario, in which basic HTML page creation is followed by adding JavaScript code to the HTML document. The page is then tested iteratively in the Web browser of choice.

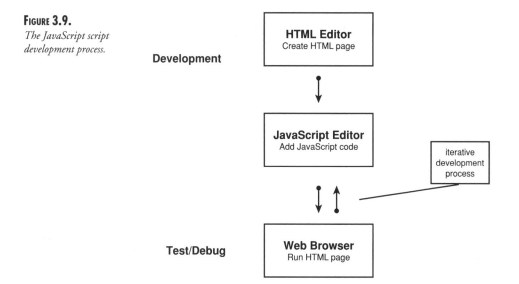

FIGURE 3.9.
The JavaScript script development process.

Server-Side JavaScript Tools

JavaScript is featured as the scripting language for two server-side Web development tools—Netscape LiveWire and Borland IntraBuilder. This section provides a brief overview of these tools.

Netscape LiveWire

LiveWire (and the enhanced LiveWire Pro) is a suite of tools that work with a Netscape server to help you administer a Web site. LiveWire includes JavaScript as a native scripting language and provides some server-side language extensions for file and database access. You can use server-side JavaScript to develop custom scripts that run on the Netscape server, eliminating the need for CGI in your applications.

RESOURCE

Check the Netscape home page at `http://home.netscape.com` for the latest information on LiveWire.

NOTE

LiveWire is in the process of becoming incorporated into Netscape Enterprise Server 3.0 and will eventually not be considered a product separate from the Web server. However, the same capabilities will still be available.

Borland IntraBuilder

Borland's IntraBuilder is a Windows-based visual development environment designed to let you create, maintain, and administer Web database applications. If you've ever worked with a Windows visual development tool, you will feel at home with IntraBuilder.

RESOURCE

Check the Borland home page at http://www.borland.com for the latest technical and support information on IntraBuilder.

IntraBuilder's programming language is an extended version of JavaScript that supports true object orientation (including inheritance) and database-related objects. Figure 3.10 shows the IntraBuilder integrated development environment (IDE). If you have used Borland's Visual dBASE, you will find that IntraBuilder has a similar look and feel.

FIGURE 3.10.

Creating Web applications using IntraBuilder.

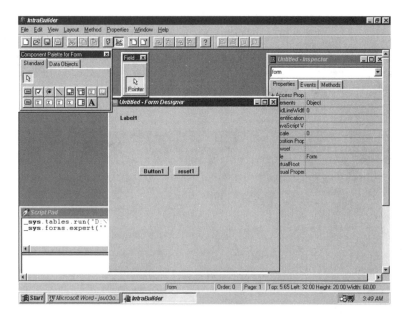

Summary

Because JavaScript is so new in the marketplace, there are no all-in-one solutions for developing client-side JavaScript applications. As a result, you are constrained to working with a host of tools that can be combined to provide a comprehensive development platform. This chapter examined the basic building blocks needed by a JavaScript programmer: a JavaScript editor, HTML editor, and Web browser. I also introduced you to two server-side products—Netscape LiveWire and Borland IntraBuilder—that feature JavaScript as their native programming language.

Using Acadia
Infuse to Create
JavaScript Scripts

IN THIS CHAPTER

CHAPTER 4

The struggles many Web developers encounter in using JavaScript have been due in part to the lack of tools available to them. Fortunately, as the technology matures, so too will the developer tools market. At the time this book was written, only one product on the market focused specifically on the JavaScript developer: Acadia Infuse. In this chapter, we will look at how you can use Infuse as an environment to create JavaScript scripts. The major topics covered include the following:

- A step-by-step guide to working with Infuse
- Additional features
- Customizing Infuse

NOTE

A trial version of Acadia Infuse 1.0 is located on the CD. Be sure to install it before continuing with this chapter.

Also, be sure to check the Acadia Infuse home page at `http://www.acadians.com/infuse` for the latest information on a new 1.1 release of Infuse, which will support JavaScript 1.2 enhancements.

A Step-by-Step Guide to Infuse

In this section, you will go through a step-by-step tutorial for Infuse, shown in Figure 4.1. Not only will this help you get to know how to use Infuse, but you will also get an idea of how to develop JavaScript scripts.

Before you begin the exercise, I will briefly introduce Infuse's visual trees. The three visual trees shown at the bottom-left quadrant of the Infuse window are, in many ways, the heart of Infuse. The first tree, called the JavaScript Object Tree (see Figure 4.2), serves several purposes for the JavaScript developer:

- Use it as a reference tool to locate the desired object, method, or property you need to use.
- Use it as a reference tool to see the interrelationships of the objects in the JavaScript object hierarchy.
- Drag and drop an object or one of its methods or properties into your code.
- Instantiate an object in your code.
- View context-sensitive Help on each object, property, or method.

FIGURE 4.1.

Acadia Infuse.

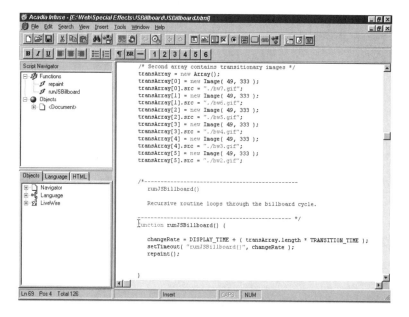

FIGURE 4.2.

JavaScript Object Tree.

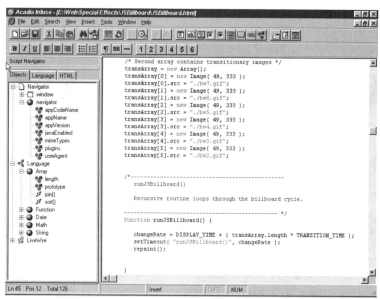

The second tree is the JavaScript Language Tree, shown in Figure 4.3, which provides access to JavaScript statements, operators, reserved words, and other language constructs. Using the JavaScript Language Tree, you can drag and drop language elements into your source document.

FIGURE 4.3.

JavaScript Language Tree.

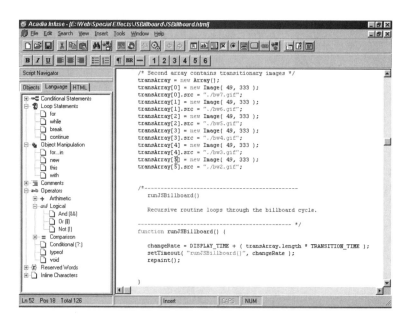

To illustrate how to use these and other Infuse capabilities, let's create a simple scripting page that allows a user to enter text using the INPUT element and then gives him the option of displaying the string in a variety of places.

TIP

Infuse integrates the official *Netscape JavaScript Authoring Guide* into its JavaScript Object and Language Trees. To receive context-sensitive Help on a language element, right-click inside the JavaScript Object or Language Tree window to display a Help cursor. Next, click on any item you want to reference. Help will be displayed on that item in a popup window.

TIP

If you want to view the JavaScript object hierarchy without the properties and methods included, select View | JavaScript Object Model. This option displays a read-only toolbox window with a visual representation of the JavaScript object model.

Creating a New File

The first step in creating a JavaScript script is to create a new HTML source file. To do so, select File | New (or click the New button on the toolbar). In the New dialog box, shown in

Figure 4.4, you can select the template on which to base the new file. The template styles are as follows:

- `JavaScript.htm` provides a basic HTML shell with a `<SCRIPT>` tag defined in the `<HEAD>` element.

- `LiveWire.htm` provides a basic HTML shell for LiveWire developers and includes a `<SERVER>` tag in the `<HEAD>` element.

- `Default.js` provides a shell file for use as an external `.js` library file.

- `Default.htm` provides a shell file with basic `<HTML>`, `<HEAD>`, and `<BODY>` elements defined. A `<SCRIPT>` tag is not included.

- (Blank) provides a blank file.

FIGURE 4.4.

Creating a new source file.

For our purposes, choose the `JavaScript.htm` and click OK.

Before going any further, save the file by selecting File | Save.

TIP

You can customize the default file templates. For more information, see the section "Customizing File Templates" later in this chapter.

Creating a Form

Once the basic HTML page outline has been constructed, begin by adding a `<FORM>` element to the body of the page. You will use this form as the container for our user interface elements: a Text element and a Select element. You can add a Form element using Infuse in one of two ways:

- The Form Object dialog box: You can create a form using the Form Object dialog box. To do so, first position your text cursor within the `<BODY>` tag and then click the Form object button from the Standard toolbar. The Form Object dialog box is displayed, as shown in Figure 4.5. Enter `exampleForm` in the Name box, and click OK. (You can ignore the other parameters for this example.)

FIGURE 4.5.

*The Form Object
dialog box.*

TIP

If you don't know which Toolbar button to click, hold the mouse over the buttons to display
a Hint denoting the purpose of the selected button.

■ Drag-and-drop: You can also define a Form object by using the JavaScript Object
Tree. You can instantiate certain JavaScript objects, such as a form, by pressing the
Ctrl key while performing a drag-and-drop action into your source document.

To do so, use the mouse to find the Form object in the JavaScript object model.
(Click the Navigator tree node, click the window object, and click the document
object. You will then see the form object.) While holding the Ctrl key, select the
Form icon with the mouse and then drag and drop the form into your code. Infuse
will insert a form "template" for you to modify, as shown here:

```
<FORM NAME="form1" TARGET="" ACTION="GET¦POST" onSubmit="">
```

NOTE

When defining objects, be sure you hold down the Ctrl key while you perform the drag-
and-drop operation. Otherwise, a dot notation reference to a form (document.form) will be
inserted rather than the <FORM> element.

Adding Text and Select Elements

The next step is to add the Text and Select elements to the form to receive user input. Within
the <FORM> tag, define the Text element using the dialog box, using drag-and-drop, or by just
entering text manually. Name the Text element userText.

Below the Text element, add a Select element. The dialog box option is preferable to use in this case because it lets you define the options at the same time, as shown in Figure 4.6. Add three options: (Select One), Message Box, Window, and Status Bar.

FIGURE 4.6.
*The Select Object
dialog box.*

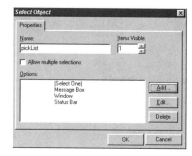

Within the <SELECT> element definition, you will want to add an onChange event handler to respond when the user selects an option from the list. (See Chapter 10, "Handling Events," for a complete discussion on event handlers.) To do that, add a new parameter to <SELECT>:

```
onChange="doAction()"
```

onChange is an event for a Select object, and doAction() is a function we will define shortly to respond to this event. After you add the event handler code, your <SELECT> element should look like this:

```
<SELECT NAME="pickList"
        SIZE=1
        onChange="doAction()">
        <OPTION>(Select One)
        <OPTION>Message Box
        <OPTION>Window
        <OPTION>Status Bar
</SELECT>
```

We have defined the basic user interface controls, but we should also add some descriptive text and formatting so that your form looks like the following:

```
<FORM NAME="exampleForm">

    <I>Enter Text Here: </I><BR>
    <INPUT TYPE="text" LENGTH=150 MAXLENGTH=150 NAME="userText">
    <BR>
    <BR>

    <I>Select Display Option:</I><BR>

    <SELECT NAME="pickList"
        SIZE=1
        onChange="doAction()">
        <OPTION>(Select One)
        <OPTION>Message Box
        <OPTION>Window
```

4

USING ACADIA
INFUSE

```
        <OPTION>Status Bar
    </SELECT>

</FORM>
```

TIP

To add basic HTML formatting tags to your source file, you can use the HTML toolbar. For example, to italicize the "Enter Text Here" label, select the text with the mouse and then click the Italics button on the toolbar. The HTML tags will be placed before and after the text you selected.

You can also insert HTML tags using two alternative methods:

- Use the HTML Tag Tree to drag-and-drop HTML tags into your source document.

- Use the HTML formatting menu commands found on the Insert menu. To use them, select the text you want to tag and then choose the desired menu command.

Responding to the User Event

The next step is to write a script that responds to the user's selection. To do so, you can define a function called doAction(). Enter the following code within the <SCRIPT> element:

```
function doAction() {

    var displayText = document.exampleForm.userText.value;
    var idx = document.exampleForm.pickList.selectedIndex;

    if ( idx == 0 ) return;
    else if ( idx == 1 ) showMessageBox( displayText );
    else if ( idx == 2 ) showWindow( displayText );
    else if ( idx == 3 ) showStatusBar( displayText );

    document.exampleForm.pickList.selectedIndex = 0;

}
```

TIP

If you would like to see the syntax for the if...else statement, go to the Language Tree. Click on the Conditional Statements tree, and then drag and drop the if...else element into your code.

> **NOTE**
>
> Notice that the JavaScript keywords (such as `function`, `var`, and `if`) are differentiated as you type them in. This is known as *color syntax highlighting,* and you can customize it by selecting Tools | Preferences.

This `doAction()` function bears closer examination. The first variable, `displayText`, is used to represent the value of our text element, while the second variable, `idx`, denotes the index value of the option that is selected. We can then evaluate the `idx` value to determine the next course of action:

- If (`Select One`) is chosen, do nothing.
- If `Message Box` is chosen, execute a `showMessageBox()` function, which we will define shortly.
- If `Window` is chosen, run a function called `showWindow()`.
- If `Status Bar` is chosen, execute `showStatusBar()`.

Notice that the `displayText` variable is passed as a parameter to the functions. Finally, the function ends by resetting the Select list back to (`Select One`).

The `doAction()` function is the main event handler in your script, but it needs the three additional functions to carry out the task. First, enter the function "shell" of `showMessageBox` by typing the following (underneath the `doAction()` function):

```
function showMessageBox( displayText ) {


}
```

When called, `showMessageBox()` is supposed to display the `displayText` variable in a message box. To enter this code, position the text cursor within the function code block and click the Add Message box button on the Standard toolbar (the last button). In the Add Message Box dialog box, shown in Figure 4.7, select Alert from the Message Box group and enter `You entered:` in the Message Text box. Click OK.

An `alert()` method will be inserted into your function. We need to add the `displayText` variable to be displayed in the message text. However, suppose you would like to separate the `You entered:` text from the `displayText` by putting them on separate lines.

> **NOTE**
>
> See Chapter 10 for more information on how to use `alert()`.

FIGURE 4.7.

The Add Message Box dialog box.

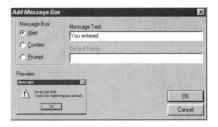

To add a carriage return and line-feed characters, go to the Language Tree and click the Inline Characters tree node to display the list of inline characters you can add to your code as variables. Drag and drop the New Line (CR/LF) item into your function definition. This defines the variable CRLF to serve as a newline character. The code should look like the following when you have finished:

```
function showMessageBox( displayText ) {

    var CRLF = "\r\n";
    alert( "You entered:" + CRLF + CRLF + displayText);

}
```

The next function to define is showWindow(), which is designed to display the text entered by the user in a separate window. Begin by entering the function code block, and then position the cursor within it. Click the Add Window open() method button on the Standard toolbar to display the dialog box shown in Figure 4.8.

FIGURE 4.8.

The Add Window open() *method dialog box.*

Within the dialog box, leave the URL blank, because we aren't connecting to another Web page. Select the desired window options in the Options group box, and click OK. (For this example, you may find it helpful to specify a small window size, such as Height=300 and Width=400.) Next, fill the rest of the function with three lines of code that insert text into the new window's document object:

```
function showWindow( displayText ) {

    newWindow = window.open( "", "JSExample", bar,menubar,scrollbars,resizable,
      status,height=300,width=400" );
    newWindow.document.open();
```

```
newWindow.document.write( displayText );
newWindow.document.close();

}
```

The final function we need to define is showStatusBar(), which places the user's text into the browser's status bar. This requires but a single line of code. We need to assign a value to the window object's status property. If you don't know the necessary syntax, you can locate the property in the JavaScript Object Tree. When you locate it, drag and drop the property into your function block and then assign it to equal the displayText variable:

```
function showStatusBar( displayText ) {

    window.status = displayText;

}
```

When you have finished, save your changes. Your source file should look like that shown in Listing 4.1.

4

USING ACADIA
INFUSE

Listing 4.1. `Stepbystep.hmtl`.

```html
<HTML>
<HEAD>
<SCRIPT LANGUAGE= "JavaScript">
<!--

    /*=========================================================================
                        Step-By-Step Example Script

                Description:
                    Displays text from a Text Input box in three different locations.

                Requirements:
                    JavaScript 1.0

                    Created By:
                        Richard Wagner, 1997

                    "Built With Acadia Infuse"
    =========================================================================*/

    /* Event handler for the Select object's onChange event */
    function doAction() {

        var displayText = document.exampleForm.userText.value;
        var idx = document.exampleForm.pickList.selectedIndex;

        if ( idx == 0 ) return;
        else if ( idx == 1 ) showMessageBox( displayText );
        else if ( idx == 2 ) showWindow( displayText );
        else if ( idx == 3 ) showStatusBar( displayText );

        document.exampleForm.pickList.selectedIndex = 0;

    }

    /* Displays text in an alert message box */
    function showMessageBox( displayText ) {

        var CRLF = "\r\n";
        alert( "You entered:" + CRLF + CRLF + displayText);

    }

    /* Displays text in a secondary window*/
    function showWindow( displayText ) {

        newWindow = window.open( "", "Example", "toolbar,menubar,scrollbars,
            resizable,status,height=300,width=400" );
        newWindow.document.open();
        newWindow.document.write( displayText );
        newWindow.document.close();

    }


    /* Displays text in the status bar of the browser */
```

```
        function showStatusBar( displayText ) {

            window.status = displayText;

        }

//-->
</SCRIPT>
</HEAD>
<BODY>
<FORM NAME="exampleForm">

    <I>Enter Text Here: </I><BR>
    <INPUT TYPE="text" LENGTH=150 MAXLENGTH=150 NAME="userText">
    <BR>
    <BR>

    <I>Select Display Option:</I><BR>

    <SELECT NAME="pickList"
        SIZE=1
        onChange="doAction()">
        <OPTION>(Select One)
        <OPTION>Message Box
        <OPTION>Window
        <OPTION>Status Line
    </SELECT>

</FORM>
</BODY>
</HTML>
```

TIP

In Figure 4.9, notice the Script Navigator in the top-left corner. This feature gives you a visual tree look at your source file and lets you quickly jump to a function or object by double-clicking it. Infuse will position the cursor at the spot of the function or object.

The Script Navigator automatically refreshes itself when you press Enter while editing the script. However, you can also manually refresh the Script Navigator by pressing F5 or selecting View | Refresh Script Navigator.

4

USING ACADIA
INFUSE

Previewing the Script

A key step in developing scripts is testing your scripts in a browser. Using Infuse, you can easily preview your script in Netscape Navigator and Microsoft Internet Explorer, but you can also add other browsers as desired.

FIGURE 4.9.

Script Navigator.

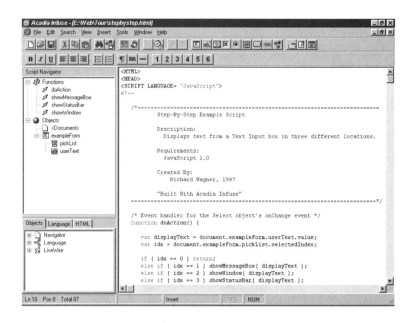

You can change the size of the preview window by selecting Tools | Preferences and then choosing the Preview tab.

If you have installed Netscape Navigator or Microsoft Internet Explorer, Infuse automatically looks for both browsers when it loads. If Infuse finds one or both of them, it activates the browser's Preview button on the toolbar. If you have Netscape Navigator installed, click the Netscape Navigator Preview button to load the source file in that browser.

Infuse looks for the latest version of Netscape Navigator and Microsoft Internet Explorer on your system and treats that as your default browser version. However, you will probably want to test under multiple versions of a browser. To add a browser, select Tools | Preferences and choose the Preview tab. You can then preview in the browser by selecting Tools | Preview, as shown in Figure 4.10.

Netscape Navigator loads your JavaScript script (see Figure 4.11), which you can then test. Try entering text in the text element, and then select each of the options. If you made a mistake entering code, you will probably see an error message. If that happens, return to Infuse, correct the mistake, save the results, and then preview the script again.

FIGURE 4.10.
The Preview dialog box.

FIGURE 4.11.
A script being run under Netscape Navigator.

NOTE

The process of debugging a script is typically an iterative process. You will probably jump back and forth between Infuse and your preview browser while you test code. Be sure to save changes in Infuse before previewing, or you won't preview the latest version of your script.

TIP

You remove the left window pane from Infuse by pressing F6 or selecting View | Full Preview. When you want to display the visual tree pane again, click F6 again.

Reusing Code with Frequent Scripts

A typical complaint of JavaScript developers is the inability to manage code reuse. You can use external .js files to serve as library files, but these are unsupported in Netscape Navigator 2.0 and Microsoft Internet Explorer 3.0. Infuse provides a utility called Frequent Scripts that lets you organize commonly used JavaScript and LiveWire code.

Inserting a Frequent Script into Your Source File

Infuse comes with 25 prebuilt JavaScript and LiveWire code snippets that you can use in your scripts. To insert a frequent script into your source document, position the text cursor in the appropriate place in your file and then click the Frequent Scripts button on the toolbar (or select Insert | Frequent Scripts). In the Frequent Scripts dialog box, shown in Figure 4.12, select the code snippet of your choice and click OK to paste the code into the current insertion point in the editor.

FIGURE 4.12.

The Frequent Scripts dialog box.

> **TIP**
>
> In an editor window, you can also select Insert Frequent Script from the popup menu to display the Frequent Scripts dialog box. Right-click to access the popup menu.

> **TIP**
>
> Frequent Scripts can be displayed in a descriptive view or code view. You can change the view by selecting Tools | Preferences and then choosing the General tab.

Adding a Frequent Script

In addition to using the prebuilt scripts, you can also use Frequent Scripts to reuse your own code. To add a routine to the Frequent Scripts library, highlight the code you want to add in the current source document and right-click to display the editor popup menu. Select the Add Frequent Script command to display the Add to Frequent Scripts dialog box, shown in Figure 4.13. Enter the information about your new script, and click OK.

FIGURE 4.13.

Adding a new frequent script.

Deleting a Frequent Script

Infuse 1.0 has no built-in support for deleting or editing frequent scripts. However, there are some workarounds to this limitation. Infuse stores frequent scripts in a text file called Fscript.dat, which is located in your main Infuse directory. You can manually work with this file to delete and edit existing scripts.

> **NOTE**
>
> Before you work with the Fscript.dat file, be sure to back it up first to prevent any accidental loss of data in case you make a mistake.

In Infuse or WordPad, locate the Fscript.dat file on your local drive and open it. Infuse treats each line as an individual record of each script, separating columns of information with tabs (see Figure 4.14).

To delete a script, locate the line on which it is defined and simply delete the entire line. Save changes and close the file. The next time you display the Frequent Scripts dialog box, your entry will be removed.

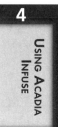

FIGURE 4.14.

Modifying the `Fscript.dat` *file.*

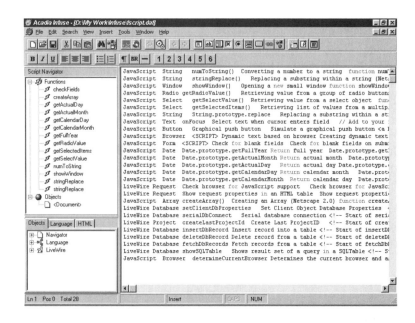

NOTE

Do not edit `Fscript.dat` using Notepad. Notepad has a limitation on line lengths and may force word wrapping. If you save the file in this state, you may cut off some of the frequent script definitions. Feel free to use WordPad as an alternative, but be sure to save the file in text format.

To modify an existing script, the best method is to insert the frequent script into a blank editor window in Infuse. Next, open `Fscript.dat` following the instructions just provided and delete the current entry. After you save changes and close the file, return to your script, make necessary changes to it, and re-add it as a new entry.

Customizing File Templates

As you learned earlier in this chapter, the New dialog box (see Figure 4.4) has file templates you can use when you create a new document. Although you can't add new templates in Infuse 1.0, you can customize the existing ones as you wish. To modify a template, locate the Templates subdirectory under your main Infuse directory. This folder contains the template files used in the New dialog box. To modify them, open them using Infuse or another editor, and customize. Be sure to save the results under the same filename.

Using Advanced Editor Options

To maximize your use of Infuse, you should be aware of several editor options. These options are discussed in the next sections.

Finding a Matching Brace

JavaScript uses braces ({}) to encapsulate portions of code, such as a complete function or the `if` and `else` portions of an `if..else` statement. Each opening brace ({) must have a matching end brace (}), or you will get a syntax error when you try to run the script. To determine a brace's match, select Search | Find Matching Brace (or click F4). Infuse will determine the appropriate match or tell you that there is none.

Setting a Bookmark

Infuse lets you set a bookmark anywhere in the current source window by choosing Search | Set Bookmark (see Figure 4.15). This action marks the current location. You can return to it by choosing Search | Find Bookmark. A bookmark remains in effect until you set a new bookmark or close the source file window.

FIGURE 4.15.
Setting a bookmark.

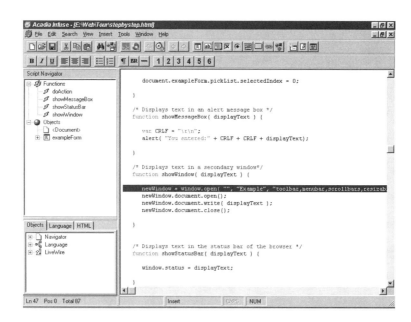

4

USING ACADIA
INFUSE

Jumping to a Line Number

You can jump to a specific line number in the current file by choosing Search | Goto Line. The Goto Line Number dialog box, shown in Figure 4.16, prompts you for the line number you want to find.

FIGURE 4.16.

Jumping to a line number in your script.

Summary

Acadia Infuse is the first editor that is devoted to creating JavaScript scripts and LiveWire applications. In this chapter, we covered the basics using Infuse to develop JavaScript scripts. We also explored some of its ancillary capabilities, such as Frequent Scripts and advanced editor options. With this as a background, you can use Infuse as you work through the rest of this book.

PART

The JavaScript Language

Fundamentals of the JavaScript Language

IN THIS CHAPTER

JavaScript is a high-level, object-based language designed to let Web authors and programmers easily create interactive Web documents. It offers the basic characteristics of an object-oriented language without the complicated features that accompany other languages such as Java and C++. JavaScript's relatively small vocabulary is easy to understand but gives way to a number of new possibilities that were previously unavailable. In this chapter, I briefly explain how JavaScript relates to two well-known Web technologies. I'll then give you the information you need to create your own JavaScript scripts.

How JavaScript Relates to CGI and Netscape Plug-Ins

You might wonder what JavaScript has to offer that using a CGI program or plug-in software doesn't. Semi-interactive Web pages were around long before JavaScript was born, thanks to CGI programs and plug-in software. I'll define these different technologies so that you can understand how JavaScript adds even more to your Web authoring toolbox.

CGI Programming

CGI (Common Gateway Interface) is the standard for the way programs interface with a Web server. Using a programming language such as Perl, C/C++, or AppleScript and complying with the CGI standard, you can create programs that pass information from the client to the Web server. For example, developers have created many search utilities using CGI to help you locate your favorite sites on the Web. Typically, the user enters a word or phrase into an HTML text element and clicks a Search button. Doing this submits the text and starts a CGI program on the server. The program searches through a master database, finding only the sites that match the search criteria. Once the CGI program is finished with the search, the program creates a new HTML document that includes a list of the results and sends it back to the user's Web browser. You'll notice that all the hard work is done by the server. If you were limited to static Web pages that had to be written ahead of time, you would have to consider every search combination possible. Creating a Web document for each query would be impractical—a ridiculous way to emulate the type of searching function that users are accustomed to. This is one problem that CGI has solved to help the Web become more interactive.

RESOURCE

For all the information you need about CGI or even links to premade CGI scripts, point your Web browser to `http://hoohoo.ncsa.uiuc.edu/cgi/overview.html`.

Netscape Plug-Ins

Clicking a Web link essentially tells the browser to download a file. If the file is a text, HTML, or graphic file, it is output to the display. If the browser doesn't recognize the file, it asks you to save the file locally (on your hard disk). Using plug-in extensions, Netscape has increased the number of files that it recognizes. Plug-ins are extra program modules that you can add to deal with files that Netscape was not originally designed to understand. Such files might include audio, animation, Acrobat, and VRML files. For example, if you click a link that points to a .WAV file, Netscape looks for a plug-in module that is configured to deal with .WAV files. If it finds one, Netscape starts the plug-in module and begins playing the audio clip for you. The integration of the browser and audio player is practically seamless.

> **RESOURCE**
>
> There are plenty of Netscape plug-ins to enhance your browsing experience. You can find a large list of them by pointing your Web browser to `http://home.netscape.com/comprod/products/navigator/version_2.0/plugins/index.html`.

JavaScript

What is unique about JavaScript is that you can use it to write programs that run on the server side (see Part V, "Programming Techniques") or on the client side within the browser. Suppose you have created an HTML document to collect data from people visiting a particular Web page. You could start out with a form that includes three text elements for their name, company, and telephone number. At the bottom of the form, you can include a standard submit button to send the visitor's information back to a database on your Web server. You also decide to require that each user complete every field and include the area code with their telephone number. After the user clicks the submit button, all the data in the form is passed to a CGI program for processing. If the CGI program notices that the user left out some information, you can have it respond with a new HTML document, asking for the required data to be re-entered. The user can then submit the form again with all the required data in the correct format. Once the CGI program is satisfied with what the visitor has typed, the program can continue by posting the data to the database. Handling required entries like these can add up to substantial delays, which are now avoidable with JavaScript. You can perform the data validation on the client side with JavaScript so that the Web server doesn't have to. Handling data validation is one example of how JavaScript can complement a CGI program by offering a quicker response to errors while freeing up more resources on the server. Chapter 10, "Handling Events," presents an in-depth look at data validation.

Embedding a Script in an HTML Document

You can implement JavaScript in one of two ways: either embedded in an HTML document between a set of <SCRIPT> tags, or inserted inside an HTML tag to respond to an event. Each time an HTML page is downloaded, JavaScript is interpreted by the client's browser. Depending on the actions of the user and other events that occur while the HTML document is being viewed, portions of the embedded script or scripts are executed.

Events

One of the key characteristics of JavaScript is its capability to catch a limited number of user actions, known to most programmers as *events*. Some HTML elements already react to events such as clicking the familiar link element that brings you to another HTML document. As you move the mouse pointer over the text or graphic that makes up the link, the pointer changes from an arrow to a small pointing hand. Some browsers also respond by displaying the destination URL in the status bar. JavaScript calls this the MouseOver event and reacts whenever you move the mouse pointer over the element. If you click any part of the link, the browser responds by sending you to a different location on the Web or opening a new file. This action is cleverly called the Click event, which is triggered whenever you click the link. HTML catches these events, and the browser always reacts the same way.

With JavaScript, you can now create custom reactions to many events that can occur while the user views an HTML document. Chapter 10 shows you how to handle events more in depth.

Basic Syntax Issues

JavaScript is embedded into HTML documents by means of a beginning and ending script tag. The browser starts by finding the first script tag:

```
<SCRIPT LANGUAGE="JavaScript">
```

It then reads everything that follows until the ending script tag:

```
</SCRIPT>
```

JavaScript translates each line of code into instructions to perform in the same way, for example, that you might follow directions to a seminar on JavaScript. Just as you would read each instruction and act on it by turning or driving your car in the appropriate direction, JavaScript follows each of your instructions in order. On your way to the seminar, you might need to stop at a red light until the signal turns green, or you might need to stop and pick up a friend. You can also emulate this with JavaScript if you want the computer to sit idle until something happens. Listing 5.1 shows how to embed JavaScript in the body section of an HTML document.

Listing 5.1. Embedding JavaScript inside an HTML document.

```
<HTML>
<HEAD>
<TITLE>JavaScript Unleashed</TITLE>
</HEAD>
<BODY>
<CENTER><H2>JavaScript brings the Web to life!</H2></CENTER>
<SCRIPT LANGUAGE = "JavaScript">
<!-- begin hiding from old browsers
document.write("Hello World Wide Web!")
// end hiding -->
</SCRIPT>
</BODY>
</HTML>
```

Figure 5.1 shows a basic HTML page that sets the title bar of your browser to "JavaScript Unleashed" and begins the page with the header "JavaScript brings the Web to life!" After the first script tag, you need to include HTML comment tags before and after the script. By surrounding the JavaScript code with these, you prevent it from showing up as plain text in older Web browsers that don't understand the `<SCRIPT>` tags.

FIGURE 5.1.

*A short sentence
displayed using
JavaScript.*

The keywords `document` and `write` are recognized by JavaScript and used together to perform an action. To be more specific, the `write()` method places the greeting onto the HTML document before it is viewed by the client's browser. An entire HTML page can be generated this way. You must use lowercase when typing the words `write` and `document`, because JavaScript is case-sensitive. If you accidentally capitalize any letters, JavaScript will simply display an error. Ideally, you should plan to test your scripts before letting others access them. That way, you can easily correct the mistake and reload the HTML document into your browser. The extra blank lines and indentation within the script don't have any effect because JavaScript ignores white space. Thoughtful use of white space provides for easy reading as your scripts become longer. The sentence "Hello World Wide Web!" within the parentheses could be any phrase you want to display, or the result of a calculation. The statement ends with a semicolon, which is not required. However, you could use a semicolon to separate statements that might need to appear on the same line. Otherwise, as long as you start a new line, JavaScript knows that you're starting a new set of statements.

Versions of JavaScript

As Netscape has been improving JavaScript, it has been releasing new versions of the language with its new versions of Netscape Navigator. This book covers up to JavaScript version 1.2. Netscape 2.0 through 2.02 and Microsoft Internet Explorer 3.0 implement JavaScript 1.0. Netscape Navigator 3.0 implements JavaScript 1.1. The Netscape Communicator package containing Navigator 4.0 implements JavaScript 1.2. As a JavaScript developer, you must know the platform you are targeting so that you can develop for the correct version of JavaScript. Once this is decided, you can specify the version you want to use with the LANGUAGE attribute of the SCRIPT tag. For example, if your application must run on Netscape Navigator versions 2.0 and above along with Microsoft Internet Explorer 3.0, you would choose to write scripts for JavaScript version 1.0. An example of how to specify JavaScript version 1.0 is shown in Listing 5.1. However, if your target platform is Netscape 4.0 and you would like to take advantage of its advanced features, you would use the following tag to activate version 1.2:

```
<SCRIPT LANGUAGE = "JavaScript1.2">
```

To specify version 1.1, use this:

```
<SCRIPT LANGUAGE = "JavaScript1.1">
```

To specify version 1.0, use this:

```
<SCRIPT LANGUAGE = "JavaScript">
```

> **NOTE**
>
> Do not try to use "JavaScript1.0" or "JavaScript1" as the language in order to specify version 1.0. These will not be recognized, and your script will be ignored.

Navigator 4.0 will use any version of JavaScript you specify up to version 1.2. Navigator 3.0 can use versions 1.1 or 1.0. If you specify a version of JavaScript that Navigator doesn't understand, Navigator ignores the entire script; it won't not try to use an earlier version of JavaScript. However, Navigator won't ignore any advanced features used by a program just because an older version is specified. So even if you specify JavaScript1.1, Navigator 4.0 will still allow you to use all the features that are available with JavaScript1.2. An exception to this rule is when you use equality operators, which is explained in Chapter 6, "Operators."

Tokens

Tokens are the smallest individual words, phrases, or characters that JavaScript can understand. When JavaScript is interpreted, the browser parses the script into these tokens while ignoring comments and white space. JavaScript tokens fall into five categories: identifiers, keywords, literals, operators, and separators. As with all computer languages, you have many ways to arrange these tokens to instruct a computer to perform a specific function. The *syntax* of a language is the set of rules and restrictions for the way you can combine tokens.

Identifiers

Identifiers are simply names that represent variables, methods, or objects. They consist of a combination of characters or a combination of characters and digits. Some names are already built into the JavaScript language and are therefore reserved (see the next section). Aside from these keywords, you can define your own creative and meaningful identifiers. Of course, there are a couple of rules to follow. You must begin all identifiers with either a letter or an underscore (_). You can then use letters, digits, or underscores for all subsequent characters. Letters include all uppercase characters, A through Z, and all lowercase characters, a through z. Digits include the characters 0 through 9. Table 5.1 shows some examples of valid and invalid identifiers.

Table 5.1. Examples of user-defined JavaScript identifiers.

Valid	*Invalid*
current_WebSite	current WebSite
numberOfHits	#ofIslands
n	2bOrNotToBe
N	return

5

FUNDAMENTALS OF THE JAVASCRIPT LANGUAGE

Notice that `current WebSite` is invalid because it contains a space. JavaScript tries to interpret this as two identifiers instead of one. If a space is needed, it is standard practice to use an underscore in its place. `#ofIslands` is invalid because the pound sign is not included in the set of characters that are valid for identifiers. `2bOrNotToBe` is not valid because it begins with a number. The `return` identifier is already used by JavaScript for another purpose. Attempting to use it as your own identifier would produce errors when you tried to run the script. Also, both n and N are valid identifiers, not to mention different from each other. JavaScript is case-sensitive and therefore considers identifiers with different case to be unique even though they might be spelled the same.

Keywords

Keywords are predefined identifiers that make up the core of a programming language. In JavaScript, they perform unique functions, such as declaring new variables and functions, making decisions based on the present state of the computer, or starting a repetitive loop inside your application. Keywords, which are built into JavaScript, are always available for use by the programmer but must follow the correct syntax. The keyword var is the first that I describe in detail later in this chapter. As you progress through this book, I'll show you how you can use other keywords to create more dynamic programs. The following list shows the available keywords:

break	if	this
continue	in	true
else	int	var
false	new	while
for	null	with
function	return	

JavaScript version 1.1 added the following keywords:

```
typeof
void
```

JavaScript version 1.2 adds the following keywords:

```
do
labeled
switch
while
```

Reserved Words

Reserved words are identifiers that you may not use as names for JavaScript variables, functions, objects, or methods. This includes keywords (described in the preceding section), along with identifiers that are set aside for possible future use. The following is a complete list of the reserved words for JavaScript:

abstract	else	int	super
boolean	extends	interface	switch

break	false	labeled	synchronized
byte	final	long	this
case	finally	native	throw
catch	float	new	throws
char	for	null	transient
class	function	package	true
const	goto	private	try
continue	if	protected	typeof
default	implements	public	var
delete	import	return	void
do	in	short	while
double	instanceof	static	with

Literals

Literals are data comprised of numbers or strings used to represent fixed values in JavaScript. They are values that don't change during the execution of your scripts. The following five sections describe the different types of literals you can use.

Integer Literals

Integers can be expressed in either decimal (base 10), octal (base 8), or hexadecimal (base 16) format. An integer literal in decimal format can include any sequence of digits that does not begin with a 0 (zero). A zero in front of an integer literal designates octal form. The integer itself can include a sequence of the digits 0 through 7. To designate hexadecimal, 0x (or 0X) is used before the integer. Hexadecimal integers can include digits 0 through 9 along with the letters a through f or A through F. Here are some examples:

Decimal	33, 2139
Octal	071, 03664
Hexadecimal	0x7b8, 0X395

Floating-Point Literals

Floating-point literals represent decimal numbers with fractional parts. They can be expressed in either standard or scientific notation. With scientific notation, use either e or E to designate the exponent. Both the decimal number and exponent can be either signed or unsigned (positive or negative) as shown in the examples:

3405.673

−1.958

8.3200e+11

8.3200e11

9.98E–12

Boolean Literals

JavaScript implements boolean data types and therefore supports the two literals, `true` and `false`. They represent the Boolean values `1` and `0`, respectively. If you are new to programming, you will soon realize how often true and false values are needed. This is why JavaScript has built them into the language. The `true` and `false` keywords must appear in lowercase. As a result, the capitalized words `TRUE` and `FALSE` are left open to define as your own identifiers, but doing so is not recommended.

String Literals

A string literal is zero or more characters enclosed in double quotes (`"`) or single quotes (`'`). JavaScript gives you this option, but you must use the same type of quote to surround each string. The following are examples of string literals enclosed in quotes:

```
"virtual communities"

'virtual communities'

"#12-6"

"Look, up in the sky!"
```

The use of either type of quotation mark is handy if you have a preference for one or the other. When you learn about JavaScript's built-in methods in Chapter 9, "The JavaScript Object Model," be careful to note the guidelines that you must follow when using string literals as parameters. In some instances, in order to use the method properly, you might have to use both types of quotations when enclosing a string literal inside another. This is different from using escape codes, which is described in the next section.

Special Characters

When writing scripts, you might sometimes need to tell the computer to use a special character or keystroke, such as a tab or a new line. To do this, use a backslash in front of one of the escape codes, as shown in the following list:

`\b` indicates a backspace.

`\f` indicates a form feed.

`\n` indicates a new line.

`\r` indicates a carriage return.

`\t` indicates a tab.

`\\` indicates a backslash.

\' indicates a single quote.

\" indicates a double quote.

If you want to emulate a tab key to align two columns of data, you must use the tab character (\t). Listing 5.2 shows how to align text using tabs. The script itself can be harder to read after you add special characters, but as Figure 5.2 shows, the results look much better.

Listing 5.2. Using special characters in JavaScript.

```
<HTML>
<HEAD>
<TITLE>JavaScript Unleashed</TITLE>
</HEAD>
<BODY>
<PRE><!-- Notice: Special characters do not take effect unless
enclosed in a pre-formatted block -->
<SCRIPT LANGUAGE = "JavaScript">
<!-- begin hiding from old browsers
document.writeln("\tPersonnel")
document.writeln("Name\t\tAddress")
document.writeln("Jeff\t\tjeff@company.com")
document.writeln("Bill\t\tbill@company.com")
document.writeln("Kim\t\tkim@company.com")
// end hiding -->
</SCRIPT>
</PRE>
</BODY>
</HTML>
```

FIGURE 5.2.

Aligning text using the tabs in JavaScript.

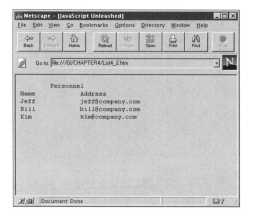

NOTE

Special characters take effect only when used in a formatted text block; therefore, your script must be within tags such as `<PRE>` and `</PRE>`.

If you need to represent quotation marks within a string literal, precede them with a backslash:

```
document.write("\"Imagination is more important than knowledge.\"")

document.write(", Albert Einstein")
```

The preceding script would display the following line of text:

```
"Imagination is more important than knowledge.", Albert Einstein
```

Variables

A *variable* is the name given to a location in a computer's memory where data is stored. The first computer programmers spent much of their time translating data such as the "Hello World Wide Web" message into binary data. They would then find an empty area in the computer's memory to put all of the 1s and 0s while remembering where the data began and ended. By knowing this location (address), they were able to find, update, or retrieve the data as needed during the rest of the program. This basically meant keeping track of a lot of numbers! Variables have made this process of storing, updating, and retrieving information much easier for the modern programmer. With variables, you can assign meaningful names to locations where data is stored while the computer handles the rest.

Naming Variables

The name of a JavaScript variable is made up of one or more letters, digits, or underscores. It can't begin with a digit (0 through 9). Letters include all uppercase characters, A through Z, and all lowercase characters, a through z. JavaScript is case-sensitive and therefore considers the following two examples to be different variable names:

```
internetAddress

internetaddress
```

The following are also valid variable names:

```
_lastName

n

number_2
```

Declaring Variables

To let JavaScript know you're going to use an identifier as a variable, you must first declare it. To declare variables in JavaScript, use the keyword var followed by the new variable name. This action reserves the name as a variable to be used as a storage area for whatever data you might want to hold with it. In the following examples, notice that you can also declare more than one variable at a time by using a comma between variable names:

```
var internetAddress
var n
var i, j, k
var isMouseOverLink, helloMessage
```

Once a variable is declared, it is then ready to be filled with its first value. This *initializing* is done with the assignment operator, =.

> **NOTE**
>
> The equals sign (=) is used to assign a value to a variable. You can read more about the assignment operator in Chapter 6.

You can initialize a variable at the same time you declare it or at any point thereafter in your script. Assigning a value when the variable is declared can help you remember what type of value you originally intended the variable to hold. The following shows the previous example rewritten to include all initializations:

```
var internetAddress = "name@company.com"
var n = 0.00
var i = 0, j = 0, k
var isMouseOverLink = false
var helloMessage = "Hello, thank you for coming!"
k = 0
```

Notice that all variables have been initialized and declared at the same time except for k, which is initialized soon after. JavaScript reads from the top down, stepping through each line of code and performing the instructions in order. Until the program reaches the initializing step, the variable is said to be *undefined,* and you can't extract a value from it. Reading a value from a variable before it is initialized causes an error in your application when you execute it. JavaScript allows you to check if a variable has been assigned using the typeof operator. This is explained in Chapter 6.

JavaScript offers one other way of declaring a variable: by simply initializing it without using the var keyword. By assigning a value to a new variable before declaring it with var, JavaScript will automatically declare it for you. It's important to note that doing so will automatically declare the variable to be *global* in scope. Although this can be a shortcut, it's good programming practice to declare all variables specifically. Using the var keyword maintains the scope of the variable. Under special circumstances, you can avoid using var to declare a variable to be global when it would otherwise be declared *local* in scope. This is covered in more detail in the section "Scope of Variables."

Variable Types

When storing a piece of data (more commonly known as a *value*), JavaScript automatically categorizes it as one of the five JavaScript data types. Table 5.2 shows the different types of data that JavaScript uses.

Table 5.2. JavaScript data types.

Type	Examples
number	`-19, 3.14159`
Boolean	`true, false`
string	`"Elementary, my dear Watson!", ""`
function	`unescape, write`
object	`window, document, null`

A variable of the `number` type holds either an integer or a real number. A `boolean` variable holds either the value `true` or `false`. String variables can hold any string literal that is assigned to it, including the empty string. Table 5.2 shows how to represent an empty string with two double quotes. Functions are either user-defined or built-in. For example, the `unescape` function is built into JavaScript. You can learn how to create user-defined functions in Chapter 8, "Functions." Functions that belong to objects, called *methods* in JavaScript, are also classified under the function data type. Elements such as the `window` or `document` are of the object data type. Object variables, or simply "objects," can store another object. A variable that holds the `null` value is said to be of the object type. This is because JavaScript classifies the value `null` as an object. Initializing a variable with `null` is a great way to prevent errors if you're not sure whether the variable will be used.

Typically, programming languages require that you define the type of data a new variable will represent. Throughout your program, any value assigned to that variable is expected to be of its defined data type. Furthermore, an error occurs when you make an attempt to assign a different data type to the variable. This doesn't happen with JavaScript, which is classified as a loosely typed language. You are not required to define data types, nor are you prevented from assigning different types of data to the same variable. JavaScript variables can accept a new type of data at any time, which in turn changes the type of variable they are. The following example shows valid uses of JavaScript variables:

```
var carLength
carLength = 4 + 5
document.writeln(carLength)
carLength = "9 feet"
document.writeln(carLength)
```

After you declare the variable, `carLength` is assigned the value of `4 + 5`. JavaScript stores the number 9 as the `number` type. However, when you reassign `carLength` to `"9 feet"`, JavaScript lets you store a new type of value, a `string`, in `carLength`. This eliminates the extra steps that are usually needed by other computer languages to let the computer know that you are switching data types.

Scope of Variables

The *scope* of a variable refers to the area or areas within a program where a variable can be referenced. Suppose you embed one script in the head of an HTML document and another script (using another set of script tags) in the body of the same HTML document. JavaScript considers any variables declared within these two areas as being in the same scope. These variables are considered to be *global,* and they are accessible by any script in the current document. Later in this chapter, I'll formally introduce functions, which are separate blocks of code. Variables declared within these blocks are considered *local* and are not always accessible by every script.

Local

A variable declared inside a function is local in scope. Only that function has access to the value that the variable holds. Each time the function is called, the variable is created. Likewise, each time the function ends, the variable is destroyed. Another function declaring a variable with the same name is considered a different variable by JavaScript. They each address their own block of memory.

Global

If you want more than one function to share a variable, declare the variable outside of any functions (but, of course, inside the <SCRIPT> tags). With this method, any part of your application, including all functions, can share this variable. I recommend that you declare global variables in the head of an HTML page to ensure that they are loaded before any other part of your application. Listing 5.3 demonstrates how a global variable is declared and implemented. To show the difference between scopes, I included two functions in this program. You do not need to understand how functions work, but realize that they are like separate parts of a script enclosed by curly braces ({}). If you are unfamiliar with functions, you can find this listing on the CD-ROM and load it into your browser. For more information on functions, refer to Chapter 8.

Listing 5.3. Global versus local scope of a variable.

```
<HTML>
<TITLE>JavaScript Unleashed</TITLE>
<HEAD>
<SCRIPT LANGUAGE = "JavaScript">
<!-- begin hiding from old browsers
//Global Variable
var globalString = "A"
//Functions
function changeToB() {
    document.outputForm.beforeB.value = globalString
    globalString = "B"
    document.outputForm.afterB.value = globalString
}
```

5

FUNDAMENTALS OF
THE JAVASCRIPT
LANGUAGE

continues

Listing 5.3. continued

```
function changeToC() {
    document.outputForm.beforeC.value = globalString
    globalString = "C"
    document.outputForm.afterC.value = globalString
}
// end of hiding from old browsers -->
</SCRIPT>
</HEAD>
<BODY>

<SCRIPT LANGUAGE = "JavaScript">
<!-- begin hiding from old browsers
document.write("The initial value of globalString is \"" +
 globalString + "\".")
// end of hiding from old browsers -->
</SCRIPT>
<BR>
<FORM NAME="outputForm">
<INPUT
    NAME="changeButtonA"
    TYPE="button"
    VALUE="Change To B"
    onClick= "changeToB()">
<INPUT
    NAME="changeButtonB"
    TYPE="button"
    VALUE="Change To C"
    onClick= "changeToC()">
<BR> <BR>
Value of globalString<BR>
<BR>
<INPUT
    NAME="beforeB"
    TYPE="TEXT"
    SIZE=5,1>
Before clicking on "Change To B"<BR>
<INPUT
    NAME="afterB"
    TYPE="TEXT"
    SIZE=5,1>
After clicking on "Change To B"<BR>
<INPUT
    NAME="beforeC"
    TYPE="TEXT"
    SIZE=5,1>
Before clicking on "Change To C"<BR>
<INPUT
    NAME="afterC"
    TYPE="TEXT"
    SIZE=5,1>
After clicking on "Change To C"<BR>
</FORM>
</BODY>
</HTML>
```

In this example, the initial value of globalString is displayed first. This shows that even though the variable was declared in the <HEAD> block of the document, a script inside the <BODY> block of the document can use it. If you click the Change to B button, the function changeToB() first displays the initial value of globalString, changes it to B, and then displays the new value that globalString holds. To demonstrate that all functions in the document can use the same variable, I added a second button to call a different function. Clicking on the Change to C button displays the current value of globalString, which is now B, and then changes globalString to C. Figure 5.3 shows the final output.

FIGURE 5.3.

The difference between local and global scopes.

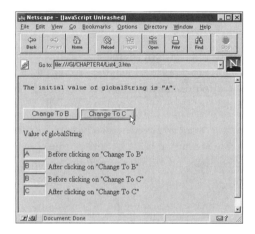

To Declare or Not to Declare?

So far, you have declared all your variables with the keyword var. JavaScript actually allows you to skip this step and create a variable by merely initializing it. I do not recommend skipping this step, because it can have a different effect on the scope of the variable. When you skip or forget to declare a variable and begin by initializing it, JavaScript assumes that the variable is global regardless of whether it was initialized inside a function. This action is exactly the same as declaring the variable outside a function, except for one point—a global variable declared outside a function can be used by the whole application as soon as the document is loaded. A global variable initialized inside a function can't be used by any part of the application until that function is actually called and executed.

Naming Conventions

When naming variables with a single word in JavaScript, it is common practice to use all lowercase letters. When using two or more words to name a variable, it is common to use lowercase letters for the first word and capitalize the first letter of all words thereafter.

I make it a practice to use two or more words when naming variables to give myself and others a better idea of what the variable was created to do. For example, suppose you need a variable to hold a boolean value (`true` or `false`) that will let you know if a visitor to your Web page is finished typing his name into a text field. If you chose a variable name such as `finish`, another programmer (or you, a couple of months down the road) could look at it and wonder, "Was this a flag that can be checked to find out if the visitor is done? Or was it a string stating what to write when the visitor was done, such as a thank-you message?" The variable name `isDone` would be a better choice in this case. By using the word `is` as a prefix, you can indicate that this variable is posing a yes-or-no question, which indicates that the variable will store a boolean value. If the visitor is done entering his name, `isDone` is assigned the value `true`. Otherwise, it's assigned the value `false`.

Although the length of a JavaScript variable is limited only by a computer's memory, it's a good idea to keep variables to a practical length. I recommend between 1 and 20 characters or two to three words. Try to prevent running over the end of a line while writing your scripts. Large variable names make this easy to do and can ruin the look and structure of your code.

Some traditional one-word and even single-character variables represent program or mathematical values. The most common are `n` for any number; `x`, `y`, and `z` for coordinates; and `i` for a placeholder in a recursive function or a counter in a loop. Again, these methods for using variables are simply traditional, and you may use them for whatever purpose you see fit.

There is a good chance that at some point, especially in the professional environment, your code will need to be read by other people. Using consistent and meaningful naming conventions can be a big help to someone who is maintaining your scripts. Poorly thought-out conventions cause big headaches and can significantly affect a company's bottom line.

Constants

A constant is a variable that holds the same value throughout a program's execution. You can be sure that a constant will always hold the same value. JavaScript uses built-in constants to represent values used by common mathematical operations such as pi. They can be accessed through the Math object. They are explained in Chapter 14, "Built-In Language Objects." You could call `true` and `false` constants, but Netscape categorizes them as keywords.

User-Defined Constants

User-defined constants are variables that are defined by the programmer and whose values cannot change. Constants are usually represented by capitalized words and are defined at the beginning of a program. JavaScript does not support constants in the traditional sense. Typically, a programming language that supports user-defined constants ensures that no other part of your application can change the value of a constant once it is defined. Attempting a change causes an error. JavaScript will not do this checking for you. Even though there is no way to have JavaScript ensure that a variable is not altered, you can still use variables to hold values that are used repeatedly throughout a script. By replacing the multiple instances of a common value with a variable, you make it easier to update a script at a later time. All you have to do is change the initialization of the variable, and the entire script is updated.

Colors

JavaScript supports the colors that are used in HTML. To specify a color in your application—for example, to set the color of a font—you can choose from the list of colors in Table 5.3. These values are string literals (not constants) that you can assign to specific object properties. Listing 5.4 shows how you can use these values to set the color of strings that are written to the display. Notice that you can use either the name of the color or its hexadecimal equivalent. This method might look somewhat strange, but it simply sets the `fontcolor` property of the string literal that is written to the display. You can learn more about changing this and other properties of a string in Chapter 14. An invitation to the company picnic can be seen in Figure 5.4.

> **NOTE**
>
> You can't change the color of text once it has been displayed in the browser window. The document would have to be reloaded with a different font color specified.

The hexadecimal string for each color is actually a combination of the RGB (red/green/blue) values that are used to make up each color. For example, the hexadecimal value for aqua is #00FFFF. This RGB value has 00 for the red value, FF for the green value, and FF for the blue value. Two digits in hexadecimal allows for 256 degrees of each color. For the color aqua, the red is set to zero, which means that there is no red. As for the green and blue degrees, they are each turned up all the way. An equal amount of green and blue is combined to create the color aqua. With 256 combinations for red, green, and blue, over 16 million colors are possible, but not all are supported by JavaScript. The full list of supported colors is shown in Table 5.3.

Listing 5.4. Using colors in JavaScript.

```
<HTML>
<HEAD>
<TITLE>JavaScript Unleashed</TITLE>
</HEAD>
<BODY BGCOLOR = "WHITE">
<CENTER><PRE><H2>
<SCRIPT LANGUAGE = "JavaScript">
<!-- begin hiding from old browsers
document.writeln("Company Picnic!".fontcolor("crimson"))
// end hiding -->
</SCRIPT>
</H2><H4>
```

5

FUNDAMENTALS OF THE JAVASCRIPT LANGUAGE

continues

Listing 5.4. continued

```
<SCRIPT LANGUAGE = "JavaScript">
<!-- begin hiding from old browsers
document.writeln("July 19th at 1pm".fontcolor("blue"))
document.writeln("Bring your family!".fontcolor("#008000"))
// end hiding -->
</SCRIPT>
</H4></PRE>
</CENTER>
</BODY>
</HTML>
```

FIGURE 5.4.

Changing the color of text in JavaScript.

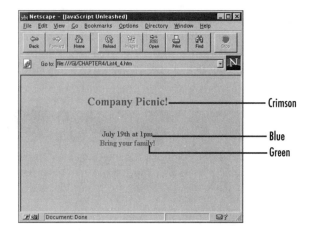

Table 5.3. Color values with hexadecimal equivalents.

Color	Red	Green	Blue	Color	Red	Green	Blue
aliceblue	F0	F8	FF	antiquewhite	FA	EB	D7
aqua	00	FF	FF	aquamarine	7F	FF	D4
azure	F0	FF	FF	beige	F5	F5	DC
bisque	FF	E4	C4	black	00	00	00
blanchedalmond	FF	EB	CD	blue	00	00	FF
blueviolet	8A	2B	E2	brown	A5	2A	2A
burlywood	DE	B8	87	cadetblue	5F	9E	A0
chartreuse	7F	FF	00	chocolate	D2	69	1E
coral	FF	7F	50	cornflowerblue	64	95	ED
cornsilk	FF	F8	DC	crimson	DC	14	3C
cyan	00	FF	FF	darkblue	00	00	8B
darkcyan	00	8B	8B	darkgoldenrod	B8	86	0B

Color	Red	Green	Blue	Color	Red	Green	Blue
darkgray	A9	A9	A9	darkgreen	00	64	00
darkkhaki	BD	B7	6B	darkmagenta	8B	00	8B
darkolivegreen	55	6B	2F	darkorange	FF	8C	00
darkorchid	99	32	CC	darkred	8B	00	00
darksalmon	E9	96	7A	darkseagreen	8F	BC	8F
darkslateblue	48	3D	8B	darkslategray	2F	4F	4F
darkturquoise	00	CE	D1	darkviolet	94	00	D3
deeppink	FF	14	93	deepskyblue	00	BF	FF
dimgray	69	69	69	dodgerblue	1E	90	FF
firebrick	B2	22	22	floralwhite	FF	FA	F0
forestgreen	22	8B	22	fuchsia	FF	00	FF
gainsboro	DC	DC	DC	ghostwhite	F8	F8	FF
gold	FF	D7	00	goldenrod	DA	A5	20
gray	80	80	80	green	00	80	00
greenyellow	AD	FF	2F	honeydew	F0	FF	F0
hotpink	FF	69	B4	indianred	CD	5C	5C
indigo	4B	00	82	ivory	FF	FF	F0
khaki	F0	E6	8C	lavender	E6	E6	FA
lavenderblush	FF	F0	F5	lawngreen	7C	FC	00
lemonchiffon	FF	FA	CD	lightblue	AD	D8	E6
lightcoral	F0	80	80	lightcyan	E0	FF	FF
lightgoldenrodyellow	FA	FA	D2	lightgreen	90	EE	90
lightgrey	D3	D3	D3	lightpink	FF	B6	C1
lightsalmon	FF	A0	7A	lightseagreen	20	B2	AA
lightskyblue	87	CE	FA	lightslategray	77	88	99
lightsteelblue	B0	C4	DE	lightyellow	FF	FF	E0
lime	00	FF	00	limegreen	32	CD	32
linen	FA	F0	E6	magenta	FF	00	FF
maroon	80	00	00	mediumaquamarine	66	CD	AA
mediumblue	00	00	CD	mediumorchid	BA	55	D3
mediumpurple	93	70	DB	mediumseagreen	3C	B3	71

continues

5

Table 5.3. continued

Color	Red	Green	Blue	Color	Red	Green	Blue
mediumslateblue	7B	68	EE	mediumspringgreen	00	FA	9A
mediumturquoise	48	D1	CC	mediumvioletred	C7	15	85
midnightblue	19	19	70	mintcream	F5	FF	FA
mistyrose	FF	E4	E1	moccasin	FF	E4	B5
navajowhite	FF	DE	AD	navy	00	00	80
oldlace	FD	F5	E6	olive	80	80	00
olivedrab	6B	8E	23	orange	FF	A5	00
orangered	FF	45	00	orchid	DA	70	D6
palegoldenrod	EE	E8	AA	palegreen	98	FB	98
paleturquoise	AF	EE	EE	palevioletred	DB	70	93
papayawhip	FF	EF	D5	peachpuff	FF	DA	B9
peru	CD	85	3F	pink	FF	C0	CB
plum	DD	A0	DD	powderblue	B0	E0	E6
purple	80	00	80	red	FF	00	00
rosybrown	BC	8F	8F	royalblue	41	69	E1
saddlebrown	8B	45	13	salmon	FA	80	72
sandybrown	F4	A4	60	seagreen	2E	8B	57
seashell	FF	F5	EE	sienna	A0	52	2D
silver	C0	C0	C0	skyblue	87	CE	EB
slateblue	6A	5A	CD	slategray	70	80	90
snow	FF	FA	FA	springgreen	00	FF	7F
steelblue	46	82	B4	tan	D2	B4	8C
teal	00	80	80	thistle	D8	BF	D8
tomato	FF	63	47	turquoise	40	E0	D0
violet	EE	82	EE	wheat	F5	DE	B3
white	FF	FF	FF	whitesmoke	F5	F5	F5
yellow	FF	FF	00	yellowgreen	9A	CD	32

Data Types

Although I have already discussed the basic data types that you can assign to variables, you should know that functions and objects are special types of data. They offer interesting ways to store and act upon the data that your scripts deal with. You will learn how to take advantage of these aspects of the language in Chapter 8, which is dedicated to functions, and Part III, "JavaScript Objects."

Expressions

Expressions are a set of statements that, as a group, evaluate to a single value. This resulting value is then categorized by JavaScript as one of the five data types: `number`, `string`, `logical`, `function`, or `object`.

An expression can be as simple as a number or variable by itself, or it can include many variables, keywords, and operators joined together. For example, the expression `x = 10` assigns the value `10` to the variable x. The expression as a whole evaluates to 10, so using the expression in a line of code such as `document.writeln(x = 10)` is valid. JavaScript would rather see a string between the parentheses and simply display it, but in this case, it finds some work to do before moving on. It must first evaluate what is between the parentheses and then display the value. In this case, the number 10 is displayed.

Once the work is done to assign 10 to x, the following is also a valid expression: x. In this case, the only work that JavaScript needs to do is read the value from the computer's memory; no assignment needs to be performed. In addition to the assignment operator, there are many other operators you can use to form an expression (see Chapter 6).

Comments

So far, I have used HTML comment tags for surrounding scripts, which ensures that old browsers don't read scripts that they can't understand. What if you want to place comments in your JavaScript code that JavaScript will ignore? The two solutions available to you are the same methods used in the C and C++ languages. Here is the syntax:

```
//Here are some comments about my JavaScript program.
```

For larger blocks of comments, use the following:

```
/*multiple lines of
comments */
```

The two forward slashes (//) hide text that follows it until the end of the current line. White space is ignored, so the following are valid:

```
//       comments

/*       multiple lines

comments              */
```

Listing 5.5 demonstrates the usage of each type of comment. Two forward slashes do not hide code from older browsers. To avoid giving old browsers a headache, continue to use <!-- and --> to surround all of your scripts. Anything that is commented in Listing 5.5 is not output to the display, as shown in Figure 5.5.

Listing 5.5. Using JavaScript comment tags.

```
<HTML>
<HEAD>
<TITLE>JavaScript Unleashed</TITLE>
</HEAD>
<BODY>
<PRE>
<SCRIPT LANGUAGE = "JavaScript">
<!-- begin hiding from old browsers
//variables
var firstName = "Jon",
lastName = "Simpson",
internetAddress = "jsimpson@company.com"
/*Display the user's first and last name
along with their e-mail address */
document.writeln(firstName + " " + lastName) //combine three strings
document.writeln("e-mail address: " + internetAddress)
// end hiding -->
</SCRIPT>
</PRE>
</BODY>
</HTML>
```

FIGURE 5.5.

Comments are not displayed in the browser.

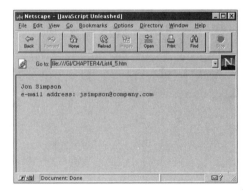

Being able to hide code from JavaScript gives you the ability to document your scripts. It is considered good programming practice to add design notes, friendly reminders, or warnings throughout your program. This can help you and others see what the different sections of your program were meant to do. Another use of comments is debugging your scripts. You can hide your code to track down problems and then easily replace it when you're done by simply removing comment identifiers. Doing this instead of deleting parts of your script helps save time.

Operators

Operators are symbols or identifiers that represent the way in which a combination of expressions is evaluated or manipulated. The most common operator you have used thus far is the assignment operator. In the example x = 10, both 10 by itself and the variable x are expressions. When JavaScript sees an assignment operator between two expressions, it acts according to the rules of the assignment operator. In this case, it takes the value from the expression on the right side and assigns it to the variable on the left side. Along with the common arithmetic operators, JavaScript supports over 30 others. I'll cover these more thoroughly in Chapter 6.

Functions

In its simplest form, a function is a script that you can call by name at any time. This enhances JavaScript in two ways. When an HTML document is read by a JavaScript-enabled Web browser, the browser will find any embedded scripts and execute the instructions step-by-step. This is fine unless you would rather have part or all of your program wait before executing. Writing this part of your program in a function and assigning it a name is a great way to set up a script to be run at a later time. When a specific event occurs, you can run this script by using the name that you gave to the function. Another advantage of functions is the ability to reuse scripts without typing in the same code repeatedly. Instead, you can just use the name given to the function to execute the group of code contained within.

Listing 5.6 shows how JavaScript executes a function. The first thing to notice is where the function is declared. Just as other variables need to be declared, so do functions. Be sure to enclose all function declarations within <SCRIPT> tags. I recommend declaring your functions in the <HEAD> block of the HTML document. Doing this ensures that the function is loaded by the browser before it is executed by the body. To use the function, just place the name of it anywhere in your program. The main program is placed within the body and is surrounded by its own set of <SCRIPT> tags.

Listing 5.6. Embedding a JavaScript function.

```
<HTML>
<HEAD>
<TITLE>JavaScript Unleashed</TITLE>
```

continues

Listing 5.6. continued

```
<SCRIPT LANGUAGE = "JavaScript">
function displayMessage() {
    document.write("JavaScript functions are easy to use!")
    document.write("<BR>")
}
<!-- begin hiding from old browsers
// end hiding -->
</SCRIPT>
</HEAD>
<BODY>
<PRE>
<SCRIPT LANGUAGE = "JavaScript">
<!-- begin hiding from old browsers
document.write("Calling a JavaScript function...<BR>")
displayMessage()
document.write("Done.<BR>")
// end hiding -->
</SCRIPT>
</PRE>
</BODY>
</HTML>
```

Starting with the main script, JavaScript executes the first line as always and then arrives at the `displayMessage()` function call. It looks up the function in memory and begins with the first line of `displayMessage()`. After writing `JavaScript functions are easy to use!`, a line break is displayed. The end of the function is reached, and program execution returns to where it left off in the main script. As you can see in Figure 5.6, each line of text is displayed in this sequence. If you have a lengthy program that displays this message many times, you can insert the function call in each place where you need it. If at a later time there is a need to update the message, you need only change the message in one place. Change it within the function declaration, and your whole application is updated. You can learn more about functions and their advantages in Chapter 8.

FIGURE 5.6.

Calling a function in JavaScript.

Summary

JavaScript is a great addition to the Web author's tool kit. It makes some things possible that CGI and plug-ins do not. It offers direct interaction with the user while an HTML document is being viewed.

Scripts are placed directly into HTML documents and surrounded by <SCRIPT> tags. Use the correct type of comments to have either the browser or JavaScript itself ignore particular sections of your scripts.

Starting from the first line of code, the JavaScript interpreter reads the script line by line. Tokens are the smallest individual words, phrases, or characters that JavaScript can understand. Tokens can be literals, identifiers, or operators.

The different data types available include the number, boolean, string, function, and object types. Variables can store one of these data types at a time. To declare a variable, use the var keyword or simply initialize the variable. Initializing a variable without first declaring it will always create a global variable. Try to use meaningful names for variables to make your scripts easier to read.

Expressions are a set of statements that evaluate to a single value. The most common expressions are ones that assign values to variables. The assignment operator, =, is used to assign the value of its right operand to the variable that is its left operand. JavaScript supports all standard math operations either through operators or by using the built-in Math object.

Use comments to help document your scripts. This will make it easy to for you and for others to maintain.

Operators are symbols or identifiers that represent the way in which a combination of expressions is evaluated or manipulated. Operators are covered thoroughly in Chapter 6.

Functions are scripts that you can execute at any time before or after an HTML document is viewed by the user. With functions, you can set aside a script to be executed at any time and as often as you like. Using functions can also make your scripts easier to maintain. Chapter 8 explains functions in greater detail.

In the next chapter, I'll take a closer look at the built-in tools JavaScript offers to handle and manipulate data. If you're familiar with C and C++-style operators, you could use Chapter 6 as a reference and move onto Chapter 7, "Control Structures and Looping," to find out how to make decisions with JavaScript.

Operators

IN THIS CHAPTER

CHAPTER 6

The whole idea of writing a script is to input, evaluate, manipulate, or display data. Until now, you have concentrated on displaying data with JavaScript. To create more useful programs, you need to evaluate or even change the data that your scripts are dealing with. The tools for this job are called *operators*. They are the symbols and identifiers that represent either the way that the data is changed or the way a combination of expressions are evaluated. JavaScript supports both binary and unary operators. Binary operators require that there be two operands in the expression, such as 9 + x, whereas unary operators only need one operand. One example is x++.

Both of the examples used here are arithmetic operators, and their use will come naturally to those who understand basic math. Other types of JavaScript operators deal with strings and logical values. They don't act as intuitively, but they're easy to learn and very handy when you're dealing with large amounts of text over the Internet. This chapter takes a close look at each type of JavaScript operator.

NOTE

Netscape offers a type-in mode that allows you to type in expressions and have their values displayed immediately. I have found it to be an excellent way to quickly check the value of an expression and an easy way to experiment. To enter this mode, choose File | Open Location and enter the following text in the location field:

```
JavaScript:
```

Press Enter, and your screen will be split into two sections. You may now type in just about any line of JavaScript. This includes declaring variables, functions, and objects along with evaluating expressions. I have shown an example of using this feature in Figure 6.1. I entered 12<<1 into the typein field and pressed Enter. The result was then displayed in the main browser window.

FIGURE 6.1.

Using Netscape's typein feature.

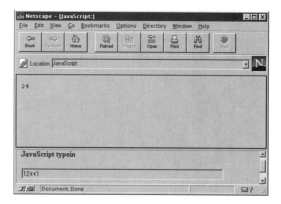

Assignment Operators

An operator you're already familiar with is the assignment operator. Its most basic function is assigning a value to a variable, thereby placing the value in memory. For example, the expression x = 20 assigns the value 20 to the variable x. When JavaScript encounters the assignment operator (=), it first looks to the right for a value. It then looks to the left and ensures that there is a place to store the number. If it finds a variable, it assigns the value to it. In this case, x holds the value of 20. It always works from right to left, so the expression 20 = x causes an error in JavaScript by trying to assign a new value to 20. This is not allowed, because 20 is not a variable, but an integer whose value can't be changed.

JavaScript supports 11 other assignment operators that are really a combination of the assignment operator and either an arithmetic or bitwise operator. These shorthand versions follow:

The Combination of Assignment and Arithmetic Operators

x += y is short for x = x + y

x -= y is short for x = x - y

x *= y is short for x = x * y

x /= y is short for x = x / y

x %= y is short for x = x % y

The Combination of Assignment and Bitwise Operators

x <<= y is short for x = x << y

x >>= y is short for x = x >> y

x >>>= y is short for x = x >>> y

x &= y is short for x = x & y

x ^= y is short for x = x ^ y

x ¦= y is short for x = x ¦ y

Arithmetic Operators

When working with numbers, you use arithmetic operators. The most basic operators of the group include the plus sign (+), which adds two values; the minus sign (-), which subtracts one value from another; the asterisk (*), which multiplies two values together; and the forward slash (/), which divides one value by another. When JavaScript encounters one of these operators, it looks to the right and left sides of the operator to find the values to work on. In the example 7 + 9, JavaScript sees the plus operator and looks to either side of it to find 7 and 9. The plus operator then adds the two values together, resulting in the expression as a whole equating to

16. Using arithmetic operators with the assignment operator, you can assign a variable the value of an expression. The following assignment uses the expression from the last example:

```
x = 7 + 9
```

x will now equal 16 and can be used again, even to give itself a new value:

```
x = x + 1
```

Follow the last two examples in order. x is first assigned the value 16. Next, x is reassigned the present value of x (which, at that moment, is still 16) plus 1. It is a very common operation to increment the value of a variable and then reassign that value to itself. It is used so often in computer programs that some languages incorporate special shorthand operators to increment and decrement the values that variables hold more easily. JavaScript is one such language. It uses ++ to increment and -- to decrement a value by 1. Note the following syntax:

> ++i is the same as using i = i + 1
>
> --i is the same as using i = i - 1

You can use these operators as either a prefix or a suffix. This way, you can change the order in which a value is returned by the expression and when the new value is assigned. Listing 6.1 demonstrates how increment and decrement operators work.

Listing 6.1. Examples of using increment and decrement operators.

```
<HTML>
<HEAD>
<TITLE>JavaScript Unleashed</TITLE>
</HEAD>
<BODY>
<PRE>
<SCRIPT LANGUAGE = "JavaScript">
<!-- begin hiding from old browsers
var i = 0,  result = 0
document.writeln("If i = 0,")
document.write("\t++i returns the value of i")
document.write(" after incrementing  : ")
result = ++i //increment prefix
document.writeln(result)

i = 0 //reset variable
document.write("\ti++ returns the value of i")
document.write(" before incrementing : ")
result = i++ //increment suffix
document.writeln(result)

i = 0 //reset variable
document.write("\t--i returns the value of i")
document.write(" after decrementing  : ")
result = --i //decrement prefix
document.writeln(result)

i = 0 //reset variable
document.write("\ti-- returns the value of i")
```

6

```
document.write(" before decrementing : ")
result = i-- //decrement suffix
document.writeln(result)
// end hiding -->
</SCRIPT>
</PRE>
</BODY>
</HTML>
```

The important thing to notice in Listing 6.1 is whether i is incremented before or after the expression is evaluated.

In the first example, result is set to the original value of i plus 1. In the second example, result is immediately set equal to the original value of i before i is incremented. The next two examples work the same way, but demonstrate the decrement operator. The results of these four examples are shown in Figure 6.2. Although these might seem like unnecessary ways to allow the operator to be used, they can come in handy when writing scripts that repeat a part of the program. This is shown in Chapter 7, "Control Structures and Looping."

FIGURE 6.2.

The increment and decrement operators shown in Listing 6.1.

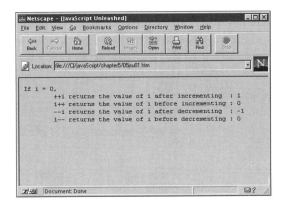

The unary negation operator (-) is used to change a value from positive to negative or vice versa. It is unary because it operates on only one operand. If, for example, you assign the value 5 to a variable x (x = 5), and then negate x and assign the value to y (y = -x), y will equal -5. The opposite is also true when negating a negative number; the result will be positive. In both instances, the negation operator does not negate the value of x. The value of x remains equal to 5.

The modulus operator is symbolized by the percent sign (%). To find the modulus of two operands is to find the remainder after dividing the first operand by the second. In the example x = 10 % 3, x is assigned the number 1, because 10 divided by 3 is equal to 3 with one third left over. With the modulus operator, you can easily determine that one number is the multiple of another if the modulus of the two numbers is equal to 0. This would be true for the expression x = 25 % 5. 25 divided by 5 is equal to 5 with no remainder, which leaves x equal to 0.

CAUTION

In some cases, Netscape Navigator returns an incorrect value when dealing with fractions. For example, 10/3 should return 3 1/3. If you use Netscape's typein feature to evaluate 10/3, you will see that the result is 3.3333333333333335. The small inaccuracy at the sixteenth decimal place occurs due to the way in which fractions are stored in a computer's memory. Microsoft's Internet Explorer uses a workaround to this problem by displaying only 14 decimal places. Displaying the result of the same calculation shows 3.33333333333333.

Comparison Operators

Comparison operators are used for just that—comparing. Expressions that use comparison operators are essentially asking a question about two values. The answer can either be `true` or `false`.

Two equal signs (==) make up the equal operator. When you use the equal operator in the middle of two operands, you're trying to determine whether the values of these two operands are equal. Listing 6.2 shows how to display the result when asking if two variables are equal.

Listing 6.2. Using the equal operator.

```
<HTML>
<HEAD>
<TITLE>JavaScript Unleashed</TITLE>
</HEAD>
<BODY>
<PRE>
<SCRIPT LANGUAGE = "JavaScript">
<!-- begin hiding from old browsers
var x,y,z
x = 5
y = 5
z = 10
//output to display
document.writeln("x = "+x)
document.writeln("y = "+y)
document.writeln("z = "+z)
document.write("Is x equal to y,(x==y)? ")
document.writeln(x==y)
document.write("Is y equal to z,(y==z)? ")
document.writeln(y==z)
// end hiding -->
</SCRIPT>
</PRE>
</BODY>
</HTML>
```

Be sure to use the correct operator for the job. Again, the equal operator (==) tests to see whether two values are equal, but the assignment operator (=) sets a variable equal to a value. If you happen to make a mistake and use the wrong one, the JavaScript interpreter is good about letting you know! Figure 6.3 shows the display after Listing 6.2 is executed.

FIGURE 6.3.

The equal operator from Listing 6.2.

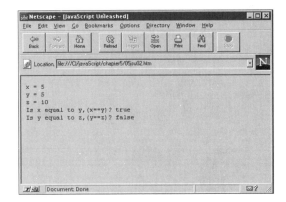

Here is a list of all the comparison operators:

==	The equal operator. Returns true if both of its operands are equal.
!=	The not-equal operator. Returns true if its operands are not equal.
>	The greater-than operator. Returns true if its left operand is greater in value than its right operand.
>=	The greater-than-or-equal operator. Returns true if its left operand is greater than or equal to its right operand.
<	The less-than operator. Returns true if its left operand is less than the value of its right operand.
<=	The less-than-or-equal operator. Returns true if its left operand is less than or equal to its right operand.

Comparison operators are usually used in JavaScript for making decisions. With them, you can ask, "What path in my script do I want to take?" Chapter 7 goes into detail on this topic.

Comparison Operators in JavaScript 1.2

Up until JavaScript 1.1, the language was very forgiving when comparing operands of different data types. For example, when comparing the number 7 with the string "7", JavaScript would first convert or *cast* the string operand to a number and then compare the two. JavaScript would then find them equal. As of version 1.2, it is up to the programmer to first cast the string as a number or cast the number as a string. If you don't, JavaScript will never find them equal. Listing 6.3 demonstrates a way to compare strings and numbers that returns the same results for all versions of JavaScript. Figure 6.4 shows how JavaScript 1.2 reacts to the three different scripts. Listing 6.3 can only be fully executed within a JavaScript 1.2-enabled browser, such as Netscape Navigator 4.0.

Listing 6.3. Testing different JavaScript versions.

```
<HTML>
<HEAD>
<TITLE>JavaScript Unleashed</TITLE>
</HEAD>
<BODY>
<BR>
<SCRIPT LANGUAGE= "JavaScript">
<!--
var x = "3"
var y = 7
document.write('x = "3"')
document.write("<BR>")
document.write("y = 7")
document.write("<BR><HR>")
document.write("JavaScript versions prior to 1.2<BR>")
document.write("x == 3 : ")
document.write(x == 3)
document.write("<BR>")
document.write('y == "7" : ')
document.write(y == "7")
//-->
</SCRIPT>
<BR><BR>
<SCRIPT LANGUAGE= "JavaScript1.2">
<!--
document.write("JavaScript version 1.2<BR>")
document.write("x == 3 : ")
document.write(x == 3)
document.write("<BR>")
document.write('y == "7" : ')
document.write(y == "7")
//-->
</SCRIPT>
<BR><BR>
<SCRIPT LANGUAGE= "JavaScript">
<!--
document.write("Accomodate all versions.<BR>")
document.write("x-0 == 3 : ")
document.write(x-0 == 3)
document.write("<BR>")
document.write('"" + y == "7" : ')
document.write("" + y == "7")
//-->
</SCRIPT>
</BODY>
</HTML>
```

FIGURE 6.4.

The comparison strings and integers shown in Listing 6.3.

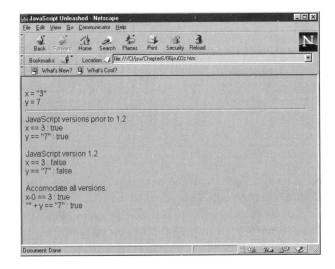

String Operators

The set of string operators available in JavaScript includes all comparison operators, along with the concatenation operator (+). Using the concatenation operator, you can easily attach strings together to make a longer string, as shown in Listing 6.4.

Listing 6.4. Concatenating strings.

```
<HTML>
<HEAD>
<TITLE>JavaScript Unleashed</TITLE>
</HEAD>
<BODY>
<PRE>
<SCRIPT LANGUAGE = "JavaScript">
<!-- begin hiding from old browsers
var a, b, c, sumOfParts, address1, address2
a = "www"
b = "company"
c = "com"
document.writeln("Part a is equal to \""+a+"\".")
document.writeln("Part b is equal to \""+b+"\".")
document.writeln("Part c is equal to \""+c+"\".\n")
sumOfParts = a + "." + b + "." + c
address1 = "WWW.COMPANY.COM"
address2 = "www.company.com"
//output to display
document.write("Is sumOfParts equal to "+address1+"? ")
document.writeln(sumOfParts == address1)
```

continues

Listing 6.4. continued

```
document.write("Is sumOfParts equal to "+address2+"? ")
document.writeln(sumOfParts == address2)
document.write("Is sumOfParts greater than "+address1+"? ")
document.writeln(sumOfParts > address1)
// end hiding -->
</SCRIPT>
</PRE>
</BODY>
</HTML>
```

To begin, the script initializes three variables to hold three parts of an Internet Web address. Next, all three parts are added together, separated by the appropriate dots found in all Web addresses. To test if `sumOfParts` holds a specific Internet address, the script compares it to two possibilities. Figure 6.5 shows that JavaScript is case-sensitive when comparing strings, and that it returns `true` only when comparing addresses with the same case. JavaScript goes from left to right, comparing the ASCII codes of each character in both strings. If all character codes match each other, the strings are equal. All uppercase letters have values less than their lowercase equivalents, which explains why the last comparison in Listing 6.3 returns `true`.

FIGURE 6.5.

The concatenation of strings shown in Listing 6.4.

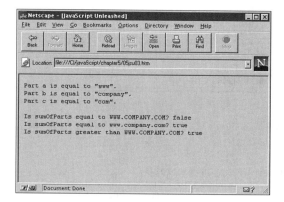

Conditional Operators

JavaScript uses the set of two operators, `?` and `:`, to form conditional expressions. If you're familiar with immediate if statements, the JavaScript conditional operators perform the same operation. Conditional expressions return one of two values based on the logical value of another expression. You might recognize this type of expression as an immediate if statement. For example, you can use the following conditional expression to alert the user if he is the millionth person to view the page:

```
resultMsg = (numHits==1000000)?"You have won!" : "You lost. Try again!"

alert(resultMsg)
```

Provided that numHits is set equal to 1000000 elsewhere in the program, this expression returns the string You have won!; otherwise, it returns You lost. Try again!. The second line of the previous example displays the result to the user using the built-in alert() function. If numHits is equal to one million, an alert dialog box pops up to let the visitor know. Otherwise, the expression returns false, and a sympathetic message is displayed.

A conditional expression can be used to return any data type, such as a number or Boolean. The following expression returns either a string or a number, depending on whether useString is true or false:

```
result = useString ? "seven" : 7
document.write(result)
```

Boolean Operators

Boolean operators (also called logical operators) are used in conjunction with expressions that return logical values. The best way to understand these is to see them used with comparison operators. The following is a list of the three Boolean operators. The examples are shown with either the syntax *Expression1 [operator] Expression2* or *[operator] Expression*:

&&   The logical and operator returns true if both *Expression1* and *Expression2* are true. Otherwise, it returns false. Examples:

    (1>0) && (2>1) returns true.

    (1>0) && (2<1) returns false.

¦¦   The logical or operator returns true if either *Expression1* or *Expression2* is true. If neither *Expression1* nor *Expression2* is true, it returns false. Examples:

    (1>0) ¦¦ (2<1) returns true.

    (1<0) ¦¦ (2<1) returns false.

!   The logical not operator is a unary operator that returns the opposite value of a Boolean *Expression*. If *Expression* is true, it returns false, and if *Expression* is false, it returns true. This will not permanently change the value of *Expression*, because it works the same way as the arithmetic negation operator. Examples:

    !(1>0) returns false.

    !(1<0) returns true.

The typeof Operator

The typeof operator returns the type of data that its operand currently holds. This is especially useful for determining if a variable has been defined. Note the following examples:

typeof unescape returns the string "function".

typeof undefinedVariable returns the string "undefined".

typeof 33 returns the string "number".

typeof "A String" returns the string "string".

typeof true returns the string "boolean".

typeof null returns the string "object".

CAUTION

The typeof operator was added for Navigator 3.0 (JavaScript 1.1). It will work only with JavaScript 1.1 and higher.

Function Operators

Functions are covered in Chapter 8, "Functions." There are two operators you should be familiar with when dealing with functions. The first is the call operator, which is symbolized by a set of parentheses and always follows the function name. For example, a function named displayName would be declared using the following syntax:

```
function displayName(){
    [statements]
}
```

The call operator is also used when calling the function from elsewhere in a script. It would look like this:

```
displayName()
```

The parentheses signify that a function is being used instead of any other user-defined identifier.

The second function operator is the comma. It's used to separate multiple arguments that a function can accept. Arguments are always enclosed by the call operator. Modifying the displayName() function to accept two arguments would look like the following:

```
function displayName(argument1,argument2){
    [statements]
}
```

Data Structure Operators

The operators described in this section are first used in Part III of this book, "JavaScript Objects."

Data structure operators is the term I use to classify two operators that are needed when dealing with data structures. Data structures are frameworks that are set up to store one or more basic pieces of data in an orderly fashion. In JavaScript, objects are used to group pieces of data to serve a more specific purpose. An operator to be familiar with when dealing with objects is commonly referred to as the dot. Symbolized by a period, the dot is technically called the structure-member operator. It allows you to refer to a member (a variable, function, or object) belonging to the specified object. The syntax is as follows:

```
objectName.variableName
```

or

```
objectName.functionName()
```

or

```
objectName.anotherObject
```

This way of referring to a piece of data, usually called dot notation, returns the value of the rightmost variable, function, or object.

The member operator, also known as the array subscript operator, is used to access a piece of data from an array. Symbolized by a pair of square brackets, it allows you to refer to any one element of an array. Arrays are objects in JavaScript and are introduced in Chapter 14, "Built-In Language Objects." The following is the syntax for using the member operator:

```
arrayName[indexNumber]
```

The member operator encloses an integer, shown here as `indexNumber`. `indexNumber` specifies an index into `arrayName`, allowing access to any one member of the array.

Bitwise Operators

At the lowest level, integers (along with all data) are stored in memory as bits. They are stored using the binary number system, which can represent any integer using the symbols 0 and 1. Depending on placement, a bit set to 1 represents a value equal to 2 raised to *n,* where *n* is the number of places from the right of the number. For example, the integer 12 can be represented by the binary number 1100 and takes a minimum of 4 bits to store in memory. Starting from the right and moving to the left, 1100 can be calculated using the following expression:

$$0 \times 2^n + 0 \times 2^1 + 1 \times 2^2 + 1 \times 2^3 = 12$$

A larger number such as 237 in binary, 11101101, requires 8 bits of memory to be stored. 11101101 can also be calculated in the following way:

$$1 \times 2^0 + 0 \times 2^1 + 1 \times 2^2 + 1 \times 2^3 + 0 \times 2^4 + 1 \times 2^5 + 1 \times 2^6 + 1 \times 2^7 = 237$$

JavaScript sets aside 32 bits per integer when storing integers in memory. Once in memory, 237 conceptually looks like 00000000000000000000000011101101 but is typically written as 11101101, excluding the leading zeros, which are insignificant. You can enter an integer as a decimal, octal, or hexadecimal number, and JavaScript will store it in binary form. To accommodate negative values, the leftmost bit or highest bit represents a negative value equal to $-(2^{31})$. Using the highest bit, you can start with $-(2^{31})$ and add positive values to it (represented by the remaining 31 bits) to generate any negative number greater than or equal to $-(2^{31})$. Note the following examples:

```
10000000000000000000000000000001 = -2147483648 + 1 = -2147483647

10000000000000000000000000000011 = -2147483648 + 3 = -2147483645

11111111111111111111111111111111 = -2147483648 + 2147483647 = -1

11111111111111111111111111111110 = -2147483648 + 2147483646 = -2
```

JavaScript gives you access to an integer's binary representative through bitwise operators. The simplest of bitwise operators is the unary one's complement operator, symbolized by the tilde (~). Its job is to "flip" every bit of its operand. This is classified as a negation operator because it negates each bit. If a bit is a 1, it will become a 0. If a bit is a 0, it will become a 1. Finding the one's complement of the number 6 can be visualized in the following ways:

```
x = ~6

x = ~00000000000000000000000000000110

x =   11111111111111111111111111111001

x = -7
```

Bitwise Logical Operators

When you use bitwise logical operators, JavaScript pairs up each operand bit-by-bit. It then performs the operation on each pair of bits. For example, using the bitwise and operator on the numbers 01111 and 11011 results in the number 00011. Their binary equivalents are aligned from right to left to form five pairs of bits. The pairs are then operated on separately, and a new number is generated. You can visualize this in the following way:

```
01111        & 10011

1            & 1 = 1

1            & 1 = 1

1            & 0 = 0

1            & 0 = 0

0            & 1 = 0
```

& The bitwise and operator returns 1 if both operands are 1. Otherwise, it returns 0. Example: 15 & 27 returns 11 (01111 & 11011 returns 01011).

¦ The bitwise or operator returns 1 if either operand is 1. Otherwise, it returns 0. Example: 15 ¦ 27 returns 31 (01111 ¦ 11011 returns 11111).

^ The bitwise exclusive or operator returns 1 if one but not both operands are 1. Otherwise, it returns 0. Example: 15 ^ 27 returns 20 (01111 ¦ 11011 returns 10100).

Bitwise Shift Operators

All bitwise shift operators take two operands. The left operand is an integer whose bits are to be shifted. The right operand is the number of bits to shift the binary representation of the integer.

<< The left-shift operator returns the value of an integer if its bits were shifted a number of places to the left. All void rightmost bits are filled in with zeros. The following examples shift the number 15 to the left by 1 and then by 2, respectively.

15 << 1 returns 30 (1111 << 1 returns 11110).

15 << 2 returns 60 (1111 << 2 returns 111100).

Note that shifting a positive integer to the left n times is equivalent to multiplying the value by 2 n times. In most cases, a computer can perform a left-shift faster than multiplying by 2. For this reason, it is common to see the bitwise left-shift chosen over its higher-level counterpart when having the computer perform many multiplications. Any small increase in efficiency could result in a noticeable advantage. Using the left-shift on a negative integer could result in either a negative or positive integer, depending on the state of the highest bit after the left-shift has been performed.

>> The sign-propagating right-shift operator returns the value of an integer if its bits were shifted a number of places to the right. All void bits are filled in with a copy of the leftmost bit (also called the sign bit). Copying the leftmost bit ensures that the integer will stay either positive or negative. This is also a more efficient way to divide a positive, even integer by 2 n times. In the case of a positive odd integer, a right-shift is the same as dividing by 2 n times, but it throws away remainders. Note the following examples:

15 >> 1 returns 7 (1111 >> 1 returns 0111).

-15 >> 1 returns -8 (11111111111111111111111111110001 >> 1 returns 11111111111111111111111111111000)

>>>   The zero-fill right-shift operator returns the value of an integer if its bits were shifted a number of places to the right. All void high-order bits are filled in with zeros. When operating on positive integers, the zero-fill right-shift operator produces the same result as using the sign-propagating right-shift operator. This is due to the fact that the sign bit being copied is always zero for positive integers. As for negative integers, any zero-fill right-shift will change the highest bit from a 1 to a 0. The result will always be an integer that is greater than or equal to 0. Note the following examples:

15 >>> 1 returns 7 (1111 >>> 1 returns 0111).

-15 >>> 1 returns 2147483640 (11111111111111111111111111110001 >> 1 returns 01111111111111111111111111111000).

Why Mess with Bits?

Bitwise operators aren't needed in most scripts. It's possible that you may never have to deal with bits for your entire JavaScript career. However, there are special cases where dealing with data at its lowest level becomes practical or even necessary. An example of when bitwise operators are needed is when converting a number from base 10 (decimal) to base 16 (hexadecimal). This takes a little extra effort, because JavaScript only allows you to display the decimal representation of a number stored in memory. There is no built-in way to display the number in an alternative base. Using bitwise operators, the solution to this obstacle is relatively easy. For instance, if you store the value 0xDC in a variable x, JavaScript converts it to binary. If you try to display x using the following lines of code, the number is displayed in decimal as 220:

```
x = 0xDC
```

```
document.writeln(x)// will write "220" to the display
```

JavaScript doesn't offer a method of displaying 220 as its hexadecimal equivalent, DC. This is a useful function if you are performing operations on HTML color values that are in hexadecimal. The easiest way to accomplish this is to use the binary value of the integer and translate it into hexadecimal.

Hexadecimal values are easily represented in binary. Four bits of memory can store 16 values. Because hexadecimal uses 16 digits, it takes 4 bits to store the value of each hexadecimal digit. In a 32-bit integer, the rightmost 4 bits of memory represent the rightmost digit of a hexadecimal integer. The next 4 bits store the next digit, and so on. To convert a 32-bit integer into hexadecimal, you can do this eight times, matching each 4-bit value to its hexadecimal equivalent.

To read in only 4 bits at a time, use the & operator with a control value. The control value should have a 1 in each bit location that you would like to copy from the integer being converted. Because you want the value of the first 4 bits, the control value should have a 1 in its first 4 bits. All other bits should be set to 0. The control value in this case must equal 1111 (15 or 0xF). This operation conceptually appears as the following:

Control: 00000000000000000000000000001111 &

Integer to convert: 00000000000000000000000011011100 =

Result: 00000000000000000000000000001100

The result is a copy of the first 4 bits of the integer you're converting. You can easily compare this to each of the 16 hexadecimal digits to find that it is equal to C. To find the next hexadecimal digit, copy the next 4 bits out of the integer. I have chosen to do this by shifting all the bits in the integer 4 bits to the right while using the same control. This will work as in the following:

Control: 00000000000000000000000000001111 &

Integer to convert: 00000000000000000000000000001101 =

Result: 00000000000000000000000000001101

Again, you can use the result to match up against the second digit, D. If the original integer was larger, you could continue this process up to six more times.

Listing 6.5 shows this algorithm in action. Using only the operators discussed up to this point, it can convert any 8-bit value into a string representing its hexadecimal equivalent. The value to be converted is first assigned to the variable intValue. I then display the value to show that JavaScript will return only the decimal value of DC, which is 220. The program proceeds to translate the binary form of 220 into hexadecimal and displays the result. The output is shown in Figure 6.6.

Listing 6.5. Converting base 10 to base 16 using bitwise operators.

```
<HTML>
<HEAD>
<TITLE>JavaScript Unleashed</TITLE>
</HEAD>
<BODY>
<PRE>
<SCRIPT LANGUAGE = "JavaScript">
<!-- begin hiding from old browsers
var originalInt
var intValue = 0xDC //intValue can be any 8 bit value.
var controlValue = 0xF, fourBitValue
var hexChar = "", hexString = ""
document.writeln("When displaying integers from memory,")
document.writeln("JavaScript always uses their decimal ")
document.writeln("equivalent: " + intValue)
originalInt = intValue
fourBitValue =  controlValue & intValue
hexChar = (fourBitValue == 0x0) ? "0" : hexChar
hexChar = (fourBitValue == 0x1) ? "1" : hexChar
hexChar = (fourBitValue == 0x2) ? "2" : hexChar
```

continues

Listing 6.5. continued

```
hexChar = (fourBitValue == 0x3) ? "3" : hexChar
hexChar = (fourBitValue == 0x4) ? "4" : hexChar
hexChar = (fourBitValue == 0x5) ? "5" : hexChar
hexChar = (fourBitValue == 0x6) ? "6" : hexChar
hexChar = (fourBitValue == 0x7) ? "7" : hexChar
hexChar = (fourBitValue == 0x8) ? "8" : hexChar
hexChar = (fourBitValue == 0x9) ? "9" : hexChar
hexChar = (fourBitValue == 0xA) ? "A" : hexChar
hexChar = (fourBitValue == 0xB) ? "B" : hexChar
hexChar = (fourBitValue == 0xC) ? "C" : hexChar
hexChar = (fourBitValue == 0xD) ? "D" : hexChar
hexChar = (fourBitValue == 0xE) ? "E" : hexChar
hexChar = (fourBitValue == 0xF) ? "F" : hexChar
//build hexString placing digits from right to left
hexString = hexChar + hexString
//shift intValue four bits right
intValue = intValue >> 4
//extract the next four bit value
fourBitValue =  controlValue & intValue
//find the matching hex value and assign its string
//equivalent to hexChar.
hexChar = (fourBitValue == 0x0) ? "0" : hexChar
hexChar = (fourBitValue == 0x1) ? "1" : hexChar
hexChar = (fourBitValue == 0x2) ? "2" : hexChar
hexChar = (fourBitValue == 0x3) ? "3" : hexChar
hexChar = (fourBitValue == 0x4) ? "4" : hexChar
hexChar = (fourBitValue == 0x5) ? "5" : hexChar
hexChar = (fourBitValue == 0x6) ? "6" : hexChar
hexChar = (fourBitValue == 0x7) ? "7" : hexChar
hexChar = (fourBitValue == 0x8) ? "8" : hexChar
hexChar = (fourBitValue == 0x9) ? "9" : hexChar
hexChar = (fourBitValue == 0xA) ? "A" : hexChar
hexChar = (fourBitValue == 0xB) ? "B" : hexChar
hexChar = (fourBitValue == 0xC) ? "C" : hexChar
hexChar = (fourBitValue == 0xD) ? "D" : hexChar
hexChar = (fourBitValue == 0xE) ? "E" : hexChar
hexChar = (fourBitValue == 0xF) ? "F" : hexChar
hexString = hexChar + hexString
document.write(originalInt +" displayed in")
document.write(" hexadecimal :")
document.writeln(hexString)
// end hiding -->
</SCRIPT>
</PRE>
</BODY>
</HTML>
```

> **NOTE**
>
> The previous example uses multiple conditional expressions to find a match. More efficient ways to compare a range of numbers are possible using loops. Loops are discussed in Chapter 7.

FIGURE 6.6.

Converting base 10 to base 16, as shown in Listing 6.5.

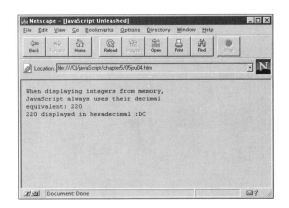

Notice from the previous discussion how many zeros are left unused when storing a relatively small number. This is another area where bitwise operators can prove useful. Using bitwise operators, you can conserve memory by storing data in the unused portion of any variable. For example, if your script uses a large group of positive integers less than or equal to 255, you could store four of them within one 32-bit word. Using a simple bitwise operation, you could then extract any number at will. With the amount of RAM most computers have today, it is usually not worth the extra coding effort. However, because JavaScript is designed to run on many platforms, you never know who will be running your script and who might run out of memory. Even so, you would have to be storing a lot of data in memory to begin worrying about this.

Operator Precedence

When creating expressions that use more than one operator, you should be aware that JavaScript doesn't necessarily evaluate an expression from right to left or vice versa. Each part of an expression is evaluated in an order based on a predefined precedence for each operator. Note the following example:

```
x = a * b + c
```

a is multiplied by b; the result is added to c. The result of the addition is finally assigned to x. The multiplication operator has a higher precedence than the addition operator and therefore is evaluated first. If, however, you need the addition to be evaluated first, you can surround the expression with parentheses:

```
x = a * (b + c)
```

Parentheses are operators that boost the precedence of the expression that they enclose. When an expression has more than one operator of the same kind, JavaScript evaluates from left to right.

The following list shows operators in order of their precedence from lowest to highest:

Comma	,
Assignment	= += -= *= /= %= <<= >>= >>>= &= ^= ¦=
Conditional	? :
Logical or	¦ ¦
Logical and	&&
Bitwise or	¦
Bitwise xor	^
Bitwise and	&
Equality	== !=
Comparison	< <= > >=
Bitwise shift	<< >> >>>
Addition/subtraction	+ -
Multiplication/division	* / %
Negation/increment	! ~ - ++ --
Call, data structure	() [] .

One effect that operator precedence can have is determining the type of value that is returned by an expression. This becomes apparent when trying to concatenate strings and numbers, as shown in Listing 6.6.

Listing 6.6. Operator precedence and different data types.

```
<HTML>
<HEAD>
<TITLE>JavaScript Unleashed</TITLE>
</HEAD>
<BODY>
<PRE>
<SCRIPT LANGUAGE = "JavaScript">
<!-- begin hiding from old browsers
carLength = 4 + 5
document.writeln(carLength)
carLength = 4 + 5 + " feet"
document.writeln(carLength)
carLength = "Length in feet: " + 4 + 5
document.writeln(carLength)
carLength = "Length in feet: " + (4 + 5)
document.writeln(carLength)
// end hiding -->
</SCRIPT>
</PRE>
</BODY>
</HTML>
```

When expressions have operators of the same precedence, JavaScript evaluates from left to right. The addition operator has the same precedence as the concatenate operator; therefore, JavaScript will evaluate all additions and concatenations from left to right throughout the statement. Notice in Figure 6.7 that the first two examples work as you would want them to. The third example shows what can happen when JavaScript works as designed. With the first + symbol, it converts the number 4 to a string and concatenates it to the end of `"Length in feet: "`. The result of this is the string `"Length in feet: 4"`. It then does the same with the number 5 to produce `"Length in feet: 45"`. If, however, you want to display the sum of 4 and 5 instead, you can use parentheses to increase the precedence of 4 + 5. In this case, both operands are numbers, and JavaScript performs an addition rather than a string concatenation. Figure 6.7 shows this as the fourth example.

FIGURE 6.7.

Operator precedence and different data types, as shown in Listing 6.6.

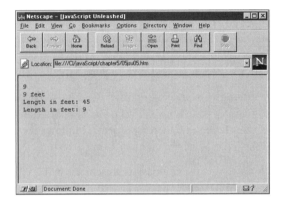

Summary

Assignment operators assign values to variables. Along with the simple assignment operator, JavaScript supports 11 combination assignment operators that combine either arithmetic or bitwise operators with the simple assignment operator.

Arithmetic operators let you perform basic math operations in JavaScript. These include addition, subtraction, multiplication, division, and modulus. JavaScript also includes increment and decrement operators as shortcuts to two common math operations. More advanced math operations are also built into JavaScript, but they must be accessed through the Math object. This is covered in Chapter 14.

Comparison operators compare two values and return a value of `true` or `false`. You can check to see if one value is equal to another, greater or less than another, or any combination of these.

The conditional operators let you return one of two values that you can define to be of any data type. The value returned is decided by the value of a logical expression that you also define.

String operators include the concatenation operator and all comparison operators. The concatenation operator is used to append one string to another to form a new string. Comparison operators can be used with strings to compare their ASCII values. Starting with the leftmost character of each string and moving right, a pair of characters are compared at a time. The returned value is either `true` or `false`.

Boolean operators are used with logical expressions to form another logical expression. The and operator returns `true` if both of its operands are `true`. Otherwise, it returns `false`. The or operator returns `true` if at least one of its operands are `true`. Otherwise, it returns `false`. The not operator returns `true` if its operand is `false`, and it will return `false` if its operand is `true`.

The `typeof` operator was added in version 3.0 of Netscape's Navigator Web browser. It is now a built-in operator for JavaScript used to return a string representing the type of data that its operand holds. This is especially useful when determining if a variable has been defined yet.

Two operators are involved to declare and use JavaScript functions. The call operator always follows a function name and surrounds any arguments that the function might accept. The comma operator is used to separate arguments if the function accepts more than one.

When you're dealing with arrays and other objects, two operators are needed. The dot is used to reference a member of an object. This is the standard dot notation. The member operator is used to index one element of an array object. It follows the array name and encloses a integer that refers to the location of the element being accessed.

JavaScript allows access to the binary representation of any integer through its bitwise operators. The one's complement operator is used to flip each bit of an integer. Bitwise logical operators are included to compare two integers. The binary form of each operand is used to pair up the bits in each integer. The logical operation is then performed on each pair of bits to return the resulting integer. Bitwise shift operators shift the bits of an integer to the right or left n number of places. When shifting to the right, JavaScript allows you to specify either sign-propagating or zero-fill shifting.

When all operations in the expression are of the same precedence, JavaScript interprets from right to left when evaluating expressions. Otherwise, the operation with the highest precedence is performed first and then the next highest, and so on. The precedence of each operator is predefined by JavaScript.

CHAPTER 7

Control Structures and Looping

IN THIS CHAPTER

Designing a script to make decisions during runtime can be the most interesting part of JavaScript. When you have a script make a decision based on its present state, you're simply telling it to ask a question and then choose a path to take based on the answer. For example, consider my morning commute to work. I can take a couple of different routes, and I choose one based on certain factors. I seldom cook, so the most important question I ask myself in the morning is whether I'm hungry. If I am, I choose the route that passes by the bagel shop. By the time I've finished picking up my breakfast, I'm usually running a little late. To make up for lost time, I drive directly to the highway where I can quickly accelerate to just under the speed limit. On the other hand, if I'm not hungry, which is hardly ever the case, I choose to drive past the bagel shop and continue to work at a steady 10 miles per hour below the speed limit.

Using the same idea, you can design your JavaScript programs to perform specific operations based on one or more factors. For example, in Chapter 6, "Operators," you learned how to test whether a variable is equal to a particular value or even a range of values. Using control structures, you can now make your program take one or more different paths based on the result of such a test. This is the first topic I'll cover in this chapter.

As your programs become larger, one thing to watch for is the length of time it could take for the client to download them. One way to cut down on the amount of source code in a script is to use looping statements. Using a loop, you can make your scripts perform many similar operations with only a few lines of code. This can help you shrink the size of your scripts and avoid typing the same commands repeatedly. Also in this chapter, I'll demonstrate ways to make your scripts more efficient.

Conditional Statements

In Chapter 6, I covered two conditional operators—? and :. These operators are used to create a two-step process. First, an expression is evaluated to be either `true` or `false`. Then, based on the result, one of two values is returned. You can also have the script make a decision based on an expression using the `if` and `else` statements. However, the result is different. Instead of returning a value based on the result, the program takes one of two paths. With this ability, you can make JavaScript perform many different functions based on any information you have available.

If

You use the `if` statement in the following way:

```
if (condition) {
    [statements]
}
```

The *condition* can be any logical expression. If the result of *condition* is `true`, the `statements` are executed, and program execution continues. If the condition returns `false`, JavaScript ignores the `statements` and continues. In Listing 7.1, I emulate the type of influence an over-bearing marketing department might have on a company's Web site. The script begins by setting the value of `visitorInterest` to one of two values. I selected `"Technical Support"` for this example and commented out the alternative assignment. Next, the script reaches the first `if` statement, which checks whether the value of `visitorInterest` is equal to the string `"New Products"`. The resulting value of this expression is `false`, and the block of code immediately following the `if` statement is ignored. The script then reaches the second `if` statement and checks the value of `visitorInterest` against `"Technical Support"`. The expression returns `true`, and the code that is enclosed in curly braces is executed. Regardless of what value `visitorInterest` is equal to, the last statement always executes, and Frank Zealous sends his sales pitch to the visitor. The entire display is shown in Figure 7.1. If you switch the value of `visitorInterest`, the output will change.

Listing 7.1. Using the `if` statement to make decisions.

```
<HTML>
<HEAD>
<TITLE>JavaScript Unleashed</TITLE>
</HEAD>
<BODY>
<IMG SRC="file:///C¦/javaScript/CHAPTER6/frank.gif" ALIGN=RIGHT>
<BR>
<PRE>
<SCRIPT LANGUAGE = "JavaScript">
<!-- begin hiding from old browsers
var visitorInterest
//visitorInterest = "New Products"
visitorInterest = "Technical Support"
document.writeln("Hello, my name is Frank Zealous!")
if (visitorInterest == "New Products") {
    document.writeln("Thank-you for inquiring about our products!")
}
if (visitorInterest == "Technical Support") {
    document.writeln("Technical support is now available.")
    document.write("But first, let me introduce you to our ")
    document.writeln("newest products!")
}
document.write("Our newest products will satisfy all of your ")
document.writeln("business needs!")
// end hiding -->
</SCRIPT>
</PRE>
</BODY>
</HTML>
```

FIGURE 7.1.

*Frank gives a
customized sales pitch.*

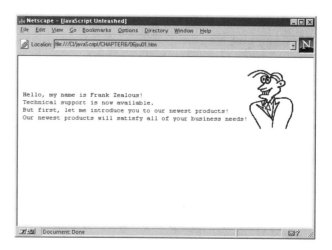

It's common practice to indent the set of statements enclosed in curly braces. This helps give your scripts a logical look and proves especially helpful when you nest if statements (that is, when you use an if statement within another if statement). Listing 7.2 demonstrates how you can use logical variables by themselves to determine the path a script can take. The first if statement evaluates the variable needsInfo. needsInfo was set to true, so JavaScript enters the first if block and continues by displaying Our products are used all over the world. Next, the second, or nested, if block is reached, and needsMoreInfo is evaluated. Again, the value returned is true, and the statements within the second block are executed. The end of the nested if block is completed, and JavaScript picks up where it left off with the first block. Notice how the indentation helps distinguish the separate blocks of code that may or may not be executed. Figure 7.2 shows that JavaScript performed each line of code in sequence. By resetting the values of needsInfo and needsMoreInfo, you can create three different results. One important thing to realize is that if needsInfo is false, the second if block is never reached. In this case, it doesn't matter if needsMoreInfo is set to true or false, because it will never have a chance to be evaluated. Sorry, Frank, but if they don't need information, they certainly don't need more information.

Listing 7.2. Nested if statements.

```
<HTML>
<HEAD>
<TITLE>JavaScript Unleashed</TITLE>
</HEAD>
<BODY>
<IMG SRC="file:///C¦/javaScript/CHAPTER6/frank.gif" ALIGN=RIGHT>
<BR>
<PRE>
<SCRIPT LANGUAGE = "JavaScript">
<!-- begin hiding from old browsers
var needsInfo, needsMoreInfo
```

```
//set either of the following to false and the output notice the change.
needsInfo = true
needsMoreInfo = true
document.writeln("I work for Best Products International!")
if (needsInfo) {
    document.writeln("Our products are used all over the world.")
    if (needsMoreInfo) {
        document.write("I don't know how you have managed")
        document.writeln(" without them.")
    }
document.writeln("\nOrdering is easy using our on-line service.")
}
// end hiding -->
</SCRIPT>
</PRE>
</BODY>
</HTML>
```

FIGURE 7.2.

One of three possible outcomes.

If...Else

Sometimes using the `if` statement alone is not enough. You can also reserve a set of statements to execute if the conditional expression returns `false`. You do this by adding an `else` block of statements immediately following the `if` block:

```
if (condition) {
    statements
} else {
    statements
}
```

Nothing is worse than a nagging computer, but Listing 7.3 demonstrates how interactive a Web page can be with only a few lines of code. Again I have hard-coded the key value, `purchaseAmount`, which determines the outcome of the script. To truly interact with the users of your script, you need to be able to receive input from them. This way, `purchaseAmount` can end up being any value, depending on what the customer orders. You can do this using JavaScript and standard HTML input objects such as checkbox and text objects. Chapter 13, "Form Objects," covers this topic in more detail.

In this example, the user hasn't spent enough money to satisfy Frank. The `if` statement evaluates to `false`, and the `else` block is executed. Figure 7.3 shows how the user's purchase is questioned by a pushy salesman.

Listing 7.3. The `else` block responds to a `false` value.

```
<HTML>
<HEAD>
<TITLE>JavaScript Unleashed</TITLE>
</HEAD>
<BODY>
<IMG SRC="file:///C¦/javaScript/CHAPTER6/frank.gif" ALIGN=RIGHT>
<BR>
<PRE>
<SCRIPT LANGUAGE = "JavaScript">
<!-- begin hiding from old browsers
var purchaseAmount
purchaseAmount = 10.00
if (purchaseAmount > 500.00) {
document.write("Thank-you for your purchase!")
} else {
    document.writeln("Thank-you, but surely there is something ")
    document.writeln("else you would like to purchase.")
}
// end hiding -->
</SCRIPT>
</PRE>
</BODY>
</HTML>
```

FIGURE 7.3.

One of two possible outcomes.

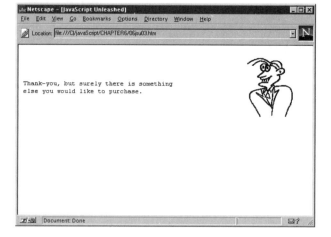

Looping Statements

Creating a loop inside a script can serve many purposes. One simple but very common use of a loop is counting. For example, writing a program that displays the numbers 0 through 9 is a quick and easy task. You could simply write 10 commands to display each number:

```
document.writeln("0")
document.writeln("1")
...
document.writeln("9")
```

This works for counting from 0 to 9, but what if you needed to count to 1,000? You can do this in the same manner, but the code takes much more time to write and download. The best way to count to 1,000 or any number is to use the same display statement with a variable in place of the string literal. By counting like this, the only thing you need is a way to increment the variable and repeat the display statement. JavaScript gives you the tools to handle this and other looping operations.

for

You use the `for` statement to start a loop in a script. Before taking a closer look at the `for` statement in Listing 7.4, examine the following syntax:

```
for ([initializing_expr]; [condition_expr]; [loop_expr]) {
    statements
}
```

The three expressions enclosed in parentheses are optional, but if you omit one, the semicolons are still required. This keeps each expression in its appropriate place. You typically use the initializing expression to initialize and even declare a variable to use as a counter for the loop. Next, the condition expression must evaluate to `true` before each execution of the statements enclosed in curly braces. Finally, the loop expression typically increments or decrements the variable that is used as the counter for the loop.

Listing 7.4 demonstrates the use of a `for` statement to count from 0 to 99 while displaying each number. To fit the output on a standard page, I added a line break after each set of 10 numbers. The output is shown in Figure 7.4.

Listing 7.4. A `for` loop used to count from 0 to 99.

```
<HTML>
<HEAD>
<TITLE>JavaScript Unleashed</TITLE>
<BODY>
<PRE>
<SCRIPT LANGUAGE = "JavaScript">
```

continues

Listing 7.4. continued

```
<!-- begin hiding from old browsers
document.writeln("Numbers 0 through 99 : ")
for (var i = 0 ; i < 100; ++i) {
    if(i%10 == 0) {
        document.writeln()
    }
    document.write(i + " ")
}
document.writeln("\n\nAfter completing the loop, i equals : " + i)
// end hiding -->
</SCRIPT>
</PRE>
</BODY>
</HTML>
```

FIGURE 7.4.

The output after looping through the same code 100 times.

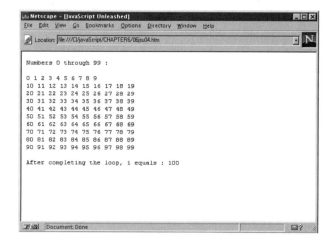

In Listing 7.4, the order of execution is as follows: The initializing expression declares the variable i and sets it to 0. The variable i is then tested to ensure that it's less than 100. Where i is still equal to 0, the condition expression returns true, and the program executes the statements between the curly braces. Once the program executes all the statements and reaches the ending curly brace, it evaluates the loop expression, ++i. This increments i by 1, thus concluding the first full loop, and the process begins again from the top. This time, JavaScript knows not to perform the initializing section of the for loop. Instead, the condition expression is evaluated again. Where i is still less than 100, another loop is allowed to occur. This continues, and the set of statements inside the for block is repeated until i reaches 100.

At 99, the condition expression returns true, and the program executes the statements one last time. Once again, i is incremented and set to 100. When the condition expression is evaluated, it returns false, and the loop breaks. Program execution picks up immediately after the ending curly brace. Because i was incremented to 100 before the loop was broken, 100 is the resulting value of i after the loop is finished. Notice also that the scope of i extends outside the `for` loop, obeying the rules of scope discussed in Chapter 5, "Fundamentals of the JavaScript Language."

> **NOTE**
>
> If the condition expression returns `false` on the first loop, the statements between the curly braces are never executed.

As with `if` statements, `for` loops can also be nested. Listing 7.5 shows how to step through each coordinate of a 10-by-10 grid. For each iteration of the first loop, there are 10 iterations of the nested loop. The result is that the nested loop is executed 100 times.

x is first assigned the value of 0. JavaScript reaches the nested loop and also assigns 0 to y. The nested loop displays the values of x and y and then increments y by 1. The nested loop continues until y is no longer less than 10. At this point, 10 sets of coordinates have been generated. The nested loop breaks, and control returns to the outer loop. x is incremented by 1, and again the nested loop starts. JavaScript knows that the nested loop is starting from the beginning and that the initializing expression must be evaluated again. This resets y to 0, and the statements are run another 10 times. The entire process continues until x is no longer less than 10 and the outer loop finally breaks. This displays 100 sets of coordinates, as shown in Figure 7.5. You aren't limited to a single nested loop, so you can increase the number of coordinates to three or even four. You can also use this same method to visit each element of a multidimensional array. Arrays are discussed in Chapter 14, "Built-In Language Objects."

Listing 7.5. A demonstration of a nested loop.

```
<HTML>
<HEAD>
<TITLE>JavaScript Unleashed</TITLE>
</HEAD>
<BODY>
<PRE>
<SCRIPT LANGUAGE = "JavaScript">
<!-- begin hiding from old browsers
document.writeln("All x,y coordinates between (0,0) and (9,9) :\n")
for (var x = 0; x < 10; ++x) {
    for (var y = 0; y < 10; ++y) {
        document.write("("+x + "," + y +") ")
    }
    document.writeln()
}
document.writeln("\nAfter completing the loop, x equals : " + x)
document.writeln("After completing the loop, y equals : " + y)
// end hiding -->
</SCRIPT>
</PRE>
</BODY>
</HTML>
```

FIGURE 7.5.

One hundred sets of coordinates generated by two loops.

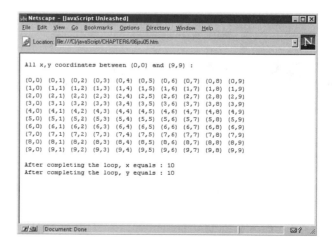

```
All x,y coordinates between (0,0) and (9,9) :

(0,0) (0,1) (0,2) (0,3) (0,4) (0,5) (0,6) (0,7) (0,8) (0,9)
(1,0) (1,1) (1,2) (1,3) (1,4) (1,5) (1,6) (1,7) (1,8) (1,9)
(2,0) (2,1) (2,2) (2,3) (2,4) (2,5) (2,6) (2,7) (2,8) (2,9)
(3,0) (3,1) (3,2) (3,3) (3,4) (3,5) (3,6) (3,7) (3,8) (3,9)
(4,0) (4,1) (4,2) (4,3) (4,4) (4,5) (4,6) (4,7) (4,8) (4,9)
(5,0) (5,1) (5,2) (5,3) (5,4) (5,5) (5,6) (5,7) (5,8) (5,9)
(6,0) (6,1) (6,2) (6,3) (6,4) (6,5) (6,6) (6,7) (6,8) (6,9)
(7,0) (7,1) (7,2) (7,3) (7,4) (7,5) (7,6) (7,7) (7,8) (7,9)
(8,0) (8,1) (8,2) (8,3) (8,4) (8,5) (8,6) (8,7) (8,8) (8,9)
(9,0) (9,1) (9,2) (9,3) (9,4) (9,5) (9,6) (9,7) (9,8) (9,9)

After completing the loop, x equals : 10
After completing the loop, y equals : 10
```

for...in

You need a basic understanding of JavaScript objects to use a `for...in` loop. After reading Chapter 9, "The JavaScript Object Model," you should be able to use the `for...in` construct with ease.

With `for...in`, you can execute a set of statements for each property in an object. You can use the `for...in` loop with any JavaScript object, regardless of whether it has properties. One iteration is executed for each property, so if the object doesn't have any properties, no loops occur. The `for...in` loop also works with custom objects. A variable of a custom JavaScript object is considered a property and therefore executes a loop for each one. Here is the syntax:

```
for (property in object) {
    statements
}
```

property is a string literal generated for you by JavaScript. For each loop, *property* is assigned the next property name contained in *object* until each one is used. Listing 7.6 uses this function to display each property name of the document object, along with each of the property's values. The results are shown in Figure 7.6.

CAUTION

The `for...in` loop works only with Netscape Navigator version 3.0 and later. It doesn't work properly in older versions of Navigator or in Microsoft Internet Explorer version 3.0.

Listing 7.6. Using a `for...in` loop in JavaScript.

```html
<HTML>
<HEAD>
<TITLE>JavaScript Unleashed</TITLE>
</HEAD>
<BODY>
<PRE>
<SCRIPT LANGUAGE = "JavaScript">
<!-- begin hiding from old browsers
var anObject = document
var propertyInfo = ""
for (var propertyName in anObject) {
    propertyInfo = propertyName + " = " + anObject[propertyName]
    document.writeln(propertyInfo)
}
// end hiding -->
</SCRIPT>
</PRE>
</BODY>
</HTML>
```

FIGURE 7.6.

Each property and its value for the document object.

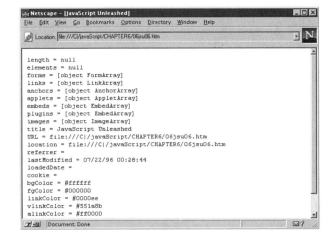

while

The `while` statement acts much like a `for` loop but doesn't include the function of initializing or incrementing variables in its declaration. You must declare variables beforehand and increment or decrement the variables within the *statements* block. The syntax follows:

```
while (condition_expr) {
    statements
}
```

Listing 7.7 shows how you can use a logical variable as a flag in determining whether to continue looping. This variable, status, is declared ahead of time and set to true. Once i is equal to 10, status is set to false, and the loop breaks. The result of Listing 7.7 is the sum of the integers from 0 to 10, as you can see in Figure 7.7.

Listing 7.7. Using the while loop in JavaScript.

```
<HTML>
<HEAD>
<TITLE>JavaScript Unleashed</TITLE>
</HEAD>
<BODY>
<PRE>
<SCRIPT LANGUAGE = "JavaScript">
<!-- begin hiding from old browsers
var i = 0,
    result = 0,
    status = true
document.write("0")
while (status) {
    result = result + ++i
    document.write(" + " + i)
    if(i == 10) {
        status = false
    }
}
document.writeln(" = " + result)
// end hiding -->
</SCRIPT>
</PRE>
</BODY>
</HTML>
```

FIGURE 7.7.

The results of Listing 7.7: 11 iterations of a while *loop.*

do...while

With the release of JavaScript version 1.2, the language now offers the do...while construct. This works exactly like the while statement, except that it doesn't check the conditional expression until after the first iteration. This guarantees that the script within the curly braces will be executed at least once. Listing 7.8 shows an example where it's unknown what the exact value of userEntry might be (if it were actually entered by the user). A value of 0 is given to userEntry to demonstrate that the user might not enter a value that satisfies the conditional statement. Yet the user's entry is still displayed.

Listing 7.8. The do...while statement ensures at least one iteration.

```
<HTML>
<HEAD>
<TITLE>JavaScript Unleashed</TITLE>
</HEAD>
<BODY>
<PRE>
<SCRIPT LANGUAGE = "JavaScript1.2">
<!-- begin hiding from old browsers
var userEntry = 0
var x = 1
do {
     document.writeln(x)
     x++
} while (x <= userEntry)
// end hiding -->
</SCRIPT>
</PRE>
</BODY>
</HTML>
```

break and continue

A loop usually doesn't stop repeating itself until the specified condition returns false. Sometimes, you might want to exit the loop before reaching the ending curly brace. You can do this by adding either break or continue to the statements block of a loop. break terminates the loop altogether, whereas continue skips the remaining statements for the current loop, evaluates the loop expression (if one exists), and begins the next loop. You can see the difference between these two statements in Listing 7.9. This script takes a very basic approach to finding the approximate square root of a number, n. Starting with i set to 0, the for loop begins by displaying the value of i. Next, the script checks to ensure that n is not negative. If n is negative, the loop is broken, and program execution resumes after the ending curly brace. If n is positive, i is multiplied by itself, and the result is compared to n. If the result is less than n, i is stored as the highest number so far to be equal to or less than the square root of n. The continue statement then skips the rest of the current loop and resumes from the top of the loop after incrementing i. As soon as i squared is greater than n, the script passes the continue statement and reaches the break statement, which stops the loop completely. The approximate square root of 175 is shown in Figure 7.8.

Listing 7.9. Using the `continue` **and** `break` **statements.**

```
<HTML>
<HEAD>
<TITLE>JavaScript Unleashed</TITLE>
</HEAD>
<BODY>
<PRE>
<SCRIPT LANGUAGE = "JavaScript">
<!-- begin hiding from old browsers
var highestNum = 0
var n = 175 //any number will do.
for (var i = 0; i < n; ++i) {
    document.writeln(i)
    if (n < 0) {
        document.write("n cannot be negative.")
        break
    }
    if (i * i <= n) {
        highestNum = i
        continue
    }
    document.writeln("Finished!")
    break
}
document.write("The integer less than or equal to the Square Root")
document.writeln(" of " + n + " = " + highestNum)
// end hiding -->
</SCRIPT>
</PRE>
</BODY>
</HTML>
```

FIGURE 7.8.

The display after break *is reached and the loop stops.*

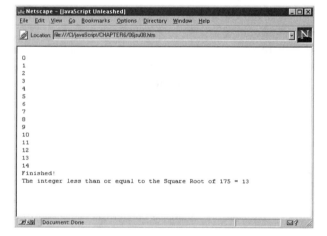

labeled

With the release of JavaScript version 1.2, the language now offers a way to be more specific when using the break or continue statements. You can see its use in Listing 7.10.

Listing 7.10. Using the `labeled` statement.

```
<HTML>
<HEAD>
<TITLE>JavaScript Unleashed</TITLE>
</HEAD>
<BODY>
<PRE>
<SCRIPT LANGUAGE = "JavaScript1.2">
<!-- begin hiding from old browsers
var stopX = 3
var stopY = 8
document.writeln("All x,y pairs between (0,0) and ("+stopX+","+stopY+") :\n")
loopX:
for (var x = 0; x < 10; ++x) {
    for (var y = 0; y < 10; ++y) {
        document.write("("+x + "," + y +") ")
        if(x == stopX && y == stopY) {
            break loopX
        }
    }
    document.writeln()
}
document.writeln("\nAfter completing the loop, x equals : " + x)
document.writeln("After completing the loop, y equals : " + y)
// end hiding -->
</SCRIPT>
</PRE>
</BODY>
</HTML>
```

The `labeled` statement can be placed before any control structure that can nest other statements. In Listing 7.9, a `for` loop is labeled with the user-defined identifier `loopX`. This lets you break out of or continue in this `for` loop, regardless of how nested the program is at that time. `loopX` is added to the `break` statement to stop both `for` loops from continuing. Without the label, the `break` statement would have stopped only the loop generating values for y. (Listing 7.9 was modified from Listing 7.5.) Figure 7.9 displays the results when the x and y values reach 3 and 8, respectively.

FIGURE 7.9.

Using the labeled
statement to break out
of a nested for *loop.*

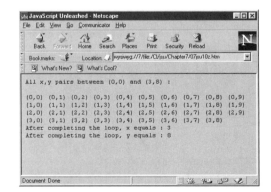

with

The `with` statement is used to avoid repeatedly specifying the object reference when accessing properties or methods of that object. Any property or method in a `with` block that JavaScript doesn't recognize is associated with the object specified for that block. Here is the syntax:

```
with (object) {
    statements
}
```

`object` specifies which object reference to use in the absence of one in the `statements` block. This is quite useful when you're using advanced math functions that are available only through the `math` object. The `math` object isn't covered until Chapter 14, so instead I'll demonstrate the `with` statement using the `document` object, which you're more familiar with. When using the `write()` or `writeln()` methods associated with the `document` object, I include the prefix `document.`, as in the following line:

```
document.writeln("Hello!")
```

When you display a large amount of data using this technique, it's not uncommon to use the same `document.writeln()` statements many times over. To cut down on the amount of code needed, enclose all statements that reference the `document` object within a `with` block, as shown in Listing 7.11. This way, you can eliminate the `document` prefix when using a document's methods or properties. Notice that `title` and `URL` are properties of the document object and would normally be written as `document.title` and `document.URL`. Using the `with` statement, you need to reference the object only once to produce the same results as typing each line. Figure 7.10 shows the results.

CAUTION

Internet Explorer version 3.0 doesn't support the `with` statement.

Listing 7.11. Using the `with` statement in JavaScript.

```
<HTML>
<HEAD>
<TITLE>JavaScript Unleashed</TITLE>
</HEAD>
<BODY>
<PRE>
<SCRIPT LANGUAGE = "JavaScript">
<!-- begin hiding from old browsers
with (document) {
    writeln("Hello!")
    writeln("The title of this document is, \"" + title + "\".")
    writeln("The URL for this document is: " + URL)
    writeln("Now you can avoid using the object's prefix each time!")
}
```

```
// end hiding -->
</SCRIPT>
</PRE>
</BODY>
</HTML>
```

FIGURE 7.10.

Displaying information using the with statement.

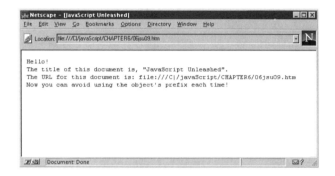

switch

The switch statement is used to compare one value against many others. This task can be accomplished using many if statements, but the switch statement is more readable and allows you to specify a default set of statements to execute in case a match isn't found. Listing 7.12 assumes that the variable request could change, depending on what the user has asked for. For this example, request is assigned "Names" as the value to compare to each case. The second case is equal to request, and it executes the statements that follow.

Listing 7.12. The switch statement.

```
<HTML>
<HEAD>
<TITLE>JavaScript Unleashed</TITLE>
</HEAD>
<BODY>
<SCRIPT LANGUAGE= "JavaScript1.2">
<!--
var request = "Name"
switch (request) {
    case "Logo" :
        document.write('<IMG src="logo.gif" alt="Logo" height=45 width=45>')
        document.write("<BR>")
        break
    case "Name" :
        document.write("Acadia Software Inc.")
        document.write("<BR>")
        break
```

continues

Listing 7.12. continued

```
    case "Products" :
          document.write("Acadia Infuse")
          document.write("<BR>")
          break
    default :
          document.write("www.acadians.com")
          break
}
//-->
</SCRIPT>
</BODY>
</HTML>
```

The break statement is used to stop any further execution of the code remaining in the switch statement. If no break statements were used, the remaining code for each case would be executed, regardless of a match between request and that case. Figure 7.11 simply shows that request matched the value "Name" and displayed the company name.

FIGURE 7.11.

Using the switch
statement.

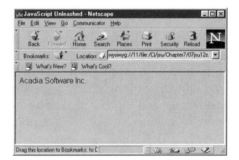

Summary

To make decisions in JavaScript, use the conditional statements if and else. You can use if by itself to execute a section of code based on the condition of an expression. If the expression returns true, the code will be executed; otherwise, it will not.

Use the else statement immediately after the if block to have JavaScript execute code when the expression from the if block returns false.

JavaScript lets you nest if and if...else statements within each other. Using this method, you can ask questions based on the answers to previous questions.

Use for loops to repeat a section of your script. In the declaration, you have the option of initializing a variable to be used inside the loop. You can also specify how to change the variable each time a loop is completed. Based on the conditional expression of the for loop, you can specify the reason for the loop to stop.

Use the `for...in` loop to perform a set of operations for each property of an object. JavaScript automatically assigns the name of the property to a variable that you specify. Using this variable, you can perform operations on that property.

Use the `while` loop to repeat a section of your script. You only need to specify a conditional expression that needs to return `true` before each loop is executed.

The `break` and `continue` statements are used to stop the execution of any loop. `break` stops the loop completely, and `continue` stops only the current iteration of the loop and skips to the beginning of the next iteration.

The `with` statement is used in conjunction with JavaScript objects. It allows you to reference an object once rather than each time you access a property or method of the object. Inside the `with` block, you can use the property and method names of an object without their object reference prefix.

Functions

IN THIS CHAPTER

CHAPTER 8

Performing a function, or many functions, is the purpose of all JavaScript programs. In its simplest form, a script can read or take in data, perform operations on a set of data, or display and send out data. As you have seen in previous examples, you can use a combination of these basic tools or merely one of them to serve an overall purpose. To entertain a casual browser, you might first inquire about his interests and then point him in the right direction. To welcome someone back to your Web page, you might let her know what is new and exciting. If you have products to sell, JavaScript can easily quote a price for any combination of items that interest the user while storing this data for your marketing department.

Accomplishing tasks such as these requires writing many lines of JavaScript code. Some sections of the script might need to execute as soon as a Web page is loaded into the browser. Other parts of the script might be most useful if they are delayed until an HTML form accepts data from the client. Sometimes, you might need parts of a script more than once or even an unlimited amount of times, and intermittently repeating a section of code could become necessary. These issues bring about the idea of splitting a script into smaller parts to serve an individual, specific purpose. A specific purpose might be to signal a "direct hit" during a game developed with JavaScript. Validating data entered in an HTML form is another task you might want a script to run more than once while someone is viewing your Web page.

It makes a lot of sense to logically split a script into sections that each serve a single purpose. When the time comes, one particular section of a script can be called to execute. JavaScript gives you this ability through a structure known as a *function*.

Understanding Functions

A JavaScript function is simply a script that is sectioned off as a separate piece of code and given a name. Using this name, a script can then call this separate script to execute at any time and as often as it needs to. Many programming languages, such as C and C++, also use functions, whereas others incorporate the same tools but call them procedures or subroutines. They all do basically the same thing, but they do have differences.

Functions are meant to serve a single purpose to help split up the many tasks that one script is designed to do. You can think of this process as telling JavaScript to perform this list of related instructions and tell you when it's done.

Functions can receive values from their calling statements, called *arguments*. You can then use the arguments as *variables* within the statements block.

Creating Functions

The following code fragment shows the syntax for declaring a function:

```
function functionName ([argument1] [...,argumentN]) {
     [statements]
}
```

The keyword `function` is used to specify a name, *functionName*, which serves as the identifier for the set of statements between the curly braces. Enclosed in parentheses and separated by commas are the argument names, which hold each value that a function receives. Technically, arguments are variables that are assigned to literal values, other variables, or objects that are passed to the function by the calling statement. If you don't specify any arguments, you must still include an empty set of parentheses to complete the declaration. The statements, which are the core of the function, are executed each time the function is called. For better readability, statements within the statement block are typically indented.

Where to Declare Functions

You can declare functions anywhere inside a `<SCRIPT>` block except within other functions or control structures. Keep in mind that just as different blocks of an HTML document are loaded ahead of others, so are any scripts that are embedded in these HTML blocks. For this reason, it is recommended that you declare functions inside a script that is embedded in the `<HEAD>` block of a document. Declaring all your functions here ensures that the functions are available if another script needs to use them immediately.

Inside the <HEAD> Section

Listing 8.1 shows a function named `defaultColors()` declared inside the `<HEAD>` block of an HTML document. This function is then called once within the `<BODY>` block of the document.

Listing 8.1. Declaring a function in the <HEAD> block.

```
<HTML>
<HEAD>
<TITLE>JavaScript Unleashed</TITLE>
<SCRIPT LANGUAGE = "JavaScript">
<!-- begin hiding from old browsers
function defaultColors() {
    document.fgColor = "black"
    document.bgColor = "white"
    document.writeln("Inside of defaultColors()")
}
// end hiding -->
</SCRIPT>
</HEAD>
<BODY>
<PRE>
<SCRIPT LANGUAGE = "JavaScript">
<!-- begin hiding from old browsers
document.writeln("Functions are scripts just waiting to run!")
defaultColors()
document.writeln("All done.")
// end hiding -->
</SCRIPT>
</PRE>
</BODY>
</HTML>
```

8

Calling Functions

Listing 8.1 shows how the function `defaultColors()` is called from the second script block. This is an example of calling a function that takes no arguments. When the HTML document is loaded, the function is loaded into memory and "put on hold." The function is not executed until the main script block calls it with the following statement:

```
defaultColors()
```

At this point, program execution jumps immediately to the first line of the `defaultColors()` function. After executing all three lines of code, the program jumps back to where it left off and finishes what is left. This results in the same effect as if you had inserted all the function's statements directly into that position in your code. Now that a name is assigned to this function, all you need to do to run the same statements is use its name again. You can view the results of this process in Figure 8.1. Reusing code like this is the ideal way to use functions.

FIGURE 8.1.

Reusing code.

> **NOTE**
>
> Unlike a string's `fontcolor` property, you can change a document's `fgcolor` and `bgcolor` properties without refreshing or reloading the page into the browser.

Working with Arguments

Setting up functions to accept arguments can be very useful. Doing so lets you reuse the function in several ways while serving the same general purpose. For example, you might want to create a function to be used many times throughout your program; however, one of the values inside the function might need to change each time the function is called. One way to solve this problem without arguments is to use global variables that can be modified both outside and inside the function. This can get confusing if you happen to use the same variable names inside more than one function. The best thing to do is set up the function to accept an argument for each value you want it to receive. Listing 8.2 shows a function that takes advantage of using arguments.

Listing 8.2. Using an argument with a JavaScript function.

```
<HTML>
<HEAD>
<TITLE>JavaScript Unleashed</TITLE>
<SCRIPT LANGUAGE = "JavaScript">
<!-- begin hiding from old browsers
function getBinary(anInteger) {
    var result = "" // full 32-bit result
    var shortResult = "" // without leading zeros
    for(var i=1; i <= 32; i++) {
        if(anInteger & 1 == 1) {
            result = "1" + result
            shortResult = result
        } else {
            result =  "0" + result
        }
        anInteger = anInteger >> 1
    }
    return(shortResult)
}
// end hiding -->
</SCRIPT>
</HEAD>
<BODY>
<PRE>
<SCRIPT LANGUAGE = "JavaScript">
<!-- begin hiding from old browsers
var binaryString = ""
x = 9
binaryString = getBinary(x)
document.write("The number " + x + " in binary form is : ")
document.writeln(binaryString)
x = 255
binaryString = getBinary(x)
document.write("The number " + x + " in binary form is : ")
document.writeln(binaryString)
document.writeln("The variable x is still equal to : " + x)
// end hiding -->
</SCRIPT>
</PRE>
</BODY>
</HTML>
```

8

FUNCTIONS

When the function is called with the statement getBinary(x), the function receives a copy of the value that is stored in x. This process is called *passing by value*. The value is then assigned to anInteger, a variable local to the function. Notice that you don't need to declare anInteger using the var keyword. JavaScript automatically declares a new variable every time the function is called. You can then use the variable throughout the statement block as a local variable. If anInteger changes value while inside the function, it doesn't affect the value of the variable x, which was passed as an argument, as shown in Figure 8.2.

FIGURE 8.2.

Passing by value doesn't affect the original variable.

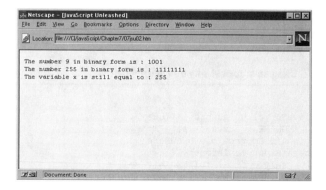

The last statement given in the getBinary() function is return(shortResult). Just as a function can receive a value, it can also return a value. The return statement returns a single value to the location in the program that first called the function. Returning a value from a function works in the same way as returning a value from an expression. The following statement assigns the value returned by getBinary() to the variable binaryString:

```
binaryString = getBinary(x)
```

In this case, the final value of shortResult ends up assigned to binaryString.

You can use functions that return values anywhere you use a normal expression. Some functions return the result of a set of calculations, whereas others return a logical value just to let you know if everything went all right. This technique is demonstrated in Listing 8.3. The function call isPhone(userInput) is used as the condition expression of an if statement. The function isPhone() is a function that returns a logical value. The value returned lets the caller know if a phone number was entered in the correct format. This is useful for validating data that the user has entered in an HTML form. Figure 8.3 shows that the phone number was entered correctly, and an appropriate message is displayed. You can find more information about validating data entry in Chapter 20, "Forms and Data Validation."

Listing 8.3. Functions that return values can be used in expressions.

```
<HTML>
<HEAD>
<TITLE>JavaScript Unleashed</TITLE>
<SCRIPT LANGUAGE = "JavaScript">
<!-- begin hiding from old browsers
function isPhone(aString) {
    var aChar = null
    var status = true
    if(aString.length != 13) {
        status = false
    } else {
        for(var i = 0; i <= 12; i++) {
            aChar = aString.charAt(i)
```

```
                    if ( i == 0 && aChar == "(" )
                        continue
                    else
                        if( i == 4 && aChar == ")" )
                            continue
                        else
                            if( i == 8 && aChar == "-" )
                                continue
                            else
                                if( parseInt(aChar,10) >= 0 &&
                                    parseInt(aChar,10) <= 9 )
                                    continue
                                else {
                                    status = false
                                    break
                                }
            }
        }
        return(status)
}
// end hiding -->
</SCRIPT>
</HEAD>
<BODY>
<PRE>
<SCRIPT LANGUAGE = "JavaScript">
<!-- begin hiding from old browsers
var userInput = "(800)555-1212"
if(isPhone(userInput)) {
    document.writeln("Thank you for your phone number.")
document.writeln("I will have a representative get you")
    document.writeln("more information.")
} else {
    document.writeln("Please re-enter your phone number")
    document.writeln("using the format (###)###-####")
}
// end hiding -->
</SCRIPT>
</PRE>
</BODY>
</HTML>
```

8

FUNCTIONS

FIGURE 8.3.

*Using a function as a
conditional expression.*

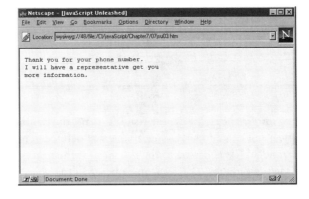

Varying the Number of Arguments

A function is set up to accept a certain number of arguments. Although it's good programming practice to pass the same number of arguments that were declared, it's sometimes practical to allow a different number of arguments. This is common when calling a function that usually uses the same parameter each time but is set up to handle special cases. In this case, you might want to use a default value inside the function if no arguments are passed. This lets you use the function without arguments or lets you specify a value other than the default. In Listing 8.4, I set up a function to display a very basic welcome message when the user arrives at a Web page.

Listing 8.4. Accepting either one or no arguments.

```
<HTML>
<HEAD>
<TITLE>JavaScript Unleashed</TITLE>
<SCRIPT LANGUAGE = "JavaScript">
<!-- begin hiding from old browsers
//userName is optional
function welcomeMessage(userName) {
    if (userName != null) {
        document.writeln("\"Hello again, " + userName + ".\"")
      } else {
        document.writeln("\"Welcome to our Web site!\"")
        document.write("\nIf a value is not passed to this ")
        document.writeln("function, displaying the")
        document.write("variable \"userName\" would show : ")
        document.writeln(userName)
      }
}
// end hiding -->
</SCRIPT>
</HEAD>
<BODY>
<PRE>
<SCRIPT LANGUAGE = "JavaScript">
<!-- begin hiding from old browsers
document.writeln("First call to welcomeMessage(),\n")
welcomeMessage("Mr. President")
document.writeln("<HR>\nSecond call to welcomeMessage(),\n")
welcomeMessage()
// end hiding -->
</SCRIPT>
</PRE>
</BODY>
</HTML>
```

Depending on whether it knows the visitor's name, the program displays one of two messages. If userName is not equal to null, the variable was defined. This is possible only if a value, such as "Mr. President," was passed to the function. If the function is equal to null, the program avoids using the variable in the welcome message altogether. Using it displays unwanted data, as shown in Figure 8.4. Depending on your Web browser, the unwanted data will be displayed as undefined or will be left blank.

FIGURE 8.4.

The results of passing either one or two arguments.

TIP

JavaScript now supports the `typeof` operator, which could be used to check if `userName` is undefined rather than `null`. This is the ideal way to check but is not yet supported by all browsers.

RESOURCE

For an up-to-date summary of new JavaScript features, follow this link to Netscape's authoring guide:

`http://home.netscape.com/eng/mozilla/3.0/handbook/javascript/#summary`

Another possibility is that a function gets passed more arguments than were specified in the declaration. The extra values aren't lost; they're stored in an array named `arguments`, which is a property of every function. All arguments stored in the array can be extracted within the statements block. For example, to get the first argument passed to the `welcomeMessage` function, you can use the following statement:

```
firstArg = welcomeMessage.arguments[0]
```

JavaScript arrays are indexed starting at 0. To find the second item in the array, you would use 1, and so on. To find the total number of arguments that were passed, you can use the following statement to find the length of the array:

```
numArgs = welcomeMessage.arguments.length
```

8

FUNCTIONS

Using these features, I modified the welcomeMessage() function to accept a variable number of arguments and included it in Listing 8.5. The welcomeMessage() function can therefore accept the following syntax:

```
welcomeMessage([userName] [,extraMessage1] [,extraMessage2]...)
```

Listing 8.5. A function can be set up to accept a variable number of arguments.

```
<HTML>
<HEAD>
<TITLE>JavaScript Unleashed</TITLE>
<SCRIPT LANGUAGE = "JavaScript">
<!-- begin hiding from old browsers
//Use this syntax for welcomeMessage function:
//welcomeMessage([userName] [,extraMessage1] [,extraMessage2]...)
function welcomeMessage(userName) {
    if (userName != null) {
        document.writeln("\"Hello again, " + userName + ".\"")
    } else {
        document.writeln("\"Welcome to our Web site!\"")
    }
    numArgs = welcomeMessage.arguments.length
    //If more arguments than the userName were sent,
//display each one.
    if (numArgs > 1) {
        for(var i = 1; i < numArgs; i++) {
            document.writeln("\""+welcomeMessage.arguments[i]+"\"")
        }
    }
}
// end hiding -->
</SCRIPT>
</HEAD>
<BODY>
<PRE>
<SCRIPT LANGUAGE = "JavaScript">
<!-- begin hiding from old browsers
var userName = "David", extraMsg = "It has been a long time!"
var userName2 = null
var extraMsg1 = "Would you like to become a member?"
var extraMsg2 = "You can enroll online!"
welcomeMessage(userName, extraMsg)
document.writeln("<HR>")
welcomeMessage(userName2, extraMsg1, extraMsg2)
// end hiding -->
</SCRIPT>
</PRE>
</BODY>
</HTML>
```

Notice that Listing 8.5 can still handle the situation in which the userName is unknown but extra messages need to be displayed. The variable userName2 is assigned null to fill the first element in the arguments array so that a message isn't displayed as the user's name. Figure 8.5 shows the resulting output.

FIGURE 8.5.

*Accepting multiple
arguments to display
many messages.*

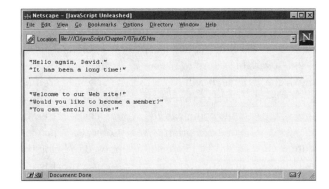

When you're developing with a group of people, it's important to document the intricacies of your scripts so that others can understand the full potential of what you have written. Without descriptive comments, reading through an application takes much more time to understand.

Using Global and Local Variables

In Chapter 5, "Fundamentals of the JavaScript Language," I described the difference between local and global variables. I demonstrated how global variables can be modified from anywhere in a document, whereas local variables can be modified only within the function where they're declared. You can choose which type of variable to use by following these guidelines:

- If the value of a variable is meant to be used and possibly modified by any part of a program, both inside and outside functions, the variable should be declared outside any function. This has the effect of making it global and modifiable by any part of the program. The best place to declare a global variable is in the <HEAD> block of an HTML document to ensure that it's declared before being used. The variable need not be declared again inside any function.

- If the variable is needed only within a particular function, it should be declared inside that function. Be sure to use the keyword var when declaring the variable. This ensures that its value can be changed only within the function. This also ensures that JavaScript looks at this variable as unique and separate from any global variables that might have the same name. It's not necessary to use the var keyword to declare argument variables. Variables that are specified in the declaration of the function are automatically considered local, as if they were declared with the var keyword.

- If you want to use a variable only in the main script and not within any functions, declare the variable somewhere outside all functions. Unfortunately, nothing prevents the script from using the variable inside functions, because the variable is still considered global. If you aren't careful, this can lead to overwriting values held by variables with the same name. To avoid this problem completely, always follow the preceding guideline.

8

FUNCTIONS

■ If you want the value of a variable to be modifiable by one function, but you need to use the variable in another function, pass the variable as an argument to that function. This has the effect of making a copy of the variable and assigning its value to the argument variable set up to receive it. As the function works and modifies its own copy of the variable, it will not affect the original. Argument variables are automatically declared as local to that function. Even if the argument variable has the same name as the variable being passed, making changes to it doesn't affect the variable that was passed. The one exception to this is objects. When an object is passed as an argument, it's passed by reference, as opposed to being passed by value. Instead of making a copy of the object, the function uses the original object. Changes made to an object's properties within the function have an effect on the original object.

To see examples of passing variables by value, look at Listing 8.6. I made it a point to demonstrate how JavaScript considers some variables with the same name to be different. This is shown when the variable numberB is passed to the function doublePassedVar(). JavaScript automatically creates a local variable also named numberB. Even though this local variable has the same name as the global variable, modifications to it don't affect the global variable. Figure 8.6 shows the results.

Listing 8.6. The effects of local and global variables.

```
<HTML>
<HEAD>
<TITLE>JavaScript Unleashed</TITLE>
<SCRIPT LANGUAGE = "JavaScript">
<!-- begin hiding from old browsers
var numberA //Global variable modified in any function
var numberB //Global variable only modified in main script
function doubleGlobalVar() {
    numberA *= 2  // This will change the value of the
                  // global variable.
}
function tripleLocalVar() {
    var numberA = 1 // This uses the same name as the
                    // global variable, but is considered
                    // different by JavaScript.
    numberA *= 3
}
function doublePassedVar(numberB) {
    // I purposely gave the argument variable the same
    // name as the variable being passed. This shows that
    // JavaScript considers them to be different.
    numberB *= 2
}
// end hiding -->
</SCRIPT>
</HEAD>
<BODY>
<PRE>
<SCRIPT LANGUAGE = "JavaScript">
<!-- begin hiding from old browsers
numberA = 1
```

```
document.writeln("Initial value of numberA: " + numberA)
doubleGlobalVar()
tripleLocalVar()
document.writeln("Final value of numberA: " + numberA)
numberB = 1
document.writeln("Initial value of numberB: " + numberB)
doublePassedVar(numberB)
document.writeln("Final value of numberB: " + numberB)
// end hiding -->
</SCRIPT>
</PRE>
</BODY>
</HTML>
```

FIGURE 8.6.

The resulting values of the numberA *and* numberB *variables.*

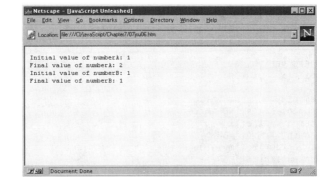

Passing Objects by Reference

A formal introduction to creating custom JavaScript objects is given in Chapter 15, but when dealing with functions, it's important to know what happens when you use an object as one of the arguments for a function call. When a simple data type such as a string, number, or boolean is passed to a function, it's passed by value. This means that a copy of the variable instead of the original is used by the function. Any changes made to the copy don't affect the original. On the other hand, when an object is passed to a function, it's passed by reference. This allows the function to alter the original version of the object. Knowing this, you have the ability to wrap simple data types inside an object if you would rather pass the variable by reference. Listing 8.7 demonstrates how to do this.

Listing 8.7. Passing by reference versus passing by value.

```
<HTML>
<HEAD>
<TITLE>JavaScript Unleashed</TITLE>
<SCRIPT LANGUAGE= "JavaScript">
<!--
//wrap and integer inside an object
function intObject() {
```

continues

Listing 8.7. continued

```
        this.i
        return this
}
function start() {
    //declare two ways to store an integer
    var i
    var myIntObject = new intObject()

    //assign initial values
    i = 0
    myIntObject.i = 0

    //display current values
    document.write("<BR>Before<BR>")
    document.write("i = " + i)
    document.write("<BR>")
    document.write("myIntObject = " + myIntObject.i)
    document.write("<BR>")

    //pass variables
    modify(i, myIntObject)

    //display current values
    document.write("<BR>After<BR>")
    document.write("i = " + i)
    document.write("<BR>")
    document.write("myIntObject = " + myIntObject.i)
    document.write("<BR>")
}
function modify(n, obj) {
    n++
    obj.i++
}
//-->
</SCRIPT>
</HEAD>
<BODY>
<SCRIPT LANGUAGE="JavaScript">
<!--
start()
//-->
</SCRIPT>
</BODY>
</HTML>
```

The function `intObject()` is actually used to wrap the variable `i` inside an object. An instance of the object is created with the line

```
var myIntObject = new intObject()
```

`myIntObject` can now be used to access the variable `i` with the code

```
myIntObject.i
```

This also allows you to pass the number by reference if you pass the entire object to the function. The `modify()` function is used to show the difference between modifying a simple data type and modifying an object. In Figure 8.7, you can see that the original value of n was not affected, while the original value of `myIntObject.i` was.

FIGURE 8.7.

*Passing a custom
JavaScript object
by reference.*

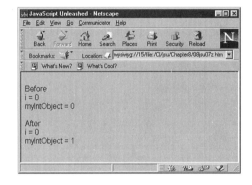

Reusing Functions

Functions are great for separating an application into its logical parts, but their best advantage is promoting the reuse of code. Functions are unlike sections of code enclosed in loops to be repeated many times in succession; you can reuse a function at any given time by simply calling its name. Creating functions that serve one purpose but that are useful in many situations takes practice and a little foresight. For example, in Listing 8.4, the `welcomeMessage()` function serves one purpose on more than one occasion throughout the execution of the program. By allowing a more flexible argument list in Listing 8.5, the `welcomeMessage()` function became useful in more situations. The function still serves the same purpose, but it's a better candidate for reuse in its more flexible form.

Recursive Functions

JavaScript functions can be *recursive,* which means that a function can call itself. Solving factorial equations is a common way to demonstrate how recursion works. Since JavaScript doesn't offer a factorial operator, I have included an example of how to solve factorials using a recursive function. To find the factorial of any positive integer n, you simply find the product of all integers 1 through n. To find the factorial of 7, written 7!, calculate the following:

$6! = 6 \times 5 \times 4 \times 3 \times 2 \times 1$

$= 720$

To calculate 7!, you would use the following:

$7! = 7 \times 6 \times 5 \times 4 \times 3 \times 2 \times 1$

Comparing these two calculations, you can produce a general formula to use in your function. Notice that 7! is equal to 7 × 6!. For any positive integer n greater than 0, n! = n × (n - 1)!. The first iteration would process this:

$$7! = 7 \times (7 - 1)!$$
$$= 7 \times 6!$$

From here, you have to stop and calculate 6! before continuing with the rest of the calculation. This occurs six more times before you can back out of each one and find the final solution. Instead of doing that, you can use a recursive function such as the following:

```
function getFactorial(n) {
    var result
    if(n > 0)
        result = n * getFactorial(n - 1)
    else if(n==0)
            result = 1
        else
            result = null
    return(result)
}
```

The function first checks to see if n is greater than 0, which happens the majority of the time. If this is true, the function multiplies n by the result returned from calling the function again with a different argument—in this case, n-1. This continues to put many getFactorial functions on hold until n is equal to zero. At this point, the most nested occurrence of the function finishes and returns the first value. JavaScript then backs out and finishes each nested function until it reaches the original call to getFactorial, and then it returns the final result.

Developing useful functions can be one of the most rewarding and interesting aspects of programming. After you see a function in action, it's common to go back and modify it to make it more flexible. If you do this, be sure that the function still serves one purpose and doesn't do more than you expect from reading the name. Becoming experienced in writing functions prepares you for the next exciting step in JavaScript programming—creating custom objects. This is covered in Chapter 15, "Creating Custom JavaScript Objects." For now, there is much to be learned about the objects that are already built into HTML and JavaScript, which is the focus of Part III, "JavaScript Objects." JavaScript also includes functions that are built into the language and can be used at any time. These are covered in Chapter 14, "Built-In Language Objects."

Summary

JavaScript functions serve a few purposes. They let you put code on hold so that it doesn't execute immediately when the document is loaded. They let you duplicate code easily and use the same code to perform the same operations on different sets of data. The latter is done with arguments.

A *function* is a set of JavaScript code that is grouped and given a name. To declare a function, use the `function` statement followed by the name you wish to give it, a set of parentheses, and the script that you want the function to include. Function names must adhere to the rules applied to all variables.

Functions can be declared anywhere inside an HTML document, as long as the declaration is surrounded by `<SCRIPT>` tags. It is suggested that functions be declared in the `<HEAD>` of the document.

To call a function, use its name followed by a set of parentheses. The parentheses enclose any arguments that the function can accept.

JavaScript arguments are passed by value. Functions can accept a variable number of arguments regardless of how the function was declared. Each function has an array named `arguments` associated with it. This array can be used to extract an argument that might have been passed to the function.

JavaScript functions can return values. Functions that return values can be used as expressions or in other expressions.

Argument variables don't need to be declared. They are automatically declared as local variables each time the function is called. To declare a global variable within a function, don't use the `var` keyword. Instead, just initialize the variable.

Functions that serve one purpose but are flexible enough to deal with different pieces of data are the most reusable functions.

In JavaScript, functions can call themselves. Functions that do call themselves are called *recursive functions*.

8

FUNCTIONS

PART

IN THIS PART

JavaScript Objects

The JavaScript
Object Model

IN THIS CHAPTER

So far in this book, you have looked at the basic language elements of JavaScript. But you can't stop there. Undoubtedly, the heart and soul of client-side JavaScript is its built-in object model. With that in mind, this chapter takes a top-level view of JavaScript's object model.

However, before diving into JavaScript objects, you should first take a brief high-level look at some of the basic concepts of object-oriented programming (OOP). JavaScript isn't object-oriented in the same way that Java and C++ are, but it is object-based. Therefore, understanding OO terminology is fundamental to a good understanding of how to maximize your use of JavaScript objects.

After the OOP primer, this chapter continues by looking exactly at what the JavaScript object model is and, just as important, what it is not. Finally, I conclude by providing a brief description of all the objects in the model.

RESOURCE

If you want to learn more about object-oriented programming, check out the following resources on the Web:

> *Object-Oriented System Development* by Champeaux, Lea, and Faure, Addison-Wesley, 1993, at `http://g.oswego.edu/dl/oosdw3`.

> The Global Network Academy offers a free C++ tutorial called "Introduction to OOP Using C++" at `http://uu-gna.mit.edu:8001/uu-gna/text/cc/index.html`.

> The University of Vienna publishes an electronic book about object orientation. Visit `http://ravel.ifs.univie.ac.at/ISOO/isoohome.html`.

> One online magazine about object orientation is *Object Currents,* at `http://www.sigs.com/objectcurrents/`.

> The Object-Oriented Page is an index page where you can find many other links to specific object-oriented information on the Web. Its URL is `http://galaxy.einet.net/galaxy/Engineering-and-Technology/Computer-Technology/Object-Oriented-Systems/ricardo-devis/oo.html`.

Talking the "Object Talk"

If you're new to object-oriented concepts, you might find that developers who are comfortable with OOP seem to be speaking a different language. After all, terms such as "OOP," "method," and "property" may initially be confusing if you're used to programming functions or macros. However, once you take a moment to understand OO, you will find it to be really very intuitive. In this section, I'll look at some of the basic OO concepts, including objects, properties, and methods.

Objects

Programs are developed for executing a particular business case. For example, an order management system handles customer orders. The business tasks of an application in addition to the end-user requirements form the "problem world" or "problem space" of a software system. This area also includes technical components such as a graphical user interface.

In constructing OO software applications, objects are considered the central logical building blocks. Objects in program code are often representations of real-world objects found in the problem space. Additionally, you can build technical helper-objects for solving special computer science problems.

An object can be any of the following:

- A tangible or visible thing in the problem space—for example, an order or a customer. If you are developing software for a car dealer business, probable objects are the cars to be sold, car models, employees, customers, and so on.

- An abstract concept in the mind of the developer or something that can be comprehended intellectually. For example, if you are building an application for chemists, you might need chemical structures for objects such as molecules, atoms, chemical models, and the like. Date and time might be considered intellectual objects, too, because they are certainly not tangible. The math object in JavaScript is another good example of a purely logical concept. The math object provides advanced mathematical functions (arithmetic and trigonometric) for processing numbers in JavaScript.

- Visible GUI objects are also considered objects in the object-oriented model. JavaScript has many different GUI objects such as windows, frames, buttons, input fields, and so on.

- Historically, the object-oriented model stems from inventing the concept of data structures. Think of a data structure as a more complex data type. A data structure is very similar to the idea of an object. It is a model of an abstract concept in computer science for solving primitive technical programming tasks. A data structure is a container of corresponding data variables together with the operations defined for it. Many examples cited as objects in computer science books are essentially data structures, such as records, arrays, complex numbers, or a stack. A stack is a storage container of data values and works basically like a stack of paper. A stack can store only a single data item at a time, which is always put on top of the other data items. Moreover, you can remove a data item only from the top position of the stack. Other popular data structures are strings and dates, which are also implemented in JavaScript as built-in objects. A string is a collection of single characters. A string is considered a single entity, even though some string functions extract substrings out of strings. A date object contains the data values resembling date and time.

An object includes the data values needed to describe its nature (its properties) and the functions it can perform (its methods). You can consider an object an entity with a defined boundary, as shown in Figure 9.1. The kernel of an object is built by its data values. The data items of an object describe the object's special characteristics and its identity. In object-oriented jargon, object data are called properties (or attributes).

Figure 9.1.

A graphical view of an object.

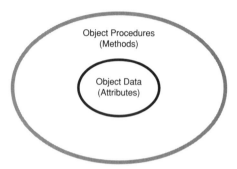

Generally, an object supports several functions. The functions of an object visible to the outside form the behavior of an object. In object-oriented terms, an object function is often called a method. A *method* is a chunk of source code performing one single task that is an important feature for the object. A method is a function of the object that could be called. In other words, the methods of an object represent its behavior, which is its outwardly visible and testable activity.

Figure 9.1 shows the popular donut view of an object. The methods of an object are drawn in the outer circle because they are visible to other objects. This means these functions could be called and executed on the object. The attributes are in the inner circle.

One example of an object is my car. My car is represented as the object `myCar` in the object-oriented world. It is a red Renault 19 built in 1992, so its data attributes include the following:

make	Renault
model	19
age	1992
color	red

My car can park or drive. Those are the important functions it provides. Figure 9.2 shows a graphical image of my car as an object in the donut-view perspective.

FIGURE 9.2.

A graphical view of my car as an object.

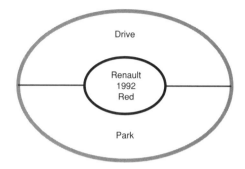

In addition to specific characteristics and identifying values, an object's attribute can also represent the state of the object or a role that an object could play at a given time. State and role are special time-dependent object characteristics. A *state* is a kind of data item that changes over time and generally shows a current value for the object. Add to the list of `myCar` attributes another attribute, `position`, which always contains the current geographic position of my car. The attribute `position` is a typical example of a state attribute.

An employee might be a team leader or department head at any given time in his professional career. An employee object can contain an attribute for professional status that stores the different roles (such as team leader, department head, and so on) an employee could fulfill.

Let's look at an example that uses factorials. Figure 9.3 shows a simple graphical user interface for computing factorials. The source code for constructing this form is shown in Listing 9.1, which contains the body of an HTML document.

FIGURE 9.3.

A graphical user interface for computing n!.

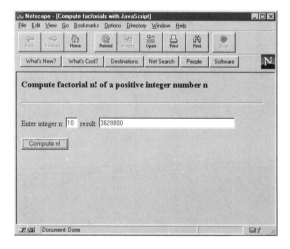

Listing 9.1. guifactorials.htm.

```
<BODY>
<FORM>
<H3>
Compute factorial n! of a positive integer number n
</H3>
<P>
<HR>
<P>
Enter integer n:
<INPUT TYPE="text" NAME="fn" SIZE=2>
    result:
<INPUT TYPE="text" NAME="fresult" SIZE=40>
<P>
<INPUT TYPE="button" NAME="compute"
  VALUE="Compute n!" onClick="xcompute(this.form)">
<BR>
</FORM>
</BODY>
```

In JavaScript, an object's attributes are referred to as the object's *properties*. For example, the pushbutton fn in the example is a GUI object in JavaScript. A pushbutton has the JavaScript properties name and value. In the HTML document example (see Listing 9.1), the properties are specified by the uppercase tags NAME and VALUE. The user can click a GUI button, so the object fn supports the function click. The function click presents a way to trigger the object fn through the programmed script instead of through a user action. All the functions of an object build its behavior. In object-oriented terms, an object's function is often called a method. In JavaScript, however, the respective keyword is function. Figure 9.4 shows a JavaScript object drawn in the graphical donut view.

Figure 9.4.

A graphical view of a JavaScript object.

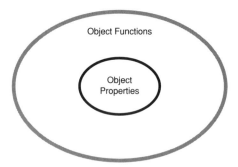

The built-in object string is a special object type. You can simply create the string myString with the var statement. The var statement creates new variables in JavaScript, as shown here:

```
var myString = "This is my text. It resembles a string object";
```

MyString has the property length, which all strings possess. The attribute length contains the length of the string myString—in this case, the number 45. Strings feature several different methods (see Chapter 14, "Built-In Language Objects," for details), including blink(), which results in a blinking string. This statement has the same effect as the following HTML tag:

```
<BLINK>  sample text </BLINK>
```

The following statement makes the text "This is my text. It resembles a string object" blink on-screen:

```
myString.blink();
```

An object's properties can contain simple variable types such as characters, integers, and so on, as well as other objects. Figure 9.5 illustrates this idea. For example, the object myCar can be defined through attributes such as make, model, year, and owner, where owner is a person object defined through attributes such as name, age, and address. The inclusion of objects in the data attributes of the containing object is often called *aggregation* or a *whole-part* relationship. The expression whole-part signifies a typical example for containment where a machine consists of several smaller parts, as in a car with an engine, four wheels, and so on.

FIGURE 9.5.

A graphical view of object containment.

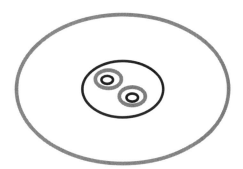

JavaScript has many different built-in objects, such as string, date, button, and math. The developer can use all those objects. In fact, you can have several different objects of one type. For example, your HTML form can have various pushbuttons. Every button possesses the same properties and methods; that is, every button has a value and supports a click method. A button is only a kind of construction plan for creating new existing buttons in a form. Such a construction specification is called a class in object-oriented terms. (See the section "Classes" later in this chapter for more details.) The different built-in objects in JavaScript actually form a set of classes that you can reuse. Such a set of classes is called a *class library*. Because JavaScript doesn't really deal with classes in the way object-oriented languages do, the built-in objects in JavaScript as a whole are often called the *JavaScript object library*.

TIP

To save development time and programming effort, use as many of the built-in JavaScript objects as suitable. Study the JavaScript object library carefully. Don't invent your own object types if it isn't necessary. Reusing already existing software components is a beneficial strategy when you're programming the object-oriented way.

Encapsulation

The data attributes and functions of an object form one inseparable entity, as shown in Figure 9.6. The information about the inner workings of an object should be hidden.

FIGURE 9.6.

A graphical view of an object as one encapsulated entity.

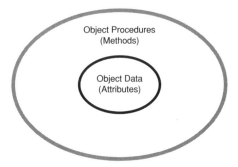

An object presents itself to the world through its published public methods, which form the interface. Take another look at the object myCar. The published methods of the object myCar are park and drive, which are the functions the object myCar supports. They are called public because the methods are accessible from the outside. They can be invoked by other objects to perform their tasks. The interface of an object is the set of public methods it offers. The opposite of a public method is a private method. Private methods are helper functions for an object. They are only used inside the object methods itself. Private methods can't be called from the outside. JavaScript has no private methods, so all functions declared in an object are public.

Even the attributes of an object should not be manipulated outside the object itself. In software engineering, this principle is called *information hiding*. Return to the object myCar, and extend the list of attributes make, model, age, and color with additional ones such as engine and wheels. I'm not particularly interested in the type of engine or what kind of wheels myCar has. The only thing that is important to me is the fact that my car works all right and can drive. If I have a car mechanic change the type of car engine, it should not change the working condition of myCar. Moreover, the type of new engine doesn't interest me. I only want to drive around with myCar.

The abstraction of an object should precede the decisions of its implementation. The source code specifying the inner part of an object should be changeable without interfering with the abstract view. For a better and simpler software design, no part of a complex application should depend on the internal details of any object declared in it.

You can gain a couple of important benefits through encapsulation and information hiding:

- Consider an object a small software component. You could easily use it in many situations and places in a program. Reusing software components is highly supported through encapsulation. Possible reuse is one of the great advantages of object orientation. Rightly used, it could save a lot of time and money in developing software projects.

- Hiding the object's implementation details gives the programmer the opportunity to modify the data representation later without changing the object's representation to the outside world. The same applies to changes inside methods. The object's interface stays the same. The source code of collaborating objects remains as is. This means maintenance efforts are greatly reduced and the architecture of the software system is far more stable than in conventionally made applications.

What is the importance of these theoretical remarks to programming in JavaScript? Most objects used in JavaScript are the built-in data structures created by Netscape. As a result, the software engineers at Netscape gain the advantage of quicker development and better software quality. This is also a benefit to the programmer and user.

Messages

If you want an object to do something for you, you send a message to it. A message invokes an object's function. Figure 9.7 illustrates message passing between objects.

FIGURE 9.7.
A graphical view of object messaging.

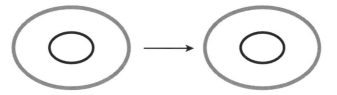

For example, if you need the current time in your application, you create a new object `currTime` of type `date` and set it to the current date and time:

```
var currTime = new Date ();
```

The statement `var` simply creates a new variable in JavaScript. New objects are created with the `new` method of the object type. The `new` method for the object type `date` creates a new object of type `date`. This new object automatically contains the current date and time. Because of the assignment (=) in the previous statement, the variable currTime contains an object of type date set with the current date and time.

You might want to extract the current time in hours and minutes:

```
var     hours;
var     minutes;

hours   = currTime.getHours ();
minutes = currTime.getMinutes ();
```

What you do is to send the message getHours to your object currTime to extract the number of hours. Then, you use the message getMinutes to get the number of minutes, respectively. In JavaScript, messages are essentially function calls. You know from the documentation of the built-in JavaScript objects that an object of type date understands the messages getHours and getMinutes. This means the object type date includes an implementation of the functions getHours() and getMinutes().

When creating custom-made objects, you define object methods as well. Inside one method, you might need other objects to accomplish a certain task. For example, in a car dealer application, you have an object currSale resembling a car sale with a method getSaleData() extracting data about the sale. Inside the function getSaleData(), you address an object of type Car and another of type Customer. Both objects are sent messages to get the necessary information. If you take this concept further, you'll see that an object-oriented software application consists of a world of objects communicating through messages.

Classes

Objects are concrete, existing software entities in a program. For example, the okButton or myWindow or a special data structure such as currTime are all objects. An object is a concrete entity that exists in time and space; a class represents only an abstraction of several similar objects, as shown in Figure 9.8.

FIGURE 9.8.
*A graphical view
of a class.*

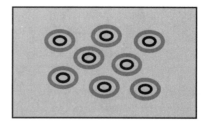

Objects with the same properties and behavior form a class or object type. A class features a construction plan for the objects contained in it. This means a class defines the number, name, and structure of data attributes and methods. Additionally, a class provides the behavior (implementation) of the functions. New objects are created due to the primarily defined construction plan. Every object is a member of a certain class; the object is said to be an instance of this class. Object properties are also called instance variables of a class or an object.

For example, your car, my car, and your neighbor's car are all cars, although they have different makes, ages, and colors. All cars have a make, model name, model year, and color. Moreover, all cars can stand in a parking space or drive. The features and possible functions are the same. The class car describes the data characteristics and methods for cars.

JavaScript is not a class-based, object-oriented language, because there is no class statement. However, JavaScript includes a similar concept: an object type. First, the built-in object types include the different GUI objects or data structures such as `date`, `string`, or `math`. New objects are created with the `new` method of the object type. This is true for all objects. For example, the following statement creates the object `currTime` as an new instance of the object type `date`:

```
var currTime = new Date ();
```

In JavaScript, you can define your own object type. For example, if your system should display time values, you might want to implement a new object type `clock`. A `clock` object should know the hours and minutes it is set to, so the properties of the `clock` object are `hours` and `minutes`. The methods a `clock` object should implement are `displayTime()` and `setTime()`. The following segment shows the definition of the object type `clock`:

```
function Clock (hours, minutes)
{
   this.hours          = hours;
   this.minutes        = minutes;
   this.setTime        = setTime;
   this.displayTime = displayTime;
 }

function setTime (hours, minutes)
{
   this.hours      = hours;
   this.minutes  = minutes;
}

function displayTime ()
{
   var line = this.hours + ":" + this.minutes;
   document.write ("<HR><P>Time of clock:   " + line);
}
```

JavaScript an instance-based language, because there is no class construct. *Instance-based* is an object-oriented term that means that the programming language has objects but no classes. JavaScript is not very well structured in this context. It has no classes, but it does have a concept like an object type. Moreover, new objects aren't constructed through existing objects; instead, they get created with the statement new. Netscape itself calls JavaScript an instance-based programming language.

I want to point out that the `function` statement in JavaScript serves many purposes. Creating a new object type means defining a function with the name of the object type as the function name. The result is a source code that always looks a little confusing to the reader. The properties of the new object type are declared as parameters of the defining function. This means there is only one constructor for a new class. As the name already points out, a constructor is a method of a class that creates a new object from the class template. A constructor initializes the new object with the given data values in the parameter part of the constructor method. The following code shows a template for declaring a new object type in JavaScript:

```
function ObjectType (instVar1, instVar2, ...)
{
    this.property1 = instVar1;
    this.property2 = instVar2;
    ...
    this.method1 = function1;
    this.method2 = function2;
    ...
}

function1 ( param1, param2, ...)
{
    here goes the implementation
}

function2 ( param1, param2, ...)
{
    here goes the implementation
}
```

The special object `this` addresses the current object in the object type declaration. The properties and methods of the new object are defined with assignments to `this`. The initial properties for the new object are given as parameters of the creating function; in the template, they are named `instVar1` and `instVar2`. In the object type definition, only the method names (`method1` and `method2`) are present. The implementation for the methods as JavaScript functions (`function1` and `function2`) is given later.

Declarations of new object types are best placed in the <HEAD> section of the HTML document so that they are read at the beginning of the document-loading process. This ensures that the class declarations are known when the rest of the program is interpreted. You usually put the action tasks in the <BODY> segment of the HTML document.

To give you a better understanding of classes, Listing 9.2 shows a short description of the `clock` class in a simple but complete HTML document.

Listing 9.2. `clock.htm`.

```
<HTML>
<HEAD>
<SCRIPT>
function Clock (hours, minutes)
{
    this.hours          = hours;
```

```
  this.minutes      = minutes;
  this.setTime      = setTime;
  this.displayTime = displayTime;
 }

function setTime (hours, minutes)
{
  this.hours      = hours;
  this.minutes   = minutes;
}

function displayTime ()
{
  var line = this.hours + ":" + this.minutes;
  document.write ("<HR><P>Time of clock:   " + line);
}
</SCRIPT>
</HEAD>
<BODY>
<SCRIPT>
var currTime = new Date;
myClock = new Clock (currTime.getHours (), currTime.getMinutes ());
myClock.displayTime ();
</SCRIPT>
</BODY>
</HTML>
```

The new clock object myClock is created and initialized with the current system time in the <BODY> section of the document with the following statement:

```
myClock = new Clock (currTime.getHours (), currTime.getMinutes ());
```

NOTE

Because JavaScript is an instance-based language, you can extend any existing object with new properties and methods at runtime. This adds a new feature to only one particular object and doesn't affect the other objects of the same object type.

Is JavaScript an Object-Oriented Language?

As discussed at the start of this chapter, JavaScript is not an object-oriented language, but an object-based language. It follows the notions of objects, properties, methods, and encapsulation. It is loosely typed, because variables aren't declared in conjunction with an object type. For example, you declare the variable currTime with the following statement:

```
var currTime;
```

You provide no variable type (such as int or char) or other object type. You could put any variable or object type in the variable currTime.

Interpretation is always done through dynamic binding at runtime. Dynamic binding means that the types of all the variables and expressions are not known until the program is actually executed.

JavaScript doesn't implement the class concept and is, instead, largely instance-based. (See the section "Classes" earlier in this chapter.) Still more significant is the lack of inheritance. Therefore, JavaScript falls into the category of object-based programming languages.

Objects and Dot Notation

In JavaScript, you access the properties and methods of an object through dot notation:

```
objectName.propertyName
objectName.methodName (arguments)
```

The current object is addressed through the special variable this. In the method declaration of an object type (class), you address the object itself with the variable this. The object itself, meaning the current object, is the object for which you are declaring the method.

In an object type defining complex numbers, you write a method for adding two complex numbers as follows:

```
// add x + z  giving rz

function add (z)
{
   var a, b, rz;

   a = this.real + z.getReal (z);
   b = this.img  + z.getImg  (z);
   rz = new Complex (a,b);
   return rz;
}
```

The numbers x and y are then summed with the following statement:

```
x.add(y);
```

In the method add, the term this.real addresses the property real of the current object—in this case, x.real. Similarly, this.img addresses the property img—that is, x.img, which is the img part of x.

Properties

Properties in JavaScript resemble the data attributes of an object. The properties of an object explain the characteristics and identity of the given object. In addition to specific characteristics and identifying values, an object's attribute can also represent the state of the object or a role that an object could play at a given time. State and role are special time-dependent characteristics. A state is a kind of data item that changes over time and generally shows a current value for the object. For example, the object `myCar` can be defined through properties such as `make`, `model`, and `year`. Add to the list another attribute `position`, which always contains the current geographic position of `myCar`. The attribute `position` is a typical example of a state attribute.

An employee might be a team leader or department head at any given time in his professional career. An employee object can contain an attribute for professional status that stores the different roles (for example, team leader, department head, and so on) an employee could fulfill.

When modeling projects, you could define the object type `Project` as follows:

```
function Project (members, leader, currentMilestone, time)
{
   this..members            = members;
   this.leader               = leader;
   this.currentMilestone  = currentMilestone;
   this.time                 = time;
 }
```

You would then create the particular software project `myProject` as follows:

```
myProject = new Project (memberGroup, "Claudia", "starting",  currTime);
```

The object `myProject` consists of a group of persons described in the object `memberGroup`. The project leader is `"Claudia"` and the current milestone is `"starting"` because the project just recently began. The variables `memberGroup` and `currTime` contain other objects that are not described here.

In addition to the dot notation, you have other ways to access the properties of an object. The following example shows the array notation:

```
objectName ["propertyName"]
```

The next line demonstrates indexing through ordinal numbers:

```
objectName [integerIndex]
```

This technique returns the attribute of number `integerIndex`.

Outside an object itself, you might not want to access an object's attributes directly because it damages the principle of encapsulation. (See the section "Encapsulation" earlier in this chapter.)

9

THE JAVASCRIPT
OBJECT MODEL

Methods

A method denotes a service the class offers to other objects. Generally, methods belong to one of the following four categories:

- Modifier: A method that changes the state of an object. This method changes the value of one or more data attributes of the object. A popular modifier method is a `set` function that sets the value of one particular object attribute.

- Selector: A method that accesses the data attributes of an object but makes no changes. An important selector is a `get` function that returns (gets) the value of one particular object attribute.

- Iterator: A method that accesses all the parts of an object, such as all the data attributes, in some defined order. As the name denotes, an iterator method iterates over the data attributes of an object.

- Constructor: A constructor is a method of an object type that creates a new object from the class template. A constructor initializes the new object with the given data values in the parameter part of the constructor method.

In JavaScript, object methods are normal JavaScript functions. You access them through dot notation:

```
objectName.functionName (arguments)
```

Generally, an HTML file includes a `<BODY>` section that creates the special document object in JavaScript. The document object supports the method `write`. With this method, you can dynamically extend the text layout of your HTML page through JavaScript. The following statement prints a horizontal rule and the string `"This is sample text"`:

```
document.write ("<HR><P>This is sample text");
```

When constructing new object types in JavaScript, you use a source code template such as the one presented here:

```
function ObjectType (instVar1, instVar2, ...)
{
    this.property1 = instVar1;
    this.property2 = instVar2;
    ...
    this.method1 = function1;
    this.method2 = function2;
    ...
}

function1 ( param1, param2, ...)
{
    here goes the implementation
}

function2 ( param1, param2, ...)
{
    here goes the implementation
}
```

The special object `this` addresses the current object in the object type declaration. The properties and methods of the new object are defined with assignments to `this`. The initial properties for the new object are given as parameters of the creating function; in the template, they are named `instVar1` and `instVar2`. In the object type definition, only the method names (`method1` and `method2`) are present.

The implementation for the object methods is given later in a function declaration following the rules for regular JavaScript functions. The arguments of a function can be strings, numbers, or complete objects. The following segment shows an example of defining a class representing complex numbers:

```
// define complex numbers

function Complex (real, img)
{
   this.real          = real;
   this.img           = img;
   this.getReal       = getReal;
   this.getImg        = getImg;
   this.add           = add;
   this.subtract      = subtract;
   this.multiply      = multiply;
   this.divide        = divide;
}

// get real part
function getReal ()
{
   return this.real;
}

// get img part
function getImg ()
{
   return this.img;
}

// add x + z  giving rz
function add (z)
{
   var a, b, rz;

   a = this.real + z.getReal (z);
   b = this.img  + z.getImg  (z);
   rz = new Complex (a,b);
   return rz;
}

// methods subtract, multiply and divide not yet implemented
```

The object method `add` takes one argument of type `Complex`. You can add two complex numbers x and y as follows:

```
var x = new Complex (a,b);
var y = new Complex (c,d);

var z = x.add (y);
```

Inside a function declaration, you can refer to the properties of the current object with the special object `this`, as shown here:

```
a = this.real + z.getReal (z);
```

Events

Often, JavaScript statements create or manipulate graphical user interface elements such as forms or windows. Figure 9.9 shows a simple graphical user interface.

FIGURE 9.9.

A graphical user interface.

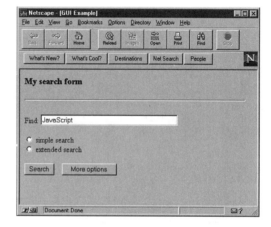

Listing 9.3 serves only for generating a form. Other parts are not fully programmed yet and generally produce Not yet implemented messages.

Listing 9.3. guiexample.htm.

```
<HTML>
<HEAD>
<TITLE>
GUI Example
</TITLE>

<SCRIPT LANGUAGE="JavaScript">
function fsearch (aForm)
{
   // search function not yet implemented
   // here: create display of result list
   alert ("Sorry, search function not yet implemented");
}
function foptions (aForm)
{
   // display of options not yet implemented
   alert ("Sorry, no options available");
}
</SCRIPT>
</HEAD>
<BODY>
<FORM>
<H3>
My search form
</H3>
<P>
```

```
<HR>
<P>
Find:
<INPUT TYPE="text"   NAME="tfield" SIZE=40>
<P>
<INPUT TYPE="radio">
simple search
<BR>
<INPUT TYPE="radio">
extended search
<BR>
<P>
<INPUT TYPE="button" NAME="bsearch"
  VALUE="Search" onClick="fsearch (this.form)">
  
<INPUT TYPE="button" NAME="boptions"
  VALUE="More options" onClick="foptions (this.form)">
<BR>
</FORM>
</BODY>
</HTML>
```

In the context of a graphical user interface, an event is a result of a user action. It takes place when the application's user does something. For example, when the user clicks a button on the user interface, the event "button clicked" occurs. Other GUI events include clicking a checkbox, selecting a string in a list box, double-clicking an item, opening or closing a window, and so on.

The best way to control GUIs is through event-driven programming. Events automatically trigger JavaScript functions as a result of user action. JavaScript has a language concept called event handlers. Event handlers are based on HTML tags. (See Chapter 10, "Handling Events," for more information.)

Generally, events are not considered object-oriented features, although some object-oriented programming languages also support events. Most GUI elements, such as windows, buttons, text fields, checkboxes, and so on, react to certain events. These elements exist in JavaScript as built-in object types. For example, you can create a button in JavaScript to trigger the onClick event when the button is clicked:

```
<SCRIPT>
<FORM>
<INPUT  TYPE="button",  VALUE="press me" onClick="myfunc ()">
</FORM>
</SCRIPT>
```

In this example, the function myfunc is executed when the user clicks the "press me" button. Some built-in objects feature methods that emulate an event. For example, the object type checkbox defines a click () method that emulates the checkbox being clicked. The same applies to the object type button. The event-emulation method doesn't trigger an event-handler declared elsewhere for the object. If you need the event-handler action, you have to call the event-handler method explicitly.

9

THE JAVASCRIPT
OBJECT MODEL

Because event handlers are allowed only for HTML tags, newly created object types have no event handlers. See the next chapter on events and event handlers in JavaScript for a more detailed description of this subject.

Exploring the JavaScript Object Model

JavaScript objects are truly objects in the sense that they have properties and methods and can respond to events. However, as you have learned in this chapter, JavaScript doesn't have the same true OOP capabilities of inheritance. When you look at the JavaScript object model, it is critical that you look at it in that context. Rather than a class hierarchy that is inheritance-based, the JavaScript object model is a containership hierarchy, as shown in Figure 9.10. If you are experienced in object-oriented programming languages, such as Java, C++, or Delphi, that might be the biggest adjustment you need to make in your thinking when developing with JavaScript.

FIGURE 9.10.

The JavaScript built-in object model hierarchy.

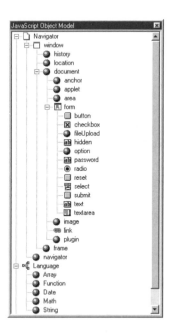

Containership is the principle of one object containing another object. If you look again at Figure 9.10, you can see that the relationship between the form object and the radio object is not one of ancestor-descendant (or class-subclass), but one of container-contained. Stated differently, there is no bloodline between these objects because one did not descend from the other. As a result, no object can inherit properties and methods from another object, nor can you subclass an object in the hierarchy.

Containership in JavaScript

Containership is an important term to understand as you develop JavaScript scripts and applications—not only in terms of how one object relates to another, but in practical terms of how you reference an object. Recall from the discussion of dot notation earlier in this chapter that when you reference an object's properties or methods, you use a dot to denote ownership. For example, in the following command, the `write` method is said to be owned by the document object:

```
document.write("<H1>A cow jumping over the moon.</H1>")
```

However, you can extend this to include not only properties and methods of an object, but also objects contained by that object. If you wanted to return the name of a button object to a variable, you would use the following command:

```
buttonName = document.formMain.okButton.name
```

`document` is the default name of the document object, and `formMain` is the name of the form object, which contains the `okButton` button.

An important fact to understand when you work with objects is knowing when you need to reference a container object and when you don't. For example, the window object is essentially the highest-level object you work with in your code. Most of the references you make are to objects within its containership. You could also write the previous `document.write` example like this:

```
window.document.write("<H1>A cow jumping over the moon.</H1>")
```

Although you can ignore the window reference in most cases, it is necessary when you deal with multiple windows or frames. For instance, Listing 9.4 creates a window object in the `showStats()` function and then closes it in the `closeWindow()` function.

Listing 9.4. `WindowWorks.htm`.

```
<HTML>
<HEAD>
<SCRIPT LANGUAGE = "JavaScript">
<!--
    var windowObject

    function showStats() {
        windowObject = window.open("", "ViewStats", "toolbar=0,width=100,
            height=50,resizable=0")
        windowObject.document.write("<H2>We outperformed all goals\
            this month. Congratulations!</H2>")
```

continues

Listing 9.4. continued

```
    }

        function closeWindow() {
            windowObject.close()
        }
// -->
</SCRIPT>

<BODY OnUnload="closeWindow()">
<H1>Click the following button to view the monthly stats.</H1>
<FORM>
<INPUT
    Type="button"
    Value="Show Stats"
    OnClick="showStats()"
    </INPUT>
</FORM>
</BODY>
```

The window object is the only one that provides any leniency in object references. For example, if you want to reference a form within an HTML page, you must add its parent object (document) for JavaScript to understand which object you are referencing. If you want to reference the first form within the document object and retrieve the number of elements in it, you use the following command:

```
num = document.forms[0].length
```

Even if the form had a name attribute, you still need to add the parent reference:

```
num = document.queryForm.length
```

An Overview of JavaScript Objects

When you begin to look closely at the JavaScript object hierarchy, you can see that each object falls into one of two categories: Navigator objects or built-in language objects. This section looks at these sets and introduces you to each of the objects within them.

Navigator Objects

Most of the functionality built into JavaScript centers on what you can do with HTML pages. The first set of objects—I'll call them Navigator objects—generally has a correlation to the browser and HTML tags within it. Figure 9.11 shows HTML source for a Web page and highlights the JavaScript objects in it.

FIGURE 9.11.
Many JavaScript objects match HTML tags.

As you can see, most JavaScript objects are object representations of HTML tags. Table 9.1 lists the Navigator objects and the corresponding HTML tags for these objects.

Table 9.1. JavaScript built-in objects and HTML tags.

JavaScript Object	Corresponding HTML Tag
window	N/A
frame	`<FRAME>`
document	`<BODY>`
form	`<FORM>`
button	`<INPUT TYPE="button">`
checkbox	`<INPUT TYPE="checkbox">`
hidden	`<INPUT TYPE="hidden">`
fileUpload	`<INPUT TYPE="file">`
password	`<INPUT TYPE="password">`
radio	`<INPUT TYPE="radio">`
reset	`<INPUT TYPE="reset">`
select	`<SELECT>`
submit	`<INPUT TYPE="submit">`
text	`<INPUT TYPE="text">`

9

THE JAVASCRIPT
OBJECT MODEL

continues

Table 9.1. continued

JavaScript Object	Corresponding HTML Tag
textarea	`<TEXTAREA>`
link	`<A HREF="">`
anchor	`<A NAME="">`
applet	`<APPLET>`
image	`<IMG>`
plugin	`<EMBED>`
area	`<MAP>`
history	N/A
location	N/A
navigator	N/A

If you have developed applications with a fourth-generation language (4GL) such as Visual Basic or PowerBuilder, or another visual tool such as Delphi, the names of some of the objects, such as text and reset, might be counterintuitive. Table 9.2 lists some of the JavaScript objects that are better known in the 4GL world under a different name.

Table 9.2. Common 4GL vernacular for JavaScript objects.

JavaScript Object	Common 4GL Term
Window	Window/form
Frame	Panel
Document	Page
Button	Button
Checkbox	Checkbox
Radio	Radio button
Reset	Button
Select	Drop-down list box
	Selection list
Submit	Button
Text	Edit field
Textarea	Memo field
Navigator	Application

As you explore each of these objects, you'll look at the various ways they are presented to users and developers: user interface view, HTML tag, and JavaScript object code.

The Window Object

A Web browser—whether it's Netscape Navigator, Microsoft Internet Explorer, or whatever—is presented to the user in a window. Everything a user does with the browser is performed within that window. Moreover, every screen element is also contained inside that window. The window object provides a direct corollary to this metaphor (see Figure 9.12). It is considered the highest-level object of all objects in the JavaScript object hierarchy and contains all other Navigator objects (except for the navigator object itself). Just as you can have multiple windows open in your browser, you can work with multiple window objects at once in your code.

FIGURE 9.12.
A window object contains all other elements—both visually as well as in your code.

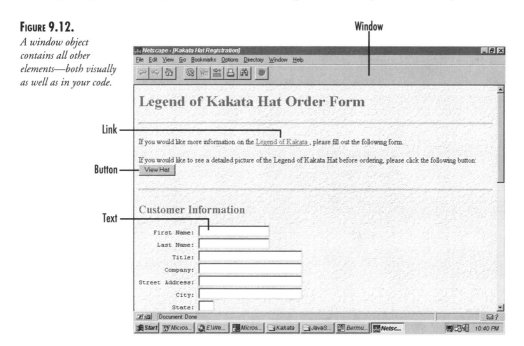

The window object has no HTML tag equivalent, although you do define its event handlers (onLoad, onUnload) in the <BODY> tag. Within JavaScript code, you work with a window object as shown in the following example. Suppose you want to add text to the status bar of the window. The code follows:

```
window.status = 'Welcome to the Acadia home page.';
```

9

THE JAVASCRIPT
OBJECT MODEL

The Frame Object

As you will learn in this book, frames are especially important objects to use to enhance the presentation of your Web application. The frame object represents a frame within a frameset, as shown in Figure 9.13. In a multiframe presentation, your window object is the page that contains the <FRAMESET> definition, whereas the other pages are considered frames in that context. The relationship between the frame and window object is a special one that is explored in depth in Chapter 11, "Navigator Objects."

FIGURE 9.13.

Frame objects are contained by the window object.

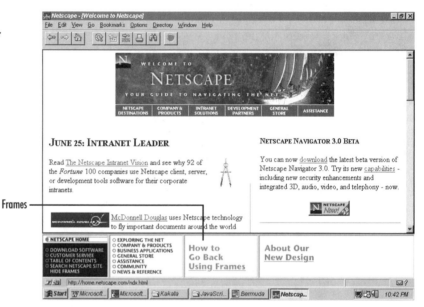

The Location Object

The Web is all about content presentation. Every window object is designed to display content to the user, but that content must come from somewhere. The origin of the page is thus contained in the location object. The location object is used to store all URL information for a given window. Although users see URL information in the Location box on-screen, as shown in Figure 9.14, you can work with that same information with the location object.

FIGURE 9.14.

Users work with the Location box, and you can work with the location object.

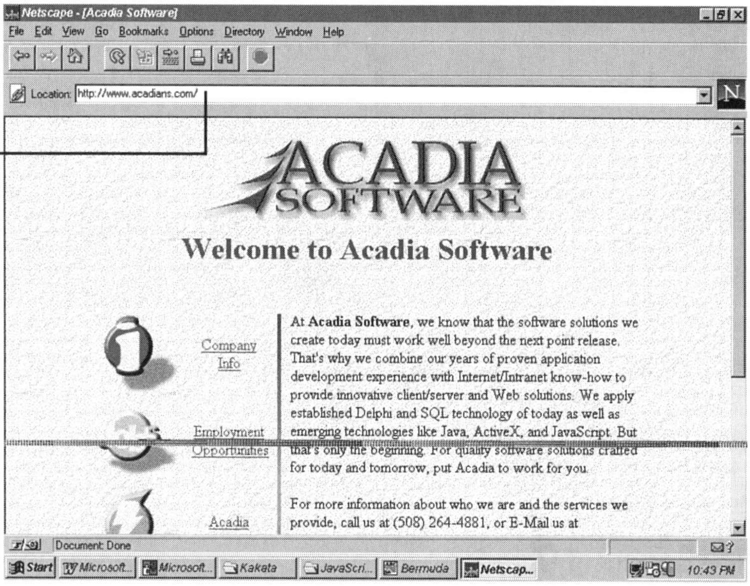

Location ——

If you want to retrieve the protocol portion of the current URL and evaluate it, you use the following:

```
function evalProtocol(){
    curProtocol = window.location.protocol
    if (curProtocol == "http:") {
    alert("The document comes from the Web.") }
    else {
      if (curProtocol == "file:") {
        alert("This document comes from your hard drive.")}
      else {
        alert("This document comes from somewhere else.")}
    }
}
```

The History Object

A long-time feature in browser software is the capability to track where you have surfed within a given session. This feature has come to be known as a *history list,* and it's available in both Navigator and Internet Explorer's Go menus (see Figure 9.15). The history object is the JavaScript equivalent to this list. You can work with it as a user might, moving forward or backward in a list to navigate where a user has been.

FIGURE 9.15.
The history list is accessible through JavaScript.

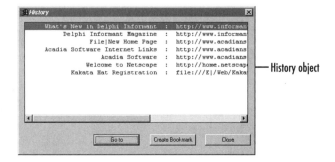
— History object

Suppose you wanted to go back two pages in your history list when the user clicked a button. The event handler would look like this:

```
function goBackTwoPages() {
    window.history.go(-2)
}
```

The Document Object

Although the window object is the top-level object in the hierarchy, the document object is arguably the most important. The document object, shown in Figure 9.16, is responsible for all the actual content displayed on a given page. You can work with the document object to display dynamic HTML pages. Also contained within the document are all the typical user interface (UI) elements of a Web application.

FIGURE 9.16.
The document object is focused on content.

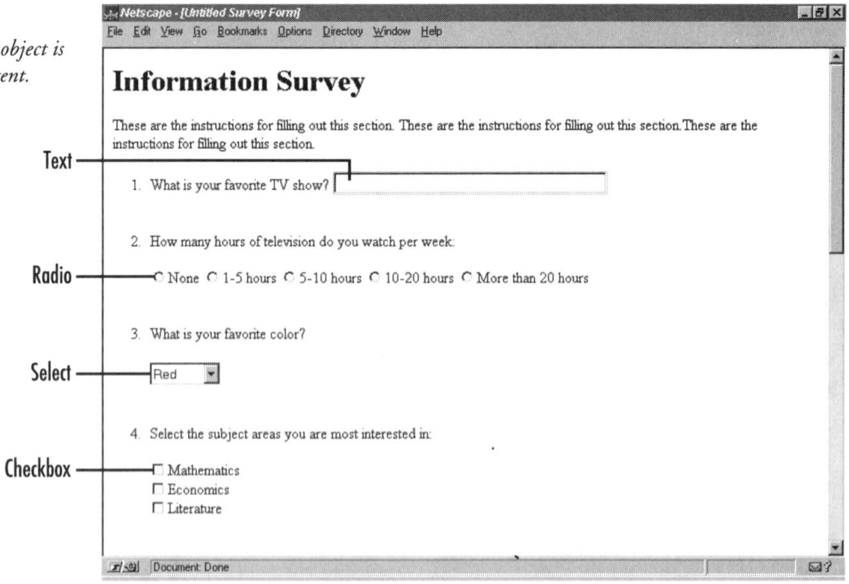

Text —

Radio —

Select —

Checkbox —

A common use of the document object is generating HTML pages through JavaScript. You can do this using the `write()` or `writeln()` methods. For example, the following code displays the HTML text specified as the `method` parameter:

```
<HTML>
<HEAD>
<SCRIPT LANGUAGE = "JavaScript">
   document.write("<h1>Text created by JavaScript</h1>");
</SCRIPT>
</HEAD>
```

The Form Object

Forget for a moment such add-ins as Java applets or ActiveX controls that can interact with the user. If you think only in terms of the HTML world, the only way to interact with the user is through a form and its elements (see Figure 9.17). Forms give life to static pages by providing an interface users can interact with through controls. You can only place a button, text, or other UI object within the confines of a form. The form object is your means of interacting with this HTML element in your scripts.

FIGURE 9.17.
Forms create interactive HTML pages.

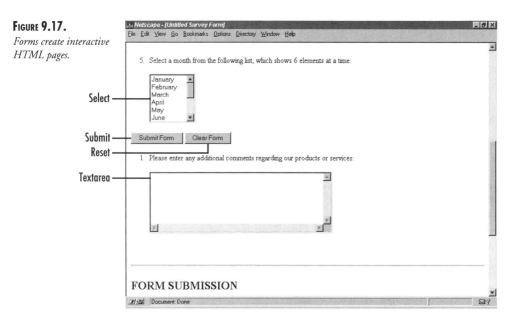

The Button Objects: Button, Submit, and Reset

Unless you jumped into Web development from a character-based environment, you're un-doubtedly familiar with pushbuttons. JavaScript has three button objects: button, submit, and reset. Each of these is an object representation of an HTML tag. The button object is a generic button to which you need to add code in order for it to be useful. The submit button is a specialized version of a button whose default action is to submit the form of which it is a part. Similarly, the reset button is hard-coded to reset the values of all controls within a form. You could use a button object to serve the same role as the submit object (by calling the form's `submit()` method). These three look identical, as shown in Figure 9.18, and you have control over how they are labeled.

Figure 9.18.

UI objects contained in a form.

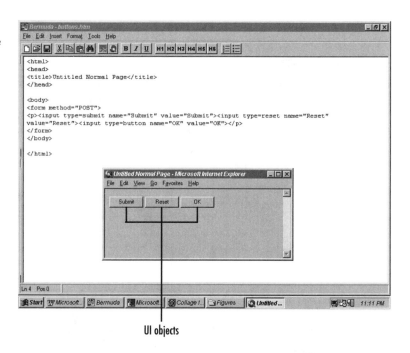

UI objects

TIP

The width of the button is determined by the length of the text within the LABEL= parameter. To enlarge a button's width, add spaces around the text:

```
<INPUT type=button label="   OK   " onClick="doThis()">
```

The Select Object

Another common control in windowed environments is a drop-down list or selection list box, both of which let the user select from a predefined list of values. The difference is that the user can select only one value from a drop-down list, whereas he can select multiple choices from a selection list. The select object encapsulates the behavior of both of these UI elements. In other words, it can appear as a drop-down list (default) or a selection list (if its multiple property is set to true), as shown in Figure 9.17.

The Checkbox Object

Another industry-wide standard UI control is the checkbox. This element allows the user to specify a yes/no or true/false value by clicking the checkbox control (see Figure 9.16).

The Radio Object

Radio buttons are a set of mutually exclusive controls, such that if one radio button is selected, all other buttons in the set become unselected. The radio object provides this element in an HTML form (see Figure 9.16). You define a set of radio buttons by giving them the same name property.

> **NOTE**
>
> Radio buttons are grouped based on a common name property.

The Text Object

A principal element for any data entry application is a field in which the user can input data. The text object serves as this data-capturing device as the objectified representation of the text input HTML tag (see Figure 9.16).

The Textarea Object

Related to the text object is the textarea object, which allows you to enter multiple lines of text as opposed to a single line (see Figure 9.17). If you've worked with other programming environments, it might be helpful to think of the textarea object as a memo field.

The Password Object

If JavaScript supported inheritance, the password object would be a subclass of the text object. The only difference between the two is that all the characters entered into the password object are displayed as asterisks.

The Hidden Object

Another field object, the hidden object, is like a text object with a visible property set to false. It's used to store values to pass to a server process. The hidden object comes from the pre-JavaScript days of HTML, when there were no such things as variables, arrays, or objects to store values. Although you might still want to employ them for transferring data among pages of a multiple-page data entry application, much of the data storage value of hidden objects is no longer needed with JavaScript.

The FileUpload Object (JavaScript 1.1 and Higher)

The fileUpload object is the JavaScript equivalent to the HTML file upload element. You can't do much with this object in JavaScript, however, other than reference its properties. The `fileUpload` method has no methods to act on.

The Link Object

Lest you forget, the whole reason the Web was developed back in 1989 was the simple hypertext link of an HTML page. Perhaps overlooked in the latest Web application craze, the link remains the very heart of Web technology. The link object lets you work with links in JavaScript code. Because a link simply references another HTML page or other destination, it's very similar to the location object (which contains the same information for the current HTML page).

> **NOTE**
>
> In Netscape 3.0, images defined with the IMG tag are now accessible through JavaScript. Images in a document are treated as an array of images and are accessible only by specifying an element in the array. Because you can't work with images outside this document array structure, they are perhaps better considered properties of a document rather than discrete object entities.

The Anchor Object

The anchor object is a piece of text or an image in the HTML page that can be the target of a hypertext link. In practical terms, you use the anchor object very little with JavaScript, making it perhaps the least important of all built-in objects.

The Image Object (JavaScript 1.1 and Higher)

JavaScript 1.1 added the image object as an encapsulation of an HTML image. Perhaps the most effective use of this object type is to cache images you want to display. You can construct an image object in your code and download the image data from the server before it is needed for display by the browser. When the image is requested, you can pull the image from cache rather than from the server.

The Area Object (JavaScript 1.1 and Higher)

The area object lets you define an area of an image as an image map. An area's HREF reference is loaded in a target window when it is clicked by the user.

The Applet and Plugin Objects (JavaScript 1.1 and Higher)

The applet and plugin objects represent the JavaScript equivalent of the `<APPLET>` and `<EMBED>` HTML tags, respectively. In a generic sense, these JavaScript objects have no methods associated with them, but that is really irrelevant, because you can use JavaScript to access the specific methods of a given Java applet or ActiveX control. (See Chapter 26, "LiveConnect: Integrating JavaScript and Java," for more information.)

The Navigator Object

Boldly named by the developers of JavaScript (Netscape), the navigator object is an object representing the browser software in use. Using this object, you can retrieve information about the name and version of the browser in use. Both Netscape Navigator and Microsoft Internet Explorer support the navigator object.

Built-In Language Objects

The second set of objects never appear visually, but you work with them within your JavaScript code. You can call them built-in language objects because they are simply constructs of the JavaScript language. Anyone who has worked with any programming language before has worked with the types of objects described in this section.

The String object represents a value you assign to a variable of an object property. JavaScript treats both assigned variables and string literals as string objects. For example, both the variable `myString` and the literal `"Banana bread"` are considered string objects:

```
function showFavoriteFood()
{
    var myString = "Angel food cake";
    myWindow = window.open()
    myWindow.document.write("<H1>Favorite Foods</H1>");
    myWindow.document.write("<H2>" + myString + " and " + "Banana
      bread" + "</H2>");
}
```

> **NOTE**
>
> The String object was enhanced in JavaScript 1.1 such that you can reference a string object property or method using standard dot notation:
>
> ```
> "I am President".bold()
> ```

The Array object is an object representation of the traditional programming construct. An array is an ordered set of data elements, and every index number in an array contains a value. You can have as many indexes in the array as you want.

Arrays are powerful, and your JavaScript scripts can use them in a variety of ways. The following code segment shows a simple example, the result of which is shown in Figure 9.19:

```
<HTML>
<HEAD>
<SCRIPT LANGUAGE = "JavaScript">

     theJs = new Array(3)
     theJs[1] = "Jordan"
     theJs[2] = "Jared"
     theJs[3] = "Justin"

     document.write("<H1>The three Js are:</H1>")

     document.write("<OL>")
     for (var i = 1; i < 4; i++) {
         document.write("<LI>" + theJs[i])
     }
     document.write("</OL>")
</SCRIPT>
</HEAD>
</HTML>
```

FIGURE 9.19.

Using an array object.

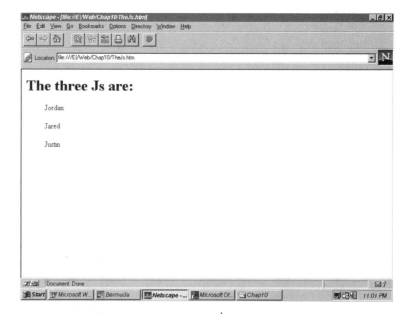

> **NOTE**
>
> The Array object was added in JavaScript 1.1. Although you could work with arrays in Netscape 2.x, you can now use the new operator to create true array objects.

The Math object is used for standard mathematical calculations. Rather than using generic math functions in JavaScript, these functions are implemented as methods of the math object. Suppose you wanted to evaluate two numbers that the user entered. Listing 9.5 shows how you could use the math object's max() method to do this.

Listing 9.5. Wizard.htm.

```
<html>
<head>
<title>Wizard</title>
<SCRIPT LANGUAGE="JavaScript">

    function calculateValues() {
      num1 = parseFloat(document.forms[0].Number1.value)
      num2 = parseFloat(document.forms[0].Number2.value)
      result = Math.max(num1, num2)
      alert('The wizard says ' + result + ' is the greatest value');
      }

</SCRIPT>
</head>
<body>
<h1>Stump the Wizard</font></h1>
<p>Without connecting to a backend server or using a Java applet,
the Browser Wizard will tell you which number is greater...</p>
<form method="POST">
<pre>First Number:  <input type=text size=5 maxlength=5 name="Number1"></pre>
<pre>Second Number: <input type=text size=5 maxlength=5 name="Number2"></pre>
<p><input
    type=button
    name="WizButton"
    value="Submit"
    onClick="calculateValues()"></p>
</form>
</body>
</html>
```

On first take, the fact that JavaScript has no "date" data type seems like a limitation. JavaScript largely makes up for this by providing a Date object. The date object allows you to work with both date and time values by providing a host of methods, such as getMonth(), setDay(), and getTimezoneOffset(), which are used to work with time zones. One example of how to use the date object is making an on-screen clock. Listing 9.6 shows the code, and Figure 9.20 shows the results.

Listing 9.6. Clock.htm.

```
<HTML>
<HEAD>
<SCRIPT LANGUAGE="JavaScript">
```

continues

Listing 9.6. continued

```
<!--
    function dailyTask() {
        var tod = new Date()
        tod.getTime()
        document.TimeForm.TimeOfDay.value = tod.toString()
        timerID = setTimeout("dailyTask()",1000)
    }
//-->
</SCRIPT>
</HEAD>

<BODY onLoad="dailyTask()">
<form method="POST" name="TimeForm">
Current time:   <input type=text size=50 maxlength=50 name="TimeOfDay">
</form>
</BODY>
</HTML>
```

FIGURE 9.20.

The on-screen clock.

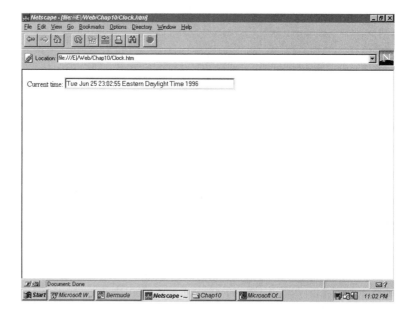

Added in JavaScript 1.1, the Function object is a powerful object that allows you to declare a function at runtime. Using the Function object, you could change the behavior of a function based on runtime conditions. The Function object uses string literals or variables to define the body of the function you are creating.

Summary

JavaScript's navigator and built-in language objects serve as the fundamental tools by which you can construct scripts. This chapter took a high-level view of the JavaScript object hierarchy and each of the JavaScript objects.

Much of the object model consists of HTML elements that are "objectified," allowing you to work with HTML tags in an object-oriented manner. If you come from an HTML background, begin to think of these elements not just as tags, but as objects. Chapter 10 covers events, and Chapters 11 through 15 build on the information in this chapter by exploring JavaScript objects in complete detail.

Handling Events

IN THIS CHAPTER

CHAPTER 10

If you've developed software in the 1990s, you probably have worked with event-driven programming languages. Procedural programs of the past dictated which task a user could perform at any given time. However, the graphical, windowed environments of today have a completely different paradigm and require applications to respond to events initiated by users rather than the other way around.

Given JavaScript's object-based nature (discussed in Chapter 9, "The JavaScript Object Model"), it should come as no surprise that JavaScript is primarily an event-driven language. This chapter discusses JavaScript events and how you can respond to them and thus create interactive applications.

Understanding Events and Event Handlers

Much of the code you write in JavaScript will respond to an event performed by either the user or the browser software. This event-driven environment lets you focus only on the events that affect your application; what the browser performs in between events is its burden, not yours. In addition, you don't need to concern yourself with all the events performed by the user— only those to which you care to respond.

Each JavaScript event has a corresponding *event handler* that is charged with the responsibility of automatically responding to the event when it occurs. When you work with an event, you never add code to or modify the event itself; rather, you manage the event handler to which that event corresponds.

JavaScript Event Handlers

If you've created HTML pages, you know that each element on a form has a tag and attributes associated with it. For example, you would define a text input in the following way:

```
<input
    type=text
    size=30
    maxlength=30
    name="LastName">
```

JavaScript implements event handlers by embedding them as attributes of HTML tags. For example, suppose you want to perform a method you created each time the value of the text object changes. To do so, assign the method (called `checkField()`) to the text object's `onChange` event handler:

```
<input
    type=text
    size=30
    maxlength=256
    name="LastName"
    onChange="checkField(this)">
```

Within the quotes, you can either write in-place JavaScript code or call a separate function. Although the previous example calls the `checkField()` method, the following code is also valid:

```
<input
    type=text
    size=30
    maxlength=256
    name="LastName3"
    onChange="if (confirm('Are you certain you wish to change this value?')){
        alert('Changed')}">
```

TIP

If you use in-place code, you can place multiple lines within the event-handler assignment by using a semicolon to separate each JavaScript command. However, use multiple lines of code with caution. It's much easier to work with code separated as a function rather than work within the event handler itself. For example, if the code is located in a central location, it becomes much easier to make changes to it over the life of your application.

JavaScript has nine built-in events to which certain objects can respond. Table 10.1 summarizes the events and objects that can respond to them.

Table 10.1. Object event handlers.

Object	onClick	onSubmit	onChange	onFocus	onBlur	onLoad	onUnload	onMouseOver	onSelect	onAbort	onError	onMouseOut	onReset
button	■												
reset	■												
submit	■												
radio	■												
checkbox	■												
link	■							■				■	
form		■											■
text			■	■	■				■				
textarea			■	■	■				■				
select			■	■	■								
image										■	■		
area	■							■				■	
window						■	■				■		

> **NOTE**
>
> Not all JavaScript objects can respond to events. The anchor, `frame`, `hidden`, `navigator`, and password objects do not have event handlers.

As you proceed through this chapter, you will examine each of the events individually, paying particular attention to the events for which you will most often want to trap. In doing so, you will take a typical HTML form (shown in Figure 10.1) and add life to it by adding code to its event handlers. The form you will use initially is a sample order form for a fictitious company.

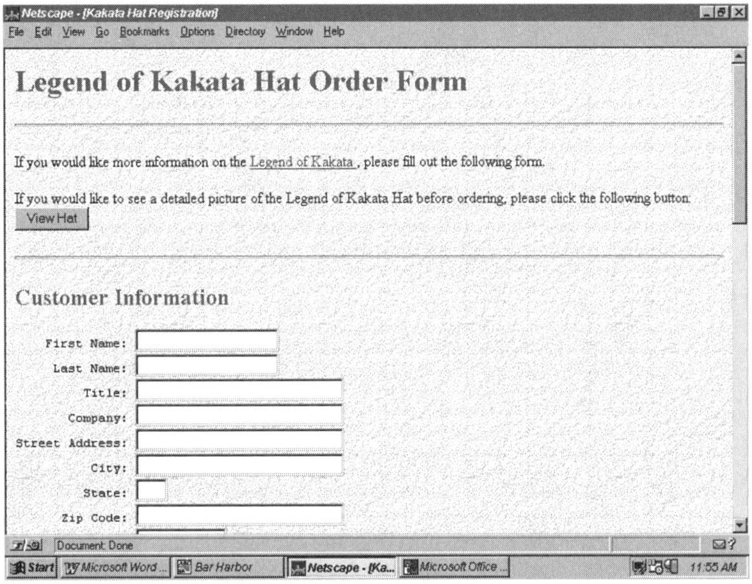

FIGURE 10.1.
A sample HTML form.

Clicking an Object (`onClick`)

One of the most common uses of JavaScript is to enhance HTML forms to provide a greater degree of interactivity. If that is true, perhaps the single most common event many developers will work with is the `click` event. The `click` event is triggered when the user clicks a clickable object. These objects include the following:

- Buttons (button, submit, and reset)
- Checkbox
- Radio
- Link

As is standard for most computer environments, the `click` event is triggered only after the default mouse button is pressed and released. A user holding the mouse button down without releasing it on the object will not cause the object's `click` event to be triggered.

When a `click` event occurs, the `onClick` event handler for the object that is clicked executes one or more JavaScript commands or calls a custom function. For example, note the View Hat button in Figure 10.1. Suppose you would like to add code that displays a second browser window showing an image of the hat when the button is clicked.

In the HTML source, the button object is defined as follows:

```
<input
    type=button
    name="ViewHat"
    value="View Hat"
    OnClick="displayHat()">
```

In the <HEAD> section of the HTML file, you can then write the `displayHat()` method that will be called when the button's `onClick` event handler is triggered:

```
<HEAD>
<SCRIPT LANGUAGE="JavaScript">
<!--

    //onClick event handler
    function displayHat() {
       hatWindow = window.open("http://www.acadians.com/
         javascript/examples/kakata.htm", "ViewHat",
         "toolbar=0,width=200,height=400,resizable=0");
    }
</SCRIPT>
</HEAD>
```

When the user clicks the button, the event handler uses the `open()` method for the window object to display a window showing the hat image, as shown in Figure 10.2.

The `onClick` event handler isn't just for buttons; you can use it to respond to clicks of checkboxes, radio buttons, and link objects. Because of the nature of these controls, a customized `click` event for them is much less common. Checkboxes and radio buttons are often used for data entry and evaluated at a later point rather than when a control is clicked. Also, the link object is used primarily as a reference to the location specified in its HREF property, so adding code is often not necessary unless you want to modify its default behavior.

FIGURE 10.2.

The second window is displayed using the open() method.

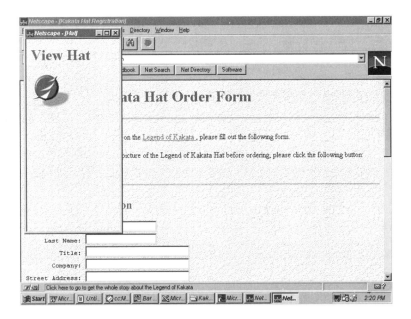

For checkboxes, links, radio buttons, and reset and submit buttons, Navigator 3.0 lets you return a false value from the onClick event handler to cancel the triggered action. For example, if you wanted to confirm whether or not to check a checkbox, you could add the following code to its onClick event handler:

```
<INPUT TYPE="checkbox" NAME="checkbox1" VALUE="DeluxeRoom"
onClick="return confirm('Deluxe rooms are very expensive.
➡Are you sure?')">Deluxe Room
```

Because the appearance of a Web page is important, you might want to use images rather than buttons to respond to click events. Although an image can't actually respond to any event, you can imitate a click event through the smart use of a link object. I'll demonstrate this by using an image, rather than the View Hat button, to execute the displayHat() method from the previous example. To do so, you can define the link object as follows:

```
<a
    href="JavaScript:displayHat()">
    <img src="minihat.gif"
        align=bottom
        border=0
        width=89
        height=75></a>
```

10

HANDLING EVENTS

Rather than add code to the link's onClick event handler, I used JavaScript: as the protocol for the HREF property. Using JavaScript:*JavaScriptExpression* as the HREF property tells the browser to execute a JavaScript expression rather than navigate to a defined link.

Submitting a Form (onSubmit)

As discussed in Chapter 1, "JavaScript and the World Wide Web," one of the advantages of using JavaScript in HTML forms is that you can perform data validation on the client side rather than pass this task onto an overloaded server. You can perform validation on a field-by-field basis or on a form-wide basis. Depending on the context, you might want to use one or both methods.

For form-wide data validation as well as for other tasks, the submit event is your primary concern. This event occurs just before the submission of an HTML form. Adding code to the onSubmit event handler of a form object enables you to check the submission and either allow it to proceed or block it and notify the user.

The submit event will occur unless a false value is returned from the onSubmit event handler. Any other value (true or otherwise) will cause the submission to occur. For example, suppose you want to display a simple confirmation message to the user of the Kakata Hat order form before processing the submittal. The form is defined in the HTML source as follows:

```
<form action="process.cgi" method="POST" onSubmit="return confirmOrder()">
```

The confirmOrder() method referenced in the form's onSubmit event handler is declared in the <HEAD> section of the file:

```
//onSubmit event handler
function confirmOrder() {
    return confirm('Are you certain you wish to order the Kakata hat?');
}
```

When triggered, the confirmOrder() method displays a Confirm dialog box with buttons labeled OK and Cancel. If the user clicks OK, the dialog box is closed, and a true value is returned to the onSubmit event handler. If the user clicks Cancel, false is returned. The return statement in the onSubmit event handler examines the incoming value and determines whether the form should continue to process. The return in the event-handler assignment is essential for the code to work correctly. Assigning onSubmit="confirmOrder()" to the event handler causes the form to process regardless of the returned value from the dialog box.

The onSubmit event handler is similar to an onClick event handler of a submit object. Both of these are events you can use to trap a form before it's processed. As shown in Figure 10.3, the submit object's onClick event handler is triggered first, followed by the form's onSubmit.

FIGURE 10.3.
Event sequencing on a form submittal.

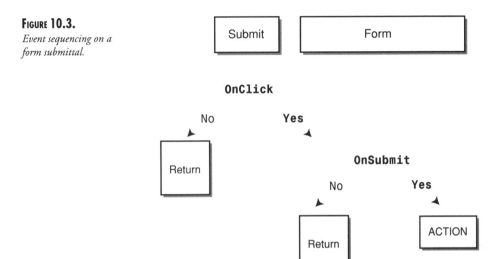

The onSubmit event handler is an ideal location to place form-level data validation before it is sent to a server or other process. See Chapter 16, "Creating Special Effects with JavaScript," for an example of using onSubmit to validate data.

Resetting a Form (onReset)

You might have to trigger an event when a form is submitted, as well as when it is reset. The onReset event handler triggers JavaScript code when a reset event occurs. Just as with onSubmit, onReset is an event handler of a form object.

To illustrate, look again at the Kakata hat order form used in the last section. After you add a new event handler to the form object's definition, the code would look like this:

```
<form action="process.cgi" method="POST"
onSubmit="return confirmOrder()"
onReset="return confirmReset()">
```

The confirmReset() method referenced in the form's onReset event handler is declared in the <HEAD> section of the file:

```
//onReset event handler
function confirmReset() {
    return confirm('Are you certain you wish to clear the order form?');
}
```

NOTE

The onReset event handler is supported in JavaScript 1.1 and higher.

Modifying Data (onChange)

As mentioned with the submit event, when your JavaScript applications deal with data, you'll typically want to preprocess the data entered by the user to avoid validation problems when the data is sent to a server. Although submit is designed for form-wide verification, the change event is typically the most important event for field-level validation. The change event occurs when the value of a field object changes and the field itself loses focus. Here's a list of the objects that can respond to change events:

- text
- textarea
- select

> **CAUTION**
>
> The onChange event handler doesn't work in all platform versions of Netscape 2.0.

You use the onChange event handler to execute JavaScript code or call a function to handle the event. Suppose you want to add a basic validity-checking routine to the Kakata Hat data entry form. Specifically, you want to ensure that the State field is always uppercase. The text object is defined as follows:

```
<input
    type=text
    size=3
    maxlength=2
    name="State"
    onChange="convertToUppercase(this)">
```

The convertToUppercase() method converts the value of the State field to uppercase using the string method toUpperCase():

```
function convertToUppercase(fieldObject) {
  fieldObject.value = fieldObject.value.toUpperCase()
}
```

Receiving Focus (onFocus)

The focus event is triggered when a field object receives focus—when the user either tabs into the object or clicks it with the mouse, or when you call an object's focus() method (discussed later in this chapter). Only one object can receive focus at a given time. Similar to the change event, the focus event can be handled by the following objects:

- text
- textarea
- select

> **NOTE**
>
> JavaScript 1.1 and higher expands the scope of onFocus to include it as an event handler for window, frame, and frameset objects. For each of these objects, the onFocus event handler specifies the action that should execute when the window receives focus.
>
> The onFocus event handler should be placed in the <BODY> tag of the window, frame, or frameset.

You can add an onFocus event handler to these objects to trigger an action. For an example, enhance the standard behavior of the text objects on the form. When you move onto a text object, an insertion point appears by default. However, a standard in many environments (such as Windows) is that if the field already has a value, the contents are selected when the object receives focus. To code this behavior, you need to add an onFocus event handler for each of the text objects, as well as the textarea object:

```
<pre>    First Name: <input
                       type=text
                       size=20
                       maxlength=20
                       name="FirstName"
                       onFocus="selectContents(this)">
     Last Name: <input
                       type=text
                       size=20
                       maxlength=20
                       name="LastName"
                       onFocus="selectContents(this)">
         Title: <input
                       type=text
                       size=30
                       maxlength=256
                       name="Title"
                       onFocus="selectContents(this)">
       Company: <input
                       type=text
                       size=30
                       maxlength=256
                       name="Company"
                       onFocus="selectContents(this)">
Street Address: <input
                       type=text
                       size=30
                       maxlength=256
                       name="StreetAddr"
                       onFocus="selectContents(this)">
          City: <input
                       type=text
                       size=30
                       maxlength=256
                       name="City"
                       onFocus="selectContents(this)">
```

10

HANDLING EVENTS

```
        State: <input
                        type=text
                        size=3
                        maxlength=2
                        name="State"
                        onFocus="selectContents(this)"
                        onChange="convertToUppercase(this)">
     Zip Code: <input
                        type=text
                        size=30
                        maxlength=10
                        name="ZipCode"
                        onFocus="selectContents(this)">
    Telephone: <input
                        type=text
                        size=12
                        maxlength=12
                        name="Phone"
                        onFocus="selectContents(this)">
          FAX: <input
                        type=text
                        size=12
                        maxlength=12
                        name="FAX"
                        onFocus="selectContents(this)">
       E-mail: <input
                        type=text
                        size=30
                        maxlength=256
                        name="Email"
                        onFocus="selectContents(this)">
          URL: <input
                         type=text
                         size=30
                         maxlength=256
                         name="URL"
                         onFocus="selectContents(this)"></pre>

<textarea
       name="worthyBox"
        rows=3
        cols=49
        onFocus="selectContents(this)">
</textarea>
```

Although you could write separate event handlers for each of these fields, it would be unwise to do so unless the processes were completely different. Instead, the selectContents() method takes advantage of the this keyword to reference the object making the call. The following function is then used as a global function for all the objects:

```
function selectContents(fieldObject) {
    fieldObject.select();
}
```

When any of the text or textarea objects calls the selectContents() method, the method uses the fieldObject parameter as a reference to the calling object. The select() method then selects the input area of the specified object.

Losing Focus (onBlur)

The blur event (the inverse of the focus event) is triggered when an object loses focus. The following data entry objects can respond to blur events:

- text
- textarea
- select

> **NOTE**
>
> As with the onFocus event handler, JavaScript 1.1 and higher expands the scope of onBlur to include it as an event handler for window, frame, and frameset objects. For each of these objects, the onBlur event handler specifies the action that should execute when the window loses focus.
>
> The onBlur event handler should be placed in the <BODY> tag of the window, frame, or frameset.

For example, suppose that on the data entry form you want to ensure that the Email text object is not left blank by the user. You could add this check to the onBlur event handler of the object. Because this affects a single field of the form, you can just add the JavaScript code to the text object definition:

```
<input
    type=text
    size=30
    maxlength=256
    name="Email"
    onFocus="selectContents(this)" onBlur="if (this.value == ''){
        alert('You must enter something.');this.focus();}">
```

If the user tries to tab out of the object without entering text, an alert dialog box notifies the user not to leave the field blank. The next command returns focus to the Email text object. If that command hadn't been used, the cursor would have moved on to the next tab stop.

As you have probably noticed, onChange and onBlur are similar. When should you use one over the other? onChange is best for checking or analyzing the content of an object and has the advantage of not being called if the user doesn't change the value. On the other hand, for required fields, you might want to use onBlur.

The sequencing of the onChange, onBlur, and onFocus event handlers is important to understand before you use them. As Figure 10.4 illustrates, onFocus occurs when you enter the field. As you leave, onChange is called, followed by the onBlur event handler, and finally by the onFocus handler of the next input object. Keep in mind that the code you might add, for example, to the onChange event handler could have an impact on an onBlur event handler of the same object. As a general rule, you should use these three events conservatively.

FIGURE 10.4.
*Event sequencing from
one text object to
another text object.*

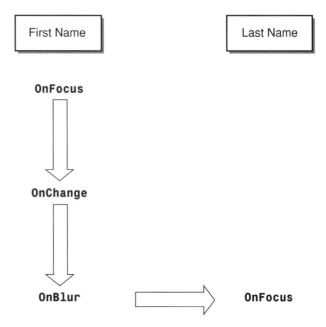

Selecting Text (onSelect)

The next JavaScript event is the select event, which occurs when the user selects text from a text or textarea object. The object's onSelect event handler either executes JavaScript code or calls a predefined function.

> **CAUTION**
>
> As with onChange, the onSelect event handler doesn't work in all platform versions of Netscape 2.0.

Regardless of whether it works, the select event's scope is rather limited for most purposes, and most developers will have little occasion to use it.

Moving the Mouse Over Objects (onMouseOver and onMouseOut)

If you are an experienced Web user, you have come to expect that the act of moving your mouse over link text displays the link's target destination (typically a URL address). However, no matter how much a power user might want to see the URL address, beginning users usually want something less esoteric. This is particularly the case in intranet environments where the destination URL is probably not thasœ"d¿éingful. Trapping the `mouseOver` and `mouseOut` event lets you change the default text in the status bar.

> **NOTE**
>
> The `onMouseOver` and `onMouseOut` event handlers are also supported by the area object in JavaScript 1.1 and higher.

The `mouseOver` event takes place when the user moves the mouse cursor over a link or area object. As you might expect, `onMouseOut` behaves in much the same way, except that it occurs each time a mouse pointer leaves an area or link. These objects' `onMouseOver` or `onMouseOut` event handlers can then change the default behavior of the browser. If you want to set the window's `status` and `defaultStatus` properties, you need to return a value of `true` to the event handler.

For example, suppose you want to display the following text in the status bar when a `mouseOver` event occurs for the Kakata Hat link:

```
Click here to get the whole story about the Legend of Kakata.
```

To do this, add the `onMouseOver` event handler to the link tag:

```
<a href="http://www.acadians.com/javascript/kakata/kakata.htm"
   name="linker"
   onMouseOver="return updateStatusBar()"
   >Legend of Kakata</a>
```

The `updateStatusBar()` method is defined as follows:

```
// onMouseOver event handler
function updateStatusBar() {
   window.status = 'Click here to get the whole story about the
      Legend of Kakata';
   return true
}
</textarea>   window.status = 'Click here to get the whole story about the
      Legend of Kakata';
   return true
```

Each of the examples discussed in this chapter is contained in the `Register.htm` file. Listing 10.1 lists the complete source code for the examples.

Listing 10.1. Source code for `Register.htm`.

```
<html>
<head>
<title>Kakata Hat Registration</title>
```

continues

Listing 10.1. continued

```
<SCRIPT LANGUAGE="JavaScript">
<!--

    var noticeWindow

    //onClick event handler
    function displayHat() {
       hatWindow = window.open("http:/../kakata/viewhat.htm",
       "ViewHat" ,"toolbar=0,width=200,height=400,resizable=0");
    }

    //onSubmit event handler
    function confirmOrder() {
      return confirm('Are you certain you wish to order the Kakata hat?');
    }

    //onChange event handler
    function convertToUppercase(fieldObject) {
       fieldObject.value = fieldObject.value.toUpperCase();
    }

    // onFocus event handler
    function selectContents(fieldObject) {
       fieldObject.select();
    }

    // onMouseOver event handler
    function updateStatusBar() {
      window.status = 'Click here to get the whole story
         about the Legend of Kakata';
      return true
    }

    // onSelect event handler
    function accessText() {
       alert('Success');
    }

// -->
</SCRIPT>
</head>
<body background="lt_rock.gif">
<h1><font color="#008000">Legend of Kakata Hat Order Form</font></h1>
<hr>

<p>If you would like more information on the <a
    href="http://www.acadians.com/javascript/kakata/kakata.htm"
    name="linker"
    onMouseOver="return updateStatusBar()">Legend of Kakata </a>, please
    fill out the following form. </p>

<form method="POST">
<p>If you would like to see a detailed picture of the Legend of Kakata
Hat before ordering, please click the following button: <input
type=button name="ViewHat" value="View Hat" onClick=displayHat()></p>
</form>
```

```
<hr>
<form
    action="JavaScript:alert('order')"
    method="POST"
    name="MainForm"
    onSubmit="return confirmOrder()">
<h2><font color="#008000">Customer Information</font></h2>
<pre>    First Name: <input
                        type=text
                        size=20
                        maxlength=20
                        name="FirstName"
                        onFocus="selectContents(this)">
     Last Name: <input
                        type=text
                        size=20
                        maxlength=20
                        name="LastName"
                        onFocus="selectContents(this)">
         Title: <input
                        type=text
                        size=30
                        maxlength=30
                        name="Title"
                        onFocus="selectContents(this)">
       Company: <input
                        type=text
                        size=30
                        maxlength=30
                        name="Company"
                        onFocus="selectContents(this)">
Street Address: <input
                        type=text
                        size=30
                        maxlength=30
                        name="StreetAddr"
                        onFocus="selectContents(this)">
          City: <input
                        type=text
                        size=30
                        maxlength=30
                        name="City"
                        onFocus="selectContents(this)">
         State: <input
                        type=text
                        size=3
                        maxlength=2
                        name="State"
                        onFocus="selectContents(this)"
                        onChange="convertToUppercase(this)">
      Zip Code: <input
                        type=text
                        size=30
                        maxlength=10
                        name="ZipCode"
                        onFocus="selectContents(this)">
```

10

HANDLING EVENTS

continues

Listing 10.1. continued

```
        Telephone: <input
                                type=text
                                size=12
                                maxlength=12
                                name="Phone"
                                onFocus="selectContents(this)">
                FAX: <input
                                type=text
                                size=12
                                maxlength=12
                                name="FAX"
                                onFocus="selectContents(this)">
            Email: <input
size=30
                                maxlength=50
                                name="Email"
                                onFocus="selectContents(this)">
                URL: <input
                                 type=text
                                 size=30
                                 maxlength=100
                                 name="URL"
                                 onFocus="selectContents(this)"></pre>
        <hr>

        <p><strong>Are you &quot;Kakata worthy&quot;? Please use the space below to
        enter a thorough reason for your order.</strong></p>
        <blockquote>
        <p><textarea
             name="worthyBox"
              rows=3
              cols=49
              onFocus="selectContents(this)">
        </textarea></blockquote></p>

        <h2><font color="#008000">Form Submission</font></h2>
        <p><em>Please click the Order button to order your free Legend of Kakata hat.
        You will receive email confirmation of your order in 24 hours.</em></p>
        <p><input
             type=submit
             value="Order"
             onClick="confirmOrder('Submit object')">
        <input
             type=reset
             value="Clear Form"
             onClick="alert('Clearing!')"></p>
        <p> </p>
        <p>
        </form>

        <hr>
        <h5>Developed by Richard Wagner for <em>JavaScript Unleashed</em>.<br>
        </h5>
```

```
<a
   href="JavaScript:displayHat()">
   <img src="ball.gif" align=bottom border=0 width=16 height=16>
</a>

</body>
</html>
```

TIP

If you're trapping for multiple mouseOver and mouseOut events in an area object, onMouseOut will be triggered when you leave an area, followed by onMouseOver when you enter the next area.

Loading a Document (onLoad)

The initial opening of a window or frameset can be an important time to perform a JavaScript process. The load event lets you harness this by adding an onLoad event handler to a single-frame window's <BODY> tag or a multiframe window's <FRAMESET> tag. The load event is executed when the browser finishes loading a window or all frames within a frameset. The window object is the only object that can handle this event.

To illustrate, suppose you want to ensure that all intranet users in your company are using the correct version of Netscape Navigator. You could evaluate the browser being used in the onLoad event handler and then notify the user if his or her software version is incorrect. In the <BODY> tag for the document, you would add the onLoad event handler:

```
<body onLoad="checkBrowser()">
```

Next, the checkBrowser() method is defined in the document's <HEAD> tag as follows:

```
//onLoad event handler
function checkBrowser() {
  ((navigator.appName == 'Netscape') &&
  (navigator.appVersion == '3.0b3 (Win95; I)')) {
noticeWindow = window.open("", "NoticeWindow",
      "toolbar=0,width=300,height=100,resizable=0");
  noticeWindow.document.write("<HEAD><TITLE>Upgrade Notice</TITLE></HEAD>");
  noticeWindow.document.write("<CENTER><BIG><B>Your Web Browser needs
  to be updated. Please see your supervisor before noon.
  </B></BIG></CENTER>")}
}
```

When the document is loaded, the JavaScript method is executed. Figure 10.5 shows the Upgrade Notice window displayed for versions that don't pass the test.

FIGURE 10.5.
The Upgrade Notify window is opened during the onLoad *event handler.*

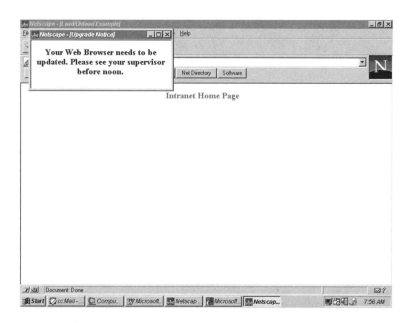

Exiting a Document (onUnload)

The unload event, which is the counterpart to the load event, is triggered just before the user exits a document. As with onLoad, you can add an onUnload event handler to a single-frame window's <BODY> tag or a multiframe window's <FRAMESET> tag. If you have a frameset and multiple onUnload event handlers, the <FRAMESET> event handler always happens last.

One example of how you can use the onUnload event handler is cleaning up the browser environment before continuing to the next page. For instance, suppose you want to close the View Hat window when leaving the Kakata Order page. You can add onUnload to the <BODY> tag as follows:

```
<body onLoad="checkBrowser()" onUnload="clean()">
```

Next, you can define the clean() method:

```
// onUnload event handler
function clean() {
   noticeWindow.close();
}
```

noticeWindow is a global variable declared in the <HEAD> tag of the document and refers to the Upgrade Notice window displayed in the onLoad event handler. If open, the Upgrade Notice window is closed when the user exits the current page.

Listing 10.2 provides the complete source code for the onLoad and onUnload examples.

Listing 10.2. The source code for LoadUnload.htm.

```
<html>
<head>
<title>Load/Unload Example</title>

<SCRIPT LANGUAGE="JavaScript">
<!--

   var noticeWindow

//onLoad event handler
function checkBrowser() {
  ((navigator.appName == 'Netscape') &&
   (navigator.appVersion == '3.0b3 (Win95; I)')) {
noticeWindow = window.open("", "NoticeWindow",
       "toolbar=0,width=300,height=100,resizable=0");
    noticeWindow.document.write("<HEAD><TITLE>Upgrade Notice</TITLE></HEAD>");
    noticeWindow.document.write("<CENTER><BIG><B>Your Web Browser needs
     to be updated. Please see your supervisor before noon.
     </B></BIG></CENTER>")}
}

// onUnload event handler
   function clean() {
     noticeWindow.close();
   }

// -->
</SCRIPT>
</head>
<body onLoad="checkBrowser()" onUnload="clean()">
<font color="#008000">
<CENTER><BIG><B>Intranet Home Page</B></BIG></CENTER>
</body>
</html>
```

Handling Errors (onError)

The window and image objects have an onError event handler that lets you trap for errors occurring during the loading of a document or image. The error that will be trapped will be either a JavaScript syntax or runtime error, not a browser error (such as an unresponsive server message). See Chapter 22, "Error Handling and Debugging in JavaScript," for full coverage of trapping errors with onError.

> **NOTE**
>
> The onError event handler is supported in JavaScript 1.1 and higher.

Aborting an Image Load (onAbort)

Depending on their size, loading of HTML images can be a time-intensive process. As a result, users may become impatient and stop the image load before it has been completed. For example, a user may abort the loading process by clicking a link to another page or the browser's Stop button.

> **NOTE**
>
> The image object and onAbort event handler are supported in JavaScript 1.1 and higher.

However, having the user work with a partially downloaded HTML file may not be what you would like to occur and will likely have some ramifications on any image-specific code in your script. The onAbort event handler lets you react to this aborting of an image load and trigger a JavaScript function as a response. For example, suppose you wanted to alert your user that the entire HTML document hasn't been downloaded. You would add the following event handler to your <IMG> tag:

```
<IMG NAME="mapworld" SRC="global.gif"
     onAbort="alert('You have not downloaded the entire document.')">
```

Changing Event Handlers

In JavaScript 1.1 and higher, you can change an event handler defined in the HTML tag definition. For example, in the following code, the optionA() function is assigned by the <INPUT> definition to be the event handler for the button1 object. However, the second script defined evaluates the choice variable. If choice isn't equal to "A," the code changes the event handler assignment to the optionB() function.

```
<SCRIPT LANGUAGE="JavaScript">      var choice = "A"
    function optionA() {
       ...
    }
```

```
        function optionB() {
            ...
        }
        ...
</SCRIPT>
<BODY>

<FORM NAME="form1">
<INPUT TYPE="button" NAME="button1"
    onClick="optionA()">
</FORM>

<SCRIPT LANGUAGE="JavaScript">

    if (choice != "A") {
        document.form1.button1.onclick=optionB
    }

</SCRIPT>
</BODY>
```

Notice that event handlers are function references and therefore do not have parentheses added to them when defined in code. If the code had been defined as follows, the `optionB()` function would have been triggered, not assigned as an event handler:

```
document.form1.button1.onclick=optionB()
```

Triggering Events in Code

So far, this chapter has discussed responding to events generated by either the user (such as a `click` event) or the system (such as an `onUnload` event). In most cases, you will design your code to respond to these events as they occur. However, as a JavaScript developer, you don't have to rely on external forces to cause an event to happen. In fact, you can trigger some of these events to occur within your code.

For example, you can simulate a `click` event for a `button` object by calling its `click()` method. Although this is valid for a `button` object, a `link` object—which has an `onClick` event handler— doesn't have a `click()` method.

However, if you have assigned an `onClick` event handler to this button, it may or may not be called, depending on the browser you're using. With Netscape 2.x and Navigator 3.0, the event handler isn't triggered for the button. In contrast, with Microsoft Internet Explorer 3.0, the event handler is triggered just as if the user had clicked the button. Because of this inconsistency, it's highly recommended that you call the JavaScript method that the event handler is calling directly rather than trigger the event itself.

Table 10.2 lists the JavaScript events and the methods that can trigger them.

Table 10.2. Events that can be triggered by a JavaScript method.

Object	click()	submit()	focus()	blur()	select()
button	■				
reset	■				
submit	■				
radio	■				
checkbox	■				
link					
form		■			
text			■	■	■
textarea			■	■	■
select			■	■	
window					

Timer Events

Many event-driven programming environments use a `timer` event, which is an event triggered every time a given time interval elapses. Although JavaScript offers no event called `timer`, you can use the `window` object's `setInterval` method to serve the same function.

NOTE

The `setInterval` method is supported in JavaScript 1.2 and higher.

The `setInterval` method repeatedly calls a function or evaluates an expression each time a time interval (in milliseconds) has expired. This method continues to execute until the window is destroyed or the `clearInterval` method is called.

For example, in Listing 10.3, the `setInterval` method is executed when the document opens and begins to call the `dailyTask()` function every 10,000 milliseconds. The `dailyTask()` function evaluates the time each time it is called, and when it is 8:30 a.m., the code within the `IF` statement is called, alerting the user and then clearing the interval. Once the `clearInterval` method is called, the `setInterval` halts execution.

Listing 10.3. Source code for `Timer12.htm`.

```
<HEAD>
<SCRIPT LANGUAGE="JavaScript">
<!--
    function dailyTask() {
       var tdy = new Date();
       if ((tdy.getHours() == 8) && (tdy.getMinutes() == 30)) {
          alert('Good morning sunshine!')
          clearInterval(timerID)
       }
    }

//-->

timerID = setInterval('dailyTask()', 10000)

</SCRIPT>
</HEAD>
```

If you're using JavaScript 1.1 or earlier, you can perform a similar process, albeit in a much less straightforward way, using the `setTimeout()` and `clearTimeout()` methods.

You usually use the `setTimeout()` method to evaluate an expression after a specific amount of time. This evaluation is a one-time process that is not repeated an infinite number of times. However, because you can make recursive function calls in JavaScript, you can use recursion to create a *de facto* timer event.

Suppose you want to perform the same task just shown each morning at 8:30 a.m. You could have a timer evaluate the time of day; when that time is reached, the process is spawned. The `dailyTask()` method is defined as follows:

```
function dailyTask() {
  var tdy = new Date();
  if ((tdy.getHours() == 8) && (tdy.getMinutes() == 30)) {
    performProcess()}
  timerID = setTimeout("dailyTask()",10000)
}
```

The method creates a `date` object to get the current time using `getHours()` and `getMinutes()`. If these evaluate to 8:30 a.m., the `performProcess()` method is called. The next line—the heart of the `timer` process—uses the `setTimeout()` method to call the `dailyTask()` method recursively every 10,000 milliseconds.

CAUTION

This example demonstrates a "kludge" method of using a timer, but you would probably want to be careful implementing such a solution in the real world. Implementing a continuous looping process like that in a browser could lead to resource constraints over time.

To trigger this `timer` initially when the document is loaded, you can add an `onLoad` event handler to the `<BODY>` tag of the HTML document:

```
<BODY onLoad="dailyTask()">
```

Listing 10.4 provides the entire source code listing for this example.

Listing 10.4. Source code for `Timer11.htm`.

```
<HEAD>
<SCRIPT LANGUAGE="JavaScript">
<!--
    function performProcess() {
        alert('Good morning sunshine!
');
    }

    function dailyTask() {
        var tdy = new Date();
        if ((tdy.getHours() == 8) && (tdy.getMinutes() == 30)) {
        performProcess()}
        timerID = setTimeout("dailyTask()",10000)
        }
//-->
</SCRIPT>
</HEAD>

<BODY onLoad="dailyTask()">
</BODY>
```

Summary

Given JavaScript's event-driven nature, a solid understanding of its built-in events is key to maximizing the power of JavaScript. This chapter discussed events and their associated event handlers. I focused on the events that are most useful to you, as well as specific examples of how you can use them. Having this foundation in place will assist you over the next few chapters as you look in depth at JavaScript's built-in events.

Navigator Objects

IN THIS CHAPTER

CHAPTER 11

The navigator objects are the highest-level objects in the JavaScript object hierarchy. These objects don't deal with the nuts and bolts of HTML; instead, they deal primarily with browser issues, such as opening a new browser window, traversing the history list, or obtaining the hostname from the current URL.

This chapter looks at the major navigator objects in JavaScript. We'll start by looking at the highest-level object in the object hierarchy—the window—and then we'll look at the frame, location, and history objects. We'll close the chapter by looking at the application-level navigator object.

The Window Object

As discussed in Chapter 9, "The JavaScript Object Model," the window object is the top-level object in the JavaScript object hierarchy. Unlike other objects that may or may not be present, the window object is always there, whether it's in a single or multiframe display. However, the window object is unusual in that you can often simply ignore it, for two reasons.

First, if you're working in a single-frame environment, you can ignore explicit referencing of the window object. JavaScript infers the reference to the current window. For example, the following two statements are equivalent and produce the same results:

```
myTitle = window.document.title
```

```
myTitle = document.title
```

Second, because of the structure of the JavaScript language, some "system"-level methods, such as displaying message boxes or setting a timer, are assigned to the window object. However, you don't need to reference the window itself when calling these methods; the reference to the window is implicit.

Working with window objects is important when programming in JavaScript because of the way people use browser windows. Although most people browsing the Web typically use only one instance of the browser, having two or more windows open is sometimes beneficial. You can compare pages from different sites, enter information into a form using data from a different Web page, and conduct research from a list on one page and look at the references with another browser instance.

The term *browser window* is often shortened to just *window,* although you should be careful not to confuse separate copies of the browser with frames, which are also referred to as windows (subwindows of the browser window). The browser window is also called the *top window,* because frames are subwindows of the browser. Browsers that support JavaScript let you programmatically open and close browser windows and navigate through these windows. A site with separate windows can provide several simultaneous views of the site's content, increase access to the information and features, and offer new ways to fully interact with the site.

NOTE

JavaScript 1.2 added several new window methods: `moveBy`, `moveTo`, `resizeBy`, `resizeTo`, `scrollBy`, and `scrollTo`. Refer to Chapter 16, "Creating Special Effects with JavaScript," for additional information on these new capabilities.

In many cases, frames might be better for simultaneous viewing. However, multiple browser windows can be individually resized and positioned by the user. Users can also minimize and maximize the window, move the window to the foreground or background as needed, and typically keep all the tools and other features (menu bar, location field, status bar, bookmarks, and so on) with each instance of the browser.

TIP

Many users might find it distracting and annoying if you unexpectedly open new browser windows, especially if they have to keep closing them. Let the visitor know that an action will cause a window to open—for example, a short note next to a link. In the following sentence, Spike is a link that opens a new window:

```
See a picture of my dog Spike. (new window)
```

Opening and Closing Windows

NOTE

As a user, you can always open a new window by selecting File | New Browser (or a similar option). However, any window opened by a user in this way can't be referenced by JavaScript in other windows.

You can use JavaScript to open and close browser windows. As a developer, you can create a new window with a particular document loaded into it, based upon specific conditions. You can also specify, for example, the size of the new window and the options that are available in the window, and you can assign names for referencing it. Although the act of opening a window is similar to creating a new window object, you don't use the `new` constructor. Instead, you use the following syntax:

```
windowVar = window.open(URL, windowName, [, windowAttributes])
```

The parameters for the open() method are

- *URL*: The URL of the target window. This parameter is optional. If the URL is an empty string (""), the browser opens a blank window, allowing you to use the write() method to create dynamic HTML.

- *windowName*: The name of the window object. *Name* is also optional; however, to target the window with a link or a form, you need a name. You can provide a name at a later time by assigning the window.name property.

- *windowAttributes*: A list of display attributes for the browser window.

If successful, the open() method returns a handle to a window object. If open() fails, it returns a null value.

NOTE

The two names that can refer to a window aren't the same functionally. Consider the following code:

```
myWindow=window.open("","newWindow");
```

myWindow is a variable of the object that opened the newWindow. newWindow is the new window's name. The new window's properties can be referenced through the variable myWindow. Links and forms can be targeted to the new window with its name newWindow.

Specifying Window Content

The URL parameter specifies what content appears in the new window. If you specify a value, the browser attempts to locate and display the specified document:

```
newWindow = window.open("http://www.acadians.com", "AcadiaPage", "")
```

Alternatively, you can display a blank page by specifying an empty string ("") as the URL parameter. Use this technique if you want to create an HTML page dynamically using JavaScript:

```
newWindow = window.open("", "DynamicPage", "")
newWindow.document.write("<H1>Document created using JavaScript.</H1>")
newWindow.document.close()
```

See Chapter 12, "Document Objects," for complete details on using the document object's write() method to create dynamic HTML.

Specifying Window Attributes

The *windowAttributes* parameter is important as you display windows, because it lets you customize the look of the window you're opening. The *windowAttributes* parameter is optional; not including it gives you a window identical to the current one with respect to attributes. Table 11.1 lists the possible attributes that you can specify.

Table 11.1. The open() method's window display attributes.

Attribute	Description
width	Width of the Navigator client area in pixels
height	Height of the Navigator client area in pixels
toolbar	Shows/hides the browser toolbar
menubar	Shows/hides the browser menu bar
scrollbars	Shows/hides the browser horizontal and vertical scrollbars
resizable	Allows/disallows resizing of the browser window
status	Shows/hides the browser status bar
location	Shows/hides the URL location box
directories	Shows/hides a secondary toolbar (Netscape)
copyhistory	Copies the current window's Go history for new window
outerWidth	Width of the Navigator window in pixels (JavaScript 1.2)
outerHeight	Height of the Navigator window in pixels (JavaScript 1.2)
left	Distance in pixels from the left side of the screen (JavaScript 1.2)
top	Distance in pixels from the top of the screen (JavaScript 1.2)
alwaysRaised	Creates a browser window that floats on top of other windows, regardless of whether it is active or not (JavaScript 1.2)
z-lock	Creates a new browser window that doesn't rise above other windows when given focus (JavaScript 1.2)

11

NAVIGATOR OBJECTS

NOTE

The alwaysRaised and z-lock attributes added in JavaScript 1.2 work only on Windows and Macintosh platforms.

The width and height attributes specify the dimensions of the window in pixels. The remaining attributes are set by using Boolean values: true values are either 1, yes, or the attribute alone; false values are either 0, no, or, more simply, leaving the attribute out altogether. For example, if you want to display the new window with only a toolbar and menu bar, you use the following syntax:

```
newWindow = window.open("", "myWindow", "toolbar=1,menubar=1")
```

The following syntaxes are also valid:

```
newWindow = window.open("", "myWindow", "toolbar=yes,menubar=yes")

newWindow = window.open("", "myWindow", "toolbar,menubar")
```

As you see, you can simply leave out attributes that aren't specified. They are assumed to have `false` values.

NOTE

The `outerWidth`, `outerHeight`, `left`, and `top` attributes added in JavaScript 1.2 let you provide absolute positioning of browser windows on your desktop.

TIP

A bug in certain varieties of the Netscape Navigator browser prevents the display of a document with the `window.open()` method. The workaround for this bug is to repeat the window-opening statement:

```
myWindow = window.open("new.html","newWindow");
myWindow = window.open("new.html","newWindow");
```

Repeating the statement forces the display of newWindow and its document in all varieties of the Netscape Navigator browser.

NOTE

In addition to the window `open()` method, you can also provide a link attribute of `TARGET="_blank"` or even a target attribute value of any name (window or frame) not currently in use to open a new window. The link `<A HREF="foo.html" TARGET="bar">foo </A>` opens a browser window, names the window bar, and loads the document `foo.html` in it, as long as one of the current windows or frames in use isn't named bar (window and frame names are case-sensitive).

Additionally, the link `TARGET="_blank"` creates an unnamed window, which makes it difficult to update the window. With a target of _blank, a link (whether the same link or a different one) simply adds another new window, instead of updating the previously opened window.

Closing Windows

To close a window, you can use the window object's `close()` method. If you're closing the current window, your method call is simply `window.close()`. Unlike other window object methods, such as `alert()` or `setTimer()`, the `close()` method must always accompany an object reference. If you use `close()` by itself, you could close the current document rather than the window, depending on the context of the method call. The reason is that the document object has a `close()` method, too.

NOTE

Later versions of Netscape prevent the `window.close()` from closing a window that wasn't created by JavaScript. This security measure prevents pranksters from inserting the code in poorly written guest books and the like. This measure shouldn't affect any legitimate use of the `window.close()` method.

A function or event handler with `window.close()` closes the window containing it:

```
<FORM>
<INPUT TYPE="BUTTON" VALUE="Close Window" onClick="top.close()">
</FORM>
```

NOTE

For an event handler, such as `onClick`, you must specify a window name, such as `window`, `parent`, `top`, `self`, or an assigned variable name such as `myWindow`, as in `window.close()` or `myWindow.close()`. Simply using `close()` in an event handler implies `document.close()`.

You can close a window by reference, in the same window that opened it, through the variable assigned to the new window:

```
myWindow = window.open("new.html","newWindow");
.....
<FORM>
<INPUT TYPE="BUTTON" VALUE="Close Window" onClick="myWindow.close()">
</FORM>
```

NOTE

`newWindow.close();` won't work. You can use the name `newWindow` in the preceding example to identify the window (the `window.name` property) and target the window in links and forms. However, you can't use `newWindow` to reference the new window and its properties.

TIP

A good use of the `window.close()` method is to provide a button or link for users to easily close a new window when they're finished with it. (Some users, especially new ones, might not know how to close the window or might mistakenly exit the browser instead of closing

continues

continued

the window.) You can use a conditional statement to provide a close button or link if the document is loaded in an explicitly named window (a new window):

```
<SCRIPT LANUAGE="JavaScript">
<!--
//newWindow is the name given the new window
if(top.name == "newWindow"){
  document.write('<A HREF="javascript:top.close()>close</A>"'  +
                 " this window to return to previous window.");
     }     //  For clarity the angle brackets
           // are not encoded, unescape("%3C"), unescape("%3E").
 //However in actual code they would be encoded to
 //prevent misinterpretation as comment tags by older browsers.
// -->
</SCRIPT>
```

The form in Figure 11.1 demonstrates the various aspects of opening and closing windows. By filling out the form, you can specify the options of how you want the new window to look.

FIGURE 11.1.

A Window Open sample form.

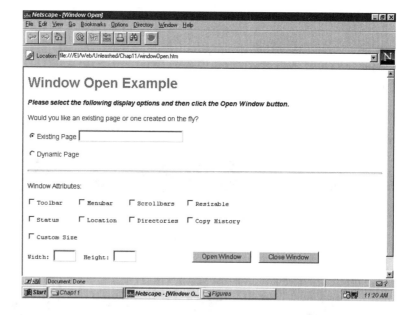

In the first section, you can specify the URL parameter—to use an existing URL or create a page on-the-fly. The second section lets you specify each of the window attributes available. By default, all are unchecked. You can check all the ones you want to display. By checking the Custom Size box, you can specify the dimensions of the new window.

By clicking the Open Window button, you can see the new window that is created, as shown in Figure 11.2.

FIGURE 11.2.

The new window is displayed.

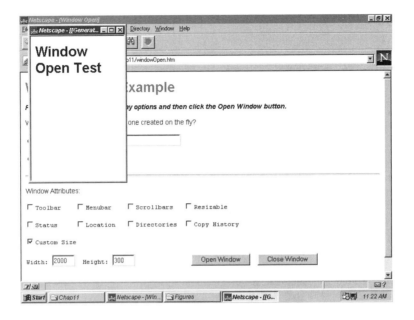

Listing 11.1 provides the source code for this example.

Listing 11.1. OpenWindow.htm.

```html
<html>
<head>
<title>Window Open</title>
<SCRIPT LANGUAGE="JavaScript">
<!--
    var newWindow

    // Open Window based on user defined attributes
    function openWindow() {

        // Build the windowAttributes parameter list
        var winAtts = ""
        if (document.winOptions.toolbarOption.checked) {
            winAtts += "toolbar=1," }
        if (document.winOptions.menubarOption.checked) {
            winAtts += "menubar=1," }
        if (document.winOptions.scrollbarsOption.checked) {
            winAtts += "scrollbars=1," }
        if (document.winOptions.resizableOption.checked) {
            winAtts += "resizable=1," }
        if (document.winOptions.statusOption.checked) {
            winAtts += "status=1," }
        if (document.winOptions.locationOption.checked) {
            winAtts += "location=1," }
        if (document.winOptions.directoriesOption.checked) {
            winAtts += "directories=1," }
```

continues

Listing 11.1. continued

```
            if (document.winOptions.copyHistoryOption.checked) {
                winAtts += "copyhistory=1," }
            if (document.winOptions.customSizeOption.checked) {
                winAtts += "height=" + document.winOptions.heightBox.value + ","
                winAtts += "width=" + document.winOptions.widthBox.value + ","
            }
            winAtts = winAtts.substring(0, winAtts.length-2)

            // Determine URL and show window
            if (document.winOptions.pageType[1].checked) {
                var urlVar = ""
                urlVar = document.winOptions.urlBox.value
                newWindow = window.open(urlVar,"newWindow",winAtts) }
            else {
                newWindow = window.open("","newWindow",winAtts)
                newWindow.document.write("<H1>Window Open Test</H1><p>")
            }
        }

    // Close Window
    function closeWindow() {
        newWindow.close()
    }
// -->
</SCRIPT>
</head>

<body background="../lt_rock.gif">
<h1><font color="#008040">Window Open Example</font></h1>
<p><i><b>Please select the following display options and then click
the Open Window button. </i></B></p>
<form name="winOptions" method="POST">
<p>Would you like an existing page or one created on the fly?</p>
<input
    type=radio
    checked
    name="pageType"
    value="existing">Existing Page
    <input
        type=text
        size=30
        maxlength=256
        name="urlBox"></p>
    <input
        type=radio
        name="pageType"
        value="dynamic">Dynamic Page</p>
<hr>
<p>Window Attributes:</p>
<pre><input
    type=checkbox
    name="toolbarOption"
    value="ON"
    >Toolbar     <input
    type=checkbox
    name="menubarOption"
    value="ON">Menubar      <input
```

```
            type=checkbox
            name="scrollbarsOption"
            value="ON">Scrollbars    <input
            type=checkbox
            name="resizableOption"
            value="ON">Resizable</pre>
<pre><input
            type=checkbox
            name="statusOption"
            value="ON">Status      <input
            type=checkbox
            name="locationOption"
            value="ON">Location    <input
            type=checkbox name="directoriesOption"
            value="ON">Directories   <input
            type=checkbox name="copyHistoryOption"
            value="ON">Copy History</pre>
<pre><input
            type=checkbox
            name="customSizeOption"
            value="ON">Custom Size</pre>
<pre>Width: <input
            type=text
            size=5
            maxlength=5
            name="widthBox">  Height: <input
            type=text
            size=5
            maxlength=5
            name="heightBox">                <input
            type="button"
            name="OpenButton"
            value="Open Window"
            onClick="openWindow()">  <input
            type="button"
            name="CloseButton"
            value="Close Window"
            onClick="closeWindow()"></pre>
</form>
<p> </p>
</body>
</html>
```

Navigating Between Windows

It's possible to have a number of windows open during a session; however, only one window can be active, or have focus, at a time. Having focus means that the window can directly receive and respond to user input. Also, the window with the focus is typically the top window on the display, the one in the foreground overlapping the other windows. (In UNIX and X Window, the window with focus can be in the background.)

The user can navigate between the windows by using the mouse. Often, clicking the window gives the window focus. With some varieties of UNIX, moving the mouse cursor on a window is enough to give a window focus; conversely, moving the cursor off the window blurs (removes focus, or deactivates) the window.

Relying on user action isn't the only way, nor at times the best way, to give focus to a window and blur others. JavaScript and HTML provide several methods to focus and blur windows automatically through code. This automatic focusing and blurring allows navigation through the windows with little or no user action. Instead of providing a message to tell the user to click a window, the code can focus the window automatically for the user. The intent isn't to remove user control of the session but to assist the user—as cruise control in an automobile does.

Although many sites don't need multiple windows, sites that do might benefit by controlling these windows programmatically. JavaScript provides a good means of controlling windows through the opening and closing techniques previously described and through techniques to apply and remove window focus. All these techniques for controlling the windows combine to provide a programmatic window navigation system.

In JavaScript, merely specifying an object of the window or its document, or even changing a property in the window, doesn't give the window focus. You can give focus to a window in two ways:

- Indirectly, by giving focus to an object in the window
- Directly, by giving focus to the window

Indirect Focus

A window opened with a variable `myWindow`, containing a document with a form named `myForm` and an input element named `myInput`, can receive focus through the window that opened it by using the following code:

```
myWindow.document.myForm.myInput.focus();
```

The input element, `myInput`, gains focus, and as a result, `myWindow`, which contains `myInput`, also gets focus.

A new window can give focus to the window that opened it through its `opener` property:

```
window.opener.focus();
```

> **NOTE**
>
> The opener property is supported in JavaScript 1.1 and higher.

To provide focus from a new window to the window that opened it in early versions of JavaScript-capable browsers, the new window needs a variable to reference the opening window:

```
myWindow = window.open("new.html","newWindow");
myWindow.oldWindow = top;
```

The new window can reference the old window and indirectly give it focus:

```
oldWindow. document.myForm.myInput.focus();
```

Direct Focus

A window receives focus directly if you use the `window.focus()` method. If the window can reference another window through a variable such as `myWindow`, it can give focus to the other window:

```
myWindow.focus();
```

A new window can give focus to the window that opened it through its `opener` property:

```
window.opener.focus();
```

A call to a function in a window can provide focus to the window if the function contains `window.focus()`:

```
function focusDemo(){
    top.focus;
    ... rest of function
    }
```

> **NOTE**
>
> The methods `window.focus()` and `window.blur()`, like the `opener` property, are supported only in JavaScript 1.1 and higher. To support the early versions of the browser, you have to use the indirect focusing technique.

Removing Focus

To blur, or remove focus from, a window just gives focus to another window. Because only one window can have focus at a time, giving focus to a window directly or indirectly blurs the other windows.

A window can directly lose focus without another window gaining the focus through the `window.blur()` method. You can use any of the means that you employ with `window.focus()` for `window.blur()` as well.

> **NOTE**
>
> According to Netscape documentation, you're supposed to give focus to a window by targeting a link at the window:
>
> ```
> <A HREF="some.html" TARGET="myWindow">My Window</A>
> ```

continues

continued

Clicking the link should load the document some.html in the window myWindow and give focus to myWindow. If myWindow doesn't exist, a new window is opened with some.html loaded in it, and the new window has the focus.

This technique doesn't always work in every version of the browser. If the window is already open, it might not gain focus.

Displaying Message Boxes

Dialog boxes are typically an important part of an application environment. If you've used Windows much, you know that dialog boxes are a given in this and other graphical user interfaces. JavaScript can display standard dialog boxes to either notify a user or receive information before proceeding. However, because of the nonmodal nature of the Web, I recommend that you not use dialog boxes. You can usually communicate with the user in some other way rather than resorting to dialog boxes.

TIP

Modal dialog boxes are common in Windows applications. If you come from a Windows 4GL background, be sure to adjust your thinking about their use.

The JavaScript language itself not so subtly enforces this notion by adding a prefix to the messages you display. For alert messages, "JavaScript Alert" appears before the message you specify. For confirm dialog boxes, it's "JavaScript Confirm"; in prompt dialog boxes, you see "JavaScript Prompt." One reason for this is that the user can better determine the source of the dialog box that is displayed.

NOTE

Other than providing the message itself, you can't customize the look of JavaScript message boxes. The title and icons are always the same.

Simple Notification

You use the window object's alert() method to display information to the user. The alert dialog box displays a message to the user with a single OK button to close the box. It is modal, so the user must close the dialog box before continuing in the browser (even in multiframe documents). No value is returned when the dialog box is closed. Its syntax follows:

```
[window.]alert(message)
```

You can display information about the current window in an alert message with the code shown in Listing 11.2.

Listing 11.2. DisplayWindowInfo.htm.

```
<HTML>
<HEAD NAME = "WindowPane">
<SCRIPT LANGUAGE = "JavaScript">

    function displayWindowInfo() {
        var winInfo = ""
        winInfo = "Number of frames: " + window.length + "\r"
        winInfo += "Window object name: " + window.window + "\r"
        winInfo += "Window parent name: " + window.parent + "\r"
        winInfo += "URL: " + window.location + "\r"
        alert(winInfo)
    }

</SCRIPT>
</HEAD>

<BODY>
<FORM>
<INPUT
    Type="button"
    Value="Display Window Information"
    OnClick="displayWindowInfo()"
</INPUT>
</FORM>
</BODY>
```

Figure 11.3 shows the alert dialog box that is displayed when the user clicks the button.

Although it's typically a string, the message parameter of the alert() method isn't required to be. Because JavaScript isn't a strongly typed language, you can display other data type information without converting the data to a string. You can even use an object as a parameter, as shown in Listing 11.3. Figure 11.4 shows the result.

Listing 11.3. DisplayWindowInfo.htm.

```
<HTML>
<HEAD>
<SCRIPT LANGUAGE = "JavaScript">

    function Application(Title, ProgramName, Path, Vendor) {
        this.Title = Title
```

continues

Listing 11.3. continued

```
        this.ProgramName = ProgramName
        this.Path = Path
        this.Vendor = Vendor
    }

    function displayApp() {
        alert(Application)
    }

</SCRIPT>
</HEAD>
<BODY>
<H1></H1>
<FORM>
<INPUT
    Type="button"
    Value="Display Object Definition"
    OnClick="displayApp()"
</INPUT>
</FORM>
</BODY>
```

Figure 11.3.
The Alert dialog box.

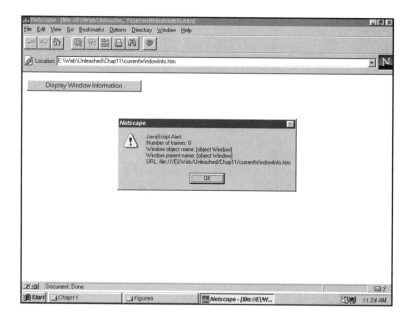

Yes/No Confirmation

In addition to simply displaying information in a dialog box, you can also ask a question using the window object's confirm() method. The confirm dialog box features OK and Cancel buttons, each returning a value. OK returns true, and Cancel returns false. As the method's name implies, you typically use a confirmation dialog box to confirm an action the user is about to take. Here is its syntax:

```
returnValue = [window.]confirm(message)
```

Figure 11.4.

The object definition displayed in an alert dialog box.

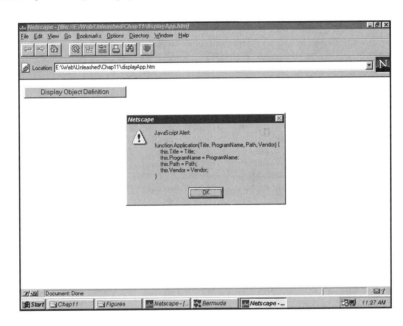

A common use of the confirmation dialog box is to ask the user to confirm a form submission or send an e-mail message. Listing 11.4 shows how you can use `confirm()` to return a value to the form's `onSubmit` event handler. If the user clicks OK, the form is e-mailed to the specified address. If the Cancel button is clicked, the submit event is canceled.

Listing 11.4. JavaScriptChronicles.htm.

```html
<html>
<head>
<title>Untitled Normal Page</title>
<SCRIPT LANGUAGE="JavaScript">

    function confirmAction() {

        return confirm("Do you really want this subscription?
                The magazine is not really that good.")
    }

</SCRIPT>
</head>

<body>
<h2><em>JavaScript Chronicles -- Free Subscription Form</em></h2>
```

continues

Listing 11.4. continued

```
<form
      action="mailto:subscribe@jschronicles.com"
      method="POST"
      name="SubscribeForm"
      onSubmit="return confirmAction()">
<ol>
<li>What other magazines do you currently subscribe to?
<pre><input type=checkbox name="C1-SKU01" value="SKU01">PC Week
<input type=checkbox name="C1-SKU04" value="SKU04">DBMS
<input type=checkbox name="C1-SKU07" value="SKU07">Wired
<input type=checkbox name="C1-SKU10" value="SKU10">Yahoo
<input type=checkbox name="C1-SKU02" value="SKU02">InfoWorld
<input type=checkbox name="C1-SKU05" value="SKU05">Databased Advisor
<input type=checkbox name="C1-SKU08" value="SKU08">Web Publisher
<input type=checkbox name="C1-SKU11" value="SKU11">Internet Advisor
<input type=checkbox name="C1-SKU03" value="SKU03">PC Magazine
<input type=checkbox name="C1-SKU06" value="SKU06">Delphi Informant
<input type=checkbox name="C1-SKU09" value="C1-SKU09">Web Informant
<input type=checkbox name="C1-SKU12" value="SKU12">JavaWorld
</pre>

</li>
<li>Please enter the reason you would like to subscribe to
<em>JavaScript Chronicles:</em><br>
<br>
<textarea
      name="Comments"
      rows=6
      cols=46>
      </textarea></li>
</ol>
<p>
<input
      type=submit
      name="Submit"
      value="Submit">

</form>
</body>
</html>
```

Figure 11.5 shows the confirm message box that is displayed when the user clicks the Submit button.

User Input

A third message box that you can use for obtaining user input is invoked with the prompt() method of the window object. Use the prompt dialog box when you want to obtain a value from a user. This dialog box features a message, an edit box for user input, and OK and Cancel buttons. The prompt() method has the following syntax:

```
returnValue = [window.]prompt(message, defaultReply)
```

FIGURE 11.5.
The confirm dialog box returns the user's response.

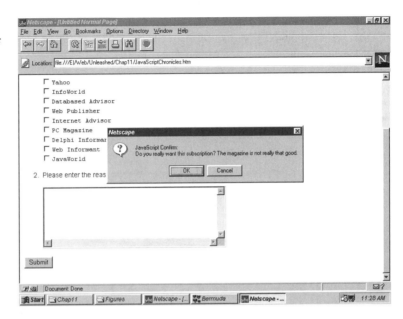

As you can see, in addition to specifying the message of the dialog box, you need to specify a *defaultReply* parameter. This value becomes the default text inserted in the edit box of the message box. You must specify this parameter, even if you have no default value.

> **NOTE**
>
> Be sure to always use a default reply when displaying a prompt dialog box. If you don't add this parameter, JavaScript places <Undefined> in the edit box, which can be confusing for users. If you have no default value, use an empty string ("") for the parameter.

If the user clicks OK, the prompt() method returns the string value entered by the user. If nothing is entered in the edit box, an empty string ("") is returned. However, if the user clicks Cancel, a null value is returned.

> **CAUTION**
>
> Don't assume that the user will always click OK in the prompt dialog box. Every time you use the prompt() method, you should first ensure that a non-null value is returned before proceeding to evaluate it. Otherwise, if the user clicks Cancel, you will be working with a string value of "null" rather than what the user actually entered.

Listing 11.5 shows one example of how you can use the prompt message box. The user is asked to enter text in the box, as shown in Figure 11.6. This text is then used in a new window, as shown in Figure 11.7.

FIGURE 11.6.

The prompt message box.

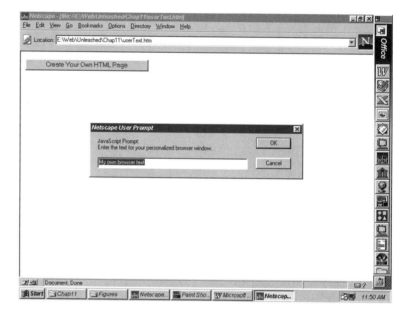

FIGURE 11.7.

The new window displays content provided by the user.

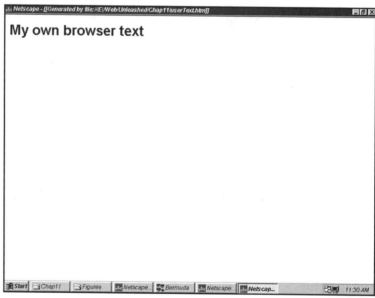

11

Listing 11.5. UserText.htm.

```
<HTML>
<HEAD>
<SCRIPT LANGUAGE = "JavaScript">

    function showBox() {
            userText = prompt("Enter the text for your " +
              personalized browser window.","My own browser text")
          if (userText != null) {
            userWindow = window.open("", "userTextWindow", "toolbar=0")
            userWindow.document.write("<h1>" + userText + "</h1>") }
    }

</SCRIPT>

<BODY>
<FORM>
<INPUT
    Type="button"
    Value="Create Your Own HTML Page"
    OnClick="showBox()"
</INPUT>
</FORM>
</BODY>
```

The return value is always a string. If you want to treat it as another value, you must convert it first. For example, if you want to calculate a total price based on a user-defined interest rate, you could get that value using the prompt() method, as shown in Figure 11.8. Next, you could convert the value into a float using parseFloat() before calculating. Listing 11.6 shows the code.

FIGURE 11.8.

Retrieving input from the user.

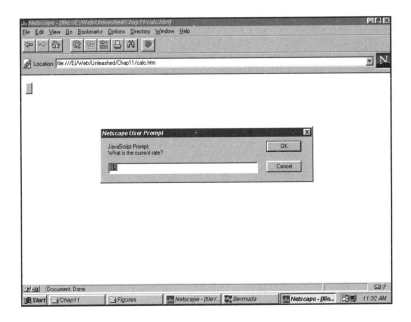

Listing 11.6. Calc.htm.

```
<HTML>
<HEAD>
<SCRIPT LANGUAGE = "JavaScript">

    function getPercentageRate() {
       percent = prompt("What is the current rate?", "8.5")
       if (percent != null) {
          totalPrice = parseFloat(percent) * 20000
          alert(totalPrice) }
    }

</SCRIPT>
<BODY>
<FORM>
<INPUT
    Type="button"
    Value="Calculate Total Price"
    OnClick="getPercentageRate()"
</INPUT>
</FORM>
</BODY>
```

Working with Status Bar Messages

The status bar of a browser can be an important means of communicating with the user. You can use two properties of the window object—defaultStatus and status—to control the text that is displayed.

Generally, there are two ways to use the status bar. First, you can display a default message on the status bar. The user sees this message without performing any action. You can display a default message using the defaultStatus property. The defaultStatus property can be set at any time—either upon loading the window or while the window is already open.

Second, you can display a "temporary" message that overrides the default text. In practice, this message usually appears when a user performs an event, such as moving a mouse over a jump. You can set this message using the status property.

Figure 11.9 demonstrates the use of the defaultStatus and status properties.

The code behind this page shows three actions that you code to change the status bar message. First, a default message is set when the window opens using the following code:

```
window.defaultStatus = "Welcome to the large URL page."
```

Second, when the user passes over the "Go" link, its onMouseOver event handler calls the following function:

```
function changeStatus() {
   window.status = "Click me to go to the Acadia Software home page."
}
```

FIGURE 11.9.

Setting the
defaultStatus *and*
status *properties.*

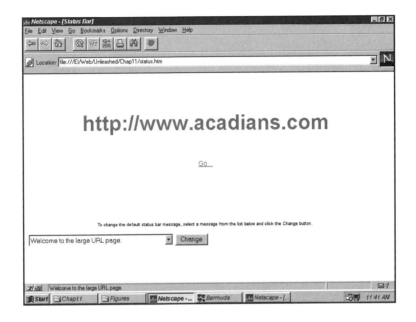

Third, to change the text of the default status message, the user can select a different message from the select object. When the Change button's onClick event handler is triggered, it executes the following function:

```
function changeDefaultStatus() {
    window.defaultStatus = window.document.statusForm.messageList.
    options[window.document.statusForm.messageList.selectedIndex].
    text
}
```

Listing 11.7 provides the complete source code for this example.

Listing 11.7. Status.htm.

```
<html>
<head>
<title>Status Bar</title>
<SCRIPT LANGUAGE="JavaScript">
<!--
    window.defaultStatus = "Welcome to the large URL page."

    function changeStatus() {
        window.status = "Click me to go to the Acadia Software" +
        + " home page."
    }

    function changeDefaultStatus() {
        window.defaultStatus = window.document.statusForm.messageList.
        options[window.document.statusForm.messageList.
        selectedIndex].text
    }
```

continues

Listing 11.7. continued

```
//-->
</SCRIPT>
</head>

<body>
<p> </p>
<p> </p>
<p align=center>
<font color="#008040">
<font size=7>
<strong>http://www.acadians.com</strong></font></font></p>
<p align=center>
<a href="http://www.acadians.com" onMouseOver="changeStatus()
    ;return true">Go...</a></p>

<form name="statusForm" method="POST">
<p><br>
<br>
<br>
<br>
</p>
<p align=center>
<font size=1>To change the default status bar message, select
a message from the list below and click the Change button. </font></p>
<p align=center><select
    name="messageList"
    size=1>
    <option selected>Welcome to the large URL page.</option>
    <option>En route to Acadia Software</option>
    <option>This page intentionally left (nearly) blank.</option>
    <option>An exciting example of changing status bar text.</option>
    </select>
<input
    type=button
    name="Change"
    value="Change"
    onClick="changeDefaultStatus()"></p>
</form>
</body>
</html>
```

The Frame Object

Along with JavaScript, frames were introduced in Netscape Navigator 2.0. Frames quickly became popular because they could display multiple documents simultaneously in the same window. The window is divided into several subwindows called frames, which are based on the designer's specification. Each frame can contain a separate document (HTML, text, image, and so on), each one individually addressable and scrollable. As with windows, you can name and reference frames. You can load documents in a frame without affecting the documents in the other frames.

Frames provide a means to view and interact with a site that isn't accessible otherwise. Users can have a permanently displayed index or navigation bar that provides quick and effective location of content in the site. You can simultaneously display the input and output of forms, as well as view multiple documents. You can select different image files from a menu for viewing. A new window can open to provide an expanded view of a document and close when it's no longer needed. You can give slide show presentations. The possible uses and implementations of a framed site are limited only by the Web site author's imagination.

CAUTION

Some visitors find frames and new windows distracting, and, especially with small monitors, too much of the display area is lost due to frames. A framed-site author should make sure that using frames provides a benefit to the visitor and should make an alternative no-frame version of the site available. For more information, visit `http://edbo.com/frames/why.html`.

JavaScript greatly enhances a frame site and adds to the interaction of the site with the user. You can open and close new windows programmatically. You can update and synchronize frames through the script without relying on a server-side program. Image maps and links can be dynamic, changing with different configurations and uses of the site. Documents in different frames and windows can pass information to, and interact with, each other.

RESOURCE

You can find online resources for JavaScript and frames at the Netscape site `http://home.netscape.com/` and at `http://edbo.com/frames/`.

A real benefit of using frames is the capability to provide a permanent navigation menu for the site. Instead of hopping from one page to another to navigate, a user can readily select a page from the menu and see the page appear in another frame (a main display frame). Some variations of the navigation menu include keeping a table of contents in one frame and document display in another or presenting a button bar frame along one edge of the window from which the user can click the buttons to load different portions of the site in the display frame.

TIP

Using frames does have some drawbacks. The major drawback is that the area to display each document is reduced. Users with small monitors, laptop computers, or palmtop computers might have difficulty viewing some of the documents in frames. It's considered a good idea to provide frame and no-frame versions of a site and give frame-capable users the option of viewing either version (which is fairly easy to accomplish with JavaScript).

The frame object is essentially the same element as a window object, and you can deal with it in a similar manner. If you're working with a single window, the window object is the top-level object. If you're working within a frameset, the top-level window is considered the parent window, whereas its child windows are considered frame objects.

Creating Frames

Frames are created with `<FRAMESET>` tags and specified with `<FRAME>` tags.

```
<FRAMESET COLS="60%,*">
     <FRAME SRC="doc1.html" NAME="frame1">
     <FRAME SRC="doc2.html" NAME="frame2">
</FRAMESET>
```

> **TIP**
>
> Indenting the `<FRAME>` tags isn't necessary but is frequently done to provide the Web author a better view of the tags and the frame hierarchy within the code.

`<FRAMESET>` Tags

The `<FRAMESET>` tag has an attribute that describes how to divide the window into frames. This attribute is either COLS or ROWS (for columns or rows), but not both. The author can specify the number of rows or columns in the window and the size of each. Each row or column can be specified as an absolute size in pixels, a relative size in percent of the window, or the remainder of the window. The following line creates two frames as columns, one with 60 percent of the window and the other with the remainder (specified by *) of the window's width (in this case, 40 percent):

```
<FRAMESET COLS="60%,*">
```

The next code line creates the two frames as before, but without the percent sign, the width of the first frame is an absolute value of 60 pixels wide:

```
<FRAMESET COLS="60,*">
```

The second frame still has the remainder of the window's width.

The following line creates four frames as columns; three of the frames each take 30 percent of the screen width, and the fourth takes the remainder:

```
<FRAMESET COLS="30%,30%,30%,*">
```

You could replace the * with 10% in this case. You aren't required to use *. However, if you specify all the frames with percentages, they must add up to 100 percent of the window width.

The next code line creates two frames as rows, the first with 70 percent of the window's height and the second with 30 percent:

```
<FRAMESET ROWS="70%,30%">
```

The frame sizes can be a mix of absolute, relative, and remainder, but if the total size of all the frames doesn't equal the window size, the results are unpredictable. Specifying frame sizes with just a * might seem obvious; however, you can use a * for each frame. The following line creates three equal frames, each with one third of the window's height:

```
<FRAMESET ROWS="*,*,*">
```

<FRAME> Tags

The <FRAME> tag attributes specify the document to be loaded in the frames, the name of the frame, frame margins, scrollbars, and the resizing option. All the following attributes of the <FRAME> tag are optional:

■ The SRC attribute is the URL (relative or absolute) of the document to be loaded in the frame. The document can be from the same server as the frameset file or from another server. If you don't use the SRC attribute, the frame contains just blank space. This blank space might be what you want, especially if you use JavaScript to write content to the frame.

■ The NAME attribute, if specified, provides a means to reference the frame from other frames and with JavaScript. JavaScript can also reference the frame through the frames array, which is covered in the section "Referencing Windows and Frames" later in this chapter. The value for the NAME attribute must begin with an alphanumeric character.

■ You set the margins with two attributes, MARGINWIDTH and MARGINHEIGHT:

MARGINWIDTH controls the side margins of the frame. Its value, in pixels, can be as low as 1. The maximum value is limited only by the size of the frame. (You can't set the margin in such a way as to leave no room to display the document.)

The MARGINHEIGHT attribute is the same as the MARGINWIDTH, except that it controls the top and bottom margins.

Both MARGINWIDTH and MARGINHEIGHT, if not specified, default to a value determined by the browser.

■ The SCROLLING attribute controls whether the frame has scrollbars. The values for SCROLLING are YES, NO, and AUTO. A value of YES causes scrollbars to always be present in the frame. NO prevents scrollbars from displaying. AUTO displays scrollbars only if the document is larger than the frame; otherwise, scrollbars are suppressed. The default value for SCROLLING is AUTO.

■ NORESIZE prevents the user from resizing the frame. There is no value specified for this attribute. By default, all frames are resizable unless you specify this attribute. Frames that border a frame with the NORESIZE attribute can't be resized along the common border.

> **TIP**
>
> If possible, it's best to let the user resize the frame by not specifying this attribute.

Use the following code segment to name a frame `frame1`, load the document `doc1.html`, set the side margins to 5 pixels, set the upper and lower margins to 10 pixels, always display scrollbars, and prevent the user from resizing the frame:

```
<FRAME SRC="doc1.html" NAME="frame1" MARGINWIDTH=5
MARGINHEIGHT=10 SCROLLING=YES NORESIZE>
```

Netscape and Microsoft are introducing more advanced features for their latest browsers. Visit the Web sites for these companies to find detailed information on the attributes (`http://home.netscape.com/` and `http://www.microsoft.com/`, respectively).

Tag Placement

You usually place the `<FRAMESET>` and `<FRAME>` tags in the body of the document. However, in several versions of Netscape Navigator, enclosing them in `<BODY>` and `</BODY>` tags prevents the browser from reading the `<FRAMESET>` tags. Because the `<BODY>` tags are optional, place the `<FRAMESET>` tags after the head section of the document and omit the `<BODY>` tags, as shown here:

```
<HTML>
<HEAD>
<TITLE>Frame Demo</TITLE>
</HEAD>
<FRAMESET COLS="60%,*">
      <FRAME SRC="doc1.html" NAME="frame1">
      <FRAME SRC="doc2.html" NAME="frame2">
</FRAMESET>
</HTML>
```

This code sets up the frames and loads the appropriate documents. Actually, you can make the file smaller, because the `<HTML>`, `<HEAD>`, and `<BODY>` tags are optional; the file can contain only the `<TITLE>`, `<FRAMESET>`, and `<FRAME>` tags, as shown in the next segment. (The title's opening and closing tags are the only tags required by HTML specification to be in every HTML document.)

```
<TITLE>Frame Demo</TITLE>
<FRAMESET COLS="60%,*">
      <FRAME SRC="doc1.html" NAME="frame1">
      <FRAME SRC="doc2.html" NAME="frame2">
</FRAMESET>
```

The <NOFRAMES> Tag

Many authors also include a set of <NOFRAMES> tags to display a message for non-frame–capable browsers:

```
<NOFRAMES>
code and text content to display to nonframe-capable browsers
</NOFRAMES>
```

The content can contain HTML tags as well as text. A frame-capable browser ignores the content between the <NOFRAMES> and </NOFRAMES> tags, whereas a non-frame–capable browser ignores the <FRAMESET>, <FRAME>, and <NOFRAMES> tags and displays the content between the <NOFRAMES> and </NOFRAMES> tags. You place the <NOFRAMES> tags within <FRAMESET> tags:

```
<TITLE>Frame Demo</TITLE>
<FRAMESET COLS="60%,*">
        <FRAME SRC="doc1.html" NAME="frame1">
        <FRAME SRC="doc2.html" NAME="frame2">
<NOFRAMES>
code and text content to display to nonframe-capable browsers
</NOFRAMES>
</FRAMESET>
```

> **TIP**
>
> A number of authors actually duplicate the main document of the site in the <NOFRAMES> tags for a nonframe version. However, it isn't usually necessary to use this technique because you can create a framed version of the site with JavaScript from the same pages that are displayed to non-frame–capable users.

It's interesting to note that you can include the <BODY> tags in the <NOFRAMES> tags, using the attributes of background, bgcolor, text, and so on for the noframes version of the document. The non-frame–capable browser ignores the <FRAMESET> tags and initiates the body section at the first appropriate content (that is, a <BODY> tag) in the <NOFRAMES> tag. The frame-capable browser initiates the body section at the first <FRAMESET> tag and ignores the contents of the <NOFRAMES> tag. Of course, the frame-capable browser loads the documents specified by the <FRAME> tags, and the <BODY> tags of these documents are properly recognized by the browser.

Nested Frames

You can create nested frames where a frame is divided into more frames. Of the two different ways to create nested frames, both display the same, but there's a big difference in the frame hierarchy and the way that nested frames are referenced.

The following code creates frames with multiple framesets in a single window. Figure 11.10 shows the frames, and Figure 11.11 shows the structure (hierarchy).

```
<FRAMESET COLS="30%,*">
    <FRAME SRC="doc1.html" NAME="frame1">
    <FRAMESET ROWS="*,20%">
        <FRAME SRC="doc2.html" NAME="frame2">
        <FRAME SRC="doc3.html" NAME="frame3">
    </FRAMESET>
</FRAMESET>
```

FIGURE 11.10.

Creating frames with multiple framesets in a single window.

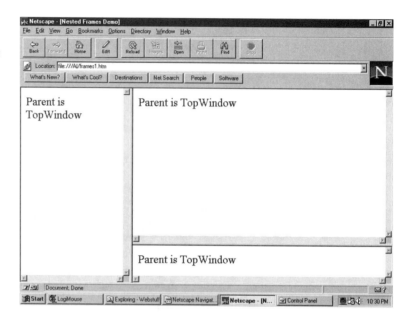

FIGURE 11.11.

The frame hierarchy of multiple framesets in a single window.

The following code creates frames with multiple framesets in two windows. (A frame is considered a window.) Figure 11.12 shows these frames, and Figure 11.13 shows the hierarchy.

```
<FRAMESET COLS="30%,*">
    <FRAME SRC="doc1.html" NAME="frame1">
    <FRAME SRC="frame2.html" NAME="frame2">
</FRAMESET>
```

The file `frame2.html` contains the following additional frameset information:

```
<FRAMESET ROWS="*,20%">
        <FRAME SRC="doc2.html" NAME="frame3">
        <FRAME SRC="doc3.html" NAME="frame4">
</FRAMESET>
```

FIGURE 11.12.

Creating frames with multiple framesets in two windows.

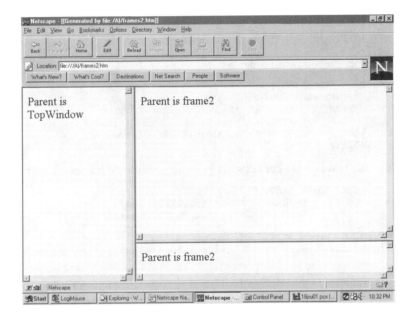

FIGURE 11.13.

The frame hierarchy of multiple framesets in two windows.

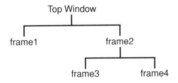

The two codes produce frames that display exactly the same, as shown in Figures 11.10 and 11.12. However, the structures, as shown in Figures 11.11 and 11.13, are completely different. In the code for Figure 11.11, all three frames have the same parent, the top window. In the code for Figure 11.13, only frame1 and frame2 have the top window as parent; frame3 and frame4's parent is frame2. This can make a big difference in how the frames are referenced, as discussed in the following sections.

Adding JavaScript Code to Frames

The frameset files and most of the files of the documents that display in frames are HTML files. As a result, you can use JavaScript in them, as you do in other HTML files. The only difference is that JavaScript can easily reference properties of other documents in frames and use certain features to reference those properties.

You can refer to the top window and its frames by their relationships to each other. A window (frames are considered windows) can be referenced with the window properties top, parent, window, and self. The top property refers to the main window (the browser window); parent refers to the window (frame) containing the frameset for a particular frame. For frames with a frameset in the top window, parent and top are the same. The properties self and window both refer to the particular frame or window.

Consider the following code:

```
<FRAMESET COLS="10%,*">
     <FRAME SRC="doc1.html" NAME="frame1">
     <FRAMESET COLS="50%,*">
          <FRAME SRC="frame2.html" NAME="frame2">
          <FRAME SRC="doc3.html" NAME="frame3">
</FRAMESET>
```

The file frame2.html contains the following additional frameset information:

```
<FRAMESET ROWS="*,20%">
          <FRAME SRC="doc4.html" NAME="frame4">
          <FRAME SRC="doc5.html" NAME="frame5">
</FRAMESET>
```

The parent of frame1, frame2, and frame3 is top because the frameset for each of these frames is in the top window. The parent for frame4 and frame5 is frame2 because the frameset for these two frames is in the window (or frame) of frame2. To reference the top frame from the document in frame4, you use the top property; to reference frame2, you use the parent property; and finally, to reference its own frame, you use self or window.

You can refer to functions, variables, and other properties with the relational window properties:

```
<HTML>
<HEAD>
<TITLE>Frame Demo</TITLE>
<SCRIPT LANGUAGE="JavaScript">
<!--
a1 = 2;
function addA1(){
    a2 = a1 + 1;
    return a2;
 }
 // -->
</SCRIPT>
</HEAD>
<BODY>
<FRAMESET COLS="10%,*">
     <FRAME SRC="doc1.html" NAME="frame1">
     <FRAMESET COLS="50%,*">
          <FRAME SRC="frame2.html" NAME="frame2">
          <FRAME SRC="doc3.html" NAME="frame3">
</FRAMESET>
.....
```

The file frame2.html contains additional frameset information:

```
<HTML>
<HEAD>
<TITLE>Frame Demo</TITLE>
<SCRIPT LANGUAGE="JavaScript">
<!--
```

```
b1 = 2;
function addB1(){
    b2 = b1 + 1;
    return b2;
 }
 // -->
</SCRIPT>
</HEAD>
<BODY>
 <FRAMESET ROWS="*,20%">
            <FRAME SRC="doc4.html" NAME="frame4">
            <FRAME SRC="doc5.html" NAME="frame5">
 </FRAMESET>
```

To access variable a1 and function addA1() from frame1, frame2, or frame3, you could use either top.a1 or parent.a1 and either top.addA1() or parent.addA1(). However, from frame4 or frame5, you can use only top.a1 and top.addA1 because parent refers to frame2. You can access variable b1 and function addB1() from frame4 and frame5 with parent.b1 and parent.addB1(). I hope you aren't thoroughly confused. I'll discuss more ways of referring to various frames and windows in the section "Referencing Windows and Frames" later in this chapter.

You must exercise several precautions when dealing with framed documents and JavaScript. Your script can produce errors if a referenced frame doesn't contain the correct document or doesn't even exist.

Trying to access top.a1 from any of the documents in the previous example when the document isn't in frames causes an error. However, JavaScript offers the means to prevent such errors, as discussed in the next section.

Synchronizing Frames

As I mentioned, not having the right documents or the right frames loaded can cause errors and other problems. A session can stop dead in its tracks if it can't find one variable. Furthermore, the problem might be that the documents haven't finished loading. Synchronizing the frames ensures that the frames and documents have finished loading before they are needed or that alternative actions are taken.

Verifying Frames

A common potential problem concerns a page containing JavaScript that can be viewed either in or out of frames. The window.length property is quite useful for letting JavaScript determine whether a document is being viewed in frames. The length property is equal to the number of frames a window or frame contains. You can set a conditional statement that performs an action if frames are being used:

```
if( top.length != 0 ){
    document.write("Frames are being used");
    }
```

You usually use `top` or `parent` instead of `window`, because `window` implies the frame containing the code, which doesn't contain frames unless the document is a frameset file. If a window or frame does have frames, its length is greater than zero. However, writing > for "greater than" could be misinterpreted as the end of an HTML comment by older browsers, so using != (not equal to) is preferable.

The short-circuit feature of the `if` statement is useful for preventing an error when a document that isn't in frames attempts to access a variable in another frame or frameset. If the top frameset contains a variable a1 that is used in a conditional statement by a framed document, an error is produced if the document is viewed as a stand-alone (no-frame) document. However, if the `length` property is checked first in the conditional and found to be `false`, the statement ends, which prevents an error from attempting to access a nonexistent variable.

The first part of the following statement, `parent.length != 0`, is `false` when frames aren't used, so further evaluation is stopped and the error doesn't occur:

```
if( (parent.length != 0) && (top.a1 == x ) )
```

Verifying Documents Loaded

Various techniques have been developed to synchronize the frames—some rather simple, others rather complex. One of the easiest techniques is to use JavaScript to verify that a particular document is present in a certain frame before proceeding with the rest of the code. The frames array lets you specify a frame as an element of the array. (Refer to the section "Referencing Windows and Frames" later in this chapter for information on the frames array.) Consider the following code line:

```
if( (parent.length == 3)&&(parent.frames[1].title == "My Page") )
```

The `if` statement verifies that the right frame structure is present (in this case, three frames) and that the document in the second frame (which, in this case, is to be referenced) is the correct one. If the frame structure is incorrect, the conditional evaluation stops, and no further action is taken or an alternative action is taken. If the frame structure is correct but the wrong document is present, the script initiates no action or an alternative action. Initiating no further action simply maintains the session at its current position, allowing the user to proceed with other actions or retry a failed action. (Perhaps the page wasn't finished loading and another attempt will be successful.) An alternative action could include providing an alert to the user, loading the correct page, and proceeding or proceeding with the action but skipping the steps that require the missing document.

The previous example checked a simple frame structure (three frames). You can check more complex structures using the frames array of various windows or frames in a multipart `if` statement. The multipart `if` statement has to verify the structure from top down; otherwise, referencing a missing frame causes an error. Note the following line of code:

```
if(top.length==3)&&(top.frames[1].length==2)&&(top.frames[1].frames[1]==3)...
```

If a portion of the frame structure isn't present, the `if` statement stops at that point, and the script can perform an alternative action by using an `else` statement or perform no action at all.

In verifying that the correct document is present, the code can check other properties besides the title, such as the frame's `location.href`. You can assign a common variable in each document a unique name or number and then check this document identity variable instead of the document title or other properties.

Registering Documents

Simply verifying that the required document is present can get complicated with larger sites and doesn't necessarily verify that the document is loaded. Another technique involves having the documents indicate when they are loaded and unloaded. Using the `onLoad()` and `onUnload()` events, the documents record their presence in a top window variable or a cookie. (See Chapter 25, "Cookies and State Maintenance," for more information about cookies.) The following code shows that you don't have to use the title to identify the document; you could use another property or an identity variable:

```
<BODY onLoad="top.funRecord(document.title)"
   onUnload="top.funRemove(document.title)">
```

The following example shows a simple document registration scheme. The first code segment contains the top frameset file:

```
<SCRIPT LANGUAGE="JavaScript">
<!--
var a4 = "";   // variable for document registration string

function funRecord(a){ // add the document to the registration string on load
   a4 += a;
}

function funRemove(a){        // remove document registration on unload
  a4 = a4.substring( 0,a4.indexOf(a) ) +
         a4.substring(a4.indexOf(a)+a.length,a4.length);
}

function funCheck(a){   // check whether document is registered or not
  if( a4.indexOf(a) != -1)  return true;
  else   return false;
 }
// -->
</SCRIPT>
```

The next code segment shows the document file:

```
<HTML>
<TITLE>The Harley FXSTC</TITLE>
<SCRIPT LANGUAGE="JavaScript">
<!--
function funRegister(a){
  // check that top frameset is present to register document, else ignore
  if( ( top.length != 0 )&&(top.document.title == "Main Frameset") )
```

```
      if( a ="R") top.funRecord(document.title);
      else top.funRemove(document.title);
 }
 function funCheck(a){   // check whether document is registered or not
   if( ( top.length != 0 )&&(top.document.title == "Main Frameset") )
      return top.funCheck(a);
  else return false;
 }
 // -->
 </SCRIPT>
 <BODY onLoad="top.funRecord(document.title)"
      onUnload="top.funRemove(document.title)">
```

The following code checks whether the document is registered:

```
if( funCheck("The Softtail Series") )
      top.frames[2].fxnames();   // document registered, proceed with action
else                            // document not registered, take alternative action
      top.location.href = "http://www.foo.com/fx.html;
```

Extensive Registration Schemes

More complex schemes not only register the document but also register the document's position in the frame structure hierarchy. If a document position changes due to different possible loading scenarios or a site update, the code dependent on referencing the document can locate the document through the document's registration information. Instead of using a single variable or a cookie to hold registration information, some schemes employ an array of variables with each element (variable) containing identity and position information for a registered document. These schemes are complex to set up; however, they do provide great benefit in very large sites where a small change in the structure could throw off the code references in many of the documents.

The hIdaho Frameset (`http://hidaho.com/frameset/`) is a registration scheme that is effective for large, complex frame structures. It registers functions and locations of functions within the frame structure. It determines the location by passing its frame name (`self.name`) to its parent, which attaches its own name and passes the information to its parent. The process continues upwards, parent by parent, until the top window is reached. Also included are functions to unregister a particular function (all functions must have a unique name) and unregister a frame name (all the functions that were located in that frame) on a document's unload.

Also included in the hIdaho Frameset is a function to check whether a specified function is registered (it returns `false` if the specified function isn't registered) and a function, `Exec()`, that calls other functions and passes parameters to the other functions. Because all function names must be unique, the author can call a particular function without knowing its location and pass parameters to it through `Exec(function,parameter1,parameter2,...)`.

Updating Frames

A significant benefit of frames is the capability to update or change the document in a frame while other frames remain unchanged. Whether a frame gets updated from user input in another frame or gets updated programmatically, you can provide the means to direct the changes to the appropriate frame through several techniques. These techniques can employ HTML (with certain Netscape extensions), JavaScript, or a combination of both.

Links

Perhaps the simplest updating technique is using a link to update (by loading a new document) its own frame. To direct the new document into another frame, the anchor tag has a target attribute for which you can specify either a value of a frame name or a relational name. The relational words (called magic target names by Netscape) correspond to the relational window properties discussed previously. The relational names used for targeting links all begin with an underscore and are always lowercase. These names are _top, _parent, and _self, which correspond to the window properties top, parent, and self. There is no _window, however.

The following code represents frames in which a link in one frame must update another frame:

```
<FRAMESET COLS="10%,*">
     <FRAME SRC="doc1.html" NAME="frame1">
     <FRAMESET COLS="50%,*">
          <FRAME SRC="frame2.html" NAME="frame2">
          <FRAME SRC="doc3.html" NAME="frame3">
</FRAMESET>
```

The file frame2.html contains the following additional frameset information:

```
<FRAMESET ROWS="*,20%">
          <FRAME SRC="doc4.html" NAME="frame4">
          <FRAME SRC="doc5.html" NAME="frame5">
</FRAMESET>
```

To load a new document in frame2 from a link in doc4.html (in frame4), write the link as follows:

```
<A HREF="new.html" TARGET="_parent">
```

Use the following line to load the document in the top window and basically clear all the frames:

```
<A HREF="new.html" TARGET="_top">
```

Dynamic Links

Because links are objects in JavaScript and href and target are properties of links, you can create a dynamic link by reassigning the values of href and target:

```
<A HREF="#" TARGET="_top" onClick='this.href="new.html";this.target="_self";'>
```

For JavaScript-enabled browsers, the document `new.html` loads in the current frame; otherwise, the current document loads in the top window. (A fragment specifier, #, without a URL and an anchor name, or fragment identifier, refers to the current document.) This reassignment of the link's `href` and `target` properties can be more dynamic if you combine the assignment statements with conditional and other statements. For example, load a frameset file in the parent if frames are being used; otherwise, load the main document of the frameset:

```
<A HREF="main.html" TARGET="_top"
   onClick='if( top.length != 0 ){this.href="frameset1.html";
                                  this.target="_parent";}'>
```

Watch those quotes; the event handler must be enclosed in a set of quotes (either double or single).

You don't need to reassign both the `href` and `target` properties for every dynamic link. The previous example could have had the target attribute set to _parent.

For the no-frame user, _parent and _top are equivalent. If the user doesn't have a frame-capable browser, the `target` attribute is ignored. The example could be written:

```
<A HREF="main.html" TARGET="_parent"
   onClick='if( parent.length != 0 ){this.href="frameset1.html";}'>
```

The link tag can get pretty long and cumbersome as you add more statements to the event handler. To help simplify the link, you can use function calls:

```
<A HREF="main.html" TARGET="_top" onClick='this.href=theHref();
                                  this.target=theTarget;'>
```

`theHref()` is a user-defined function that determines the conditions and returns the appropriate value for the `href` property. Likewise, `theTarget()` returns the appropriate value for the `target` property. These functions must return a value regardless of whether the evaluated condition is `true` or `false`; only the non-JavaScript–enabled browser uses the default values set by the HREF and TARGET attributes. For our frame-to-noframe examples, consider the following code:

```
function theHref(){
    if( top.length != 0 )
      a = "frameset1.html";
    else
      a = "main.html";
    return a;
}
```

`theTarget()` would be similarly constructed. You could also use the functions for other links on the page by passing the appropriate URLs and target names in the function calls. You could use one or two generic functions for a number of links.

You will often find that dynamic links aren't necessary. Typically, a page is loaded into the current frame, or the links appear on a navigational menu that isn't seen by no-frame users and can always be targeted to a particular frame. However, for the few circumstances when they're necessary, dynamic links can be quite effective. Also, the frame/no-frame condition isn't the only case where dynamic links might be necessary; you can set up these links for any circumstance you can imagine.

The `location.href` Property

Another way to update a frame that doesn't necessarily require a link is by using the `href` property of the location object. You can also use the `href` property in conjunction with a form button event handler or a function. Don't confuse the location object with the `location` property of the document. `document.location` is a read-only property, but you can write to `window.location.href`. The following statements are equivalent and update the current frame with the home page of `http://www.mcp.com/`:

```
location.href = "http://www.mcp.com/";
self.location.href = "http://www.mcp.com/";
window.location.href = "http://www.mcp.com/";
```

The following statements update the parent and top frames, respectively:

```
parent.location = "http://www.mcp.com/";
top.location = "http://www.mcp.com/";
```

Instead of using relational window properties, you can use a frame name:

```
parent.frame3.location.href = "http://www.mcp.com/";
```

In addition to writing the `href` property, you can also write the `pathname` property of the location object, which lets you specify the path or file name from the server root. (Of course, the host name, as well as the protocol and port, remains unchanged from the current location.) Use the following code to load the document `http://www.abc.com/foo/doc2.html` in `frame1`, which currently has `http://www.abc.com/index.htm`:

```
frame1.location.pathname="/foo/doc2.html";
```

However, if the current document is `http://www.def.org/home.html` or `ftp://ftp.abc.com/pub/abc.txt`, you must use the `href` property.

The `write()` Method

A third way to update a frame is using the `write()` or `writeln()` methods. JavaScript can dynamically generate a document in a frame:

```
<HTML>
<HEAD>
<TITLE>Updating Demo Frameset</TITLE>
</HEAD>
<FRAMESET COLS="40%,*">
    <FRAME SRC="doc1.html" NAME="frame1">
    <FRAME SRC="doc2.html" NAME="frame2">
</FRAMESET>
</HTML>

file doc1.html
```

The file `doc2.html` can be any file, even empty. However, you should place at least a space or carriage return in the file so that you don't cause a `Document contains no data` error.

Dynamically uploading a frame can be interactive with the user through links or forms:

```
<HTML>
<HEAD>
<TITLE>Updating Demo frame1</TITLE>
<SCRIPT LANGUAGE="JavaScript">
<!--
function docWrite(){
    top.frame2.document.clear();
    top.frame2.document.write("<HTML><HEAD>" +
        "<TITLE>Updating Demo frame2</TITLE>");
    top.frame2.document.write(" </HEAD><BODY BGCOLOR=\"" +
                    document.form1.bginput.value + "\">");
    top.frame2.document.write("<H1>Updated Page</H1>");
    top.frame2.document.write("Update by " + document.form1.input1.value);
    top.frame2.document.write("</BODY></HTML>");
    top.frame2.document.close();
  }
// -->
</SCRIPT>

</HEAD>
<BODY>
<FORM NAME="form1">
<INPUT TYPE="TEXT" NAME="input1">
<P>
Select a Background Color<BR>
<INPUT TYPE="RADIO" NAME="radio1" VALUE="white" CHECKED
    onClick='document.form1.bginput.value="white"'>White<BR>
<INPUT TYPE="RADIO" NAME="radio1" VALUE="red"
    onClick='document.form1.bginput.value="red"'>Red<BR>
<INPUT TYPE="RADIO" NAME="radio1" VALUE="blue"
    onClick='document.form1.bginput.value="blue"'>Blue<BR>
<INPUT TYPE="RADIO" NAME="radio1" VALUE="green"
    onClick='document.form1.bginput.value="green"'>Green<BR>
<P>
<INPUT TYPE="HIDDEN" NAME="bginput" VALUE="white">
<P>
<INPUT TYPE="BUTTON" VALUE="Update frame2" onClick="testW()">
</FORM>
</BODY>
</HTML>
```

The JavaScript code used to update a frame can be very sophisticated. You can use conditional statements, calculations, or any script imaginable to create a document to update the frame. Games, slide shows, highlighted maps, and database query results are some examples of what you can use to update the frame.

Caching Files

Image files to be included in an updated frame can be cached ahead of time to prevent the download from delaying the update. You use the image object to cache an image until it's needed.

However, this object isn't available in early versions of JavaScript-capable browsers. Another technique is to use a document in a hidden frame to download the images:

```
<HTML>
<HEAD>
<TITLE>Hidden Frame to Cache Images</TITLE>
</HEAD>
<FRAMESET COLS="100%,*">
    <FRAME SRC="doc1.html" NAME="frame1">
    <FRAME SRC="cache.html" NAME="frame2">
</FRAMESET>
</HTML>
```

The following file, `cache.html`, is a nondisplayed document just for downloading images so that the image files are stored in the cache:

```
<HTML>
<HEAD>
<TITLE>Updating Demo frame1</TITLE>
<SCRIPT LANGUAGE="JavaScript">
<!--
var a1 = 0;
// -->
</SCRIPT>
</HEAD>
<BODY onLoad="a1 = 1;">
<IMG SRC="image1.gif" WIDTH=100 HEIGHT=200>
<IMG SRC="image2.jgp" WIDTH=300 HEIGHT=120>
<IMG SRC="image3.gif" WIDTH=200 HEIGHT=200>
</BODY>
</HTML>
```

TIP

You should size the image tags to prevent problems when the script executes in certain browser versions.

Although good practice usually dictates that you use the `alt` attribute with image tags, the attribute isn't necessary here because the document doesn't display to any browser—let alone a nongraphical browser.

Variable `a1` is a flag that is set when the images are downloaded. You aren't required to use this flag, but it's useful to prevent the execution of a frame update script until the images are downloaded:

```
if(top.frame2.a1 !=1 ){
   alert("Please wait, images are still downloading");
   }
else{
   ...continue with rest of script
```

Scripting Image Map Frames

Netscape Navigator 2.0 began implementing client-side image maps (although Netscape wasn't the first browser to do so) along with frames and JavaScript. The client-side image maps (CSIM) offered enormous benefit over the server-side image maps used previously. With CSIM, you can include the map file in the document with the image or reference it as a separate file. No longer do you have to send a request to the server for processing and redirecting the appropriate URL. Users can see in the status bar the URLs associated with the map. Furthermore, you can use CSIMs in conjunction with the older server-side image maps for downward compatibility with older browsers.

Image Map Properties

Image maps have several objects and properties. The area tags in the map are JavaScript objects. The `href` and `target` attributes are properties of the area object that can change programmatically with JavaScript. The area object has event handlers such as `onClick`, `onMouseOver`, and `onMouseOut`. In fact, the area object has all the same properties and events as the link object. The area tag also has a `nohref` attribute that prevents the loading of the document URL assigned to the `href` attribute.

> **NOTE**
>
> The image map objects and properties aren't available in early versions of JavaScript-capable browsers. The area object and its properties were introduced in JavaScript 1.1. Furthermore, in JavaScript 1.1, the `onClick` event handler and the `nohref` attribute aren't functional for all platforms.

Referencing Area Objects

You can reference the area objects with the links array. The links array consists of all the link and area objects in the document. The elements are numbered from zero to one less than the total number of link and area tags. The following code is an example of a document with a link and a CSIM for explaining the links array in the next paragraph:

```
<HTML>
<HEAD>
<TITLE>CSIM DEMO</TITLE>
</HEAD>
<BODY>
<A HREF="doc1.html" target="frameA">The Softtails</A>
<MAP NAME="map1">
<A NAME="areaA" COORDS="20,20,80,80" HREF="doc2.html" TARGET="frameA">
<A NAME="areaB" COORDS="100,20,180,80" HREF="doc3.html" TARGET="frameA">
<A NAME="areaC" COORDS="20,100,80,180" HREF="doc4.html" TARGET="frameA">
<A NAME="areaD" COORDS="100,100,180,180" HREF="doc5.html" TARGET="frameA">
</MAP>
```

```
<IMG SRC="map1.gif" WIDTH=200 HEIGHT=200 ALT="Menu" USEMAP="#map1">
<!-- Code for alternative server-side map and a text menu for
non-graphical browsers omitted for clarity in the above example -->.
</BODY>
</HTML>
```

In the preceding example, the link is referenced by document.links[0] because it's the first link or area tag in the document. Area areaA is referenced by document.links[1] because it's the second link or area tag. areaB is document.links[2], areaC is document.links[3], and areaD is document.links[4].

The href and target properties of the area objects, as with the link objects, can be referenced and assigned new values through the links array. The following line changes the value of areaB's href property so that when its area of the image map is clicked, the document doc6.html loads instead of doc3.html:

```
document.link[2].href="doc6.html"
```

Likewise, you can change the target property:

```
document.link[2].target="frameB"
```

The target attribute and property must be specified as a frame name or one of the special relational frame words (_top, _parent, _self, or _blank) and not with a JavaScript property (top, parent, and so on).

You can open and name new windows by assigning to the target a name that isn't already in use. A new window opened in this manner has the name specified as the value of the target attribute.

Calling Functions

The area tags don't always have to reference a document. You can make function calls by using a protocol of javascript: followed by the function name:

```
<A NAME="areaA" COORDS="20,20,80,80" HREF="javascript:fun1()">
```

The script calls the user-defined function fun1() instead of a document. You can also use JavaScript methods and statements. This technique is particularly suited for a framed version of a site in which the image map server is a navigation button bar. The function can perform various statements to determine whether frames are used and certain flags are set or perform a calculation or evaluation. The function can then take the appropriate action, such as loading a certain document, or take no action at all.

The following code segments contain a rather simple slide show script with a button bar image map that allows the user to cycle forward and backward through slides. The image map also contains buttons to return to the menu so the user can select another slide show or return to the home page. Each slide show has a sequence name that forms the first part of the file names of the slides in the sequence. The second part of the file name is a sequential number unique to each slide in the sequence. Each of the slide files has three variables: the sequence name, the sequential number of the slide, and the total number of slides in the sequence. The script reads these three variables to load the next slide file based upon which portion of the image map was clicked.

The following segment is the frameset file:

```
<HTML>
<HEAD>
<TITLE>Slide Show Main Frameset</TITLE>
</HEAD>
<FRAMESET ROWS="*,55">
     <FRAME SRC="slide1.html" NAME="frameA">
     <FRAME SRC="button.html" NAME="frameB">
</HTML>
```

The next segment is the slide1 file:

```
<HTML>
<HEAD>
<TITLE>Slide Show - First Slide</TITLE>
<SCRIPT LANGUAGE="JavaScript">
<!--
var a1 = "slide";    //first portion of slide file names
var a2 = 1;             // sequential number of the slide
var a3 = 3;             // total number of slides
// -->
</SCRIPT>
</HEAD>
<BODY>
<IMG SRC="slide1.gif" WIDTH=300 HEIGHT=200
     ALT="The 1992 FXSTC, Softtail Custom">
</BODY>
</HTML>
```

The following segment contains the button bar file:

```
<HTML>
<HEAD>
<TITLE>Slide Show Demo Image Map</TITLE>
<SCRIPT LANGUAGE="JavaScript">
function fun1(a){
  a1 = top.frames[0].a1; // root file name for series of slides
  a2 = top.frames[0].a2; // sequential slide number
  a3 = top.frames[0].a3; // number of slides
  if( a == "f" )
    if(a2 == a3)
      a2 = 0;
  if( a == "r" )
    if(a2 == 1)
      a2 = a3 - 1;
    else
      a2 = a2 - 2;
  a2 = a2 + 1;
  a1 += a2;
  a1 += ".html";
  top.frames[0].location.href = a1;
 }
```

```
</SCRIPT>
</HEAD>
<BODY BGCOLOR="000000">
<MAP NAME="map1">
  <AREA COORDS="1,1,75,50" HREF='javascript:fun1("f")'
  onMouseOver='window.status="Cycle forward through slide show";
  return true'>
  <AREA COORDS="76,1,150,50" HREF="menu.html" TARGET="frameA"
    onMouseOver='window.status="Return to Menu to Select Another Slide Show";
    return true'>
  <AREA COORDS="151,1,225,50" HREF="home.html" TARGET="_top"
    onMouseOver='window.status="Quit Slide Show and Return to Home Page";
    return true'>
  <AREA COORDS="226,1,300,50" HREF='javascript:fun1("r")'
    onMouseOver='window.status="Cycle backward through slide show";
    return true'>
</MAP>
<IMG SRC="buttons.gif" WIDTH=300 HEIGHT=50 USEMAP="#map1">
</BODY>
</HTML>
```

Working with Frame URLs

There are no real differences between frame and no-frame documents regarding URLs. Within the entire window, however, you can use different sites and base hrefs. One frame might contain a document from a certain directory on a server, another frame might have a document from another directory, and a third frame could have a document from a different server. Regardless of which frame is targeted, a relative URL in a link is referenced from the document containing the link. You can use the base tag <BASE HREF="http://www.foo.com/some.html"> in a document to set all links relative to the base href, if needed. You can override the base href by specifying an absolute URL in the link.

As with the href attribute of the <BASE> tag, you can also specify a base target. <BASE TARGET="frameA"> directs all links in the document to the specified frame. You can also override the base target with the target attribute in the link. For example, <A HREF="some.html" TARGET="_self"> overrides the base target and loads the document into its own frame.

NOTE

You must place the base tag <BASE HREF="some.html" TARGET="someframe"> in the head section of the document. No content or closing tag is associated with the base tag. The base tag with both the HREF and TARGET attributes is shown in the following example:

```
<HTML>
<HEAD>
<TITLE>Base Demo</TITLE>
<BASE HREF="http://www.foo.com/home.html" TARGET="frameA">
</HEAD>
<BODY>
...
```

You can find additional information on using URLs in frames throughout this chapter, especially in the next section and the section "Updating Frames."

Referencing Windows and Frames

When working with single and multiple frames in your JavaScript application, you probably need to use additional ways to reference windows. JavaScript provides four references to windows. Each of the references are implemented as properties of the window object.

> **NOTE**
>
> Separate browser windows don't have a hierarchy structure; however, the window containing the code that opens another window is often referred to as the parent window. The new window is often referred to as the child window. Any new window can assign a variable in other windows so that other windows can reference it and its properties. To reference a property in the new window, you simply use `windowName.property`.
>
> Consider the following code:
>
> ```
> newWindow = window.open();
> newWindow.location.href = "http://www.mcp.com/";
> ```
>
> Although this segment doesn't exhibit the most efficient way to write the code, it demonstrates referencing a child window's property. The new window is opened and named (in this case, `newWindow`). Then, the new window's `location.href` is referenced and assigned.

The Current Window

Chapter 9 discussed using `window` to reference the current window. However, what wasn't said at the time is that the window object also contains a property called `window` that can be used as a self-referencing tool. In addition, the `self` property of the window object is another means of referring to the current or active window. For example, the following two code lines are functionally the same:

```
window.defaultStatus = "Welcome to the Goat Farm Home Page"
```

```
self.defaultStatus = "Welcome to the Goat Farm Home Page"
```

Because both window and self are synonyms of the current window, you might find it curious that both are included in the JavaScript language. As shown in the previous example, the rationale is simply flexibility; you can use `window` or `self` as you want.

However, as useful as `window` and `self` can be, it can easily become confusing to think about the logic behind it all. After all, an object's property that is used as an equivalent term for the object itself is rather unusual. Consequently, you might find it helpful to think of `window` or `self` as "reserved words" for the window object rather than its properties.

Because window and self are properties of the window object, you can't use both window and self in the same context. For example, the following code doesn't work as desired:

```
window.self.document.write("<h1>Test.</h1>")
```

Finally, in multiframe environments, window and self always refer to the window in which the JavaScript code is executed.

> **NOTE**
>
> In some object-oriented or object-based languages, self might refer to the active object, no matter what type it is. In JavaScript, self refers only to the active window or frame object—nothing else.

Parent to Child

A child frame is referenced by the parent in one of two ways. First, you can use a frame's name, which is defined by the NAME parameter of the <FRAME> tag. For example, in the following code, the myFrameFlicka variable references the name of the frameA frame:

```
<HTML>
<HEAD>
<TITLE>Parent to Child Demo</TITLE>
<SCRIPT LANGUAGE="JavaScript">
function childCall(){
    var myFrameFlicka = self.frameA.name
}
</SCRIPT>
</HEAD>
<FRAMESET COLS="50%,*">
    <FRAME SRC="doc1.html" NAME="frameA">
    <FRAME SRC="doc2.html" NAME="frameB">
</FRAMESET>
</HTML>
```

You can also reference child frames using the frameset's frames array. Every frame in the window, or parent frame, is an element of the array. The frames array's elements are referenced by frames[i], where i is the number corresponding to the order in which the frame is created in the parent window. The frames are numbered starting with zero up to one less than the total number of frames. The following frameset contains four frames:

```
<FRAMESET ROWS="25%,25%,25%,25%">
    <FRAME SRC="doc1.html" NAME="frameA">
    <FRAME SRC="doc2.html" NAME="frameB">
    <FRAME SRC="doc3.html" NAME="frameC">
    <FRAME SRC="doc4.html" NAME="frameD">
</FRAMESET>
```

The window's frames array has four elements:

`frames[0]` for frame `frameA`

`frames[1]` for frame `frameB`

`frames[2]` for frame `frameC`

`frames[3]` for frame `frameD`

Note the plural, frames, when referring to an element in the frames array.

Child to Parent

As you've learned in this chapter, frames are the same as window objects within a frameset. Within this multiframe setting, you need to distinguish between the various frames displayed in the browser. The parent property of a window object helps you do that by referencing its parent—the window containing the `<FRAMESET>` definition. For example, if you want to retrieve some information about the current window's parent, you use the following example in Listing 11.8.

Listing 11.8. `childWindow.htm`.

```
<html>
<head>
<title>Child Window</title>
</head>
<SCRIPT LANGUAGE="JavaScript">
<!--
    function getParentInfo() {
        myParentTitle = parent.document.title
        alert("My daddy's name is " + myParentTitle)
    }
// -->
</SCRIPT>
<form>
<input
    type="button"
    value="Get Info"
    onClick="getParentInfo()">
</form>
</body>
</html>
```

Not only can you retrieve property values, but you can also access the parent's methods. For example, Listing 11.9 shows the HTML source for a parent window in a frameset with a `showInfo()` method defined with no means of implementation in it. Listing 11.10 shows how the child window accesses this method. When the user clicks the `childButton` button object, its `onClick` event handler calls `runDadMethod()` using the `this` keyword as its parameter. The `runDadMethod()` in turn calls the parent object's `showInfo()` method, passing the current object's name as the parameter. Figure 11.14 shows the result.

Listing 11.9. parentWindow.htm.

```
<html>
<head>
<title>Parent Window Title</title>
<SCRIPT LANGUAGE="JavaScript">

    function showInfo(objectName) {
        alert(objectName)
    }

</SCRIPT>
</head>
<Frameset Cols="35%,65%">
<Frame Name = "FRAME1" SRC="childWindow.htm">
<Frame Name = "FRAME2" >
</Frameset>
</html>
```

TIP

To define a blank frame, simply leave off the SRC attribute in the <FRAME> definition.

Listing 11.10. anotherChildWindow.htm.

```
<html>
<head>
<title>Child Window</title>
</head>
<SCRIPT LANGUAGE="JavaScript">
<!--
    function runDadMethod(curObject) {
        parent.showInfo(curObject.name)
    }

// -->
</SCRIPT>
<form>
<input
    type="button"
    name="childButton"
    value="Run Dad's Method"
    onClick="runDadMethod(this)">
</form>
</body>
</html>
```

The parent is often the topmost window within a multiframe window environment, but not necessarily. You can have nested levels of framesets, as you will see in the following discussion on the top property. Therefore, the parent property refers to the current window's immediate parent. If you wanted to access the parent's parent (the "grandparent" window), you could use the following:

```
myGranddadTitle = parent.parent.document.title
```

FIGURE 11.14.

Calling a method of a parent.

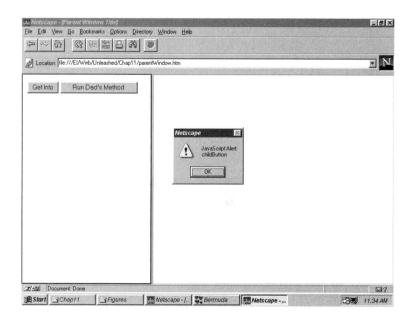

In more complex frame structures, all the frames can still be referenced by their positions in the structure, as shown in Figure 11.15 and Table 11.2.

FIGURE 11.15.

The hierarchy of a complex nested frame site.

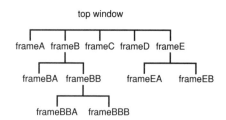

Table 11.2. Referencing other frames from `frameBBB`.

Frame	*Reference*
`frameA`	`top.frameA` or `top.frames[0]`
`frameBA`	`top.frames[1].frameBA` or `top.frames[1].frames[0]`
`frameBB`	`parent`, `top.frames[1].frameBB`, or `top.frames[1].frames[1]`
`frameEA`	`top.frames[4].frameEA` or `top.frames[4].frames[0]`

Use the following line to reference the title of the document in `frameEA` and assign it to a variable `a1`:

```
a1 = top.frames[4].frames[0].document.title;
```

Other properties are referenced similarly.

> **NOTE**
>
> It's important to note the hierarchy differences that can exist between two similar-looking frame structures, as mentioned in the section "Creating Frames" earlier in this chapter.

JavaScript 1.1 and higher supplies the `opener` property, which is used to reference the window (the parent) that opened the current window. From the new (child) window, you can reference a property of the opener (parent) window with the `top.opener.property`.

To reference the opener window from the new window in JavaScript 1.0, you can use an assignment technique. The samples here use the window property `top`; however, you can use `self`, `parent`, or `window` instead of `top` if necessary. The property `top` is used in the following code segment because the code might appear in any frame of the windows. Using `top` ensures that the appropriate property of the top window is identified. `self`, `parent`, or `window` could be any frame in the top window.

```
newWindow = window.open("doc1.html");
newWindow.oldWindow = top;
```

Use the following syntax to reference a property in the opener window from the new window:

```
top.oldWindow.property
```

Child to Child

The `parent` property is important not only for accessing a child window's parent window, but also for referencing another object in one of its "sibling" windows. As shown in Figure 11.16, any communication between child frames must go through their parent.

Frames on the same level with different parents must be referenced by the absolute position in the frame structure:

```
<FRAMESET COLS="50%,*">
    <FRAME SRC="doc1.html" NAME="frameA">
    <FRAME SRC="doc2.html" NAME="frameB">
</FRAMESET>
```

The following segment contains `doc1.html`:

```
<FRAMESET ROWS="50%,*">
    <FRAME SRC="doc3.html" NAME="frameAA">
    <FRAME SRC="doc4.html" NAME="frameAB">
</FRAMESET>
```

FIGURE 11.16.

Using the parent property to reference siblings.

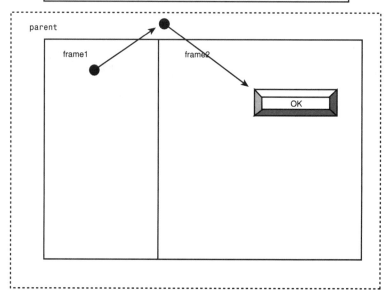

In this example, frame1 wants to reference the value of the OK button in frame2. Using the `parent` property, it could do that with the following code:

```
buttonLabel = parent.frame2.document.form[0].okButton.value
```

The next segment contains `doc2.html`:

```
<FRAMESET ROWS="50%,*">
    <FRAME SRC="doc5.html" NAME="frameBA">
    <FRAME SRC="doc6.html" NAME="frameBB">
</FRAMESET>
```

`frameAB` is referenced by `frameBB` as in the following:

```
top.frames[0].frameAB
```

You can also use the following line:

```
top.frames[0].frames[0]
```

There is no intermediate level between top and parent, such as grandparent, to reference frames. It's probably a good thing that parent is the only term borrowed from genealogy; imagine referring to a frame as `third.cousin.twice.removed`.

If browser windows are always assigned a name when opened, it's no problem for one of the new (child) windows to reference another child window through the opener (parent window). The name of the window is simply referenced as described in the previous sections. If a window was assigned a variable name of `myWindow` when it was opened, another child window can reference it like this:

```
top.opener.myWindow
```

You can synchronize the window with the same techniques employed for frames. However, because there is no one top browser window or window hierarchy, one window, such as the opener for the other windows, has to serve as the synchronization point. The following code segment is an example of a script used to synchronize windows:

```
<HTML>
<TITLE>The Harley FXSTC</TITLE>
<SCRIPT LANGUAGE="JavaScript">
<!--
function funRegister(a){
  // check that page is in its own window and that the opener
  //window contains the correct document
 if( (top.name=="newWindow1") && (top.opener.document.title=="Main Frameset") )
    if( a ="R") top.opener.funRecord(document.title);
    else top.opener.funRemove(document.title);
}
function funCheck(a){   // check whether document is registered or not
 if( (top.name=="newWindow1") && (top.opener.document.title=="Main Frameset") )
    return top.opener.funCheck(a);
 else return false;
}
// -->
</SCRIPT>
<BODY onLoad="top.funRecord(document.title)"
    onUnload="top.funRemove(document.title)">
...
```

The following code checks whether the document is registered:

```
if( funCheck("The Softtail Series")
   newWindow2.frames[2].fxnames(); // document registered, proceed with action
else                          // document not registered, take alternative action
     top.location.href = "http://www.foo.com/fx.html;
...
```

As with frames, you can use more complex schemes to register the location information for the document. These schemes employ the same scripts as those for frames but would extend one level to incorporate separate browser windows.

The Top Window

Similar in function to the parent property, the window object's top property allows you to reference the topmost window within a frameset or set of framesets. If you're working with a single frameset, the top and parent properties refer to the same window. However, if you have nested levels of framesets, top refers to the highest level window, whereas parent may or may not refer to that same window.

> **TIP**
>
> The top and parent windows can be excellent locations for storing global methods.

This difference is best illustrated through an example. Suppose you have two framesets. The first frameset divides the window horizontally using 80 percent, 20 percent (as shown in Figure 11.17). Divided into four quadrants, the second frameset (shown in Figure 11.18) is intended for the lower 20 percent of the top-level frameset.

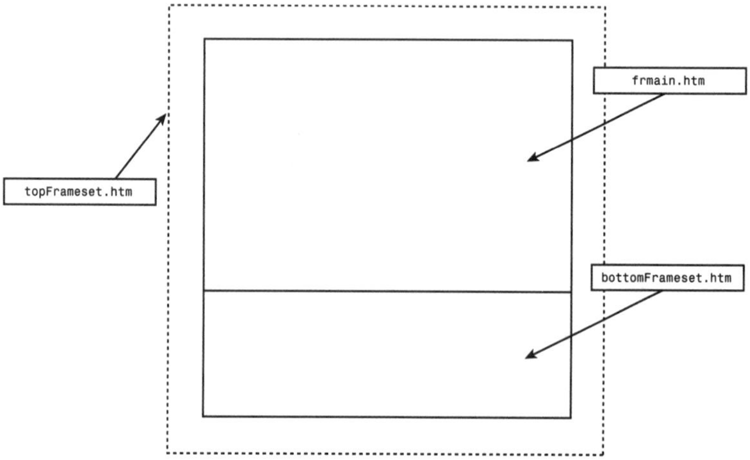

FIGURE 11.17.

A top-level frameset.

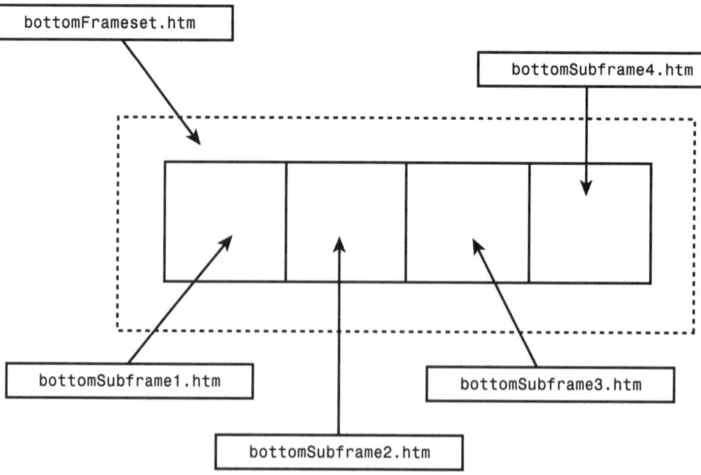

FIGURE 11.18.

A lower-level frameset.

For each of the "child" frames, suppose you want to get the titles of its respective top and parent windows. To do so, you can define a common function called getName() that returns this information to the calling window. Just as child windows can access a method in a parent window, all frames in a multiframeset window can access methods in the top window. Therefore, the top window serves as a good repository for functions you want to be globally available to all windows. The `getName()` method is defined as follows:

```
function getName(callingObject, relation, parentName) {
 callingObject.document.write("My " + relation + "'s name is " +
  parentName +".")
}
```

The `callingObject` parameter represents the window that is calling the function. Using dot notation, you can then assign the `document.write` command to be performed within the window in question. The `relation` and `parentName` parameters are strings provided by the calling window but aren't manipulated in this function.

This `getName()` method is called by the child frames upon loading. You can do this by putting the following code in each of the child frames:

```
<SCRIPT LANGUAGE="JavaScript">
    top.getName(self, "parent", parent.document.title)
    document.write("<p>")
    top.getName(self, "top", top.document.title)
</SCRIPT>
```

The script uses `top` to access the `getName()` method, `self` to identify itself as the calling window, and `parent` and `top` to retrieve the titles for both windows. Figure 11.19 shows the result when the frameset is loaded.

FIGURE 11.19.

The top *and* parent *properties.*

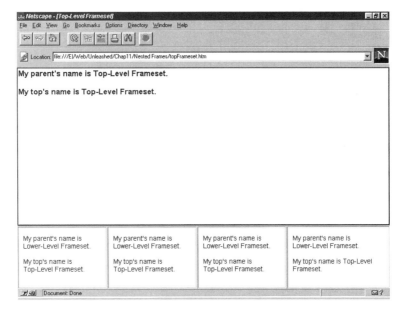

Listings 11.11, 11.12, and 11.13 provide the source code for the top-level frameset (topFrameset.htm), lower-level frameset (bottomFrameset.htm), and one of the bottom child frames (bottomSubframe1.htm).

Listing 11.11. topFrameset.htm.

```
<HTML>
<HEAD>
<TITLE>Top-Level Frameset</TITLE>
<SCRIPT LANGUAGE="JavaScript">

     function getName(callingObject, relation, parentName) {
     callingObject.document.write("My " + relation +
       "'s name is " + parentName +".")
     }

</SCRIPT>
</HEAD>
<FRAMESET ROWS="80%,20%">
  <FRAME SRC="frmain.htm"
         NAME="main"
         MARGINWIDTH="1"
         MARGINHEIGHT="1">
  <FRAME SRC="bottomFrameset.htm"
         NAME="footnotes"
         MARGINWIDTH="1"
         MARGINHEIGHT="1">
  <NOFRAMES>
Warning text should go here for browsers with no frame support.
<BODY>
</BODY>
</NOFRAMES>
</FRAMESET>
</HTML>
```

Listing 11.12. bottomFrameset.htm.

```
<HTML>
<HEAD>
<TITLE>Lower-Level Frameset</TITLE>
</HEAD>
<FRAMESET COLS="24%,24%,24%,28%">
  <FRAME SRC="bottomSubframe1.htm">
  <FRAME SRC="bottomSubframe2.htm">
  <FRAME SRC="bottomSubframe3.htm">
  <FRAME SRC="bottomSubframe4.htm">
</FRAMESET>
</HTML>
```

Listing 11.13. bottomSubframe1.htm.

```
<HTML>
<HEAD>
<TITLE>Footnotes Frame in Bottom Frameset</TITLE>
<SCRIPT LANGUAGE="JavaScript">
     top.getName(self, "parent", parent.document.title)
     document.write("<p>")
     top.getName(self, "top", top.document.title)
</SCRIPT>
</HEAD>
<BODY>
</BODY>
</HTML>
```

NOTE

A possible concern about referencing documents in other frames and windows is a security restriction that prevents JavaScript from accessing the properties of documents from a different server. Starting with Netscape Navigator 2.02, this restriction was implemented to keep people from accessing information on the user's history, passwords in HTML forms, directory structure, and other confidential items. Netscape Navigator 3.0 incorporates a security measure called *data tainting,* which permits people to access a different server's documents without the possible security risk. With data tainting, JavaScript code can access and use properties of documents from different servers. The data obtained is marked (tainted) so that it can't be sent to a different server (a security and privacy concern) without user confirmation. You can find more information on data tainting in Chapter 24, "JavaScript and Web Security."

The Location Object

The location object encapsulates the URL of the current page. Its purpose is twofold, allowing you to do the following:

- Set the location object to move to a new URL.
- Extract specific elements of the URL and work with them. Without the location object, you would be forced to perform string manipulations on a URL string to get at the information you need.

The basic structure of a URL is as follows:

protocol//hostname: port pathname search hash

A typical URL could look something like the following:

```
http://www.acadians.com/javascript/search/Hats?qt=RFC+1738+&col=XL
```

The location object has the properties shown in Table 11.3, each of which is an element in the URL.

Table 11.3. Location object properties.

Attribute	Description
href	Complete URL
protocol	Initial element of a URL (before and including colon)
hostname	Host and domain name or IP address
host	*Hostname:port* element of a URL
port	Communications port of the server
pathname	Path element of a URL
search	Query definition portion of a URL (begins with a ?)
hash	Anchor name of a URL (begins with an #)

NOTE

It's important to distinguish the location object from the document object's `location` property. Although you can set the location object, the document object's location property is read-only.

Opening a New URL

Instead of using a specific method to go to a new URL in a window, you can open a new URL by setting the value of the location object. Interestingly, you can do this by either assigning a URL to the object itself or assigning a URL to the location object's href property. For example, the following two lines perform the same action:

```
window.location = "http://www.acadians.com/"
```

```
window.location.href = "http://www.acadians.com/"
```

For example, to roughly simulate a browser's location edit box using JavaScript, you could use the code in Listing 11.14.

Listing 11.14. moveTo.htm.

```html
<HTML>
<HEAD>
<SCRIPT LANGUAGE = "JavaScript">

    function moveon() {
        var urlAddress = ""
        urlAddress = document.forms[0].Edit1.value
        window.location = urlAddress
    }

</SCRIPT>
</HEAD>
<BODY>
<FORM>
<INPUT type="text" name="Edit1">
<INPUT type="button" value="move" onClick="moveon()">
</FORM>
</BODY>
</HTML>
```

In multiframe windows, you can specify the value of the location object in other frames by referring to the appropriate window name. For example, Figure 11.20 displays a multiframe window in which you can change the URL based upon the entry of the form in the footnote frame. Listing 11.15 shows the source code for the footnote frame.

FIGURE 11.20.

Using the location object to change another frame's URL.

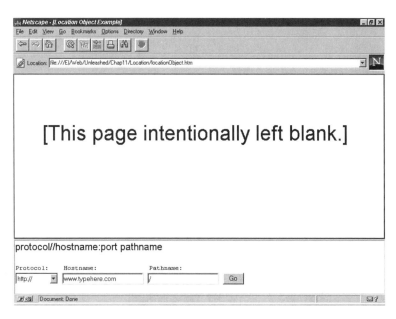

Listing 11.15. `frfootno.htm`.

```html
<html>
<head>
<title>Footnotes Frame in Location Object Example</title>
<SCRIPT LANGUAGE="JavaScript">
<!--
    function gotoPage() {
       parent.frames[0].location.href = window.document.loc.ProtocolField.
        options[window.document.loc.ProtocolField.selectedIndex].text
        + document.loc.HostnameField.value + document.loc.PathnameField.value
    }
//-->
</SCRIPT>
</head>

<body>
<p><font size=5>protocol//hostname:port pathname</font></p>
<form name="loc" method="POST">
<pre>Protocol:    Hostname:              Pathname:
<select name="ProtocolField" size=1>
<option>http://</option>
<option>file://</option>
<option>javascript:</option>
<option>ftp:</option>
<option>mailto:</option>
<option>gopher:</option>
<option>about:</option>
</select> <input
    type=text
    size=23
    maxlength=256
    name="HostnameField"
    value="www.typehere.com"> <input
    type=text
    size=20
    maxlength=100
    name="PathnameField"
    value="/"> <input
    type=button
    name="Go"
    value="Go"
    onClick="gotoPage()"></pre>
</form>
</body>
</html>
```

Working with the `protocol` Property

The `protocol` property of the location object lets you specify the type of URL with which you're working. Table 11.4 lists the most common protocols used.

Table 11.4. Location object protocols.

URL Type	Protocol
Web	http:
File	file:
FTP	ftp:
MailTo	mailto:
Usenet	news:
Gopher	gopher:
JavaScript	javascript:
Navigator	about:

The History Object

If you've done much Web surfing, you're probably very familiar with a browser's history list. Just as the history list lets the user traverse where she has been, JavaScript's history object lets you as a JavaScript developer maneuver through previously visited Web pages.

Determining the Size of the List

You can use the length() property of the history object to determine the number of entries in the list. For example, suppose you want to track the number of history list entries in the right frame of a multiframe window. The left frame contains the following code:

```
<HTML>
<HEAD>
<SCRIPT LANGUAGE = "JavaScript">

    function moveon() {
       var urlAddress = ""
       urlAddress = document.forms[0].Edit1.value
       parent.frames[1].location = urlAddress
       document.forms[0].Edit2.value = parent.frames[1].history.length
     }

</SCRIPT>
</HEAD>

<BODY>
<FORM>
<INPUT type="text" name="Edit1">
<INPUT type="button" value="move" onClick="moveon()">
<INPUT type="text" name="Edit2">
</FORM>
</BODY>
</HTML>
```

The user can use the Edit1 text object to enter a URL to move to. As the user clicks the Move button to move to the URL, the Edit2 text object is updated to provide the length of the history list for the right frame.

Navigating the History List

Just knowing the length of the history list is rarely useful, but it can become useful when you want to navigate a list using the history object methods back(), forward(), and go().

Moving Back a Page

The back() method is the functional equivalent of clicking the back (left-arrow) button on the browser's toolbar. For example, the following code moves a window to its previous position:

```
window.history.back()
```

Moving Forward a Page

As you would expect, the forward() method is the same as clicking the right-arrow button on the browser's toolbar. It is used as follows:

```
window.history.forward()
```

Going to a Specific Page Based on a Number

The go() method jumps to a specific place in the history list. Its syntax follows:

```
[window.]history.go(delta ¦ "location")
```

The *delta* parameter is a positive or negative integer that can specify the number of places to jump. For example, the following line moves to the next document in the history list (the equivalent of using the forward() method):

```
window.history.go(1)
```

The following list details the *delta* value:

delta < 0	Moves backward *delta* number of entries
delta > 0	Moves forward *delta* number of entries
delta = 0	Reloads the current document

Going to a Specific Page Based on a String

Alternatively, you can use the *location* parameter to specify a specific URL in the list. Note that this doesn't have to be an exact URL—only a substring. The following example moves to the URL in the history list that contains "www.acadians.com/filenew":

```
window.history.go("www.acadians.com/filenew")
```

You can add the `back()`, `forward()`, and `go()` to the earlier example to provide a more fully functional multiframe navigating system. Figure 11.21 shows the frameset. Listing 11.16 provides the HTML source for the parent frameset page, and Listing 11.17 provides the HTML source for the heart of this example, the history list. The right pane contains no JavaScript code related to this example.

FIGURE 11.21.

The history frame example.

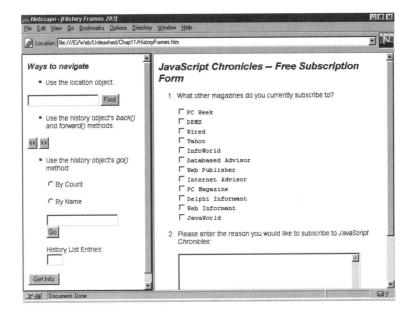

Listing 11.16. HistoryFrames.htm.

```
<html>
<head>
<title>History Object Example</title>
</head>
<Frameset Cols="35%,65%">
<Frame Name = "FRAME1" SRC="History.htm">
<Frame Name = "FRAME2" SRC="JavaScriptChronicles.htm">
</Frameset>

</html>
```

Listing 11.17. History.htm.

```
<html>
<head>
<title>History Page</title>
</head>
<body bgcolor="#FFFFFF">
```

continues

Listing 11.17. continued

```
<SCRIPT LANGUAGE="JavaScript">
<!--
    function goPrev() {
       parent.frames[1].history.back()
    }

    function goNext() {
       parent.frames[1].history.forward()
    }

    function moveOn() {
       var urlAddress = ""
       urlAddress = document.forms[0].LocationBox.value
       if (urlAddress != "") {
          parent.frames[1].location = urlAddress
          document.forms[0].ListLen.value = parent.frames[1].history.length }
       else {
          alert("Please enter a URL before clicking the Go button.")
       }
    }

    function jump() {
       if (document.forms[0].goParam[1].checked) {
          var goVal = 0
          goVal = parseInt(document.forms[0].GoBox.value) }
       else {
          var goVal = ""
          goVal = document.forms[0].GoBox.value
       }
       parent.frames[1].history.go(goVal)
    }
// -->
</SCRIPT>

<form method="POST">
<h3><em>Ways to navigate</em></h3>
<ul>
<li>Use the location object.</li>
</ul>
<p><input
    type=text
    size=20
    maxlength=50
    name="LocationBox"> <input
    type="button"
    value="Find"
    onClick="moveOn()"> </p>
<ul>
<li>Use the history object's <em>back()</em> and<em> forward() </em>methods.
</li>
</ul>
<p align=center><input
    type="button"
    value="&lt;&lt;"
```

```
onClick="goPrev()"> <input
        type="button"
        value="&gt;&gt;"
        onClick="goNext()"></p>
<ul>
<li>Use the history object's <em>go()</em> method:</li>
</ul>
<blockquote>
<p><input type=radio name="goParam" value="ByCount">By Count</p>
<p><input type=radio name="goParam" value="ByName">By Name</p>
<p><input
        type=text
        size=20
        maxlength=30
        name="GoBox"> <input
        type="button"
        value="Go"
        onClick="jump()"> </p>
<p>History List Entries: <input
        type=text
        size=3
        maxlength=4
        name="ListLen"> </p>
</blockquote>
</form>
</body>
</html>
```

The Navigator Object

The navigator object is the one object that just doesn't seem to fit into the JavaScript built-in object hierarchy. On first glance, it would seem to be the top level of the pyramid, because the browser software—the element the navigator object represents—contains windows and any other object. However, the navigator object has no real connection to any other object in the hierarchy; it really stands alone, providing only a way to obtain information about the current Web browser.

> **NOTE**
>
> Keep in mind that you can't use the navigator object to obtain information from browsers that don't support JavaScript. If the browser doesn't support JavaScript, it doesn't process the request for information. You obviously couldn't use a JavaScript routine to determine whether the browser supports JavaScript.

The navigator object has four properties, as shown in Table 11.5.

Table 11.5. Properties of the navigator object.

Property	Description
appName	Name of the browser
appVersion	Version of the browser
appCodeName	Code name for the browser
userAgent	User-agent header for the browser

Both Netscape Navigator and Microsoft Internet Explorer support the navigator object. Listing 11.18 provides an example of displaying browser information in a dialog box when the user clicks the Show Browser Info button. Figures 11.22 and 11.23 show the alert message boxes that appear when the script is run in both Netscape and Internet Explorer.

Listing 11.18. navigatorInfo.htm.

```
<HTML>
<HEAD>
<SCRIPT LANGUAGE = "JavaScript">

    function displayBrowserInfo() {

        var browserStr = ""
        browserStr += "Browser: " + navigator.appName + "\r"
        browserStr += "Version:" + navigator.appVersion + "\r"
        browserStr += "Codename: " + navigator.appCodeName + "\r"
        browserStr += "User agent: " + navigator.userAgent + "\r"
        alert(browserStr)
    }

</SCRIPT>

<BODY>
<H1></H1>
<FORM>
<INPUT
    Type="button"
    Value="Show Browser Information"
    OnClick="displayBrowserInfo()"
</INPUT>
</FORM>
</BODY>
</HTML>
```

11

FIGURE 11.22.

*Netscape Navigator
browser information.*

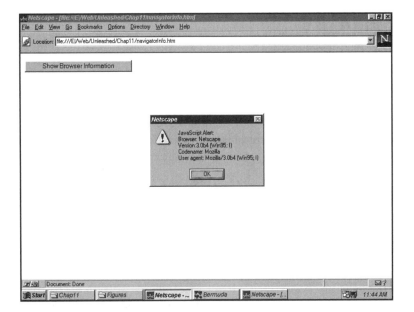

FIGURE 11.23.

*Microsoft Internet
Explorer browser
information.*

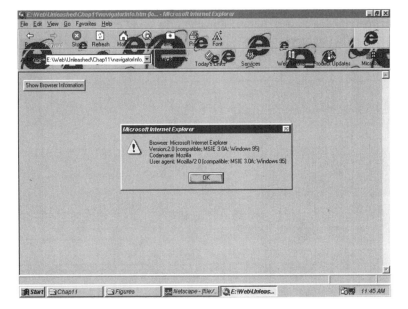

Summary

This chapter dived into the top level of the JavaScript object hierarchy. The objects I discussed have much less to do with HTML tags than with various aspects of a browser window. As the top-level object in the hierarchy, the window object is charged with many responsibilities—both in single and multiframe windows. The frame, location, and history list objects are all properties of the window object and provide a means to work with their respective browser counterparts. The navigator object, much different in purpose from the other JavaScript objects, lets you retrieve information about the current browser being used.

This chapter also discussed how to use JavaScript to reference objects and properties in other frames and browser windows. I outlined basic window creation and frame setup and covered referring to properties in different frames and windows. I also explained updating frames and synchronizing frames and windows, providing a few examples of windows and frames interacting with each other through JavaScript. Frame synchronization, the slide show, and updating frames are just a few examples of the interaction possible.

Although using JavaScript in a framed site might be a little more complex than using it in a no-frames site, the benefits are often worth the small amount of added complexity. I only touched upon a few examples of JavaScript with frames and windows. The possible uses and implementations of a framed site are limited only by the Web site author's imagination and the depth of his or her perseverance.

Document Objects

IN THIS CHAPTER

Chapter 11, "Navigator Objects," began the look at JavaScript objects by examining the first object tier. This chapter continues that discussion by looking at the second tier of Navigator objects in the JavaScript hierarchy—document objects. This set of objects includes the document object and three of its "child" objects: link, anchor, and image. The form object is a child of the document object as well; Chapter 13, "Form Objects," discusses the form object in depth.

> **TIP**
>
> See Chapters 26, 27, and 28 for complete information on how to work with the applet and plug-in objects in JavaScript.

The Document Object

The window object is the highest-level object for built-in JavaScript objects. In this role, it serves as a container, but it doesn't have any content associated with it per se. It leaves the content of a Web document up to the document object. The document object serves as the JavaScript equivalent of an HTML document, as shown in Figure 12.1.

FIGURE 12.1.

Working with the document object.

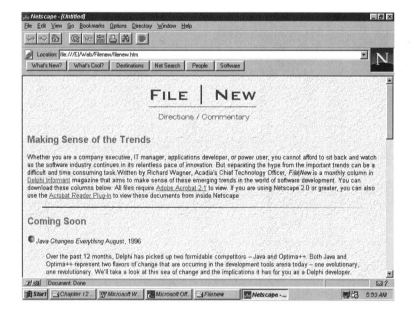

In this role, the document object is a container for all HTML-related objects that is associated with both the <HEAD> and <BODY> tags. The document object gets its `title` property from the <TITLE> tag (located within the <HEAD> section) and several color-related properties from the <BODY> section, which is shown here:

```
<BODY
    [BACKGROUND="backgroundImage"]
    [BGCOLOR="backgroundColor"]
    [TEXT="foregroundColor"]
    [LINK="unfollowedLinkColor"]
    [ALINK="activatedLinkColor"]
    [VLINK="followedLinkColor"]
    [onLoad="methodName"]
    [onUnload="methodName"]>
</BODY>
```

> **NOTE**
>
> Although onLoad and onUnload events are associated with the <BODY> tag, they are events of the window object, not the document object.

The document object is critical as you work with JavaScript and HTML, because all the action happens on a Web page within a document. Because of this scope, you need to refer to the document object when you access an object within it. For example, if you want to access a form object named `invoiceForm`, you must preface your reference with `document`:

```
document.invoiceForm.submit()
```

If you don't, JavaScript can't locate the object within the page.

Creating HTML Documents Programmatically

As you will see throughout this book, you can use JavaScript to react to events generated on static Web pages. You can also use it to generate HTML pages on-the-fly. In fact, you can use each of the methods of the document object somehow to alter documents programmatically:

- `open(["mimeType"])` prepares a stream for `write()` and `writeln()` statements. Its parameter can be one of several MIME types (`text/html` is the default):

  text/html
  text/plain
  image/gif
  image/jpeg
  image/x-bitmap
  plugIn (any Netscape plug-in MIME type)

- ■ `write(JavaScriptExpression)` writes a JavaScript expression to a document.

- ■ `writeln(JavaScriptExpression)` also writes a JavaScript expression to a document but appends a newline character to the end of the expression.

- ■ `close()` closes the stream that was opened by the `open()` method.

- ■ `clear()` clears the contents of the document.

Whereas `open()`, `close()`, and `clear()` prepare or close a generated document, the `write()` and `writeln()` methods give the document content. You can use any valid JavaScript expression as their parameters, including a string literal, variable, integer value, and so on. For example, each of the following are valid uses of `write()`:

```
var loc = "Ashford, Kent"
document.write("The castle is located in " + loc)
document.write("I stayed in the Robert Courtneys room.")
document.write("I would like " + 70 + "copies of that report.")
```

Keep in mind that you are writing HTML, not straight text. You can use HTML tags just as if you were writing the document in an HTML editor, as in the following example:

```
document.write('<h3>Return to the <a
href="http://www.acadians.com">Acadia Software</a> home
page.</h3><p>')
```

Figure 12.2 shows the result.

FIGURE 12.2.

A link generated using JavaScript.

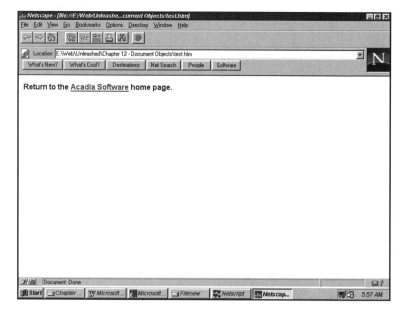

The one key limitation you need to keep in mind when using write() or writeln() is that you can't change the contents of the current document without completely reloading the window. The following sections describe the three valid contexts in which you can create HTML documents on-the-fly.

Creating a Document in the Current Window Upon Loading

You can create a new document in the current window when the document loads. You typically place this code within a <SCRIPT> tag either in the <HEAD> section or else by itself if it stands alone. For example, if you want to evaluate the browser and change the text based on its type, you can use the script shown in Listing 12.1.

Listing 12.1. writeCurrent.htm.

```
<SCRIPT LANGUAGE = "JavaScript">

    var browser = navigator.appName
    document.open()
    if (browser == "Netscape") {
        document.write("<h2>Welcome <a href='http://home.netscape.com'>
        Netscape</a>
         user.</h2><p><p>")}
    else {
        if (browser == "Microsoft Internet Explorer") {
            document.write("<h2>Welcome <a href='http://www.microsoft.com'>
              Microsoft</a>Internet Explorer user.</h2><p><p>") }
        else {
            document.write("<h1>Welcome. But what browser are you using?
              </h1><p><p>")
        }
    }
    document.write("We are glad you came to our Web site.<p><p>")
    document.write("Don't you wish you knew how we knew your browser type?")
    document.close()

</SCRIPT>
```

Figure 12.3 shows the result in Netscape Navigator 3.0, and Figure 12.4 shows the result in Internet Explorer 3.0.

Creating a Document in a Frame

You can also generate a new document in another frame of a multiframe window. The techniques are similar to those used in the preceding example, but you must reference the correct document using dot notation. For example, to reference the first frame of a frameset, you could use the following code:

```
parent.forms[0].document.write("test")
```

FIGURE 12.3.

A customized Netscape page.

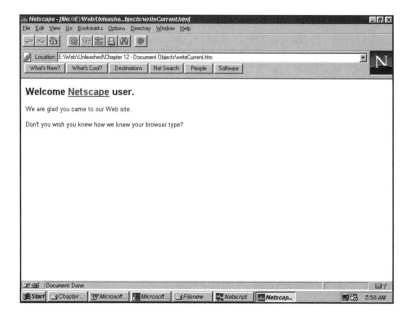

FIGURE 12.4.

A customized Internet Explorer page.

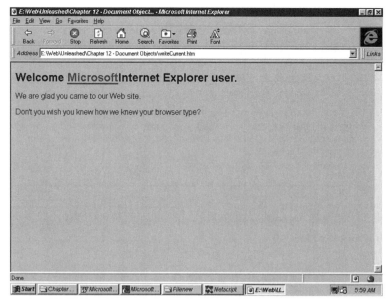

Listing 12.8, which you'll see later in this chapter, has an example of setting a frame document programmatically.

Creating a Document in a Separate Window

The third technique for creating documents on-the-fly is opening a new window and writing to its document. If you wanted to enumerate a list of installed plug-ins for the browser in a separate window, you could use the code shown in Listing 12.2.

Listing 12.2. writeWindow.htm.

```
<HTML>
<HEAD>
<SCRIPT LANGUAGE = "JavaScript">

    function showWindow() {
        var len = navigator.plugins.length

        newWin = window.open("", "", "height=300,width=400")
        newWin.document.write("<h2>Plug-In Info:</h2><p><p>")

        for (var i=0; i<len; i++) {
            newWin.document.write("<li>" + navigator.plugins[i].description
                + "</li>")
        }

        newWin.document.close()
    }

</SCRIPT>
</HEAD>
<BODY>
<form>
<input type=button value="Show Plug-In Information" onClick="showWindow()">
</form>
</BODY>
</HTML>
```

Figure 12.5 shows the result of the script.

Clearing a Window's Contents

You can clear the contents of a window by issuing either a document's `clear()` method or its `write()` method with no parameter. Either way, the effect is the same. Both methods empty a document and display a blank window. To illustrate, imagine that you are "Q" from a James Bond movie trying to relay a message to your best agent, James Bond, 007. After he reads the message, you want to be sure he erases the contents of the document before anyone else can read it. (I know—the scenario falls apart when you think of the realities of the Web, but play along on this one.) Figure 12.6 shows the top-secret message. Listing 12.3 shows the code for `007message.htm`.

FIGURE 12.5.

Generating a new document in a separate window.

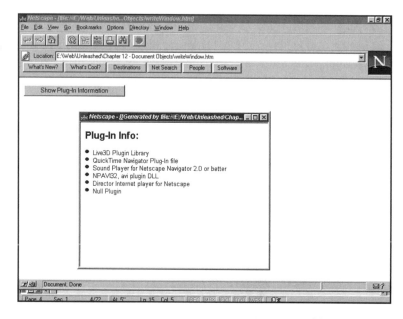

FIGURE 12.6.

A secret message that needs to be cleared.

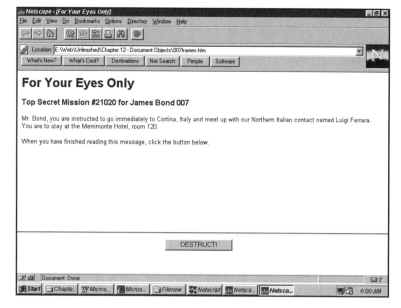

Listing 12.3. 007message.htm.

```
<HTML>
<BODY>
<h1>For Your Eyes Only</h1><p><p>
<h3>Top Secret Mission #21020 for James Bond 007</h3><p><p>
```

```
Mr. Bond, you are instructed to go immediately to Cortina, Italy
and meet up with our Northern Italian contact named Luigi Ferrara.
You are to stay at the Merrimonte Hotel, room 120.<p><p>
When you have finished reading this message, click the button below.<p><p>
</BODY>
</HTML>
```

> **NOTE**
>
> I have found that clear() performs inconsistently in both Netscape Navigator and Microsoft Internet Explorer. Therefore, I use the alternative empty write() method in this example.

Listing 12.4 shows the source code for the frameset document. It contains a JavaScript function named destroyContents() that empties the contents of the top frame, named "message".

Listing 12.4. 007frames.htm.

```html
<HTML>
<HEAD>
<TITLE>For Your Eyes Only</TITLE>
<SCRIPT LANGUAGE="JavaScript">

    function destroyContents() {
        self.message.document.write()
        self.message.document.close()
    }

</SCRIPT>
</HEAD>
<FRAMESET ROWS="80%,20%">
  <FRAME SRC="007message.htm" NAME="message" MARGINWIDTH="10" MARGINHEIGHT="10">
  <FRAME SRC="007control.htm" NAME="control" MARGINWIDTH="10" MARGINHEIGHT="10">
  <NOFRAMES>
<BODY>
<P>This web page uses frames, but your browser doesn't support them.</P>
</BODY>
</NOFRAMES>
</FRAMESET>
</HTML>
```

Listing 12.5 shows the HTML source from the bottom frame, which contains the button. As you can see, it simply calls the parent window's destroyContents() method when Bond clicks the DESTRUCT! button.

Listing 12.5. 007control.htm.

```
<HTML>
<BODY>
<FORM>
<DIV align="center"><INPUT type=button value="   DESTRUCT!   " onClick=
  "parent.destroyContents()"></DIV>
</FORM>
</BODY>
</HTML>
```

Changing Document Attribute Colors

Color settings for documents are usually set by a user in his browser configuration, but JavaScript gives you the ability to change these color settings programmatically. The document object has five properties that reflect the colors of various attributes within the document—alinkColor, bgColor, fgColor, linkColor, and vlinkColor. These are described in Table 12.1.

Table 12.1. Document color-related properties.

Property	HTML Tag	Description
alinkColor	ALINK=	The color of an activated link (after mouse down and before mouse up)
bgColor	BGCOLOR=	The background color of the document
fgColor	TEXT=	The foreground color of document
linkColor	LINK=	The color of unvisited links
vlinkColor	VLINK=	The color of visited links

These properties are expressed either as string literals or as hexadecimal RGB triplet values. For example, if you wanted to assign a background color of chartreuse to a document, you could use the string literal chartreuse:

```
document.bgColor = chartreuse
```

You could also use the equivalent hexadecimal RGB triplet value:

```
document.bgColor = "7fff00"
```

NOTE

You can find the JavaScript color values table in Table 5.3 in Chapter 5, "Fundamentals of the JavaScript Language." It lists the color values as both string literals and hexadecimal RGB triplets.

A hexadecimal RGB triplet is a combination of three hexadecimal values representing red, green, and blue, respectively. When combined, the values form a hexadecimal RGB triplet. The number should take one of two case-sensitive forms:

```
rrggbb
```

```
#rrggbb
```

When applying color changes to a document attribute, you must follow the same principles that apply to changing a document's text. You can make the changes only when the page is set, such as in a `document.write()` statement—not on a page that has already been "painted" in the browser window.

To see how to set these color settings, look at the example shown in Figure 12.7. The bottom frame has a selection list with all the colors and a group of radio buttons associated with the document attribute color options. You can select a color and the property you want to use and then click the Apply button. A JavaScript code reloads the top frame based on your setting.

FIGURE 12.7.

Changing color of a frame on-the-fly.

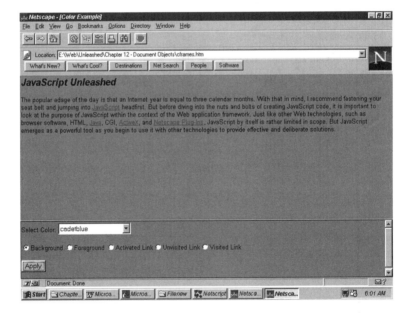

Listing 12.6 provides the HTML source of the frameset document. Listing 12.7 shows the code for `dummy.htm`. Listing 12.8 lists the code from the lower frameset that performs this process. When the user clicks the Apply button, the `refreshMain()` method assigns a value to the `newColor` variable based on the currently selected option in the selection list. Next, using dot notation, the document of the upper frame is referenced (`parent.main.document`) and reloaded based on the `write()` and a color property assignment.

Listing 12.6. cframes.htm.

```
<HTML>
<HEAD>
<TITLE>Color Example</TITLE>
</HEAD>
<FRAMESET ROWS="80%,20%">
  <FRAME SRC="dummy.htm" NAME="main" MARGINWIDTH="1" MARGINHEIGHT="1">
  <FRAME SRC="colordef.htm" NAME="colorDef" MARGINWIDTH="1" MARGINHEIGHT="1">
  <NOFRAMES>
<BODY>
<P>This web page uses frames, but your browser doesn't support them.</P>
</BODY>
</NOFRAMES>
</FRAMESET>
</HTML>
```

Listing 12.7. dummy.htm.

```
<html>
<head>
</head>
<body>
<h2><em>JavaScript Unleashed</em></h2>
<p>The popular adage of the day is that an Internet year is equal to three
calendar months. With that in mind, I recommend fastening your seat belt
and jumping into <a href="http://home.netscape.com">JavaScript</a> headfirst.
But before diving into the nuts and bolts of creating JavaScript code, it is
important to look at the purpose of JavaScript within the context of the Web
application framework. Just like other Web technologies, such as browser
software, HTML, <a href="http://java.sun.com">Java</a>, CGI, <a href=
"http://www.microsoft.com/activex">ActiveX</a>, and <a href=
"http://home.netscape.com">Netscape Plug-Ins</a>, JavaScript by itself is
rather limited in scope. But JavaScript emerges as a powerful tool as you
begin to use it with other technologies to provide effective and deliberate
solutions.</p>
<p> </p>
</body>
</html>
```

Listing 12.8. colordef.htm.

```
<html>

<head>
<title>Color Definition</title>
<SCRIPT LANGUAGE="JavaScript">
var graf = '<body><h2><em>JavaScript Unleashed</em></h2><p>The popular
adage of the day is that an Internet year is equal to three calendar
months. With that in mind, I recommend fastening your seat belt and
jumping into <a href="http://home.netscape.com">JavaScript</a> headfirst.
But before diving into the nuts and bolts of creating JavaScript code, it
is important to look at the purpose of JavaScript within the context of the
```

Web application framework. Just like other Web technologies, such as browser
software, HTML, `<a href="http://java.sun.com">Java</a>`, CGI, `<a
href="http://www.microsoft.com/activex">ActiveX</a>`, and `<a
href="http://home.netscape.com">Netscape Plug-Ins</a>`, JavaScript by
itself is rather limited in scope. But JavaScript emerges as a powerful tool
as you begin to use it with other technologies to provide effective and
deliberate solutions.</p></body>'

```
    function refreshMain() {

        var newColor = document.form1.colorList.options[document.form1.
            colorList.selectedIndex].text
        var selProp = null

        with (parent.main.document) {
            open()
            write(graf)
            if (document.form1.type[0].checked) {
                bgColor = newColor }
            else {
                if (document.form1.type[1].checked) {
                    fgColor = newColor }
                else {
                    if (document.form1.type[2].checked) {
                        alinkColor = newColor }
                    else {
                        if (document.form1.type[3].checked) {
                            linkColor = newColor }
                        else
                            if (document.form1.type[4].checked) {
                                vlinkColor = newColor }
                    }
                }
            }
            close()
        }
```

</SCRIPT>
</head>

```
<body bgcolor="tomato">
<form name="form1" method="POST">
<p>Select Color: <select name="colorList" size=1>
<option>aliceblue</option>
<option>antiquewhite</option>
<option>aqua</option>
<option>aquamarine</option>
<option>azure</option>
<option>beige</option>
<option>bisque</option>
<option>black</option>
<option>blanchedalmond</option>
<option>blue</option>
<option>blueviolet</option>
<option>brown</option>
<option>burlywood</option>
<option>cadetblue</option>
```

continues

Listing 12.8. continued

```
<option>chartreuse</option>
<option>chocolate</option>
<option>coral</option>
<option>cornflowerblue</option>
<option>cornsilk</option>
<option>crimson</option>
<option>cyan</option>
<option>darkblue</option>
<option>darkcyan</option>
<option>darkgoldenrod</option>
<option>darkgray</option>
<option>darkgreen</option>
<option>darkkhaki</option>
<option>darkmagenta</option>
<option>darkolivegreen</option>
<option>darkorange</option>
<option>darkorchid</option>
<option>darkred</option>
<option>darksalmon</option>
<option>darkseagreen</option>
<option>darkslateblue</option>
<option>darkslategray</option>
<option>darkturquoise</option>
<option>darkviolet</option>
<option>deeppink</option>
<option>deepskyblue</option>
<option>dimgray</option>
<option>dodgerblue</option>
<option>firebrick</option>
<option>floralwhite</option>
<option>forestgreen</option>
<option>fuchsia</option>
<option>gainsboro</option>
<option>ghostwhite</option>
<option>gold</option>
<option>goldenrod</option>
<option>gray</option>
<option>green</option>
<option>greenyellow</option>
<option>honeydew</option>
<option>hotpink</option>
<option>indianred</option>
<option>indigo</option>
<option>ivory</option>
<option>khaki</option>
<option>lavender</option>
<option>lavenderblush</option>
<option>lawngreen</option>
<option>lemonchiffon</option>
<option>lightblue</option>
<option>lightcoral</option>
<option>lightcyan</option>
<option>lightgoldenrodyellow</option>
<option>lightgreen</option>
<option>lightgrey</option>
<option>lightpink</option>
```

```
<option>lightsalmon</option>
<option>lightseagreen</option>
<option>lightskyblue</option>
<option>lightslategray</option>
<option>lightsteelblue</option>
<option>lightyellow</option>
<option>lime</option>
<option>limegreen</option>
<option>linen</option>
<option>magenta</option>
<option>maroon</option>
<option>mediumaquamarine</option>
<option>mediumblue</option>
<option>mediumorchid</option>
<option>mediumpurple</option>
<option>mediumseagreen</option>
<option>mediumslateblue</option>
<option>mediumspringgreen</option>
<option>mediumturquoise</option>
<option>mediumvioletred</option>
<option>midnightblue</option>
<option>mintcream</option>
<option>mistyrose</option>
<option>moccasin</option>
<option>navajowhite</option>
<option>navy</option>
<option>oldlace</option>
<option>olive</option>
<option>olivedrab</option>
<option>orange</option>
<option>orangered</option>
<option>orchid</option>
<option>palegoldenrod</option>
<option>palegreen</option>
<option>paleturquoise</option>
<option>palevioletred</option>
<option>papayawhip</option>
<option>peachpuff</option>
<option>peru</option>
<option>pink</option>
<option>plum</option>
<option>powderblue</option>
<option>purple</option>
<option>red</option>
<option>rosybrown</option>
<option>royalblue</option>
<option>saddlebrown</option>
<option>salmon</option>
<option>sandybrown</option>
<option>seagreen</option>
<option>seashell</option>
<option>sienna</option>
<option>silver</option>
<option>skyblue</option>
<option>slateblue</option>
<option>slategray</option>
<option>snow</option>
<option>springgreen</option>
```

12

DOCUMENT OBJECTS

continues

Listing 12.8. continued

```
<option>steelblue</option>
<option>tan</option>
<option>teal</option>
<option>thistle</option>
<option>tomato</option>
<option>turquoise</option>
<option>violet</option>
<option>wheat</option>
<option>white</option>
<option>whitesmoke</option>
<option>yellow</option>
<option>yellowgreen</option>
</select>
<p><input type=radio name="type" value="bgColor" checked>Background <input
type=radio name="type" value="fgColor">Foreground <input type=radio
name="type" value="alinkColor">Activated Link<input type=radio name="type"
value="linkColor">Unvisted Link<input type=radio name="type"
value="vlinkColor">Visited Link<p>
<input type=button name="Apply" value="Apply" onClick="refreshMain()"></p>
</form>
</body>
</html>
```

Although this is a limited example, you can build on this base to develop some much more flexible scripts to change colors on-the-fly.

RESOURCE

For a comprehensive example of using colors in your documents, see the hIdaho Color Center at http://www.hidaho.com/colorcenter/.

The Link Object

Perhaps love makes the world go 'round, but what makes the World Wide Web go 'round are links. HTML links are the core elements of any Web document, allowing you to jump to another Web page with the click of a mouse. The location of the document is immaterial; it could be on the same Web server or thousands of miles away. All that matters is that the URL is valid. The link object is the JavaScript equivalent of the hypertext link, which is defined in HTML syntax as

```
<A HREF=locationOrURL
   [NAME="objectName"]
   [TARGET="windowName"]
   [onClick="methodName"]
   [onMouseOver="methodName"]>
   linkText
</A>
```

The link object has several properties that are the same as the parameters for the location object. These include `hash`, `host`, `hostname`, `href`, `pathname`, `port`, `protocol`, and `search`. See Chapter 11 for more information on these properties.

Referencing Link Objects

Link objects don't have a name property, so you can't refer to a specific link object by itself. The only way you can refer to a link object in your JavaScript code is by using the links array. The links array is a collection of all the links within the current document. The order of the array is based on the order in which the links are located within the source file. I'll present an example that demonstrates how you can use the link array to deal with individual link objects.

Suppose you want to extract the URLs from each link on a page and list them on another page. Using a triple-frame frameset, you can set the bottom frame to be the "free" window that is used for browsing, the top frame to contain a button to set off the process, and the middle frame to list the URLs. Figure 12.8 shows the triple-frame frameset in a Netscape window after this process is performed.

FIGURE 12.8.

Getting URL information using the links array.

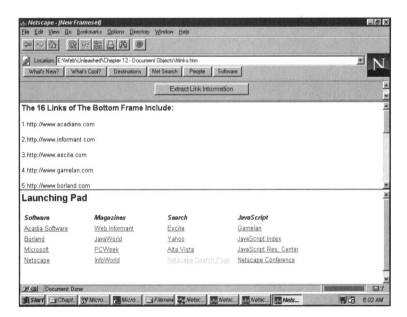

12

DOCUMENT OBJECTS

Listing 12.9 displays the frameset source code, Listing 12.10 shows the code for frbottom.htm, and Listing 12.11 lists the JavaScript source code for the top frame, which contains the processing power for this example. Clicking the Extract Link Information button triggers the getLinkInfo() method. This method references the links array of the bottom frame (named bFrame) and sets the len variable to equal to its length. While writing to the middle frame, the method loops through each element in the links array and retrieves the href property value.

Listing 12.9. frlinks.htm.

```
<HTML>
<HEAD>
<TITLE>New Frameset</TITLE>
</HEAD>
<FRAMESET ROWS="10%,35%,*">
  <FRAME SRC="frtop.htm" NAME="tFrame" MARGINWIDTH="2" MARGINHEIGHT="4">
  <FRAME SRC="frmiddle.htm" NAME="mFrame" MARGINWIDTH="5" MARGINHEIGHT="2">
  <FRAME SRC="frbottom.htm" NAME="bFrame" MARGINWIDTH="5" MARGINHEIGHT="2">
  <NOFRAMES>
<BODY>
<P>This web page uses frames, but your browser doesn't support them.</P>
</BODY>
</NOFRAMES>
</FRAMESET>
</HTML>
```

Listing 12.10. frbottom.htm.

```
<html>

<head>
</head>

<body>
<h2>Launching Pad </h2>
<table width=80%>
<tr><td width=25%><em><strong>Software</strong></em></td><td width=25%><em>
<strong>Magazines</strong></em></td><td width=25%><em><strong>Search</strong>
</em></td><td width=25%><em><strong>JavaScript</strong></em></td></tr>
<tr><td width=25%><a href="http://www.acadians.com">Acadia Software</a></td>
<td width=25%><a href="http://www.informant.com">Web Informant</a></td><td
width=25%><a href="http://www.excite.com">Excite</a></td><td width=25%><a
href="http://www.gamelan.com">Gamelan</a></td></tr>
<tr><td width=25%><a href="http://www.borland.com">Borland</a></td>
<td width=25%><a href="http://www.javaworld.com">JavaWorld</a></td><td
width=25%><a href="http://www.yahoo.com">Yahoo</a></td><td width=25%><a
href="http://www.c2.org/~andreww/javascript/">JavaScript Index</a></td></tr>
<tr><td width=25%><a href="http://www.microsoft.com">Microsoft</a></td><td
width=25%><a href="http://www.pcweek.com">PCWeek</a></td><td width=25%><a href=
"http://www.altavitsa.digital.com">Alta Vista</a></td><td width=25%><a
href="http://www.intercom.net/user/mecha/java/index.html">JavaScript Res.
Center</a></td></tr>
```

```
<tr><td width=25%><a href="http://home.netscape.com">Netscape</a></td>
<td width=25%><a href="http://www.infoworld.com">InfoWorld</a></td><td
width=25%><a href="http://home.netscape.com/escapes/search/search4.html">
Netscape Search Page</a></td><td width=25%><a href="http://home.netscape.com/
misc/developer/conference/proceedings/">Netscape Conference</a></td></tr>
</table>
<p> </p>
</body>
</html>
```

Listing 12.11. `frtop.htm`.

```
<html>
<head>
<base target="middle">
<SCRIPT LANGUAGE="JavaScript">

    function getLinkInfo() {
        var len = parent.bFrame.document.links.length
        with (parent.mFrame.document) {
            open()
            write("<h3>The " + len
              + " Links of The Bottom Frame Include:</h3><p>")
            for (var i=0; i<len; i++) {
                write((i+1) + "." + parent.bFrame.document.links[i].href
                    + "<p>")
            }
            close()
        }
    }

</SCRIPT>
</head>
<body bgcolor="crimson">
<form method="POST">
<p>
<DIV align=center><input type=button name="Extract" value="Extract Link
Information"
  onClick="getLinkInfo()"></DIV>
</form>
</body>
</html>
```

Executing JavaScript Code Using Links

Using `javascript:` as the protocol element of the link's `href`, you can perform a JavaScript expression in place of a typical link action, such as jumping to a new Web page or sending a mail message. However, the code you execute must be self-contained. You can't call another method, as you would with an event handler, nor can you reference other objects outside of their context, such as another window.

You could use a link to evaluate the type of browser in use, such as in the following code:

```
<A HREF="javascript:if (navigator.appName != 'Netscape')
{ alert('You should not have clicked this link!') } else
{ alert('Thanks for clicking.')} ">All Netscape users, click me</A>
```

As a second example, I set up the table of contents for the first edition of this book in an HTML document and added links to each of the part names. For the HREF= parameter of these links, I placed a description of each part in an alert message box. Because of the nature of the javascript: protocol, I was forced to use a message box rather than write the text to another frame or window. Listing 12.12 shows the HTML code for this example, and Figure 12.9 shows the result of clicking the Part III link. (In the real world, a better solution would be to separate the text into one or more HTML documents and use the links in a traditional method to jump to their locations.)

Listing 12.12. jsLinks.htm.

```
<html>
<head>
<title>JavaScript Unleashed Table of Contents</title>
</head>
<body>
<p><a href="javascript:alert('In this first section, you will get a complete
introduction to JavaScript. Chapter 1 takes a unique look at JavaScript,
focusing on how and where it fits into the Web application development
framework. You will also see how it relates to other Web technologies both on
the client- and server-side. Next, in Chapter 2, you will learn about the
relationship between JavaScript and Hypertext Markup Language (HTML) and how
the browser interprets your code at runtime. Chapter 3 looks at the software
tools you need to develop in JavaScript.')"><font size=4>Part I: Getting
Started with JavaScript</font></a><font size=4> </font></p>
<blockquote>
<p><font size=4>1) JavaScript and the World Wide Web <br>
2) How JavaScript and HTML Work Together <br>
3) Assembling Your JavaScript Toolkit </font></p>
</blockquote>
<p><a href="javascript:alert('The second part presents a thorough look at
the JavaScript language. In Chapters 4-7, you will learn about language
basics, control structures, operators, and functions.')"><font size=4>Part II:
The JavaScript Language </font></a></p>
<blockquote>
<p><font size=4>4) Fundamentals of the JavaScript Language<br>
5) Control Structures and Looping <br>
6) Operators<br>
7) Functions</font></p>
</blockquote>
<p><a href="javascript:alert('Part three dives into the heart of JavaScript--
objects. After an introduction to object-oriented concepts in Chapter 8,
Chapter 9 looks at how you can handle user and system events. Chapter 10 then
looks at the built-in JavaScript hierarchy and introduces you to each of
the Navigator and Built-in language objects. Chapters 11-14 continue where
the previous chapter left off by exploring in-depth each of the built-in
```

JavaScript objects. Chapter 15 rounds out the discussion on objects, focusing on how you can create your own. It includes many innovative ideas related to custom object development within JavaScript.')"><font size=4>Part III: JavaScript Objects</font></a></p>
<blockquote>
<p><font size=4>8) Fundamentals of Object-Orientation
9) Handling Events
10) JavaScript Built-In Object Model
11) Navigator Objects
12) Document Objects
13) Form Objects
14) Built-in Language Objects
15) Creating Custom JavaScript Objects </font></p>
</blockquote>
<p><a href="javascript:alert('The next section builds upon everything you learned up to that point to look at specific areas of interest to the JavaScript developer. Chapter 16 explores how you can enhance HTML forms with JavaScript, such as providing client-side data validation. Both Chapters 17-18 really focus on frames and how you can use JavaScript in multi-frame windows. I have found frame management to be perhaps the most common use of JavaScript on the Web. Chapter 19 looks at yet another key topic, cookies and other techniques for handling and maintaining state in the stateless environment of the Web.')"><font size=4>Part IV: JavaScript Programming </font></a></p>
<blockquote>
<p><font size=4>16) Enhancing Forms with JavaScript
17) Working with Frames and Windows
18) Scripting Outlines and Table of Contents
19) Cookies &amp; State Maintenance </font></p>
</blockquote>
<p><a href="javascript:alert('While Parts I-IV focused on client-side JavaScript, this section focuses on its server-side counterpart. Within Netscape LiveWire and other products such as Borland IntraBuilder, you can use JavaScript as a server-side scripting language. In doing so, you are freed from writing CGI scripts and dealing with such languages as PERL. Chapter 20 looks at server-side JavaScript, focusing on LiveWire and IntraBuilder. Chapter 21 takes look at the issue of how to architect client/server applications on the Web. Covered are many of the issues you will encounter as you plan such an application.')"><font size=4>Part V: JavaScript on the Server</font></a></p>
<blockquote>
<p><font size=4>20) Server-Based JavaScript
21) Partitioning Client and Server Applications </font></p>
</blockquote>
<p><a href="javascript:alert('Part VI explores five advanced subjects, many of which are emerging as key topics as JavaScript matures. Chapter 22 dives into Error Handling and Debugging JavaScript applications. Chapter 23-24 cover the hot topic of integrating JavaScript with Netscape Plug-Ins and ActiveX controls. Chapter 25 looks at integrating JavaScript with VRML and multimedia data. Chapter 26 closes the section by looking at a more conceptual topic—JavaScript security. The chapter not only looks at the key issues surrounding this subject, but provides some helpful advice as you consider using JavaScript for your Web site.')"><font size=4>Part VI: Advanced JavaScript</font></a><font size=4> </font></p>
<blockquote>

12

DOCUMENT OBJECTS

continues

Listing 12.12. continued

```
<p><font size=4>22) Error Handling and Debugging in JavaScript <br>
23) Working with Netscape Plug-ins <br>
24) ActiveX Scripting with JavaScript <br>
25) VRML and Multimedia <br>
26) JavaScript and Web Security </font></p>
</blockquote>
<p><a href="javascript:alert('JavaScript is an important tool to glue HTML
and Java applets. In this section, we will look at Java from a JavaScript
perspective in Chapter 27 and see how similar or different the language is
for JavaScripters. Chapter 28 provides a good introduction on how to build
a Java applet, while Chapter 29 is where the rubber meets the road when it
focuses on integrating Java and JavaScript.')"><font size=4>Part VII: Java
and JavaScript </font></a></p>
<blockquote>
<p><font size=4>27) Java from a JavaScripter Perspective <br>
28) Building Java Applets<br>
29) Integrating JavaScript with Java </font></p>
</blockquote>
<p><a href="javascript:alert('Many corporations will use the Web as a way
to get at their data. As a result, how JavaScript can access data will be
an increasingly important topic as the technology matures. In this section,
we will look at how you can work with data both on the client-side and
server-side. Chapter 30 introduces the notion of maintaining lookup tables
on the client side to lessen the need to access the server. Chapter 31 then
gets into how you can use JavaScript to access server-side data. LiveWire
and IntraBuilder will again be used in this context.')"><font size=4>Part
VIII: JavaScript Database Applications</font></a></p>
<blockquote>
<p><font size=4>30) Using Client-Side Tables in JavaScript <br>
31) Working with Server-Side Database Objects </font></p>
</blockquote>
<p><a href="javascript:alert('The final section provides some extra
information that will assist you as you read the book. Appendixes A-B
provide basic references on the JavaScript and HTML respectively. Appendix C
looks at how VBScript and JavaScript compare. Appendix D lists JavaScript
resources that are available online.')"><font size=4>Part IX: Appendixes
</font></a></p>
<blockquote>
<p><font size=4>A) JavaScript Language Summary <br>
B) Fundamentals of HTML <br>
C) Comparing JavaScript with Microsoft&#146;s VBScript <br>
D) JavaScript Resources on the Internet <br>
</font></p>
</blockquote>
</body>
</html>
```

FIGURE 12.9.
*Clicking a link displays
a message box.*

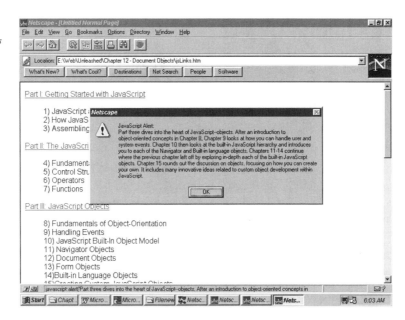

The Anchor Object

You most often use a link object to jump to another Web page or another location within the current document. Within the current document, the link locates a specific place in the text, called an *anchor*. This is defined in HTML syntax as

```
<A [HREF=locationOrURL]
   NAME="objectName"
   [TARGET="windowName"]>
   anchorText
</A>
```

You could say that the anchor object is "JavaScript-challenged," because you can do little in JavaScript with anchors. By itself, an anchor object has no properties, methods, or events. The only way you can really use them in JavaScript is through the anchors array of the document object. You can use the anchors array to determine the number of anchors in a document and iterate through them as desired.

The Image Object

NOTE

The image object is supported in JavaScript 1.1 and later. It is not supported in JavaScript 1.0 and JScript 1.0.

If you've spent much time on the Web, you probably realize how important graphics are to the Web. You can hardly go to a page without seeing several graphics scattered throughout. New to Netscape Navigator 3.0, the image object represents an HTML image, which is defined in the following format:

```
<IMG
    [NAME="objectName"]
    SRC="Location"
    [LOWSRC="Location"]
    [HEIGHT="Pixels"¦"Value"%]
    [WIDTH="Pixels"¦"Value"%]
    [HSPACE="Pixels"]
    [VSPACE="Pixels"]
    [BORDER="Pixels"]
    [ALIGN="left"¦"right"¦ "top"¦
        "absmiddle"¦"absbottom"¦
        "texttop"¦"middle"¦"baseline"¦
        "bottom"]
    [ISMAP]
    [USEMAP="Location#MapName"]
    [onAbort="methodName"]
    [onError="methodName"]
    [onLoad="methodName"]>
```

TIP

For more information on image object events, see Chapter 10.

For example, to display an image called dot.gif in HTML, you would use the following syntax:

```
<IMG SRC='dot.gif' height="200" width="200">
```

Instantiating an Image Object

You can create an instance of an image object using the new operator, as shown here:

```
companyLogo = new Image()
companyLogo.src = "logo.gif"
```

You can set the dimensions of the graphic as a parameter to the Image() constructor. For example, if you wanted to display the logo in a 200×300 pixel format, you could use the following:

```
companyLogo = new Image(200,300)
companyLogo.src = "logo.gif"
```

By assigning a value to the src property, you can change the image that is displayed. However, if you do this, the new URL or graphic loads in the image area.

Because you still define an image using the <IMG> tag, an image object you create serves a rather limited purpose. You can use it to retrieve an image before it's actually needed for display purposes. Because this image is now in memory, it would be much quicker to display it when a document is reloaded. The most common example is an animation-like series of images that are retrieved using the Image() object and then displayed later while they are in memory.

> **TIP**
>
> See Chapter 16, "Creating Special Effects with JavaScript," for more information on how you can use image objects.

Summary

The document objects discussed in this chapter are the JavaScript equivalent of some of the most basic HTML elements around. These objects include the HTML document, link, anchor, and image. Although you can use JavaScript to enhance or retrieve information from these objects, much of the JavaScript interaction usually comes from working with forms. Therefore, the next chapter looks closely at form objects.

CHAPTER 13

Form Objects

IN THIS CHAPTER

One of the key milestones in the evolution of the Web was the emergence of HTML forms from the world of static pages. With forms, the Web could actually be more than a one-directional mode of communication. Forms provided a means by which any user on any machine could transfer data to a server for processing. With JavaScript, HTML forms grow even more powerful. Not only can you preprocess form data before it's sent to the user, but you can also use forms in an application that is completely contained on the client side. This chapter discusses the form object and the numerous objects it can contain.

> **NOTE**
>
> The form objects discussed in this chapter can exist only within a form—not outside one.

The Form Object

One of the principal uses of JavaScript is providing a means to interact with the user on the client side. Most of the time, this interaction with the user happens through an HTML form. As a result, the JavaScript form object is an important object within the JavaScript object model. When you work with the form object, you don't do that much with a form object in and of itself. Rather, the form object provides a container by which you can retrieve data from the user.

In HTML, the form object is defined as

```
<FORM
    [NAME="formName"]
    [ACTION="serverURL"]
    [ENCTYPE="encodingType"]
    [METHOD=GET ¦ POST]
    [TARGET="windowName"]
    [onSubmit="methodName"]>
</FORM>
```

To define a form, follow standard HTML conventions:

```
<FORM NAME="form1" ACTION="http://www.acadians.com/js/script.jfm" METHOD=GET>

  <!-- Enter form objects here -->

</FORM>
```

> **NOTE**
>
> For more information on using forms in JavaScript, see Chapter 20, "Forms and Data Validation."

Submitting Forms to the Server

Before JavaScript came along, the only real purpose of an HTML form was to send the data elements gathered on the client side to the server. Because the client side itself wasn't powerful enough to intelligently process the data, it was up to the server to then react to the information it received. JavaScript lets you add a great deal of front-end processing to your HTML forms, but that doesn't eliminate the need to submit a form to a server for more industrial-strength purposes.

You can submit a form using one of two processes. You can call the form object's `submit()` method, or you can click a Submit button, which automatically submits the form with which it is associated.

> **NOTE**
>
> See Chapter 10, "Handling Events," and Chapter 16, "Creating Special Effects with JavaScript," for more information on performing validity checks using JavaScript before submitting a form.

Many of the form object properties deal with additional information that is sent to the server from the form. These properties include the following:

- `action` (same as the `ACTION=` parameter): The `action` property specifies the server URL to which the form is sent:

```
form1.action = "http://www.acadians.com/js/surv.cgi"
```

This is usually a CGI program, a LiveWire application, or an IntraBuilder .JFM file.

- `enctype` (same as the `ENCTYPE=` parameter): The `enctype` property specifies the MIME encoding of the form. The default is `application/x-www-form-urlencoded`, as shown here:

```
if (form1.enctype == "application/x-www-form-urlencoded") {
    alert("Encoding type is normal.") }
```

- `method` (same as the `METHOD=` parameter): The `method` property defines how the form is sent to the server. The value of `GET` is used most often, but you can use `POST` as well. This parameter is based on the server-side process, so as you design the HTML form, you need to check the server program's requirements. The following code shows an example of using the `method` parameter:

```
var methodType
methodType = form1.method
alert("The method type for this form is: " + methodType)
```

- `target` (same as the `TARGET=` parameter): The `target` property specifies the destination window that the server should send information back to. If the `target` property isn't specified, the server displays results in same window that submitted the form. If you're using a frameset, the `target` property can be a frame specified by the NAME parameter of the <FRAME> tag. You can also use one of the following reserved window names: _top, _parent, _self, and _blank. Keep in mind that you are in HTML for this specification, not JavaScript. You can't use a JavaScript window object name, such as parent.resultsWindow. The following code shows an example:

```
if (document.form1.newWindowCheckBox.checked) {
    document.form1.target = "resultsForm" }
else {
    document.form1.target = "_self" }
```

The HTML form shown in Listing 13.1 uses a combination of HTML tags and JavaScript code to submit a form. Note that if the user checks the Rush Order checkbox, the form's action property changes to a new value during the form's onSubmit event. Setting the action property programmatically overrides the default value.

Listing 13.1. formSubmit.htm.

```
<html>
<head>
<title>For More Information</title>
<SCRIPT LANGUAGE="JavaScript">

    function checkType() {
        if (document.form1.rush.checked) {
            document.form1.action = "http://www.acadians.com/js/rush.cgi" }
    }
</SCRIPT>
</head>

<body>
<h1>Order Form</h1>
<hr>
<form name="form1" action="http://www.acadians.com/js/order.cgi"
method="POST" onSubmit="checkType()">
<p>Please provide the following contact information:</p>
<blockquote>
<pre><em>        First name </em><input type=text size=25 maxlength=256
name="Contact_FirstName">
<em>        Last name </em><input type=text size=25 maxlength=256
name="Contact_LastName">
<em>            Title </em><input type=text size=35 maxlength=256
name="Contact_Title">
<em>     Organization </em><input type=text size=35 maxlength=256
name="Contact_Organization">
<em>       Work Phone </em><input type=text size=25 maxlength=25
name="Contact_WorkPhone">
<em>              FAX </em><input type=text size=25 maxlength=25
name="Contact_FAX">
<em>           E-mail </em><input type=text size=25 maxlength=256
name="Contact_Email">
<em>              URL </em><input type=text size=25 maxlength=25
name="Contact_URL">
</pre>
</blockquote>
```

```
<p>Please provide the following ordering information:</p>
<blockquote>
<pre><strong>QTY      DESCRIPTION
</strong><input type=text size=6 maxlength=6
name="Ordering_OrderQty0">
<input type=text size=45 maxlength=256 name="Ordering_OrderDesc0">
<input type=text size=6 maxlength=6 name="Ordering_OrderQty1">
<input type=text size=45 maxlength=256 name="Ordering_OrderDesc1">
<input type=text size=6 maxlength=6 name="Ordering_OrderQty2">
<input type=text size=45 maxlength=256 name="Ordering_OrderDesc2">
<input type=text size=6 maxlength=6 name="Ordering_OrderQty3">
<input type=text size=45 maxlength=256 name="Ordering_OrderDesc3">
<input type=text size=6 maxlength=6 name="Ordering_OrderQty4">
<input type=text size=45 maxlength=256 name="Ordering_OrderDesc4">

<em>                </em><strong>BILLING</strong>
<em>Purchase order # </em><input type=text size=25 maxlength=256
name="Ordering_PONumber">
<em>   Account name </em><input type=text size=25 maxlength=256
name="Ordering_POAccount">

<em>                </em><strong>SHIPPING</strong>
<em>  Street address </em><input type=text size=35 maxlength=256
name="Ordering_StreetAddress">
<em> Address (cont.) </em><input type=text size=35 maxlength=256
name="Ordering_Address2">
<em>            City </em><input type=text size=35 maxlength=256
name="Ordering_City">
<em>  State/Province </em><input type=text size=35 maxlength=256
name="Ordering_State">
<em> Zip/Postal code </em><input type=text size=12 maxlength=12
name="Ordering_ZipCode">
<em>         Country </em><input type=text size=25 maxlength=256
name="Ordering_Country">
</pre>
<pre><input type=checkbox name="rush" value="ON">Rush Order!</pre>
</blockquote>
<p><input type=submit value="Submit Form"> <input type=reset
value="Reset Form"> </p>
</form>
</body>
</html>
```

13

FORM OBJECTS

NOTE

For more information on the onSubmit event handler, see Chapter 10.

Checking Elements on a Form

The form acts as a container object for all objects on a form. Because these types of objects, such as text or button objects, are for user interaction, you can refer to them as *user interface objects* or *UI objects*. The form object has an `elements` property that you can use to either refer to an element on a form or check all elements on a form to perform a particular task. The order of the array is based purely on the order in which the elements of the HTML form are defined in the source file. The first element listed is `element[0]`, the second is `element[1]`, and so on.

You can refer to each form element either by name or by its index in the `elements` array. For example, if the text object named `LastName` was the first element defined on the form, it could be accessed using the following code:

```
custLastName = form1.elements[0].value
```

You could also use this:

```
custLastName = form1.LastName.value
```

You could also use the `elements` property to do something with each object within the form. For example, suppose you wanted to make sure that each field on your form wasn't blank. Using the `elements` property, you could use a `for` loop to iterate through each array element and check the values. This code is shown in Listing 13.2.

Listing 13.2. `formElements.htm`.

```
<html>
<head>
<title>Online Registration</title>
<SCRIPT LANGUAGE="JavaScript">
<!--
    function checkFields() {
        var num = document.form1.elements.length
        var validFlag = true
        for (var i=0; i<num; i++) {
            if ((document.form1.elements[i].value == null ||
                document.form1.elements[i].value == "") &&
                (typeof document.form1.elements[i] != 'submit' ||
                typeof document.form1.elements[i] != 'reset'))
    {
                validFlag = false
                alert("The " + document.form1.elements[i].name +
                    " field is blank. Please enter a value.")
                break }
        }
        return validFlag
    }
// -->
</SCRIPT>
</head>

<body>
<form name="form1" method="POST" onSubmit="return checkFields()">
<h2>Online Registration</h2>
<p>Username:<br>
<input type=text size=25 maxlength=256 name="Username"><br>
Category of Interest:<br>
<input type=text size=25 maxlength=256 name="Category"><br>
```

```
Starting Year:<strong><br>
</strong><input type=text size=25 maxlength=256 name="StartYear"><br>
Email address:<strong><br>
</strong><input type=text size=25 maxlength=256 name="EmailAddress"></p>
<h2><input type=submit value="Register"> <input type=reset value="Clear"></h2>
</form>
<p> </h5>
</body>
</html>
```

Notice that the `checkFields()` method uses the `elements.length` property to determine the number of iterations in the `for` loop. Next, because the `elements` array includes all objects in the form, including the two button objects, the `typeof` operator is used to qualify the element before checking its value. Figure 13.1 shows the alert message box that displays if a field is blank.

FIGURE 13.1.

Checking the values of fields on a form.

13

FORM OBJECTS

The Text Object

For most tasks, the text object is the element you use most often to gather data entered by the user. The text object is used for capturing single-line, free-flow information. For information that spans multiple lines, use the textarea object, discussed in the section "The Textarea Object." As with other form objects, the text object is the "objectified" version of an HTML tag, and it has the following syntax:

```
<INPUT
    TYPE="text"
    [NAME="objectName"]
```

```
[VALUE="value"]
[SIZE=size]
[MAXLENGTH=size]
[onBlur="methodName"]
[onChange="methodName"]
[onFocus="methodName"]
[onSelect="methodName"]>
```

For example, to define a text object for a last name, you could use the following:

```
<INPUT TYPE="text" NAME=LastName SIZE=20 MAXLENGTH=25>
```

> **NOTE**
>
> For more information on the text object events, such as onBlur, onChange, onFocus, and onSelect, see Chapter 10.

Assigning a Default Value to a Text Object

There might be times when you want to assign a default value to a text object. If you're creating an HTML document on-the-fly, you can do this by setting the VALUE= parameter of the <INPUT type=text> tag. To illustrate, suppose you wanted to automatically check the type of the navigator object and fill it in a form. The code shown in Listing 13.3 generates the form shown in Figure 13.2. Notice that the Browser field is automatically filled in for the user when the script checks the appName property of the navigator object.

Listing 13.3. textDefaultValueWrite.htm.

```
<SCRIPT LANGUAGE="JavaScript">
var browserVar = navigator.appName
document.write('<body>')
document.write('<form name="form1" method="POST">')
document.write('<h2>Online Registration</h2>')
document.write('<p>Username:<br>')
document.write('<input type=text size=25 maxlength=256 name="Username"><br>')
document.write('Browser used:<br>')
document.write('<input type=text size=25 maxlength=256
name="Browser" value="' + browserVar + '"><br>')
document.write('Email address:<strong> <br>')
document.write('</strong><input type=text size=25 maxlength=256')
document.write('name="EmailAddress"></p>')
document.write('<h2><input type=submit value="Register">  ')
document.write('<input type=reset value="Clear"></h2>')
document.write('</form>')
document.write('</body>')
document.write('</html>')
// -->
</SCRIPT>
```

FIGURE 13.2.

The default value is set for the user.

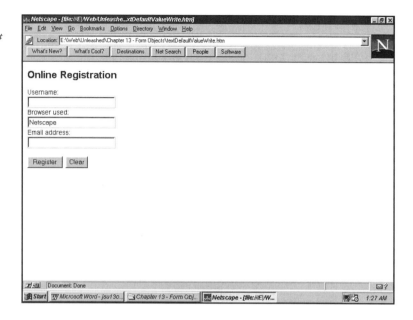

A second way to assign a default value to a text object already generated is to set its value property. For example, you could create the same form using the code shown in Listing 13.4. In this example, the window's onLoad event handler assigns a value to the Browser field.

Listing 13.4. textDefaultValue.htm.

```
<html>
<head>
<title>Online Registration</title>
<SCRIPT LANGUAGE="JavaScript">
<!--
    function findBrowser() {
        document.form1.Browser.value = navigator.appName
    }
// -->
</SCRIPT>
</head>

<body onLoad="findBrowser()" >
<form name="form1" method="POST">
<h2>Online Registration</h2>
<p>Username:<br>
<input type=text size=25 maxlength=256 name="Username"><br>
Browser used:<br>
<input type=text size=25 maxlength=256 name="Browser"><br>
Email address:<strong> <br>
</strong><input type=text size=25 maxlength=256 name="EmailAddress"></p>
<h2><input type=submit value="Register"> <input type=reset value="Clear"></h2>
</form>
</body>
</html>
```

13

FORM OBJECTS

Paradoxically, the `defaultValue` property isn't used in this example. Although you can assign a value to the `defaultValue` property, the form isn't updated when you do so. Therefore, you should use the `value` property, as shown in this example.

> **TIP**
>
> The `defaultValue` property is most useful for obtaining the default value of a text object, not for setting the default value.

Selecting Text Upon Focus

By default, when you enter a text object, the cursor is an insertion point. If the field currently has text you want to type over, you have to explicitly select the text, delete it, and retype a value. You can change this behavior by using the `select()` method of the text object. Listing 13.5 shows an HTML form with four text objects, each of which calls `this.select()` when the `onFocus` event is triggered. As a result, when the user enters each of these fields, any existing text is highlighted automatically. Figure 13.3 shows the result.

Listing 13.5. `textSelect.htm`.

```
<html>
<head>
<title>Online Registration</title>
</head>

<body>
<form name="form1" method="POST">
<h2>Online Registration</h2>
<p>Username:<br>
<input type=text size=25 maxlength=256 name="Username"
onFocus="this.select()"><br>
Browser used:<br>
<input type=text size=25 maxlength=256 name="Browser"
onFocus="this.select()"><br>
Email address:<strong> <br>
</strong><input type=text size=25 maxlength=256 name="EmailAddress"
onFocus="this.select()"></p>
<h2><input type=submit value="Register"> <input type=reset value="Clear"></h2>
</form>
</body>
</html>
```

Figure 13.3.

Highlighting text automatically.

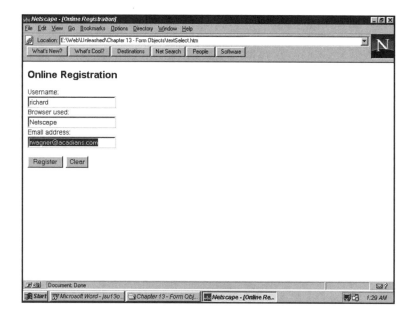

The Textarea Object

All the other form objects that you work with are designed for capturing data of limited size (less than 256 characters). The textarea object provides a means for capturing information that doesn't lend itself to simple text fields, radio buttons, or selection lists. You can use the textarea object to enter free-form data that spans several lines. You're limited to displaying ASCII text, but such basic formatting as paragraphs is allowed. The textarea object is defined using the standard HTML syntax:

```
<TEXTAREA
    NAME="objectName"
    ROWS="numRows"
    COLS="numCols"
    [WRAP="off¦virtual¦physical"]
    [onBlur="methodName"]
    [onChange="methodName"]
    [onFocus="methodName"]
    [onSelect="methodName"]>
    displayText
</TEXTAREA>
```

For example, to define a textarea for submitting online comments, you could define the object as follows:

```
<textarea name="Comments" rows=12 cols=78></textarea>
```

Figure 13.4 shows the results in a form.

FIGURE 13.4.

The textarea object.

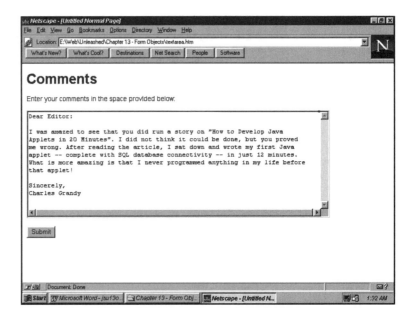

NOTE

For more information on textarea events, such as onBlur, onChange, onFocus, and onSelect, see Chapter 10.

Wrapping Text in a Textarea Object

By default, text doesn't wrap in a textarea object. The user must manually enter a new line using the Enter key. However, working with such an element can be frustrating for the user, so you can set text wrapping options with the WRAP= parameter of the <TEXTAREA> HTML tag. Besides off, the default setting, you have two additional options:

- virtual: If the WRAP= parameter is set to virtual, the lines wrap on-screen at the end of the textarea object, but a new line is defined only when you actually enter a carriage return.

- physical: If the WRAP= parameter is set to physical, the lines wrap on-screen, but a carriage return is automatically placed at the end of each on-screen line when it is sent to the server.

The Button Objects: Submit, Reset, and Button

Because graphical operating environments have become dominant over the past decade, the pushbutton is perhaps the most ubiquitous of all user interface components. HTML has three types of buttons you can use in your forms: button, submit, and reset. As you can see, two are specialized forms of the more generic button object. Using conventional HTML syntax, a button is defined as

```
<INPUT
   TYPE="button¦submit¦reset"
   [NAME="objectName"]
   [VALUE="labelText"]
   [onClick="methodName"]>
```

The three button types have different purposes:

- The submit button submits the form in which it is contained to the server, based on the parameters of the form. No JavaScript code is needed to perform this action, because its behavior is built into the object itself.

- The reset button clears the values in the fields of the current form, restoring any default values that might have been set. As with the submit button, no JavaScript code is used for this.

- The button object is a generic object with no predefined behavior built into it. In order for this object to do anything, you need to add an onClick event handler to the button.

If you're new to HTML, you might be wondering about the reasons for the submit and reset buttons, because you could use a button object to perform these same tasks. These originated before the days of JavaScript, when you couldn't use a generic button because you had no way to make it do anything. Additionally, although not all browsers support JavaScript (and thus the button object), all modern browsers do support the reset and submit buttons. For compatibility reasons, it's usually best to use the submit and reset buttons unless JavaScript support is a requirement for accessing your page. In that case, it wouldn't matter.

> **NOTE**
>
> For more information on the onClick event for the button type objects, see Chapter 10.

Listing 13.6 shows an example of how you can use all three buttons. As you would expect, the submit and reset buttons are used to submit or clear the form, although their VALUE= parameters were changed to reflect a more user-friendly verbiage. The button object is used to display a Help window that tells users how to fill out the registration form.

Additionally, in the Help window that is generated by the showHelp() method, a button object is defined using the document's write() method. Let me point out two things about this

13

FORM OBJECTS

button. First, to center the button on the page, I used the <DIV ALIGN=> tag. Second, to add a little "beef" to the width of the button, I added a few blank spaces before and after the OK in the VALUE= parameter. Figure 13.5 shows the form that is generated by the HTML.

Listing 13.6. buttons.htm.

```
<html>
<head>
<title>Online Registration</title>

<SCRIPT LANGUAGE="JavaScript">

      function showHelp() {

            helpWin = window.open("", "Help", "height=200,width=400")
            helpWin.document.write("<body><h2>Help on Registration</h2>")
            helpWin.document.write("1. Please enter your product
               information into the fields.<p>")
            helpWin.document.write("2. Press the Register button
               to submit your form.<p>")
            helpWin.document.write("3. Press the Clear button to clear the
               form and start again.<p>")
            helpWin.document.write("<p>")
            helpWin.document.write("<form><DIV ALIGN='CENTER'>")

            helpWin.document.write("<input type=button value='  OK  '
               onClick='window.close()'>")
            helpWin.document.write("</DIV></form></body>")

      }

</SCRIPT>

</head>

<body>
<h1>Online Registration</h1>
<form method="POST">
<p>Please provide the following product information:</p>
<blockquote>
<pre><em>    Product name </em><input type=text size=25 maxlength=256
name="ProductName">
<em>           Model </em><input type=text size=25 maxlength=256
name="Product_Model">
<em>  Version number </em><input type=text size=25 maxlength=256
name="Product_VersionNumber">
<em>Operating system </em><input type=text size=25 maxlength=256
name="Product_OperatingSystem">
<em>   Serial number </em><input type=text size=25 maxlength=256
name="Product_SerialNumber">
</pre>
</blockquote>
<p><input type=submit value="Register"> <input type=reset value="Clear">
<input type=button value="Help" onClick="showHelp()"></p>
</form>
</body>
</html>
```

FIGURE 13.5.

The button (OK), reset (Clear), and submit (Register) buttons are used in this application.

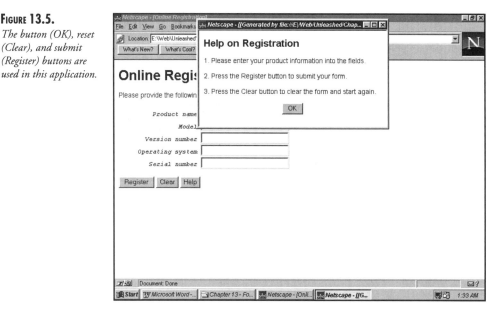

The Checkbox Object

The checkbox object is the form object that is best equipped to denote logical (true or false) data. It acts as a toggle switch that can be turned on or off either by the user or by your JavaScript code. To define a checkbox, use the following HTML syntax:

```
<INPUT
    TYPE="checkbox"
    [NAME="objectName"]
    [VALUE="value"]
    [CHECKED]
    [onClick="methodName"]>
    [displayText]
```

For example, the following checkbox lets users specify their foreign-language proficiencies:

```
<input type=checkbox name="language">I speak multiple languages.
```

Following user interface conventions, a checkbox shouldn't usually cause a "processing action" to be performed (à la button objects). As a result, you probably won't use its onClick event handler extensively. However, the exceptions to this rule include changing the state of other objects on the form.

NOTE

For more information on the onClick event for the checkbox object, see Chapter 10.

13

FORM OBJECTS

Determining Whether a Checkbox Object Is Checked

Perhaps the most important property of the checkbox object is its checked property. You can evaluate this property to determine whether the user has checked a checkbox. You shouldn't use the value property to test a checkbox object, as clarified in the following caution.

> **CAUTION**
>
> The value property can be misleading at first. Unlike some environments, the value property is static and doesn't change in response to the checkbox's change of state. Therefore, don't check the value property to determine whether a checkbox is checked.

To illustrate, I'll build on an example I used in the discussion of text objects earlier in this chapter. As you'll recall, one of the examples automatically highlighted the entire content of a text object by calling the text object's select() method. Suppose you wanted to give users the option of having the text selected or not. You could use a checkbox to achieve this result. Listing 13.7 shows this code. Figure 13.6 shows the resulting form.

Listing 13.7. checkboxSelect.htm.

```
<html>
<head>
<title>Online Registration</title>
<SCRIPT LANGUAGE="JavaScript">

    function selectText(currentObject) {
        if (document.form1.selectBox.checked) {
            currentObject.select()
        }
    }

</SCRIPT>
</head>

<body>
<form name="form1" method="POST">
<h2>Online Registration</h2>
<p>Username:<br>
<input type=text size=25 maxlength=256 name="Username"
onFocus="selectText(this)"><br>
Browser used:<br>
<input type=text size=25 maxlength=256 name="Browser"
onFocus="selectText(this)"><br>
Email address:<strong> <br>
</strong><input type=text size=25 maxlength=256 name="EmailAddress"
onFocus="selectText(this)"></p>
<h2><input type=submit value="Register"> <input type=reset value="Clear"></h2>
<p><input type=checkbox name="selectBox">Activate field selection.
</form>
</body>
</html>
```

FIGURE 13.6.

Using a checkbox.

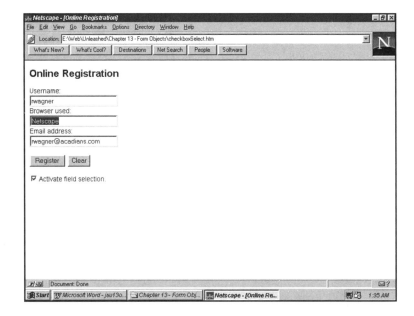

> **NOTE**
>
> The example shown in Listing 13.7 is useful in demonstrating how to evaluate the checked property during a process. However, it should be noted that this code doesn't necessarily work as you would expect. Once the checkbox is checked, text is highlighted from that point on, regardless of whether you uncheck the checkbox. This is because once a `select()` method is called for a text object, the highlighted state remains in effect until the page is reloaded.
>
> Interestingly, if you reload the page using Netscape Navigator's Reload toolbar command, it works fine thereafter without erasing the contents of the form. If you try to use Netscape Navigator 3.0's `reload()` method, your existing values are cleared.

The Radio Object

You use the radio object to let a user select a single option from a group of options. If one option within a set is selected, no others can be selected at the same time. The act of clicking a radio button deselects any other radio button that was selected.

The radio object is different from the other form objects you have worked with. Whereas other form objects have a one-to-one correspondence with an HTML tag, a radio object has a one-to-many relationship with a set of `<INPUT type="radio">` elements within the HTML source code. Each element of a radio object is defined like this:

```
<INPUT
   TYPE="radio"
   [NAME="groupName"]
   [VALUE="value"]
   [CHECKED]
   [onClick="methodName"]>
   [displayText]
```

You don't group each of these elements as you do with the items in a select object (discussed later in this chapter). The way they are grouped is based on the NAME= parameter of the radio buttons. Each element in a radio object must use the same value in that parameter. For example, the following set of radio buttons is treated as a single radio object called `weekdays`:

```
<INPUT TYPE="radio" NAME="weekdays" VALUE="Monday">Monday
<INPUT TYPE="radio" NAME="weekdays" VALUE="Tuesday">Tuesday
<INPUT TYPE="radio" NAME="weekdays" VALUE="Wednesday">Wednesday
<INPUT TYPE="radio" NAME="weekdays" VALUE="Thursday">Thursday
<INPUT TYPE="radio" NAME="weekdays" VALUE="Friday">Friday
<INPUT TYPE="radio" NAME="weekdays" VALUE="Saturday">Saturday
<INPUT TYPE="radio" NAME="weekdays" VALUE="Sunday">Sunday
```

> **NOTE**
>
> For more information on the `onClick` event for the radio button, see Chapter 10.

Determining the Value of the Selected Radio Button

One of the most common programming needs you will have when using a radio object is retrieving the value of the currently selected radio button. To do so, you must determine which of the radio buttons is selected and then return its value. Rather than custom coding each time you need this routine, you could more easily use a generic function I call `getRadioValue()`, which returns the value of the radio object used as the method's parameter.

Look at the code shown in Listing 13.8. The `songs` radio object lists a set of three songs. The Show Selected button object displays the currently selected object by calling the `getRadioValue()` method using the `songs` object as the function's parameter. The `getRadioValue()` method performs a `for` loop to analyze which of the radio buttons is checked (selected). It uses the `length` property of the radio object to determine the number of iterations. When the `for` loop encounters the checked value, it assigns the variable the value of the radio button, breaks the loop, and then returns the value to the button event handler.

Listing 13.8. radio.htm.

```
<HTML>
<HEAD>
<SCRIPT LANGUAGE = "JavaScript">
    function getRadioValue(radioObject) {
        var value = null
        for (var i=0; i<radioObject.length; i++) {
            if (radioObject[i].checked) {
                value = radioObject[i].value
                break }
        }
        return value
    }
</SCRIPT>
</HEAD>
<BODY>
<FORM name="form1">
<p><input type=radio name="songs" value="Liquid">Liquid</p>
<p><input type=radio name="songs" value="Flood">Flood</p>
<p><input type=radio name="songs" value="World's Apart">World's Apart</p>
<input type=button value="Show Selected"
onClick="alert(getRadioValue(this.form.songs))">
</FORM>
</BODY>
</HTML>
```

Figure 13.7 shows the result of clicking the Show Selected button.

FIGURE 13.7.

Determining the value of the radio object.

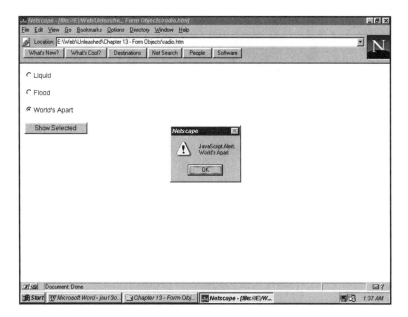

13

FORM OBJECTS

> **NOTE**
>
> Listings 13.12 and 13.13, which you'll see later in this chapter, show how to check a radio button automatically.

The Select Object

The select object is one of the most useful and flexible of all the form objects. You can use it in instances where you might otherwise use a radio object. The select object can take up less real estate than a radio object, which needs space for each of its radio buttons. Here is the basic HTML syntax for a select object:

```
<SELECT
    [NAME="objectName"]
    [SIZE="numberVisible"]
    [MULTIPLE]
    [onBlur="methodName"]
    [onChange="methodName"]
    [onFocus="methodName"]>
    <OPTION VALUE="optionValue" [SELECTED]>displayText</OPTION>
    [<OPTION VALUE="optionValue">displayText</OPTION>]
</SELECT>
```

The select object is flexible and can take three different forms: a selection list, a scrolling list, and a multiselection scrolling list.

> **NOTE**
>
> For more information on select object events, see Chapter 10.

Creating a Selection List

A selection list is a drop-down list of options in which the user can select a single item from the list. A selection list usually displays a single value at a time, as shown in Figure 13.8, but it expands to show a list when the user clicks its arrow, as shown in Figure 13.9. Unlike combo boxes in the Windows world, you can't enter a value in the box; you can only select from an existing array of values.

FIGURE 13.8.

A selection list in its normal state.

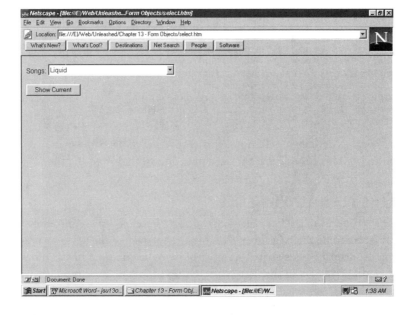

FIGURE 13.9.

A selection list in an expanded state.

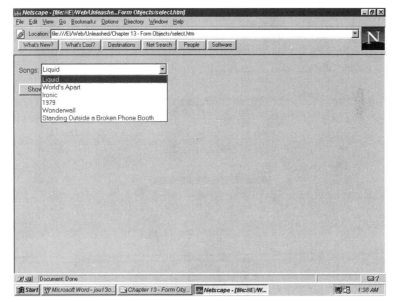

13

FORM OBJECTS

The selection list shown in Figures 13.8 and 13.9 can be defined like this:

```
<select NAME="songs" SIZE=1>
<option VALUE="Liquid">Liquid</option>
<option VALUE="World's Apart">World's Apart</option>
<option VALUE="Ironic">Ironic</option>
<option VALUE="1979">1979</option>
<option VALUE="Wonderwall">Wonderwall</option>
<option VALUE="Standing Outside a Broken Phone Booth">
Standing Outside a Broken Phone Booth</option>
```

The key to defining a selection list is to give the SIZE= parameter a value of 1 (or leave it out entirely). This ensures that the list shows only a single line at a time.

Creating a Scrolling List

The second form a select object can take is a scrolling list—commonly known in many operating environments as a *list box*. Rather than retract all the items in a drop-down list, a scrolling list displays a designated number of items at one time in a list format. The scrolling list includes scrollbars so the user can scroll up or down to see more than what fits in the space provided.

To define a scrolling list, the only change you make to the HTML <select> definition is in the SIZE= parameter. Making this value greater than 1 transforms the select object into a scrolling list. For example, when you change the SIZE= parameter of the previously defined songs object from 1 to 5, the list takes on a new look, as shown in Figure 13.10. As with the selection list, a scrolling list lets you select a single value from the list.

FIGURE 13.10.

A scrolling list.

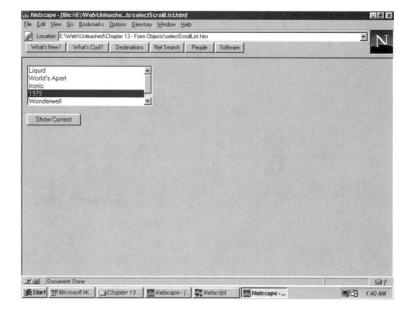

Creating a Multiselection List

The final form a select object can take is a multiselection list. It looks the same as a normal scrolling list but has different behavior. You can select one or more items from this type of select object. The task of selecting multiple items depends on the operating environment. In most cases, you can either drag the mouse across multiple contiguous items or hold the Shift or Ctrl key while you click an item.

To define a multiselection list, you simply add the MULTIPLE parameter to the select object definition:

```
<select NAME="songs" SIZE=5 MULTIPLE>
<option VALUE="Liquid">Liquid</option>
<option VALUE="World's Apart">World's Apart</option>
<option VALUE="Ironic">Ironic</option>
<option VALUE="1979">1979</option>
<option VALUE="Wonderwall">Wonderwall</option>
<option VALUE="Standing Outside a Broken Phone Booth">
Standing Outside a Broken Phone Booth</option>
```

Determining the Value or Text of the Selected Option

In a selection or scrolling list, you can determine the value of the selected option by using a combination of the options and selectedIndex properties of the select object. For example, if I wanted to determine the song that was selected in our songs object example, I could use the following:

```
favorite = document.form1.songs.options[document.form1.songs.selectedIndex].
   value
```

The options property is an array containing each option defined within a select object. Using this property, you can access the properties of each option. You can use the selectedIndex property to return the index of the selected option. When options and selectedIndex are used in combination, you can return the value of the currently selected option.

With JavaScript's dot notation requirements, trying to retrieve the currently selected value can involve long code lines. You can avoid this by making a generic getSelectValue() method to use instead. Listing 13.9 shows how to define this method. As you can see, the select object is passed as the getSelectValue() method's parameter when the user clicks the Show Current button. The selectObject variable is treated as an object type variable and retrieves the value of the currently selected option. This value is passed back to the button object's event handler and displayed in an alert message box.

Listing 13.9. select.htm.

```
<HTML>
<HEAD>
<SCRIPT LANGUAGE = "JavaScript">
```

continues

Listing 13.9. continued

```
function getSelectValue(selectObject) {
    return selectObject.options[selectObject.selectedIndex].value
}

</SCRIPT>
</HEAD>
<BODY>
<FORM name="form1">
Songs: <select NAME="songs" SIZE=1>
<option VALUE="Liquid">Liquid</option>
<option VALUE="World's Apart">World's Apart</option>
<option VALUE="Ironic">Ironic</option>
<option VALUE="1979">1979</option>
<option VALUE="Wonderwall">Wonderwall</option>
<option VALUE="Standing Outside a Broken Phone Booth">
Standing Outside a Broken Phone Booth</option>
</SELECT><p>
<input type=button value="Show Current"
onClick="alert(getSelectValue(this.form.songs))">
</FORM>
</BODY>
</HTML>
```

One important difference between the select and radio objects is that the select object has a `text` property in addition to the `value` property. If the value you want to define is the same as what is being displayed to the user—as in Listing 13.9—you can return the `text` value of the currently selected object rather than the `value` property. If the select object were defined like this:

```
<select NAME="songs" SIZE=1>
<option>Liquid</option>
<option>World's Apart</option>
<option>Ironic</option>
<option>1979</option>
<option>Wonderwall</option>
<option>Standing Outside a Broken Phone Booth</option>
```

you could use the `text` property rather than the `value` property to return the song name:

```
function getSelectValue(selectObject) {
    return selectObject.options[selectObject.selectedIndex].text
}
```

Determining the Values of Multiselection Lists

In lists where a single option is selected at any given time, the `selectedIndex` property efficiently returns information you need from the currently selected option. If you have a multiselection scrolling list, however, `selectedIndex` returns only the first option that is selected, not all of them. When you use multiselection lists, you must use the `selected` property of the options array to determine the status of each option in the list. Listing 13.10 shows an example of this in its showSelection() method. In this function, a for loop iterates through each option in the select object and tests to see whether the selected property is true. If it is, the value of the element's text property is added to the list variable. The results are then presented in a second window, as shown in Figure 13.11.

Listing 13.10. selectMultiple.htm.

```
<HTML>
<HEAD>
<SCRIPT LANGUAGE = "JavaScript">

    function showSelection(objectName) {
        var list = ""
        for (var i=0; i<objectName.length; i++) {
            if (objectName.options[i].selected) {
                list += objectName.options[i].text + "<p>"
            }
        }
        selWindow = window.open("", "Selections", "height=200,width=400")
        selWindow.document.write("<h2>You picked the following songs:
            </h2><p><p>")
        selWindow.document.write(list)
    }

</SCRIPT>
</HEAD>
<BODY>
<FORM name="form1">
Pick Your Favorite Songs From the List:<p>
<select NAME="songs" SIZE=5 MULTIPLE>
<option>Fortress Around Your Heart</option>
<option>Breakfast at Tiffany's</option>
<option>Flood</option>
<option>The Chess Game</option>
<option>Liquid</option>
<option>World's Apart</option>
<option>Ironic</option>
<option>1979</option>
<option>Wonderwall</option>
<option>Standing Outside a Broken Phone Booth</option>
</SELECT><p>
<input type=button value="Show Selection"
onClick="showSelection(this.form.songs)">
</FORM>
</BODY>
</HTML>
```

13

FORM OBJECTS

FIGURE **13.11.**

Displaying multiple selections.

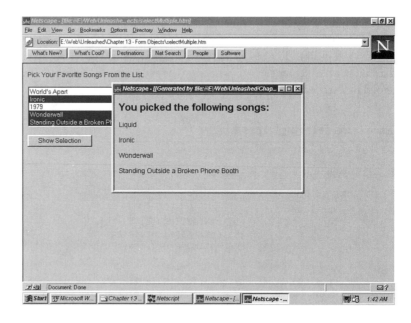

Selecting an Option Using JavaScript

You can select an option programmatically by setting the `selected` property of a select object's options array. Suppose you have a Favorite Band field and a list of songs. If the value of the Favorite Band field is Oasis, you want to locate a song written by that group in the Songs field. Listing 13.11 shows this example.

Listing 13.11. selectSelected.htm.

```
<HTML>
<HEAD>
<SCRIPT LANGUAGE = "JavaScript">

    function quickSelect() {
        var bnd = document.form1.band.value
        bnd = bnd.toUpperCase()
        if (bnd == "OASIS") {
            document.form1.songs[4].selected = "1"
        }
    }

</SCRIPT>
</HEAD>
<BODY>
<FORM name="form1">
Favorite Band: <input type=text name="band" size=20 onBlur="quickSelect()"><p>
Songs: <select NAME="songs" SIZE=1>
<option VALUE="Liquid">Liquid</option>
<option VALUE="World's Apart">World's Apart</option>
<option VALUE="Ironic">Ironic</option>
```

```
<option VALUE="1979">1979</option>
<option VALUE="Wonderwall">Wonderwall</option>
<option VALUE="Standing Outside a Broken Phone Booth">
Standing Outside a Broken Phone Booth</option>
</SELECT><p>
<input type=button value="Show Current" onClick="quickSelect()">
</FORM>
</BODY>
</HTML>
```

The Password Object

As you can tell from its name, the password object has but a single purpose: to capture a password value from a user. A password object is similar to a text object but displays any character the user types in the field as an asterisk (*). It can be defined in HTML syntax like this:

```
<INPUT
    TYPE="password"
    [NAME="objectName"]
    [VALUE="defaultPassword"]
    [SIZE=integer]>
```

The following line shows an example:

```
<INPUT TYPE="password" NAME="passwordField" SIZE=15>
```

JavaScript has little control over the password object. For example, you can't retrieve the value of the text entered by the user to evaluate it; you can only retrieve default text that has been defined using the VALUE= parameter of the <INPUT type=password> tag. Part of the reason JavaScript can't access this is that JavaScript code is currently embedded into the HTML document so that the user can access it. As JavaScript matures, it might get more control over this form object.

The Hidden Object

As one might infer from its name, the hidden object is invisible to the user. The hidden object is a hidden text field that you can use to store values that you don't want to present to the user with a normal text field. You can then pass this information to the server for processing. You can define a hidden object in HTML using the following syntax:

```
<INPUT
    TYPE="hidden"
    NAME="objectName"
    [VALUE="value"]>
```

The following line shows an example:

```
<INPUT TYPE="hidden" NAME="hiddenField1">
```

In a pure HTML world, hidden fields played an important role in holding specific bits of information on the user side that the server could use later. With the advent of JavaScript, the hidden object makes less sense to use in combination with JavaScript. The reason is that a JavaScript global variable serves the same purpose as the hidden object, and it's much easier to manipulate.

The following two examples demonstrate this. Figure 13.12 shows a set of radio buttons the user can click. However, you want to add code to the Undo Last button so that the user can undo the last selection he made. You can't use a reset button for this, because that will either clear the radio buttons or return the default value. Instead, you need to add JavaScript code to perform this task. The code shown in Listings 13.12 and 13.13 are charged with performing this task. Listing 13.12 uses a set of hidden fields to carry this out, whereas Listing 13.13 uses global variables. Keep in mind that neither of these methods is incorrect; both are valid techniques.

Figure 13.12.

Storing the last value using a hidden object.

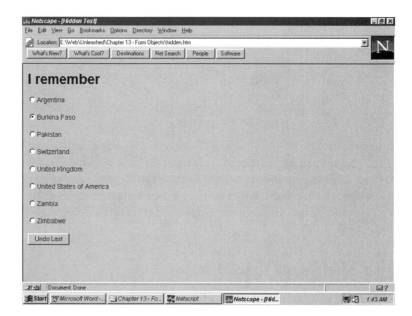

Listing 13.12. `hidden.htm`.

```
<html>
<head>
<title>Hidden Test</title>
<SCRIPT LANGUAGE="JavaScript">

    function postData(value) {
        document.form1.holder2.value = document.form1.holder.value
        document.form1.holder.value = value
    }

    function resetValue() {
```

```
            var len = document.form1.ctyList.length
            for (var i=0; i<len; i++) {
                if (document.form1.ctyList[i].value ==
                    document.form1.holder2.value) {
                        document.form1.ctyList[i].checked = "1"
                        break }
            }
        }

</SCRIPT>
</head>

<body>
<h1>I remember</h1>
<form name="form1" method="POST">
<p><input type=radio name="ctyList" value="Argentina"
onClick="postData(this.value)">Argentina</p>
<p><input type=radio name="ctyList" value="Burkina Faso"
onClick="postData(this.value)">Burkina Faso</p>
<p><input type=radio name="ctyList" value="Pakistan"
onClick="postData(this.value)">Pakistan</p>
<p><input type=radio name="ctyList" value="Switzerland"
onClick="postData(this.value)">Switzerland</p>
<p><input type=radio name="ctyList" value="United Kingdom"
onClick="postData(this.value)">United Kingdom</p>
<p><input type=radio name="ctyList" value="United States of America"
onClick="postData(this.value)">United States of America</p>
<p><input type=radio name="ctyList" value="Zambia"
onClick="postData(this.value)">Zambia</p>
<p><input type=radio name="ctyList" value="Zimbabwe"
onClick="postData(this.value)">Zimbabwe</p>
<p><input type=button name="UndoLast" value="Undo Last"
onClick="resetValue()"></p>
<INPUT TYPE="hidden" NAME="holder" value="">
<INPUT TYPE="hidden" NAME="holder2" value="">
</form>
</body>
</html>
```

13

FORM OBJECTS

In this first example, each time the user clicks a radio button, the postData() method places the current radio button value in the hidden object called holder and the current holder value into the holder2 object. This value is then retrieved when the user clicks the Undo Last button and the appropriate radio button is selected.

Listing 13.13. hiddenVars.htm.

```
<html>
<head>
<title>Hidden Var Test</title>
<SCRIPT LANGUAGE="JavaScript">

    var holder = ""
    var holder2 = ""
```

continues

Listing 13.13. continued

```
function postData(value) {
    holder2 = holder
    holder = value
}

function resetValue() {
    var len = document.form1.ctyList.length
    for (var i=0; i<len; i++) {
        if (document.form1.ctyList[i].value == holder2) {
            document.form1.ctyList[i].checked = "1"
            break }
    }
}
</SCRIPT>
</head>

<body>
<h1>I remember</h1>
<form name="form1" method="POST">
<p><input type=radio name="ctyList" value="Argentina"
onClick="postData(this.value)">Argentina</p>
<p><input type=radio name="ctyList" value="Burkina Faso"
onClick="postData(this.value)">Burkina Faso</p>
<p><input type=radio name="ctyList" value="Pakistan"
onClick="postData(this.value)">Pakistan</p>
<p><input type=radio name="ctyList" value="Switzerland"
onClick="postData(this.value)">Switzerland</p>
<p><input type=radio name="ctyList" value="United Kingdom"
onClick="postData(this.value)">United Kingdom</p>
<p><input type=radio name="ctyList" value="United States of America"
onClick="postData(this.value)">United States of America</p>
<p><input type=radio name="ctyList" value="Zambia"
onClick="postData(this.value)">Zambia</p>
<p><input type=radio name="ctyList" value="Zimbabwe"
onClick="postData(this.value)">Zimbabwe</p>
<p><input type=button name="UndoLast" value="Undo Last"
onClick="resetValue()"></p>
</form>
</body>
</html>
```

In this second example, the `holder` and `holder2` variables are defined globally at the start of the script. This script uses these variables in place of the hidden object references of the first example.

Summary

Forms play an important role in JavaScript. Not only can you qualify and sharpen data before it's sent to the server for processing, but you can also use HTML forms to create client-side applications using JavaScript. In this chapter, you learned about form objects and the various objects that can exist only inside its borders. You also learned how to submit forms to the server and how to work with and check the values of input controls before data is sent on.

This chapter finished the in-depth discussion of the browser-related objects. Chapter 14, "Built-In Language Objects," looks at the other side of the object model.

Built-In Language Objects

IN THIS CHAPTER

CHAPTER 14

You could be justified in calling the Navigator-based objects the heart of JavaScript, but an important part of developing sophisticated JavaScript applications comes in working with its built-in language objects. In this chapter, I'll look in-depth at the String, Array, Date, Math, Boolean, Number, and Function objects. These object types are maturing in later versions of Netscape Navigator. Part of the discussion in this chapter explores the differences that exist in working with these objects in JavaScript 1.1 (and higher) and in JavaScript 1.0.

> **NOTE**
>
> The objects you will be working with in this chapter—String, Array, Date, Math, Boolean, Number, and Function—should all be capitalized when you are referring to their object types. Interestingly, this distinction is the opposite of the Navigator objects in the preceding chapters, all of which were lowercase.

The String Object

Strings are a fundamental part of any programming language. A string, which is a set of alphanumeric characters, can be either a *literal* string, such as `"Push the envelope"`, or a variable representing a string, such as `thePhrase`. You learned about strings as data types in Chapter 5, "Fundamentals of the JavaScript Language," but a string can also be treated as an object, complete with its own suite of methods and properties.

Creating a String Object

As JavaScript has matured, strings have gained more power. JavaScript 1.0 doesn't treat strings as true objects, but JavaScript 1.1 and higher does. For example, if you were creating a string and checking its length in JavaScript 1.0, you would use the following code:

```
<SCRIPT LANGUAGE = "JavaScript">

    var str = "My name is Richard"
    alert(str.length)

</SCRIPT>
```

However, in JavaScript 1.1 and higher, you could use the new operator just like another object:

```
<SCRIPT LANGUAGE = "JavaScript">

    var str = new String("My name is Richard")
    alert(str.length)

</SCRIPT>
```

If you try this using a browser that doesn't support the String object definition, you get a `String is not defined` error.

You might be wondering at this point what is the purpose of explicitly declaring a String object. Its major benefit is that the String objects can be accessed from other frames in a manner that is easier and more reliable than in JavaScript 1.0. For example, if you wanted to access a variable called `custName` from the parent window, you would use the following:

```
var customer = new String()
customer = parent.custName
```

In JavaScript 1.0, you had to add an empty string to the end of the expression to use it successfully:

```
var customer = parent.custName + ""
```

Working with Strings

Because strings are one of the primary types of data you must work with, it is critical to have ways to extract data from strings and obtain information about strings. JavaScript has the properties and methods shown in Table 14.1 to allow you to handle strings.

Table 14.1. String-handling methods and properties.

Method/Property	Description	Example
`length`	Returns an integer representing the size of the string.	`"Declare".length` returns a value of 7.
`charAt(pos)`	Returns the character at the specified index.	`"Light".charAt(0)` returns a value of `"L"`.
`indexOf(searchText [, startPos])`	Returns the index of the first occurrence of `searchText`.	`"Manners".indexOf("er")` returns a value of 4.
`lastIndexOf (searchText [, endPos])`	Returns the index of the last occurrence of `searchText`.	`"Manners".indexOf("n")` returns a value of 3.
`substring(startPos, endPos)`	Returns the substring of the string starting at `startPos` and ending at `endPos`.	`"Yahoos".substring(0,2)` returns a value of `"Yah"`.

Determining String Lengths

You can use the String object's `length` property to determine the size of a string. For example, the following code returns 17:

```
"Crazy Legs Nelson".length
```

The following code returns 16:

```
var str = "This is the day."
len = str.length
```

Searching Within Strings

You can search for text within strings by using `indexOf()` and `lastIndexOf()`. Use these methods when you want to search for a particular character or substring within a string and return the position (or index) of the occurrence within the string. Whereas `indexOf()` starts at the left of the string and moves right, `lastIndexOf()` performs the same operation but starts at the left. Both `indexOf()` and `lastIndexOf()` start at the 0 position for the first character encountered, and both return a value of -1 if the search text isn't found. For example, the following code returns a value of 3:

```
"Time and time again".indexOf("e")
```

On the other hand, the following code returns a value of 12:

```
"Time and time again".lastIndexOf("e")
```

Both methods have an optional second parameter that allows you to specify where in the string you want to start the search. For example, the script shown in Listing 14.1 searches through the variable `graf` and counts the number of occurrences of the letter e.

Listing 14.1. indexOf.htm.

```
<SCRIPT LANGUAGE = "JavaScript">

    pos = 0
    num = -1
    i = -1

    var graf = "While nearly everyone agrees on the principle of reuse,
                the priority we give it varies wildly."

    while (pos != -1) {
        pos = graf.indexOf("e",i+1)
        num += 1
        i = pos
    }

    document.write(graf)
    document.write("<p><p>")
    document.write("There were " + num + " e's in that paragraph.")

</SCRIPT>
```

Figure 14.1 shows the result of the script.

FIGURE 14.1.

The results of the
indexOf() *example.*

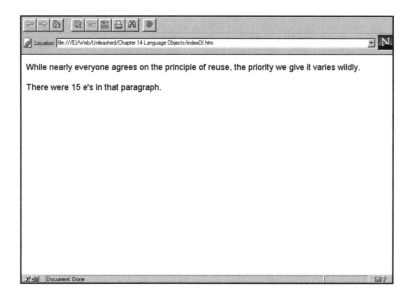

Location: file:///E|/Web/Unleashed/Chapter 14 Language Objects/indexOf.htm

While nearly everyone agrees on the principle of reuse, the priority we give it varies wildly.

There were 15 e's in that paragraph.

Document: Done

Retrieving a Portion of a String

You can retrieve a portion of a string variable or literal by using the substring() method. It has two parameters—the start position and the end position of the substring you want to return. Just like indexOf() and lastIndexOf(), this method is also zero-based, such that the first position of the string begins at 0. For example, the following code returns New:

```
"New England".substring(0,3)
```

If you want to retrieve a single character, you can use charAt(). The charAt() method returns the character at the position you specify as a parameter. For example, the following code returns a value of v:

```
"Denver Broncos".charAt(3)
```

If you specify a position that is out of the string's range, a value of -1 is returned:

```
"007".charAt(20102)
```

Replacing String Utility Code

The true power of these string-handling routines is demonstrated when you combine them to solve a problem. For an illustration of this, consider a common routine that you could want in JavaScript: a generic routine to replace specified text within a string with something else. To do this, develop a generic string-replace function that uses the length property, indexOf(), and substring(). Additionally, I will demonstrate both procedural and object-oriented approaches to solving this problem.

Using a traditional procedural approach, you could develop a `stringReplace()` function that has three parameters:

- `originalString`: The original string upon which you want to perform the replacement.
- `findText`: The string that you want to be replaced.
- `replaceText`: The string that you want to insert into the `originalString`.

The function then uses that information to perform the replacement process. You can see that Listing 14.2 uses the `indexOf()` method to look for the `findText` parameter, and the `substring()` method pulls out the strings that are before and after `findText`. The function then concatenates the `preString`, `replaceText`, and `postString` and assigns the result to the `originalString` variable. This process occurs for each occurrence of `findText` throughout the string. When `findText` is no longer found, the `originalString` value is returned to the user.

Listing 14.2. `stringReplace.htm`.

```
Replace code with the following:
<SCRIPT LANGUAGE = "JavaScript">

    function stringReplace(originalString, findText, replaceText) {
        var pos = 0
        var len = findText.length
        pos = originalString.indexOf(findText)
        while (pos != -1) {
            preString = originalString.substring(0, pos)
            postString = originalString.substring(pos+len,
            ➥originalString.length)
            originalString = preString + replaceText + postString
            pos = originalString.indexOf(findText)
        }
        return originalString
    }


    document.write(stringReplace("Richard", "ard", "ini"))


</SCRIPT>
<SCRIPT LANGUAGE = "JavaScript">

    function stringReplace(originalString, findText, replaceText) {
        var pos = 0
        pos = originalString.indexOf(findText)
        while (pos != -1) {
            preString = originalString.substring(0, pos)
            postString = originalString.substring(pos+1,
             originalString.length)
            originalString = preString + replaceText + postString
            pos = originalString.indexOf(findText)
        }
        return originalString
    }
</SCRIPT>
```

An alternative way to code this same function is to take advantage of JavaScript 1.1's object prototype capabilities and add a `replace()` method to the String object type. You can restructure the `stringReplace()` code to work within the object framework, the result of which is shown in Listing 14.3.

Listing 14.3. stringOOReplace.htm.

```
<SCRIPT LANGUAGE = "JavaScript">

     String.prototype.replace = stringReplace
          function stringReplace(findText, replaceText) {
var originalString = new String(this)
               var pos = 0
               pos = originalString.indexOf(findText)
               while (pos != -1) {
                    preString = originalString.substring(0, pos)
                    postString = originalString.substring(pos+len,
                       originalString.length)
                    originalString = preString + replaceText + postString
                    pos = originalString.indexOf(findText)
               }
               return originalString
          }

</SCRIPT>
```

To put the `replace()` method into action, you can create a String object, assign a value to it, and then use the newly created method to replace all occurrences of 1s with 2s:

```
var myVar = new String("")
myVar = "11111111111111"
myVar = myVar.replace("1", "2")
document.write(myVar)
```

Formatting Strings

JavaScript has several methods you can use to format strings. Most of these methods are simply equivalents of HTML formatting tags. Using the formatting methods gives you an object-oriented way of dealing with HTML formatting tags, and it's also easier than continuously concatenating HTML tags to strings. In other words, if you have a string literal `This is the day` and you want to add bold formatting to it, you could do so using one of two means. First, you could add HTML formatting tags:

```
"<B>" + "This is the day" + "</B>"
```

Second, you could use the String object method `bold()` to add the formatting:

```
"This is the day".bold()
```

When you use this string, the following HTML text is returned:

```
"<B>This is the day</B>"
```

If you have a string variable called dayVar that contains the "This is the day" text, you could use the same two options:

```
dayVar = "This is the day"
"<B>" + dayVar + "</B>"
```

The preceding code accomplishes the same thing as the following:

```
dayVar = "This is the day"
dayVar.bold()
```

NOTE

Keep in mind the context in which you can use the formatting methods. You can't use them outside a JavaScript script as a substitute for HTML formatting tags.

Table 14.2 lists each of the String object formatting methods.

Table 14.2. String object formatting methods.

String Method	Example	HTML Code Returned
anchor("*anchorName*")	"Section 3".anchor ("Section3")	\<A NAME="Section3">Section 3\</A>
big()	"Just save the name".big()	\<BIG>Just save the name\</BIG>
blink()	"Why ask why".blink()	\<BLINK>Why ask why\</BLINK>
bold()	"Live and learn".bold()	\<B>Live and learn\</B>
fixed()	"JavaScript code".fixed()	\<TT>JavaScript code\</TT>
fontcolor("*color*")	"Acadia Software". fontcolor("green")	\<FONT COLOR="green">Acadia Software\</FONT>
fontsize(*size*)	"Impact".fontsize(3)	\<FONT SIZE="3">Impact\</FONT>
italics()	"JavaScript Unleashed".italics()	\<I>JavaScript Unleashed\</I>
link("*URL*")	"See My Home Page".link ("http://www.myhomepage. com/")	\<A HREF="http://www. myhomepage.com/">See My Home Page\</A>
small()	"Tiny Tim".small()	\<SMALL>Tiny Tim\</SMALL>
strike()	"Game Canceled" strike()	\<STRIKE>Game Canceled\</STRIKE>

String Method	Example	HTML Code Returned
sub()	"Submarines".sub()	_{Submarines}
sup()	"Superman".sup()	^{Superman}
toLowerCase()	"See SPOT rUN". toLowerCase()	see spot run
toUpperCase()	"let's go to the BEACH".toUpperCase()	LET'S GO TO THE BEACH

Basic Formatting Methods

To demonstrate how the basic formatting methods are used in JavaScript, look at a sample JavaScript page that lets you format a user-defined string based on the options set using an HTML form. Figure 14.2 shows the form.

FIGURE 14.2.
A String object formatting page.

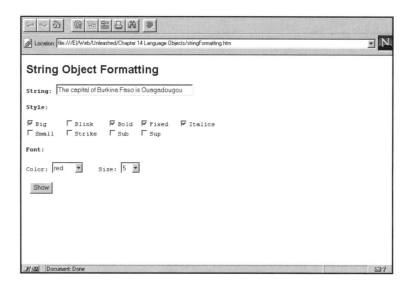

Looking at the code behind the form, you see a single JavaScript method called showWindow() that is called when the Show button is clicked. The method assigns the value of the form's text field to a string variable called txt:

```
var txt = document.form1.stringField.value
```

Each of the formatting options shown as checkboxes in Figure 14.2 is either true or false. The following code checks to see if each of the boxes is checked. If so, it calls the appropriate formatting method for the txt variable:

```
if (document.form1.bigBox.checked) {
    txt = txt.big()}

if (document.form1.blinkBox.checked) {
    txt = txt.blink() }

if (document.form1.boldBox.checked) {
    txt = txt.bold() }

if (document.form1.fixedBox.checked) {
    txt = txt.fixed()}

if (document.form1.italicsBox.checked) {
    txt = txt.italics()}

if (document.form1.smallBox.checked) {
    txt = txt.small()}

if (document.form1.strikeBox.checked) {
    txt = txt.strike()}

if (document.form1.subBox.checked) {
    txt = txt.sub()}

if (document.form1.supBox.checked) {
    txt = txt.sup()}
```

None of these formatting options are mutually exclusive—although some might cancel each other out. As a result, you can use as many of the methods at the same time as you want. JavaScript simply processes each of the methods, adding the appropriate HTML tags in sequential order.

The font color and size settings aren't simply logical settings, so they require a parameter to be set. The select boxes on the form are used to specify these settings. The following code grabs this information from the form objects and calls the fontcolor() and fontsize() methods (clr and sze variables are used to make the code easier to read):

```
clr = document.form1.colorList.options[document.form1.
    colorList.options.selectedIndex].text
txt = txt.fontcolor(clr)
sze = document.form1.sizeList.options[document.form1.
    sizeList.options.selectedIndex].text
txt = txt.fontsize(sze)
```

Finally, the txt variable is used in a document.write() method on a new window that is created. Based on the settings shown in Figure 14.2, the txt variable returns the following value:

```
<FONT SIZE="5"><FONT COLOR="red"><I><TT><B><BIG>The capital
of Burkina Faso is Ouagadougou</BIG></B></TT></I></FONT></FONT>
```

Because the code uses multiple tags, JavaScript places each successive tag outside of all previous ones. As a result, the <BIG> tags are the innermost tags in the formatting definition because the big() method is the first one that was called. The tags of the last method called —fontsize()— are on the outside.

Figure 14.3 shows the result window based on the settings shown in Figure 14.2.

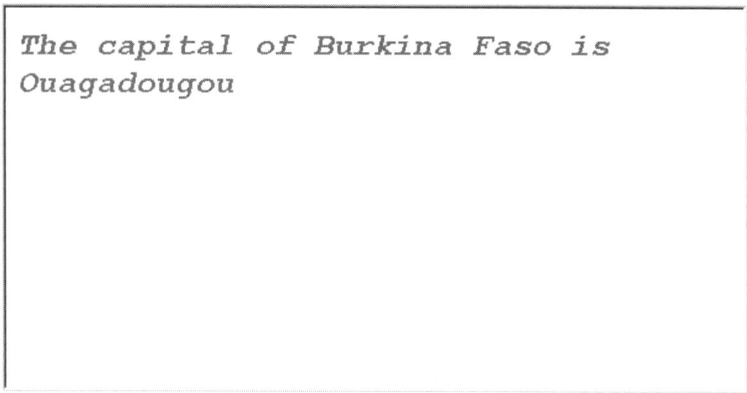

FIGURE 14.3.
The results of the string formatting options.

The capital of Burkina Faso is
Ouagadougou

Listing 14.4 shows the entire source code for this example.

Listing 14.4. stringFormatting.htm.

```
<html>
<head>
<title>String Object Formatting</title>
</head>
<body>
<SCRIPT LANGUAGE="JavaScript">
<!--

    function showWindow() {
        var txt = document.form1.stringField.value
        var clr = ""
        var sze = ""

        if (document.form1.bigBox.checked) {
            txt = txt.big()
        }

        if (document.form1.blinkBox.checked) {
            txt = txt.blink()
        }

        if (document.form1.boldBox.checked) {
            txt = txt.bold()
        }

        if (document.form1.fixedBox.checked) {
            txt = txt.fixed()
        }

        if (document.form1.italicsBox.checked) {
            txt = txt.italics()
        }
```

continues

14

Listing 14.4. continued

```
            if (document.form1.smallBox.checked) {
                txt = txt.small()
            }

            if (document.form1.strikeBox.checked) {
                txt = txt.strike()
            }

            if (document.form1.subBox.checked) {
                txt = txt.sub()
            }

            if (document.form1.supBox.checked) {
                txt = txt.sup()
            }

            clr = document.form1.colorList.options[document.form1.
                    colorList.options.selectedIndex].text
            txt = txt.fontcolor(clr)
            sze = document.form1.sizeList.options[document.form1.
                    sizeList.options.selectedIndex].text
            txt = txt.fontsize(sze)

            objWindow = window.open("", "","width=600,height=300")
            objWindow.document.write(txt)
            objWindow.document.close()
        }
// -->
</SCRIPT>
<h1>String Object Formatting</h1>
<form method="POST" name="form1">
<pre><strong>String: </strong><input type=text size=40 maxlength=256
name="stringField"></pre>
<pre><strong>Style: </strong></pre>
<pre><input type=checkbox name="bigBox" value="ON">Big      <input
type=checkbox name="blinkBox" value="ON">Blink     <input type=checkbox
name="boldBox" value="ON">Bold   <input type=checkbox name="fixedBox"
value="ON">Fixed    <input type=checkbox name="italicsBox" value="ON">Italics
<input type=checkbox name="smallBox" value="ON">Small    <input type=checkbox
name="strikeBox" value="ON">Strike    <input type=checkbox name="subBox"
value="ON">Sub    <input type=checkbox name="supBox" value="ON">Sup</pre>
<pre><strong>Font: </strong></pre>
<pre>Color: <select name="colorList" size=1>
<option selected>black</option>
<option>green</option>
<option>red</option>
</select>    Size: <select name="sizeList" size=1>
<option selected>1</option>
<option>2</option>
<option>3</option>
<option>4</option>
<option>5</option>
<option>6</option>
<option>7</option>
</select></pre>
```

```
<pre> <input type="button" name="Show" value="Show"
onClick="showWindow()"></pre>
</form>
</body>
</html>
```

Case-Changing Formatting Methods

The `toUpperCase()` and `toLowerCase()` methods work just as you would expect. They are help-ful to use when you need to compare text without concerning yourself with the case of the text. For example, if you want to compare user-entered text with a string literal, it is helpful to use all uppercase or all lowercase when making the evaluation:

```
myVar = document.form1.field1.value
if (myVar.toUpperCase() == "SHAGGY") {
    doMethod() }
```

Hypertext Formatting Methods

You can use the String object's `anchor()` and `link()` methods to create anchor and link ob-jects. These methods make it much easier to work with anchors and links in your code, avoid-ing painful string concatenations of HTML tags. To illustrate, we can use an idea similar to the previous formatting example to work with hypertext formatting. Figure 14.4 shows an HTML form you can use to specify the elements of a hypertext link: text, anchor/link designa-tion, and URL/anchor to associate with the underlined text.

FIGURE 14.4.
String object hypertext formatting.

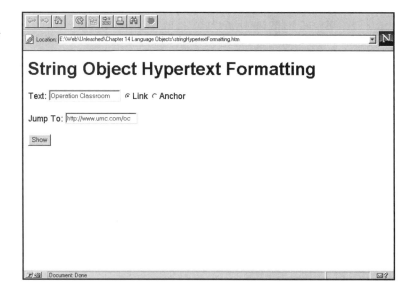

14

BUILT-IN
LANGUAGE
OBJECTS

A similar showWindow() method (triggered by the Show button's onClick event handler) processes the user-entered options and calls either the link() or anchor() method of the txt variable.

```
var txt = document.form1.stringField.value

if (document.form1.hypertext[0].checked) {
      txt = txt.link(document.form1.jumptoField.value) }
else {
 if (document.form1.hypertext[1].checked) {
      txt = txt.anchor(document.form1.jumptoField.value) }
}
```

Figure 14.5 shows the resulting window with a new hypertext link created.

FIGURE 14.5.

A Link object created using the link() *method.*

Listing 14.5 shows the entire source code.

Listing 14.5. stringHypertextFormatting.htm.

```
<title>String Object Hypertext Formatting</title>
</head>
<body>
<SCRIPT LANGUAGE="JavaScript">
<!--

    function showWindow() {
        var txt = document.form1.stringField.value

        if (document.form1.hypertext[0].checked) {
            txt = txt.link(document.form1.jumptoField.value) }
        else {
         if (document.form1.hypertext[1].checked) {
            txt = txt.anchor(document.form1.jumptoField.value) }
        }

        objWindow = window.open("", "","width=600,height=300")
        objWindow.document.write(txt)
        objWindow.document.close()
    }
//-->
</SCRIPT>
<h1>String Object Hypertext Formatting</h1>
<form method="POST" name="form1">
```

```
<p>   Text: <input type=text size=20 maxlength=256 name="stringField"> <input
type=radio name="hypertext" value="Link" checked>Link <input
type=radio name="hypertext" value="Anchor">Anchor </p>
<p>Jump To: <input type=text size=20 maxlength=256 name="jumptoField"></p>
<input type="button" name="Show" value="Show" onClick="showWindow()">
</form>
</body>
</html>
```

Working with Special Characters

When working with strings in any language, you will discover certain characters that are difficult to use. JavaScript lets you work with these special-case characters by using a backslash character (\) followed by the character or its code. Table 14.3 lists the JavaScript inline symbols.

Table 14.3. Inline symbols.

Symbol	Description
\t	Tab
\n	New line
\r	Carriage return
\f	Form feed
\\	Backslash
\b	Backspace
\"	Double quote
\'	Single quote

For example, if you want to use a backslash in a string literal, you use the following method:

```
"Your file is located in C:\\WINDOWS\\TEMP"
```

When displayed, it looks like this:

```
Your file is located in C:\WINDOWS\TEMP
```

> **TIP**
>
> Use the \r inline symbol to add a carriage return to an alert() message box message. Figure 14.6 shows the result of the following example:
>
> ```
> alert("Follow these steps:\r\r1. Choose Print from the File menu.\r2.
>     Click the OK button to print.")
> ```

FIGURE 14.6.

New lines in message boxes.

Because these inline symbols can be confusing to use, you might find it helpful to assign variables to them. In fact, if you use them often, you can pull these defined "constants" from a JavaScript code library and use them over and over. Listing 14.6 shows these inline characters treated as constants and shows how to use them in a `write()` method.

Listing 14.6. `inlineConstants.htm`.

```
<SCRIPT LANGUAGE = "JavaScript">
    // Inline Character Constants
    var TAB = "\t"
    var CR = "\r"
    var LF = "\n"
    var CRLF = "\r\n"
    var FF = "\f"
    var DQUOTE = '\"'
    var SQUOTE = "\'"
    var BACKSLASH = "\\"
    var BACKSPACE = "\b"

    document.write("Column1" + TAB + "Column2" + TAB + "Column3")
</SCRIPT>
```

In addition to these inline symbols, you also have other ways of working with non-alphanumeric values in JavaScript. If you need to convert a non-alphanumeric value to an ASCII-encoded value, you can use the built-in `escape()` method. One example is the following code:

```
escape("Jim's Favorite ASCII character is the tilde(~)")
```

This code returns the following value:

```
Jim%27s%20Favorite%20ASCII%20character%20is%20the%20tilde%28%7E%29
```

If you need to convert an ASCII-encoded string—perhaps a string retrieved from a server—you can use the `unescape()` method. The following code is a good illustration:

```
unescape("email%20me%20at%20rwagner@acadians.com%21")
```

This code returns the following string value:

```
email me at rwagner@acadians.com!
```

Converting Strings to Numbers

JavaScript provides two built-in methods that you can use to convert strings to numbers: parseInt() and parseFloat(). Both functions take strings as their parameters and attempt to convert the string data into a numeric value. parseInt() tries to convert it into an Integer value, and parseFloat() attempts to convert it into a floating-point value. For example, the following code returns 123:

```
parseInt("123.88888")
```

The following code returns 1234.0012121:

```
parseFloat(„1234.0012121")
```

Both of these routines start the conversion from the left side of the string and convert until they come to something other than a numeric digit (0 to 9), a decimal (.), or a plus or minus sign (+/-). If the routine does encounter a nonnumeric character, the rest of the string is ignored. For example, the following code returns 1234.01:

```
parseFloat("1234.01 is the total price")
```

However, the following code returns a 0 value because the dollar sign is a nonnumeric value:

```
parseFloat("$1234.01 is the total price")
```

These conversion functions are very useful when you're working with text objects. Because the value property of a text object returns a string, you must convert this data any time you want to treat text entered by the user as a numeric value. Suppose, for example, that you want to take a number entered by the user and use it in a calculation. You could use parseInt() for this task:

```
stateTax = .06
subtotal = parseInt(document.form1.subtotal.value)
total = subtotal + (stateTax * subtotal)
```

Converting Numbers to Strings

You can also convert numeric values to strings, but there are no built-in methods to do so. Instead, you perform this task based on how JavaScript processes the addition (+) operator. As JavaScript adds elements of an expression and it encounters a string, the whole expression is treated as a string from that point on. For example, 35 + 100 returns a numeric value of 135. If the "100" is a string, however, 35 + "100" returns a string value of "35100".

14

> **NOTE**
>
> If you're working with a Number object, you can use its toString() method to convert it to a string value.

Interestingly, because JavaScript processes the additional operator from left to right, you could actually add two numeric digits together before the expression is converted into a string. For example, 10 + 20 + "40" returns a string value of "3040" because the 10 + 20 pair is added before its result is added to the next string value. In contrast, "40" + 10 + 20 returns a string value of "401020" because the string is on the left of the numeric values.

In most programming languages, you must convert a numeric value before you can use it in the context of a string value. As you can see, the only thing you need to do is either use it in a string expression with other string values or add an empty string to it. For example, the expression 1300 + "" returns a string value of "1300". Rather than add an empty string each time you want to perform this conversion, you could use a simple conversion function to do this for you:

```
function numToString(number) {
    number += „"
    return number
}
```

Listing 14.7 shows a sample script that demonstrates this function. The first alert message box displays "Number" as the data type for the number variable. After the numToString() function is performed, the second alert box displays "String" as number's data type.

Listing 14.7. numToString.htm.

```
<SCRIPT LANGUAGE = "JavaScript">

    function numToString(number) {
        number += „"
        return number
    }

    var number = 100
    alert (typeof number)
    number = numToString(number)
    alert (typeof number)

</SCRIPT>
```

The Array Object

An array is a programming construct fundamental to nearly all modern languages. JavaScript is no different, providing the capability to construct and work with arrays. An *array* is simply a container holding a set of data elements. Each of the elements in an array is a separate value, but they exist as part of the array and cannot be accessed except by going through the array.

> **NOTE**
>
> Although strongly typed languages require that all array values be of the same type, JavaScript does not. Consequently, your array can contain mixed data types, just as an object can have properties of varying types.

To define or access a particular element, you need to add brackets and an index value to the array variable. For example, you can define an array called `coffee` as follows:

```
coffee[0] = "Ethiopian Sidamo"
coffee[1] = "Kenyan"
coffee[2] = "Café Verona"
coffee[3] = "Sumatra"
coffee[4] = "Costa Rica"
coffee[5] = "Columbian"
coffee[6] = "Bristan"
```

If you wanted to use any of these elements within a script, you could access them using the array variable along with an index value representing the location of the element within the array. Therefore, if you wanted to write the following line:

```
My favorite coffee is Ethiopian Sidamo
```

You would code the following:

```
document.write("My favorite coffee is " + coffee[0])
```

If arrays are new to you, you might find it helpful to think of an array as JavaScript's equivalent of a numbered list. It's really no more complicated than that. For example, suppose you have a list of 10 items:

1. JavaScript
2. Java
3. Delphi
4. C++
5. Visual Basic
6. Oracle Power Objects
7. SmallTalk
8. PowerBuilder
9. Paradox
10. Access

If you wanted to assemble this group of items in a JavaScript array, it would look like this:

```
devTools[0] = "JavaScript"
```

14

```
devTools[1] = "Java"
devTools[2] = "Delphi"
devTools[3] = "C++"
devTools[4] = "Visual Basic"
devTools[5] = "Oracle Power Objects"
devTools[6] = "SmallTalk"
devTools[7] = "PowerBuilder"
devTools[8] = "Paradox"
devTools[9] = "Access"
```

Creating an Array Object

Unlike a string, an array is not recognized as a data type in JavaScript, but you can work with it as an object. The way in which you create Array objects varies, depending on the browser you're using.

Array Objects with JavaScript 1.1 (and Higher)

JavaScript 1.1 and higher lets you work with arrays as true JavaScript objects. You can create instances of an Array object using the new operator. For example, if you wanted to create the coffee array defined earlier, you would define it as follows:

```
var coffee = new Array()
coffee[0] = "Ethiopian Sidamo"
coffee[1] = "Kenyan"
coffee[2] = "Café Verona"
coffee[3] = "Sumatra"
coffee[4] = "Costa Rica"
coffee[5] = "Columbian"
coffee[6] = "Bristan"
```

The new operator creates an Array object, and the statements following fill the array with data elements.

> **TIP**
>
> An alternative way to define an Array object is to specify the data elements as parameters of the new call. For example, the following line is the functional equivalent of the previous example:
>
> ```
> var coffee = new Array("Ethiopian Sidamo", "Kenyan", "Café Verona",
> "Sumatra", "Costa Rica", "Columbian", "Bristan")
> ```

Notice that you didn't specify a size of the array, as is common in many programming languages. JavaScript doesn't require that you specify the size of the array, which allows you to incrementally expand the array as you add each new data element. However, if you want to, you can specify the size of the array initially as a parameter in the new expression:

```
var coffee = new Array(7)
```

Alternatively, you could also resize an array simply by defining a data element at the n position. If n is the highest number defined in the array, the new array size is expanded to $n + 1$. Note the following example:

```
var javaDrinks = new Array()
javaDrinks[0] = "Regular coffee"
javaDrinks[1] = "Decaf coffee"
javaDrinks[2] = "Café Mocha"
javaDrinks[3] = "Café au Lait"
javaDrinks[199] = "Café Latte"
```

The size of the javaDrinks array is 200, even though only five data elements are defined. Each undefined element returns a null value if you access it.

You can retrieve the size of the array using the Array object's length property. For example, if you wanted to iterate through each element in an array object, you could use the script shown in Listing 14.8.

Listing 14.8. coffeeArrayObject.htm.

```
<SCRIPT LANGUAGE = "JavaScript">

    var coffee = new Array()
    coffee[0] = "Ethiopian Sidamo"
    coffee[1] = "Kenyan"
    coffee[2] = "Café Verona"
    coffee[3] = "Suma2tra"
    coffee[4] = "Costa Rica"
    coffee[5] = "Columbian"
    coffee[6] = "Bristan"


    document.write("Coffees of the World:<p>")
    for (var i=0; i<coffee.length; i++) {
        document.write(i + 1 + "." + coffee[i] + "<p>")
    }

</SCRIPT>
```

Figure 14.7 shows the result.

14

BUILT-IN
LANGUAGE
OBJECTS

> **CAUTION**
>
> The Array object's length property is read-only. As a result, you can't resize an array by assigning a value to the length property.

FIGURE 14.7.
*Using JavaScript to
display a coffee list.*

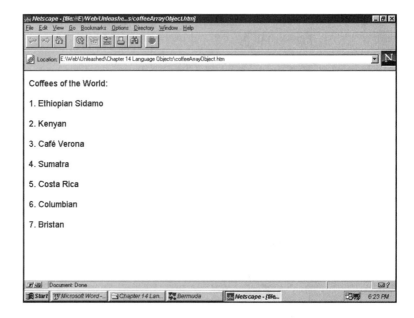

Basic Arrays with JavaScript 1.0

If you are working with JavaScript 1.0, you can't take advantage of the Array object. Because an array isn't a distinct data type, you need to create one through a rather inelegant process (or, if you're frank, you can call it a work-around). Although Chapter 15, "Creating Custom JavaScript Objects," is devoted to creating custom objects, I'd like to describe this process here. To create an array, you need to create your own custom routine that emulates an array object "constructor." Using a custom function called `createArray()`, you can create the array as a custom object:

```
function createArray(size) {
   this.length = size;
   for (var i = 1; i <= size; i++) {
     this[i] = null }
     return this
     }
}
```

The `createArray()` function uses its `size` parameter to define the length of the array. Notice that the length actually becomes the first element in the array. Although the `length` property of the JavaScript 1.1 Array object is maintained internally, the `length` property of the custom-made array must be maintained by you. Also, as the first element in the array, it occupies the `array[0]` position. When you work with these array elements, you should always start with 1 as the initial position; otherwise, you'll overwrite the length value. Obviously, because everything else in JavaScript is zero-based, this can be confusing.

> **CAUTION**
>
> In order for the `length` property to have any meaning, you need to manually update this setting when you resize an array. If you don't, it will be outdated.

After the `length` property is set, the `createArray()` function uses a `for` loop to assign a null value to each element of the array.

> **NOTE**
>
> Here is the official Netscape recommendation for working with arrays in JavaScript 1.0:
>
> ```
> function MakeArray(n) {
>    this.length = n;
>    for (var i = 1; i <= n; i++) {
>    this[i] = 0 }
>    return this
>    }
> }
> ```
>
> The only difference between the Netscape version and the `createArray()` function shown in this book is that `createArray()` more closely resembles the functionality of the Array object—undefined data elements have a null value.

Using this process, the `coffee` Array object example shown in the preceding section would be coded as shown in Listing 14.9.

Listing 14.9. `coffeeArrayOrig.htm`.

```
<SCRIPT LANGUAGE = "JavaScript">

    function createArray(size) {
       this.length = size;
       for (var i = 1; i <= size; i++) {
         this[i] = null }
         return this
     }

    var coffee = new createArray(7)

    coffee[1] = "Ethiopian Sidamo"
    coffee[2] = "Kenyan"
    coffee[3] = "Café Verona"
    coffee[4] = "Sumatra"
    coffee[5] = "Costa Rica"
    coffee[6] = "Columbian"
    coffee[7] = "Bristan"
```

14

BUILT-IN LANGUAGE OBJECTS

continues

Listing 14.9. continued

```
document.write("Coffees of the World:<p>")

for (var i=1; i<=coffee.length; i++) {
    document.write(i + ". " + coffee[i] + "<p>")
}
```

```
</SCRIPT>
```

Working with Multidimensional Arrays

The array examples I have shown so far deal with single-dimensional arrays. That is, a single value is associated with each index of the array. Some languages let you create multidimensional arrays so that you can store two or more values per array index. You can think of a multidimensional array as a database table with multiple fields (columns).

JavaScript doesn't provide explicit support for multidimensional arrays, but you can simulate them by creating an array of custom objects.

The Date Object

The Date object is the means by which you work with date and time values in JavaScript. You should understand three significant facts regarding the Date object before using it:

- Following the UNIX convention, JavaScript considers January 1, 1970 to be the baseline date. Consequently, you can't work with dates prior to that time frame.

- When you create a Date object, the time reflected within the object is based on the client machine. You are thus dependent on the client computer to have a working and accurate clock. Keep this dependency in mind as you consider time-sensitive code in your JavaScript scripts.

- JavaScript keeps track of date/time values in the form of milliseconds since the baseline date (1/1/70).

Encapsulated within the Date object are an impressive array of methods to get and set date values and convert them into various forms. Tables 14.4 through 14.7 list the Date object methods based on method type.

Table 14.4. Get methods of the Date object.

Method	*Description*
getDate()	Returns date within month (1 to 31)
getDay()	Returns day within week (0 to 6)

Method	Description
getHours()	Returns hour within day (0 to 23)
getMinutes()	Returns minutes within hour (0 to 59)
getMonth()	Returns month within year (0 to 11)
getSeconds()	Returns seconds within minute (0 to 59)
getTime()	Returns number of milliseconds since 1/1/70 00:00:00
getYear()	Returns number of years since 1900
getTimeZoneOffset()	Returns minutes offset from GMT/UTC

Table 14.5. Set methods of the Date object.

Method	Description
setDate(*value*)	Sets date within month (1 to 31)
setHours(*value*)	Sets hour within day (0 to 23)
setMinutes(*value*)	Sets minutes within hour (0 to 59)
setMonth(*value*)	Sets month within year (0 to 11)
setSeconds(*value*)	Sets seconds within minute (0 to 59)
setTime(*value*)	Sets number of milliseconds since 1/1/70 00:00:00
setYear(*value*)	Sets number of years since 1900

Table 14.6. To methods of the Date object.

Method	Description
toGMTString()	Returns date string in universal format
toLocalString()	Returns date string in local system's format

Table 14.7. Static parse methods of the Date object.

Method	Description
parse("*stringDate*")	Converts *stringDate* to milliseconds
UTC(*value1*,*value2*,...*value5*)	Converts comma-delimited values to milliseconds of GMT date

NOTE

Like almost everything else in JavaScript, relative date values are also zero-based. This is perhaps counterintuitive, because days of the week are 0 to 6 rather than 1 to 7, and months of the year are 0 to 11 rather than 1 to 12. As you process these values in your code, you need to account for these zero-based values.

However, note that the date within the month is an exception (1 to 31), because this is an absolute value.

Creating a Date Object

Creating a Date object is similar to creating String or Array objects. You can create as many Date objects as you want in your scripts. Using the new operator, you can define a Date object as follows:

```
var dateVariable = new Date([parameters])
```

You can include several parameters, as shown in Table 14.8.

Table 14.8. Date object parameters.

Parameter	Description	Example
Nothing	Creates an object with the current date and time.	`var today = new Date()`
`"month dd, yyyy hh:mm:ss"`	Creates an object with the specified date and time in the string. (All omitted time values are automatically set to zero.)	`var jaredBirthday = new Date("September 22, 1992")`
`yy, mm, dd`	Creates an object with the specified date of the set of integer values (zero-based).	`var justinBirthday = new Date(94,1,0)`
`yy, mm, dd, hh, mm, ss`	Creates an object with the specified date and time of the set of integer values (zero-based). (All omitted time values are automatically set to zero.)	`var jordanBirthday = new Date(90,7,12,7,10,29)`

Working with Date Values

Once a Date object is created, you can use one of several methods to either get or set date values. For example, to return the date of the current month, you would code the following:

```
var today = new Date()
result = today.getDate()
```

To change the month defined for the Date object appt, you can use the following:

```
var appt = new Date(1996,06,12)
result = appt.setMonth(7)
```

I discussed earlier how zero-based date values can make it difficult to work with getting dates. You can get around this annoyance by extending the Date object methods by prototyping more user-friendly get methods. If you recall, JavaScript 1.1 lets you extend the capabilities of built-in objects by letting you prototype new methods or properties. All objects of this type will inherit this new prototype. Add five new methods to the Date object:

- getFullYear() returns a year in *yyyy* format.

- getActualMonth() returns the actual numeric value for the month.

- getCalendarMonth() returns the name of the month.

- getActualDay() returns the actual numeric value of the day of week.

- getCalendarDay() returns the name of the day of week.

Listing 14.10 shows the method definitions for each of these prototype methods.

Listing 14.10. dateGetActual.htm.

```
<SCRIPT LANGUAGE="JavaScript">

     //////////////////////////////////////////////
     //     Date Object Enhanced Get Methods     //
     //////////////////////////////////////////////
     Date.prototype.getFullYear = getFullYear
     Date.prototype.getActualMonth = getActualMonth
     Date.prototype.getActualDay = getActualDay
     Date.prototype.getCalendarDay = getCalendarDay
     Date.prototype.getCalendarMonth = getCalendarMonth

          function getFullYear() {
               var n = this.getYear()
               n += 1900
               return n
          }

          function getActualMonth() {
               var n = this.getMonth()
               n += 1
               return n
          }
```

14

BUILT-IN
LANGUAGE
OBJECTS

continues

Listing 14.10. continued

```
function getActualDay() {
    var n = this.getDay()
    n += 1
    return n
}

function getCalendarDay() {
    var n = this.getDay()
    var dow = new Array(7)
    dow[0] = "Sunday"
    dow[1] = "Monday"
    dow[2] = "Tuesday"
    dow[3] = "Wednesday"
    dow[4] = "Thursday"
    dow[5] = "Friday"
    dow[6] = "Saturday"
    return dow[n]
}

function getCalendarMonth() {
    var n = this.getMonth()
    var moy = new Array(12)
    moy[0] = "January"
    moy[1] = "February"
    moy[2] = "March"
    moy[3] = "April"
    moy[4] = "May"
    moy[5] = "June"
    moy[6] = "July"
    moy[7] = "August"
    moy[8] = "September"
    moy[9] = "October"
    moy[10] = "November"
    moy[11] = "December"
    return moy[n]
}

/////////////////////////////////////////////
//          End Date Object Prototype        //
/////////////////////////////////////////////

var today = new Date()

document.write("<h2>I hereby declare that on " +
today.getCalendarDay() + ", the " + today.getDate()
+ "th day of " + today.getCalendarMonth() + " in the year "
+ today.getFullYear() + " A.D. at the " + today.getHours()
+ "th hour of the day, absolutely nothing is happening.</h2>")

</SCRIPT>
```

After the methods are declared, the script creates a Date object and then generates an HTML document using a combination of the prototype methods. Figure 14.8 shows the result.

FIGURE 14.8.

Using the enhanced Get *methods.*

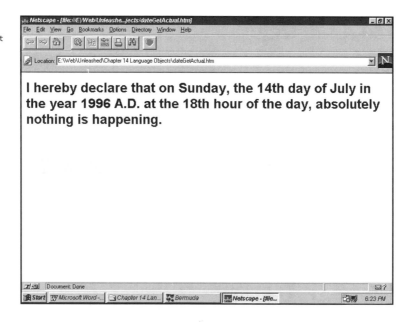

Working with Time Zones

Given that JavaScript is an application for the World Wide Web, it is only fitting that it include some date functions to deal with time zones. getTimezoneOffset() returns the number of minutes difference between the client computer and GMT (Greenwich Mean Time). For example, as I write this, I am in the U.S. Eastern time zone. If I want to return the number of time zone offset hours, I could use the following code:

```
var today = new Date()
offset = today.getTimezoneOffset()/60
if (offset == -5) {
    alert("You are in the Eastern Timezone")
}
```

Figure 14.9 shows the result when I run the script.

FIGURE 14.9.

Using
getTimezoneOffset()
to determine the time zone.

Calculating with Dates

You can perform calculations between date values, determining such things as the number of days until the end of the century. When you perform calculations with dates, it's important to keep the dates in their "native" millisecond format during the calculation and then extract the relevant data later.

The Math Object

For mathematical calculations, JavaScript encapsulates a host of mathematical constants and procedures into a single entity—the Math object. The Math object is quite different from the other built-in objects. First, you can perform basic arithmetic calculations (addition, subtraction, multiplication, and division) outside a Math object, so unless you regularly require advanced math functions, you might rarely use it.

> **NOTE**
>
> Few developers might need to tap into the true power of the Math object, but for those who do, its capabilities are vital. Rather than pass values back to the server to perform mathematical calculations, you can use the Math object to perform advanced math processing on the client side.

Second, although you can create instances of String, Array, and Date objects using `new`, you work with a built-in instance of the Math object. This quality of the Math object parallels the Navigator object, for example, which is not created on-the-fly. Consequently, the Math object is commonly referred to as a *static* object.

The Math object's properties are really nothing more than a list of common mathematical constants, as shown in Table 14.9. Note the case of the constants. Although nearly all JavaScript properties are lowercase or mixed-case, these properties are all uppercase.

Table 14.9. Math object properties.

Property	Description	What It Returns
E	Euler's constant	2.718281828
LN2	Natural log of 2	0.693147181
LN10	Natural log of 10	2.302585093
LOG2E	Log base –2 of E	1.442695041
LOG10E	Log base –10 of E	0.434294482
PI	Pi	3.141592654
SQRT1_2	Square root of 0.5	0.707106781
SQRT2	Square root of 2	1.414213562

Table 14.10 shows the methods of the Math object.

Table 14.10. Math object methods.

Method	*What It Returns*
abs*(value)*	Absolute value of *value*
acos*(value)*	Arc cosine of *value* (in radians)
asin*(value)*	Arc sine of *value* (in radians)
atan*(value)*	Arc tangent of *value* (in radians)
ceil*(value)*	Next integer >= *value*
cos*(value)*	Cosine of *value*
exp*(value)*	Euler's constant to the power of *value*
floor*(value)*	Next integer <= *value*
log*(value)*	Natural logarithm of *value* (base e)
max*(value1, value2)*	The highest number of *value1* or *value2*
min*(value1, value2)*	The lowest number of *value1* or *value2*
pow*(value1, value2)*	*value1* to the *value2* power
random()	A random number between 0 and 1
round*(value)*	*n* + 1 (if *value* >= *n*.5; else *n*)
sin*(value)*	Sine of *value* (in radians)
sqrt*(value)*	Square root of *value*
tan*(value)*	Tangent of *value* (in radians)

The Boolean Object (JavaScript 1.1 and Higher)

Boolean values are an important part of any programming language. JavaScript 1.1 and higher supports a Boolean object, which is used to convert a non-Boolean value into a Boolean value. You can then use the Boolean object as if it were a normal Boolean value (true or false).

You can create a Boolean object using the now familiar new operator with the following syntax:

```
booleanObjectName = new Boolean(initialValue)
```

The initialValue parameter specifies the initial setting of the Boolean object. If initialValue is false, 0, null, or an empty string (""), or if it is omitted altogether, initialValue is set to false. All other values will set the object to true.

> **TIP**
>
> Keep in mind that the `initialValue` parameter is assumed to be `false` if it is not included or if it is set to 0, null, `false`, or `""`. But if `initialValue` is set to the string `"false"`, the parameter is set to `true`.

For example, the following code sample uses the Boolean object `bool` to assist in the evaluation process of the current browser:

```
<HTML>
<HEAD>
<SCRIPT LANGUAGE= "JavaScript">
<!--

    var browser = navigator.appName

    bool = new Boolean(true)

    if (browser != "Netscape") {
        bool = false
    }

    if (bool) {

        document.write("Welcome Netscape user.")
        document.close()

    }

// -->
</SCRIPT>
</HEAD>
</HTML>
```

The Number Object (JavaScript 1.1 and Higher)

The Number object, supported in JavaScript 1.1 and higher, does for number values what the String object does for string values. However, in practice, it is typically much less used. You will find the Number object useful when you need to access certain constant values, such as the largest and smallest representable numbers, positive and negative infinity, and the Not-A-Number value. JavaScript represents these values as Number object properties, as shown in Table 14.11.

Table 14.11. Number object properties.

Property	What It Returns
MAX_VALUE	Largest representable number
MIN_VALUE	Smallest representable number

Property	What It Returns
NaN	Special "Not-A-Number" value
NEGATIVE_INFINITY	Special negative infinite value; returned on overflow
POSITIVE_INFINITY	Special infinite value; returned on overflow
prototype	Adds properties to the Number object

Number objects are instantiated in your script using the new operator with the following syntax:

```
numberObjectName = new Number(initialValue)
```

You can create Number objects when you need to add properties to them. For example, the code in Listing 14.11 demonstrates a scenario in which Number objects would be very useful. This scenario avoids the necessity of making several string-to-number conversions.

Listing 14.11. NumberObjects.htm.

```
<HTML>
<HEAD>
<SCRIPT LANGUAGE= "JavaScript">
<!--

        // Add description property to Number objects
        Number.prototype.description = null

        // Speed Limit Numbers
        slHighway         = new Number(65)
        slCity            = new Number(35)
        slSchoolZone      = new Number(25)

        // Add Descriptions
        slHighway.description = "Interstate Highway Speed Limit"
        slCity.description = "City Speed Limit"
        slSchoolZone.description = "School Zone Speed Limit"

        // Subtract num2 from num1 and display the value of
        // the difference between the two along with the original
        // number descriptions.
        function tellDifference(num1, num2) {
            diff = num1 - num2
            document.write("The speed difference between " + num1.description +
                " and " + num2.description + " is " + diff)
        }

        // Call function
        tellDifference(slHighway, slCity)

//-->
</SCRIPT>
</HEAD>
</HTML>
```

14

BUILT-IN LANGUAGE OBJECTS

This script will generate the following line of text:

```
The speed difference between Interstate Highway Speed Limit
and City Speed Limit is 30
```

The Function Object (JavaScript 1.1 and Higher)

The last built-in object is the Function object. The Function object lets you define a string at runtime and compile it as a function. Here is the syntax for declaring a Function object:

functionObjectName = new Function ([arg1, arg2, ... argn], functionBody)

Keep in mind that a Function object and a standard JavaScript function are similar, but also different. The object name of a Function object is considered a *variable* representing the current value of the function defined with new Function(), whereas a name of a standard JavaScript function is not a variable, just the name of a function.

> **NOTE**
>
> Function objects are evaluated each time they are used. Not surprisingly, they are slower in execution than normal JavaScript functions.

You can use a Function object as an event handler, as shown in the following code:

```
window.onload = new Function("document.bgColor = 'aqua'")
```

Summary

You can think of the built-in language objects as the nuts and bolts of JavaScript, because much of the hard programming work is performed within the constructs of these objects. In this chapter, you learned about how to use language objects and the differences that exist when working with different versions of browser software. In the next chapter, you will apply what you learned about arrays in this chapter as you examine how to create custom objects.

Creating Custom JavaScript Objects

CHAPTER 15

IN THIS CHAPTER

This chapter's discussion is a natural follow-up to the previous chapters. Chapter 9 covered many basics of object-oriented programming, and Chapters 10 through 14 discussed the entire spectrum of built-in objects within the JavaScript language. But if you stop there, you limit a great deal of the power that JavaScript has: letting you create your own custom objects. In this chapter, I discuss how to create custom objects in JavaScript, the major capabilities of JavaScript, and its limitations.

Creating an Object

Custom objects in JavaScript have a close association with arrays. Arrays are a means of structuring data into a container. Yet, as powerful as arrays are, they fail to meet the needs of everything you would like to do as a JavaScript developer. Although they store data, they cannot store behavior. As discussed in Chapter 9, "The JavaScript Object Model," an object contains both data, known as *properties,* and behavior, known as *methods.* Therefore, although an array is essentially the same thing as an object with properties, it doesn't store information on how the array can respond to messages. Our mission, then, is to create an entity that can encapsulate data elements and responses to messages.

To create a JavaScript object, you need to create a *constructor.* A constructor is a special JavaScript function that defines what the object will look like and how it will act. The constructor doesn't actually create the object; instead, it provides a template for what an instantiated object will look like. (Creating an instance of an object is called *instantiating* an object.) The following is the basic structure of an instantiated object:

```
function object(paramter1, parameter2,...) {
     this.property1 = parameter1
     this.property2 = parameter2
     this.property3 = parameter3
  ®  this.property4 = parameter4
     this.method1 = function1
     this.method2 = function2
}
```

As you can see, the actual structure of the constructor is relatively straightforward. First, you name the method itself. The name of the function will serve as the name of your object type. Therefore, it's critical for clarity's sake to give your constructor method a descriptive name. If you're creating an object to represent an invoice, call it `invoice`. I've seen some people name their constructor in a verb format, such as `createInvoice`. This practice can lead to confusing and hard-to-read code, because a property of the object would look like this:

```
myDate = createInvoice.date
```

Even worse, if you had `create()` as a method of the object, your code would look like this:

```
createInvoice.create()
```

A much clearer method of presentation is to use a noun-based approach, which would make the preceding two lines much more readable:

```
myDate = invoice.date
```

and

```
invoice.create()
```

Second, add parameters to the function for all the properties of the object. With this approach, when you instantiate the object, you pass the property values to the function as parameters.

Third, assign the value of the incoming parameters to the properties of the object. The this keyword comes in handy here; it's used to represent the object as you define the properties.

Fourth, define the methods that the object type will have. Whereas properties are assigned values by parameters of the constructor itself, methods are created as functions outside of the constructor and are assigned to the method definition of the object.

To illustrate, suppose I wanted to create a custom object in which I could store information on my favorite books. In particular, I would like to track a book's title, author, ISBN, subject, and a personal rating. The constructor can be defined as follows:

```
function book(title, author, ISBN, subject, rating) {
    this.title = title
    this.author = author
    this.ISBN = ISBN
    this.subject = subject
    this.rating = rating
}
```

Also, I want to add a method called show(), which displays the information on the instantiated object to the user. Therefore, I need to create a function, separate from the constructor itself, to do this:

```
function show() {
    objWindow = window.open("", "", "width=600,height=300")
    objWindow.document.write("<h1>Object Description</h1>")
    objWindow.document.write("<p>")
    objWindow.document.write("Book Title: " + this.title + "<p>")
    objWindow.document.write("Author: " + this.author + "<p>")
    objWindow.document.write("ISBN: " + this.ISBN + "<p>")
    objWindow.document.write("Subject: " + this.subject + "<p>")
    objWindow.document.write("Rich's Rating: " + this.rating + "<p>")
    objWindow.document.close()
}
```

Even though this code is outside of the constructor, you can consider it a part of the object declaration. Therefore, you can use the this keyword and have it refer to the object instance that is being called.

I can then add a new entry to my constructor for the method:

```
function book(title, author, ISBN, subject, rating) {
    this.title = title
    this.author = author
    this.ISBN = ISBN
    this.subject = subject
    this.rating = rating
    this.show = show
}
```

Notice two details about the show() method declaration. First, although the object method name is the same as the associated external function, it doesn't have to be. You can name each object method anything you like. For readability, some developers prefer to use identical names, and others prefix the external function with the object name, such as book_show(). Second, the external function doesn't include parentheses in the constructor, only the function name itself.

In older versions of Netscape Navigator, you needed to place a method definition above the object constructor, because all references were executed in a top-down format. This is no longer the case in Netscape Navigator 3.0 and later. The placement of the show() method vis-à-vis the constructor method isn't important from JavaScript's point of view. I find it helpful to take advantage of this new capability and make the code easier to read by placing any method definitions immediately under the object constructor. I also use comments to keep the set of functions together and treated as a unit. Listing 15.1 shows the complete object declaration for the book object.

Listing 15.1. The book object definition.

```
////////////////////////////
//        Book Object      //
////////////////////////////
function book(title, author, ISBN, subject, rating) {
    this.title = title
    this.author = author
    this.ISBN = ISBN
    this.subject = subject
    this.rating = rating
    this.show = show
}
    function show() {
        objWindow = window.open("", "", "width=600,height=300")
        objWindow.document.write("<h1>Object Description</h1>")
        objWindow.document.write("<p>")
        objWindow.document.write("Book Title: " + this.title + "<p>")
        objWindow.document.write("Author: " + this.author + "<p>")
        objWindow.document.write("ISBN: " + this.ISBN + "<p>")
        objWindow.document.write("Subject: " + this.subject + "<p>")
        objWindow.document.write("Rich's Rating: " + this.rating + "<p>")
        objWindow.document.close()
    }

////End Book Object Defition////
```

Gary Griffin, one of this book's co-authors and my colleague at Acadia Software, came up with an innovative way to use a custom object as a means to control a set of buttons on a page. After having problems working with an array of buttons, he decided to create a custom `buttonSet` object. The `buttonSet` object gave him a way to add buttons to a set on-the-fly, place a `buttonSet` in any document object, space buttons, and conditionally display individual buttons. The constructor for the `buttonSet` object is shown in Listing 15.2.

Listing 15.2. `buttonSet` object constructor.

```
//////////////////////////////////////////////
//  buttonSet object contructor            //
//  Created by Gary Griffin, Acadia Software //
//////////////////////////////////////////////
function buttonSet(name) {
   this.name = name
   this.length = 0
   this.addBtn = addBtn
   this.print = print
   this.index = 4    // Point at which to add additional
                     // members to this object. If this
                     // must be changed, reflect it in
                     // this.print()
   return this
}
// print() method for buttonSet object
// dObj is a document object
// spaceInt enables you to adjust spacing of buttons
function print(dObj) {
   var spaceInt
   for(var i = 5; this.index >= i; i++) {
     if(eval(this[i].condition)) {
       dObj.writeln('<A HREF = "'+this[i].url+'"><img src="' +
            this[i].file+'" alt="'+this[i].alt +
            '" width="44" height="46" border=0></A>')
       // Add space if specified.
       spaceInt = 0 + this[i].spacer
       if(navigator.appName == "Microsoft Internet Explorer") {
          spaceInt = spaceInt + 3 }
       if(spaceInt != 0) {
          dObj.write('<img src="images/space.gif" width=' + spaceInt +
             'height=46 border=0>')
       }
         }
   }
}
```

Instantiating Objects

To use the object I have declared in the book() constructor method, I need to create an instance of it in my JavaScript code. The new operator is used for this purpose. It has the following syntax:

```
objectInstance = new objectType(parameter1, parameter2, parameter3,...)
```

Using the new operator, I create a book object using the following code:

```
dbBook = new book("Cost of Discipleship", "Dietrich Bonhoeffer",
                  "1-57521-118-1", "Grace", 5)
```

I can now refer to this object anywhere in my code using the dbBook variable. The instance will exist in memory as long as the page is loaded in my browser. After the user moves to a new page or closes the browser, the instance of the object disappears. This is important to understand when you start assigning values to object properties. If you want to save the objects persistently, you will need to pass them to the server for processing.

> **NOTE**
>
> Persistence is a buzzword of the object community. In a nutshell, it means the ability to create an object instance and save the state of the object, so that the next time the object is accessed, it is retrieved in its saved state.
>
> You can't persistently store objects using client-side JavaScript.

To demonstrate what has been developed so far, the following code creates an instance of the book object and calls its show() method. Figure 15.1 shows the result.

```
<SCRIPT LANGUAGE = "JavaScript">

    // Book object defined here

    dbBook = new book("Cost of Discipleship", "Dietrich Bonhoeffer",
     "1-57521-118-1",  "Grace", 5)
    dbBook.show()

</SCRIPT>
```

FIGURE 15.1.

*Book object informa-
tion is displayed in a
new window.*

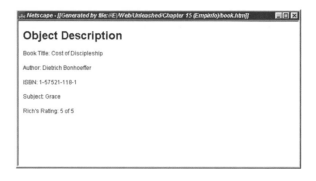

Working with Object Instances

After an object instance is created, you can work with it by assigning values to it or by performing one of its methods. You can also connect objects to user interface elements. For example, suppose you wanted to create a form that would let you change the rating for books, as well as display the book information form for each of the book objects you have instantiated. You can define the book object as shown earlier and create five book instances using the following code:

```
dbBook = new book("Cost of Discipleship", "Dietrich Bonhoeffer", "1-57521-118-1",
          "Grace", 5)
fkBook = new book("The Once and Future King", "T.H. White", "1-57521-112-1",
          "Camelot", 5)
olBook = new book("On Liberty", "John Stuart Mill", "1-53221-118-1",
          "Political Philosophy", 4)
iaBook = new book("Icarus Agenda", "Robert Ludlum", "1-53221-118-1",
          "Political Thriller", 2)
cnBook = new book("Chronicles of Narnia", "C.S. Lewis", "1-53231-128-1",
          "Children's Fiction", 5)
```

For the form itself, use a select object with an \<OPTION> defined for each of the books, as well as one for the rating (a range of 1 to 5). Add two buttons—one for making the rating assignment, and another for displaying the book information form. The form code looks like the following (and is shown in Figure 15.2):

```
<body>
<h1>Book Objects </h1>
<form name="form1">
<p>Select a book: </p>
<p><select name="bookList" size=1>
<option value="dbBook">Cost of Discipleship</option>
<option value="fkBook">The Once and Future King</option>
<option value="olBook">On Liberty</option>
<option value="iaBook">Icarus Agenda</option>
<option value="cnBook">Chronicles of Narnia</option>
</select>      </p>
<p>Assign a rating: </p>
<p><select name="rating" size=1>
<option>1</option>
<option>2</option>
<option>3</option>
<option>4</option>
<option>5</option>
</select> </p>
<p>Click to assign: </p>
<p><input type="button" name="Assign" value="Assign" onClick="assignRating()">
</p>
<p>Click to show: </p>
<p><input type="button" name="Show" value="Show" onClick="showBook()">
</p>
</form>
</body>
```

15

CREATING CUSTOM
JAVASCRIPT
OBJECTS

FIGURE 15.2.

The book object form.

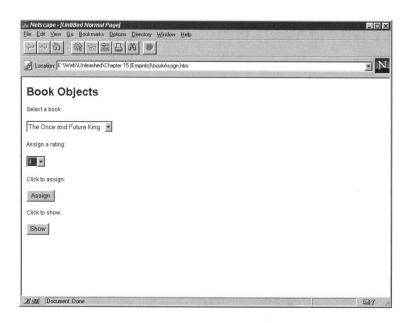

The heart of this example is in the event handlers for the Assign and Show buttons. The `assignRating()` method assigns the value of the selected rating to the selected book:

```
function assignRating() {
    selectedBook = document.form1.bookList.options[document.form1.bookList.
      selectedIndex].value
    selectedBook = eval(selectedBook)
    selectedBook.rating = document.form1.rating.options[document.form1.
      rating.selectedIndex].text
}
```

Looking at this more closely, you can see that the method retrieves the value of the selected `bookList` option and assigns it to the `selectedBook` variable. To get this value, I use the `bookList` object's `options` property, along with its `selectedIndex` property. I now have the name of the book object contained in the `selectedBook` variable, but JavaScript looks at this as a string value, not as a reference to an object instance. Therefore, the `eval()` method is used to convert the variable to an object reference. The last line of the method uses the `selectedBook` variable to assign its rating property the value of the currently selected option in the rating select object.

NOTE

You can use the `typeof` operator to test a variable's type during a method's execution. For example, you could display an alert message box showing the `selectedBook` variable's type using the following code:

```
alert(typeof selectedBook)
```

The showBook() method uses the same techniques to call the object's show() method:

```
function showBook() {
    selectedBook = document.form1.bookList.options[document.form1.bookList.
        selectedIndex].value
    selectedBook = eval(selectedBook)
    selectedBook.show()
}
```

Listing 15.3 gives the entire source code for this example.

Listing 15.3. Source code for the showBook() example.

```
<html>
<head>
<title>Untitled Normal Page</title>
<SCRIPT LANGUAGE = "JavaScript">

    ////////////////////////////////
    //          Book Object       //
    ////////////////////////////////
    function book(title, author, ISBN, subject, rating) {
        this.title = title
        this.author = author
        this.ISBN = ISBN
        this.subject = subject
        this.rating = rating
        this.show = show
    }

        function show() {
            objWindow = window.open("", "", "width=600,height=300")
            objWindow.document.write("<h1>Object Description</h1>")
            objWindow.document.write("<p>")
            objWindow.document.write("Book Title: " + this.title + "<p>")
            objWindow.document.write("Author: " + this.author + "<p>")
            objWindow.document.write("ISBN: " + this.ISBN + "<p>")
            objWindow.document.write("Subject: " + this.subject + "<p>")
            objWindow.document.write("Rich's Rating: " + this.rating
                + " of 5<p>")
            objWindow.document.close()
        }

    ////End Book Object Definition////


    function assignRating() {
        selectedBook = document.form1.bookList.options[document.form1
            bookList.selectedIndex].value
        selectedBook = eval(selectedBook)
        selectedBook.rating = document.form1.rating.options[document.form1.
            rating.selectedIndex].text
    }
```

15

CREATING CUSTOM
JAVASCRIPT
OBJECTS

continues

Listing 15.3. continued

```
function showBook() {
    selectedBook = document.form1.bookList.options[document.form1.
      bookList.selectedIndex].value
    selectedBook = eval(selectedBook)
    selectedBook.show()
}


// Execute on loading
dbBook = new book("Cost of Discipleship", "Dietrich Bonhoeffer",
          "1-57521-118-1", "Grace", 5)
fkBook = new book("The Once and Future King", "T.H. White",
          "1-57521-112-1", "Camelot", 5)
olBook = new book("On Liberty", "John Stuart Mill",
          "1-53221-118-1", "Political Philosophy", 4)
iaBook = new book("Icarus Agenda", "Robert Ludlum",
          "1-53221-118-1", "Politcal Thriller", 3)
cnBook = new book("Chronicles of Narnia", "C.S. Lewis",
          "1-53231-128-1", "Children's Fiction", 5)


</SCRIPT>
</head>

<body>
<h1>Book Objects </h1>
<form name="form1">
<p>Select a book: </p>
<p><select name="bookList" size=1>
<option value="dbBook">Cost of Discipleship</option>
<option value="fkBook">The Once and Future King</option>
<option value="olBook">On Liberty</option>
<option value="iaBook">Icarus Agenda</option>
<option value="cnBook">Chronicles of Narnia</option>
</select>     </p>
<p>Assign a rating: </p>
<p><select name="rating" size=1>
<option>1</option>
<option>2</option>
<option>3</option>
<option>4</option>
<option>5</option>
</select> </p>
<p>Click to assign: </p>
<p><input type="button" name="Assign" value="Assign" onClick="assignRating()">
</p>
<p>Click to show: </p>
<p><input type="button" name="Show" value="Show" onClick="showBook()">
</p>
</form>
</body>
</html>
```

Creating Complex Objects

The objects covered so far have been *simple objects,* or ones with a single level of properties and methods. JavaScript also supports *complex objects,* which let you have an object's property be an object itself. Complex objects let you structure your code in a more logical manner rather than being forced to dump all data into a single-level object. Suppose you would like to track information on employees, their current projects, and their related clients. Obviously a client address really shouldn't be part of an employee object definition, so JavaScript's complex objects let you structure the data around three separate but related entities: employee, project, and client.

In the employee constructor, define the basic properties (name, phone, and e-mail address) and a method called `showSummaryInfo()`. However, for project information, define a `Project` property in the employee object. You would define this in much the same way you would a normal property, except that the `project` parameter is actually a reference to another object rather than a string value:

```
function employee(FirstName, LastName, HomePhone, Ext, EmailAddress, project) {
    this.FirstName = FirstName
    this.LastName = LastName
    this.HomePhone = HomePhone
    this.Ext = Ext
    this.EmailAddress = EmailAddress
    this.Project = project
    this.showSummaryInfo = summaryInfo
}
```

Define the `project` object type in a similar manner, using the `client` object as a property:

```
function project(ProjectName, client, DevTool) {
    this.ProjectName = ProjectName;
    this.Client = client;
    this.DevTool = DevTool;
}

function client(ClientName, Address, City, State, Zip) {
    this.ClientName = ClientName
    this.Address = Address
    this.City = City
    this.State = State
    this.Zip = Zip
}
```

To show how these nested objects can be referenced, define the `showSummaryInfo()` method of the employee object. This method opens a new window to display an employee summary information sheet—essentially a listing of all the properties for the employee object and the objects contained within it.

```
function summaryInfo() {
    objWindow = window.open("", "", "width=600,height=400")
    objWindow.document.write("<h1>Employee Summary Information Sheet</h1>")
    objWindow.document.write("<p>")
    objWindow.document.write("<h2>" + this.FirstName + " " + this.LastName
        + "<p></h2>")
    objWindow.document.write("<p>")
    objWindow.document.write("<EM><STRONG>Contact Information</STRONG>
        </EM><p>")
    objWindow.document.write("Home Phone: " + this.HomePhone + "<p>")
    objWindow.document.write("Ext.: " + this.Ext + "<p>")
    objWindow.document.write("Email: " + this.EmailAddress + "<p>")
    objWindow.document.write("<p>")
    objWindow.document.write("<EM><STRONG>Project Information</STRONG>
        </EM><p>")
    objWindow.document.write("Current Project: " + this.Project.ProjectName
        + "<p>")
    objWindow.document.write("Client: " + this.Project.Client.ClientName
        + "<p>")
    objWindow.document.write("Client: " + this.Project.Client.Address
        + "<p>")
    objWindow.document.write("Client: " + this.Project.Client.City + ", " +
        this.Project.Client.State + " " + this.Project.Client.Zip + "<p>")
    objWindow.document.write("Developmnt Tool Used: " + this.Project.DevTool
        + "<p>")
    objWindow.document.close()
}
```

Child objects are referenced using familiar dot notation, so that the client's address is referenced with `this.Project.Client.Address`.

Now that the constructors are defined for each of these object types, you can instantiate a sample employee, project, and client object:

```
CoastTech = new client("Coastal Technology", "100 Beacon Hill", "Boston",
            "MA", "01220")
Coastal = new project("Coastal01", CoastTech, "JavaScript")
Richard = new employee("Richard", "Wagner", "617/555-1212", "100",
            "rwagner@acadians.com", Coastal)
```

The `project` parameter in the employee definition and the `client` parameter in the project definition are not strings; they are the names of the newly created objects. Also, notice the order in which these objects are created. Because the `Richard` object uses the `Coastal` project object as a parameter, `Coastal` must be instantiated first, or you will get an error. The same principle applies to creating the `CoastTech` instance of the client object before creating the `Coastal` project.

After the object instances are created, call `Richard.showSummaryInfo()` to display the window shown in Figure 15.3.

FIGURE 15.3.

The Employee Summary Information Sheet.

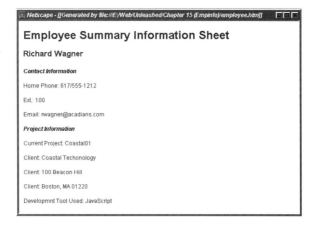

Listing 15.4 provides the entire source code for this example.

Listing 15.4. employee.htm.

```javascript
<SCRIPT LANGUAGE="Javascript">
<!--

    // Complex Custom Objects Example
    // Created by Richard Wagner
    // JavaScript Unleashed

    /////////////////////////////
    //      Employee Object      //
    /////////////////////////////

    // Employee object constructor
    function employee(FirstName, LastName, HomePhone, Ext, EmailAddress,
        project) {
        this.FirstName = FirstName
        this.LastName = LastName
        this.HomePhone = HomePhone
        this.Ext = Ext
        this.EmailAddress = EmailAddress
        this.Project = project
        this.showSummaryInfo = summaryInfo
    }
        function summaryInfo() {
            objWindow = window.open("", "", "width=600,height=400")
            objWindow.document.write("<h1>Employee Summary " +
                "Information Sheet</h1>")
            objWindow.document.write("<p>")
            objWindow.document.write("<h2>" + this.FirstName + " "
                + this.LastName + "<p></h2>")
            objWindow.document.write("<p>")
            objWindow.document.write("<EM><STRONG>Contact Information" +
                "</STRONG></EM><p>")
```

continues

Listing 15.4. continued

```
                objWindow.document.write("Home Phone: " + this.HomePhone
                    + "<p>")
                objWindow.document.write("Ext.: " + this.Ext + "<p>")
                objWindow.document.write("Email: " + this.EmailAddress
                    + "<p>")
                objWindow.document.write("<p>")
                objWindow.document.write("<EM><STRONG>Project Information"+
                    "</STRONG></EM><p>")
                objWindow.document.write("Current Project: " +
                    this.Project.ProjectName + "<p>")
                objWindow.document.write("Client: " +
                    this.Project.Client.ClientName+ "<p>")
                objWindow.document.write("Client: " + this.Project.Client.Address
                    + "<p>")
                objWindow.document.write("Client: " + this.Project.Client.City
                    + ", " + this.Project.Client.State + " " +
                    this.Project.Client.Zip + "<p>")
                objWindow.document.write("Developmnt Tool Used: "
                    + this.Project.DevTool + "<p>")
                objWindow.document.close()
        }

    ////End Employee Object////


    ////////////////////////////
    //      Project Object      //
    ////////////////////////////

    function project(ProjectName, client, DevTool) {
        this.ProjectName = ProjectName;
        this.Client = client;
        this.DevTool = DevTool;
    }


    ////////////////////////////
    //      Client Object       //
    ////////////////////////////
    function client(ClientName, Address, City, State, Zip) {
        this.ClientName = ClientName
        this.Address = Address
        this.City = City
        this.State = State
        this.Zip = Zip
    }

    CoastTech = new client("Coastal Techonology", "100 Beacon Hill", "Boston",
                "MA", "01220")
    Coastal = new project("Coastal01", CoastTech, "JavaScript")
    Richard = new employee("Richard", "Wagner", "617/555-1212",
                "100", "rwagner@acadians.com", Coastal)

    Richard.showSummaryInfo()

// -->
</SCRIPT>
```

Dynamic Creation of Objects

The ability to create your own objects in code gives the JavaScript developer power and flexibility, but all the examples I've shown so far have dealt with objects being created as the window loads using the new operator. You might be wondering what ability you have to dynamically create objects at runtime. After all, with other object-oriented programming environments, you can create object instances on-the-fly.

JavaScript does allow you to create object instances on-the-fly, but with certain definite limitations. Initially, my plan was to create a generic instantiator function that created an object instance each time it was called. If this were successful, you could avoid using new statements that have already been defined and create objects based on input from the user. The idea was that the method would look like this:

```
function addEmployee(ObjectName,FirstName, LastName) {
     ObjectName = new employee(FirstName, LastName)
}
```

Ideally, this method would instantiate an object and give the object's name based on the ObjectName parameter. Unfortunately, no matter what was tried, JavaScript wouldn't allow the name of the object instance to be a variable. Instead, it used ObjectName as the name of the object. In contrast, the following is valid as long as Frank has already been defined as the object reference:

```
function addFrank(FirstName, LastName) {
     Frank = new employee(FirstName, LastName)
}
```

Therefore, although you can't dynamically name an object being instantiated, you can create an object as an element of a container array. You could, therefore, have an employeeList array that stores each employee object that is created. Therefore, if you modify the addEmployee() method, you could use the following:

```
function addEmployeeObject(FirstName, LastName, HomePhone, Ext, EmailAddress) {
    empList[i] = new employee(FirstName, LastName, HomePhone, Ext, EmailAddress)
}
```

Using this method, you can actually create object instances based on user input and dynamically create the object by calling the addEmployeeObject() method. For example, the form shown in Figure 15.4 allows a user to enter basic information on an employee. When the user clicks the Add button, a new object instance is created. Listing 15.5 shows the source code for this sample form.

Listing 15.5. employeeDynamic.htm.

```
<HTML>
<HEAD>
<TITLE>Intranet Employee Database</TITLE>
<SCRIPT LANGUAGE="JavaScript">
```

continues

Listing 15.5. continued

```
// Dynamic Object Creation Example
// JavaScript Unleashed (Sams.net Publishing)
// Created by Richard J. Wagner (rwagner@acadians.com)

// Global variables
var i = 0

// Create Array objects
var empList = new Array()

///////////////////////////////
//     Employee Object       //
///////////////////////////////

// Employee object constructor
function employee(FirstName, LastName, HomePhone, Ext, EmailAddress) {
    this.FirstName = FirstName
    this.LastName = LastName
    this.HomePhone = HomePhone
    this.Ext = Ext
    this.EmailAddress = EmailAddress
    this.show = show
}
    function show() {
        alert(this.FirstName + "/n" +
            this.LastName + "/n" +
            this.HomePhone + "/n" +
            this.Ext + "/n" +
            this.EmailAddress)
    }

function addEmployeeObject(FirstName, LastName, HomePhone, Ext,
        EmailAddress) {
    empList[i] = new employee(FirstName, LastName, HomePhone, Ext,
      EmailAddress)
}

function insertRecord() {
    FirstName = document.form1.FirstName.value
    LastName = document.form1.LastName.value
    HomePhone = document.form1.HomePhone.value
    Ext = document.form1.Ext.value
    EmailAddress = document.form1.EmailAddress.value
    i++
    addEmployeeObject(FirstName, LastName, HomePhone, Ext, EmailAddress)
}

function showAll() {
    objWindow = window.open("", "", "width=600,height=300")
    objWindow.document.write("<h1>Object Description</h1>")
    objWindow.document.write("<p>")
    for (var q=1; q<empList.length; q++) {
        objWindow.document.write("<strong>"+ empList[q].FirstName
            + " " + empList[q].LastName + "</strong><p>")
        objWindow.document.write(empList[q].HomePhone + "<p>")
        objWindow.document.write(empList[q].Ext + "<p>")
```

```
                objWindow.document.write(empList[q].EmailAddress + "<p>")
                objWindow.document.write("<p>")
            }

            objWindow.document.close()
        }

</SCRIPT>
</HEAD>
<BODY>
<h1>Dyanamic Object Creator </h1>
<p>Enter employee information in the form below and click the Add button.
Press the Show All button to view a list of all
employees you have entered. </p>
<form name="form1">
<pre>First Name:       <input type=text size=20 maxlength=256 name="FirstName">
<pre>Last Name:        <input type=text size=20 maxlength=256 name="LastName">
<pre>Home Phone:       <input type=text size=20 maxlength=256 name="HomePhone">
<pre>Ext.:           <input type=text size=20 maxlength=256 name="Ext">
<pre>Email Address:      <input type=text size=20 maxlength=256
   name="EmailAddress">
<pre>            <input
                type="button"
                name="Add"
                value="Add",
                onClick="insertRecord()">  <input
                type="button"
                name="ShowAll"
                value="Show All"
                onClick="showAll()"></pre>
</form>
</BODY>
</HTML>
```

FIGURE 15.4.
Dynamic object creation.

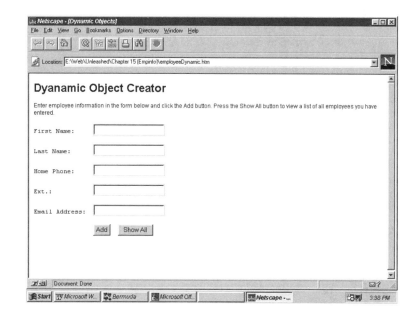

The Show All button lets you see all the objects that have been created during that session. Figure 15.5 shows a list of employee objects that have been instantiated.

> **NOTE**
>
> Array objects are supported in Netscape Navigator 3.0 and later. Version 2.0 does not support them.

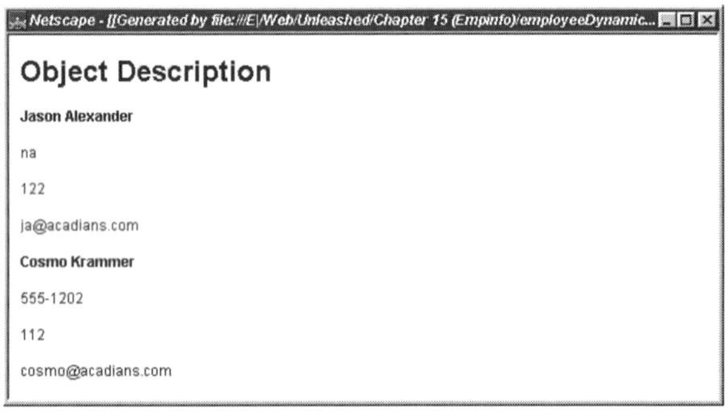

FIGURE 15.5.

A list of dynamically created objects.

Object Description

Jason Alexander

na

122

ja@acadians.com

Cosmo Krammer

555-1202

112

cosmo@acadians.com

Extending Instantiated Objects

Just as JavaScript is a loosely typed language in terms of data types, it's also flexible in terms of object definitions. You can extend the definition of any object instance by declaring the new property and assigning it a value. Using the `book` object example from earlier in this chapter, suppose you wanted to add a series property to the `cnBook` object after it has been defined. As you recall, it is defined as follows:

```
cnBook = new book("Chronicles of Narnia", "C.S. Lewis",
    "1-53231-128-1", "Children's Fiction", 5)
```

Later in the script, add a `Series` property to it using the following code:

```
cnBook.Series = "True"
```

This technique applies to that object instance only, not to the object type. However, Netscape Navigator 3.0 lets you extend objects you already created using an object prototype. Its syntax is as follows:

```
objectType.prototype.propertyName
```

An object prototype lets you add a property or method to each instance of an object type. Therefore, if you wanted to add a new `recommended` property to each `book` object and it had the value of `true`, you could use the following line:

```
book.prototype.recommended = True
```

You can test this by calling alert(iaBook.recommended). The result is shown in Figure 15.6.

Indexing Object Properties

The ability to index object properties depends on the version of the browser you're using. Netscape Navigator 2.0 lets you deal with an object's properties through their ordinal index. For example, in Netscape Navigator 2.0, the following two lines of code are equivalent:

```
employee.FirstName = "Richard"
```

```
employee[0] = "Richard"
```

However, Netscape is moving away from this practice. In Netscape Navigator 3.0, if you define an object using property names, you must always reference by name.

Summary

JavaScript supports the ability to create custom objects in your client-side scripts. This capability adds a great deal of power and flexibility to JavaScript and allows you to structure your code in an object-based manner. In this chapter, you learned all about the various aspects of creating and instantiating object types. You also learned about how to extend the power of normal objects by creating complex objects, which can also be referred to as "objects within objects." You can use complex objects to encapsulate data that spans multiple levels, much in the same way a relational database does with one-to-many table relationships. Finally, you learned how to extend objects that have already been instantiated by using the prototype operator. As you proceed through the rest of this book, you will find many instances where custom objects are used.

IN THIS PART

IV
PART

Visual Programming Techniques

Creating Special Effects with JavaScript

CHAPTER

16

Web technologies such as JavaScript and Java are important primarily because of the practical purposes they serve in the realm of Web application development. At the same time, some of the primary reasons JavaScript and Java are so popular are the "cool" things you can do with them on your Web site. Think back: As Java was gaining popularity, how many meaningless Java marquees and other applets did you see spread across the Web? And, in the JavaScript realm, as the language has matured, you can do many more exciting things with JavaScript. In this chapter, you'll learn how you can create special effects using JavaScript to enliven your Web site. Specifically, I'll show you how to create each of the following using JavaScript:

- Scrolling marquees
- Billboards
- Color fading
- Animated pushbuttons

Scrolling Marquees

A scrolling marquee is a popular effect for Web site developers. The purpose for it is related to relaying the latest news or tidbit to visitors of your Web site. The "marquee" or "ticker tape" was first popularized with the first Java applets. You can create a scrolling marquee in JavaScript as well, although the visual appearance is typically less stunning than a Java applet. This is because you're forced to use a Text object as the container for the scrolling text, and none of the HTML form objects are going to dazzle you with their visual look. Nonetheless, JavaScript marquees don't require a separate applet to be used and can be created quickly and easily, so you may find them very useful in a variety of situations.

To create a JavaScript marquee, you need to do three things:

1. Create an HTML form with an embedded text object.
2. Write a function that scrolls text within the text object.
3. To set the wheels in motion, associate this function as an event handler of the window's onLoad event.

To begin, create a form and text object within it. As you do so, it's helpful to name these objects appropriately. Because they are created specifically for the marquee and are irrelevant to other forms on the page, I often label the form "marqueeForm" and text "marqueeText", or something to that effect. Next, enter the marquee message as the value for the <INPUT> VALUE attribute. (Alternatively, you can assign the value to the text object using its value parameter.) Here is the form definition code:

```
<FORM NAME="marqueeForm">
<CENTER>
<INPUT
    NAME =  "marqueeText"
    SIZE =  50
```

Creating Special Effects with JavaScript

CHAPTER 16

427

16

CREATING SPECIAL
EFFECTS WITH
JAVASCRIPT

```
        VALUE = "THIS JUST IN...JavaScript is selected as official
                scripting language of the 1998 Winter Olympics..."
   >
</CENTER>
</FORM>
```

Once we have the "marquee container" defined, we can get to the heart of the matter. We first want to define two global "constants" to use in the marquee: the rate (in milliseconds) at which to scroll, and the number of characters to scroll at a time. Also, we will create a string object called `marqueeMessage` that we will use as well:

```
var SCROLL_RATE = 100;
var SCROLL_CHARS = 1;
var marqueeMessage = new String();
```

The next task is to create a function, called `JSMarquee()`, that transforms your ordinary text object into the look of a marquee. Because a marquee requires continuous updating, you will need to make `JSMarquee()` recursive by calling `setTimeout()` at the start of the function. (See Chapter 10, "Handling Events," for more information on the `setTimeout()` method, as well as the "Billboard" section of this chapter.) The global variable `SCROLL_RATE` is used as the method parameter to determine how often to call the function.

The heart of the `JSMarquee()` function is to first get the value of the text object and assign it to the `marqueeMessage` string. You can then simulate the word wrapping by chopping off a chunk of the message at the front and placing it on the end of the string. The String object's `substring()` method is used to do this, as shown here:

```
function JSMarquee() {

    setTimeout('JSMarquee()', SCROLL_RATE);
    marqueeMessage = document.marqueeForm.marqueeText.value;
    document.marqueeForm.marqueeText.value =
        marqueeMessage.substring( SCROLL_CHARS ) +
        marqueeMessage.substring( 0, SCROLL_CHARS );
}
```

Figures 16.1 and 16.2 show the scrolling effect of the marquee as it runs continuously while you are on the page.

The complete source code for the marquee example is shown in Listing 16.1.

NOTE

The code shown in Listing 16.1 adds a little extra JavaScript code to the example so you can define the text of the message to be a global variable. If you change the scrolling text message often, you may find it easier to maintain with such an implementation.

FIGURE 16.1.
The start of the scrolling marquee.

FIGURE 16.2.
JavaScript simulates the word-wrapping effect of a marquee.

Listing 16.1. JSMarquee.html.

```
<HTML>
<HEAD>
<SCRIPT LANGUAGE= "JavaScript">
<!--
```

```
/*======================================================================
            JSMarquee

        Description:
            Provides a marquee using a text object.

        Requirements:
            JavaScript 1.0

======================================================================*/

        var SCROLL_RATE = 100;
        var SCROLL_CHARS = 1;
        var MESSAGE = "THIS JUST IN...JavaScript is selected as" +
            "official scripting language of the 1998 Winter Olympics...";
        var marqueeMessage = new String();


        function JSMarquee() {

            setTimeout( 'JSMarquee()', SCROLL_RATE );

            marqueeMessage = document.marqueeForm.marqueeText.value;
            document.marqueeForm.marqueeText.value =
                marqueeMessage.substring( SCROLL_CHARS ) +
                marqueeMessage.substring( 0, SCROLL_CHARS );
        }
//-->
</SCRIPT>
</HEAD>
<BODY onLoad="JSMarquee()">
<FORM NAME="marqueeForm">
<CENTER>
<INPUT
    NAME =   "marqueeText"
    SIZE =   50
 >
</CENTER>
<SCRIPT LANGUAGE= "JavaScript">
        document.marqueeForm.marqueeText.value = MESSAGE;
</SCRIPT>
</FORM>
</BODY>
</HTML>
```

Billboards

Billboards are another common component found on Web pages. They are eye-catching teasers often used for advertising, as shown in Figure 16.3. Invariably, their mission is to be interesting enough to be noticed and tantalizing enough to get a user to click them. Using JavaScript image objects, you can create professional-caliber billboards without the need for animated GIFs or Java applets.

FIGURE 16.3.

Billboards are in-creasingly becoming a standard part of popular Web sites.

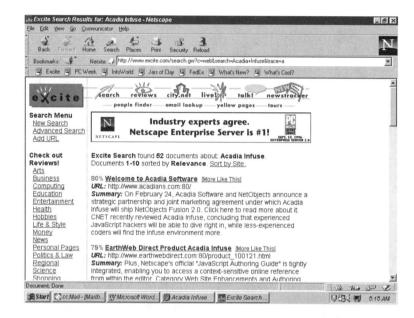

Once your billboard GIF files are ready, you need to follow these steps to create a JavaScript billboard:

1. Create an image placeholder on your Web page.
2. Define an array to hold your primary images and one to hold your transitional images.

Creating Special Effects with JavaScript

CHAPTER 16

431

16

CREATING SPECIAL
EFFECTS WITH
JAVASCRIPT

3. Develop a routine to manage image presentation.

4. Associate this function as an event handler of the window's onLoad event.

To begin, create an image object on your Web page that will serve as the placeholder for all the action. Because billboards typically take you somewhere once they're clicked, you'll probably want to put the <IMG> tag inside a link:

```
<A HREF = "http://www.acadians.com"
        onMouseOver = "window.status='http://www.acadians.com';" +
            "return true;"
        onMouseOut = "window.status = ''; return true;">
    <IMG NAME = "billboard"
        HEIGHT = 49
        WIDTH  = 333
        SRC    = "./visjs.gif">
    </A>
```

NOTE

Note the onMouseOver and onMouseOut event handlers that are defined in the link object. Although they aren't needed if you're hardcoding the URL, they become useful if each of the primary images in your billboard has a different URL destination. You would then create a URL array and have the mouseOver text dependent on the active image.

Within your <HEAD>, you need to add a <SCRIPT> tag and define a series of variables and objects. You have two global "constants" for the amount of time (in milliseconds) to display the primary images and an additional constant for the amount of time to display the transitional images. Two additional variables are defined for use later:

```
/* Global constants */
var DISPLAY_TIME = 3500;
var TRANSITION_TIME = 50;

/* Global variables */
var primaryIdx = 0;
var transIdx = 0;
```

Two arrays should now be defined to hold the information about both the primary and transitional image sets. For each array element, the image src property is declared:

```
/* First array contains primary images */
JSBillboardArray = new Array( 3 );
JSBillboardArray[0] = new Image( 49, 333 );
JSBillboardArray[0].src = "./visjs.gif";
JSBillboardArray[1] = new Image( 49, 333 );
JSBillboardArray[1].src = "./url.gif";
JSBillboardArray[2] = new Image( 49, 333 );
JSBillboardArray[2].src = "./bltwith.gif";

/* Second array contains transitionary images */
transArray = new Array( 6 );
```

```
transArray[0] = new Image( 49, 333 );
transArray[0].src = "./bw7.gif";
transArray[1] = new Image( 49, 333 );
transArray[1].src = "./bw6.gif";
transArray[2] = new Image( 49, 333 );
transArray[2].src = "./bw5.gif";
transArray[3] = new Image( 49, 333 );
transArray[3].src = "./bw4.gif";
transArray[4] = new Image( 49, 333 );
transArray[4].src = "./bw3.gif";
transArray[5] = new Image( 49, 333 );
transArray[5].src = "./bw2.gif";
```

The main function used to run the billboard is called runJSBillboard(). First, it determines the rate of change for each billboard cycle, and then it uses that value in a recursive setTimeout() method call. The runJSBillboard() function then calls a second function called repaint():

```
function runJSBillboard() {

    changeRate = DISPLAY_TIME + ( transArray.length * TRANSITION_TIME );
    setTimeout( "runJSBillboard()", changeRate );

    repaint();

}
```

The repaint() function is the nuts and bolts of a JavaScript billboard. It determines which image to display in this cycle. First up are the transitional images, and repaint() begins by checking to see their state and determining whether they have completed cycling. If they are, the if section of code is processed, displaying the current primary image. If they have not, the else section of code is executed:

```
function repaint() {

  if ( transIdx > transArray.length - 1 ) {

    primaryIdx++;
    transIdx = 0;

    if ( primaryIdx > JSBillboardArray.length - 1 ) primaryIdx = 0;

      document.billboard.src = JSBillboardArray[primaryIdx].src;

      return;
  }

  else {

        document.billboard.src = transArray[transIdx].src;
        setTimeout( "repaint()", TRANSITION_TIME );

  }

  transIdx++;
}
```

The repaint() function deserves a closer look. The if section is designed to display a primary image—specifically, the one that is current in the JSBillboardArray. When it does so, it resets the transIdx variable to 0 so that the transitional cycle will begin the next time through repaint(). After checking to see if the primaryIdx should be reset as well, it returns control to the calling function runJSBillboard().

Because runJSBillboard() is recursive, the repaint() function is immediately processed again. Because the if clause was processed last time, you can be assured that the else clause will kick in this time around. This section of code displays the current transitional image from the transArray array. It then calls setTimeout() to recursively call repaint(). For each transitional cycle, the else clause is triggered until the last transitional image is displayed. The next time repaint() is called (by itself), the if clause resets everything when it executes.

NOTE

Recursion can be a difficult programming concept to understand. But, as this example shows, you can use it for some powerful coding techniques.

Figures 16.4, 16.5, and 16.6 show snapshots of the billboard cycling process.

FIGURE 16.4.

The initial primary image.

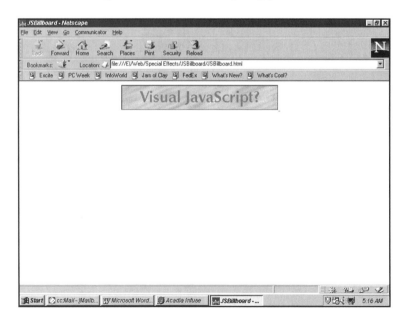

FIGURE 16.5.
One of the five transitional images.

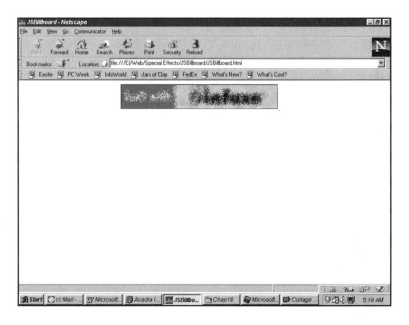

FIGURE 16.6.
The second primary image.

Listing 16.2 provides the full source code for the billboard example.

Listing 16.2. JSBillboard.html.

```
<HTML>
<HEAD>
<TITLE>JSBillboard</TITLE>
<SCRIPT LANGUAGE= "JavaScript">
<!--
        /*=======================================================
                JSBillboard

                Description:
                        Creates a billboard using JavaScript.

                Requirements:
                        JavaScript 1.1 or higher

        =====================================================*/

        /* Global constants */
        var BB_URL = 'http://www.acadians.com';
        var DISPLAY_TIME = 3500;
        var TRANSITION_TIME = 50;

        /* Global variables */
        var primaryIdx = 0;
        var transIdx = 0;


        /* First array contains primary images */
        JSBillboardArray = new Array( 3 );
        JSBillboardArray[0] = new Image( 49, 333 );
        JSBillboardArray[0].src = "./visjs.gif";
        JSBillboardArray[1] = new Image( 49, 333 );
        JSBillboardArray[1].src = "./url.gif";
        JSBillboardArray[2] = new Image( 49, 333 );
        JSBillboardArray[2].src = "./bltwith.gif";

        /* Second array contains transitional images */
        transArray = new Array();
        transArray[0] = new Image( 49, 333 );
        transArray[0].src = "./bw7.gif";
        transArray[1] = new Image( 49, 333 );
        transArray[1].src = "./bw6.gif";
        transArray[2] = new Image( 49, 333 );
        transArray[2].src = "./bw5.gif";
        transArray[3] = new Image( 49, 333 );
        transArray[3].src = "./bw4.gif";
        transArray[4] = new Image( 49, 333 );
        transArray[4].src = "./bw3.gif";
        transArray[5] = new Image( 49, 333 );
        transArray[5].src = "./bw2.gif";
```

continues

Listing 16.2. continued

```
/*--------------------------------------------------
    runJSBillboard()

    Recursive routine loops through the billboard cycle.

-------------------------------------------------- */
function runJSBillboard() {

  changeRate = DISPLAY_TIME +
      ( transArray.length * TRANSITION_TIME );
  setTimeout( "runJSBillboard()", changeRate );

  repaint();

}


/*--------------------------------------------------
    repaint()

    if clause paints the primary images
    else clause paints the transitional images

-------------------------------------------------- */
function repaint() {

  if ( transIdx > transArray.length - 1 ) {

    primaryIdx++;  // Increment primary image index
    transIdx = 0;  // Reset transitional image index

    if ( primaryIdx > JSBillboardArray.length - 1 )
        primaryIdx = 0;  // Reset primary index
    document.billboard.src = JSBillboardArray[primaryIdx].src;

    return; // Return to runJSBillboard()
  }

  else {

    // Display transitional image
    document.billboard.src = transArray[transIdx].src;

    // Run repaint() recursively through cycle
    setTimeout( "repaint()", TRANSITION_TIME );
  }

  transIdx++; // Increment transitonary index
  }
//-->
</SCRIPT>
</HEAD>

<BODY onLoad = "runJSBillboard()">
<CENTER>
```

```
<A HREF = "http://www.acadians.com"
        onMouseOver = "window.status = BB_URL; return true;"
        onMouseOut = "window.status = ''; return true;">
    <IMG NAME = "billboard"
         HEIGHT = 49
         WIDTH  = 333
         SRC    = "./visjs.gif">
    </A>
</CENTER>
</BODY>
</HTML>
```

Color Fading

So far in this chapter, we have looked at how you can use JavaScript to simulate a control, such as a billboard or marquee, which is typically implemented using Java. However, ignore the hype you read in the press: Java can't do everything. A case in point is the next technique—fading the color of an HTML page. Because JavaScript has an ability to control an HTML document that Java doesn't, it works best for techniques such as this.

Color fading is performed by gradually changing the value of the document object's bgColor property. This property is either a hexadecimal RGB triplet or a string literal representing an RGB triplet, such as "aqua" or "red." Although string literals are easy to work with when setting the bgColor property on a one-time basis, you need to use an hexadecimal RGB triplet value in the format rrggbb.

Using JavaScript, you can create a function called JSFade() to perform the color fading and then simply make a call to that function when the document loads. The JSFade() function has seven parameters:

- Initial RGB values for red, green, and blue
- Ending RGB values for red, green, and blue
- The number of milliseconds to perform the fading process

Next, a for loop is used to step through the fading process. It's dependent on the delay parameter to determine the actual number of times the for loop is processed. Two variables are defined: finishPercent tells the percentage of the process left until the process is finished, and startPercent tells the percentage of the process that has completed. The heart of the color fade process is in the next statement, which assigns a value to the document.bgColor property based on adding the quotient of the starting red value times the startPercent variable and the quotient of the finishing red value times the finishPercent variable. This process is repeated for both the green and blue sets as well.

```
function JSFade(startRed, startGreen, startBlue, finishRed,
                finishGreen, finishBlue, delay) {
```

```
for ( var i=1; i<=delay-1; i++ ) {

    var finishPercent = i/delay;
    var startPercent = 1 - finishPercent;

    document.bgColor =

        Math.floor( startRed * startPercent + finishRed *
                FinishPercent )*256*256 +
        Math.floor( startGreen * startPercent + finishGreen *
                FinishPercent )*256 +
        Math.floor( startBlue * startPercent + finishBlue *
                FinishPercent );

    }
}
```

You can then call this in your script. For example, to fade from off-white to teal green, you would use the following:

```
JSFade( 255,255,240,0,128,128,170 );
```

To fade from blue to red, you would use this:

```
JSFade( 0,0,198,196,2,40, 170 );
```

Finally, to fade from black to white, you would use this:

```
JSFade( 0,0,0,255,255,255, 170 );
```

Listing 16.3 provides the source code for this color fade example.

Listing 16.3. JSFade.html.

```
<HTML>
<HEAD>
<SCRIPT LANGUAGE= "JavaScript">
<!--
    /*=========================================================
                JSFade

        Description:
                Progressively fades the colour of the HTML document.

        Requirements:
                JavaScript 1.0
                Quirky in JScript

    =========================================================*/

    function JSFade(startRed, startGreen, startBlue, finishRed,
        finishGreen, finishBlue, delay) {

        for ( var i=1; i<=delay-1; i++ ) {
```

```
        var finishPercent = i/delay;
        var startPercent = 1 - finishPercent;

        document.bgColor =

            Math.floor( startRed * startPercent + finishRed *
               finishPercent )*256*256 +
            Math.floor( startGreen * startPercent + finishGreen *
               finishPercent )*256 +
            Math.floor( startBlue * startPercent + finishBlue *
               finishPercent );

    }
}


    JSFade( 255,255,240,0,128,128,170 );

//-->
</SCRIPT>
</HEAD>
</HTML>
```

Animated Pushbuttons

The look and feel of the Web has come a long way over the past three years. Originally a text-based technology medium, the Web today sports graphics, multimedia, and sophisticated page layouts. However, one aspect of the old "ugly" look is form objects, such as text input boxes and pushbuttons. After all, you can't even specify the font for these controls yet. It isn't surprising, therefore, that many Web developers are looking to JavaScript to provide alternatives to one of the most common UI controls today: buttons. Although no graphical button objects are available yet, with the image object, JavaScript does a remarkably good job of simulating the behavior of a pushbutton.

NOTE

As with the billboard example from earlier in this chapter, you need to first assemble the appropriate GIF files to use on your Web page.

In this example, I'll show you how to use JavaScript to simulate the look and feel of the new Windows 97 style of buttons, first popularized with Microsoft Internet Explorer 3.0. This new style looks flat until you place the mouse cursor on top of them, at which point they take on a three-dimensional effect. With that in mind, you will add Previous and Next buttons to the page to simulate the Prev and Next buttons of any browser.

To create animated pushbuttons like these, you need to do the following:

1. Create image placeholders on your Web page for each of the buttons.

2. Define image objects and associate a GIF or JPG file with these language constructs.

3. Create a routine to display images on demand.

4. Add handlers for `onMouseOver` and `onMouseOut` events.

5. Add handler code for the link object's click event.

To use image objects to serve as button replacements, you can define the `<IMG>` tags. However, because image objects don't respond to events, you need to encapsulate each of the images in a link object. This is shown in the following code:

```
<A HREF=""
    <IMG SRC="./prev_off.gif"
        BORDER  = 0
        WIDTH   = 52
        HEIGHT  = 42
        NAME    = "Prev">
</A

<A HREF=""
    <IMG SRC="./next_off.gif"
        BORDER  = 0
        WIDTH   = 52
        HEIGHT  = 42
        NAME    = "Next">
</A>
```

Within a `<SCRIPT>` tag in the `<HEAD>` section of the HTML document, you need to define image objects for each of the four images to be used: two representing the flat button look, and two representing the 3D look. At this time, you also associate the image object with an external source:

```
var prevBtnOff = new Image( 42, 52 );
prevBtnOff.src = "./prev_off.gif";

var prevBtnOn =  new Image( 42, 52 );
prevBtnOn.src = "./prev_on.gif";

var nextBtnOff = new Image( 42, 52 );
nextBtnOff.src = "./next_off.gif";

var nextBtnOn =  new Image( 42, 52 );
nextBtnOn.src = "./next_on.gif";
```

So far we have defined placeholder `<IMG>` tags for both the Previous and Next buttons and instantiated the associated image objects for both their "off" and "on" states. Next, we can add a function called `highlightButton()` that changes the "state" of an image being displayed on demand.

The `highlightButton()` function has two parameters: One is the name of the `<IMG>` image placeholder, and one is the name of the image object to be displayed. You can use the built-in `document.images` array to reference the `<IMG>` image placeholder:

```
function highlightButton(placeholder, imageObject) {
  document.images[placeholder].src = eval( imageObject + ".src" )
}
```

We now need to return to the `<IMG>` tag definitions to add the appropriate event handler code to them. For both animated buttons, when a mouse cursor passes over them, we want the buttons to reflect an "on," 3D-like state; otherwise, we want them to appear flat. You can add `onMouseOver` and `onMouseOut` event handlers to do just that. Therefore, when a `onMouseOver` event is triggered, the `highlightButton()` function is called for that button. Then, when the `onMouseOut` event is called, the `highlightButton()` function is called again for the "off" state image to appear:

```
<A HREF="javascript:history.back()"
    onMouseOver = "highlightButton( 'Prev', 'prevBtnOn'
                  );window.status='Previous';return true;"
    onMouseOut = "highlightButton( 'Prev', 'prevBtnOff'
                  );window.status='';return true;" >
     <IMG SRC="./prev_off.gif"
            BORDER  = 0
            WIDTH   = 52
            HEIGHT  = 42
            NAME    = "Prev">
</A>

<A HREF="javascript:history.forward()"
    onMouseOver = "highlightButton( 'Next', 'nextBtnOn'
                  );window.status='Next';return true;"
    onMouseOut = "highlightButton( 'Next', 'nextBtnOff'
                  );window.status='';return true;" >
     <IMG SRC="./next_off.gif"
            BORDER  = 0
            WIDTH   = 52
            HEIGHT  = 42
            NAME    = "Next">
</A>
```

The final step is to add code to respond to the clicking of an animated button. Because the image object can't respond to a click event, you need to use the `javascript:` protocol in the `<A>` link object's HREF property. As shown in the preceding code, the history object's `back()` and `forward()` methods are employed to provide the desired capabilities.

As a last "cleanup," you need to add some additional code to the `onMouseOver` and `onMouseOut` event handers to customize the message in the browser's status bar. If you don't do this, the `javascript:` protocol is shown.

Figures 16.7 and 16.8 show the code in action.

Figure 16.7.

Buttons in their normal flat state.

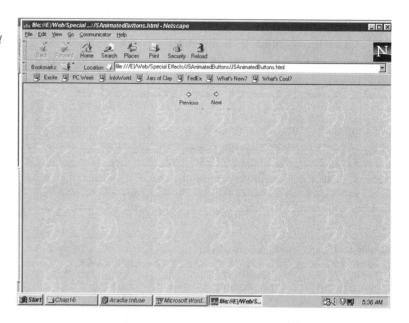

Figure 16.8.

Previous button changes to the 3D state when the mouse cursor is over it.

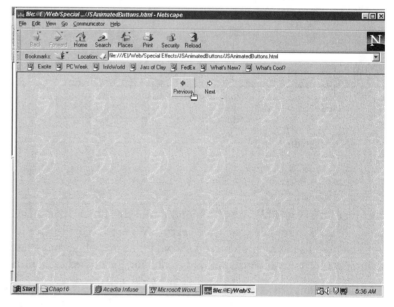

Listing 16.4 provides the complete source code.

Listing 16.4. JSAnimatedButtons.html.

```
<HTML>
<HEAD>
<SCRIPT LANGUAGE= "JavaScript">
<!--

    /*=======================================================

      JSAnimatedButtons

        Description:
          Creates animated "Windows 97" Previous and Next buttons.

        Requirements:
          JavaScript 1.1 or higher

    =======================================================*/

          /* Define image objects */
          var prevBtnOff = new Image( 42, 52 );
          prevBtnOff.src = "./prev_off.gif";

          var prevBtnOn =  new Image( 42, 52 );
          prevBtnOn.src = "./prev_on.gif";

          var nextBtnOff = new Image( 42, 52 );
          nextBtnOff.src = "./next_off.gif";

          var nextBtnOn =  new Image( 42, 52 );
          nextBtnOn.src = "./next_on.gif";


      /* Changes image being displayed. */
          function highlightButton(placeholder, imageObject) {
            document.images[placeholder].src = eval( imageObject + ".src" )
          }

//-->
</SCRIPT>
</HEAD>
<BODY background="./aiback.gif">
<CENTER>
<A HREF="javascript:history.back()"
    onMouseOver = "highlightButton( 'Prev', 'prevBtnOn' );window.status=
      'Previous';return true;"
    onMouseOut = "highlightButton( 'Prev', 'prevBtnOff' );window.status='';
     return true;" >
    <IMG SRC="./prev_off.gif"
           BORDER  = 0
           WIDTH   = 52
           HEIGHT  = 42
           NAME    = "Prev">
</A>
```

continues

Listing 16.4. continued

```
<A HREF="javascript:history.forward()"
    onMouseOver =
        "highlightButton( 'Next', 'nextBtnOn' );window.status='Next';return true;"
    onMouseOut =
        "highlightButton( 'Next', 'nextBtnOff' );window.status='';return true;" >
    <IMG SRC="./next_off.gif"
            BORDER  = 0
            WIDTH   = 52
            HEIGHT  = 42
            NAME    = "Next">
</A>
</CENTER>
</BODY>
</HTML>
```

Summary

Let's be honest: Many Web sites are boring to look at and have little visual appeal. After all, HTML by itself can do nothing more than place a flat image on a page and display it. Many people are using Java applets to add "life" to HTML, but as JavaScript matures, it's becoming an increasingly popular option as well.

JavaScript 1.1 and 1.2 have added several capabilities that let you visually enhance the appearance of your Web site. In this chapter, you looked at four of the most popular examples of using JavaScript to create special effects: marquees, billboards, animated buttons, and fading backgrounds. In the next chapter, the special effects discussion continues by looking at how you can use Netscape's new layers technology to create textured pages under Netscape Navigator and how JavaScript can be used to control them programmatically.

Controlling Layers
with JavaScript

CHAPTER 17

Until recently, one of the fundamental limitations of Web pages has been the inability to precisely position text or images on a page. Additionally, there was no way to overlap HTML elements on a page. Products such as FutureTense Texture and others were built mainly to provide a way around this restriction by producing layered text and graphics as a single image that HTML could understand.

One of most innovative aspects of Netscape Navigator 4.0 is its support for layers. Layers let you define overlays of transparent or solid content in an HTML document, which can be positioned precisely where you want them. Layers are implemented using the new HTML elements <LAYER> and <ILAYER> (the I stands for *inflow*), which let you encapsulate HTML elements inside of them. Moreover, you have considerable power to control layers from within JavaScript, which is of primary concern to you as a JavaScript developer. This chapter looks at how to manipulate layers using JavaScript by exploring the following topics:

- Accessing layers from JavaScript
- Managing overlaying layers
- Creating animation effects

Accessing Layers Using JavaScript

Layers are defined in an HTML document using the <LAYER> and <ILAYER> tags. <LAYER> elements let you precisely position a layer on a page, whereas <ILAYER> elements appear in the natural flow of the document. The HTML definition for the <LAYER> tag is as follows (<ILAYER> has same definition):

```
<LAYER
        NAME="layerName"
        LEFT=xPosition
        TOP=yPosition
        Z-INDEX=layerZ
        WIDTH=layerWidth
        CLIP="x1_offset, y1_offset, x2_offset, y2_offset"
        ABOVE="layerName"
        BELOW="layerName"
        VISIBILITY=SHOW ¦ HIDE ¦ INHERIT
        BGCOLOR="rgbColor"
        BACKGROUND="imageURL">

</LAYER>
```

In JavaScript, layers are treated like other HTML elements, such as form or frame objects. Layer objects are created implicitly as the <LAYER> elements are defined in HTML. A layer object has the properties listed in Table 17.1.

Table 17.1. Layer object properties.

Property	Read-Only?	Description
name	Yes	The name of <LAYER>.
width	Yes	The width of the layer in pixels.
height	Yes	The height of the layer in pixels.
left	No	The x-axis position of the layer in pixels, relative to the origin of its parent layer.
top	No	The y-axis position of the layer in pixels, relative to the origin of its parent layer.
zIndex	No	The relative z-order of the layer, relative to its siblings and parent.
visibility	No	Defines whether or not the layer is visible. show will display the layer, hide will hide the layer, and inherit will inherit the visibility of its parent layer.
clip.top, clip.left, clip.right, clip.bottom, clip.width, clip.height	No	Clip properties define the "clipping rectangle," which defines the region of the layer that is made visible. Anything outside of this rectangle is clipped from view.
background	No	The URL of an image to use as the background for the layer.
bgColor	No	The background color for the layer.
siblingAbove	Yes	The layer object above this one in z-order, among all layers within the same parent layer (null if this layer is topmost).
siblingBelow	Yes	The layer object below this one in z-order, among all layers within the same parent layer (null if this layer is bottommost).
above	Yes	The layer object above this one in z-order, among all layers in the document (null if this layer is topmost).
below	Yes	The layer object below this one in z-order, among all layers in the document (null if this layer is bottommost).
parentLayer	Yes	The layer object that contains this layer (null if this layer is not within another layer).

17

CONTROLLING
LAYERS WITH
JAVASCRIPT

continues

Table 17.1. continued

Property	Read-Only?	Description
layers	Yes	The array enumerating all child layer objects by both name and index (null if no child layers exist).
src	Yes	The URL for the layer's content source.

Layer object methods are defined in Table 17.2.

Table 17.2. Layer object methods.

Method Name	Description
offset(x, y)	Alters the position of the layer by applying the x,y deltas in pixels.
moveTo(x, y)	Changes the layer position to the specified x,y pixel coordinates.
resize(width, height)	Resizes the layer to the specified height and width values in pixels. Existing content might be clipped if it falls outside the specified dimensions.
moveAbove(layer)	Stacks this layer above the specified layer. (After restacking, both layers will have the same parent layer.)
moveBelow(layer)	Stacks this layer below the specified layer. (After restacking, both layers will have the same parent layer.)

Managing Overlying Layers

The visible property of the layer object can be effectively used to produce some interesting visual effects. For example, suppose you wanted to display some chart report data on a Web page. Your goal is to have one chart displayed at a time while giving the user the option of viewing one of the other charts. Perhaps if you were working in a Windows environment, you could imagine the use of a tabbed window for this purpose, with each chart being shown on a separate tab. Layers make it possible to have a similar effect on a Web page.

> **NOTE**
>
> For our example, you could achieve similar results using dynamic image objects in Java-Script 1.1, but layers are far more powerful. They let you present any arbitrary HTML you like, not just images.

Defining the <LAYER> Elements

For this example, four GIF images are used to display charts within a tabbed page control. (You can see the image showing the 1997 chart in Figure 17.1.) Each of these images is assigned to a separate layer within our HTML document. The <LAYER> elements are given the same LEFT and TOP parameters so that they will lie directly on top of each other.

FIGURE 17.1.

The GIF image used in the example.

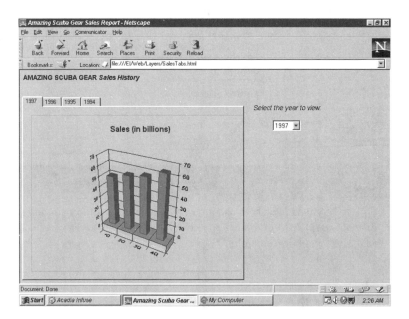

```
<LAYER NAME="tab3" LEFT=5 TOP=55>
    <IMG SRC="./1994tab.gif">
</LAYER>
<LAYER NAME="tab2" LEFT=5 TOP=55>
    <IMG SRC="./1995tab.gif">
</LAYER>
<LAYER NAME="tab1" LEFT=5 TOP=55>
    <IMG SRC="./1996tab.gif">
</LAYER>
<LAYER NAME="tab0" LEFT=5 TOP=55>
    <IMG SRC="./1997tab.gif">
</LAYER>
```

NOTE

Layers use the concept of "The last shall be first" (or, at least, "highest"). In the preceding code, notice that the 1997 tab was defined last in the sequence of the HTML file. The final layer element defined is considered the highest and will be lain on top of the others.

In order to provide some user interaction, we can define another layer containing a form with a select list. The user can then select a tab to view from this list. We can define an onChange event handler to execute a function called showTab() and send the selected option as its parameter. Here is the code:

```
<LAYER NAME="Select" LEFT=500 TOP=55 WIDTH=150>
    <CENTER>
      <P><I>Select the year to view:</I></P>
      <FORM NAME="selectForm">
          <SELECT NAME="pickYear" SIZE=1
                  onChange="showTab(this.selectedIndex); return false;">
                <OPTION SELECTED>1997
                <OPTION>1996
                <OPTION>1995
                <OPTION>1994
          </SELECT>
      </FORM>
    </CENTER>
</LAYER>
```

> **NOTE**
>
> Optimally, you would like an image map defined for the tab boundaries of the images. By associating an onClick event handler with these areas, you could simulate the feel of a typical tabbed page control.

Displaying the Selected Tab

We can now create the showTab() function, which is used to display the selected tab. To do this, we first need to hide all layers, and then we can make the selected layer visible. (As of this writing, there was no bringToTop() method for a layer.) The following code uses the document.layers array to step through each layer in the document, hiding each of the layers (except the Select form layer). Next, the selected tab is assigned the inherit value to make it visible.

```
function showTab( idx ) {
    for ( var i=1; i<document.layers.length; i++ ) {
        if ( document.layers[i].name != 'Select' ) {
                document.layers[i].visibility = 'hide';
        }

    }
    document.layers["tab"+idx].visibility = 'inherit';
}
```

Viewing the Results

When we view and test the code, we can select a year from the Select list to display the corresponding tab. Figure 17.2 shows the result of the 1996 option's being selected from the Select list.

FIGURE 17.2.

The 1996 layer is made visible.

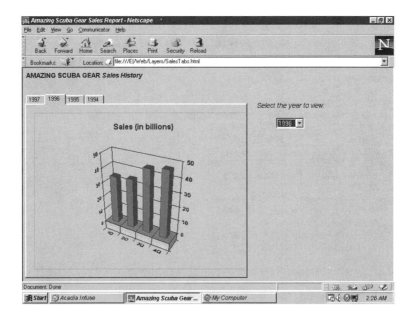

Listing 17.1 provides the complete source code for this example.

Listing 17.1. SalesTabs.html.

```
<HTML>
<HEAD>
<TITLE>Amazing Scuba Gear Sales Report</TITLE>
<SCRIPT LANGUAGE= "JavaScript">
<!--
      /*=====================================================
            SalesTabs
            Description:
                  Simulates tabbed notebook.
            Requirements:
                  JavaScript 1.2 or higher


      ===================================================*/
      /*---------------------------------------------
            showTab()

            Display appropriate tab based on index value.

      --------------------------------------------- */
```

continues

Listing 17.1. continued

```
            function showTab( idx ) {

                    for ( var i=1; i<document.layers.length; i++ ) {
                        if ( document.layers[i].name != 'Select' ) {
                                document.layers[i].visibility = 'hide';
                        }


                    }
                    document.layers["tab"+idx].visibility = 'inherit';
            }
//-->
</SCRIPT>
</HEAD>
<BODY BGCOLOR="Silver">
<h4>AMAZING SCUBA GEAR <i>Sales History</i></h4>
<LAYER NAME="tab3" LEFT=5 TOP=55>
    <IMG SRC="./1994tab.gif">
</LAYER>
<LAYER NAME="tab2" LEFT=5 TOP=55>
    <IMG SRC="./1995tab.gif">
</LAYER>
<LAYER NAME="tab1" LEFT=5 TOP=55>
    <IMG SRC="./1996tab.gif">
</LAYER>
<LAYER NAME="tab0" LEFT=5 TOP=55>
    <IMG SRC="./1997tab.gif">
</LAYER>
<LAYER NAME="Select" LEFT=500 TOP=55 WIDTH=150>
   <CENTER>
     <P><I>Select the year to view:</I></P>
     <FORM NAME="selectForm">
         <SELECT NAME="pickYear" SIZE=1
                     onChange="showTab(this.selectedIndex); return false;">
                     <OPTION SELECTED>1997
                     <OPTION>1996
                     <OPTION>1995
                       <OPTION>1994
         </SELECT>
     </FORM>
   </CENTER>
</LAYER>
</BODY>
</HTML>
```

Creating Animation Effects

One of the most intriguing aspects of layers is the way you can use them to create animations. Because JavaScript lets you dynamically position layers, you can create recursive routines in which layers can appear to slide or jump across the document. The possibilities are endless. Let's look at an example. Suppose we would like to create a bouncing ball animation on a page, in which three balls move independently within specified boundaries.

Defining the <LAYER> Elements

To create this animation, we can use three different GIF images to represent a green ball, a red ball, and a multicolored ball. Once we have the images, we want to enclose each one in separate <LAYER> elements:

```
<BODY>
<LAYER NAME="greenball" WIDTH=13 HEIGHT=13 LEFT=5 TOP=1>
     <IMG SRC="./grnball.gif">
</LAYER>
<LAYER NAME="redball" WIDTH=13 HEIGHT=13 LEFT=25 TOP=135>
     <IMG SRC="./redball.gif">
</LAYER>
<LAYER NAME="colourball" WIDTH=13 HEIGHT=13 LEFT=255 TOP=115>
     <IMG SRC="./clrball.gif">
</LAYER>
</BODY>
```

The WIDTH and HEIGHT parameters of the <LAYER> elements have the same dimensions as the GIF images. The LEFT and TOP parameters are random numbers positioned within a "canvas" that we will arbitrarily define as 400 pixels wide by 200 pixels deep. These are the coordinates from which the balls will start.

Specifying Global Variables

After adding a <SCRIPT> element within the <HEAD> section of the document, we can define some global variables used throughout our animation routines. For each of the balls, we will be using the layer object's offset() method, which lets you change the layer's position by applying a delta of x,y values. With that in mind, we want to have a pair of x,y delta values for each ball:

```
var grnX = 2;
var grnY = 2.5;

var redX = 2;
var redY = -2;

var colourX = 2;
var colourY = 3;
```

Therefore, when applied later in the offset(), these variables call for the green ball to move 2 pixels to the left and 2.5 pixels down from its current position, the red ball to move 2 pixels left and 2 pixels up, and the multicolored ball to move 2 pixels left and 3 pixels down.

We also want to specify within this script for a new property of the window object called flickerFree to be set to true. This property helps provide for smoother animation effects:

```
window.flickerFree = true;
```

Accessing Layer Objects

Before working with the <LAYER> elements in our JavaScript code, we need to reference each layer and assign it to a variable. Within the <BODY> section of the document, add a new <SCRIPT> element and place the following code in it:

```
<SCRIPT LANGUAGE="JavaScript1.2">
<!--
        var green = document.layers["greenball"];
        var red = document.layers['redball'];
        var colour = document.layers['colourball'];
//-->
</SCRIPT>
```

Using the document.layers array, we can access each of the layers by name and assign a variable to represent them in the script.

> **NOTE**
>
> Unlike the number variables defined earlier, you can't place this layer object assignment code in the <HEAD> script, because it references elements that are defined later in the <BODY>. Therefore, this assignment code must be processed after the <LAYER> elements have been defined.

Defining the Animator Functions

Our next step is to create the script to actually perform the animations. Our purpose is rather simple to start: Set each ball in motion based on its offset() value specified earlier. However, in reality, there is much to do around the periphery of this core functionality.

Specifically, we need to continually monitor the x,y position of each ball before each call to offset(). If we don't, the balls will quickly move beyond the boundaries of the 400×200 canvas and beyond the HTML document itself. Therefore, if the layer object's LEFT property is between 0 and 400 and its TOP property is between 0 and 200, the offset() method should be executed. But if the layer fails in that boundary check, send it in a reverse direction, giving the appearance of a ricochet effect.

Let's look at how this logic is implemented in our script. We are using two functions:

- ■ startTheBallRolling() is the main recursive function, and it's responsible for calling each ball to animate. It also performs necessary correction of the offset values when the ball tries to move beyond the canvas.

- ■ moveBall() is in charge of moving the ball within the canvas boundaries. It analyzes the top and left properties of the ball and performs an offset() action if they pass the test. If the check fails, this function tells startTheBallRolling() which boundary is being violated.

While moveBall() is invoked by startTheBallRolling(), perhaps it makes the most sense to look at moveBall() first and then work our way back to startTheBallRolling(). The moveBall() function has three parameters: a reference to a ball object, and its x,y offset values. Performing the logic discussed earlier, it checks the ball's LEFT and TOP properties and does one of the following:

■ Performs the offset() and returns a value of 'ok' to startTheBallRolling().

■ Returns a value of 'topBoundary' to the calling function, denoting that the TOP property is being violated.

■ Returns a value of 'leftBoundary' to the calling function, denoting that the LEFT property is being violated.

The code is as follows:

```
function moveBall(ball, offsetX, offsetY) {
        if (( ball.left < 400 )  && ( ball.left > 0 )) {

            if (( ball.top < 200 ) && ( ball.top > 0 )) {
                    ball.offset( offsetX, offsetY );
                    return 'ok';  }

            else {

                 return 'topBoundary';
            } }

        else {

                 return 'leftBoundary';

        }
}
```

Now, let's look at the function that calls moveBall(). For each of the three ball objects, startTheBallRolling() calls moveBall() and then analyzes the success or failure of the attempt. For the green ball, the code is as follows:

```
if ( moveBall( green, grnX, grnY ) == 'topBoundary' ){
    grnY = 0 - grnY;
    green.offset( grnX, grnY ); }
else {
   if ( moveBall( green, grnX, grnY ) == 'leftBoundary' ) {
        grnX = 0 - grnX;
         green.offset( grnX, grnY ); }
}
```

If moveBall() is successful and returns an 'ok' value, the script moves on. However, if 'topBoundary' (or 'leftBoundary') is returned, we know we need to correct the y (or x) offset value. To do this, we assign a new value to the offending offset value, making it equal to zero minus its current value. An offset() action is then performed, setting the ball on its way in the inverse direction. This same code is duplicated for the red ball and the multicolored ball:

```
if ( moveBall( red, redX, redY ) == 'topBoundary' ){
    redY = 0 - redY;
```

```
        red.offset( redX, redY ); }
else {
   if ( moveBall( red, redX, redY ) == 'leftBoundary' ) {
        redX = 0 - redX;
         red.offset( redX, redY ); }
}
if ( moveBall( colour, colourX, colourY ) == 'topBoundary' ){
     colourY = 0 - colourY;
     colour.offset( colourX, colourY ); }
else {
   if ( moveBall( colour, colourX, colourY ) == 'leftBoundary' ) {
         colourX = 0 - colourX;
          colour.offset( colourX, colourY ); }
}
```

Finally, setTimeout() is called to make this entire process recursive:

```
setTimeout("startTheBallRolling()", 2);
```

The final step is to actually start the ball rolling by assigning startTheBallRolling() to serve as the event handler for the window's onLoad event:

```
<BODY onLoad="startTheBallRolling()">
```

Viewing the Animated Layer Script

After defining the animator functions, the final step is to view and test the code. Figures 17.3 and 17.4 show the animated action.

FIGURE 17.3.

The balls in motion.

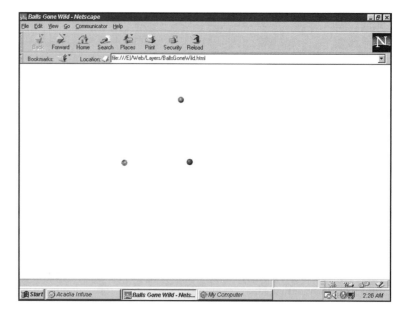

FIGURE 17.4.

Continued action.

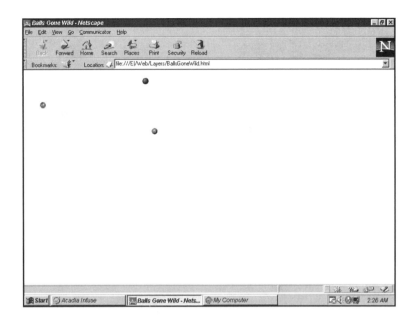

Listing 17.2 provides the entire source file for the BallsGoneWild demo.

Listing 17.2. BallsGoneWild.html.

```
<HTML>
<HEAD>
<TITLE>Balls Gone Wild</TITLE>
<SCRIPT LANGUAGE= "JavaScript1.2">
<!--
        /*=======================================================
                BallsGoneWild
            Description:
                Creates a bouncing ball demo using layers.
            Requirements:
                    JavaScript 1.2 or higher


        =====================================================*/


        /* Global variables */
        var grnX = 2;
        var grnY = 2.5;

        var redX = 2;
        var redY = -2;

        var colourX = 2;
        var colourY = 3;
        /* Smooth animation effects */
        window.flickerFree = true;
```

continues

Listing 17.2. continued

```
/*------------------------------------------------
    moveBall()

        Moves ball within the canvas boundaries. It analyzes
        the top and left properties of the ball and performs
        an offset() action if they pass the test. If the check
        fails, this function notifies startTheBallRolling()
        which boundary is being violated.

        Called only by startTheBallingRolling(), not
        directly.

------------------------------------------------ */
function moveBall(ball, offsetX, offsetY) {
    if (( ball.left < 400 ) && ( ball.left > 0 )) {

        if (( ball.top < 200 ) && ( ball.top > 0 )) {
                ball.offset( offsetX, offsetY );
                return 'ok';    }

        else {

            return 'topBoundary';
        } }

    else {

            return 'leftBoundary';

    }
}
/*------------------------------------------------
    startTheBallRolling()

        Recursive function that is responsible for calling
        each ball to animate. It also performs necessary
        correction of the offset values when the ball tries
        to move beyond the canvas.

------------------------------------------------ */
function startTheBallRolling() {
    if ( moveBall( green, grnX, grnY ) == 'topBoundary' ){
        grnY = 0 - grnY;
        green.offset( grnX, grnY ); }
    else {

        if ( moveBall( green, grnX, grnY ) == 'leftBoundary' ) {
            grnX = 0 - grnX;
            green.offset( grnX, grnY ); }
    }
    if ( moveBall( red, redX, redY ) == 'topBoundary' ){
        redY = 0 - redY;
        red.offset( redX, redY ); }
    else {

        if ( moveBall( red, redX, redY ) == 'leftBoundary' ) {
```

```
                        redX = 0 - redX;
                         red.offset( redX, redY ); }
                }
                if ( moveBall( colour, colourX, colourY ) == 'topBoundary' ){
                    colourY = 0 - colourY;
                    colour.offset( colourX, colourY ); }
                else {

                    if ( moveBall( colour, colourX, colourY ) == 'leftBoundary' ) {
                        colourX = 0 - colourX;
                         colour.offset( colourX, colourY ); }
                }
                setTimeout("startTheBallRolling()", 2);
         }
// -->
</SCRIPT>
</HEAD>
<BODY onLoad="startTheBallRolling()">
<LAYER NAME="greenball" WIDTH=13 HEIGHT=13 LEFT=5 TOP=1>
    <IMG SRC="./grnball.gif">
</LAYER>
<LAYER NAME="redball" WIDTH=13 HEIGHT=13 LEFT=25 TOP=135>
    <IMG SRC="./redball.gif">
</LAYER>
<LAYER NAME="colourball" WIDTH=13 HEIGHT=13 LEFT=255 TOP=115>
    <IMG SRC="./clrball.gif">
</LAYER>
<SCRIPT LANGUAGE="JavaScript1.2">
<!--
        /* Define layer objects */
        var green = document.layers["greenball"];
        var red = document.layers['redball'];
        var colour = document.layers['colourball'];
// -->
</SCRIPT>
</BODY>
</HTML>
```

Summary

Layers are potentially one of the most significant advancements in HTML over the past two years. They let you move beyond the sequential word-processor-like world of HTML and into the world of graphical layout and design. JavaScript significantly adds to the power of layers by giving the developer full control over their behavior. The results can be powerful and stunning. The biggest caveat for their use is that layers will initially be a Netscape-specific technology, making widespread use across the Net more difficult until Microsoft Internet Explorer supports them.

JavaScript Style Sheets

IN THIS CHAPTER

The introduction of cascading style sheets into HTML has given developers a more powerful way to express style, enhance presentation, and define more consistent styles in the HTML documents. A style sheet consists of one or more style definitions for HTML properties (fonts sizes, font styles, text alignment, font and background colors, margins, padding, line height, and so on) that can be linked to an HTML document to give consistent styles throughout the document.

JavaScript Style Sheets (JSSS), introduced in Netscape Navigator 4.0, go one step beyond the functionality of cascading style sheets by introducing style sheets that can be attached to HTML documents using JavaScript. Adding JavaScript to style sheets expands the functionality of basic style sheets by allowing the developer to create JavaScript functions and variables that access the Style Sheets. Applying JavaScript with style sheets also allows the developer to change styles at runtime based on user input or other HTML changes.

CAUTION

The JavaScript Style Sheets implementation in the current prerelease of Netscape Navigator 4.0 is not yet complete. Some JSSS definitions may change, and new definitions may be added before the final release of 4.0. Go to

```
http://home.netscape.com/eng/mozilla/3.0/handbook/javascript/index.html
```

or

```
http://developer.netscape.com/library/documentation/communicator/stylesheets/
➥jssindex.htm
```

to get the most up-to-date information on the current style sheet implementation.

Basic JavaScript Style Sheet Concepts

JavaScript Style Sheets are implemented within your HTML document, using methods similar to linking generic JavaScript statements to the document. JSSS definitions may be completely contained within the HTML document itself, or they may be defined in external files and linked from within the HTML document. The external storage and retrieval of style sheets is similar to the external storage of JavaScript code.

The benefit of keeping style sheets defined external to your HTML document is that you can use the JSSS for multiple documents and thus maintain a consistent style throughout a group of HTML documents or even entire Web sites. You can now have a corporate template that uses JavaScript with all HTML documents. Your Web site can now be more consistent and take advantage of JavaScript programming at the same time.

Defining Styles Within Documents

Styles defined with HTML documents are contained in the `<STYLE>` `</STYLE>` elements. The `type` attribute of the `<STYLE>` element is where the style is defined to be accessible through JavaScript. Using the element definition `<STYLE TYPE="text/javascript">`, you are telling the browser that the style sheet being defined is a JSSS.

Listing 18.1 shows a simple JavaScript Style Sheet definition that will make all H1 headers green and italic as the default, and text in the document in 12-point font height as the default.

Listing 18.1. Defining simple styles for <H1> tags and all fonts.

```
<HTML>
<HEAD>
><STYLE TYPE="text/javascript")
document.tags.H1.color="green";
document.tags.H1.fontStyle="italic";
document.tags.all.fontSize="12";
</STYLE>
</HEAD>
<BODY>
</BODY>
</HTML>
```

Linking External Style Sheets

External JavaScript Style Sheets are built similarly to the JSSS defined within the document. The style sheet is stored as a URL containing the style definitions, and any HTML elements (`<STYLE></STYLE>`) are not needed. External JSSS can be linked to an HTML document using two different methods:

```
<LINK>
```

```
<STYLE HRF="">
```

The `<LINK>` element is used to link a JSSS into the document in the header section of the document. Using the `<LINK>` element causes the URL to the style sheets and the type of style sheet to be defined:

```
<HEAD>
<LINK REL=STYLESHEET TYPE="text/javascript"
HREF="http://www.acadians.com/stylesheets/jsunstyle">
</HEAD>
```

The `<STYLE>` element with HREF attribute reference is used to link style sheets directly into the `<STYLE>` element. This format is also useful if multiple JSSSs need to be linked to one HTML document.

18

JAVASCRIPT
STYLE SHEETS

```
<STYLE TYPE="text/javascript" SRC="http://www.acadians.com/
stylesheets/jsunsty1"></STYLE>
<STYLE TYPE="text/javascript" SRC="http://www.acadians.com/stylesheets/
jsunsty2"></STYLE>
```

Using this method, multiple <STYLE></STYLE> element pairs can be implemented to use multiple JavaScript Style Sheets.

The implementation of multiple style sheets brings up the possibility of multiple style definitions for HTML elements. Any style definitions in a style sheet will always take precedence over any styles that have been previously defined for the document.

The use of multiple style sheets can be beneficial when generic styles apply to the entire document and certain styles need to be overwritten for only a portion of the document. This is helpful when a corporate style is defined for the beginning of a document and the developer would like different styles to take precedence when used with JavaScript code.

Using Styles in Your Document

Once the styles have been defined in the JSSS, they can be used in the creation of the HTML document. Styles that are defined at the document.tags level are not explicitly called in the document. These styles are assumed to be the new default styles throughout the document. Using Listing 18.1, the H1 headers in Listing 18.2 would always appear green and italic and would have a font size of 12 points.

Listing 18.2. Using a defined style sheet to apply color to a heading.

```
<HTML>
<BODY>
<H1> This will be green and italic.</H1>
<H2> This will be default text <H2>
</BODY>
</HTML>
```

Styles that are defined by class are explicitly called with the HTML elements at each use. Style classes, as shown in Listing 18.3, can be used to override the existing document defaults or the new element's defaults set by the document.elements JSSS definitions. Figure 18.1 displays the second H1 header in yellow instead of green because the class attribute of the second H1 element overrides the previously defined tag's definition. Note that the italic style remains in effect because only the color property has been overridden.

Listing 18.3. Using classes to define overriding styles.

```
<HTML>
<HEAD>
<STYLE TYPE="text/javascript">
document.tags.H1.color="green";
```

```
document.tags.H1.fontStyle="italic";
document.tags.all.fontSize="12";
classes.newheader.H1.color = "yellow";
</STYLE>
</HEAD>
<BODY>
<H1> This header is green and italic.</H1>
<H1 class="newheader"> This header will be yellow and italic.</H1>
<H2> This will be default text <H2>
</BODY>
</HTML>
```

FIGURE 18.1.

Header text overridden with class.

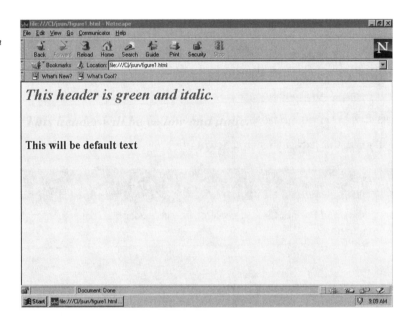

Defining styles in classes rather than generic to the document gives you more control over the usage of the styles and allows for more flexibility on a element-by-element basis. This method can also make JSSS more complicated, because the HTML document has now become more complex, with much interwoven JSSS class usage.

Selectors

The method by which you access, or call, a style sheet attribute is defined as the *selector*. It is the means by which you select the style you will use for the element. Three selectors are defined for use when implementing JavaScript Style Sheets:

- Classes
- IDs
- The style attribute of HTML elements

The fourth method of invoking style sheets within a document doesn't involve any particular call or reference for the element. Any styles defined with the tags method need not be called explicitly; they are called by default.

The innermost style defined for an element has precedence over any parent styles that have been defined.

STYLE Element Selector

The lowest-level selector involves defining a style for a particular instance of an element. This allows for very specific style definitions for each element. Styles are not often defined in this manner because of the difficulty in editing the style in the future. However, defining styles in this manner becomes extremely useful when the need to override a style occurs for only one particular instance of an element in the document.

For example, the code line

```
<H3 STYLE="lineHeight='36'">
```

will make this particular `<H3>` a height of 36.

> **NOTE**
>
> This method has not been in implemented in Netscape Communicator (Navigator 4.0) prerelease 2.

Style Sheet Classes

Using the Class attribute of the `<STYLE>` element, style classes can be defined for HTML elements, and the element will take on all applicable properties of the class to which it belongs.

```
<STYLE TYPE="text/javascript">
classes.firstclass.all.color = "yellow";
classes.secondclass.DIV.color = "blue";
classes.secondclass.H2.color = "blue";
</STYLE>
```

In this style definition, all elements belonging to the class `firstclass` will be displayed yellow, and only DIV and H2 belonging to the class `secondclass` will be displayed in blue. The style `secondclass` can be applied to other elements, but they will not inherit the style because they are not elements belonging to the class definition. Only DIV and H2 elements can belong to the class `secondclass` and take on its properties.

Defining classes of styles can be especially useful when styles need to apply to more than one type of HTML. It would be extremely tedious to define a style for multiple elements, each of which sets the color to yellow. You can uses classes to define one `yellowClass` and then use that class with any element that has the color property. Defining classes is the most effective method for making use of the flexibility of style sheets.

Class definitions can also be easily referenced in JavaScript function calls.

Listing 18.4 uses a combination of classes and tag style definitions. You can see the results in Figure 18.2. Note the paragraph that doesn't reflect any of the styles. Because no specific style is given and no style is defined for <P> tags, this paragraph will be rendered in the default properties for the <P> element.

Listing 18.4. Defining classes for use with multiple elements.

```
<HTML>
<HEAD>
<STYLE TYPE="text/JavaScript">
classes.larger.all.fontSize = "18";
tags.H1.textDecoration = "underline";
classes.nextclass.P.fontWeight = "bold";
</STYLE>
</HEAD>
<BODY>
<P CLASS="nextclass">This will be a bold paragraph</P>
<P CLASS="larger">This has a font Size of 18</P>
<BLOCKQUOTE CLASS="larger">This blockquote also has a font Size of
18</BLOCKQUOTE>
<P>This will NOT be a bold, 18 point paragraph</P>
<H1>This header is underlined</H1>
</BODY>
</HMTL>
```

FIGURE 18.2.

Multiple style definitions incorporated into a single style sheet.

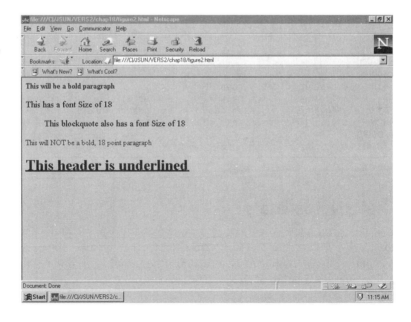

18

JAVASCRIPT STYLE SHEETS

Using IDs

Using IDs in style definitions is similar to using classes in style definitions.

```
<STYLE TYPE="text/javascript">
ids.myid.lineheight = 10;
</STYLE>
<BODY>
<P ID="myid">This line height will be 10</P>
</BODY>
```

Any element defined using the `myid` will have the style defined for the ID. `myid` is the name (similar to class names, which are given class style definitions) used when referencing the style of `lineheight = 10`. These IDs do not have to be previously defined in the document.

Mixing Selectors

Using JSSS, style selectors can be mixed and used in conjunction with each other to achieve the desired effect. Listing 18.5 demonstrates that mixing selectors of the same and different types can achieve the effects shown in Figure 18.3. Multiple attributes of the same selector (two class attributes used in conjunction) and attributes of different selector types (one class and one ID attribute) can be combined in one HTML element to achieve combined style effects.

Listing 18.5. Combining styles in a single style definition.

```
<HTML>
<HEAD>
<STYLE TYPE="text/javascript">
document.tags.H1.color="green";
classes.head2.fontStyle="italic";
ids.myid.fontSize="12";
classes.newheader.H1.color = "yellow";
</STYLE>
</HEAD>
<BODY>
<H1> This header will be green</H1>
<H1 class="newheader" ID="myid"> This header will be yellow and point size 12</H1>
<H1 class="newheader" class="head2"> This header will be yellow and italic.</H1>
<H2> This will be default text <H2>
</BODY>
</HTML>
```

Contextual Selectors

The JavaScript method `contextual()` can be used in style definitions to broaden the criteria for which styles are defined. "Contextual" means that the styles will be applied only if the context of the elements defined by `contextual()` is met. The definition of the contextual selectors can be any combination of classes, IDs, and tags.

All <BLOCKQUOTES> contained within <P> will be italic:

```
tags.contextual(tags.P, tags.BLOCKQUOTE).fontWeight = "italic";
```

All <P>s that have an ancestor of `firstclass` will be bold:

```
tags.contextual(classes.firstclass.all, tags.P).fontWeight = "bold";
```

All <P>s that have an ancestor of `myid` will be bold:

```
tags.contextual(ids.myid, tags.P).lineHeight = "10";
```

Contextual styles can be useful when you want a style to be applied in a document, but only if certain styles have preceded it. For instance, you may want <BLOCKQUOTE> text to be displayed in bold throughout a document, except if it is within a <P> (paragraph) tag, in which case you would want it in italic to stand out more.

The context of an HTML tag in relation to the previous tags and styles in a document can now be used to determine style definitions. You have functionality similar to an `if...then..else` statement without ever defining any JavaScript functions.

FIGURE 18.3.
Mixed and matched selectors.

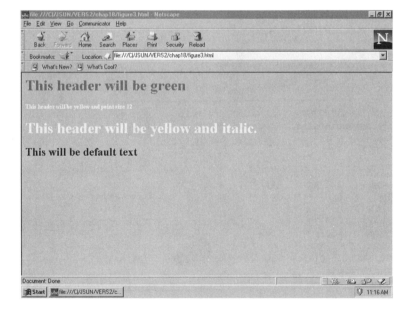

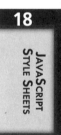

Defining with JavaScript Functions

Because JavaScript is a programming language, JavaScript style sheet definitions need not be completely text-driven. Styles can be applied in JSSS using function calls and assigned values. The function in Listing 18.6 is called to evaluate the style applied to <BLOCKQUOTE> elements based on the background color of the document. In Listing 18.6, the function get_style() is called when a BLOCKQUOTE is encountered, and the styles are applied based on the results of the function. In this example, the size of the font for the BLOCKQUOTE is based on whether the background of the document is white. The font size is 20-point if the background is white and 10-point if it is not. The font will also be italic if the background is white. The BLOCKQUOTE that is a member of the pointsize class has its font overridden by the pointsize font size, but it will still take on the italic property if the background is white.

Listing 18.6. Defining styles within JavaScript functions.

```
<HTML>
<HEAD>
<SCRIPT LANGUAGE = "JavaScript">
function default_colors() {
document.bgColor = "white"
}
</SCRIPT>
<STYLE type="text/JavaScript">

function get_style(){
if (document.bgcolor = "white") {
tags.BLOCKQUOTE.fontSize="20";
tags.BLOCKQUOTE.fontStyle="italic";
}
else{
tags.BLOCKQUOTE.fontSize="10";
}
}

tags.BLOCKQUOTE.apply  = get_style();
classes.pointsize.BLOCKQUOTE.fontSize = "28";
</STYLE>
</HEAD>

<BODY>
<SCRIPT LANGUAGE = "JavaScript">
default_colors()
</SCRIPT>
<BLOCKQUOTE> This is a 20 point line if the background if white, otherwise it
is 14 point.
</BLOCKQUOTE>
<BLOCKQUOTE class="pointsize"> This is a 28pt line
</BLOCKQUOTE>
</BODY>
</HTML>
```

The results of this example when the background is white are shown in Figure 18.4.

Figure 18.4.

The results when the background is white.

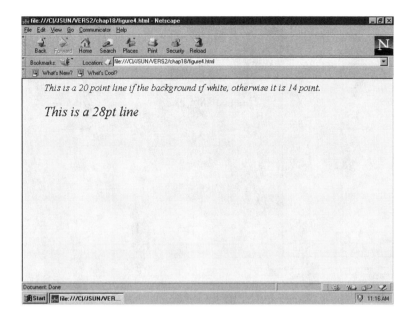

This basic example demonstrates the power and flexibility available when combining JavaScript and style sheets. By changing the function from

```
if (document.bgcolor = "white") {
```

to

```
if (document.bgcolor == "white") {
```

you're calling the `else` part of the function. You see the result shown in Figure 18.5.

The ability to use JavaScript function calls and assigned values in style sheets is the center of JSSS. Developers now have the capability to base styles on user input and to programmatically select and change styles based on the document itself. JSSS means that styles don't have to be static following page generation; instead, they can be updated as the document requires.

18

JavaScript Style Sheets

FIGURE 18.5.

The else *clause is called when the background is not white.*

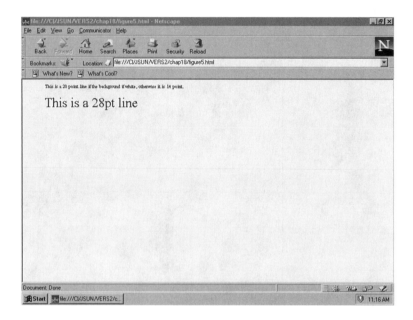

Inheritance

It's important to remember the concept of inheritance when defining styles. The term *inheritance* is used to describe the concept by which a child has the same properties as the parent. For the definitions used here, *parent* and *child* refer to HTML elements that are grouped or contained within other elements. The <BODY> element can have many children within it, including <H1> or <P>, whereas the <P> element will have fewer children (<EM> is an example). For the majority of styles, the styles of a parent are inherited by the child if the child has the same properties.

Style sheets give you the ability to set global styles for your documents and allow those styles to be passed to other elements within the document, thus saving you the time of defining styles for each element. You can safely assume that a <P> within the <BODY> will reflect the font size of the <BODY> unless the <P> specifically overrides it. Styles are inherited inside containers for which they are defined. This functionality gives the document a more consistent look and feel.

Font sizes, text placement, and margins are excellent examples of how style sheets can help give a Web site consistency. When you define these styles generically in the parent elements, the styles will be inherited in the children of the document. Each document can have the same look and feel while still giving the developer the option of manipulating and overriding the styles during runtime if desired.

Styles are inherited by default, but, by using JavaScript and input from the user, these styles can be changed as applicable.

> **NOTE**
>
> For the most part, styles that aren't inherited will be obvious. If the child doesn't have the same property as the parent, the child can't inherit the style.

A style that is defined (or redefined) for a child will always take precedence over and override the parent style. To override globally set styles, the child style can be redefined in the style sheet definition or at the element level. Listing 18.7 shows how to define an overriding style class for the H1 element.

Listing 18.7. Defining overriding class styles.

```
<HTML>
<HEAD>
<STYLE TYPE="text/javascript">
document.tags.BODY.fontSize ="12";
classes.newheader.H1.fontSize ="20";
</STYLE>
</HEAD>
<BODY>
<H1> This header is 12pt because it is inherited from the parent</H1>
<H1 class="newheader"> This header is 20pt because it is overriden
by a style definition in the child</H1>
<H1 STYLE="fontSize = '24'"> This header would be 24 if supported in release</H1>
</BODY>
</HTML>
```

18

JAVASCRIPT
STYLE SHEETS

In Figure 18.6, note the font size defined in the body. In Listing 18.7, this font size is inherited by the first H1 (the child). In the second H1, it's overridden by a class-defined style for that child. In the final H1, it displays in the parent style.

> **NOTE**
>
> In future releases, the definitions of styles in the element tag will be allowed, and the third H1 header would have been in the 24-point size as described.

FIGURE 18.6.

Inheritance of styles.

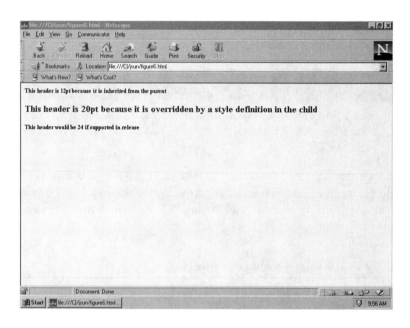

JavaScript Style Sheet Properties

Table 18.1 shows the properties that are available for definition in JavaScript Style Sheets.

Table 18.1. Style sheet properties.

Property Name	What It Applies To	Possible Values	Value Definitions
		Font Properties	
fontSize	All elements	Absolute sizes	x-small, small, medium, large, x-large, point size
		Relative sizes	smaller, larger
		Percentage	150% bigger
fontStyle	All elements		normal, italic, oblique, small-caps
		Text Properties	
lineHeight	Block-level elements	Number	Units to increase height by
		Length	Absolute value of line height
		Percentage	Percentage of parent
verticalAlign	All elements		baseline, sub, sup, top, text-top middle, bottom, text-bottom
textDecoration	All elements		none, underline, overline, line-through, blink

Property Name	What It Applies To	Possible Values	Value Definitions
		Text Properties	
textTransform	All elements		capitalize, uppercase, lowercase, none
textAlign	Block-level elements		left, right, center, justify
textIndent	Block-level elements	Length	Numerical units to indent
		Percentage	Percentage of parent
		Block-Level Properties	
padding()	All elements	Number	Number of units of padding
		Percentage	Percentage of parent
borderWidth()	All elements	Number	Number of units for width of border
margins()	All elements	Length	Margins in number of units
		Percentage	Percentage of parent
		Auto	Document autosizes margins
borderStyle	All elements		none, solid, 3D
width	Block-level elements	Length	Width in units
		Percentage	Percentage of parent
		Auto	Document autosizes width
length	Block-level elements	Length	Length in units
		Auto	Document autosizes length
align	All elements		left, right, none
		Color Properties	
color	All elements	Color	color names, RGB colors
backgroundImage	All elements		url
backgroundColor	All elements	Color	color names, RGB colors
		Classification Properties	
display	All elements		block, inline, list-item, none
listStyleType	Elements with display		disc, circle, square, property decimal, lower&upper-roman, lower&upper-alpha, none
whiteSpace	Block-level elements		Normal and pre

18

JAVASCRIPT STYLE SHEETS

Margins and Padding

Not only can text properties be defined with JavaScript Style Sheets, but padding, borders, and margins for block-level elements can also be defined. Block-level elements are elements such as <H1> and <P>, which always start on a new line.

The following are all the margin and padding properties that can be set in JavaScript Style Sheets for the block-level elements:

```
marginTop

marginBottom

marginRight

marginLeft

margins()

borderTopWidth

borderRightWidth

borderBottomWidth

borderLeftWidth

borderWidths()

paddingTop

paddingRight

paddingBottom

paddingLeft

paddings()
```

paddingTop, paddingRight, paddingBottom, and paddingLeft can each be set separately, or this group of properties can be defined together using the padding() style and referencing all four styles in a comma-delimited list. margins() and borderWidths() are also available to define a comma-delimited list of margin sizes and border widths.

```
tags.H1.margins(10,20,30,40)
```

is the same as

```
tags.H1.marginTop = 10;
tags.H1.marginRight = 20;
tags.H1.marginBottom = 30;
tags.H1.marginLeft = 40;
```

> **CAUTION**
>
> When defining units of width in JSSS, watch the sum of the horizontal properties. The total of all horizontal properties can't exceed the defined width of the document. If the width is exceeded, JSSS will auto-calculate values that rank lowest in horizontal property priority. Here is the ranking priority for calculating horizontal widths in JavaScript:
>
> 1. Left border
> 2. Right border
> 3. Left padding
> 4. Right padding
> 5. Width
> 6. Left margin
> 7. Right margin

Using JSSS to evaluate and redefine margins and borders is useful when document layout needs to be adjusted based on user input. A user's request may drastically change the manner in which a document should be displayed. (See Chapter 13, "Form Objects," for the methodology of accepting and processing user input with JavaScript.) Also, by adjusting the styles for particular elements, you can accomplish the changes fairly seamlessly.

Comments

As in all coding, comments are important in your code. Writing comments in JSSS is similar to defining comments in other well-known programming languages. For example, both

```
/* comment type 1 */
```

and

```
// second comment type
```

are acceptable comment formats in JSSS.

> **TIP**
>
> Comments in JavaScript Style Sheets can't be nested.

18

JAVASCRIPT
STYLE SHEETS

HTML and JavaScript Additions and Changes

JSSS brings with it new HTML elements, additional attributes for existing HTML elements, and new JavaScript object properties. These changes are specific to JavaScript Style Sheets and thus will not be applicable in browsers that don't yet support JSSS. Older browsers that don't support JSSS will ignore all style sheet definitions, tags, and attributes and display the document using the default document style.

As with any JavaScript implementation, JavaScript Style sheet implementations must take into account browsers that don't support JavaScript (or JSSS) and account for the differences.

HTML Elements

Three new HTML elements have been introduced to attach style sheets to the HTML document. `<LINK>`, `<STYLE>`, and `<SPAN>` are used to define and reference JavaScript Style Sheets in HTML documents.

<LINK>

`<LINK>` is the element used to link external style sheets to a document. The attributes of the `<LINK>` element, `Type` and `HREF`, are used to define the type of link (text or JavaScript) and the URL where the external style sheet can be located.

<STYLE>

`<STYLE>` is used to define style sheets within the document itself. `<STYLE>` also uses the `Type` attribute to distinguish JavaScript style sheets from cascading style sheets. `<STYLE>` tags are always contained within the `<HEAD>` section of the document and contain all the style definitions for the document.

<SPAN>

`<SPAN>` and `</SPAN>` are used to mark a specific piece of text to which a style will be applied. This element is used when a section of text within an element (not the entire element) needs to have a style applied.

```
<STYLE>
classes.italicclass.fontStyle = "italic"
</STYLE>
<P>This section of text is normal <SPAN class="italicclass">except for
this section will be display
in italic </SPAN>unlike the rest of the text</P>
```

NOTE

For more explicit definitions of these elements, see Appendix B, "Fundamentals of HTML."

HTML Attributes

STYLE, CLASS, and ID are new element attributes that are used to define the specific style for an element. These attributes (also defined in Appendix B) give greater style functionality to existing HTML tags, such as H1, P, BLOCKQUOTE, and BODY.

STYLE

STYLE defines a new style to be used for a particular element only. This allows each element to have its own style, independent of any style defined in the current style sheet.

CLASS

CLASS defines the style class to be applied to the element. Classes must have been previously defined in the JavaScript Style Sheet declaration.

ID

ID defines the ID reference to the style to be applied. IDs must also have been previously defined in an existing JSSS declaration.

WARNING

The STYLE attribute is not implemented in Netscape Navigator 4.0 (Communicator) prerelease 2.0.

JavaScript Objects

Three new JavaScript objects—tags, classes, and id—have been introduced for use with JavaScript style sheets. These objects are used in JSSS statements to define the types of styles. Currently, three available style types can be defined. These objects can be defined in external style sheets, which are linked to the HTML document, or they can be defined in the document itself, within the <STYLE> and </STYLE> elements.

18

JAVASCRIPT STYLE SHEETS

tags

The tags object is a reference to HTML tags. The full syntax of this definition is `document.tags`, but because the tags object always applies to the current document, the document object is unnecessary. Thus, the following two statements are identical:

```
document.tags.BLOCKQUOTE.fontSize = "20";

tags.BLOCKQUOTE.fontSize = "20";
```

Following the tags object in the definition is the element to which it applies (`BLOCKQUOTE` in the preceding example), or the element `ALL` can be used to apply to all tags. After the element definition is the style for the element that is being defined.

classes

The classes object defines the JavaScript style sheet classes of styles. A style class can apply to one particular element:

```
classes.fontclass.BLOCKQUOTE.fontSize = "20";
```

or it can be defined to be accessible to all elements:

```
classes.fontclass.all.fontSize = "20";
```

Following the classes object in the dot notation is the name of the class, and then the element to which the class is defined for. Classes defined as `ALL` can be applied to all elements.

id

The id object is similar to classes, except that any element that references an id will be rendered with the style defined in the id.

```
id.myid.fontSize = "20";
```

The id object tag is followed by the name of the ID, and, unlike the classes and tags objects, it doesn't take the element name (or `ALL`) as part of the definition. id objects can be used with any element to which they apply.

Style Precedence Order for Classes, Tags, and IDs

To find the value or precedence of a style for an element (and property), you must follow these rules:

1. Locate all references to the element by any selector.
2. Sort the references by explicit weight.

3. Sort by origin of style sheet: Default values are overridden by user style sheets, which are overridden by author style sheets.

4. Sort by specificity: Give one point for each of the following three options, and then sum the points to get specificity:

   ■ The number of id attributes

   ■ The number of class attributes

   ■ The number of tag names referenced

5. Sort by the order specified. For two rules with identical weights, the latter rule will take precedence.

Using these five rules, you can accurately determine and account for the style that will be applied for an element when you're developing documents using JSSS.

Summary

JavaScript Style Sheets offer the Web developer greater control over the style of documents that are created. Default styles can be defined both internally and externally to the document and can be applied against a wide range of elements.

Styles can be defined using tags, classes, and IDs; a wide range of style properties are currently available. New HTML elements and attributes have been added to incorporate JavaScript Style Sheets into the HTML document.

JSSS allows styles to change within an interactive document, and the developer can have control over how and when to implement the changes.

18

JAVASCRIPT
STYLE SHEETS

V

PART

Programming Techniques

Site Navigation with JavaScript

CHAPTER 19

Navigation Techniques

JavaScript transfers much of the burden of content delivery and formatting to the browser rather than having the server deal with it. One of the benefits of this client-side control is improved navigation. Instead of merely providing static links that connect Web pages within a site, Webmasters can use JavaScript to control the display of a site's information.

Before frames were available, it was difficult to add navigational aids to a Web page without limiting the site's layout and its content in several ways. For example, displaying a map showing a view of your site at all times could be done only by adding it to each page. First, the map would need to be small enough to avoid distracting the user. Second, if the page being viewed was too long, the map would often be unavailable as the user scrolled through the page. Limiting your Web site to one-page documents may not have been an option, and a site map that was available only part of the time looked unprofessional.

Frames can solve this problem. Splitting the browser into more than one window lets you keep a site map visible at all times while the user scrolls through the many pages of an HTML document. Using links on the site map, a new page can be displayed in the other frame. It doesn't take JavaScript to do this. Simply use the TARGET attribute of the anchor tag to point to any frame you want. However, what if the page currently being displayed contains a data entry form and needs to be submitted before moving onto another page? Submitting the form using a submit button is fine, but it brings the user to a new page, leaving him somewhere off the map. In some cases, it may be ideal to allow the user to move throughout the site entering data without requiring him to click a submit button on each page. This can be done using JavaScript by submitting the forms across frames.

If your site map is rather large, it may be your preference to display only part of the map at a time. Updating the map then becomes necessary. How do you update a map, submit a form, display the resulting document, and keep track of where the user is with one click? Using JavaScript is the easiest way. The navigation techniques in this chapter demonstrate how to create and use a dynamic toolbar and a table of contents.

Scripting a Dynamic Toolbar

Toolbars are a common user interface used to navigate through any software program. In relation to JavaScript, a "dynamic" toolbar is one that can change itself while the user interacts with it. As an example, I have written a toolbar that controls a simple slide show. Four buttons on the toolbar are used to move forward or backward through an array of slides. Two other buttons are used to start or stop an automatic cycle through all of the slides. One logical way to program this is to create two custom objects—a button object and a toolbar object. The entire Slide Show application can be found on the CD-ROM as SlideShw.htm, but it is also split up into different parts throughout the first half of this chapter.

Writing a Custom Toolbar Object

A toolbar can be thought of as a set of buttons, so I have named the toolbar object buttonSet. Listing 19.1 shows the buttonSet constructor used to set up all of the properties and methods available to a toolbar.

Listing 19.1. The buttonSet object constructor.

```
function buttonSet(name) {
  /*
   * Description: button object constructor.
   * Arguments: name - The variable name of the buttonSet.
   */
  // Properties
  this.name = name
  this.startIndex = 7
  this.length = 7
  this.isBusy = false
  // Methods
  this.addBtn = addBtn
  this.print = print
  this.clear = clear
  return this
}
```

The addBtn method creates and adds a new button object to the buttonSet. The print method writes the buttonSet out to an HTML document. The clear method resets all buttons contained within the buttonSet to their original state of either disabled or enabled. These methods are described in detail in the following sections.

The Button Object

The buttonSet object is used to keep track of one or more button objects. Each button object holds the information needed for when it is clicked or displayed as an HTML <IMG> element. Listing 19.2 shows the two functions used to create a new button.

Listing 19.2. The button object's click method and constructor.

```
function click() {
  /*
   * Description: Method of button. Executes command for this button.
   * Arguments: None.
   */
  eval(this.command)
}

function button(name, file, alt, url, spacer, condition, command) {
  /*
   * Description: button object.
   * Arguments:
   *   name - The name used as this button's HTML element name.
   *   file - The button image's source url.
   *   alt  - The alt attribute for the button.
   *   url - The url which can reference(across frames) the
   *         buttonSet that holds this button.
   *   spacer - number of pixels of horizontal spacing used
   *            after the button being added.
   *   condition - conditional statement that determines
   *               whether or not to display this button.
   *   commmand - The command to be executed by this button.
   */
  // Properties
  this.name = name
  this.file = file
  this.alt = alt
  this.url = url
  this.spacer = spacer
  this.condition = condition
  this.command = command
  // Methods
  this.click = click
  return this
}
```

The name property becomes its HTML name. The button's file property is the source URL for the button's image. The alt property is used as the HTML alt attribute. The url property is used as the HREF property of the anchor associated with the button's image. Using a transparent graphic file, the spacer property specifies how much space to leave before placing another button image to the right of this one. This allows you to easily create different sections within the toolbar or compensate for button images with different widths. A button will be displayed only if its conditional expression evaluates to true. This is the key to knowing which buttons are displayed and available to the user. Whenever a buttonSet object is written to an HTML page, it looks at each button's conditional expression to determine if the button is enabled. If a button is enabled and the user clicks it, the command is executed. The command string can be any JavaScript statement, as long as it can be executed from the document where the buttonSet is created.

Instantiating a Toolbar

Using the following lines of code, the Slide Show program creates a new buttonSet object and resets its current state.

```
Toolbar = new buttonSet("Toolbar")
Toolbar.clear()
```

It is important when creating a new buttonSet that the argument passed to the constructor be equal to the variable name of the object being created. This allows the buttonSet object to create JavaScript commands using its own name. The clear() method is used to set or reset the global variables used by the buttonSet to determine which of its buttons are enabled. Listing 19.3 shows the clear() method that was written for the Slide Show application.

Listing 19.3. The clear() method of the buttonSet() object.

```
function clear() {
  /*
   * Description: Method of buttonSet object. Used to reset any global
   *              variables on which any buttons in the buttonSet rely
   *              on for their condition statements.
   * Arguments: None.
   */
  gIsRunning=false
}
```

Once the new buttonSet has been created, the Slide Show application creates each button by using the addBtn() method. The first button created is shown in the following code:

```
Toolbar.addBtn("First","graphics/first.gif","First Picture",0,"true",
  "changeSlide('first')")
```

Listing 19.4 shows the complete addBtn() method, which simply creates a new button object and then adds it to the buttonSet.

Listing 19.4. The addBtn() method of the buttonSet object.

```
function addBtn(name,file,alt,spacer,condition,command) {
  /* Description: Method of the buttonSet object used to add a new button to
   *              the end of the button set.
   * Arguments: name - (string) The name used as this button's HTML element name.
   *            file - (string) The button image's source url.
   *            alt  - (string) The alt attribute for the button.
   *            spacer - (integer) number of pixels of horizontal spacing used
   *                     after the button being added.
   *            condition - (string) conditional statement determines
   *                        whether or not to display the button.
   *            commmand - (string) The command to be executed.
   *
   */
  var i = this.length
```

continues

Listing 19.4. continued

```
this[i] = new button(
        name,
        file,
        alt,
        "javascript:parent."+this.name+"["+i+"]"+".click()",
        spacer,
        condition,
        command)
    this.length++
}
```

The `url` argument specified for the `button` constructor in Listing 19.4 is worth noting. This string will be used as the HREF property of the button's image. The following example is the resulting HTML generated for the first Slide Show button:

```
<a HREF = "javascript:parent.Toolbar[7].click()">
<img src="graphics/first.gif" alt="First Picture" width="24" height="24" border=0>
</a>
```

When the user clicks this image, the `click()` method of the seventh property of the Toolbar object is called. The seventh item in the Toolbar object (essentially an array) is where the first `button` object was stored using the `addBtn()` method. This is the best way to call the `click()` method across frames while working in both Netscape and Microsoft browsers. The `buttonSet` object is set up in such a way that the programmer using it doesn't need to keep track of how the buttons are indexed.

Displaying the Toolbar

The global variable `gIsRunning` is `true` when the slide show is automatically stepping through each slide; otherwise, it is `false`. This variable is used by four button objects to display two buttons at a time. One is for an active state, and the other is for its disabled state (its face is grayed out). The following examples show two buttons that depend on `gIsRunning`:

```
Toolbar.addBtn("Start", "graphics/auto.gif", "Start Slideshow", 0,
            "gIsRunning==false", "changeSlide('start')")
Toolbar.addBtn("StartGrey", "graphics/autoGrey.gif", "Start Slideshow", 0,
            "gIsRunning==true", "")
```

The `StartGrey` button will be displayed only if `gIsRunning` is equal to `true`. On the other hand, if `gIsRunning` is equal to `false`, the `Start` button will be displayed. If the `Start` button is enabled and the user clicks it, the following code is executed within the `changeSlide()` function:

```
if(command == "start") {
    gIsRunning = true
    Toolbar.print(window.frames[2].document)
    gTimer = window.setTimeout("startAuto()",1500)
}
```

gIsRunning is set to true, and the toolbar is printed to the document object specified. The current toolbar is eliminated, and a new HTML page is created containing a new toolbar, which then takes into account the new state of gIsRunning. This means that the StartGrey button will be enabled, while the Start button is never even written into the new page. This gives the illusion of graying out the start button when, in fact, it is a different button. Listing 19.5 shows the print() method, which is responsible for writing the new HTML page.

Listing 19.5. The print() method of the buttonSet object.

```
function print(dObj) {
  /*
   * Description: Method of buttonSet object.
   * Arguments: dObj - document object receiving buttonSet.
   */
  this.isBusy = true
  var spaceInt
  var DQUOTE = '\"'
  var topBase = ""
  var basePath = ""+window.location.pathname
  var baseDir = ""
  var baseFile = basePath.substring(basePath.length-10,basePath.length)

  baseDir = basePath.substring(0,basePath.length-12)
  topBase=window.location.protocol+"//"+window.location.host+baseDir

  dObj.open()
  dObj.bgColor = parent.frames[0].document.bgColor
  dObj.writeln('<!DOCTYPE HTML PUBLIC "-//IETF//DTD HTML//EN">')
  dObj.writeln('<html><head>')
  dObj.writeln('<title>Toolbar</title>')
  dObj.writeln('<BASE href = '+DQUOTE+topBase+DQUOTE+'>')
  dObj.writeln('<SCRIPT LANGUAGE="JavaScript">')
  dObj.writeln('</SCRIPT>')
  dObj.writeln('</head>')
  dObj.writeln('<body bgcolor="'+parent.frames[0].document.bgColor.toUpperCase()+
    '">')
  dObj.writeln('<center>')
  dObj.writeln('<table width="100%" border="0">')
  dObj.writeln('<tr><td align="center">')

  //Print each button. Start at property index i.
  for(var i = this.startIndex; this.length > i; i++) {
    if(eval(this[i].condition)) {
      dObj.write('<A HREF = "'+this[i].url+'">')
      dObj.write('<img src="'+this[i].file+'" alt="'+this[i].alt+
        '" width="24" height="24" border=0>')
      dObj.write('</A>')
      // Add space if specified.
      spaceInt = 0 + this[i].spacer
      if(spaceInt != 0) {
        dObj.write('<img src="graphics/space.gif" width='+spaceInt+
          ' height=24 border=0>')
      }
    }
  }
}
```

continues

Listing 19.5. continued

```
dObj.writeln('</td></tr></table>')
dObj.writeln('</center>')
dObj.writeln('</body></html>')
dObj.close()
this.isBusy = false
}
```

The print() method begins by setting the isBusy flag to true to prevent the user from clicking other buttons while the toolbar is refreshing. Next, a base URL is formed that is equal to the base URL of the current window. This is stored in the topBase variable and is used to generate a <BASE> tag for the new toolbar document. This assumes that the filename for the frameset HTML document is 12 characters long, as is the case with SlideShw.htm. This is to accommodate Netscape Navigator versions prior to 3.0.

> **WARNING**
>
> If you fail to specify a base URL for a JavaScript-generated HTML document, Netscape Navigator versions prior to 3.0 will not correctly resolve unqualified URLs.

The print() method continues by opening access to the destination document. It then writes each line of HTML required to build a Web page that looks like a toolbar. I use a table to center all the buttons within it. A for loop is used to print each button that is stored within the buttonSet. If a space was specified, a blank graphic will be inserted and "stretched" to the designated number of pixels. Finally, the document is closed, and the browser window is refreshed.

Refreshing the Toolbar

As you can see, refreshing the toolbar is as easy as calling its print() method. Simply set the global variables on which the buttons depend, and call print(). Documents within other frames can also refresh the toolbar. For example, you can modify the slide show application so that the user cannot start the slide show from the last slide. To do this, add a new global variable to the clear() method called canStart, and set it equal to false. Modify the addBtn calls for the Start and StartGrey buttons to take gCanStart into account. The new code would look like this:

```
Toolbar.addBtn("Start", "graphics/auto.gif", "Start Slideshow", 0,
    "gIsRunning==false && gCanStart==true", "changeSlide('auto')")
Toolbar.addBtn("StartGrey", "graphics/autoGrey.gif", "Start Slideshow", 0,
    "gIsRunning==true ¦¦ gCanStart==false", "")
```

Then insert the following script into the <HEAD> block of the last slide document:

```
<SCRIPT LANGUAGE="JavaScript">
<!--
var savedState
savedState = parent.gCanStart
```

```
parent.gCanStart=false
parent.Toolbar.print(parent.frames[2].document)
parent.gCanStart=savedState
//-->
</SCRIPT>
```

Next, add another call to the Toolbar's print method when the document unloads. This would look like the following:

```
<BODY onUnload="parent.Toolbar.print(parent.frames[2].document)">
```

This will return the toolbar to its previous state after moving to another slide.

If you have every slide set the global variables and reset the toolbar, you can eliminate the need to refresh the toolbar using the onUnload event handler. Using this approach, you can have every document specify which buttons to display, knowing that it will be reset the next time a different document is loaded.

Using the Slide Show Application

On the CD-ROM included with this book, you will find a directory containing all the files needed for the slide show application. Simply load slideshow.htm into the browser to activate the frameset. The toolbar is used to move through each slide and its corresponding description. Figure 19.1 shows what the slide show application looks like when loaded into the browser.

FIGURE 19.1.
A toolbar used with the slide show application.

Five slides are included with the program. You can use the toolbar to advance or move back by one slide using the second and third buttons, respectively. You can also use the first and fourth buttons to move to the first and last slides in the slide show. The last two buttons on the right will start and stop the program from stepping through each slide for you. Notice how the last button is grayed out. This is the StartGrey button. After clicking the start button, shown as a right-pointing arrow followed by an ellipse, the slide show begins to cycle through each pair of

HTML documents. Figure 19.2 shows a snapshot of the browser during the show. Notice how the stop button is enabled while the show is running, and the start button is grayed out.

FIGURE 19.2.

A snapshot of the slide show in progress.

Extra Features

The core `buttonSet` object could be altered to handle even more situations. For example, it could be modified to support vertical toolbars instead of horizontal ones, or even both. Simply modify the `print()` method to add the `<BR>` tag after each button. Another thought would be to create the toolbar in a separate browser window. It could be used as a navigation tool or a even a help menu. No modifications would be necessary. Simply pass the document object of the new window to the `print()` method.

> **RESOURCE**
>
> A reusable version of the `buttonSet` object can be found in the JavaScript libraries included with Acadia Infuse for Windows 95 and Windows NT. Acadia Infuse is a JavaScript development tool available on the CD-ROM included with this book. You can insert the `buttonSet` object framework into your script by selecting Insert | Frequent Script or by pressing F2. For more information on Infuse, see Chapter 4, "Using Acadia Infuse to Create JavaScript Scripts."

Scripting a Dynamic Table of Contents

The second tool I have written to show how JavaScript can be used for navigation is the Table of Contents application. It offers a tree view similar to a directory structure, where each "branch" of the tree may or may not have other branches extending from it. The user can expand or reduce the level of detail in the table of contents displays by clicking the individual branches.

Why Not Just Use Links?

A table of contents consisting of nothing more than links might work well enough, even when you use frames. A shortcoming of this approach, however, is revealed in how the user sees what you present. If the information you are presenting follows a logical pattern and flow of ideas, one spawning from another, shouldn't your overview display the ideas with that same flow?

Trying to show the parent/child relationships between ideas using HTML alone becomes a frustrating process. Either you show the table of contents formatted with <PRE> and </PRE>— somewhat of an aesthetic nightmare—or you use tables to convey the structure. Tables can get tricky if someone accesses your site using a different screen resolution than what you used. Screen resolution is also an issue if your listing is long, requiring the user to constantly scroll up and down, trying to compare the information associated with different links. JavaScript lets you create a table of contents whose entries are nested, thus giving a visual clue to the organization of information, as well as providing a way to expand and condense the topic tree.

Another advantage of doing it this way is in the familiarity of the user interface. Since the creation of windowing computer systems (Macintosh, Motif, and others), the visual metaphor of information nested by topic appears as a familiar, normal way of categorizing things.

Some Application Examples

Using a dynamic table of contents works with any situation in which information should be presented in a clear manner while showing dependencies and relationships. For example, Joe's Widget Shop stocks many different kinds of widgets, some of which are further subclassified by size. Joe, who serves as his own Webmaster, can easily provide specifications and prices in the form of one large HTML file with anchors, or he could devise another system to let the user navigate his site. Instead, Joe decides to use a dynamic table of contents, so when his customers need to quickly find out how much force they can exert on a Number 43 Reverse Kretchmer widget, the answer is only a click away.

The dynamic table of contents can also function well in an intranet setting. If a company's reports are all organized by month and then further classified by division, users can switch between March and November general accounting reports without needing a great deal of screen real estate.

Figure 19.3 demonstrates that, by organizing the natural flow of ideas using this technique, educators can present a context for the lessons they teach. If the students actually see the evolution of concepts, the learning process becomes a matter of finding the connections between the concepts.

Figure 19.3.

The dynamic table of contents in action.

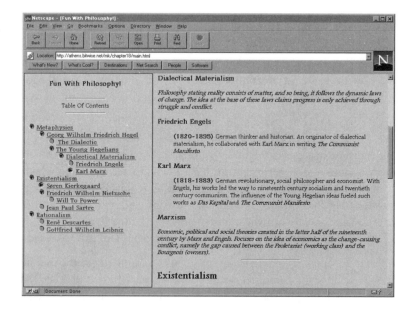

The Files for the Project

Because the Table of Contents works within a series of frames, a number of files are used in the project. Although all the HTML files are necessary for the project, only one contains the JavaScript necessary to make it work.

The Main Frame

Before going on to scripting, you must first create the `<FRAMESET>` for the table of contents and the actual information you want to present. You see it in Listing 19.6, `main.html`.

Listing 19.6. `main.html`.

```
<HTML>
<HEAD>
<TITLE>Fun With Philosophy!</TITLE>
</HEAD>
<FRAMESET COLS="35%,*">
<NOFRAMES>
<CENTER><H3>Sorry!</H3>
<P>
If you want Fun With Philosophy, you'll have to get
 <A HREF="http://home.netscape.com/">Netscape 2.0</A> or better!
<FRAME NAME="TOCFrame" SRC="toc.html">
<FRAME NAME="ContentFrame" SRC="fun.html">
</FRAMESET>
</HTML>
```

This `<FRAMESET>` refers to two separate files: `toc.html`, which holds the JavaScript code, and `fun.html`, which I use merely as a splash page. You can put the HTML file of your information here if you like, but I chose to keep the text separate until the user follows a link to a subject.

The Splash Page

The splash page also serves another purpose: It contains references to the images you use later for icon representations of the different levels of the table of contents. See Listing 19.7.

Listing 19.7. `fun.html`.

```
<HTML><HEAD><TITLE>Fun With Philosophy! Intro</TITLE></HEAD>
<BODY><CENTER>
<H1>Fun With Philosophy!</H1><P>
<IMG SRC="open.jpg" ALIGN=MIDDLE WIDTH="15" HEIGHT="15">
<IMG SRC="end.jpg" ALIGN=MIDDLE WIDTH="15" HEIGHT="15">
<IMG SRC="open.jpg" ALIGN=MIDDLE WIDTH="15" HEIGHT="15">
<HR WIDTH = 150>
<P>
That's right, now you can combine JavaScript with the complexities of the
world's greatest thinkers all in a space-saving user interface!
<P>
Sound too good to be true? Continue on and find out!
<P>
<HR WIDTH = 150>
<IMG SRC="open.jpg" ALIGN=MIDDLE WIDTH="15" HEIGHT="15">
<IMG SRC="end.jpg" ALIGN=MIDDLE WIDTH="15" HEIGHT="15">
<IMG SRC="open.jpg" ALIGN=MIDDLE WIDTH="15" HEIGHT="15">
</CENTER></BODY></HTML>
```

Placing the images on the splash page increases the speed of loading the page. If the images are all shown initially, they get held in the browser's cache directory. As the JavaScript dynamically updates the table of contents, the user doesn't need to wait for the images to download from the server.

The Information

With this project, I've elected to use one larger HTML file to display my information. If you want, you can link to several different files, but for smaller chunks of text under each table of contents listing, one file works well. Listing 19.8 shows an excerpt from `contents.html`.

Listing 19.8. `contents.html`.

```
<A NAME="exist">
<H2>Existentialism</H2></A>
<CITE>Philosophy of the nineteenth and twentieth centuries. Claims that since
there are no objective, universal truths,
```

continues

Listing 19.8. continued

```
man's existence precedes his essence, thereby allowing individual choice to
determine the outcome of life. This realization of free will and no ultimate
truths induces human anxiety.</CITE>
<A NAME="kierk">
<H3>S&oslash;ren Kierkegaard</H3></A>
<DL><DD><B>(1813-1855)</B> Danish religious thinker, large influence on later
existentialists. Believed that "truth is
subjectivity", and an individual's relationship with God required a "leap of
faith". Also defined human anxiety as angst.
</DL>
<A NAME="subject">
<H3>Subjectivism</H3></A>
<CITE>Belief that all morality is based on individual thought and to label an
action as "good" or "bad" outside of this realm of human subjectivity was
irrelevant.
</CITE>
```

> **NOTE**
>
> Besides using the structure of the table of contents, I use different formatting for each type of information. A school of thought falls under the <CITE></CITE> tags, whereas a philosopher's name uses the <DL></DL> markup. This is purely a design decision to better differentiate subject matter.

The Table of Contents

Listing 19.9, toc.html, shows the frame that handles all the JavaScript functionality. In it, you'll create and populate an array for the information that the table of contents needs in order to display the proper images and text. You also create the links to contents.html. To do this, you use some concepts from earlier in this book (control structures, the onClick() event handler, and many Navigator objects, to name a few). You also use the properties of the browser's *cookie,* an instrument that stores information about what the user has done. If you're unclear about all this cookie talk, don't worry. Chapter 25, "Cookies and State Maintenance," goes into more detail. For now, the manipulation of the cookie isn't too complex, so in-depth coverage is unnecessary.

Now let's step through toc.html.

Listing 19.9. toc.html.

```
<HTML><HEAD>
<TITLE>Fun With Philosophy! TOC</TITLE>
<SCRIPT LANGUAGE="JavaScript">
<!--
/*****
```

```
** Create an array in the browser's memory. This is used to hold all the
** subsequent table of content entries by "newing" the array.
*****/
function TOCArray( length )
{
    var i = 0;
    this.length = length;
    for ( i = 1; i < length; i++ )
    this[i] = 0;
    return this;
}
```

This function constructs the array used to hold the table of contents records. By setting `length` number of elements equal to zero, you ensure a populated array; if, later on, you only partially fill the array and reference one of the non–filled-in elements, you won't generate a runtime error.

```
/*****
** Create the table of content entry object, to be stored in the array.
** Called by "newing", the TOCEntry breaks down like this:
**          TOCEntry.parent (whether or not the entry has child entries)
**          TOCEntry.text (the link text to be displayed)
**          TOCEntry.URL (the link's URL)
**          TOCEntry.nesting (how deep is the entry)
*****/
function TOCEntry( parent, text, URL, nesting)
{
    this.text = text;
    this.URL = URL;
    this.parent = parent;
    this.nesting = nesting;
    return this;
}
```

Here you build the structures that are added as records to the TOCArray. By accessing the internal structure of these records, you get all the information needed to display the entries in the table of contents. Access is provided by using the index of the record in the array and then using a dot (.) to retrieve the field you need. In practice, the reference looks like this:

```
arrayEntry[index].value
```

This somewhat bizarre syntax stems from JavaScript's inability to handle multidimensional arrays. You'll see how to use this to your advantage later in the script.

```
/*****
** New an array to hold n many table of content entries.
*****/
var toc = new TOCArray(17);
```

This creates a global array that is 17 members long. The reason it is declared outside a function is to keep it in scope for all JavaScript within the file.

```
/*****
** Newing the TOCEntry for insertion into the TOCArray.
```

```
*****/
toc[1] = new TOCEntry( "Metaphysics", "contents.html#meta", 1,  0);
toc[2] = new TOCEntry( "Georg Wilhelm Friedrich Hegel",
    "contents.html#hegel", 1, 1);
toc[3] = new TOCEntry( " The Dialectic", "contents.html#dialectic", 0, 2);
toc[4] = new TOCEntry( "The Young Hegelians", "contents.html#young", 1, 2);
toc[5] = new TOCEntry( "Dialectical Materialism", "contents.html#dm", 1, 3);
toc[6] = new TOCEntry( "Friedrich Engels", "contents.html#engels", 0, 4);
toc[7] = new TOCEntry( "Karl Marx", "contents.html#marx", 1, 4);
toc[8] = new TOCEntry( "Marxism", "contents.html#marxism", 0, 5);
toc[9] = new TOCEntry( "Existentialism", "contents.html#exist", 1, 0);
toc[10] = new TOCEntry( "S&oslash;ren Kierkegaard", "contents.html#kierk", 1, 1);
toc[11] = new TOCEntry( "Subjectivism", "contents.html#subject", 0, 2);
toc[12] = new TOCEntry( "Friedrich Wilhelm Nietzsche",
    "contents.html#nietzsche", 1, 1);
toc[13] = new TOCEntry( "Will To Power", "contents.html#will", 0, 2);
toc[14] = new TOCEntry( "Jean Paul Sartre", "contents.html#sartre", 0, 1);
toc[15] = new TOCEntry( "Rationalism", "contents.html#ration", 1, 0);
toc[16] = new TOCEntry( "Ren&eacute; Descartes",
    "contents.html#descartes", 0, 1);
toc[17] = new TOCEntry( "Gottfried Wilhelm Leibniz",
    "contents.html#leibniz", 0, 1);
```

> **NOTE**
>
> No, you're not going crazy. The ø and é you see in the preceding lines of code are part of HTML. Entities such as this provide you with many nonstandard characters, such as é.

The preceding code creates new TOCEntry structures that are added to the TOCArray. By using these structures as the primary data control mechanism for the script, you make it far easier to update and control what is shown (or not shown) in the actual table of contents. Standardized, easily maintainable data is invaluable if you need to add or remove dependencies.

```
/*****
** Set Cookie to the values needed to properly display the table
** of contents. There is no path specification, since the TOC is only
** good for where the user is at the current time, nor is there an
** expiration specified.
*****/
function SetTOC( name, value )
{
    document.cookie = name + "=" + escape( value );
}
```

This is the function you use to change the browser's cookie value. Again, the details of cookie manipulation are explained in Chapter 25. For now, you simply set a cookie named name equal to value.

When you later call this function, you are setting a cookie named TableOfContents equal to a series of 0 or 1 values, basically imitating a binary string that is as long as the number of entries you have in the `TOCArray`. `0` means that the entry hasn't been clicked, so it appears condensed; a value of `1` shows the opposite.

You could set other values here, but all you want is something that tracks the table of contents and disappears at the end of the browser session.

> **TIP**
>
> Although in this script you don't really need JavaScript's built-in `escape()` function to translate non-ASCII characters (such as spaces) into their ASCII counterparts, it's a good habit to use `escape()` and `unescape()` when dealing with cookies. It saves many headaches later.

```
/*****
** Get the value set in the Cookie in order to display table of contents
** in proper nesting order.
*****/
function GetTOC( name )
{
    var tocName = name + "=";
    var tocLength = tocName.length;
    var cookieSpan = document.cookie.length;
    var endOfCookie = "";
    var i = 0;
    var j = "";

    while (i < cookieSpan)
    {
        j = i + tocLength;

        if (document.cookie.substring( i,j ) == tocName)
        {
            endOfCookie = document.cookie.indexOf( ";", j );

            if ( endOfCookie ==     -1 )
                endOfCookie = document.cookie.length;

            return unescape( document.cookie.substring( j, endOfCookie ) );
        }
    }
    return "";
}
```

In order to show the nested relationship between parent and child in the table of contents, you need to access the cookie you set earlier. This function gives the actual value of the cookie labeled `TableOfContents` by returning the string that runs from the end of the cookie's name plus an equals sign (`TableOfContents=`) for the length of the cookie.

From this, you determine what the user has clicked; based on the position of that value in the cookie, you discover the other properties of the entry.

```
/*****
** Main action function.
** Changes the Cookie value for each table of contents entry based on whether
** or not it has been clicked. The Cookie's format is a string of ones and
** zeros, the length of which is determined by the number of entries
** in the TOCArray. The "entryPoint" is the TOCEntry position in the Cookie.
*****/
function ChangeTOC( entryPoint )
{
    if ( entryPoint != 0 )
    {
        var updatedTOC = "";
        var currentTOC = GetTOC( "TableOfContents" );
        var clicked = currentTOC.substring( entryPoint-1, entryPoint );
          // Find the value of the TOCEntry

        updatedTOC = currentTOC.substring( 0, entryPoint-1 );

        ( clicked == 1 ) ? updatedTOC += 0 : updatedTOC += 1;
          // Flip the appropriate value

updatedTOC += currentTOC.substring( entryPoint, currentTOC.length );

        SetTOC( "TableOfContents", updatedTOC );
    }
}
```

Here you handle updating individual values of cookie data (such as flipping a one to a zero or vice versa). The argument passed to this function is the numeric location of the value you want to change.

Once you have the location and the rest of the cookie, you simply reconstruct another cookie value from the old one, change the number at the location specified, and then add on the rest of the old cookie.

NOTE

For C or C++ programmers, this might appear suspiciously like string manipulation through pointer arithmetic. For all intents and purposes, this is as close as JavaScript comes to such a concept.

The final action of the function is resetting the cookie with the newly created value:

```
/*****
** Determines what image to add to the HTML based on the state and position
** of the table of contents entries.
*****/
function Image( index )
{
    var parent = toc[index].parent;
    var isOpen = GetTOC( "TableOfContents" ).substring( index-1, index );

    if ( !parent )
        return "end.jpg";
```

```
    else
    {
        if ( isOpen == 1 )
            return "open.jpg";
    }

    return "closed.jpg";
}

/*****
** Determines what status message to display based on the state and position
** of the table of contents entries.
*****/
function Status( index )
{
    var parent = toc[index].parent;
    var isOpen = GetTOC( "TableOfContents" ).substring( index-1, index );

    if ( !parent )
        return "Last Entry";
    else
    {
        if ( isOpen == 1 )
            return "Click To Hide Nested Entries";
    }
    return "Click To Show Nested Entries";
}
```

These two functions return different properties, based on either of the following situations:

- ■ The level of nesting shown by the image
- ■ The status message displayed when the user places the mouse cursor over the image

They are identical aside from their return value, which is the image or the message, depending on the function. These functions use the index into the TOCArray, as well as the cookie value at the TOCEntry position, to determine what to return.

```
/*****
** Add spacing for nested entries.
*****/
function nestSpace( nestLevel )
{
    var space = ""
    var i = "";

    for ( i = 1; i <= nestLevel; i++ )
        space += "      ";

    return space;
}
```

This function is fairly straightforward. It simply adds the necessary number of spaces for the visible nesting in the table of contents. The nestLevel value is the TOCEntry.nesting property of the TOCEntry you constructed earlier. You use five physical spaces to represent the nesting because when you display the table of contents, it is placed within the <PRE> and </PRE> tags, keeping the spaces as literals.

```
/*****
** If this is the user's first time in, the Cookie must be set with the
** proper number of entries according to the length of the TOCArray.
*****/
if ( GetTOC( "TableOfContents" ) == "" )
{
    var firstTOC = "";
    var i = "";

    for ( i = 1; i <= toc.length; i++ )
        firstTOC += "0";

    SetTOC( "TableOfContents", firstTOC );
}

// -->
</SCRIPT>
</HEAD>
<BODY>
```

This function handles the initialization of the first cookie for the user. It loops for the length of the TOCArray, setting each value in the cookie to zero.

In this case, for the TOCArray length of 17, you get a string of 17 zeroes. This is the initial view of the table of contents, where only the first-level entries (whose TOCEntries.nesting equals zero) appear.

Now you set up the display of the table of contents:

```
<SCRIPT LANGUAGE="JavaScript">
<!--

/*****
** Start using document.write() to display the table of contents
** (images, status messages and text) based on looping through
** the TOCArray and the Cookie values.
***/
var nestingShown = 0;
var showChild = 0;
var tableOfContents = "<PRE><H4>";
var i = "";

document.write("<CENTER><H3>Fun With Philosophy!</H3><HR WIDTH = 100>");
document.write("Table Of Contents<HR WIDTH = 100><P></CENTER>");
```

These calls to document.write() set the stage for the output of HTML. Keep an eye on the variable tableOfContents. That's where you add the stream of what you want to display. The controlling element in this situation is, once again, the length property of the TOCArray.

```
for ( i = 1; i <= toc.length; i++ )
{
    var image = Image( i );
    var statusMessage = Status( i );
    var nesting = toc[i].nesting;
    var opened = GetTOC( "TableOfContents" ).substring( i-1,i )

    if ( nesting == 0 || nesting <= nestingShown ||
```

```
    ( showChild == 1 && ( nesting - nestingShown == 1)))
{
    tableOfContents += nestSpace( nesting )

    tableOfContents += "<A HREF=\"javascript:history.go(0)\" onMouseOver=
➡\"window.parent.status=\'" + statusMessage +
        "\';return true;\" onClick=\"ChangeTOC(" +
        i + ")\"><IMG SRC=\"" + image +
        "\" HEIGHT=15 WIDTH=15 BORDER=0 ALIGN=TOP></A>";

    tableOfContents += " <A HREF=\"" + toc[i].URL +
        "\" TARGET= \"ContentFrame\" onMouseOver=\"window.parent.status=\'" +
        toc[i].text + "\';return true;\">" + toc[i].text + "</A><BR>";

    nestingShown = nesting;
    showChild = opened;
}
}
```

The large control statement in the preceding code displays each node of the Table of Contents as the TOCArray is looped through. It sends you into the code that builds the HTML strings, including the spacing for nesting entries. The loop also modifies the variables nestingShown and showChild, changing the way the data gets handled the next time through the loop.

As an aside, using a combination of the <PRE> </PRE> and <H4> </H4> tags, you keep the spacing but still allow for nicely formatted text.

> **CAUTION**
>
> There is a bug in the way that version 2.01 of Netscape Navigator for Macintosh handles the A HREF pointing to javascript.
>
> This version of the browser is the only one that exhibits this behavior. The functionality of the JavaScript code doesn't change, but whenever a user clicks one of the images, a runtime error creates a modal dialog box that the user must dismiss, either with a mouse click or by pressing the Enter key.

The last lines of the file send the constructed HTML string to the browser.

```
tableOfContents += "</H4></PRE>";

document.write( tableOfContents );

// -->
</SCRIPT>
</BODY>
</HTML>
```

Skipping Dessert

When you're trying to reach the widest audience possible, cookies may not be an option. Not all browsers support cookies, and users usually have the option of denying a Web page from creating the cookie. As an alternative, you can maintain the state that the table of contents is in by storing a variable in the frameset document. The variable in this case would be in place of the cookie named TableOfContents. The disadvantage of depending on a variable stored in the frameset is that once the user moves to a page that breaks the frameset, the variable is lost. This might not be a problem as long as the table of contents doesn't lead the user outside the frameset. When the user returns to the frameset, the table of contents could return to its default state.

Summary

With JavaScript's capability to perform many actions at once, it's possible to create more sophisticated navigation aids. With one click from the user, you can have JavaScript validate data, submit a form, regenerate a frame, and change the contents of another frame.

The toolbar example showed how to refresh an HTML page in order to give the illusion that buttons are being disabled or enabled as the user interacts with them. A method for changing the contents of three frames with one button click was also shown. The buttonSet object can easily be used in other page designs with little modification.

The table of contents example demonstrated how to form an expandable and collapsible tree view. The JavaScript you wrote accessed quite a few internal objects and functions, and it allowed you to create your own array and array entry objects. In the course of this construction, you manipulated images, text, HTML markup, and status messages. This chapter also delved into the document.cookie object, a topic that Chapter 25 covers in more depth.

The end result is a table of contents that reacts to user input, expanding or condensing nested information based on how far down the tree the user wants to travel.

Forms and Data Validation

IN THIS CHAPTER

CHAPTER 20

When HTML 2.0 was released, it contained a new capability that allowed Web page develop-ers to create online forms. The HTML forms capability had several advantages as a mechanism for creating online forms:

■ Client/server model: The Web browser supplies a generic graphical user interface (GUI) driven by the specific HTML script. Domain-specific processing is handled on the server side through the CGI program.

■ Platform independence: Web browsers run on multiple platforms. The developer need not be concerned about platform-specific issues when developing forms.

■ Network transparency: Network communications are built into the Web browser/ Web server pair and implemented through the HTTP protocol.

■ Standardized GUI: Forms were standardized with HTML 2.0. A user who is familiar with form elements can apply that knowledge to any form on the World Wide Web or corporate intranet.

The HTML forms interface in itself has a few deficiencies:

■ Dynamic user feedback: HTML forms have no means of providing dynamic informa-tion on required input on a per-form-element basis.

■ Client-side form validation: HTML forms can't validate a form element, group of elements, or entire form on the client side.

■ Dialog boxes: HTML forms can't dynamically alert the user about an input error or request additional input.

■ User confirmations: The forms have no way to ask for confirmation before taking irrevocable types of action.

■ Interactivity among form or window elements: In HTML forms, the interactivity is limited to CGI processing on the server side.

The JavaScript language addresses each of these deficiencies. JavaScript builds on the basic capabilities of HTML and produces a more powerful client-side GUI interface. In this chap-ter, you will learn how to implement these additional capabilities in JavaScript. The chapter ends with an application written in JavaScript that makes use of these new capabilities to imple-ment a tool for choosing combinations of text and background colors.

I make extensive use of JavaScript event handlers in this chapter. You can view event handlers as callbacks associated with a form or form element. They are explicitly specified as part of a form or form element tag. Event handlers get called when a user-triggered event occurs, and in turn, they call an appropriate JavaScript code fragment or function. Table 20.1 contains a sum-mary of JavaScript event handlers.

Table 20.1. JavaScript event handlers.

Event Handler	Object(s) It's Associated With	Triggering Event
onBlur	Select, text, textarea	Form object loses input focus
onChange	Select, text, textarea	Value of form object is modified
onClick	Button, checkbox, radio, link, reset, submit	Form object is clicked
onFocus	Select, text, textarea	Form object gains input focus
onLoad	Window	Web browser finishes loading window object
onMouseOver	Link	User moves cursor over link
onSelect	Text, textarea	User selects text within form object
onSubmit	Form	Form has been submitted
onUnload	Window	Window is terminated by user

User Feedback

With a well-designed form, the user should be able to rapidly determine what information is required. In very simple forms, you can accomplish this with well-thought-out labels adjacent to each form element. In complex forms, you should include a help facility that offers a detailed explanation of how to fill out the form. With JavaScript, you can add user prompting on a per-field basis. This allows you to supply additional information about the requirements or function of a form element at the moment the information is needed. By doing so, you can reduce the amount of text required in the form element label and simplify the form's appearance.

User prompting is implemented with JavaScript's event-handling capability and the browser's status bar. You can use the onFocus event handler to execute a user-defined function when a given text object, textarea object, or selection object gains input focus. Similarly, you can use the onMouseOver event handler to execute a user-defined function whenever the cursor is placed over a link. You can use these event handlers to call a function that displays a user prompt on the browser's status bar.

The following example illustrates how to provide user feedback on the browser status bar using JavaScript. Imagine for a moment that you are creating an HTML forms interface to a very advanced automated toaster. The goal is to produce a user interface so easy to use that the most naive user can instruct it to produce a savory toasted bread product. Figure 20.1 shows the interface.

20

FORMS AND DATA VALIDATION

FIGURE 20.1.

The automated toaster form.

The user can set the values of four input objects:

- A selection object representing the type of bread product
- A text object representing the quantity of toasted bread products desired
- A text object indicating the amount of toasting (as a numeric quantity)
- A pair of radio buttons indicating whether the bread product should be buttered

Each of the selection and text objects has associated onFocus and onBlur event handlers. These handlers display and remove appropriate user prompts associated with a given input object. The onClick event handler is used to associate user feedback with the radio buttons.

The window.defaultStatus property is set to display a default greeting message when no other messages are present.

The code for the toaster example is shown in Listing 20.1. Because you don't really have an automated toaster, the code sends mail once the form is filled in. In this listing, you need to substitute your actual e-mail address for the text *your_mail_ID*. In general, any time you see a segment of code in italic, you need to substitute user- or site-dependent information.

Listing 20.1. toaster.htm.

```
<!-- Web Page for controlling an automated toaster
  -- Note: Since we don't really have an automated toaster
  --       mail the results back to the developer -->
<html>
<head>
<title>The Amazing Automated Toaster</title>
```

```
<script language="JavaScript">
<!-- script start
function setStatus(str)
{
    window.status = str;
    return true;
}

var greeting="Hello! How about some nice toasted bread products!";
window.defaultStatus = greeting;
// script end -->
</script>
</head>

<body>
<h1>The Amazing Automated Toaster</h1>

<form action="mailto:your_mail_ID" method="post">

<font size=5>Bread Product:</font>
<select name="product"
    onFocus="setStatus('Select desired bread product from list.')"
    onBlur="setStatus('')">
<option>Bread
<option>Waffle
<option>Bagel
<option>Roll
<option>Muffin
<option>Croissant
<option>Scone
</select>
<br>

<font size=5>Quantity:</font>
<input type="text" name="quantity" value="1" size=4 maxlength=4
    onFocus="setStatus(
        'Enter quantity of bread products desired (1-1000).')"
    onBlur="setStatus('')">
<br>

<font size=5>Toastiness:</font>
<input type="text" name="toastiness" value="50" size=3 maxlength=3
    onFocus="setStatus(
'Enter degree of toastiness from 0-100 (0=untoasted 100=burnt).')"
    onBlur="setStatus('')">
<br>

<font size=5>Buttered:</font>
<font size=5>Yes</font>
<input type="radio" name="buttered" value="yes" checked
    onClick="setStatus(
        'Do you want butter on the bread product?')">
<font size=5>No</font>
<input type="radio" name="buttered" value="no"
    onClick="setStatus(
        'Do you want butter on the bread product?')">
```

20

FORMS AND DATA
VALIDATION

continues

Listing 20.1. continued

```
<hr>
<input type="submit" value="Start Toaster">
<input type="reset">

</form>
</body>
</html>
```

You would usually write a CGI program to process data submitted through a form. However, you might need to develop a form before the CGI program is available. Perhaps you want to debug the form without actually calling the real CGI program. There are several simple methods for testing a form independent of the CGI program:

- For forms that use the `get` method, a standard CGI program called `test-cgi` is available at most sites. Use the following form tag:

```
<form action="http://your_site_name/cgi-bin/test-cgi"
    method="get">
```

  When you submit your form, you will receive a page containing, among other things, the values of the form elements from the submitted page. Although the `test-cgi` CGI file is provided as standard with most servers, its availability and exact location could be site-dependent. Contact your Web site administrator for details.

- For forms that use the `post` method, a standard CGI program called `post-query` is available at most sites. Use the following form tag:

```
<form action="http://your_site_name/cgi-bin/post-query"
    method="post">
```

  When you submit your form, you will receive a page containing, among other things, the name/value pairs corresponding to the form elements from the submitted page. Although `post-query` is provided as standard with most servers, its availability and exact location might be site-dependent. Contact your Web site administrator for details.

- For forms that use the `post` method, you can specify that form results should be mailed to your account. Use the following form tag:

```
<form action="mailto:your_mail_ID" method="post">
```

  When you submit your form, you will receive an e-mail message containing name/value pairs corresponding to the form elements from the submitted page. (With Netscape Navigator 3.0, the user will receive a warning when submitting a form by e-mail. This is not an error; it is a security feature designed to warn the user that the recipient of the form will be able to view the user's e-mail address in the mail header. In other words, forms submission by e-mail is not anonymous.)

Displaying Message Boxes

JavaScript supports several methods for communicating with the user through pop-up alert messages and two types of dialog windows. You can use these methods to communicate important information to the user, confirm a choice made by the user, or request additional information. You can use alert messages as aids in debugging as well.

You use the `alert()` method to pop up a short message to the user. It is a method of the window object. You need not specify the window object to invoke it. You can use the alert method to inform the user of an input error, as shown in the following code:

```
alert("Error: value outside valid range of 0 to 240 volts.");
```

Using this code line displays the message shown in Figure 20.2.

FIGURE 20.2.

An alert message.

You can also use the `alert()` method as a debugging aid. Use it to display a string containing debugging information:

```
var dbgstr = "Value of 'wattage' = " + wattage;
alert(dbgstr);
```

You can use it to do tracing within your JavaScript program:

```
function CalculateWattage(volts,amps)
{
    var dbgstr = "CalculateWattage(" + volts + "," + amps + ")";
    alert(dbgstr);
. . .
}
```

Every time the function `CalculateWattage()` is called, an alert pops up, showing the call and the calling arguments. When you finish debugging the program, you can remove or comment out the debugging code.

The `confirm()` method is similar to `alert`, but it lets the user respond to the message. The responses are limited to OK and Cancel. The `confirm()` method returns true if the user selects OK and false if the user selects Cancel, as shown in the following code:

```
function submitCallback()
{
    if (selfDestructSelected == true)
        return confirm(
            "Invoke self-destruct mechanism in 60 seconds?");
    else return true;
}
...
<form ... onSubmit="return submitCallback()">
```

This code produces the pop-up confirmation dialog window shown in Figure 20.3.

Figure 20.3.
The confirmation dialog box.

Clicking OK allows the submit to proceed. Clicking Cancel returns `false`, which in turn returns `false` to the form object, preventing the form from being submitted.

The `prompt()` method is another window method. It allows you to prompt the user for an arbitrary value, as shown in the following code line:

```
var favColor = prompt("What\'s your favorite color?");
```

You can supply an optional second argument to be used as a default value:

```
var duration = prompt("Enter duration in months:",6);
```

This code line produces the dialog box shown in Figure 20.4.

Figure 20.4.
The prompt dialog box.

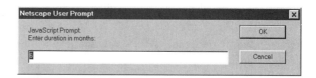

You usually ask the user for information through a form input element, but you can use the prompt dialog box when there is an infrequent need to query the user based on other input information. The following sample code queries the user about whether he wants the Texas Package—but only if he's previously indicated that he lives in Texas. The query then sets a hidden form element that is passed to the CGI program for processing:

```
function TexasQuery(formObj)
{
    var noAnswer = true;
    var ans;
    var promptStr = "Would y\'all like the Texas Package for $50"
        + "(yes or no)?"

    if (state != 'TX') return true;

    while(noAnswer) {
        ans = prompt(promptStr);
        if (ans == null ¦¦ ans.length == 0) continue;
        else {
            ans = ans.toLowerCase();
            if (ans == "yes" ¦¦ ans == "no") noAnswer = false;
        }
    }
```

```
         formObj.txPackage.value = ans;
         return true;
}
...
<form name="myform" ... onSubmit="return TexasQuery(this)">
...
<input type="hidden" name="txPackage" value="">
<input type="submit" name="submit" value="Submit">
```

Note that the user can click Cancel, which leaves the variable ans as undefined. As a result, you must test for null following the call to prompt().

> **TIP**
>
> When a message or dialog box pops up, the user is distracted from his or her task and must focus attention on the pop-up window and respond appropriately. Therefore, alert messages and dialog boxes should be used sparingly.

Status Messages

Another way to give the user feedback while data is being entered is to use status messages. Status messages are the phrases you see in the bottom bar of a window. JavaScript lets you modify what is displayed in this bar, giving you the ability to send messages to the user while he interacts with the HTML form. I find that messages displayed in the status bar are less distracting than dialog windows, but they are not always noticed. Listing 20.2 gives an example of how to give the user extra help while he is entering data into a form.

Listing 20.2. Displaying status messages.

```
<HTML>
<HEAD>
<TITLE>JavaScript Unleashed</TITLE>
<SCRIPT LANGUAGE= "JavaScript">
<!--
function statusMsg(msgType) {
   var message = ""
   if(msgType == "string") {
      message = "Any characters can be used here."
   }
   if(msgType == "integer") {
      message = "Please enter a whole number here."
   }
   else if(msgType == "dollar") {
      message = "Please enter a dollar amount here. (e.g. 19.99)"
   }
   else if(msgType == "credit") {
      message = "Please enter a credit card number here. Do not use dashes."
   }
   window.defaultStatus = message
```

20

FORMS AND DATA
VALIDATION

continues

Listing 20.2. continued

```
      window.status = message
}
//-->
</SCRIPT>
</HEAD>
<BODY onFocus="statusMsg('')">
<FORM NAME="form1" ACTION="#" METHOD="post"><BR>
First Name <INPUT TYPE="text"
           SIZE=20
           MAXLENGTH=20
           NAME="Integer"
           onFocus="statusMsg('string')"><BR>
 Last Name <INPUT TYPE="text"
           SIZE=20
           MAXLENGTH=20
           NAME="Integer"
           onFocus="statusMsg('string')"><BR>
Age <INPUT TYPE="text"
    SIZE=5
    MAXLENGTH=5
    NAME="Integer"
    onFocus="statusMsg('integer')"><BR>
Amount <INPUT TYPE="text"
       SIZE=6
       MAXLENGTH=6
       NAME="Dollar"
       onFocus="statusMsg('dollar')"><BR>
Card # <INPUT TYPE="text"
       SIZE=16
       MAXLENGTH=16
       NAME="Credit"
       onFocus="statusMsg('credit')"><BR>
<BR>
<INPUT TYPE="submit" VALUE="Submit">
</FORM>
</BODY>
</HTML>
```

When the user moves the cursor to a field, or the browser automatically moves the cursor to a field, the onFocus event handler calls the function statusMsg(). The requested type of message is then displayed in the status bar by setting the status property of the window object. The statusMsg() function also enables you to clear out the status bar by passing it an empty string. This is demonstrated when you click on the browser window anywhere outside of the text elements. This triggers the onFocus event handler for the document, which clears the status message.

NOTE

The onFocus event handler for the document was implemented in JavaScript 1.1 for Netscape Navigator 3.0. You can still use it without causing problems with browsers that aren't up to date with the latest JavaScript version.

TIP

It's a good idea to also set the defaultStatus property of the window to the same message. This ensures that your message will not easily disappear as the user moves the mouse pointer around the screen. This is most useful when you're using frames and you want the message to "stick" even though the user moves the mouse pointer to a different frame.

Validating User Input

Prior to the advent of JavaScript, form validation was handled by a CGI program. This approach was effective but required that the entire form be completed by the user and transmitted to the server prior to validation. In some environments, such as low-speed connections to the World Wide Web, a noticeable lag can occur between the time the form is submitted and the time a validation error is returned to the user. Furthermore, by waiting until the form is submitted for validation, the user doesn't receive feedback until after the entire form is completed. Immediate feedback is desirable because the user has just entered information and can place the feedback in the appropriate context. Immediate feedback might influence later behavior and reduce user errors in responding to subsequent form elements. Finally, conventional CGI programming reports input errors in a new Web page. The user must back up to the form to make changes, which interrupts the flow of the form-entry task.

Validating Free Form Input

You can use two event handlers to validate text and textarea form elements. The onBlur event handler is called when a text or textarea form element loses input focus. The onChange event handler is called when the contents of a text or textarea form element are modified.

A form element is said to have focus when any user input will be directed to that element. When a text or textarea form element has focus, a text cursor appears in that element. When the user switches to another element (by using the mouse or the Tab key), the original element is said to lose focus.

The `onBlur` handler is called any time the input field loses focus. The user may or may not have changed the data in the field. The event handler could end up calling the validation code for unchanged data or the default values in the field. You should design the validation code to deal with this possibility.

The `onChange` event handler is called only when the contents of the field are modified. If the user momentarily selects the field (perhaps to view feedback in the status bar) and then chooses another field, the user-defined callback code is not invoked. Although this is more efficient, there is a downside. Suppose that you warn a user about erroneous data in a field. If he clicks the field and then declines to modify it, or if he retypes the same erroneous data, this is not considered a change. The `onChange` event handler is not triggered. For this reason, if you choose to use `onChange`, you should also validate the input at the time of submission (through the `onSubmit` or `onClick` event handlers).

The next example provides a text field for the user to input the quantity of an item. Valid values are 100 to 1000. The `onBlur` event handler is used to call a validation function. The text input object is passed to the event handler. If the input is invalid, the following things occur:

- An alert box pops up to inform the user.
- Input focus is returned to the text field.
- The text is selected (and highlighted) so that it can be easily modified.

Note that the `onFocus` event handler is used to provide user feedback for the text field—perhaps to inform the user about minimum and maximum orders:

```
function validateQuantity(quantObj)
{
    if (quantObj.value < 100) {
        alert("Minimum order is 100 units.");
        quantObj.focus();
        quantObj.select();
    }
    else if (quantObj.value > 1000) {
        alert("Quantities greater than 1000 "
            + "units require special order.");
        quantObj.focus();
        quantObj.select();
    }
    return;
}

...

<h2>Enter number of units:</h2>
<input type="text" name="quantity" value="100" length=4
    maxlength=4 onFocus="quantFeedback()"
    onBlur="validateQuantity(this)">
```

Ensuring Consistency

Sometimes there are dependencies between several input fields. Figure 20.5 illustrates part of a form used by a business for entering a department budget. The user is prompted to enter a total budget and then allocate portions of that budget into three different categories.

FIGURE 20.5.

A form for entering a budget.

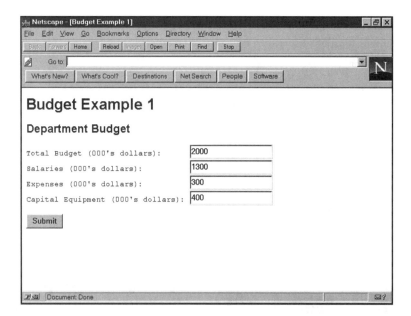

The sum of the three categories should add up to the total budget. Prior to JavaScript, the sum wouldn't have been verified until after the form was submitted and processed by a CGI program. Using JavaScript, the data can be validated prior to submission, saving the user time and preserving context (that is, the same Web page is present before and after validation). The following code segment is an implementation of the budget entry form:

```
<form name="myform" method="post" action="actionURL"
    onSubmit="return validateBudget(myform)">
<h2>Department Budget</h2>

<pre>
Total Budget (000's dollars):      <input type="text"
    name="totalBudget" value="0" onBlur="validateNumeric(this)">
Salaries (000's dollars):          <input type="text"
    name="salaries" value="0" onBlur="validateNumeric(this)">
Expenses (000's dollars):          <input type="text"
    name="expenses" value="0" onBlur="validateNumeric(this)">
Capital Equipment (000's dollars): <input type="text"
    name="capital" value="0" onBlur="validateNumeric(this)">
```

20

FORMS AND DATA VALIDATION

```
</pre>

...

<input type="submit" name="submit" value="Submit">
</form>
```

onBlur event handlers call a user-supplied validation routine that will ensure the user enters valid numeric input in each field. You must supply the following function to verify that the sum of the allocations adds up to the total amount budgeted:

```
function validateBudget(formObj)
{
    var calcBudget = parseInt(formObj.salaries.value,10)
        + parseInt(formObj.expenses.value,10)
        + parseInt(formObj.capital.value,10);
    var totalBudget = parseInt(formObj.totalBudget.value,10);

    if (calcBudget != totalBudget) {
        alert("Error: total budget is not equal to "
            + "sum of allocations.");
        return false;
    }
    else return true;
}
```

This function pops up an alert box in the event of an error and prevents the submit from being processed.

CAUTION

HTML is still an evolving language. In most cases, Web browsers ignore unknown tags or keywords. After all, they could be changes in the HTML standard or vendor-supplied HTML enhancements. This is good for users of Web browsers, because you don't want your browser to crash every time it encounters an unknown tag or keyword.

However, this is a problem for JavaScript programmers. If you misspell the name of an event handler or any other keyword within an HTML tag, your program won't function properly, and your browser won't flag the error. When using JavaScript event handlers in forms, it is prudent to visually inspect your code for typographical errors.

Handling Policy

Policies associated with a form should be indicated to the user through explanatory text within the form, a separate help document (appropriately linked to the form), or both. You can use JavaScript to validate that user input conforms to these policies.

An order form could contain a policy statement that orders can't be shipped on the weekend. Suppose the form allowed the user to specify a ship date. You could use JavaScript code to verify that the ship date is not a weekend, thus enforcing the policy. The following code segment implements these policies:

```
// Compute ship date from
//   user input.  Returns
//   date object
function calcShipDate(formObj)
{
    var day = parseInt(formObj.shipDay.value);
    var month = parseInt(formObj.shipMonth.value) - 1;
    var year = parseInt(formObj.shipYear.value) - 1900;
    var hrs = 0;
    var min = 0;
    var sec = 0;
    shipDate = new Date(year,month,day,hrs,min,sec);
    return shipDate;
}

// Validate shipping policy - don't
//   ship on weekends.  Make sure
//   date is not in past or current date
function shippingPolicy(formObj)
{
    var shipDate = calcShipDate(formObj);
    var day = shipDate.getDay();
    var currentDate = new Date();

    if (shipDate.getTime() < currentDate.getTime()) {
        alert("Error: ship date must be future date.");
        formObj.shipDay.focus();
        formObj.shipDay.select();
        return false;
    }

    if (day == 0) {
        alert("Sorry, we cannot ship on Sunday.");
        formObj.shipDay.focus();
        formObj.shipDay.select();
        return false;
    }
    else if (day == 6) {
        alert("Sorry, we cannot ship on Saturday.");
        formObj.shipDay.focus();
        formObj.shipDay.select();
        return false;
    }
    else return true;
}

...

<form name="myform" method="post" action="actionURL"
    onSubmit="return shippingPolicy(myform)">
```

If the user enters a date corresponding to a Saturday or Sunday, he is reminded of the shipping policy, focus and selection are set to the date input field, and the form is not submitted. The code also enforces the implicit policy of disallowing same-day shipping.

> **NOTE**
>
> When processing dates using JavaScript, be aware that the date and time used are based on the setting of the user's workstation or PC. It's likely that the client and server software are running in different time zones. It's also possible that the time setting on the client side is incorrect, perhaps due to the user's setting the wrong time and date on the workstation or PC. (I once received e-mail that was dated in the year 2004; I assume this was an error, because temporal anomalies are relatively rare on the Internet.)

Ensuring Completeness

Forms frequently consist of a set of mandatory and optional fields. The form can't be properly processed if the mandatory fields aren't supplied. Again, you can use JavaScript to ensure that these fields are present.

The next example is a form requesting customer contact information (see Figure 20.6). The name, address information, and home phone number are considered mandatory fields. All other fields are optional.

FIGURE 20.6.

The contact information form.

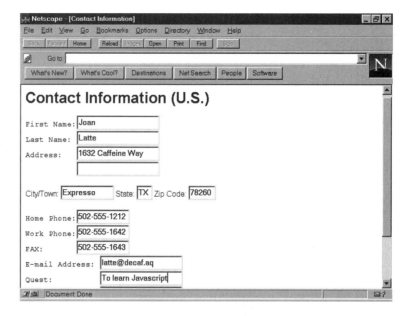

When the form is submitted, a validation function is called. If any of the mandatory fields are empty, the user is notified, and the form is not submitted. The code for the contact information form is shown in Listing 20.3.

Listing 20.3. contact.htm.

```
<html>
<head>
<title>Contact Information</title>
<script language="JavaScript">
<!-- script start
// Ensure that mandatory fields of
// form have been completed
function validateComplete(formObj)
{
    if (emptyField(formObj.firstName))
        alert("Please enter your first name.");
    else if (emptyField(formObj.lastName))
        alert("Please enter your last name.");
    else if (emptyField(formObj.address1)
        && emptyField(formObj.address2))
        alert("Please enter your address.");
    else if (emptyField(formObj.city))
        alert("Please enter your city or town.");
    else if (emptyField(formObj.state))
        alert("Please enter your state.");
    else if (emptyField(formObj.email))
        alert("Please enter your E-mail address.");
    else return true;

    return false;
}

// Check to see if field is empty
function emptyField(textObj)
{
    if (textObj.value.length == 0) return true;
    for (var i=0; i<textObj.value.length; ++i) {
        var ch = textObj.value.charAt(i);
        if (ch != ' ' && ch != '\t') return false;
    }
    return true;
}

// script end -->
</script>
</head>
<body>
<h1>Contact Information (U.S.)</h1>
<form name="myform" action="actionURL" method="post"
 onSubmit="return validateComplete(document.myform)">
<pre>
First Name:<input type="text" name="firstName">
Last Name: <input type="text" name="lastName">
Address:   <input type="text" name="address1">
           <input type="text" name="address2">
```

continues

Listing 20.3. continued

```
</pre>

City/Town:
<input type="text" name="city" size=12>
State:
<input type="text" name="state" size=2>
Zip Code:
<input type="text" name="zip" size=5>

<pre>
Home Phone:<input type="text" name="homePhone" size=12>
Work Phone:<input type="text" name="workPhone" size=12>
FAX:       <input type="text" name="FAX" size=12>
E-mail Address: <input type="text" name="email">
Quest:          <input type="text" name="quest">
Favorite Color: <input type="text" name="favColor">
</pre>
<hr>
<input type="submit" name="submit" value="Submit">
</form>
<body>
<html>
```

The code performs a very basic validation—a field is present if it is not blank. No attempt is made to determine whether the fields contain reasonable data or gibberish. You could include some additional, simple validation. For example, you could validate that the state is a two-letter abbreviation or that the phone number contains the correct number of digits. In general, you should perform simple validations on the client side and more complex validations on the server side.

> **NOTE**
>
> The preceding example is a contact form for English-speaking users in the United States. The Internet is a worldwide network. In some countries, the family name precedes the given name, states are not a political subdivision, ZIP codes don't exist, and the user's language is not English. People still have a favorite color, however. The issue of internationalization is well beyond the scope of this book; nevertheless, you should be cognizant of the potential user base when designing forms.

Calculated Fields

Prior to JavaScript, even the simplest interactive form required interaction with a CGI program on the server. With JavaScript, you can create interactive forms where the interaction is handled entirely on the client side without requiring a round trip to the server.

Interactive programming in JavaScript does have a few limitations. It would be useful to be able to change any individual element of a page dynamically. Unfortunately, you can't do that. When the Web browser renders a page and the elements are formatted, they cannot be modified by the JavaScript code. As Omar Khayyám wrote:

> The Moving Finger writes; and, having writ,
>
> Moves on: nor all thy Piety nor Wit
>
> Shall lure it back to cancel half a Line,
>
> Nor all thy Tears wash out a Word of it.
>
> (From *The Rubáiyát of Omar Khayyám*, available on the World Wide Web at `http://www.panix.com/~falcon1/omar.html`.)

If you can't change the formatting of a page once it's written, what can you do? JavaScript allows you to create interactions between the following items:

- Form elements on the same page
- Form elements and another window
- Form elements and another frame

You can use any of the techniques described earlier in this chapter—user feedback, message boxes, and input validation—to enhance a form. You can alter the entire page by completely rewriting it. In this case, the browser erases the current page and reformats the entire page from scratch. You can also change the background color of the page (a document property), but not the foreground color. The page text has already been rendered in the foreground color, so it can't be changed.

The next example, shown in Figure 20.7, is a different implementation of the budgeting example from earlier in this chapter. This example has a new text field named `remainder`. Although you can't update regular text or graphics on a page once it's written, you can update a form element. In this case, you update the `remainder` text element based on the values in the other elements. As the user types in the total budget and allocations, the `remainder` text field shows the amount of money left after the allocations are subtracted from the total budget.

FIGURE 20.7.

The calculated budget example.

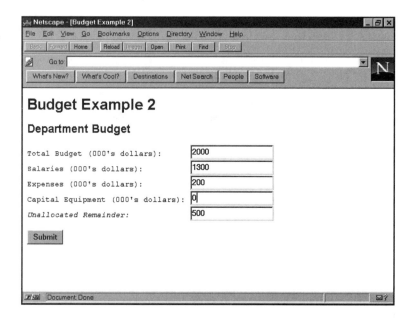

This example uses the onChange event handler to update the remainder field whenever one of the values of the other text fields is modified. When the user submits the form, the script recalculates the remainder. If it is zero, the form is submitted; otherwise, an alert dialog box is displayed. The following segment shows the code for the interactive budget example:

```
function calcRemainder(formObj)
{
    var calcBudget = parseInt(formObj.salaries.value,10)
        + parseInt(formObj.expenses.value,10)
        + parseInt(formObj.capital.value,10);
    var totalBudget = parseInt(formObj.totalBudget.value);

    var unalloc = totalBudget - calcBudget;
    formObj.remainder.value = unalloc;
}

function validateBudget(formObj)
{
    calcRemainder(formObj);
    var unalloc = formObj.remainder.value;
    if (unalloc != 0) {
        alert("Error: Total budget is not equal "
            + "to sum of allocations.");
        return false;
    }
    return true;
}

<form name="myform" method="post" action="actionURL"
    onSubmit="return validateBudget(myform)">
<h2>Department Budget</h2>
```

```
<pre>
Total Budget (000's dollars):        <input type="text"
    name="totalBudget" value="0"
    onChange="calcRemainder(myform)">
Salaries (000's dollars):            <input type="text"
    name="salaries" value="0" onChange="calcRemainder(myform)">
Expenses (000's dollars):            <input type="text"
    name="expenses" value="0" onChange="calcRemainder(myform)">
Capital Equipment (000's dollars): <input type="text"
    name="capital" value="0" onChange="calcRemainder(myform)">
<em>Unallocated Remainder:<em>                <input type="text"
    name="remainder" value="0">
</pre>

<input type="submit" name="submit" value="Submit">
</form>
```

You can use JavaScript to write small interactive applications where all the processing is done on the client side. Listing 20.4 calculates the future value of an investment. The user supplies the initial amount, an interest rate, and the number of years that the investment is compounded. Figure 20.8 shows the display after the script has been loaded into the browser. Note that the output of the JavaScript function `calculate()` is displayed through text input objects, as described earlier.

FIGURE 20.8.

The compound interest form.

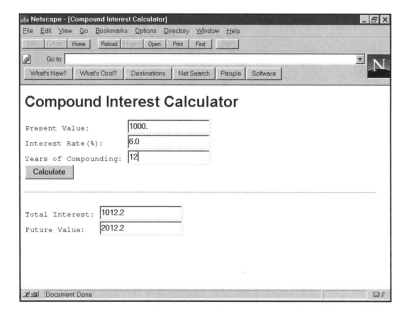

No CGI program is required, because all processing is done on the client side. Note that instead of using a `submit` input object, the form uses a `button` object. Also, instead of using an `onSubmit` event handler, the script uses an `onClick` event handler. The `submit` object and `onSubmit` event-handler semantics are used when the Web browser transmits a form to the server side.

Because you want to do the processing on the client side, you use the onClick event handler and the calculate() function when the button is pressed. The button was labeled Calculate for clarity but could have been labeled Submit. Unless the user views the source code for the page, it will appear indistinguishable from a page that uses HTML on the client side and a CGI script on the server side. The code for the compound interest form is shown in Listing 20.4.

Listing 20.4. interest.htm.

```html
<html>
<head>
<title>Compound Interest Calculator</title>
<script language="JavaScript">
<!-- script start

// script end -->
function calculate(formObj)
{
    var presentVal = parseFloat(formObj.presentVal.value);
    var intRate = parseFloat(formObj.intRate.value)/100.;
    var years = parseFloat(formObj.years.value);

    var futureVal = presentVal * Math.pow((1.0+intRate),years);
    var totalInt = futureVal - presentVal;
    futureVal = Math.round(futureVal*100.0)/100.0;
    totalInt  = Math.round(totalInt*100.0)/100.0;

    formObj.futureVal.value = futureVal;
    formObj.totalInt.value = totalInt;

    return;
}
</script>
<body>
<h1>Compound Interest Calculator</h1>
<form name="myform">
<pre>
Present Value:        <input type="text" name="presentVal">
Interest Rate(%):     <input type="text" name="intRate">
Years of Compounding: <input type="text" name="years">
<input type="button" name="calc" value="Calculate"
    onclick="calculate(myform)">
</pre>
<hr>
<pre>
Total Interest: <input type="text" name="totalInt">
Future Value:   <input type="text" name="futureVal">
<pre>
</form>
</body>
<html>
```

Frequently Used Validation Code

The following sections demonstrate ways to validate the most common types of data asked for over the Internet. The examples are especially easy to use in a code library that is stored in a separate file or in the frameset parent document. All examples accept a text element object as one of their arguments. This allows you to update the text field during data validation when necessary. If the data in need of validation is not an integer, string, dollar amount, or credit card, see the section "Advanced Validation with Pictures" for an example of how to set up more specific data validation.

> **NOTE**
>
> The validation scripts in the next five sections can be found in the code libraries of Acadia Infuse, a visual JavaScript editor found on the CD-ROM included with this book. The code libraries can be found on Infuse's Frequent Scripts menu. For more information, see Chapter 4, "Using Acadia Infuse to Create JavaScript Scripts."

Integer

Listing 20.5 is used to ensure that only whole numbers are accepted as input. The script is called when the user clicks the Validate button. The result, either `true` or `false`, is then displayed in the result text field. This specifies whether the data entered passed the validation process.

Listing 20.5. Integer validation.

```
<HTML>
<HEAD>
<SCRIPT LANGUAGE= "JavaScript">
<!--
function isInt(textObj) {
   var newValue = textObj.value
   var newLength = newValue.length
   for(var i = 0; i != newLength; i++) {
      aChar = newValue.substring(i,i+1)
      if(aChar < "0" || aChar > "9") {
         return false
      }
   }
   return true
}
//-->
</SCRIPT>
</HEAD>
<BODY>
<FORM NAME="form1">
```

20

FORMS AND DATA VALIDATION

continues

Listing 20.5. continued

```
<INPUT TYPE="text"
    SIZE=16
    MAXLENGTH=16
    NAME="data">
<INPUT TYPE="button"
    NAME="CheckButton"
    VALUE="Validate"
    onClick="document.form1.result.value = '' +
      isInt(document.form1.data)">
<BR>
Result <INPUT TYPE="text"
    SIZE=16
    MAXLENGTH=16
    NAME="result">
</FORM>
</BODY>
</HTML>
```

String

Listing 20.6 shows how to ensure that the user has entered a string of characters made up of only alphabetic and a few other characters. The other characters allowed are specified with the extraChars variable. If the user enters any characters that are neither in the alphabet nor in the extraChars variable, the function returns false. Listing 20.6 might be used to validate names, because some names contain periods, spaces, hyphens, and commas.

Listing 20.6. String validation.

```
<HTML>
<HEAD>
<SCRIPT LANGUAGE= "JavaScript">
<!--
function isString(textObj) {
    var newValue = textObj.value
    var newLength = newValue.length
    var extraChars=". -,"
    var search
    for(var i = 0; i != newLength; i++) {
        aChar = newValue.substring(i,i+1)
        aChar = aChar.toUpperCase()
        search = extraChars.indexOf(aChar)
        if(search == -1 && (aChar < "A" ¦¦ aChar > "Z") ) {
            return false
        }
    }
    return true
}
//-->
</SCRIPT>
</HEAD>
<BODY>
```

```
<FORM NAME="form1">
<INPUT TYPE="text"
   SIZE=16
   MAXLENGTH=16
   NAME="data">
<INPUT TYPE="button"
   NAME="CheckButton"
   VALUE="Validate"
   onClick="document.form1.result.value = '' +
   isString(document.form1.data)">
<BR>
Result <INPUT TYPE="text"
   SIZE=16
   MAXLENGTH=16
   NAME="result">
</FORM>
</BODY>
</HTML>
```

Dollar

Listing 20.7 uses a technique that is somewhat different from the integer and string validation examples. Instead of performing a straightforward validation, it formats a value to be displayed as an amount of money to two decimal places. This is also an example of how the function uses the text object it was given to update the object's value. If the function can't convert the data it was given into money, it defaults to an amount of 0.

Listing 20.7. Money format.

```
<HTML>
<HEAD>
<SCRIPT LANGUAGE= "JavaScript">
<!--
function moneyFormat(textObj) {
   var newValue = textObj.value
   var decAmount = ""
   var dolAmount = ""
   var decFlag = false
   var aChar = ""

   // ignore all but digits and decimal points.
   for(i=0; i < newValue.length; i++) {
     aChar = newValue.substring(i,i+1)
     if(aChar >= "0" && aChar <= "9") {
        if(decFlag) {
           decAmount = "" + decAmount + aChar
        }
        else {
           dolAmount = "" + dolAmount + aChar
        }
     }
```

20

FORMS AND DATA VALIDATION

continues

Listing 20.7. continued

```
        if(aChar == ".") {
            if(decFlag) {
                dolAmount = ""
                break
            }
            decFlag=true
        }
    }

    // Ensure that at least a zero appears for the dollar amount.
    if(dolAmount == "") {
        dolAmount = "0"
    }
    // Strip leading zeros.
    if(dolAmount.length > 1) {
        while(dolAmount.length > 1 && dolAmount.substring(0,1) == "0") {
            dolAmount = dolAmount.substring(1,dolAmount.length)
        }
    }

    // Round the decimal amount.
    if(decAmount.length > 2) {
        if(decAmount.substring(2,3) > "4") {
            decAmount = parseInt(decAmount.substring(0,2)) + 1
            if(decAmount < 10) {
                decAmount = "0" + decAmount
            }
            else {
                decAmount = "" + decAmount
            }
        }
        else {
            decAmount = decAmount.substring(0,2)
        }
        if (decAmount == 100) {
            decAmount = "00"
            dolAmount = parseInt(dolAmount) + 1
        }
    }

    // Pad right side of decAmount
    if(decAmount.length == 1) {
        decAmount = decAmount + "0"
    }
    if(decAmount.length == 0) {
        decAmount = decAmount + "00"
    }

    // Check for negative values and reset textObj
    if(newValue.substring(0,1) != '-' ||
        (dolAmount == "0" && decAmount == "00")) {
        textObj.value = dolAmount + "." + decAmount
    }
    else{
        textObj.value = '-' + dolAmount + "." + decAmount
    }
}
```

```
//-->
</SCRIPT>
</HEAD>
<BODY>
<FORM NAME="form1">
<INPUT TYPE="text"
    SIZE=16
    MAXLENGTH=16
    NAME="data">
<INPUT TYPE="button"
    NAME="CheckButton"
    VALUE="Format"
    onClick="moneyFormat(document.form1.data)">
</FORM>
</BODY>
</HTML>
```

Credit Cards

Accepting credit card orders is an important aspect of doing business over the Web. With JavaScript, you can run a preliminary check on a credit card number before it's stored on the server for final validation. Listing 20.8 demonstrates how you can run this test on credit card numbers to ensure that the card number follows the basic rules designed by credit card companies. If the card number fails this validation, you can inform the user that she may have entered the wrong number and should check again. If the user chooses not to update the card number, you can still accept it and perform the final check on the server side using an electronic commerce service.

> **WARNING**
>
> Listing 20.8 should only be used as a preliminary check for credit card validation. Using an electronic commerce service on the server side is the only way to properly validate credit cards at this time. You can find a large list of companies that offer this service at
>
> `http://www.yahoo.com/Business_and_Economy/Companies/Computers/Software/`
> `➡Financial/Electronic_Commerce/`

The isCreditCard function begins by ignoring any dashes that the user entered. It then runs the number through an algorithm that calculates a code, known as a checksum, for the credit card number. If the checksum is equal to the last digit of the credit card number, the number is valid. However, passing this test doesn't necessarily mean that an account exists for the number or that the account hasn't expired. It simply means that the number follows the rules for being a credit card number.

20

FORMS AND DATA
VALIDATION

RESOURCE

If you would like more details on how credit card checksums are calculated, you can find an excellent description at http://www.websitter.com/cardtype.html.

Listing 20.8. Credit card validation.

```
<HTML>
<HEAD>
<SCRIPT LANGUAGE= "JavaScript">
<!--
function isCreditCard(textObj) {
  /*
   *  This function validates a credit card entry.
   *  If the checksum is ok, the function returns true.
   */
  var ccNum
  var odd = 1
  var even = 2
  var calcCard = 0
  var calcs = 0
  var ccNum2 = ""
  var aChar = ''
  var cc
  var r

  ccNum = textObj.value
  for(var i = 0; i != ccNum.length; i++) {
    aChar = ccNum.substring(i,i+1)
    if(aChar == '-') {
      continue
    }
    ccNum2 = ccNum2 + aChar
  }

  cc = parseInt(ccNum2)
  if(cc == 0) {
    return false
  }
  r = ccNum.length / 2
  if(ccNum.length - (parseInt(r)*2) == 0) {
    odd = 2
    even = 1
  }

  for(var x = ccNum.length - 1; x > 0; x--) {
    r = x / 2
    if(r < 1) {
      r++
    }
    if(x - (parseInt(r) * 2) != 0) {
      calcs = (parseInt(ccNum.charAt(x - 1))) * odd
    }
```

```
    else {
        calcs = (parseInt(ccNum.charAt(x - 1))) * even
    }
    if(calcs >= 10) {
        calcs = calcs - 10 + 1
    }
    calcCard = calcCard + calcs
}

calcs = 10 - (calcCard % 10)
if(calcs == 10) {
    calcs = 0
}

if(calcs == (parseInt(ccNum.charAt(ccNum.length - 1)))) {
    return true
}
else {
    return false
}
}
//-->
</SCRIPT>
</HEAD>
<BODY>
<FORM NAME="form1">
<INPUT TYPE="text"
    SIZE=16
    MAXLENGTH=16
    NAME="data">
<INPUT TYPE="button"
    NAME="CheckButton"
    VALUE="Validate"
    onClick="document.form1.result.value = '' +
     isCreditCard(document.form1.data)">
<BR>
Result <INPUT TYPE="text"
    SIZE=16
    MAXLENGTH=16
    NAME="result">
</FORM>
</BODY>
</HTML>
```

Advanced Validation with Pictures

Picture validation is a method of validating data by comparing it to a *picture*. A picture, also known as an *edit mask,* is a string used to check each character of the data that was entered. Pictures can combine more than one type of validation, allowing you to perform a separate check for each character that was entered. For example, Listing 20.9 uses the pound sign (#) to represent any base-ten digit, 0 through 9. Knowing this, you can set up a picture to validate that phone numbers are entered using the format you need. For example, the picture

```
(###)###-####
```

would allow the user to enter any one of the following phone numbers:

```
(555)123-1234
```

```
(555)555-1212
```

```
(101)055-1212
```

However, this may not be enough of a check. For example, you may not want to allow any zeros or ones in the sixth place of the string being entered. To prevent this, Listing 20.9 allows you to specify exactly what is excepted for any one character. This is done using brackets ([]). The following example demonstrates their use:

```
(###)[23456789]##-####
```

If you specify this picture, the data will not validate unless the sixth character is a digit from 2 to 9. Here is the full list of picture characters supported by Listing 20.9:

@ Any character allowed by an HTML text element

? Any letter

Any number

$ Money characters: 0 through 9, minus sign (-), plus sign(+), and the decimal point (.)

[] Specifies a custom data set to use for the character

* Any number of the character that follows it. For example, using an asterisk followed by a question mark will allow any number of letters to be entered.

Listing 20.9. Picture validation.

```
<HTML>
<HEAD>
<SCRIPT LANGUAGE= "JavaScript">
<!--
// Globals used by isValid
var DIGITS = "0123456789"
var UPPERS = "ABCDEFGHIJKLMNOPQRSTUVWXYZ"
var LOWERS = "abcdefghijklmnopqrstuvwxyz"

function isValid(obj, picture, detailObj) {
    var status = true
    var isRepeat = false
    var pLen = picture.length
    var search = 0
    var validData = ""
    var picChar = ""
    var aChar = ""
    var newValue = obj.value
```

```
var tLen = newValue.length
var detailError = ""

for(var i = 0, j = 0; (i != newValue.length)
                   && (j != picture.length)
                   && (status==true)
                   ; i++) {
   picChar=picture.substring(j,j+1)
   if(picChar == "[") {
      validData = ""
      j++
      for(; j != picture.length; j++) {
         if(picture.substring(j,j+1) == "]") {
            break
         }
         validData = validData + picture.substring(j,j+1)
      }
   }
   else if(picChar =="@") {        // Any character
      j++
      continue
   }
   else if(picChar == "?") {       // Any letter
      validData = UPPERS + LOWERS
   }
   else if(picChar == "#") {       // Any number
      validData = DIGITS
   }
   else if(picChar =="$") {        // Money characters
      validData = DIGITS + "." + "-" + "+"
   }
   else if(picChar == "*") {
      isRepeat = true
      j++
      i--
      continue
   }
   else {
      validData = picChar
   }
   aChar = newValue.substring(i,i+1)
   search = validData.indexOf(aChar)
   if(search == -1) {
      if(isRepeat) {
         isRepeat = false
         j++
         i--
         continue
      }
      status = false
      if(aChar == " ") {
         detailError = "A space is not allowed in position #"+(i+1)+". "
      }
      else {
         detailError = "The character, " + aChar +
         ", is not allowed in position #"+(i+1)+". "
      }
   }
```

20

FORMS AND DATA
VALIDATION

continues

Listing 20.9. continued

```
        else {
            if(!isRepeat) {
                j++
            }
        }
    }
    //Check length
    if(status == true && (j < picture.length || i < newValue.length)) {
        status = false
        detailError = "incorrect length"
    }
    if(detailObj != null) {
        detailObj.value = detailError
    }
    return(status)
}

//-->
</SCRIPT>
</HEAD>
<BODY>
<FORM NAME="form1">
<INPUT TYPE="text"
    SIZE=16
    MAXLENGTH=16
    NAME="data">
<INPUT TYPE="button"
    NAME="CheckButton"
    VALUE="Validate"
    onClick="document.form1.result.value = '' +
     isValid(document.form1.data, '(###)[234$]##-####', document.form1.detail)">
<BR>
Result <INPUT TYPE="text"
    SIZE=16
    MAXLENGTH=16
    NAME="result">
<BR>
Detail <INPUT TYPE="text"
    SIZE=50
    MAXLENGTH=50
    NAME="detail">
</FORM>
</BODY>
</HTML>
```

Example: The JavaScript Color Checker

The next example, shown in Figure 20.9, uses the capabilities described in this chapter to implement a color checker. One of the challenges in designing an HTML form is choosing a background color and a text color that are aesthetically pleasing as well as legible. An enormous
number of combinations fulfill those two criteria—and an enormous number don't. The
JavaScript color checker lets the user specify two colors and view what the combination looks

like in a separate window. The window contains the HTML code for specifying the color combination. The user can then cut and paste the specification directly into her HTML code.

FIGURE 20.9.
The color checker.

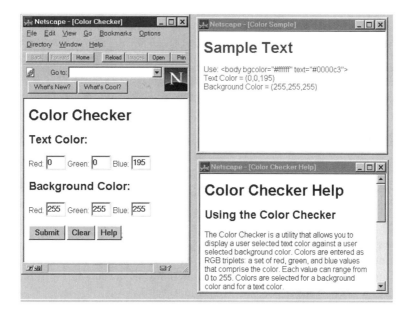

You specify color values by supplying an RGB triplet. The RGB triplet consists of three values representing the red, green, and blue components of the color. These values range from 0 to 255. For instance, the triplet (255,0,0) specifies pure red. Table 20.2 shows a few RGB color values.

Table 20.2. RGB color values.

RGB Value	Color
(0,0,0)	Black
(255,0,0)	Red
(255,255,0)	Yellow
(255,0,255)	Magenta
(0,255,0)	Green
(0,255,255)	Cyan
(0,0,255)	Blue
(128,128,128)	Dark gray
(200,200,200)	Light gray
(255,255,255)	White

As with the earlier interactive forms, all processing is done on the client side. A copy of this program is available on the CD-ROM in the file `\SOURCE\CHAP20\cchecker.htm`.

The program defines a constructor for `color` objects that hold an RGB triplet. The `color` objects have a method called `setColor()` that sets the RGB triplet and computes an equivalent hexadecimal string that can be used to set colors in conjunction with an HTML `body` tag. The program uses two instances of the `color` object: one for the text color, and one for the background color. The `onBlur` event handler calls a validation routine, `validateRGB()`, whenever one of the six color-component text input fields loses focus.

Although the program doesn't have a `submit` input object, it does have a `button` object labeled Submit. The `onClick` method calls the `processForm()` function, which does something new. It creates a window for output that is separate from the color checker program. The window is referenced by a handle named `popWin`. The `processForm()` function checks to see if `popWin` is `null` (its initial value). If it is, `processForm()` creates a separate Color Sample window using the window `open()` method.

Next, things get a little tricky; the user might close the Color Sample window. The only way to detect this is to examine the value of `popWin.document`. If `popWin` is not `null`, but `popWin.document` is `null`, the Color Sample window was closed. If this is the case, you have to re-create the Color Sample window. The `processForm()` function calls the `doSample()` function, which generates the contents of the Color Sample window.

In the body tag, you'll see an instance of the `onUnload` event handler, which is called when the main window is terminated. It calls the `closePopWin()` function, which terminates the Color Sample window if it exists. Finally, note the button named HelpButton within the form. When the user clicks this button, the program creates a new window containing help text. Listing 20.10 contains the complete source code for `cchecker.htm`.

Listing 20.10. cchecker.htm.

```
<!-- Color Checker - July 1996      -->
<!-- Written by Robert L. Platt.      -->

<html>
<head>
<title>Color Checker</title>
<script language="JavaScript">
<!-- script start

// Constructor for color object
function color(r,g,b)
{
    this.setColor = setColor;
    this.setColor(r,g,b);
}
```

```
// Color object set method
function setColor(r,g,b)
{
    this.red = r;
    this.green = g;
    this.blue = b;
    this.hex = rgb2hex(r,g,b);
}

// Convert RGB triplet to hexadecimal string
function rgb2hex(r,g,b)
{
    var str = '"#' + num2hex(r) + num2hex(g)
        + num2hex(b) + '"';
    return(str)
}

// Convert numeric string to hexadecimal string
function num2hex(n)
{
    var str = "";
    var hexstring = "0123456789abcdef";
    while(true) {
        digit = hexstring.substring((n%16),((n%16)+1));
        str = digit + str;
        n = n >> 4;
        if (n == 0) break;
    }
    // Pad string if necessary
    if (str.length < 2) str = '0' + str;
    return(str);
}

// Validate RGB component values
function validateRGB(textObj)
{
    var str = textObj.value;

    if (str.length == 0) {
        userAlert(textObj);
        return false;
    }

    for (var i = 0; i < str.length; ++i) {
        var ch = str.charAt(i);
        if (ch < "0" || ch > "9") {
            userAlert(textObj);
            return false;
        }
    }

    var value = parseInt(str,10);
    if (value < 0 || value > 255) {
        userAlert(textObj);
        return false;
    }
```

continues

Listing 20.10. continued

```
        else return true;
}

// Alert user on input error
function userAlert(textObj)
{
    alert("Please enter a value between 0 and 255.");
    textObj.focus();
    textObj.select();
}

// Write sample frame
function doSample(doc,tc,bc)
{
    var mytext="<h1>Sample Text</h1>";
    doc.open();
    doc.write("<html><head><title>Color Sample</title></head>");
    doc.write('<body bgcolor=' + bc.hex + ' text=' + tc.hex + '>');
    doc.write(mytext);
    doc.write('Use: &lt;body bgcolor=' + bc.hex + ' text='
        + tc.hex + '&gt;');
    doc.write("<br>Text Color=(",tc.red,",",tc.green,
        ",",tc.blue,")");
    doc.write("<br>Background Color=(",bc.red,",",bc.green,
        ",",bc.blue,")");
    doc.write("</body></html>");
    doc.close();
}

// Process submitted form
function processForm(myform)
{
    var winFeatures = "scrollbars,width=400,height=250";
    if ((validateRGB(myform.redtxt) &&
        validateRGB(myform.grntxt) &&
        validateRGB(myform.blutxt) &&
        validateRGB(myform.redbg) &&
        validateRGB(myform.grnbg) &&
        validateRGB(myform.blubg)) == false)
         return false;
    var textColor = new color(myform.redtxt.value,
        myform.grntxt.value,myform.blutxt.value);
    var backColor = new color(myform.redbg.value,
        myform.grnbg.value,myform.blubg.value);
    if (popWin == null)
        popWin = window.open("","PopWindow",winFeatures);
    else if (popWin.document == null)
        popWin = window.open("","PopWindow",winFeatures);

    doSample(popWin.document,textColor,backColor);    .
    return true;
}
```

```
// Reset form to initial values
function resetForm(myform)
{
    myform.redtxt.value = 0;
    myform.grntxt.value = 0;
    myform.blutxt.value = 0;
    myform.redbg.value = 255;
    myform.grnbg.value = 255;
    myform.blubg.value = 255;
    processForm(myform);
}

// Prompt for valid user input
function setPrompt()
{
    window.status="Please enter a value between 0 and 255.";
    return true;
}

// Close Pop-up Window
function closePopWin()
{
    if (popWin != null && popWin.document != null)
        popWin.close();
}

// Clear prompt
function clearPrompt()
{
    window.status="";
    return true;
}

// Initialization
var popWin = null;

// script end -->
</script>
</head>
<body bgcolor="#ffffff" text="#000000" onUnload="closePopWin()">
</script>
<h1>Color Checker</h1>
<form name="myform">

</h2>
<h2>Text Color:</h2>
Red:   <input type="text" size=3 maxlength=3 name="redtxt"
    value="0" onChange="validateRGB(this)"
    onFocus="setPrompt()" onBlur="clearPrompt()">
Green: <input type="text" size=3 maxlength=3 name="grntxt"
value="0" onChange="validateRGB(this)"
    onFocus="setPrompt()" onBlur="clearPrompt()">
Blue:  <input type="text" size=3 maxlength=3 name="blutxt"
    value="0" onChange="validateRGB(this)"
    onFocus="setPrompt()" onBlur="clearPrompt()">
<h2>Background Color:</h2>
```

continues

Listing 20.10. continued

```
Red:    <input type="text" size=3 maxlength=3 name="redbg"
        value="255" onChange="validateRGB(this)"
        onFocus="setPrompt()" onBlur="clearPrompt()">
Green:  <input type="text" size=3 maxlength=3 name="grnbg"
value="255" onChange="validateRGB(this)"
        onFocus="setPrompt()" onBlur="clearPrompt()">
Blue:   <input type="text" size=3 maxlength=3 name="blubg"
        value="255" onChange="validateRGB(this)"
        onFocus="setPrompt()" onBlur="clearPrompt()">
<p>
<input type="button" value="Submit"
        onClick="processForm(document.myform)">
<input type="reset" value="Clear"
        onClick="resetForm(document.myform)">
<input type="button" value="Help" name="HelpButton"
        onClick="window.open('cchelp.htm','CChelp',
        'scrollbars,resizable')">
</form>
</body>
</html>
```

Summary

JavaScript greatly enhances the basic form capability of HTML. Much of the processing that previously could only be performed on the server can now be done on the client side using JavaScript. The new capabilities can be summarized as follows:

- User feedback: JavaScript lets you provide feedback to the form user through a combination of event handlers and control over of the contents of the browser's status bar.

- Message boxes: By using JavaScript alert and dialog boxes, you can display a pop-up message to the user, request confirmation prior to submitting a form, and query the user for additional information.

- Validating user input: You can validate input fields, groups of fields, or the entire form by using event handlers and JavaScript functions. Users can receive feedback in the context of the current form (that is, the page is not replaced by a new page with an error message).

- You can build interactive forms where part or even all of the processing is performed on the client side.

You can use JavaScript to create forms that are easier to use and less prone to error. In turn, you can create forms that respond far more quickly than server-oriented programs, particularly when the user has a low bandwidth connection to the server.

RESOURCE

The JavaScript language is still evolving, so it wouldn't hurt to look at Netscape's JavaScript Authoring Guide, located at `http://home.netscape.com/eng/mozilla/3.0/handbook/javascript/index.htm`.

You can also find JavaScript code examples at the Gamelan Web site at `http://www.gamelan.com`.

Using Client-Side Tables in JavaScript

CHAPTER 21

IN THIS CHAPTER

The Web offers a revolutionary approach to database applications with the capability to access remote data via a Web browser and return the results to you in HTML format. Although this is now common practice with CGI scripts, you can also use JavaScript to access data as well.

When you think of Web database access, you typically think exclusively of letting the data reside on the server. However, JavaScript also lets you work with data on the client side. In this chapter, I look at how you can work with client-side tables using JavaScript and when and how these can be alternatives to CGI and server-based solutions.

Data Source: Client or Server?

Before we look at how to work with client-side databases in JavaScript, it is essential to discuss when a client-side table makes sense. A *client-side table* is a read-only set of data that can be stored in an HTML file on the client computer. For example, you might want to take data from a relational database and convert it to a structured JavaScript dataset.

Client-side tables have two major limitations. First, the database must be read-only. Because the data is actually embedded in your HTML source, you can't have users add or modify this data and save it on the client side. You could theoretically develop a process to update the same data on the server as needed, reloading the client database when a change occurs. Generally speaking, unless you jump through a lot of hoops, a client-side table is read-only.

Second, the database must be relatively small. Because the data is stored in the HTML file, it is downloaded in its entirety when the user accesses the Web page. You would obviously never want to embed a 100,000-record database in your file (or a size anywhere close to that). Even for users with direct Internet connections, the download time would be very annoying every time they wanted to access your page.

The maximum size of a dataset really depends on the context. If you create a client-side table that will be accessed over a 14.4 to 56Kbps modem, you might want to limit the size of the table to no more than 1,000 records. However, if you're creating an intranet solution in which all users have high-speed connections, you might want to push the envelope and allow many more than that.

Given these limitations, why would you ever want to use a client-side table? There are two reasons. First, for some purposes in which a dataset is relatively small and relatively static, a client-side table can provide a much simpler solution than dealing with CGI scripts or other processes on the Web server. Second, because everything resides on the client—data, searching mechanism, and user interface—you avoid the need to access the server at all. The result is that the search process is much quicker; you avoid the added load on the server to process a search and eliminate two transmissions between the client and server.

You might argue that even though the data is moved to the client for processing, the data still has to pass through the server when the page is downloaded. Of course, that's true, but the server isn't required to process a CGI search—it just sends an HTML file to a client who requests it.

As corporations roll out intranets, many small LAN-based applications will be ported to the Web. Because many of these are database-centric, it's likely that corporate Web servers' traffic will increase just to support these applications. In some cases, client-side tables could help minimize the load on the server. One such example is a company phone list application. What company doesn't have such a list, at least on paper? In this chapter, I use the phone list application as a practical and useful example of using client-side data to meet a business need.

What Is a Client-Side Table?

As a database application developer, when I hear the term *table,* I immediately envision a table of columns and rows in a relational database format. For example, Figure 21.1 shows a Paradox table. You can manipulate or search on this data in a variety of ways, depending on the capabilities of the database management software itself.

FIGURE 21.1.

A relational database table.

Unfortunately, although you can work with relational tables on the server side by accessing a database, you can't do the same using the capabilities of client-side JavaScript. You're forced to convert a database table into a structured format that your JavaScript code can use. In JavaScript, the basic organizing structure you want to use is an array. You can access each element of a JavaScript array and evaluate it—just as a relational database evaluates each record in a table during a query. Figure 21.2 shows the parallel between data in a relational table and that in an array.

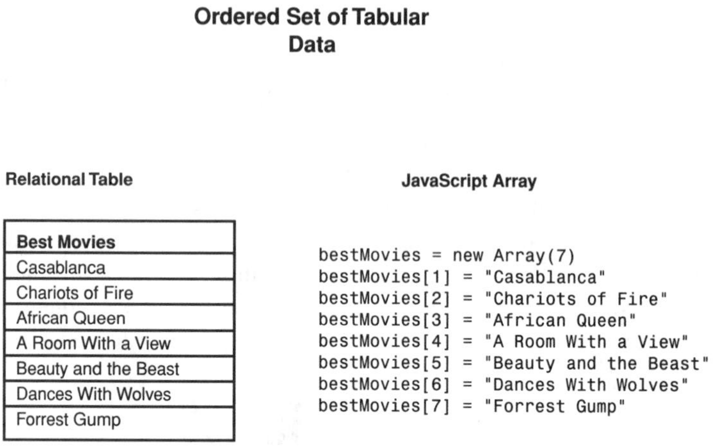

FIGURE 21.2.

You can work with tabular sets of data differently, depending on the context.

Ordered Set of Tabular Data

Relational Table

Best Movies
Casablanca
Chariots of Fire
African Queen
A Room With a View
Beauty and the Beast
Dances With Wolves
Forrest Gump

JavaScript Array

```
bestMovies = new Array(7)
bestMovies[1] = "Casablanca"
bestMovies[2] = "Chariots of Fire"
bestMovies[3] = "African Queen"
bestMovies[4] = "A Room With a View"
bestMovies[5] = "Beauty and the Beast"
bestMovies[6] = "Dances With Wolves"
bestMovies[7] = "Forrest Gump"
```

Creating a Lookup Table

The first step in using a client-side table in JavaScript is creating the table itself. A client-side table can't be an external file, so all the data must be embedded in the HTML file. However, in order for that information to be useful, you need to structure it so that the data can be searched and retrieved as desired.

As shown earlier, one option for structuring client-side data is to use a one-dimensional array. For example, if you wanted to put an entire list of employee names in an array, it would look something like this:

```
var employees = new Array(10)
employees[1] = "Richard"
employees[2] = "David"
employees[3] = "Rachel"
employees[4] = "Mark"
employees[5] = "Mellon"
employees[6] = "Margo"
employees[7] = "Darius"
employees[8] = "Dan"
employees[9] = "Dave"
employees[10] = "Pepe"
```

You could then use this array and search for individual elements within it based on what you learned in the array discussion in Chapter 15, "Creating Custom JavaScript Objects." However, a one-dimensional array is not too helpful in this context, because most lookup tables have multiple columns of data to track. In the phone list example, suppose you want to track an employee's name, title, department, phone extension, and e-mail address.

A second, more useful option is to create a custom object called `employee` and then group these employee "records" together in a one-dimensional array. Doing this lets you store multiple columns of data in an object but also work with the employee objects as a collective group.

Using Client-Side Tables in JavaScript

CHAPTER 21

551

21

USING CLIENT-
SIDE TABLES IN
JAVASCRIPT

To define the `employee` object, you must first create a constructor method, as shown here:

```
function employee(FirstName, LastName, Title, Department, PhoneExt,
        EmailAddress) {
    this.FirstName = FirstName;
    this.LastName = LastName;
    this.Title = Title;
    this.Department = Department;
    this.PhoneExt = PhoneExt;
    this.EmailAddress = EmailAddress;
}
```

The next steps after creating the object constructor method are creating the employee objects themselves and placing them in the container array called `empList`. You can perform these two steps using a single line of code for each employee. The first five employees in our complete list of 105 are shown here:

```
empList[1] = new employee("Richard", "Wagner", "Chief Technology Officer",
  "R&D", "400",
"rwagner@acadians.com")
empList[2] = new employee("Grady", "Anderson", "Programmer", "R&D", "198",
                "grady@acadians.com")
empList[3] = new employee("Thomas", "Sprat", "Marketing Manager", "Marketing",
  "656",
""tspratt@acadians.com ")
empList[4] = new employee("William", "Cleyball", "Marketing Manager",
  "Marketing", "651",
"wcal@acadians.com ")
empList[5] = new employee("Fred", "Tortallini", "Marketing Manager",
  "Marketing", "404",
"tort@acadians.com ")
```

You now have the employee data captured in a structured format that is useful for you in client-side JavaScript.

> **NOTE**
>
> Don't get discouraged as you think of the manual work that is required to migrate data stored in relational databases to a JavaScript array or object. You have many options in creating this information, apart from actually typing the text every time you want to use the data. If the data changes often, you could create a CGI script or another back-end process that generates this code automatically upon exporting a database table.

Creating the Search User Interface

The manner in which you want the users of the application to work with the client-side table will, of course, depend on the exact context of your application. This example calls for a user interface in which the users can search for employees based on text they enter. Because you have several fields in the table, you might want to also give the user the flexibility to search on the four primary searchable fields of the table: `FirstName`, `LastName`, `Title`, and `Department`.

Suppose you want the results to be presented in an HTML document upon searching. To display both the search definition and results at the same time, you could use a multiframe window. With that in mind, the phone list example uses the following files:

- employeeInfo.htm is the parent frameset window, which contains the employee database and other global information.
- searchfrm.htm is the topmost frame, which provides a user interface for entering a search request.
- result.htm is the bottom frame, which displays the search results. It is blank by default.

Figure 21.3 shows the multiframe window setup for the application.

FIGURE 21.3.

The database search user interface.

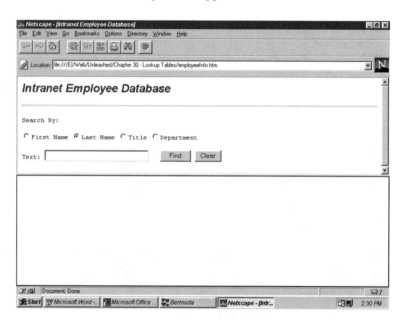

The only part of the user interface that the users will interact with is the search window (searchfrm.htm). The following segment shows the HTML source for the search definition form inside the window:

```
<body>
<form method="POST" name="form">
<pre>Search By: </pre>
<pre><input
     type=radio
     name="searchBy"
     value="FirstName">First Name <input
     type=radio
     checked
```

```
        name="searchBy"
        value="LastName">Last Name <input
        type=radio
        name="searchBy"
        value="Title">Title <input
        type=radio
        name="searchBy"
        value="Department">Department</pre>
<pre>Text: <input
        type=text
        size=30
        maxlength=30
        name="searchByText">    <input
        type=button
        size=20
        name="findButton"
        value="    Find    "
        onClick="doSearch()"> <input
        type=reset
        name="Clear"
        value=" Clear "
        onClick="clearForm()"></pre>
</form>
</body>
```

Processing the Search Request

The heart of an application based on a client-side table is the capability to search on the data. In the employee phone list example, you need to determine the field on which the search should be conducted and then pass that information along with the actual search request to the search processing method.

Search processing is done in two locations in this example. The doSearch() method in the searchForm frame prepares the search and then passes the information to the findEmployee() method of the parent window.

To do this, assign the doSearch() method to the event handler for the Find button. In this function, check to see which of the radio buttons is checked and assign the searchField variable a string value based on the result. Next, after checking to ensure that a value has been entered in the searchByText field, call the parent window's findEmployee() method using the searchField variable and value of the searchByText field as its parameters:

```
function doSearch() {
    var searchField = ""

    if (document.form.searchBy[0].checked) {
        searchField = "FirstName" }
    else {
        if (document.form.searchBy[1].checked) {
            searchField = "LastName" }
        else { if (document.form.searchBy[2].checked) {
                searchField = "Title" }
```

```
                else { if (document.form.searchBy[3].checked) {
                    searchField = "Department" }
                }
            }
        }

        if (document.form.searchByText.value == null ||
            document.form.searchByText.value == "") {
    alert("Please enter your search criteria before continuing.") }
        else {
            parent.findEmployee(searchField, document.form.searchByText.value)
        }
    }
```

In the parent window (`employeeInfo.htm`), the `findEmployee()` method takes these two parameters and uses them to evaluate the array of employee objects. A `for` loop is used to traverse the array of employee objects, checking the value of the search request (`searchWord` parameter) with the specified property (`searchField` parameter), using the string object's `indexOf()` method.

Before you get into the actual code, it's helpful to look at a more basic but equivalent example. If you wanted to search for the value of `"Richard"` in the `FirstName` property of all the employee objects, your code would look like this:

```
for (var i=1; i<empList.length; i++) {
if (empList[i].FirstName.indexOf('Richard') != -1) {
        empList[I].show() }
```

The `for` loop evaluates each object and returns a value greater than or equal to zero if the text is contained within the value of an employee object's `FirstName` property. If a match is found, the employee object's `show()` method is performed. Don't concern yourself with this method yet; it's covered in the section "Displaying the Search Results" later in this chapter.

Following the same logic, look again at the phone list application. You have to take care of a problem first: Because you want to use the `searchField` parameter to represent an object property name and not a string value, you need to use the built-in `eval()` method. The `eval()` method interprets a string value and evaluates it as a JavaScript expression. If you convert the JavaScript code to a single string, it can be evaluated using the `eval()` method:

```
function findEmployee(searchField, searchWord) {
    var str = ""

    // formatting code will go here

    for (var i=1; i<empList.length; i++) {
str = "if (empList[" + i + "]." + searchField +
        ".indexOf('" + searchWord +
"') != -1) { empList[" + i + "].show() }"
        eval(str)
    }

    // formatting code will go here
}
```

Using Client-Side Tables in JavaScript

CHAPTER **21**

555

21

USING CLIENT-
SIDE TABLES IN
JAVASCRIPT

Displaying the Search Results

The final step in the search process is to present the results of the search to the user. Use the bottom frame (`resultForm`) to display this information. You can enhance the `findEmployee()` method you looked at in the preceding section to perform this process.

Because you want to generate HTML on-the-fly, you want to use the `resultForm`'s document object as a "canvas" to write on. You first need to prepare the document canvas to accept input by using the document `open()` method. Next, to display results in a table format, you can create an HTML table using the `<table>` tag and set up the table header:

```
window.resultForm.document.open()
window.resultForm.document.write("<h2>Matches:</h2>")
window.resultForm.document.write("<table border=1>")
window.resultForm.document.
    write("<tr><td width=10%><strong>First Name</strong></td>")
window.resultForm.document.write("<td width=15%><strong>Last Name
  </strong></td>")
window.resultForm.document.write("<td width=20%><strong>Title</strong></td>")
window.resultForm.document.write("<td width=15%><strong>Department
  </strong></td>")
window.resultForm.document.write("<td width=5%><strong>Ext.</strong></td>")
window.resultForm.document.write("<td width=15%><strong>Email</strong>
  </td></tr>")
```

Now that the initial preparation of the `resultForm` is complete, you're ready to process the search as specified earlier. As you recall, each matching employee is called to execute a `show()` method. This method is used to display the employee information as a single record in the table. You therefore need to add a `show()` method to the `employee` object constructor:

```
function employee(FirstName, LastName, Title, Department, PhoneExt,
    EmailAddress) {
this.FirstName = FirstName;
    this.LastName = LastName;
    this.Title = Title;
    this.Department = Department;
    this.PhoneExt = PhoneExt;
    this.EmailAddress = EmailAddress;
    this.show = emp_show;
}
```

When an employee object's `show()` method is called, the `emp_show()` method is triggered. This method provides the location in which to place code for formatting and displaying the current employee's information. Using the `write()` method, you can place the values of each of the object's properties in separate table cells. Here is the code:

```
function emp_show() {
    window.resultForm.document.write("<tr><td width=10%>" +
      this.FirstName + "</td>")
    window.resultForm.document.write("<td width=15%>" +
      this.LastName + "</td>")
window.resultForm.document.write("<td width=20%>" + this.Title + "</td>")
    window.resultForm.document.write("<td width=15%>" + this.Department +
      "</td>")
```

```
    window.resultForm.document.write("<td width=5%>" + this.PhoneExt +
        "</td>")
window.resultForm.document.write("<td width=15%>" + "<a href='mailto:" +
        this.EmailAddress + "'>" + this.EmailAddress + "</td></tr>")
}
```

Notice that a link is defined for the employee's e-mail address. A user can then click the employee's e-mail address in the table to send a message to him or her.

The final formatting code you need to write is back in the findEmployee() method. After each of the employee records are processed, a write() method ends the table definition by sending a </TABLE> tag. Finally, the canvas is closed to additional input when a close() method is issued. Here is the complete findEmployee() method:

```
function findEmployee(searchField, searchWord) {
    var str = ""

    window.resultForm.document.open()
    window.resultForm.document.write("<h2>Matches:</h2>")
    window.resultForm.document.write("<table border=1>")
    window.resultForm.document.write("<tr><td width=10%><strong>First Name
        </strong></td>")
    window.resultForm.document.write("<td width=15%><strong>Last Name
        </strong></td>")
    window.resultForm.document.write("<td width=20%><strong>Title
        </strong></td>")
    window.resultForm.document.write("<td width=15%><strong>Department
        </strong></td>")
    window.resultForm.document.write("<td width=5%><strong>Ext.</strong></td>")
    window.resultForm.
    document.write("<td width=15%><strong>Email</strong></td></tr>")
    for (var i=1; i<=empList.length-1; i++) {
        str = "if (empList[" + i + "]." + searchField + ".indexOf('"
        + searchWord + "') != -1) { empList[" + i + "].show() }"
        eval(str)
    }
    window.resultForm.document.write("</table>")
    window.resultForm.document.close()
}
```

Running the Application

You are now ready to test the application by opening the employeeInfo.htm file in your browser. Suppose you want to search for Grady Anderson. Enter Anderson in the text field, keep the Last Name radio button selected, and click the Find button. Figure 21.4 shows the results. You can clear both the search form and the results frame by clicking the Clear button.

Listing 21.1 provides the complete source code for the employeeInfo.htm parent window, and Listing 21.2 contains the JavaScript source for the searchfrm.htm window.

Using Client-Side Tables in JavaScript

CHAPTER 21

557

21

USING CLIENT-
SIDE TABLES IN
JAVASCRIPT

FIGURE 21.4.

Search results displayed in a table.

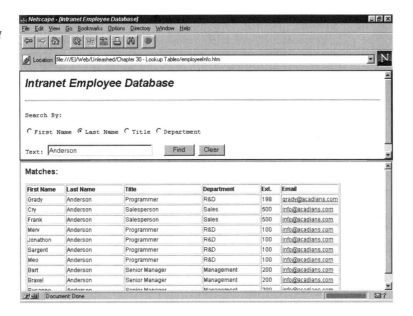

Listing 21.1. employeeInfo.htm.

```
<HTML>
<HEAD>
<TITLE>Intranet Employee Database</TITLE>
<SCRIPT LANGUAGE="JavaScript">

    // Intranet Employee Database
    // JavaScript Unleashed (Sams.net Publishing)
    // Created by Richard J. Wagner (rwagner@acadians.com)

    // Global variables
    var i = 1
    var n = 1

    // Create Array objects
    var empList = new Array()

    // show() - employee object method
    function emp_show() {
        window.resultForm.document.write("<tr><td width=10%>" +
            this.FirstName

        + "</td>")
        window.resultForm.document.write("<td width=15%>" + this.LastName
            + "</td>")
        window.resultForm.document.write("<td width=20%>" + this.Title
            + "</td>")
        window.resultForm.document.write("<td width=15%>" + this.Department
            + "</td>")
```

continues

Listing 21.1. continued

```
        window.resultForm.document.write("<td width=5%>" + this.PhoneExt
            + "</td>")
        window.resultForm.document.write("<td width=15%>" +
            "<a href='mailto:"
            + this.EmailAddress + "'>" + this.EmailAddress + "</td></tr>")
}

    // Employee object constructor
    function employee(FirstName, LastName, Title, Department,
        PhoneExt, EmailAddress) {
        this.FirstName = FirstName;
        this.LastName = LastName;
        this.Title = Title;
        this.Department = Department;
        this.PhoneExt = PhoneExt;
        this.EmailAddress = EmailAddress;
        this.show = emp_show;
    }

    // Search for employee based on field and word
    function findEmployee(searchField, searchWord) {
        var str = ""

        window.resultForm.document.open()
        window.resultForm.document.write("<h2>Matches:</h2>")
        window.resultForm.document.write("<table border=1>")
        window.resultForm.document.write("<tr><td width=10%>
          <strong>First Name</strong></td>")
        window.resultForm.document.write("<td width=15%>
          <strong>Last Name</strong></td>")
        window.resultForm.document.write("<td width=20%><strong>
          Title</strong></td>")
        window.resultForm.document.write("<td width=15%><strong>
          Department</strong></td>")
        window.resultForm.document.write("<td width=5%>
          <strong>Ext.</strong></td>")
        window.resultForm.document.write("<td width=15%><strong>
          Email</strong></td></tr>")

        for (var i=1; i<=empList.length-1; i++) {
            str = "if (empList[" + i + "]." + searchField + ".indexOf('"
            + searchWord +"') != -1) { empList[" + i + "].show() }"
            eval(str)
        }
        window.resultForm.document.write("</table>")
        window.resultForm.document.close()
    }


// Create employee objects on start up
empList[1] = new employee(
"Richard", "Wagner", "Chief Technology Officer", "R&D", "400",
    "rwagner@acadians.com")
empList[2] = new employee(
"Grady", "Anderson", "Programmer", "R&D", "198", "grady@acadians.com")
empList[3] = new employee(
```

```
"Thomas", "Sprat", "Marketing Manager", "Marketing", "656",
    "tspratt@acadians.com ")
empList[4] = new employee(
"William", "Cleyball", "Marketing Manager", "Marketing", "651",
    "wcal@acadians.com ")
empList[5] = new employee(
"Fred", "Tortallini", "Marketing Manager", "Marketing", "404",
    "tort@acadians.com ")
empList[6] = new employee(
"Smack", "Hopkins", "Marketing Manager", "Marketing", "606",
    "smack@acadians.com ")
empList[7] = new employee(
"Luey", "Gentry", "Marketing Manager", "Marketing", "450", "luey@acadians.com ")
empList[8] = new employee(
"Erwin", "Waltham", "Marketing Manager", "Marketing", "545", "ew@acadians.com")
empList[9] = new employee(
"Dallas", "Spanner", "Marketing Manager", "Marketing", "656",
    "dallas@acadians.com")
empList[10] = new employee(
"Spill", "Hopkins", "Marketing Manager", "Marketing", "120",
    "spill@acadians.com ")
empList[11] = new employee(
"Huey", "Wagner", "Marketing Asst", "Marketing", "854", "huey@acadians.com ")
empList[12] = new employee(
"Tom", "Longly", "Marketing Asst", "Marketing", "512", "info@acadians.com ")
empList[13] = new employee(
"Huck", "Starback", "Marketing Asst","Marketing", "212", "info@acadians.com ")
empList[14] = new employee(
"Crazy", "Lags", "Marketing Asst","Marketing", "122", "info@acadians.com ")
empList[15] = new employee(
"Bart", "Simpson", "Salesperson", "Sales", "500", "info@acadians.com")
empList[16] = new employee(
"Bill", "O'Reilly", "Salesperson", "Sales", "500", "info@acadians.com")
empList[17] = new employee(
"Sally", "Smatterhorn", "Salesperson", "Sales", "500", "info@acadians.com")
empList[18] = new employee(
"Kim", "Pakki", "Salesperson", "Sales", "500", "info@acadians.com")
empList[19] = new employee(
"Jacob", "Ladder", "Salesperson", "Sales", "500", "info@acadians.com")
empList[20] = new employee(
"Jared", "Gaspe", "Salesperson", "Sales", "500", "info@acadians.com")
empList[21] = new employee(
"Justus", "Argon", "Salesperson", "Sales", "500", "info@acadians.com")
empList[22] = new employee(
"Jordan", "Basker", "Salesperson", "Sales", "500", "info@acadians.com")
empList[23] = new employee(
"Lisa", "Smith", "Salesperson", "Sales", "500", "info@acadians.com")
empList[24] = new employee(
"Cry", "Anderson", "Salesperson", "Sales", "500", "info@acadians.com")
empList[25] = new employee(
"Ollie", "Ryder", "Salesperson", "Sales", "500", "info@acadians.com")
empList[26] = new employee(
"Polly", "Potts", "Salesperson", "Sales", "500", "info@acadians.com")
empList[27] = new employee(
"Xerxes", "Smith", "Salesperson", "Sales", "500", "info@acadians.com")
empList[28] = new employee(
```

continues

Listing 21.1. continued

```
"Sally Rae", "Smith", "Salesperson", "Sales", "500", "info@acadians.com")
empList[29] = new employee(
"Golden", "Driscoll", "Salesperson", "Sales", "500", "info@acadians.com")
empList[30] = new employee(
"Frank", "Anderson", "Salesperson", "Sales", "500", "info@acadians.com")
empList[31] = new employee(
"Merv", "Anderson", "Programmer", "R&D", "100", "info@acadians.com")
empList[32] = new employee(
"Manu", "Waver", "Programmer", "R&D", "100", "info@acadians.com")
empList[33] = new employee(
"Jason", "Driscoll", "Programmer", "R&D", "100", "info@acadians.com")
empList[34] = new employee(
"Ardent", "Matthews", "Programmer", "R&D", "100", "info@acadians.com")
empList[35] = new employee(
"Ortho", "Dontal", "Programmer", "R&D", "100", "info@acadians.com")
empList[36] = new employee(
"Troy", "Smith", "Programmer", "R&D", "100", "info@acadians.com")
empList[37] = new employee(
"Fred", "Barker", "Programmer", "R&D", "100", "info@acadians.com")
empList[38] = new employee(
"Richini", "Barker", "Programmer", "R&D", "100", "info@acadians.com")
empList[39] = new employee(
"Ricardo", "Bollinger", "Programmer", "R&D", "100", "info@acadians.com")
empList[40] = new employee(
"Ron", "Bollinger", "Programmer", "R&D", "100", "info@acadians.com")
empList[41] = new employee(
"Ronald", "Barker", "Programmer", "R&D", "100", "info@acadians.com")
empList[42] = new employee(
"Browser", "Tyler", "Programmer", "R&D", "100", "info@acadians.com")
empList[43] = new employee(
"Serf", "Tyler", "Programmer", "R&D", "100", "info@acadians.com")
empList[44] = new employee(
"Bill", "Tyler", "Programmer", "R&D", "100", "info@acadians.com")
empList[45] = new employee(
"William", "Smith", "Programmer", "R&D", "100", "info@acadians.com")
empList[46] = new employee(
"Billy", "Barker", "Programmer", "R&D", "100", "info@acadians.com")
empList[47] = new employee(
"Kurt", "Barker", "Programmer", "R&D", "100", "info@acadians.com")
empList[48] = new employee(
"John", "Barker", "Programmer", "R&D", "100", "info@acadians.com")
empList[49] = new employee(
"Jonathon", "Anderson", "Programmer", "R&D", "100", "info@acadians.com")
empList[50] = new employee(
"Frederick", "Barker", "Programmer", "R&D", "100", "info@acadians.com")
empList[51] = new employee(
"Smitty", "Tyler", "Programmer", "R&D", "100", "info@acadians.com")
empList[52] = new employee(
"Sargent", "Anderson", "Programmer", "R&D", "100", "info@acadians.com")
empList[53] = new employee(
"Pepe", "Potts", "Programmer", "R&D", "100", "info@acadians.com")
empList[54] = new employee(
"Leo", "Godfrey", "Programmer", "R&D", "100", "info@acadians.com")
empList[55] = new employee(
"Geo", "Stewart", "Programmer", "R&D", "100", "info@acadians.com")
empList[56] = new employee(
```

21

```
"Meo", "Anderson", "Programmer", "R&D", "100", "info@acadians.com")
empList[57] = new employee(
"Oeo", "Orefo", "Programmer", "R&D", "100", "info@acadians.com")
empList[58] = new employee(
"Jack", "Wagner", "Chief Entertainment Officer", "Exec", "300",
    "jwagner@acadians.com")
empList[59] = new employee(
"Brady", "Smith", "Programmer", "R&D", "100", "info@acadians.com")
empList[60] = new employee(
"Tristin", "Ryder", "Programmer", "R&D", "100", "info@acadians.com")
empList[61] = new employee(
"James", "Tyler", "Programmer", "R&D", "100", "info@acadians.com")
empList[62] = new employee(
"Charles", "Potts", "Programmer", "R&D", "100", "info@acadians.com")
empList[63] = new employee(
"Bill", "Potts", "Senior Manager", "Management", "200", "info@acadians.com")
empList[64] = new employee(
"Bart", "Anderson", "Senior Manager", "Management", "200", "info@acadians.com")
empList[65] = new employee(
"Ian", "Potts", "Senior Manager", "Management", "200", "info@acadians.com")
empList[66] = new employee(
"Woody", "Smith", "Senior Manager", "Management", "200", "info@acadians.com")
empList[67] = new employee(
"Mark", "Tyler", "Senior Manager", "Management", "200", "info@acadians.com")
empList[68] = new employee(
"Andrew", "Driscoll", "Senior Manager", "Management", "200", "info@acadians.com")
empList[69] = new employee(
"Andy", "Potts", "Senior Manager", "Management", "200", "info@acadians.com")
empList[70] = new employee(
"Dandy", "Driscoll", "Senior Manager", "Management", "200", "info@acadians.com")
empList[71] = new employee(
"Candy", "Potts", "Senior Manager", "Management", "200", "info@acadians.com")
empList[72] = new employee(
"Spander", "Smith", "Senior Manager", "Management", "200", "info@acadians.com")
empList[73] = new employee(
"Landry", "Potts", "Senior Manager", "Management", "200", "info@acadians.com")
empList[74] = new employee(
"Permy", "Smith", "Senior Manager", "Management", "200", "info@acadians.com")
empList[75] = new employee(
"Jostin", "Driscoll", "Senior Manager", "Management", "200", "info@acadians.com")
empList[76] = new employee(
"Justin", "Ryder", "Senior Manager", "Management", "200", "info@acadians.com")
empList[77] = new employee(
"Braxel", "Anderson", "Senior Manager", "Management", "200", "info@acadians.com")
empList[78] = new employee(
"Opene", "Smith", "Senior Manager", "Management", "200", "info@acadians.com")
empList[79] = new employee(
"Juan", "Barker", "Senior Manager", "Management", "200", "info@acadians.com")
empList[80] = new employee(
"Julios", "Driscoll", "Senior Manager", "Management", "200", "info@acadians.com")
empList[81] = new employee(
"Andre", "Barker", "Senior Manager", "Management", "200", "info@acadians.com")
empList[82] = new employee(
"Bernard", "Smith", "Senior Manager", "Management", "200", "info@acadians.com")
empList[83] = new employee(
"Susan", "Ryder", "Senior Manager", "Management", "200", "info@acadians.com")
empList[84] = new employee(
```

continues

Listing 21.1. continued

```
"Susanne", "Anderson", "Senior Manager", "Management", "200", "info@acadians.com")
empList[85] = new employee(
"Chelsey", "Barker", "Senior Manager", "Management", "200", "info@acadians.com")
empList[86] = new employee(
"Cosmo", "Krammer", "Senior Manager", "Management", "200", "info@acadians.com")
empList[87] = new employee(
"Kirby", "Tipple", "Senior Manager", "Management", "200", "info@acadians.com")
empList[88] = new employee(
"George", "Allen", "Senior Manager", "Management", "200", "info@acadians.com")
empList[89] = new employee(
"Boy", "Goeria", "Senior Manager", "Management", "200", "info@acadians.com")
empList[90] = new employee(
"Teddy", "Washington", "Senior Manager", "Management", "200", "info@acadians.com")
empList[91] = new employee(
"Tut", "Kingman", "Senior Manager", "Management", "200", "info@acadians.com")
empList[92] = new employee(
"Oil", "Larenzo", "Secretary", "Company", "800", "info@acadians.com")
empList[93] = new employee(
"Susie", "Que", "Secretary", "Company", "800", "info@acadians.com")
empList[94] = new employee(
"Trista", "Wagner", "Secretary", "Company", "800", "info@acadians.com")
empList[95] = new employee(
"Kimberly", "Smith", "Secretary", "Company", "800", "info@acadians.com")
empList[96] = new employee(
"Rachel", "McDonald", "Secretary", "Company", "800", "info@acadians.com")
empList[97] = new employee(
"Reena", "Smiles", "Secretary", "Company", "800", "info@acadians.com")
empList[98] = new employee(
"Treena", "Miles", "Secretary", "Company", "800", "info@acadians.com")
empList[99] = new employee(
"Corrina", "Triles", "Secretary", "Company", "800", "info@acadians.com")
empList[100] = new employee(
"Rosemarie", "Barlington", "Secretary", "Company", "800", "info@acadians.com")
empList[101] = new employee(
"Il", "Plage", "HR Manager", "Recruiting", "900", "info@acadians.com")
empList[102] = new employee(
"Url", "Page", "HR Manager", "Recruiting", "900", "info@acadians.com")
empList[103] = new employee(
"Youri", "Basto", "HR Manager", "Recruiting", "900", "info@acadians.com")
empList[104] = new employee(
"Pri", "Opeo", "HR Manager", "Recruiting", "900", "info@acadians.com")
empList[105] = new employee(
"Tikki", "Rodrequez", "HR Manager", "Recruiting", "900", "info@acadians.com")
</SCRIPT>

</HEAD>
<FRAMESET ROWS="35%,65%">
  <FRAME SRC="searchfrm.htm" NAME="searchForm" MARGINWIDTH="10"
MARGINHEIGHT="10">
<FRAME SRC="result.htm" NAME="resultForm" MARGINWIDTH="10" MARGINHEIGHT="10">
<NOFRAMES>
Sorry, your browser does not support frames.
</NOFRAMES>
</FRAMESET>
<BODY>
</BODY>
</HTML>
```

Listing 21.2. searchfrm.htm.

```html
<html>
<head>
<title>Search Form</title>
<SCRIPT LANGUAGE="JavaScript">

    // Intranet Employee Database
    // JavaScript Unleashed (Sams.net Publishing)
    // Created by Richard J. Wagner (rwagner@acadians.com)

    function doSearch() {
        var searchField = ""

        if (document.form.searchBy[0].checked) {
            searchField = "FirstName" }
        else {
            if (document.form.searchBy[1].checked) {
                searchField = "LastName" }
            else { if (document.form.searchBy[2].checked) {
                    searchField = "Title" }
                else { if (document.form.searchBy[3].checked) {
                    searchField = "Department" }

                }
            }
        }

        if (document.form.searchByText.value == null ¦¦
            document.form.searchByText.value == "") {
            alert("Please enter your search criteria before continuing.") }
        else {
            parent.findEmployee(searchField,
             document.form.searchByText.value)
}
    }

    function clearForm() {
        parent.resultForm.document.open()
        parent.resultForm.document.close()


    }
</SCRIPT><h1><font color="#000000"><em>Intranet Employee Database</em></font>
</h1>
</head>

<hr>
<body bgcolor="#FFFFFF">
<form method="POST" name="form">
<pre>Search By: </pre>
<pre><input
    type=radio
    name="searchBy"
    value="FirstName">First Name <input
    type=radio
    checked
```

continues

Listing 21.2. continued

```
     name="searchBy"
     value="LastName">Last Name <input
     type=radio
     name="searchBy"
     value="Title">Title <input
     type=radio
     name="searchBy"
     value="Department">Department</pre>
<pre>Text: <input
     type=text
     size=30
     maxlength=30
     name="searchByText">    <input
     type=button
     size=20
     name="findButton"
     value="   Find    "
     onClick="doSearch()"> <input
     type=reset
     name="Clear"
     value=" Clear "
     onClick="clearForm()"></pre>
</form>
</body>
</html>
```

Summary

Client-side databases are neither a replacement for larger scale SQL servers nor a means of data entry. However, although they are limited in scope, databases embedded in JavaScript code offer an innovative means of offloading some database processing that would usually take place on the server. A client can then be responsible for the entire database search and presentation process.

This chapter looked at client-side databases and explained when they should be used. It also discussed how to use JavaScript arrays as database containers that can be searched using JavaScript's built-in language constructs. A key part of the chapter was detailing a practical example of where a client-side table would be ideal.

Error Handling and Debugging in JavaScript

IN THIS CHAPTER

Although it is sometimes underestimated as a programming activity, debugging source code is a fundamental element of developing applications in any programming language. JavaScript is no exception.

Client-side JavaScript, however, is still in its infancy when it comes to support of a native or comprehensive third-party scripting and debugging environment, unlike more mature programming languages (such as C++, Visual Basic, and Java). Still, some up-and-coming new tools on the market promise to change that soon. I like to think of these tools in three categories:

- Integrated Development Environment (IDE) tools: These help you quickly construct rich and dynamic Web sites, including JavaScript-enabled pages. An example of such IDE tools includes Aimtech's Jamba. For more information, visit their site at `http://www.aimtech.com`.

- JavaScript scripting tools: These help you more efficiently develop JavaScript-enabled pages through the use of intuitive visual interface and editing techniques. One such example of these scripting tools is Acadia's Infuse, which is described in detail in Chapter 4, "Using Acadia Infuse to Create JavaScript Scripts."

- JavaScript debugging tools: These help you more effectively debug, fix, and test your code with the use of a graphical interface and commonly practiced debugging techniques (such as breakpoints and stepping into or out of code). An example of such tools is Microsoft's Script Debugger, which I will discuss in detail later in this chapter.

Error handling in general is a combination of preventive controls (identifying and fixing errors before execution), detective controls (identifying errors during execution), and corrective controls (fixing errors found during execution). JavaScript—or, more accurately, the JavaScript interpreter built into JavaScript-compliant browsers—provides automated detective error control in the form of dialog boxes that display information about the error. The introduction of new JavaScript scripting and debugging tools helps the developer take advantage of more automated preventive and—to a lesser extent—corrective controls. However, because of the immaturity and limitation of the current tools, the onus to thoroughly test and debug the JavaScript code is still firmly on the developer.

This chapter discusses methods of identifying, fixing, and testing your JavaScript, as well as techniques for writing solid and maintainable code. We will also look at Microsoft's Script Debugger—one of the first, and very few, tools currently available for debugging JavaScript.

NOTE

Microsoft Script Debugger officially supports (and debugs) JScript, Microsoft's implementation of Netscape's JavaScript. JScript is very similar to Netscape's JavaScript, but there are some subtle differences that occasionally affect page presentation, depending on which browser you use. See the section "Differences Between JavaScript and JScript," as well as Chapter 23, "JavaScript Compatibility Issues," for more information.

Types of Errors

JavaScript errors are identified by the JavaScript-compatible browser as the HTML page is loaded and can be classified in the following three types:

- Syntax errors
- Runtime errors
- Logical errors

> **CAUTION**
>
> The JavaScript interpreter doesn't identify logical errors. You must test the functionality of your code to identify potential errors in your program logic. For example, running your JavaScript code will result in a logical error if you perform an arithmetic expression on a string variable (this example is described in more detail later—see Figure 22.1).

Syntax Errors

Syntax errors, which stem from incorrectly constructed code, are often caused by typographical errors, spelling mistakes, missing punctuation, and unmatched brackets. The following example demonstrates several common syntax errors:

```
fuction errorProne() {    // "function" is misspelled
var i = o;    // should be initialized to zero "0"--not letter "o"
for (i >= 0; I =< 10; i++) {
             // variable "I" is not defined (should be small "i")
   document.write("The square of " + i + " is " + (i*i) + "<br>")
             // missing semicolon ";"
   document.write("The cube of " + i + " is ' + (i*i*i) + "<hr>");
             // double quote expected
}
// missing closing braces to end function
```

> **CAUTION**
>
> JavaScript is case-sensitive, so be careful of capitalization. In particular, when you're using JavaScript's built-in objects—and their properties, methods, and events—make sure to look up the exact syntax from the *JavaScript Language Reference Guide*.

Syntax errors are the most commonly made and easiest-to-correct errors in JavaScript. The JavaScript interpreter often does a good job of identifying the exact source of these errors in your code, and the resolution generally requires no more than a simple edit.

NOTE

Because JavaScript is interpreted and doesn't currently offer a syntax debugging tool, you identify syntax errors by running the code—loading the HTML page containing JavaScript into a JavaScript-compatible browser.

Runtime Errors

Runtime errors occur when a syntactically correct statement attempts to do a task that is impossible to perform. Common runtime error examples include invalid function calls, mismatched data types, undeclared variable assignment, and arithmetic impossibilities (such as division by zero).

Runtime errors are reported by the browser much like syntax errors are reported; however, their resolution often requires a more thorough investigation of the code. The following example demonstrates a runtime error caused by a division by zero:

```
function mismatched() {
var i = 10;
for (i <=10; i >= 0; i--) {
        // this loop will cause a division by zero and unpredictable results
document.write(i + " divided by twice its square (" +
(i*i*2) + ") = " + (i/(i*i*2)) + "<br>");
}
}
```

Logical Errors

Logical (or logic) errors occur when an application or function doesn't perform the way its users or designers intended. In other words, an application that has syntactically good code and is free of runtime errors but still produces incorrect results has logical errors. Logical errors are the hardest types of errors to identify and fix and usually demand a thorough test of the application, analysis of the results, and a review of the design. Many logical errors are propagated from a poor understanding of the requirements, bad design, and subsequent incorrect code. The following example demonstrates a logical error caused by evaluation of mismatched data types:

```
function mismatched() {
var Constant = "10";
var i = 10;
for (i <=10; i > 0; i--) {
    document.write(i + " + " + Constant + " = " + (i + Constant) + "<br>");
    }
}
```

You can see in Figure 22.1 that the results displayed are clearly incorrect, even though the code ran successfully. In this case, JavaScript evaluates the result of the expression (i + Constant) as a string and concatenates the two operands into one.

FIGURE 22.1.

An example of a logical error.

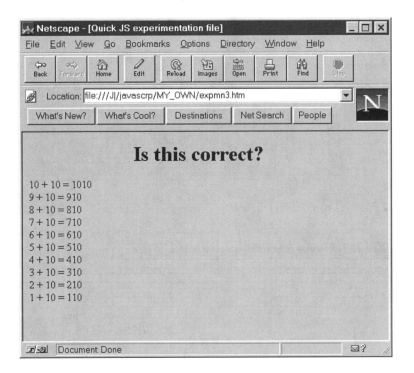

Error Messages

Once the browser recognizes an error (syntax or runtime), it displays a large dialog box, as shown in Figure 22.2. The information contained in this dialog box helps identify the approximate source and location of errors. The dialog box contains the following information:

- The URL or filename where the error occurred.

- The line number in the file where the error occurred. This is a sequential line count from the beginning of the HTML (or .JS) file—not just the JavaScript code. Don't rely too heavily on this information, because the source of the error might well be at a different place.

- A description of the error. This is valuable information in identifying the type of fix required.

- The actual code that contains the error. This is also not always reliable information, because the source of the error might well occur before this line.

- A pointer indicating where on the line the error occurred. Again, don't rely on this too heavily; try to follow the flow of nearby code.

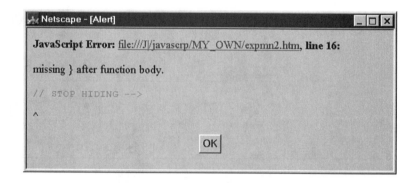

Table 22.1 summarizes the most common JavaScript error messages and their potential causes.

Table 22.1. Common JavaScript error messages.

JavaScript Error Message	Potential Causes
`item` is not defined	Named variable is not defined. Variable is misspelled. Named function is not defined. Unterminated string (regarded as an undefined variable by JavaScript).
`item` is not a function	Function is not defined. Function is misspelled. Other errors exist before function definition.
`item` cannot be converted to a function	Variable is misstated as a called function. Function (or a built-in object's method) is misspelled.
`item` has no properties	Object property is referenced incorrectly. Array is referenced incorrectly.
`item` is not a numeric literal	Variable does not contain numeric data. Other errors exist before variable assignment.
unterminated string literal	Missing quotes (around string). String value has more than 250 characters. String values include a line break.
missing) after argument list (and similar error messages)	Missing opening or closing), }, or ;.

Fixing Your Code

Even though JavaScript's error messages are helpful in identifying many program bugs, you usually need to do more investigative work yourself to fix all the errors—especially logical ones. This section outlines some common things to do to make your investigative work both easier and a little more systematic. Later in this chapter, I will also discuss how Microsoft Script Debugger can help you fix your code.

Check the HTML

Because JavaScript commonly interacts with HTML code, you must first make sure that the file has no HTML errors. Use the following list as a guideline:

- Check for starting and ending <SCRIPT> tags.
- Check for the attribute LANGUAGE = "JavaScript" inside the <SCRIPT> tag.
- Check for missing or misspelled HTML tags.
- Check for angle brackets (<>) to open and close a tag.
- Check for matching pairs of tags (for example, <SCRIPT>...</SCRIPT>).
- Check for correct use of the HTML comment tags (<!--.....-->) to hide your JavaScript.
- Make sure the form and frame names called in your JavaScript code match the names defined in the HTML files.

> **CAUTION**
>
> Don't start JavaScript code inside a table cell. This known bug in JavaScript usually causes browsers to lock up. Instead, open a <SCRIPT> tag in the desired table row (<TR>) and create the cell through JavaScript.

Use Comments to Identify Problems

You can use comments to systematically block out various lines (and functionality) in your code to identify and fix source of errors. This is an iterative process. The following list outlines the steps involved:

1. Comment out one or more lines from your code.
2. Save the code.

3. Reload the page in the browser.
4. Note the result.
5. Modify the code or comment out more lines.
6. Repeat until you've fixed the error.

Use the `alert()` Method to Trace Your Code's Progress

To identify some runtime errors and many logical errors in your code, you must be able to follow the flow of the code and imagine how it processes its data. Many debugging tools let you step into your code, execute it one line at a time, and in a side window (called the debugging window) see the impact of the executed code. You can use JavaScript's `alert()` method to simulate a similar debugging environment. `alert()` displays a dialog box that you can easily program to show various useful messages and values that help trace your code's progress. I suggest the following techniques for using `alert()`:

- Use something such as `alert("Starting Check")` to identify the starting point for debugging. As you progress further and fix errors, you can move this down in the code.

- Use `alert()` to display values of variables, arrays, and function returns. By running some simple test scenarios, you can quickly determine whether the values displayed are what you expect.

- Use `alert()` to display the results of expressions. This is particularly helpful for tracking logical errors, because many of them arise through using expressions incorrectly.

Testing Your Code

Traditionally, testing code means that you are preparing your application for production. This concept is equally true when it comes to publishing JavaScript-enhanced Web pages on the Internet—except that your "production" is now a worldwide stage with many potential users on a variety of platforms. With that as a premise, you can use many commonly practiced, traditional testing techniques to help you test your JavaScript code. You need to make some modifications to cater to the special world of JavaScript and the Internet, but not many. JavaScript is a programming language capable of producing sophisticated applications that, like applications in other, more traditional programming languages, demand solid testing.

> **NOTE**
>
> Testing is different from debugging. Testing is a means of finding errors. Debugging is a means of determining the source of errors and correcting them.

You should test your code assuming that you will find errors. If you believe there are no errors at all, you will probably test so that you don't find any! In practice, even the most thorough tests can never prove the absence of errors (you would have to run an infinite number of test cases to do that); you can only prove their existence.

To help test your code, you should write a formal test plan—one that contains both a checklist (a one-page list of all high-level testing activities) and detailed test-case scenarios to test the code with. Test-case scenarios should list specific and systematic test steps that you can perform on the application, along with expected results. Consider the following items when devising test scenarios:

- Application requirements: Tests to make sure the application satisfies the original functional requirements. Tests should include getting user (or customer) feedback on how closely the application functions to their original requirements. Users' knowledge of the underlying model for the application should lead to identification and correction of many logical errors caused by the implementation of incorrect business rules.

- Design requirements: Tests to make sure the application conforms to its proposed design. These tests should include getting feedback from the application designers on how closely the application follows their design. These tests can also identify potential flaws in the design.

- Data flow patterns: Tests to check the validity of data flow in the system, especially with respect to the design. These tests should validate the integrity of the data that is processed by your application. You need to sketch the data flow in application from input, through processing, to output, and trace how data is affected at each phase.

- Functions: You should test each function in the application for correct functionality. These tests should validate the functionality of individual functions, irrespective of the rest of the code. The success of these tests often depends on how modular (single-focused in purpose, with zero dependencies) the functions are. (Modular programming is explained in more detail later in this chapter in the section "Writing Modular Code.")

- Lines of code: You should test each line of code in the application for correct functionality. This can be done by stepping through each line of code and checking the results (for example, by using comments to isolate code).

- Bad data: Tests to see how the application performs when it receives bad data (for example, too little data, too much data, the wrong type of data, and the wrong size of data). These tests should also test for application behavior when required or optional data is missing (for instance, blank data entry fields on a form). Tests should confirm the existence of error-handling techniques to deal with these situations.

- Boundary analysis: Tests to see how the application performs at boundaries of data types, loops, and iterative function calls. These tests should ensure that the application can correctly cope with minimum and maximum values of variable ranges, and that error handling is built for the values that the application can't handle.

■ Common values: Tests to see how the application performs when given information commonly entered by the user. These tests should ensure that the application works flawlessly for common data because its failure to do so will affect the majority of users.

■ Common errors: Tests of common or previously occurring errors to ensure they have been corrected. Tests must be run to ensure that bugs that were corrected earlier (through further development) don't reappear in a later version of the code. The most common potential cause of these types of errors is poor change management (or version control), which may require follow-up tests of those procedures to identify and correct the root cause.

■ Different platforms: Tests of the application on various hardware and software platforms. The Internet consists of many users working on many different hardware platforms (such as Intel, Macintosh, and Sun) and software platforms (such as Windows 3.1, Windows 95, and different flavors of UNIX). Your code should be tested on as many different platforms as possible so you can understand its behavior, and, if necessary, modify it.

■ Minimum configurations: Tests of the application on minimum configuration client desktops. Again, users will have different resources to access the Internet. You should test to see how much demand your application puts on a client machine (for example, in terms of memory, bandwidth, processing power). This should help you understand what is the minimum configuration of each hardware and software platform on which your application will run successfully. The test should be developed to check how the code will perform under the recommended minimum configurations, and how error handling for users with less than minimum configuration is handled.

■ Different browsers: Tests of the application on different JavaScript-compatible browsers. These tests should help you identify how each browser handles your code and whether the code performs consistently. If the code doesn't perform consistently, you may need to modify your code or write some error-handling code.

NOTE

Currently, all recent Microsoft Internet Explorer (version 3.0 and higher) and Netscape Navigator (version 2.0 and higher) browsers support some level of JavaScript. However, the most recent releases of these browsers (Microsoft Internet Explorer 4.0 and Netscape Navigator 4.0) facilitate much more JavaScript functionality (such as manipulating layers) than the earlier releases. See Chapter 23 for more details on JavaScript compatibility issues across different browsers.

■ HTML compatibility with old browsers: Tests of the application to ensure that the HTML file can be read by older (non-JavaScript–compatible) browsers. You should test your code with text-only or older browsers to see how the lack of JavaScript compatibility affects the user's environment—for instance, if the browser locks up or crashes, or if the page simply fails to load. Test for whether an alternative way of reading your content is available, and how effective and reliable it is.

TIP

In many cases, because of the functionality desired, it makes sense to consciously design and implement a site around a specific base (or minimum) browser level. For instance, you may decide that the user must at least have Navigator 3.0 or Internet Explorer 3.0 in order to effectively use your application. In such a case, you must inform the users about these requirements before they enter the site and include hyperlinks to where they can download the appropriate browsers. Alternatively, you can write some JavaScript to detect the user's browser type, and, if it doesn't conform to the minimum standards, display a warning message or have the user automatically hyperlinked to an appropriate browser download site. See Chapter 23 for more details and an example of this JavaScript code.

■ Reloading: Tests of the application behavior when the HTML page is reloaded. These tests make sure that your code doesn't crash or behave oddly if the page is reloaded. If reloading affects the code, tests should confirm the existence of error-handling code and instructions to help the user avoid the problem.

■ Resizing: Tests of the application behavior when the browser window is resized. These tests confirm that your code doesn't crash or behave oddly if the page is resized. If there is an impact, your tests should confirm the existence of error-handling code and instructions to help the user avoid the problem.

■ Stress testing: Tests of the application behavior when many people use it at the same time. These tests can be done by either having several users, following a specific and detailed script, running your code, or setting up some type of automatic site launcher. You should monitor, record, and analyze the results of all tests (including response times and behavior glitches). You should also make note of how your code affects the rest of your site. If necessary, modify your code, and re-test the affected code.

■ Lost connections: Tests the application behavior when the Internet connection is lost or the page is stopped. Users commonly lose connection to a site or manually force a halt in data transmission. Your code must be able to cope with this fact and exit gracefully (without locking up or crashing the browser) when needed. You should test for this functionality.

TIP

Netscape Navigator has a built-in URL that you can use to quickly test lines of JavaScript code. In Navigator's location box, enter `javascript:` *JavaScript code*. (`mocha:` *JavaScript code* performs the same test.)

For example, entering `javascript: alert("Hello World!")` displays the string `Hello World` in an `alert()` dialog box.

Solid Programming Techniques

Like any other programmers, JavaScript authors can benefit greatly from learning and using solid programming techniques to code their applications. Even though JavaScript is still too immature to have a wealth of its own material on solid coding practices, you can adopt a good set of general guidelines from proven techniques used in other (particularly object-oriented) programming languages. The following list shows some of these techniques adopted for JavaScript:

- Building code from a high-level and detailed design
- Writing modular code
- Writing strongly cohesive code
- Writing loosely coupled code
- Writing reusable code
- Writing error-handling code
- Using strong naming conventions
- Using comments
- Declaring and initializing variables

Each of the techniques listed here is briefly explained in the following sections. Be warned, however: Consistently performing such techniques involves a stiff learning curve, not only because of the level of discipline required, but also because you might need to forget some previous bad habits and learn some new good ones!

Building Code from a High-Level and Detailed Design

Building code from a high-level and detailed design is the first step in constructing good code. A high-level design should help you identify the types of functionality required across different functions in the application. A detailed design should help you identify and name individual functions and sketch out their processes.

Good detailed design (especially if written in pseudo-code) can be transformed into code and comments without too much difficulty. You should at least be able to write function and variable declarations straight from the design. Following that, you should be able to iteratively break down the rest of the detailed design and convert each section into code.

Writing Modular Code

Writing modular code means dividing your application into several individual functions (or modules), where each function performs only one task and communicates with the other functions through function calls. You gain several benefits from such modular coding:

■ Reduced complexity: Each module focuses on only one task, so most modules remain simple.

■ Reduced duplication: If one type of functionality occurs in several different places, the code to make that happen needs to be written only once (in a function).

■ Reduced impact of change: You can change a commonly used functionality in only one place (the function where it resides) instead of several places.

■ Increased process hiding: Implementation details of functions are hidden from other functions. This means that you can change the way a function works without changing the rest of your code (by maintaining the same interface to the function).

■ Increased code reusability: You can reuse individual functions in other programs requiring the same type of functionality.

■ Improved readability: Modular programming leads to simpler and more focused components in a program, which in turn makes the program more readable and easier to maintain.

Writing Strongly Cohesive Code

Cohesion relates to how closely activities in a function are related. A strongly cohesive code means that the function is almost entirely dedicated to just one purpose. The goal is to do only one thing and do it well. An example of a perfectly cohesive function is JavaScript's `Math.sqrt(value)` function. This function simply performs the square root of the value it receives as an argument and returns the result.

Strong cohesion leads to high reliability because the scope of each function is very narrowly defined and the number of tasks it performs is extremely limited.

Writing Loosely Coupled Code

Coupling relates to how closely two functions are related. Loosely coupled code means that the relations between two functions are small, visible, and direct. This provides flexibility for either function to call the other but not depend on the other for much of its own functionality.

Writing Reusable Code

Modular style programming, along with strong cohesion and loose coupling, provides the ideal recipe for creating reusable code. You can essentially plug this code (or function) into any other code to provide a known functionality. Writing reusable code has many benefits:

- High reliability: Reusable functions are proven and tested many times.
- Low cost: There's no need to write a new function.
- Portability: You can make code available to other platforms more easily.
- Information hiding: The code's internal operations are hidden from calling objects.

Writing Error-Handling Code

A good program must be able not only to anticipate uncommon and erroneous events (for example, bad input data, unusual user behavior, and interruption of transfer) but also to deal with them all gracefully. This is where writing good error-handling code becomes a vital issue. Error handling should be built into your code to perform at least some of the following tasks:

- Check the values of all data input from external sources: You should check for the validity of the data, including data types, value ranges, and completeness. If an error occurs, the program should discard the current data and request a new submission.
- Check the value of all function parameters: You should check the validity of data coming from other functions. In case of error, the receiving function should discard the erroneous data and send a new request to the sending function.
- Perform exception handling: Exceptions should be noted by the program and logged in an exceptions log. If no solution exists, the function should exit gracefully.
- Check for other important errors: If possible, the error-handling code should prevent the errors from occurring.
- Perform graceful exits: For instance, if your code crashes or the user stops the file transmission before the page is completely loaded, the browser should remain intact (that is, not lock up or crash). This can be performed by writing an error-handling routine to check if the page is successfully loaded, or by opening a new browser window for your application, so that if it crashes it brings down only its own window.

Using Strong Naming Conventions

Using strong naming conventions refers to using appropriate, consistent, and meaningful names for all the declarations (for example, objects, properties, methods, and variables) in your code. Strong naming conventions help to reduce your code maintenance, improve readability, increase understanding, and eliminate confusing name proliferation (calling the same thing by two different names).

You can use many variations to develop a strong naming convention in your code. Here is a suggested list of things to distinctly identify in your code:

- Global variables
- Local variables
- Named constants
- Function names
- Function arguments

TIP

Use formatted compound words to enhance the meaning and readability of your names. For example, use `MaximumWeight = 200` for a variable or `findHeightInMeters(Height) {` ... for a function.

Using Comments

Comments can be a very effective form of source code communication from a programmer to the rest of the world, including other programmers who might later maintain the code. As much as good comments help dramatically increase a program's readability, bad comments can be wasteful and misleading. A certain amount of care and attention is required to write useful comments. Here are some guidelines for writing good comments:

- Include important and general program information with the source code (for example, author, date of last update, purpose of the function, and last changes). It might be the only source of documentation that is readily available or up-to-date.
- Write comments about the code that the source code itself can't (easily) explain. Comments should add value so the user can understand more than what is already apparent.
- Write comments at the level of intent of the code to explain why something is done. This means writing comments in an appropriate location (for example, right before or after a line of code) to explain the purpose of code, and not just how the code does its processing.
- Comment on global variables. What do they contain? Where do they get updated?
- Comment on unusual or hard-to-follow pieces of code. What do they do? Why are they used?

Declaring and Initializing Variables

Even though JavaScript lets you use undeclared and uninitialized variables in your code, it is good programming practice to consistently declare and initialize your variables. Declaring variables in one common place (usually at the beginning of a function or global area) makes tracking and maintaining them relatively easy. Initializing variables assures that the variables contain the correct data type throughout the remainder of the program. (For example, if `var Counter = 0;`, the variable `Counter` is set to a numeric data type.)

> **CAUTION**
>
> Don't use JavaScript's reserved keywords as variable names—this results in errors. Check JavaScript's reference guide for a list of reserved keywords.

Bulletproofing Your Code

JavaScript, like other programming languages, has a few nuances—including language bugs, obscure features, and strange behavior—that you need to recognize to write really solid code. You also need to be aware of the differences between JavaScript 1.1, as implemented in Netscape version 3.0 and higher, and JScript (the Microsoft implementation of JavaScript), as implemented in Internet Explorer version 3.0 and higher.

This section identifies some of these oddities and differences and describes proposed workarounds. Because JavaScript (and consequently JScript) is still an evolving language, the suggested list of oddities and differences isn't comprehensive. Also, the proposed workarounds may not be necessary, depending on what level of browser you choose for your base (or minimum) site requirement. You should follow Netscape's and Microsoft's frequent updates and bug fixes and online JavaScript discussion groups (such as Usenet's `comp.lang.javascript` newsgroup) for the latest information.

To bulletproof your code, pay attention to the following:

JavaScript Oddities, Known Bugs, and Helpful Tricks

■ Make sure the variable a window object is assigned to is not null before it is used. A null value means that that window object doesn't exist.

■ If the `Onload` event handler loads prematurely when you're loading forms on multiple frames, use `window.setTimeout()` to test for the existence of form elements first. If they exist, run the original script intended to run on `Onload`.

■ The on event handlers (onLoad, onClick, onFocus, and so on) sometimes cause memory leaks, which brings the system to a crawl over multiple reloads of the page. In other words, the on event handlers sometimes take browser memory but don't release it. This is a JavaScript bug (it most commonly occurs on the Windows 3.1 platform) that Netscape is aware of and is working to fix. In the meantime, to reduce the chance of this occurring, try to avoid using on event handlers if you can. When you do use them, make sure to advise users to close unnecessary open applications if they run into memory problems.

■ Divide long strings into multiple, concatenated shorter strings. JavaScript has a limit of 250 characters for strings. Shorter, concatenated strings also make your code more readable and its maintenance easier.

■ To make sure a variable contains string data type, preappend a null string ("") to the assignment expression. For example, calculatedTotal = " + TotalPrice is treated as a string.

■ Netscape currently has a bug in dealing with JavaScript's document.close() method. The browser crashes if you call this method while the browser is still loading a page. To correct this problem, use window.setTimeout() to check if the whole document is completely loaded, before executing document.close().

■ Another known bug occurs when the FileUpload object isn't properly updated to show file selection. The value of the object remains null ("") even after the user selects a file by clicking the Browse button. The filename does appears in the upload box; however, the value of the object isn't set until the user types it into the box. A workaround for Windows 95—as proposed by Netscape—is as follows:

```html
<html>
<body>
<script language="JavaScript">
function showFile(file){
file.focus();
file.blur();
alert(file.value);
}
</script>
<form>
<input type=file name=myfile>
<input type=button value=Show onClick="showFile(this.form.myfile)">
</form>
</body>
</html>
```

■ Avoid using the history.go(n) method when using frames. This is a known bug in JavaScript. Instead, use history.forward() and history.back() to go forward or backward through the browser history file.

■ If reloading the HTML page doesn't seem to show your JavaScript code changes, try reopening the file. This clears the browser's memory and loads the latest version of your code. If this doesn't seem to cure the problem (particularly when using frames), exit from the browser and restart.

- To load multiple functions from one on event, `onLoad`, you can use either of two techniques:

```
onLoad = "function one(); function two(); function three();"
onLoad = "function multipleFunction();"
```

  `function multipleFunction()` represents a function that calls several other functions.

- If you use the `document.write` method to generate HTML pages (or page elements), make certain to include the `HEIGHT` and `WIDTH` attributes on all generated `IMG` and `EMBED` tags. Otherwise, the browser crashes as the HTML layout is delayed by the unsized images, or plug-ins. This is a known JavaScript bug, and Netscape is currently working on fixing it.

- Don't use JavaScript's `Math.random()` method for generating random numbers. This method currently doesn't work consistently across different platforms. To generate random numbers, you should either make up your own routine (such as `RandomOneToTen=today.getSeconds() %10;`) or use some of the randomizer functions freely available on the Internet. For instance, try the Central Randomizer at `http://www.msc.cornell.edu/~houle/mcwtkym/randomizer.html`. This good JavaScript randomizer seems to work on all versions and platforms of Netscape Navigator.

> **TIP**
>
> To view a list of the most currently known JavaScript bugs, and potential workarounds, go to Netscape's JavaScript Known bugs page at `http://developer.netscape.com/support/bugs/known/index.html`

Differences Between JavaScript and JScript

JavaScript as implemented by Netscape (currently known as JavaScript 1.1) and JavaScript as implemented by Microsoft for its Internet Explorer browser (known as JScript) are fundamentally identical. They both support the same conditional control statements, provide for event-based programming to respond to user interaction, have defined top-level objects (such as window or document), and respond to defined functions in a similar manner. However, despite these overall similarities, there are some subtle differences between the two languages that you need to be aware of to write solid code that will work on both Microsoft and Netscape browsers. The following tips represent some of the currently known differences, as well as proposed workarounds (when available) to help you write truly bulletproof code:

- Beware of objects that are defined for Navigator but not for Internet Explorer. These objects will result in an error when the site is viewed through Internet Explorer:

  The Image object: In Netscape, this object is an array of images that contains the images in the current document. The Image object lets the developer change the images in the document using JavaScript.

The Area object: In Netscape, this object is an array of links for an image map that allows the developer to provide additional information to the user through event programming (such as `mouseOver`).

The FileUpload object: In Netscape, this object provides a simple control, including a browse button, to let the user upload a file to a designated site.

The Option object: In Netscape, this object is an array of options that can be substituted for a SELECT statement at runtime through JavaScript.

The Function object: In Netscape, this object allows the programmer to define and assign a function to a variable. The variable can be assigned to an event later.

The Applet object: In Netscape, this represents an array of applets.

The Plugin object: In Netscape, this represents an array of plug-ins contained in the page.

CAUTION

Microsoft Internet Explorer also doesn't support the Netscape `plugins` array, which contains currently installed plug-ins, or the `mimeTypes` array, which contains currently supported MIME types.

■ Beware of differences in object ownership between the two browsers. In JScript, all objects are owned by the parent object window. However, in JavaScript, information about the browser currently used is owned/contained by the `navigator` object. Also, some objects are owned by different higher-level objects in each implementation. For instance, the `history` object is owned by the `window` object in Internet Explorer, but by the `document` object in Navigator. To avoid potential problems, don't explicitly declare the `window` object in your object calls, and use parent terminology when calling browser objects within frames.

■ Beware of differences in object properties between the two browsers. Sometimes the same object will have different properties under each implementation. For instance, the `document` object has a property called URL (that is, `document.URL`) in Netscape, which returns the current site location. With Internet Explorer, the same statement returns an empty string, and the site information is contained in the `location` property. In this case, a workaround is to use `document.location`, which will work correctly for both browsers. (You can quickly test this through an alert call like this:
`alert(document.location);`.)

To significantly improve your chances of writing code that works on both browsers, you must be sure to thoroughly test your code on both browsers and avoid JavaScript that seems to work in one but not the other. If you must use code that you know won't work consistently under both environments, I recommend that you use `<SCRIPT Language="JavaScript1.1">` for Netscape-specific scripts and `<SCRIPT Language="JavaScript">` for code that will be performed equally by both browsers. If you also have Internet Explorer-specific code, you may need to rewrite that code as VBScript (Visual Basic Script) and declare it as `<SCRIPT Language="VBScript">`; currently, there is no reliable method for declaring JScript-specific code.

TIP

To read the latest information about JScript and see the differences between it and Netscape's JavaScript implementation, visit the Microsoft JScript Product documentation page at `http://www.microsoft.com/jscript/us/techinfo/jsdocs.htm`.

Using Microsoft Script Debugger

Microsoft Script Debugger (MSSD) is a freely downloadable script debugging tool that works as an integrated part of Internet Explorer (version 3.01 or later). (You can find it on the Microsoft site at `http://www.microsoft.com/`.) You can use MSSD to write, and, most importantly, debug your JavaScript (known as JScript with the Microsoft implementation) or Visual Basic Script (VBScript) code. MSSD is one of the very few Internet script debugging tools currently available, and it is designed to handle the debugging demands of ActiveX, Java, JScript, and VBScript.

An Overview of Microsoft Script Debugger Features

The following are the main features of Microsoft Script Debugger:

- A dynamic view of HTML structure: As you can see from Figure 22.3, MSSD lets you both view the whole structure of your page from the Project Explorer window and view the individual HTML files (for example, in a frameset) within their own windows.

- Multiple language integration: You can seamlessly debug JavaScript, VBScript, and Java within the same document.

- Code coloring: MSSD displays your code with standard debugging color coding to help you better identify the composition of your code and ease debugging.

- Breakpoints: You can set breakpoints anywhere in your script to stop the debugger from executing at that point.

- Stepping into code: MSSD allows you to step (execute and pause) through your code one line at a time.

- Stepping over code: This lets you step into your code, but it executes procedure calls as one unit (rather than stepping into them) and returns to the next statement.

FIGURE 22.3.

Viewing HTML files in Microsoft Script Debugger.

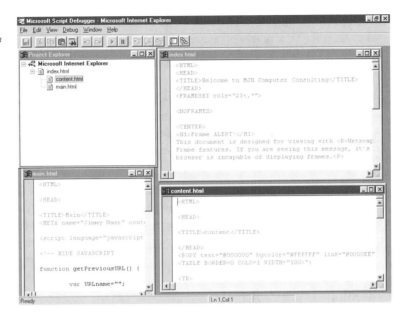

- Stepping out of code: This, as opposed to stepping over, allows you to execute the remaining lines (from the point of execution) of a called procedure, and then it returns you to the next statement after the procedure call.

- Integrated Call Stack: MSSD seamlessly integrates the Call Stack from both VBScript and JScript in your code into a single Call Stack.

- Immediate Expression Window: This allows you to immediately evaluate an expression within the Call Stack or test new code. The results from executing the line of code are displayed in the Immediate Window.

Using Microsoft Script Debugger to Debug a File

We will now walk through the steps of a sample debugging session using MSSD. During this exercise, we will be more concerned about the features of MSSD and their application than the content or functionality of the sample files. The remainder of this section assumes that you are using Microsoft Internet Explorer (version 3.01 or later) as your current browser and that you have already successfully downloaded and installed MSSD.

Starting Microsoft Script Debugger

The only way to start MSSD is to first open Internet Explorer and load the desired HTML source file. Then you can activate MSSD by choosing View | Source. (If MSSD isn't installed, viewing the source will open the source file in the Notepad editor.)

To start the debugging process, choose Edit | Break at Next Statement from Internet Explorer, or choose Debug | Break at Next Statement from MSSD, and execute the script. This starts the debugger and stops it at the first statement in the current script.

Using the Break at Next Statement Command

The Break at Next Statement command (which appears on the Edit menu of Internet Explorer and the Debug menu of MSSD) is similar to a step command, in which the debugger executes the next statement in the script and then breaks, except that you can also use it when you aren't currently running the script.

This is an important debugging feature of MSSD, because commonly a lot of JavaScript code is declared in the header (or <HEAD>) section of an HTML file, and this command is the only way to debug that code. This is because the code in the header of the file has already been executed by the time the HTML file is loaded (remember that JavaScript is interpreted). Also, any breakpoints set after the HTML file has been loaded are lost if you reload the page.

Evaluating Expressions

An expression can be evaluated with the aid of MSSD's Immediate Window and the use of the following two methods:

- `Debug.write(string)`: This method writes a specified string—commonly, the value of a variable—to the Immediate Window, with no intervening spaces or characters between each string.

- `Debug.writeln([string])`: This method is identical to the preceding method, except that a newline character is inserted after each string. Also, the string argument is optional. If it's omitted, only a newline character is written to the Immediate Window.

Figure 22.4 shows an example of using the Immediate Window to evaluate expressions (or values of variables).

Walking Through a Complete Example

To better understand the capabilities of MSSD, you should practice using it to debug your code. The following exercise should provide you with a good starting point:

1. Open Internet Explorer.
2. Select Edit | Break at Next Statement.

FIGURE 22.4.

Using the Immediate Window to evaluate expressions.

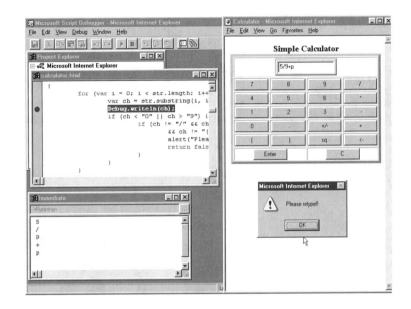

3. Open a file called `sound_test.html`. You can type its URL, drag and drop the file into the browser window, or select File | Open. The content of this file is as follows (note that you should replace the names of the .WAV files mentioned with names and paths of sound files that you have available on your system):

```
<html>
<head>
<title>Sound on JS events</title>
<script language="javascript">
<!-- Hide from old browsers

function playSound(sfile) {
// load a sound and play it
    window.location.href=sfile;
}
// Stop hiding -->
</script>
<body onLoad="playSound('Type.wav');"
onUnLoad="playSound('Glass.wav');">
<font size=+2>Sounds on JS Events</font>
<br>
<hr>
The following are example of JS event handlers used
to play sounds.
<hr>
<a href="#" onClick="playSound('Cashreg.wav');">
Click here for sound</a>
<br><br>
<form name="form1">
<input type="button" value="Press Button to play a sound"
onClick="playSound('Gunshot.wav');">
</form>
</body>
</html>
```

4. As the file is opened, MSSD is simultaneously activated, and a break occurs after the first statement is executed, as shown in Figure 22.5.

FIGURE 22.5.

MSSD breaks after reading the first statement.

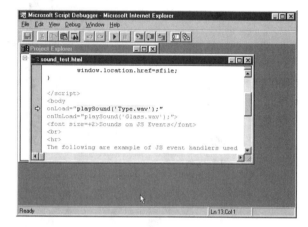

5. You can now proceed to step through your code to see the next sequence of program flow activities. Use the Step Into, Step Over, and Step Out toolbar icons to step through your code as desired. Figure 22.6 shows the next line of code that is executed after you click the Step Into button.

FIGURE 22.6.

Stepping into code using the MSSD toolbar icon.

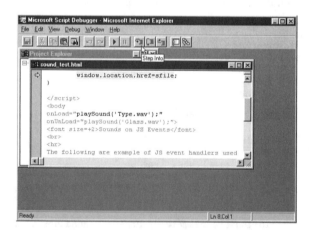

TIP

You can view the names of the icons on the MSSD toolbar by holding the mouse pointer—but not clicking—over any icon for a second or so. You can also read more detailed descriptions of all the icons and features of MSSD on the online help menu.

6. Once you have stepped through (or used the Continue icon) to where the onLoad event call has been completed, you should hear a sound file played by your system (if your PC has audio capabilities). You may need to explicitly permit the browser to open the sound file, depending on how you have your Internet Explorer browser configured. This is a security measure to safeguard you from opening unknown and potentially dangerous (virus-containing) non-HTML files. Figure 22.7 shows the file after it is completely loaded into the browser.

FIGURE 22.7.

The contents of sound_test.html *after loading is completed.*

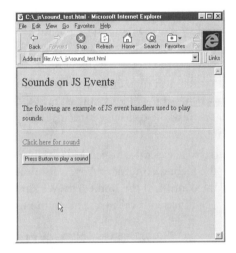

7. Select Edit | Break at Next Statement to stop code execution after the next statement. Click Press Button to play a sound on the HTML page. The debugger will stop at the onClick event handler. You can now track the executing procedure calls by opening the Call Stack window, as shown in Figure 22.8, and stepping through your code.

FIGURE 22.8.

Using the Call Stack window to see active procedure calls.

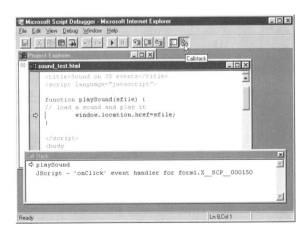

8. You can also view the value of expressions or an appropriate line of code (that is, not blank lines or comment lines, and so on) in your script using the Immediate Window:

   From MSSD, click inside the `playSound` function in your code (this is the first function declared in the header).

   If you attempt to type anything inside the function, MSSD brings up a panel asking whether you want to edit the document. Click Yes, and type `Debug.writeln(sfile);` just before the curly bracket (}) to close the function.

   Save the edited file by selecting File | Save (or by clicking the Save toolbar icon).

   You also set a manual breakpoint at the Debug line. Press F9 to set (or toggle) the breakpoint. (The breakpoint line will be highlighted in red and will have a red dot next to it in the left margin.)

   Now switch over to your browser and refresh (reload) your HTML file. (Remember that you will lose your set breakpoints after refreshing the file, so if you want to break the code at a particular line, press F9 to set the breakpoint in MSSD.)

9. As the file starts its execution, open MSSD's Immediate Window to view the current content of the Debug expression. As you continue to step through your code, you should see the content of the Immediate Window become updated every time the `Debug.writeln` function is called, as shown in Figure 22.9.

FIGURE 22.9.

Using the
`Debug.writeln` *method*
and evaluating an
expression in the
Immediate Window.

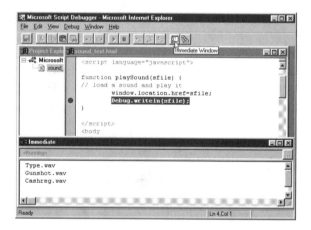

A Final Word on Microsoft Script Debugger

Microsoft Script Debugger provides a very helpful environment in which to kick-start your JavaScript debugging and testing. The tools provided in MSSD are much like tools usually found in full-blown programming language environments such as Visual Basic and C++. Also, MSSD's interface, setup, and installation are all very user-friendly and intuitive.

However, MSSD has some limitations. Among the most disturbing are the fact that it doesn't fully support JavaScript 1.1 (Netscape's implementation), that you need to frequently switch between Internet Explorer and MSSD to conduct debugging, and that you can't print source code.

To wrap up, MSSD is certainly a good tool to have in your armor, and, because it's free, it's a great value to boot. However, it can't take the place of writing solid code and systematically testing your code.

Summary

This chapter introduced you to the three types of JavaScript error—syntax, runtime, and logic—and described common JavaScript error messages and their possible causes.

You also looked at ways to fix your code and identify errors—including specific things, places, and techniques to look for to help you do so. In addition, I discussed a systematic approach for testing your code, consisting of a test plan and detailed test scenarios, including specific items to consider in creating detailed test scenarios.

I progressed to show you ways of building more preventive control into your code (so that you can spend less time debugging) by discussing proven techniques for writing solid and maintainable code. These techniques will save you many hours of work in the long run and will help you write better code.

To wrap up, I briefly covered some of the current nuances (bugs) of JavaScript and how you can avoid them to bulletproof your code. Finally, I also discussed in detail how you can use Microsoft Script Debugger to help you debug your JavaScript code.

VI

PART

IN THIS PART

Advanced JavaScript

JavaScript
Compatibility Issues

IN THIS CHAPTER

CHAPTER

23

To help introduce this chapter's topic, I want to you meet Joe. Joe is a Web developer who wants to enliven his Web site by using JavaScript for special effects, easier site navigation, animation buttons, and data validation. After spending considerable energy getting everything to work properly, he remembered that he should at least confirm that everything he developed under the current Netscape Navigator works with Microsoft Internet Explorer, as well as older versions of the Netscape browser. That's when everything broke down. His special effects relied on image objects, which aren't universally supported, and his code used a lot of array objects, which fizzle under Navigator 2.0. The end result was that his site was usable only by those who have the same version of the browser he did (see Figure 23.1).

FIGURE 23.1.

The "unknown object" error is a frequent encounter on the Web.

Although Joe is fictional, this same sad story is often repeated by developers. If you have written much JavaScript code at all, you have undoubtedly encountered similar woes.

Fortunately, Netscape and Microsoft have recognized that a JavaScript "Tower of Babel" serves no one and have submitted the language to a standardization committee called the ECMA. Therefore, in the future, we can probably expect to see fewer compatibility issues than the number we now face. However, this change isn't likely to happen overnight.

In this chapter, we will look at the issues surrounding developing JavaScript scripts within this heterogeneous environment. Specifically, we will cover the following topics:

- Comparing JavaScript dialects
- Common problem areas
- Techniques for developing "safe" scripts

Comparing JavaScript Dialects

Although we are moving toward a kinder, gentler JavaScript, this evolution is gradual and won't help us out much in 1997. Therefore, we need to look at what the various dialects of JavaScript are and which browsers provide support for the dialect.

■ JavaScript 1.2 is the latest Netscape implementation of the Web scripting language and is supported in Netscape Navigator 4.0 (Communicator 1.0). Tables 23.1 through 23.4 list the major enhancements added in JavaScript 1.2 that previous versions don't support. Internet Explorer 3.0 and above doesn't support features specific to JavaScript 1.2.

■ JavaScript 1.1 is supported in Netscape Navigator 3.0 and partially in Internet Explorer 3.0 and above. Tables 23.5 through 23.13 list the major language changes with previous JavaScript versions.

■ The base language specification, JavaScript 1.0, was first supported in Netscape Navigator 2.0. All other dialects are based on this original implementation, which was actually quite buggy.

■ JScript 1.0 and 2.0 is supported in Microsoft Internet Explorer 3.0 and higher. JScript 1.0 is roughly comparable with JavaScript 1.0, although some variations apply.

Table 23.1. Objects supported only in JavaScript 1.2 or higher.

Event

Table 23.2. Methods supported only in JavaScript 1.2 or higher.

`clearInterval`
`moveBy` (Window)
`moveTo` (Window)
`resizeBy` (Window)
`resizeTo` (Window)
`scrollBy` (Window)
`scrollTo` (Window)
`setInterval`
`setTimeout`

Table 23.3. Statements supported only in JavaScript 1.2 or higher.

`do while`
`labeled`
`switch`

Table 23.4. Other capabilities supported only in JavaScript 1.2 or higher.

Added capability to manipulate layers.

Added capability to programmatically control style sheets.

Added additional parameters to the window open() method to allow for additional customization of the opening window.

If the <SCRIPT> tag's LANGUAGE parameter is JavaScript1.2, the equality operators (== and !=) compare only like-typed operands.

Table 23.5. Objects supported only in JavaScript 1.1 or higher.

Applet

Area

Array

Boolean

FileUpload

Function

Image

MimeType

Number

Option

Plugin

Table 23.6. Properties supported only in JavaScript 1.1 or higher.

border (Image)

closed (Window)

complete (Image)

constructor (Any instantiated object)

current (History)

description (MimeType, Plugin)

domain (Document)

enabledPlugin (MimeType)

filename (Plugin)

height (Image)

hspace (Image)

`lowsrc` (Image)

`MAX_VALUE` (Number)

`MIN_VALUE` (Number)

`NaN` (Number)

`NEGATIVE_INFINITY` (Number)

`next` (History)

`opener` (Window)

`POSITIVE_INFINITY` (Number)

`previous` (History)

`prototype` (Any instantiated object)

`src` (Image)

`suffixes` (MimeType)

`type` (MimeType)

`vspace` (Image)

`width` (Image)

23

JAVASCRIPT COMPATIBILITY ISSUES

Table 23.7. Arrays supported only in JavaScript 1.1 or higher.

Applets

Embeds

History

Images

MimeTypes

Plugins

Table 23.8. Methods supported only in JavaScript 1.1 or higher.

`javaEnabled` (Navigator)

`join` (Array)

`refresh` (Plugins)

`reload` (Location)

`replace` (Location)

`reset` (Reset)

`reverse` (Array)

continues

Table 23.8. continued

scroll (Window)

sort (Array)

split (String)

taintEnabled (Navigator)

valueOf (All objects)

Table 23.9. Event handlers supported only in JavaScript 1.1 or higher.

onAbort (Window, Image)

onError (Window, Image)

onMouseOut (Area, Link)

onReset (Form)

Table 23.10. Built-in functions supported only in JavaScript 1.1 or higher.

taint

untaint

Table 23.11. Operators supported in only JavaScript 1.1 or higher.

typeof

void

Table 23.12. HTML tag enhancements supported only in JavaScript 1.1 or higher.

SRC attribute for <SCRIPT> added.

LANGUAGE attribute for <SCRIPT> can specify language version.

<NOSCRIPT> tag added.

JavaScript entities (such as &{myVar};) supported.

Table 23.13. Other capabilities supported only in JavaScript 1.1 or higher.

Added LiveConnect, or the capability for Java and JavaScript to communicate.

Added capability to detect available plug-ins.

Added object prototypes, or the capability to create properties to be shared by all objects of the same type.

Added capability for Select objects to be modified dynamically.

Added capability to pass strings among scripts in separate windows or frames.

Changed the way in which you can index object properties. If you define a property by name, you must always reference it by name. Similarly, if you define a property by an index value, you must always reference it by that index.

Changed `eval()` from a built-in function to become a method of every object.

When `write()` and `writeln()` are used, users can now print and save the dynamic HTML by using the File menu commands.

Improved behavior of three built-in functions: `isNaN`, `parseFloat`, and `parseInt`, each of which now perform similarly across platforms.

Added the capability to delete an object by setting its reference equal to null.

Added the capability to reset event handlers dynamically.

Added support of data tainting.

Added the capability to index arrays using strings.

Common Problem Areas

Fortunately, all dialects of JavaScript are derivatives of the original JavaScript implementation found in Netscape Navigator 2.0. Even JScript, which Microsoft developed by reverse-engineering JavaScript 1.0, uses essentially the same object model and language constructs. Of course, there are some important differences, but at least there is a common subset to which we can turn. By reading the language summaries shown earlier in this chapter, you can determine the specifics of what will work in any given browser, but there are some common problem areas to think about.

Images

Since their introduction in JavaScript 1.1, Image objects have proven very popular for creating animations, banners, and so on. (See Chapter 16, "Creating Special Effects with JavaScript," for some good examples of how Image objects can be used.) Unfortunately, Image objects are supported only in Netscape Navigator 3.0 and above, not in Netscape Navigator 2.x or Microsoft Internet Explorer 3.0. Most users visiting your site will typically be running Netscape Navigator 3.0 or higher, but until Microsoft JScript provides support, use Image objects with care. Feel free to use them, but be sure to do so safely, as I'll discuss later in this chapter.

Arrays

Arrays are supported by all of the current JavaScript (1.1 and higher) and JScript (1.0 and higher) versions, but they aren't explicitly supported in JavaScript 1.0. Given the fact that the vast majority of users will probably be working with something later than Netscape Navigator 2.0, you should feel fairly comfortable employing the Array object in most situations. However, if your target users are still using Netscape Navigator 2.x, you should consider using the array workaround discussed in Chapter 14, "Built-In Language Objects."

Windows

Although all dialects support the opening of a window from another window, JavaScript 1.1 provides additional support, such as adding `blur()` and `focus()` methods, easier string passing between windows, and allowing an opened window to communicate with the window that opened it. Use care if you rely on these techniques.

External .JS Library Files

JavaScript 1.1 and higher added the `SRC` parameter to the `<SCRIPT>` tag, which allows you to store JavaScript functions in an external .JS file. However, JScript and JavaScript 1.0 don't provide support for this parameter and thus will be unable to use them.

Programmable Select Objects

JavaScript 1.1 and higher lets you dynamically modify options in a Select object and display changes on the page without refreshing the entire page. However, JScript and JavaScript 1.0 don't support this capability.

Table 23.14 summarizes the problem areas I've discussed, as well as some other areas.

Table 23.14. Common areas of incompatibility.

Support for	Navigator 4.0	Navigator 3.0	Navigator 2.x	MSIE 3.0
Array object	Yes	Yes	No	Yes
Image object	Yes	Yes	No	No
`<SCRIPT> SRC` parameter	Yes	Yes	No	No
LiveConnect (Java communication)	Yes	Yes	No	Yes
Active Scripting (ActiveX communication)	No	No	No	Yes

Support for	Navigator 4.0	Navigator 3.0	Navigator 2.x	MSIE 3.0
Cookies	Yes	Yes	Yes	Yes, but not on local drives
Programmable Select objects	Yes	Yes	No	No
Plug-in detection	Yes	Yes	No	No
Layers	Yes	No	No	No
JavaScript Style Sheets	Yes	No	No	No

Techniques for Developing "Safe" Scripts

Given the varying degrees of compatibility across JavaScript dialects, it's critical that you account for this during script development. After all, a primary objective of using JavaScript is to enhance your Web site. But if you ignore the compatibility issues, users running browsers that don't support your variation of JavaScript will be disappointed. Therefore, as you design Web pages, your goal should be to develop "safe" scripts—scripts that maximize the capabilities of later versions of JavaScript but that account for browsers offering lesser support. There are two techniques you can employ, depending on the context.

The "All or Nothing" Approach

The first technique you can employ is what I call the "all or nothing" approach, which determines whether an entire script is run or ignored completely by the browser. To use this technique, specify the desired language dialect you're using in the <SCRIPT> tag's LANGUAGE parameter. Statements within a <SCRIPT> tag are ignored if the browser doesn't have the same level of JavaScript support specified. Therefore, use Table 23.15 as a guide to what each version of browser will do when it encounters a <SCRIPT> tag.

Table 23.15. Browsers' LANGUAGE attribute support.

LANGUAGE *Parameter*	*Browser Support*			
	Netscape Navigator 4.0	Netscape Navigator 3.0	Netscape Navigator 2.x	MSIE 3.0
LANGUAGE="JavaScript"	Runs	Runs	Runs	Runs
LANGUAGE="JavaScript1.1"	Runs	Runs	Ignores	Ignores
LANGUAGE="JavaScript1.2"	Runs	Ignores	Ignores	Ignores

The advantage of using this technique is that you can be confident that if the browser understands the LANGUAGE parameter, it will provide full support for the JavaScript dialect in use. The disadvantage is that unsupporting browsers will be forced to completely ignore the entire script.

> **NOTE**
>
> If you plan on using some of the new JavaScript 1.2 functionality, such as layers, JavaScript style sheets, or new language constructs such as do while or switch, you will probably want to specify "JavaScript1.2" as the LANGUAGE attribute.

The "In-Place Detection" Approach

An alternative to the "all or nothing" approach is the "in-place detection" method (sometimes also referred to as "in-situ"), a technique that requires determining the appropriate browser version within a script before making a risky, dialect-specific programming call.

Although this technique is slightly more complicated, the advantage of using it is that you can provide alternative functionality based on the level of JavaScript support you encounter. For example, the determineCurrentBrowser() function shown in the following code examines the navigator object's appName and appVersion properties and then assigns a value to a global variable called CURRENT_BROWSER:

```
/* Global variable */
var CURRENT_BROWSER = new String();

/* ------------------------------------------------------------- */
determineCurrentBrowser() {

    var bwr = navigator.appName;
    var ver = parseInt(navigator.appVersion);

    if ( bwr == "Netscape" && ver == 4 ) CURRENT_BROWSER = "Netscape 4.0";
    if ( bwr == "Netscape" && ver == 3 ) CURRENT_BROWSER = "Netscape 3.0";
    if ( bwr == "Netscape" && ver == 2 ) CURRENT_BROWSER = "Netscape 2.0";
    if ( bwr == "Microsoft Internet Explorer" && ver == 2 )
        CURRENT_BROWSER = "MSIE 3.0";

}
```

Alternatively, you could choose to forget about the browsers and focus on the highest level of JavaScript support offered. The advantage of this method is that it is often easier for comparison purposes:

```
/* Global variable */
var JS_VERSION

/* ------------------------------------- */
function JSVersionCheck() {
```

```
         var bwr = navigator.appName;
         var ver = parseInt(navigator.appVersion);

         if ( bwr == "Netscape" && ver == 4 ) JS_VERSION = 1.2;
         if ( bwr == "Netscape" && ver == 3 ) JS_VERSION = 1.1;
         if ( bwr == "Netscape" && ver == 2 ) JS_VERSION = 1.0;
         if ( bwr == "Microsoft Internet Explorer" && ver == 2 ) JS_VERSION = 1.0;


}
```

Let's look at an example to see how this might be used effectively. Chapter 16 showed you an example of how to use image objects to create animated pushbuttons. However, the problem is that if you try to run the JSAnimatedButtons example under Netscape Navigator 2.0 or Microsoft Internet Explorer 3.0, you will get an error when it encounters the image object definitions. Therefore, adding some browser detection code to this script, as shown in Listing 23.1, will allow it to function safely—albeit with less functionality for the lesser browsers.

Listing 23.1. JSAnimatedButtons-Safe.hmtl.

```
<HTML>
<HEAD>
<SCRIPT LANGUAGE= "JavaScript">
<!--
         /* Global variable */
          var JS_VERSION = 0;

         /* ------------------------------------------------------- */
         function JSVersionCheck() {

                 var bwr = navigator.appName;
                 var ver = parseInt(navigator.appVersion);

                 if ( bwr == "Netscape" && ver == 4 ) JS_VERSION = 1.2;
                 if ( bwr == "Netscape" && ver == 3 ) JS_VERSION = 1.1;
                 if ( bwr == "Netscape" && ver == 2 ) JS_VERSION = 1;
                 if ( bwr == "Microsoft Internet Explorer" && ver == 2 )
                     JS_VERSION = 1;

         }

         /* Run function */
         JSVersionCheck()

         /* Define image objects */

         if ( JS_VERSION > 1 ) {

                 var prevBtnOff = new Image( 42, 52 );
                 prevBtnOff.src = "./prev_off.gif";

                 var prevBtnOn =  new Image( 42, 52 );
                 prevBtnOn.src = "./prev_on.gif";
```

continues

Listing 23.1. continued

```
                          var nextBtnOff = new Image( 42, 52 );
                          nextBtnOff.src = "./next_off.gif";

                          var nextBtnOn =  new Image( 42, 52 );
                          nextBtnOn.src = "./next_on.gif";
                      }


          /* Changes image being displayed. */
              function highlightButton(placeholder, imageObject) {

                      if ( JS_VERSION > 1 ) {
                          document.images[placeholder].src = eval( imageObject + ".src" )
                      }
                  }

//-->
</SCRIPT>
</HEAD>
<BODY background="./aiback.gif">
<CENTER>
<A HREF="javascript:history.back()"
    onMouseOver = "highlightButton( 'Prev', 'prevBtnOn' );window.status=
        'Previous';return true;"
    onMouseOut =
        "highlightButton( 'Prev', 'prevBtnOff' );window.status='';return true;" >
    <IMG SRC="./prev_off.gif"
            BORDER  = 0
            WIDTH   = 52
            HEIGHT  = 42
            NAME    = "Prev">
</A>

<A HREF="javascript:history.forward()"
    onMouseOver =
        "highlightButton( 'Next', 'nextBtnOn' );window.status='Next';return true;"
    onMouseOut =
        "highlightButton( 'Next', 'nextBtnOff' );window.status='';return true;" >
    <IMG SRC="./next_off.gif"
            BORDER  = 0
            WIDTH   = 52
            HEIGHT  = 42
            NAME    = "Next">
</A>
</CENTER>
</BODY>
</HTML>
```

Summary

The biggest hindrance to a larger acceptance of JavaScript is the compatibility issues surrounding the various dialects coming from both Netscape and Microsoft. Although the ECMA promises a more standardized scripting language in the future, JavaScript developers will be forced to deal with these compatibility issues for the foreseeable future. In this chapter, we looked at the issues surrounding JavaScript compatibility and identified the common problem areas you should try to avoid. This chapter closed with a look at how you can develop "safe" scripts that can run in any scripting environment.

JavaScript and Web Security

IN THIS CHAPTER

CHAPTER 24

JavaScript gives the Web site developer the ability to extend static HTML pages with a dynamic, event-driven programming language. The JavaScript-enhanced Web page provides interactive client-side functionality by executing JavaScript code fragments inside the client's Web browser. The inclusion of JavaScript code fragments in the document page raises fundamental security concerns about the code integrity of the browser's script interpreter as well as about the script itself. Viewing a JavaScript-enabled page exposes the user to a greater possibility of damage than the rendering of a pure HTML document, due to the fact that the executing code fragments overlay another layer of complexity on top of the browser application.

With traditional desktop software, there is a well-defined covenant between the user and the software. Installing and using the programs requires explicit actions and decisions by the users. JavaScript code doesn't conform to accepted conventions. Script code is loaded from a remote source and executed without user confirmation. Execution of untrusted code from a remote source is analogous to receiving an apple in the mail from an unknown return address and eating it. Verifications and limitations must be placed on the use of JavaScript code in order to safeguard the user's computer from malicious or unintentional attacks on valuable information and applications. No user wants to "pull the wire" between his computer and the outside world, so knowledge of the capability for JavaScript code to attack and damage a client or server machine is necessary.

The Web was designed as an open system for publishing graphical hypertext content over the Internet. Site developers have embraced the opportunity to extend the static HTML document with dynamic, interactive capabilities through the inclusion of scripting languages in Web documents. The scripting languages are either executed on the server machine or downloaded to a client machine and executed as remote code. Security is becoming a fundamental concern, because JavaScript and Java are becoming more prevalent, thereby making them a more attractive target for attack.

Security in a connected computer network can be evaluated in terms of the "level of confidence" in a transmission. The receiving party wants to trust that the original transmission was indeed sent by the expected sender. Also, the message should not have been altered en route. In a heterogeneous computer network such as the Internet, such confidence currently can't be absolute. The Internet was designed as a distributed system whereby network traffic must pass through many different machines to reach its intended destination. The flow of the traffic through multiple host machines exposes the traffic to modification or replacement at many points. Also, the sender's return address is designated by an address, which can be spoofed (mimicked). Although the global reach and electronic structure of unsecured transmissions defy accountability, the use of encryption, digital signatures, and source code verification are attempts to raise the barrier against attack.

The user must trust that the application code will behave in a proper manner and not damage the user's system. In a typical desktop environment, code residing on the local hard drive is considered trusted, while code received from network resources, remote code, is given a lower level of trust based on the source (a corporate LAN or the site of a virus hacker). The trust engendered in the past has commonly been based on the source of the application code. The security risk taken by installing a shrink-wrapped package produced by a well-known software publisher purchased off the shelf of a retail store is perceived to be minimal when compared to downloading the latest freeware game from the Internet. Adoption of electronic distribution channels for applications (JavaScript and Java code) requires the adoption of new technology and procedures, as well as education of the expected consumer.

The computer industry is moving toward assigning digital signatures to developers and creating signed applets as a way to define accountability for JavaScript code. The identity of the JavaScript developer will likely be broadcast to the Web browser through a digital signature appended to the script file. Users, in conjunction with newer browsers, can determine whether to accept a code download from a site based on the signature received. Figure 24.1 shows a sample dialog displaying the information contained in a digital certificate.

FIGURE 24.1.

A sample view of a digital certificate.

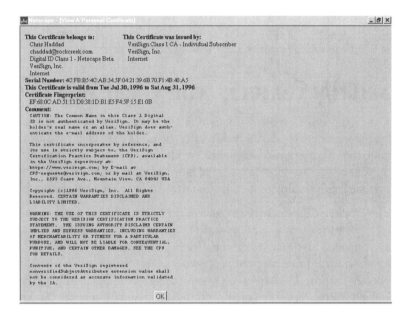

Encryption is used to prevent modification of the data transmission while en route. The browser encryption protocols, SSL (Secure Socket Layer), and SHTTP (Secure Hypertext Transport Protocol) work together to ensure that JavaScript code fragments aren't altered during transit. Last, verification of the source code is critical to providing a secure environment. Virus checkers are extended to verify that JavaScript code doesn't contain any dangerous routines.

The cost and complexity of the security measures implemented to protect a user's computer system must be balanced with the hardships proposed by their existence. The following list describes the client machine's areas of vulnerability when executing scripting code:

- Altering the file system
- Reading/writing to a file
- Reading/writing system memory
- Sending private information over the network
- Communication with other network resources
- Executing/closing programs on the local computer or an external host
- Using excessive system resources (Denial of service attacks)
- Crashing the host program (Web browser)

Programming languages are created to give the developer tools to build an application. Because of the security concerns related to executing code on network clients, Netscape has designed JavaScript without many of the functions present in traditional programming languages. The missing capabilities give Web surfers a level of protection against attack but hamper the creation of compelling application content. This chapter describes the ability of JavaScript and Java code to breach security and the steps that you can take to prevent attacks.

Security Concerns with Client-Side JavaScript

The most prevalent security risk to local machines accessing the Internet is currently related to executing remote JavaScript code on the client. The use of client-side JavaScript can be ascertained by viewing the document source. The existence of an HTML <SCRIPT> tag signifies that the page contains client-side code, and the optional tag attribute LANGUAGE="JAVASCRIPT" specifies that the page contains code conforming to the JavaScript language.

The JavaScript code may be inline with the HTML source document, or in a separate file referenced by the use of another optional <SCRIPT> tag attribute, SRC="*javafile.JS*". If JavaScript execution has been enabled for the Web browser, the script can run immediately after the page has downloaded and has been processed by the script interpreter or JIT (Just-In-Time) compiler. At the time this chapter was written, there was no mechanism to warn users that JavaScript is about to execute, nor was there a way to stop a script from executing. The ability of the browser client to selectively authorize trusted individual sites from which JavaScript code may be downloaded is also necessary but currently is unavailable in a release (nonbeta) browser application.

When viewed from the perspective of traditional desktop programmers, the implementation of client-side JavaScript currently handles security in a draconian fashion. The following security restrictions are imposed on JavaScript code when executed by Netscape Navigator:

- There is no ability to read or write files.
- There is no access to file system information.
- JavaScript can't execute programs or system commands.

■ JavaScript can't make network connections to other computers except to the machine from which the applet was downloaded.

■ There are restrictions on the access of FORM data.

JavaScript applications can't save user session information to the local hard drive, except through the cookie mechanism, communication with a plug-in, and one code trick. The trick relies on piping the information to a helper application. If a user has defined a helper application for a MIME type, the JavaScript code can open a message window and output the information to the helper application. The user can then explicitly save the information to the client machine through the helper application's File | Save option. Figure 24.2 shows what happens after data is piped to `notepad.exe` via the `test_stream` code example. The following code describes the functions necessary to perform this operation:

```
function test_stream()
{
msgwindow = window.open("","hiwin","");
msgwindow.document.open("text/plain");   // or text/sams to define a new MIME type
msgwindow.document.write("JavaScript data, save to disk drive  \nA,100,B\n");
    // write some text
msgwindow.document.write("Choose File¦Save to create a data file");
msgwindow.document.close();
msgwindow.close();
}
```

FIGURE 24.2.
Downloading data to the client from JavaScript.

CAUTION

If the document.open command is passed a parameter (mime-type) defined as Ask User or Save in the helper tab, the script doesn't save any information and generates an Out of Memory error.

Because document.write currently can't write nulls (\0) to the data stream, this example has limited use for binary files.

Access to information about the user's browser environment by the script code is critical to properly understanding the client limitations that might affect the operation of the script. The script can query the `navigator` class to ascertain the system platform as well as the browser version and type. Also, a list of registered mime-types and plug-ins can be enumerated. The navigator properties are read-only so therefore aren't a security concern. The system properties that can be acquired through access to the navigator class are listed in Table 24.1.

Table 24.1. Navigator class properties.

Description	Property Name
Browser codename	navigator.appCodeName
Browser application	navigator.appName
Browser version	navigator.appVersion
HTTP agent string	navigator.userAgent
Mime-types available	navigator.mimeTypes[]
Plug-ins installed	navigator.plugins[]

NOTE

The HTTP agent string is sent to the server during HTTP requests. Both Netscape Navigator and Microsoft Internet Explorer expose access to the navigator class.

A code example of accessing these types and attempting to change a value is in the file NAVPROPS.HTM.

JavaScript shouldn't be used to create applications that are responsible for access control. Because the user can view all JavaScript code in the document (or frame) source window, the security algorithm can be deduced easily. Even files loaded by means of the optional source tag are available for the user to download and decipher.

Denial of Service Attacks

Because a user can't terminate executing JavaScript code, denial of service attacks can currently perform the most damage. Service attacks have the capability to lock up the user interface and require the user to terminate the browser application. Common attacks include

- Stack overflow
- Infinite loops
- Infinite modal dialogs
- Using all available memory

The stack overflow condition is the easiest denial of service attack to prevent and is properly trapped by all browser implementations. A JavaScript error window is displayed with the message Out of Stack Space or Stack overflow in function_x, as shown in Figure 24.3. The following code listing demonstrates how to create a stack overflow by repeatedly calling a recursive function:

```
<HTML><HEAD>
<TITLE> Create Recursive Function Call Condition</TITLE>
<!-- File lockstack.htm -->
<SCRIPT>
function stack_lockup(){
stack_lockup();}
</SCRIPT></HEAD><BODY >
Entering Recursive Function Call
<SCRIPT LANGUAGE="JavaScript">
//<!-- comment so that JavaScript is not displayed by non-JS browsers

stack_lockup();//this line executes immediately after the document downloads
// don't forget to JS_comment the start/end of the HTML comment -->

</SCRIPT></BODY></HTML>
```

FIGURE 24.3.

The Netscape Navigator error window on stack overflow.

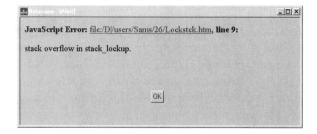

Infinite loops are the bane of all programmers, and JavaScript coders don't escape their curse. The following code fragment locks up the browser:

```
for(var i=0;;i++)
    document.write("End this message");
```

CAUTION

JavaScript code that executes infinite loops locks up all browser windows, including windows that are downloading files. According to Netscape, JavaScript code should terminate after 100,000 branches, and the user should be able to click the Stop button. However, I was unable to verify that the browser met the second specification.

JavaScript code that repeatedly displays alert boxes is an example of an infinite modal dialog box attack. The following fragment will lock up the browser's user interface:

```
for(var i=0;;i++)
    alert("Why can't i kill this script");
```

24

JAVASCRIPT AND WEB SECURITY

Netscape Navigator doesn't limit the amount of memory that JavaScript can allocate. This last attack eventually swamps the virtual memory storage and slows the machine to a crawl:

```
for(var i=0;;i++)
    str = str + "why doesn't everyone play nice";
```

A majority of these attacks are obvious and could be stopped if the user had the ability to terminate an executing script (a feature currently being investigated by Netscape). The more insidious attack is based on degradation of service. The rogue JavaScript code doesn't take over the machine, but hoards resources to the point where other browser windows appear sluggish.

Netscape Navigator 2.0 Issues

The Netscape Navigator 2.0 browser implementation takes a conservative approach toward balancing the needs of the developer with the necessity of protecting a user from security concerns. Because many security holes have been eliminated in later revisions of Netscape Navigator, valid JavaScript code developed for version 2.x doesn't often run properly on later versions of Netscape Navigator.

The balance between private and public access to JavaScript information in Navigator 2.0 was fairly clear. Navigator automatically prevented scripts from one server from accessing properties of documents residing on a different server. These security restrictions prevented a script from fetching private information that the user wouldn't want made public. Since the release of Navigator 2.0, there has been a low-level rewrite of the code related to security issues. Most importantly, the rule related to cooperation between scripts from different servers has been relaxed and codified as a new methodology—data tainting.

You should be aware of outstanding bugs in the Netscape Navigator 2.x versions and update your browser with the latest patches. Netscape has fixed numerous bugs in the 2.01 and 2.02 releases. Most bug fixes were patches to security holes in the Java implementation. I suggest that users and developers update to the latest final release version of Netscape Navigator as soon as it is available.

Later Navigator Versions

A major rewrite of the JavaScript interpreter has changed the definition of valid code compared to earlier versions. The security measures taken by the Netscape browser are currently in a state of flux as the development community determines the correct balance between language capabilities and user privacy.

The operation of the document calls have been changed to ensure that JavaScript code doesn't overwrite the original script. The presence of document.open or document.write function calls outside of the <BODY> tags that don't reference a new window result in code errors. Here is an example of an invalid script:

```
<SCRIPT LANGUAGE="Javascript">
var i;
function initialize_app()
```

```
{
i = "1";
}

function setup()
{
document.open();
document.write("My test app equals",i);
initialize_app();
document.close();
}
</SCRIPT>
<BODY onload="setup()"></BODY>
```

The browser creates a new document context and flushes out the old JavaScript. The result is the error message `initialize_app is not defined`, because the JavaScript interpreter can no longer access the function. The correct workaround to this security restriction is to either write all the text after the onload function has completed, or write the new document into another frame. The following example demonstrates the first workaround:

```
<SCRIPT>
function setup()
{
initialize_app();
}
</SCRIPT>
<BODY onload="setup()">
</BODY>
<SCRIPT>
document.write("My test app equals",i);
</SCRIPT>
```

Data Tainting

The concept of data tainting has been added to the language as a mechanism for windows originating from different servers to cooperate and share data. You enable data tainting by setting the environment variable NS_ENABLE_TAINT to any value.

When data tainting is enabled, all JavaScript objects and properties are public and accessible. The feature is necessary in order for windows to share information across servers. Windows can pull foreign form information from other accessible windows, but when the foreign information is posted to the server, a confirming dialog pops up, allowing the user to cancel or confirm the post operation. If the environment variable isn't set, references to form data on other servers generate the error message `access disallowed from scripts at` *URL1*`.htm to documents at` *URL2*`.htm`.

> **TIP**
>
> Even when data tainting is disabled, windows have the ability to call functions loaded in other windows from other servers. For instance, frame1 loaded from server1 can call a frame2 function loaded from server2.

JavaScript provides functions that let the programmer set or remove taint on objects. The function `taint()` returns a tainted reference to a property, and `untaint()` returns a copy that is untainted. For instance, the following code returns a copy of the private data that can be sent over a URL or form post operation to a server:

```
unmarked = untaint(document.forms[0].element[0].value);
```

> **CAUTION**
>
> When the NS_ENABLE_TAINT environment variable is set, JavaScript code in one window can view all document properties in other windows, including private data and session history information.

The tainting mechanism currently contains many security bugs and should be used with care. Many developers have demonstrated code that circumvents the protection mechanism by laundering the data through a sequence of data manipulations.

Internet Explorer 3.x

Because the capability to execute JavaScript and Java applets has just recently been included in Microsoft's Internet Explorer, an extensive security review hasn't been performed by independent third parties. Review of the software's application interface reveals a well-thought-out approach to security. Privacy measures and applet logging have been built into the browser and work with the user to ensure that information is only explicitly transmitted to servers. Figure 24.4 shows a dialog box that details the privacy options available in Internet Explorer.

FIGURE 24.4.

Microsoft Internet Explorer security options.

The application interface also includes the ability to restrict code downloads to only those servers deemed trustworthy. This feature relies on the use of security certificates by the server to identify trusted sites while browsing. Internet Explorer has a dialog that will display the sites that are trusted by the client browser, as shown in Figure 24.5.

FIGURE 24.5.

The Windows Software Security dialog.

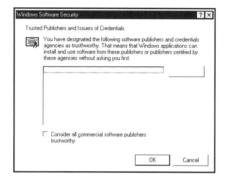

Maximizing Security Protection

Before you surf into uncharted waters, you can take steps to reduce the exposure to security attacks due to renegade JavaScript or Java code. You can determine which level of protection to use by seeing how much trust is given to the source of the Web pages visited. When visiting new sites (or visiting those listed after a query for "virus hackers"), it's advisable to totally remove the ability for the browser to execute scripting languages. Also, the network administrator can take a top-down security approach to disable execution of Java classes obtained from the Internet. The firewall can be configured to remove the capability of Java class files to pass through a proxy server into the internal network. If you keep up with the latest security bulletins and advisories, you should have a clearer understanding of the risks involved during trips outside the firewall.

Secure Sessions and Digital Signatures

As I mentioned earlier, secure sessions are initiated by the browser and establish an encrypted transmission stream between the server and the browser. The encryption is based on a digital certificate stored on the server. Further protection is achieved by digitally signing each file downloaded to the client. Verification authorities such as Verisign are working in conjunction with browser developers to create a framework for appending digital signatures for applets and script files. Later versions of Netscape Navigator and Internet Explorer will provide information about the current security level of the document or frame in addition to on-screen visual cues.

To view the security level of a document (or frame) in Netscape Navigator, choose View | Document Info or View | Frame Info. The `Security:` line gives the current security level. Figure 24.6 shows Netscape Navigator security information.

FIGURE 24.6.

The Netscape Navigator document security information window.

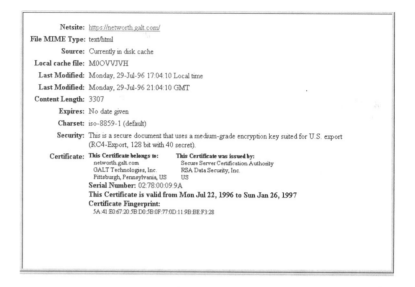

To view the security level of a document in Microsoft Internet Explorer, select File | Properties and then choose the Security tab. Figure 24.7 shows Internet Explorer security information.

FIGURE 24.7.

The Internet Explorer document security information dialog box.

Disabling Scripting Languages in the Browser

At the individual client level, the most effective way to protect the user from damaging code fragments is to simply remove the browser's ability to execute scripting code. The drawback of this approach is that many exciting capabilities are then removed from a Web site, and the Web site might not operate as intended. You should use these options when you visit untrusted sites of questionable intent.

JavaScript

To disable JavaScript in Netscape Navigator 2.01, select Options | Security Preferences and choose the General tab. Check the Disable JavaScript box, and then click the OK button.

> **NOTE**
>
> Netscape Navigator 2.0 doesn't give you the option of disabling JavaScript.

To disable JavaScript in later versions of Netscape Navigator, select Options | Network Preferences (see Figure 24.8) and choose the Languages tab. Remove the check from the Enable JavaScript box, and then click OK.

FIGURE 24.8.

Disabling JavaScript in later versions of Netscape Navigator.

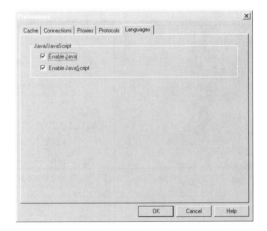

> **CAUTION**
>
> The logic statement has been reversed between versions. In Navigator 2.0, checking the box would *disable* JavaScript, whereas in later versions, checking the box *enables* JavaScript.

Currently, Internet Explorer's user interface doesn't have the ability to disable JavaScript.

Java

To disable Java in Netscape Navigator 2.01, select Options | Security Preferences and choose the General tab. Check the Disable Java box, and then click OK.

To disable Java in later versions of Netscape Navigator, select Options | Network Preferences and choose the Languages tab. Remove the check from the Enable Java box, and then click OK.

> **CAUTION**
>
> The logic statement has been reversed between versions. In Navigator 2.0, checking the box would *disable* Java, whereas in later versions, checking the box *enables* Java.

To disable Java in Internet Explorer 3.0B2, select View | Options and choose the Security tab. Remove the check from the Enable Java programs box, and then click the Apply button. Figure 24.9 shows the Internet Explorer dialog used to disable Java programs.

FIGURE 24.9.

Disabling Java in Internet Explorer.

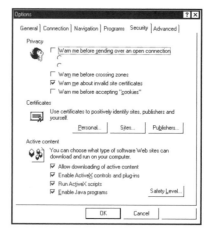

Firewall Filtering

Firewalls and/or proxy servers are commonly the first line of defense between the Internet and an internal network (WAN, LAN, or remote machine). Network administrators can configure firewall routers to filter network traffic based on various parameters and thereby ensure that users can't download a file that could cause a security breach. However, the level of filtering should be determined by balancing the benefits achieved through higher security against the cost involved to implement a solution. Router or proxy server-based high security solutions are generally expensive to implement, either from a resource or monetary standpoint, and you must be sure not to overengineer the security wall.

HTTP requests are used by the client browser to request Java and JavaScript code fragments. Because HTTP is also used for normal Web browser functionality, the proxy server can't just deny access to all HTTP requests, because that would result in no access to the Web by the browser. A filtering methodology (that can be used to remove Java downloads) is to filter URL

HTTP requests to block all files that have .class or .cla extensions. Filtering JavaScript code is more difficult because the source files may legally use any extension and because code fragments may be embedded inside Web pages.

Security Information Resources on JavaScript and Java Security

The Internet contains many sites devoted to information about security issues. Keeping informed of the latest security bulletins is a good start for making an informed decision about the risks involved in using the latest technology.

The most accurate, up-to-date information can be found at the following Web sites:

Netscape

```
http://developer.netscape.com/library/documentation/index.html
```
Information related to Netscape products.

Sun

```
http://java.javasoft.com/sfaq/
```
Information related to Java.

CERT

```
http://www.cert.org
```
Nonpartisan advisories about current security breaches.

CERT FTP

```
ftp://info.cert.org/pub/cert_advisories/
```
Search directory for files containing the name "Java."

Safe Internet Programming

```
http://www.cs.princeton.edu/sip/
```
Site of a research group at Princeton University investigating Internet scripting extensions. They are responsible for discovering the latest Java security holes.

Security Concerns for Server-Side JavaScript

The functionality of Web servers can be extended through the execution of JavaScript and Java routines as either CGI programs or server modules. Server-side JavaScript leverages existing knowledge of the JavaScript language to create applications that can reference databases and other resources residing on the server. The capability to execute server-side JavaScript in Netscape server is currently described as LiveWire technology, and it's enabled through the server administration manager. Figure 24.10 shows the Enterprise server screen that is used to activate server-side JavaScript (LiveWire).

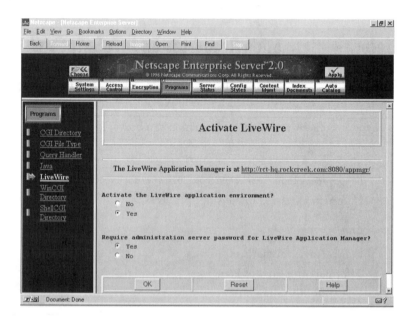

It's important to recognize that the server-side JavaScript capability must then be mapped to specific directories on the server. The necessity of authorizing server directories capable of executing server-side JavaScript helps protect the server by isolating the areas that could cause a security breach. Figure 24.11 shows the server screen that is used to activate LiveWire for a particular server subdirectory.

The LiveWire technology exposes four new JavaScript objects for use on the server: request, client, project, and server. The request object has a property, request.ip, that lets the server determine the IP address that originated the client request. This object member can be used to verify trusted clients who can be given access to confidential information. The global application data object, project, should be locked before data variable values are changed; otherwise, the integrity of application variables and counters isn't synchronized between the client processes.

The most significant security concern is the ability for server-side JavaScript to read and write directly to the hard drive. Improperly formatted data can often crash programs that read or write files. The server script code should check extensively to ensure that the user data is in a valid format before writing it to disk. Also, it's imperative that server-side JavaScript code be constructed with file-locking mechanisms to take into account that multiple processes execute on the host server. The simplest locking mechanism is to rename the file before opening it for file I/O. On all operating systems, the `rename` command is expected to be an atomic operation on any platform. The following code illustrates this principle:

```
while(rename(filename,lockname))      // rename filename to the lock filename
    ;                     // block on access to file
else
    {
// perform file i/o
rename(lockname,oldname);        // rename file to original name
}
```

FIGURE 24.11.
Activating LiveWire directories to execute JavaScript.

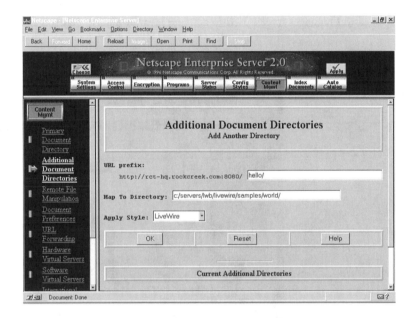

The server-side code shouldn't write to disk files in public directories that have execution capability. It's a common hacker trick to use a trusted server-side program to create a file on the server that can be used for attack later. For instance, a CGI program that uploads text files from the client to the server can be used to create a script file that can be executed. When the uploaded file is accessed by the attacker via the Web browser, the server-side code executes and can attack the server machine.

Web site administrators and code developers should be aware that server-side JavaScript can crash the production server. Excessive use of system memory, improperly locking objects, infinite loops, and improper file I/O can bring the server to a halt. All script code should be fully tested on a development server before going "live." Furthermore, code should be empirically evaluated for possible deadlock and race conditions to verify that server-side scripts won't infinitely block on a resource.

24

JAVASCRIPT AND WEB SECURITY

CAUTION

Client-side JavaScript can attempt to access any port on the originating server. A security check should be performed to ensure that a proper firewall is in place between the server and the Internet.

The Java interpreter must be explicitly activated for server directories. The server application manager is used to specify directories that can execute Java modules. Figure 24.12 shows the application manager screen used to activate Java for a particular server subdirectory.

FIGURE 24.12.

Activating Java directories on the server.

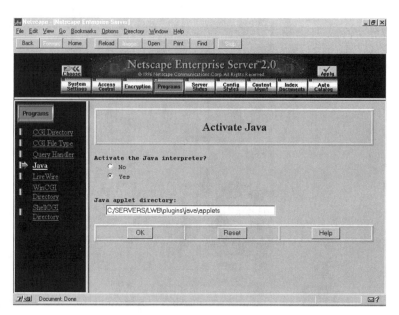

Java and Security

The Java language offers many more capabilities than JavaScript. The later versions of Netscape let the developer write a mix of Java and JavaScript code inside Java applets (LiveConnect technology). Also, JavaScript can call Java applet functions directly, passing parameters and receiving return values. The two languages can be used in tandem to create comprehensive remote client solutions.

Knowledge of Java's history is important for putting in perspective security issues related to its current implementation. The language mirrors C++ in many respects—it has common language syntax, similar keywords, and support for object-oriented programming, including inheritance. Java diverges from C++ in ways that add flexibility to the language and attempt to create a more secure environment: The code can't forge pointers, garbage collection of objects is handled automatically, and only single inheritance is implemented. The machine-independent structure of Java attempts to insulate the programmer from the target machine's operating system. Basic programming building blocks are extended with prebuilt packages capable of targeting either server or client systems.

Java was originally designed to be a language for creating embedded applications on personal appliances (desktop TV boxes, personal communicators, hand-held computers, and so on). The possibility of attack on these closed systems is much lower than it is when connecting to the largest public network with open standards.

The application programming interface proposed by Sun Microsystems for the Java language during its public alpha test phase was robust enough to handle a majority of the tasks required by traditional desktop computer applications. The goal was to allow a trusted browser or trusted Java environment to run untrusted Java class components. Java's current implementation falls short of that mandate, because its security mechanisms don't follow basic industry security standards for trusted systems. The Java language as a stand-alone definition can't be considered a secure language, because it doesn't define the most basic components of a secure architecture.

An example of accepted industry standards is documented in the *Department of Defense Trusted Computer System Evaluation Criteria* Orange Book. Java doesn't contain basic security mechanisms such as an audit capability in the class loader to document the modules loaded during an attack. Because applets can exist beyond the scope of the Web document that loaded them, a rogue applet can mount an attack without the user's drawing a correlation to its existence. A user-defined audit policy should be available that allows the logging of applet execution, applet originating network address, and applet bytecode.

Also, the implementations of Java haven't proven to be a secure language as envisioned by its creators. Many subsystems have security bugs that haven't been entirely fixed, leading to recurring security alerts. Table 24.2 details the most important of these.

Table 24.2. Java security bugs documented by Sun Microsystems in the Applet Security FAQ (`http://java.sun.com/sfaq/`).

Date	Problem	Status
June 2, 1996	Illegal type cast attack	Currently an open bug
May 18, 1996	New version of previous classloader attack	Fixed in Netscape 3.0b4
April 1996	URL name resolution attack	Fixed in Netscape 3.0b4
March 1996	Verifier implementation bug	Fixed in Netscape 2.02
March 1996	Class loader implementation bug	Fixed in Netscape 2.01
February 1996	DNS attack	Fixed in Netscape 2.01

24

JAVASCRIPT AND
WEB SECURITY

The researchers who discovered these security bugs have publicly stated that Java might have to be radically altered to meet their definition of a secure environment. The illegal type cast attack successfully circumvents the safe-type cast mechanism in Java. Successful attacks on the typecast mechanism allow Java objects to masquerade as other types. The ability of hackers to develop a rogue class loader means that untrusted application code could potentially be loaded and executed from an untrusted source without the browser's knowledge.

Security Components

The security mechanisms to control Java objects are written in Java itself. When the browser runtime system starts, no security restrictions are in place. The class that monitors security, SecurityManager, is loaded from the directory contained in the client's CLASSPATH environment variable. These trusted class files (MOZ*xxx*.ZIP in Netscape Navigator 2.0 and JAV*xxx*.ZIP in Netscape Navigator 3.x) should be protected by frequent virus checks and marked as read-only.

Bytecode Verifier

Once a Java class is downloaded from the remote host, the code is checked by a bytecode verifier. This important step ensures that the Java code conforms to known language opcodes and that the operand stack isn't subjected to overflows or underflows. All class object accesses are checked for adherence to the protection mechanism defined for the object members (private, protected, public). Furthermore, the code is verified to ensure that no illegal data conversions are present. After the verifier performs its job, the code is converted by the Java runtime compiler into machine code.

Security Manager

The SecurityManager class is used by the Java runtime system to access control authorization of Java classes. Because the SecurityManager is implemented as a Java object, when the runtime initially starts, the security manager is protected by the Java type system. If the type system has proven impenetrable, and the file system hasn't been compromised, the security manager is considered a trusted class.

The Java compilers are responsible for compiling the Java source code (a .java file) into a machine-independent bytecode (a .class file). The bytecode is transmitted over the network to the local machine and interpreted or compiled into native code by the Java runtime system. Verifying the Java bytecode is a critical step in determining the integrity of a Java applet. Just as current virus-checking programs search for illegal processor and operating system calls, bytecode should be verified to not contain any security attacks. The bytecodes must be evaluated in the context of their type. For example, the SecurityManager type should have fewer restrictions than a user-defined type.

The lack of a formal definition for the Java type system, and the need to thoroughly analyze all program execution sequences, renders this evaluation by current verifiers complicated and unreliable.

Security between applet methods is enforced by a concept of *named space*. Every Java applet should have a unique name, depending on the location from which it was downloaded. The Java documentation states that the named space of system-level objects has the ability to be shared by all other named spaces (applets), and that the runtime classloader always searches the list of system-named spaces to prevent downloaded code from overwriting a system class. Yet forging named-space hashes that inadvertently replace vital system class components like the classloader has been one of the first security bugs found in Java. Classloader bugs have been extensively documented by the researchers at Princeton University.

Security Restrictions

The basic Java language is extended by many valuable class packages that save the programmer from reinventing basic interfaces. The implementation of a package can shield the programmer from platform-specific issues, but can restrict access to certain low-level components as well. Basic access to the machine subsystems responsible for network communications, file I/O, memory access, and system resources is affected by the particular implementation of Java being used. Currently, server-side Java code has fewer security restrictions than those imposed on the client.

> **TIP**
>
> In Java code, error messages that include the term `SecurityException` indicate that a security restriction has been violated.

Network Communications

The term *sandboxing* is defined as the capability of the applet code to be restricted in its communication with other machines. A sandboxed applet can communicate only with the server from which it originated. The restriction that the code will only "play in its sandbox" is the primary line of defense against rogue applets. The security manager subjects networking calls to the restriction that they can only open communication channels between the client and the applet's originating DNS address. Because the methodology relies on the DNS subsystem to provide address verification, compromises to the DNS address server in turn invalidate the security mechanism.

According to the documentation, applets can open communication channels back to the server on any port. In reality, the Netscape Java implementation places undocumented restrictions on which ports are available.

> **TIP**
>
> Having an applet in the toolchest that queries all socket ports and returns possible communication channels saves a great deal of time when you're determining the ports that your Java implementation supports.

File I/O

Current implementations of client-side Java don't permit reading or writing to the client's hard disk. On a client machine, calls to open, read, write, and close files generate a `SecurityExceptions` or `IOExceptions` notification. Sun Microsystems' Appletviewer application uses an access control file to grant read and write permissions to the client's disk drive. It's likely that some derivation of that scheme will be adopted in the future by the Netscape browser. As I mentioned earlier in this chapter, server-side Java can access the host hard drive to perform file operations.

Memory Access

In Java, source code doesn't have the concept of memory pointers. This simplifies the implementation of language by the programmer and reduces code errors. Because data structures aren't referenced by pointers, many proponents of Java envision it to be a more secure language than C++. Also, Java programmers should be unable to forge pointers to functions.

System Resources

The ability to lock system resources is a security risk in Java. For example, in the Netscape implementation, locking the `java.net.InetAddress` class results in blocking all new network connections.

Both Java and JavaScript are revolutionary languages that help the Web site developer create interactive content. However, the ability to run remote code on client machines must be considered from the perspective of potential damage to the user's operating environment.

The goal of the Internet vendor community is the creation of a trusted environment in which users don't have to worry that an action will have damaging consequences. Ideally, the user would also know that an operation were about to occur and would be able to prevent it.

The mechanisms for creating a safe networked environment that is intuitive to the end user are still being developed. The security measures encapsulating JavaScript code might not be ready for mission-critical environments, but the fast growth of Internet technologies deserves a close watch for tomorrow's solutions.

Summary

As computer users reach beyond their desktops and communicate with business partners and friends all over the world, issues related to computer security and privacy are becoming paramount concerns. This chapter provided an introduction to the client areas that should be protected from malicious tampering and showed how users can safeguard their machines when running JavaScript and Java programs. The security methodologies are currently in a state of flux. The execution of remote code on client machines is severely restricted in the current implementations as the needs of the user and developer are balanced against concern for potential misuse. Knowledge of the limitations and features present in current technology offerings is critical when establishing a proper level of trust and proliferating dynamic and compelling applications and content throughout the Internet community.

Cookies and State Maintenance

CHAPTER 25

Web servers have very short memories. When you request a page, the server doesn't really know who you are, what you entered on a form three pages ago, or whether this is your first visit to the site or your 75th. One of the challenges of using the Hypertext Transfer Protocol (HTTP) is that it doesn't track the *state* of your interactions with the server. *State* refers to any information about you or your visit to a Web site. It's maintained as you move from page to page within the site, and it may be used by the Web server or a JavaScript program (or both) to customize your experience at the site. But if HTTP doesn't maintain the state, what does?

In this chapter, you'll learn how to get around HTTP's limitations by using cookies, URL query string parameters, and hidden form variables. Although the bulk of this chapter deals with cookies, time is spent investigating other techniques, as well where and how they may best be used.

Maintaining State

Maintaining state means remembering information while the user moves from page to page within a Web site. With this information in hand, you can set user preferences, fill in default form values, track visit counts, and do many other things that make browsing easier for users and give you more information about how your pages are used.

There are a number of ways to maintain state information:

- Store it in cookies.
- Encode it in URL links.
- Send it in hidden form variables.
- Store it in variables in other frames.
- Store it on the Web server.

There are some technical challenges regarding state maintenance. While browsing a site, a user might suddenly zoom off to another Web site and return minutes, hours, or days later, only to find that any saved state information is out of date or has been erased. He might return by clicking his browser's Back button, by using a bookmark, or by typing in the URL directly, causing state information encoded in the URL to be overwritten or lost.

The Web developer must maintain state information regardless of whether the user navigates through the site using buttons on a form or a URL link on a page. This could mean adding information to both hidden form variables and every URL <A HREF...> tag that appears on the page.

With all these difficulties to overcome, these state maintenance mechanisms had better be useful. Luckily, they are. There are many advantages to maintaining state, both within a single site visit and from one visit to the next. Consider the following scenarios:

- A shopping cart application: Users could browse through the site while selecting items and adding them to a virtual shopping cart. At any time, they can view the items in the cart, change the contents of their cart, or take the cart to the checkout counter for purchase. Keeping track of which user owns which shopping cart is essential.

- Custom home pages: Both Netscape and the Microsoft Network have set up home pages where users can customize what they see when they arrive. After giving the user a choice of layouts, color schemes, and favorite destinations, it stores the preferences on the user's own computer through the use of cookies. The user can return to the site any time and get his previously configured page.

- Frequent visitor bonuses: By storing information on the client computer, this application keeps track of how many times a browser has hit a particular page. When the user reaches a certain level of hits, he gets access to more or better services.

- Change banners: Make graphic banners and text change each time the user hits a page. This technique is often used to cycle through a list of advertisements.

- Bookmarks: Remember where a user was when he last visited the site. Was he reading a story, filling out a questionnaire, or playing a game? Let him pick up where he left off.

- Games: Remember current or high scores. Present new challenges based on past answers and performance.

Cookies: An Introduction

Cookies, sometimes called *magic cookies,* but more formally known as *persistent client state HTTP cookies,* let you store information on the client browser's computer for later retrieval. Although they have their drawbacks, cookies are the most powerful technique available for maintaining state within a Web site.

Netscape came up with the original cookie specification. Although they are sometimes called "magic cookies" (mostly on Macintosh browsers), there doesn't seem to be any good reason why Netscape chose that particular name. In fact, on their cookie specification page, they even admit that "the state object is called a cookie for no compelling reason."

In their simplest form, cookies store data in the form of `name=value` pairs. You, the developer, can pick any name and value combination you want. More advanced cookie features include the capability to set an expiration date and to specify what Web pages may see the cookie information.

Advantages of Cookies

One of the most powerful aspects of cookies is their persistence. When a cookie is set on the user's browser, it may persist for days, months, or even years. This makes it easy to save user preferences and visit information and keep this information available every time the user returns to your site.

Cookies are especially helpful when used in conjunction with JavaScript. Since JavaScript has functions for reading, adding, and editing cookies, your JavaScript programs can use them to store global information about a user as she surfs through your Web site.

Limitations of Cookies

Some limitations of cookies could prove problematic. Cookies are stored on the user's computer, usually in a special cookie file. As with all files, this cookie file might be accidentally (or purposefully) deleted, taking all the browser's cookie information with it. The cookie file could be write-protected, thus preventing any cookies from being stored there. Browser software may impose limitations on the size and number of cookies that may be stored, and newer cookies may overwrite older ones.

Because cookies are associated with a particular browser, problems come up if users switch from one browser to another. If you usually use Netscape Navigator and have a collections of cookies, they will no longer be available for you to use if you decide to switch to Microsoft Internet Explorer.

Finally, if several people use the same computer and browser, they might find themselves using cookies that belong to someone else. The reason for this is that cookie information is stored in a file on the computer, and the browser has no way to distinguish between multiple users.

Disadvantages of Cookies

There are also some problems, both real and imagined, concerning the use of cookies. Because many browsers store their cookie information in an unencrypted text file, you should never store sensitive information, such as a password, in a cookie. Anyone with access to the user's computer could read it.

Newer Web browsers, such as Netscape Navigator 3.0, might have a feature that alerts the user every time an attempt is made to set a cookie. These browsers could even be configured to prevent cookies from being set at all. This sometimes results in confusion on the user's part when a dialog box informs her that something strange involving a cookie is happening to her computer. If cookies are disabled, your carefully designed Web application might not run at all.

Cookie Myths

The biggest problem facing cookies could be a psychological one. Some savvy Web users believe that all cookies are a tool used by "Big Brother" in order to discover their innermost secrets. Perhaps I exaggerate a bit. However, considering that cookies are capable of storing information about where users have visited on a Web site, how many times they have been there, what advertising banners they have viewed, and what they have selected and placed on forms, some people think that their privacy is being invaded whenever a cookie gets set on their computer.

In reality, cookies are seldom used for these purposes. Although technically these things are possible, there are now better and easier ways of getting the same type of information without using cookies. I guess this means that you can still be paranoid—just not about cookies.

Other users complain about Web sites being able to write information to their computer and taking up space on their hard drive. This is somewhat true. Web browser software limits the total size of the cookies stored to 1.2MB, with no more than 80KB going to any one Web site. Consider, though, that this number probably is small when compared to the size of the pages and graphic images that Web browsers routinely store in their page cache.

Other users are concerned that cookies set by one Web site might be read by other sites. This is completely untrue. Your Web browser software prevents this from happening by making cookies available only to the sites that created them.

If your users understand the usefulness of cookies, this "cookie backlash" shouldn't be a problem.

> **RESOURCE**
>
> Netscape came up with the original cookie specification. You can find more information on the Netscape Web site at `http://www.netscape.com/newsref/std/cookie_spec.html`.

Using Cookies

By now you have considered the pros and cons of cookies and have decided that they are just what you need to make your JavaScript application a success.

In this section, you will find a number of handy functions for reading and setting cookies, which will help you make your Web sites smarter and more user-friendly. Also included in this section are Internet references for finding additional information concerning cookies.

Retrieving Cookie Values

Cookie names and values are stored and set using the cookie property of the document object. To store the raw cookie string in a variable, you would use a JavaScript command such as the following:

```
var myCookie = document.cookie;
```

To display it on a Web page, use the following command:

```
document.write ("Raw Cookies: " + document.cookie + "<BR>");
```

JavaScript stores cookies in the following format:

```
name1=value1; name2=value2; name3=value3
```

Individual `name=value` pairs are separated by a semicolon and a blank space. There is no semicolon after the final value.

To make it easier to retrieve a cookie, you probably want to use a JavaScript routine such as the one shown in Listing 25.1.

Listing 25.1. The GetCookie function.

```
function GetCookie (name) {
  var result = null;
  var myCookie = " " + document.cookie + ";";
  var searchName = " " + name + "=";
  var startOfCookie = myCookie.indexOf(searchName)
  var endOfCookie;
  if (startOfCookie != -1) {
    startOfCookie += searchName.length; // skip past cookie name
    endOfCookie = myCookie.indexOf(";", startOfCookie);
    result = unescape(myCookie.substring(startOfCookie, endOfCookie));
  }
  return result;
}
```

In Listing 25.1, the myCookie string helps avoid annoying boundary conditions by making sure all cookie string names start with a space and end with a semicolon.

From there, it's easy to find the start of the name= portion of the string, skip it, and retrieve everything from that point until the next semicolon.

Setting Cookie Values

The *name=value* combination is the minimum amount of information you need to set up a cookie. However, there is more to cookies than just this. Here is the complete list of parameters used to specify a cookie:

- *name=value*
- expires=*date*
- path=*path*
- domain=*domainname*
- secure

Cookie Names and Values

The *name* and *value* can be anything you choose. In some cases, you might want it to be very explanatory, such as FavoriteColor=Blue. In other cases, it could just be code that the JavaScript program interprets, such as CurStat=1:2:1:0:0:1:0:3:1:1. In any case, the *name* and *value* are completely up to you.

In its simplest form, a routine to set a cookie looks like this:

```
function SetCookieEZ (name, value) {
  document.cookie = name + "=" + escape(value);
}
```

Notice that the value is encoded using the escape function. If there were a semicolon in the string, it might prevent you from achieving the expected results. Using the escape function eliminates this problem.

Also notice that the document.cookie property works rather differently from most other properties. In most other cases, using the assignment operator (=) causes the existing property value to be completely overwritten with the new value. This isn't the case with the cookie property. With cookies, each new *name* you assign is added to the active list of cookies. If you assign the same *name* twice, the first assignment is replaced by the second.

There are some exceptions to this last statement, but these are explained in the section "Path" later in this chapter.

Expiration Date

The expires=*date* tells the browser how long the cookie will last. The cookie specification page at Netscape states that dates are in the form of

```
Wdy, DD-Mon-YY HH:MM:SS GMT
```

Here's an example:

```
Mon, 08-Jul-96 03:18:20 GMT
```

This format is based on Internet RFC 822, which you can find at http://www.w3.org/hypertext/WWW/Protocols/rfc822/#z28.

The only difference between RFC 822 and the Netscape implementation is that, in Netscape Navigator, the expiration date must end with GMT (Greenwich Mean Time). Happily, the JavaScript language provides a function to do just that. By using the toGMTString() function, you can set cookies to expire in the near or distant future.

> **TIP**
>
> Even though the date produced by the toGMTString() function doesn't match the Netscape specification, it still works under JavaScript.

If the expiration date isn't specified, the cookie remains in effect until the browser is shut down.

Here is a code segment that sets a cookie to expire in one week:

```
var name="foo";
var value="bar";
var oneWeek = 7 * 24 * 60 * 60 * 1000;
var expDate = new Date();
expDate.setTime (expDate.getTime() + oneWeek);
document.cookie = name + "=" + escape(value) + ";
    expires=" + expDate.toGMTString();
```

Deleting a Cookie

To delete a cookie, set the expiration date to some time in the past—how far in the past doesn't generally matter. To be on the safe side, a few days ago should work fine. Here is a routine to delete a cookie:

```
function ClearCookie (name) {
  var ThreeDays = 3 * 24 * 60 * 60 * 1000;
  var expDate = new Date();
  expDate.setTime (expDate.getTime() - ThreeDays);
  document.cookie = name + "=ImOutOfHere; expires=" + expDate.toGMTString();
}
```

When deleting cookies, it doesn't matter what you use for the cookie value—any value will do.

> **CAUTION**
>
> Some versions of Netscape do a poor job of converting times to GMT. Some common JavaScript functions for deleting a cookie consider the past to be one millisecond behind the current time. Although this is usually true, it doesn't work on all platforms. To be on the safe side, use a few days in the past to expire cookies.

Path

By default, cookies are available to other Web pages within the same directory as the page on which they were created. The Path parameter allows a cookie to be made available to pages in other directories. If the value of the Path parameter is a substring of a page's URL, cookies created with that path are available to that page. For example, you could create a cookie with the following command:

```
document.cookie = "foo=bar1; path=/javascript";
```

This would make the cookie foo available to every page in the javascript directory and all those directories beneath it. If, instead, the command looked like this:

```
document.cookie = "foo=bar2; path=/javascript/sam";
```

the cookie would be available to sample1.html, sample2.html, sammy.exe, and so on.

Finally, to make the cookie available to everyone on your server, use the following command:

```
document.cookie = "foo=bar3; path=/";
```

What happens when a browser has multiple cookies on different paths but with the same name? Which one wins?

Actually, they all do. When this situation arises, it's possible to have two or more cookies with the same name but different values. For example, if a page issued all the commands listed previously, its cookie string would look like the following:

```
foo=bar3; foo=bar2; foo=bar1
```

To help be aware of this situation, you might want to write a routine to count the number of cookie values associated with a cookie name. It might look like this:

```
function GetCookieCount (name) {
  var result = 0;
  var myCookie = " " + document.cookie + ";";
  var searchName = " " + name + "=";
  var nameLength = searchName.length;
  var startOfCookie = myCookie.indexOf(searchName)
  while (startOfCookie != -1) {
    result += 1;
    startOfCookie = myCookie.indexOf(searchName, startOfCookie + nameLength);
  }
  return result;
}
```

Of course, if there is a GetCookieCount function, there would need to be a GetCookieNum function to retrieve a particular instance of a cookie. That function would look like this:

```
function GetCookieNum (name, cookieNum) {
  var result = null;
  if (cookieNum >= 1) {
    var myCookie = " " + document.cookie + ";";
    var searchName = " " + name + "=";
    var nameLength = searchName.length;
    var startOfCookie = myCookie.indexOf(searchName);
    var cntr = 0;
    for (cntr = 1; cntr < cookieNum; cntr++)
      startOfCookie = myCookie.indexOf(searchName, startOfCookie + nameLength);
    if (startOfCookie != -1) {
      startOfCookie += nameLength; // skip past cookie name
      var endOfCookie = myCookie.indexOf(";", startOfCookie);
      result = unescape(myCookie.substring(startOfCookie, endOfCookie));
    }
  }
  return result;
}
```

CAUTION

There is a bug in Netscape Navigator version 1.1 and earlier. Only cookies whose path attribute is set explicitly to / are properly saved between sessions if they have an expires attribute.

In order to delete a cookie, the name and the path must match the original name and path used when the cookie was set.

Domain

Usually, after a page on a particular server creates a cookie, that cookie is accessible only to other pages on that server. Just as the Path parameter makes a cookie available outside its home path, the Domain parameter makes it available to other Web servers at the same site.

You can't create a cookie that anyone on the Internet can see. You may only set a path that falls inside your own domain. This is because the use of the Domain parameter dictates that you must use at least two periods (for example, .mydomain.com) if your domain ends in .com, .edu, .net, .org, .gov, .mil, or .int. Otherwise, it must have at least three periods (.mydomain.ma.us). Your domain parameter string must match the tail of your server's domain name.

Secure

The final cookie parameter tells your browser that this cookie should be sent only under a secure connection with the Web server. This means that the server and the browser must support HTTPS security. (HTTPS is Netscape's Secure Socket Layer Web page encryption protocol.)

If the secure parameter is not present, it means that cookies are sent unencrypted over the network.

> **NOTE**
>
> You can't set an infinite number of cookies on every Web browser that visits your site. Here are the number of cookies you can set and how large they can be:
>
> Cookies per each server or domain: 20
>
> Total cookies per browser: 300
>
> Largest cookie: 4KB (including both the name and value parameters)
>
> If these limits are exceeded, the browser might attempt to discard older cookies by tossing the least recently used cookies first.

Now that you have seen all the cookie parameters, it would be helpful to have a JavaScript routine set cookies with all the parameters. Such a routine might look like this:

```
function SetCookie (name, value, expires, path, domain, secure) {
  var expString =
            ((expires == null) ? "" : ("; expires=" + expires.toGMTString()))
  var pathString = ((path == null) ? "" : ("; path=" + path))
  var domainString = ((domain == null) ? "" : ("; domain=" + domain))
  var secureString = ((secure == true) ? "; secure" : "")
  document.cookie = name + "=" + escape (value) +
                expString + pathString + domainString + secureString;
}
```

To use this routine, you call it with whatever parameters you care about and use `null` in place of parameters that don't matter.

A Cookie Example

The JavaScript program in Listing 25.2 provides an example of cookies in use. This program allows the user to create a personalized "News-of-the-Day" page containing links to sites of general interest in a number of different categories. The user's favorite links are stored in cookies. Figure 25.1 shows what the Favorites page looks like.

Listing 25.2. The Favorites script.

```
<HTML>
<HEAD>
<SCRIPT LANGUAGE="JavaScript">
<!-- Comment out script from browsers that don't know JavaScript
// This JavaScript code should run under Netscape Navigator 3.0
// and Microsoft Internet Explorer 3.0 and above. It will not run
// locally under Internet Explorer. If you use IE, you must load
// this page from a web server.
//================================================================
// Here are our standard Cookie routines
//================================================================
//----------------------------------------------------------------
// GetCookie - Returns the value of the specified cookie or null
//             if the cookie doesn't exist
//----------------------------------------------------------------
function GetCookie(name) {
  var result = null;
  var myCookie = " " + document.cookie + ";";
  var searchName = " " + name + "=";
  var startOfCookie = myCookie.indexOf(searchName)
  var endOfCookie;
  if (startOfCookie != -1) {
    startOfCookie += searchName.length; // skip past cookie name
    endOfCookie = myCookie.indexOf(";", startOfCookie);
    result = unescape(myCookie.substring(startOfCookie,
                                              endOfCookie));
  }
  return result;
}
//----------------------------------------------------------------
// SetCookieEZ - Quickly sets a cookie which will last until the
//               user shuts down his browser
//----------------------------------------------------------------
function SetCookieEZ(name, value) {
  document.cookie = name + "=" + escape(value);
}
//----------------------------------------------------------------
// SetCookie - Adds or replaces a cookie. Use null for parameters
//             that you don't care about
//----------------------------------------------------------------
```

continues

Listing 25.2. continued

```javascript
function SetCookie(name, value, expires, path, domain, secure) {
  var expString = ((expires == null)
                   ? "" : ("; expires=" + expires.toGMTString()))
  var pathString = ((path == null) ? "" : ("; path=" + path))
  var domainString = ((domain == null)
                   ? "" : ("; domain=" + domain))
  var secureString = ((secure == true) ? "; secure" : "")
  document.cookie = name + "=" + escape(value)
                   + expString + pathString + domainString
                   + secureString;
}
//---------------------------------------------------------------
// ClearCookie  - Removes a cookie by setting an expiration date
//                three days in the past
//---------------------------------------------------------------
function ClearCookie(name) {
  var ThreeDays = 3 * 24 * 60 * 60 * 1000;
  var expDate = new Date();
  expDate.setTime (expDate.getTime() - ThreeDays);
  document.cookie = name + "=ImOutOfHere; expires="
                   + expDate.toGMTString();
}
//===============================================================
// Here are the object and the routines for our Favorites app
//===============================================================
//---------------------------------------------------------------
/* Here is our "favorite" object.
   Properties: fullName - The full descriptive name
               cook     - The code used for the cookie
               urlpath  - The full url (http://...) to the site
      Methods: Enabled  - Returns true if the link's cookie is
                          turned on
               Checked  - Returns the word "CHECKED" if the
                          link's cookie is turned on
               WriteAsCheckBox - Sends text to the document in a
                          checkbox control format
               WriteAsWebLink  - Sends text to the document in a
                          <A HREF...> format
   -----------------------------------------------------------*/
function favorite(fullName, cook, urlpath) {
  this.fullName = fullName;
  this.cook    = cook;
  this.urlpath = urlpath;
  this.Enabled = Enabled;
  this.Checked = Checked;
  this.WriteAsCheckBox = WriteAsCheckBox;
  this.WriteAsWebLink = WriteAsWebLink;
}
//---------------------------------------------------------------
// Enabled - Checks to see if the cookie exists
// returns - true if the cookie exists
//           false if it doesn't
//---------------------------------------------------------------
function Enabled() {
  var result = false;
```

```
    var FaveCookie = GetCookie("Favorites");
    if (FaveCookie != null) {
      var searchFor = "<" + this.cook + ">";
      var startOfCookie = FaveCookie.indexOf(searchFor)
      if (startOfCookie != -1)
        result = true;
    }
    return result;
  }
  //---------------------------------------------------------------
  // Checked - Checks to see if the cookie exists (using Enabled)
  // returns - 'CHECKED ' if the cookie exists
  //           "" if it doesn't
  //---------------------------------------------------------------
  function Checked () {
    if (this.Enabled())
      return "CHECKED ";
    return "";
  }
  //---------------------------------------------------------------
  // WriteAsCheckBox - The favorite may be either a regular URL or
  //                   a section title.  If the urlpath is an empty
  //                   string, then the favorite is a section title.
  //                   The links will appear within a definition
  //                   list, and are formatted appropriately.
  //---------------------------------------------------------------
  function WriteAsCheckBox () {
    // Check to see if it's a title or regular link
    if (this.urlpath == "") {
      // It's a section title
      result = '<DT><STRONG>' + this.fullName + '</STRONG>';
    } else {
      // It's a regular link
      result = '<DD><INPUT TYPE="checkbox" NAME="'
        + this.cook + '" '
        + this.Checked()
        + 'onClick="SetFavoriteEnabled(this.name, this.checked);">'
        + this.fullName;
    }
    document.write(result);
  }
  //---------------------------------------------------------------
  // Global Variable:
  // NextHeading - Sometimes we only want to print a heading if one
  //               its favorites is turned on.  The NextHeading
  //               variable helps us to do this. See WriteAsWebLink
  //---------------------------------------------------------------
  var NextHeading = "";
  //---------------------------------------------------------------
  // WriteAsWebLink - The favorite may be either a regular URL or
  //                  a section title.  If the urlpath is an empty
  //                  string, then the favorite is a section title.
  //                  The links will appear within a definition
  //                  list, and are formatted appropriately.
  //---------------------------------------------------------------
  function WriteAsWebLink() {
    var result = '';
```

continues

25

Listing 25.2. continued

```javascript
  if (this.urlpath == "") {
    NextHeading = this.fullName;        // It's must be a Title
  } else {
    if (this.Enabled() || (GetCookie("ViewAll") == "T")) {
      if (NextHeading != "") {
        result = '<P><DT><STRONG>' + NextHeading+ '</STRONG>';
        NextHeading = "";
      }
      result = result + '<DD><A HREF="' + this.urlpath + '">'
             + this.fullName + '</A>';
    }
  }
  document.write(result);
}
//================================================================
// Global Variables
//================================================================
/*-------------------------------------------------------------
FaveList will be a list of all favorite objects, which are
then declared below.  favorites with an empty urlpath property
are section headings
-------------------------------------------------------------*/
var FaveList = new Array();
// Comics Section -----------------
FaveList[1] = new favorite("Comics", "", "");
FaveList[2] = new favorite("Dilbert", "cdilb",
  "http://www.unitedmedia.com/comics/dilbert/");
FaveList[3] = new favorite("Doonesbury", "cdoon",
  "http://www.uexpress.com/cgi-bin/ups/mainindex.cgi?code=db");
FaveList[4] = new favorite("Mr. Boffo", "cboff",
  "http://www.uexpress.com/cgi-bin/ups/new_mainindex.cgi?code=mb");
// General News Section -----------
FaveList[5] = new favorite("General News", "", "");
FaveList[6] = new favorite("CNN", "ncnn", "http://www.cnn.com/");
FaveList[7] = new favorite("NPR", "nnpr",
  "http://www.npr.org/news/");
FaveList[8] = new favorite("Boston Globe Quick Read", "nbos",
  "http://www.boston.com/globe/print/print.htm");
// Computer Industry Section --------
FaveList[9] = new favorite("Computer Industry", "", "");
FaveList[10] = new favorite("PC Week", "ipcw",
  "http://www.pcweek.com/");
FaveList[11] = new favorite("Infoworld", "iinfo",
  "http://www.infoworld.com/");
FaveList[12] = new favorite("CMP TechWire", "icmp",
  "http://www.techweb.com/wire/wire.html");
// Search Engines Section ----------
FaveList[13] = new favorite("Search Engines", "", "");
FaveList[14] = new favorite("Yahoo!", "syah",
  "http://www.yahoo.com/");
FaveList[15] = new favorite("Alta Vista", "sav",
  "http://www.altavista.com/");
FaveList[16] = new favorite("excite", "sexc",
  "http://www.excite.com/");
// Misc. Section ------------------
FaveList[17] = new favorite("Misc.", "", "");
```

```
FaveList[18] = new favorite("Stock Quotes/Graphs", "mstock",
  "https://quotes.galt.com/cgi-bin/stockclnt");
FaveList[19] = new favorite("Today in History", "mtih",
  "http://www.thehistorynet.com/today/today.htm");
FaveList[20] = new favorite("Merriam-Webster's Word of the Day",
  "mwod", "http://www.m-w.com/cgi-bin/mwwod.pl");
FaveList[21] = new favorite("Quotes of the Day", "mquot",
  "http://www.starlingtech.com/quotes/qotd.html");
FaveList[22] = new favorite("Top 10 List", "mtop",
  "http://www.cbs.com/lateshow/lists/");
//===============================================================
// Page Writing Routines
//===============================================================
//---------------------------------------------------------------
// SendOptionsPage - Writes a page allowing the user to select
//                   her favorite preferences
//---------------------------------------------------------------
function SendOptionsPage() {
  document.write('<H1>Select Favorites</H1>');
  document.write('<FORM METHOD=POST>');
  // Here's the button for viewing the Favorites page
  document.write('<INPUT TYPE=button VALUE="Show Favorites" '
                 + 'onClick="'
                 +'ReloadPage()'
                 +';">');
  // The links will look nicer inside a definition list
  document.write('<DL>');
  for (var i = 1; i < FaveList.length; i++)
    FaveList[i].WriteAsCheckBox();  // Write each checkbox
  document.write('</DL><P>');
  ClearCookie("ViewAll");
  document.write('</FORM>');
}
//---------------------------------------------------------------
// LoadOptions - Sets the ShowOptions cookie, which makes the
//               option selection page appear when the page is
//               then reloaded.
//---------------------------------------------------------------
function LoadOptions() {
  SetCookieEZ("ShowOptions", "T");
  window.open(document.location.href, "_top", "");
}
//---------------------------------------------------------------
// ToggleView - Toggles ViewAll mode on and off.  When on, all
//              links will be displayed.  When off, only the
//              user's favorite selections will be displayed.
//---------------------------------------------------------------
function ToggleView() {
  if (GetCookie("ViewAll") == "T") {
    ClearCookie("ViewAll");
  } else {
    var fiveYears = 5 * 365 * 24 * 60 * 60 * 1000;
    var expDate = new Date();
    expDate.setTime (expDate.getTime() + fiveYears );
    SetCookie("ViewAll", "T", expDate, null, null, false);
  }
  window.open(document.location.href, "_top", "");
}
```

continues

Listing 25.2. continued

```
//------------------------------------------------------------------
// SendPersonalPage - Writes a page showing the categories and
//                    links which the user prefers. Only shows a
//                    heading if one of its favorites is enabled
//------------------------------------------------------------------
function SendPersonalPage() {
  if (GetCookie("ViewAll") != "T")
    document.write('<H1>Your Favorites:</H1>');
  else
    document.write('<H1>Links:</H1>');
  // Here are the buttons for viewing the options or
  // "View All" pages
  document.write('<FORM METHOD=POST>');
  if (GetCookie("ViewAll") == "T") {
    document.write('<INPUT TYPE=button VALUE="View Favorites" '
                   +'onClick="ToggleView();">')
  } else {
    document.write('<INPUT TYPE=button VALUE="View All" '
                   +'onClick="ToggleView();">');
  }
  document.write('<INPUT TYPE=button '
                 + 'VALUE="Select Personal Favorites" '
                 + 'onClick="LoadOptions();">');
  document.write('</FORM>');
  // The links will look nicer inside a definition list
  document.write('<DL>');
  for (var i = 1; i < FaveList.length; i++)
    FaveList[i].WriteAsWebLink();    // Write each link
  document.write('</DL><P>');
}
//==================================================================
// Helper Functions
//==================================================================
//------------------------------------------------------------------
// isEnabled - Returns True if the favorite identified by the
//             name parameter is enabled.
//------------------------------------------------------------------
function isEnabled(name) {
  var result = false;
  var FaveCookie = GetCookie("Favorites");
  if (FaveCookie != null) {
    var searchFor = "<" + name + ">";
    var startOfCookie = FaveCookie.indexOf(searchFor)
    if (startOfCookie != -1)
      result = true;
  }
  return result;
}
//------------------------------------------------------------------
// AddFavorite- Enables the favorite identified by the name
//              parameter.
//------------------------------------------------------------------
function AddFavorite(name) {
  if (!isEnabled(name)) {
    var fiveYears = 5 * 365 * 24 * 60 * 60 * 1000;
    var expDate = new Date();
    expDate.setTime (expDate.getTime() + fiveYears );
```

```
      SetCookie("Favorites", GetCookie("Favorites")
            + "<" + name + ">", expDate, null, null, false);
  }
}
//----------------------------------------------------------------
// ClearFavorite- Disables the favorite identified by the name
//                parameter.
//----------------------------------------------------------------
function ClearFavorite(name) {
  if (isEnabled(name)) {
    var FaveCookie = GetCookie("Favorites");
    var searchFor = "<" + name + ">";
    var startOfCookie = FaveCookie.indexOf(searchFor);
    var NewFaves = FaveCookie.substring(0, startOfCookie)
      + FaveCookie.substring(startOfCookie+searchFor.length,
                                        FaveCookie.length);
    var fiveYears = 5 * 365 * 24 * 60 * 60 * 1000;
    var expDate = new Date();
    expDate.setTime (expDate.getTime() + fiveYears );
    SetCookie("Favorites", NewFaves, expDate, null, null, false);
  }
}
//----------------------------------------------------------------
// SetFavoriteEnabled - Turns the favorite identified by the name
//                      parameter on (SetOn=true) or off
//                      (SetOn=false).
//----------------------------------------------------------------
function SetFavoriteEnabled(name, SetOn) {
  if (SetOn)
    AddFavorite(name);
  else
    ClearFavorite(name);
}
//----------------------------------------------------------------
// ReloadPage - Reloads the page
//----------------------------------------------------------------
function ReloadPage() {
  window.open(document.location.href, "_top", "");
}

// End Commented Script -->
</SCRIPT>
</HEAD>
<BODY>
<SCRIPT LANGUAGE="JavaScript">
<!-- Comment out script from browsers that don't know JavaScript
/*----------------------------------------------------------------
Here's where we select the page to send.  Normally we send the
personalized favorites page (by calling SendPersonalPage). However,
If the cookie ShowOptions is set, we'll send the options selection
page instead (by calling SendOptionsPage).
----------------------------------------------------------------*/
  if (GetCookie("ShowOptions") == "T") {
    ClearCookie("ShowOptions");
    SendOptionsPage();
  } else {
    SendPersonalPage();
  }
```

continues

Listing 25.2. continued

```
// End Commented Script -->
</SCRIPT>
<CENTER>
This is a very dull page unless you have a JavaScript
enabled browser.<BR>
</CENTER>
</BODY>
</HTML>
```

FIGURE 25.1.

The Favorites page.

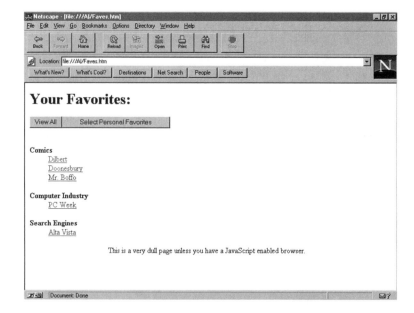

Before JavaScript, a task like this would have been handled at the server. Each hit would have involved having the server run some type of script or program to read the user's cookies and generate his page on-the-fly. With JavaScript, all this processing takes place on the client's browser. The server just downloads the static page, and it might not even do that, because the page might come from the client's local cache. When the page is loaded, all the links, selected or not, are sent. The client, with the help of cookies and JavaScript, decides which ones to show the user.

This program makes use of three different cookies. The "Favorites" cookie contains a unique code for each favored link. The "ViewAll" cookie toggles between showing the user's favorites and all possible links. The program may also display either of two pages: one for displaying the selected links, and the other for changing the configuration and options. When the "ShowOptions" cookie is set, the Options selection page is displayed. Otherwise, the regular page is shown. Figure 25.2 shows what the configuration page looks like.

FIGURE 25.2.
*The Favorites
configuration page.*

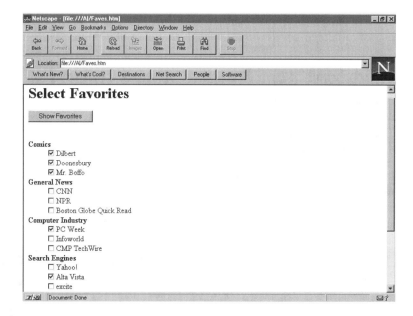

The program creates objects called—you guessed it—"Favorites." Each favorite is, in essence, a Web link to another page. The favorite contains information on the link's URL, a user-friendly page description, and the code that identifies it in the Favorites cookie string. The favorite also knows how to print itself on a Web page as a regular link for the Favorites page or in a checkbox format for the options page.

Where Are Cookies Going?

As mentioned earlier, cookies were designed and first implemented by Netscape. However, the Internet Engineering Task Force (IETF) has a committee, the Hypertext Transfer Protocol (HTTP) Working Group, whose charter is to examine, document, and suggest ways to improve HTTP.

RESOURCE

You can find a link to the HTTP Working Group's latest Internet Draft called "Proposed HTTP State Management Mechanism" at http://www.ietf.cnri.reston.va.us/html.charters/http-charter.html.

Although the draft specification resembles Netscape cookies in theory, if not in syntax, it does have a few notable differences. It doesn't encourage having cookies around much longer than the browser session. If the new specification is accepted, cookies are given a Max-Age lifetime rather than an expires date. All cookies expire when their time comes, but in all cases, they go away when the browser shuts down.

Reading the specification provides insight into the complexities that surround the inner workings of cookies; it is well worth the read, regardless of whether the specification is approved.

Which Servers and Browsers Support Cookies?

Although other ways of Web programming, such as CGI and special server interfaces, require that the server as well as the browser understand cookies, only the browser matters to JavaScript. This means that you can generally use JavaScript with impunity as long as you know your clients are JavaScript-capable.

However, many JavaScript Web applications probably mix the language with other development tools, which would require the server to understand cookies. Because new servers and browsers are coming to the Net so quickly, it's impossible for a printed book to keep up with the latest software.

RESOURCE

You can find cookie information at the following locations on the Web:

Netscape cookie spec page: `http://www.netscape.com/newsref/std/cookie_spec.html`

Browsers supporting cookies: `http://www.research.digital.com/nsl/formtest/stats-by-test/NetscapeCookie.html`

Cookie Central: `http://www.cookiecentral.com/`

Andy's cookie pages: `http://www.illuminatus.com/cookie`

Web servers that support cookies (also from Andy): `http://www.illuminatus.com/cookie_pages/servers.html`

Web browsers that support cookies from Digital: `http://www.research.digital.com/nsl/formtest/stats-by-test/NetscapeCookie.html`

Malcolm's Guide to Persistent Cookies: `http://www.emf.net/~mal/cookiesinfo.html`

Robert Brooks' Cookie Taste Test: `http://www.geocities.com/SoHo/4535/cookie.html`

Article about tracking cookies at the HotWired Web site: `http://www.arctic.org/~dgaudet/cookies`

Netscape World cookie article: `http://www.netscapeworld.com/netscapeworld/nw-07-1996/nw-07-cookies.html`

Other State Maintenance Options

As mentioned earlier in this chapter, there are a few drawbacks to using cookies. Perhaps you would rather just avoid the controversy and find some other way to maintain state from one page to the next. There are two ways of doing this. Which one you use depends on how you, the developer, will have the users get from one page to the next.

The main limitation of these methods is that they work only from one page to the page immediately following. If state information is to be maintained throughout a series of pages, these mechanisms must be used on every single page.

Query String

If most of your navigation is done through hypertext links embedded in your pages, you need to add extra information to the end of the URL. This is usually done by adding a question mark (?) to the end of your Web page URL, followed by information in an encoded form, such as that returned by the escape method. To separate one piece of information from another, place an ampersand (&) between them.

For example, if you want to send the parameters color=blue and size=extra large along with your link, you use a link like the following:

```
<a href="/mypage.html?color=blue&size=extra+large">XL Blue</A>
```

This format is the same as the format used when submitting forms using the get method. A succeeding page can read this information by using the search property of the location object. This property is called search because many Internet search engines use this part of the URL to store their search criteria.

The following is an example of how to use the location.search property. In this example, the name of the current page is sent as a parameter in a link to another page. The other page reads this property through the search property and states where the browser came from.

To start things off, Listing 25.3 shows the first page that contains the link.

Listing 25.3. Where1.htm.

```
<html>
<head>
<title>Where Was I? - Page 1</title>
</head>
<body>
<h1>Where Was I? - Demonstration</h1>
This page sets information which will allow the page it is linked
to figure out where it came from. It uses values embedded in the link
URL in order to do this
<p>
```

25

COOKIES AND STATE MAINTENANCE

continues

Listing 25.3. continued

```
We'll assume that any URL parameters are separated by an ampersand.
<p>
Notice that there doesn't need to be any JavaScript code in this page.
<p>
And now,
<a href="where2.htm?camefrom=Where1.htm
    &more=needless+stuff">Let's go to Page 2.</a>
</body>
</html>
```

Listing 25.4 shows the second page, which demonstrates how to use `location.search` to find where the browser came from.

Listing 25.4. Where2.htm.

```
<html>
<title>Where Was I? - Page 2</title>
<head>
</head>
<body>
<h1>Where Was I? - Demontration</h1>
This page reads information which allows it to figure out where it came from.
<P>
<script language="javascript">
<!-- begin script
// WhereWasI
// Reads the search string to figure out what link brought it here
function WhereWasI() {
  // Start by storing our search string in a handy place (so we don't
  // need to type as much)
  var handyString = window.location.search;
  // Find the beginning of our special URL variable
  var startOfSource = handyString.indexOf("camefrom=");
  // If it's there, find the end of it
  if (startOfSource != -1) {
    var endOfSource = handyString.indexOf("&", startOfSource+9);
    var result = handyString.substring(startOfSource+9, endOfSource);
  }
  else
    var result = "Source Unknown"; // Could not find the "camefrom" string
  return result;
}
if (WhereWasI() != "Source Unknown")
  document.write ("You just came from <b>" + WhereWasI() + "</b>.<br>")
else
  document.write ("Unfortunately, we don't know where you came from.<br>");
// end script -->
</script>
</body>
</html>
```

Hidden Form Variables

The method used in the preceding section works fine as long as the user navigates from one page to another using links. In order to do the same thing with forms, you can use hidden form variables instead of the `location.search` parameter.

Hidden form variables have the following format:

```
<input type="hidden" name="HiddenFieldName" value="HiddenFieldValue">
```

You can specify whatever you like for *HiddenFieldName* and *HiddenFieldValue*. The `value` parameter is optional.

Using hidden fields doesn't necessarily require the use of JavaScript code. They are defined instead in the `INPUT` tag of normal HTML documents. You do, however, need to have some sort of server-based script, such as a CGI program or a server API program, in order to read the values of these hidden fields.

The form containing the hidden variables is submitted to a server script, which spills out everything it knows about your browser onto a single Web page, including the form's field information. You find your hidden field information listed at the bottom of the page, where it looks like this:

```
Form Post Data:
Raw Form Data String: camefrom=where3.htm&otherStuff=I+don%27t+care
camefrom=where3.htm
otherStuff=I don't care
```

Summary

In this chapter, you learned about a number of useful techniques for maintaining state between pages of a Web application. Cookies are the most powerful method.

Cookies allow you to store information on the client computer and use it from within your Internet application to store values and other critical pieces of information. Because of the nature of cookies, they can be used for a range of reasons, from the simplest form of `name=value` pairs to the more advanced forms of cookie use.

Although cookies represent the most powerful method of accomplishing state maintenance, other approaches, such as URL query string parameters and hidden fields in forms, are also available.

VII

PART

JavaScript Connectivity

CHAPTER 26

LiveConnect: Integrating JavaScript and Java

IN THIS CHAPTER

One of JavaScript's most powerful features is its capability to interact with Java. JavaScript scripts may invoke Java methods, examine and modify Java variables, and control Java applets. Java applets, in turn, may access JavaScript methods, properties, and data structures. Applications can also use JavaScript and Java to create dynamic content. HTML can be generated on-the-fly within JavaScript scripts and Java applets and displayed in browser windows by constructing `javascript:` URLs.

Running Java Applets

JavaScript scripts communicate with Java applets running in an HTML page by accessing members (methods and fields) of the Java objects associated with those applets. Any Java method declared with the `public` modifier is available to be called from JavaScript, and any Java field declared as `public` is available to be examined or modified. The first step in communicating with a Java applet from JavaScript is to obtain a reference to the applet. Once that's accomplished, you can directly access any of the applet's public members.

Referencing Applets

Applets running in a document are reflected in JavaScript within the document's `applets` array. For example, the first applet defined in the current document could be referenced from JavaScript as `document.applets[0]`. The same applet could also be referenced by name as `document.applets["appletName"]`, or simply `document.appletName` if its name were specified in the applet tag. An applet's name can be specified in the applet tag by giving a value to the `name` attribute. For example, this tag

```
<applet name="myApplet" code="testApplet.class" width=100 height=100 MAYSCRIPT>
</applet>
```

would create an applet of class `testApplet` named `myApplet`. If that applet also happened to be the first applet on the page, it could be referenced by `document.applets[0]`, `document.applets["myApplet"]`, or `document.myApplet`.

JavaScript scripts may also reference Java applets running in other frames in the same browser window. For example, if a Java applet were running in a frame called `frame1`, it could be referenced from a sibling frame as `parent.frame1.document.myApplet`.

Controlling Applets

Once a reference to an applet has been obtained, the next step is to communicate with it by invoking one of its methods. For example, if the applet had a public method called `hello()` that took no arguments, that method could be called like this:

```
document.myApplet.hello();
```

Making that call from within JavaScript has precisely the same effect as calling the applet object's `hello()` method from within Java. As another example, suppose you have a Java applet with an audio soundtrack, and you want to turn the sound on and off from JavaScript. If the applet provided methods such as the following, you could call those methods from JavaScript to control the applet's soundtrack:

```
public void soundtrackOn();
public void soundtrackOff();
```

If you wanted to make toggling the soundtrack on and off as simple as clicking a mouse button, you could use JavaScript as "wiring" to hook up radio buttons in an HTML form to the Java applet. The following example shows how a form element's `onclick` method can be used to communicate with the applet:

```
<form>
<input type="radio" checked="true" name="sound"
onclick="document.myApplet.soundtrackOn()">On<br>
<input type="radio" name="sound"
onclick="document.myApplet.soundtrackOff()">Off<br>
</form>
```

The values for the `onclick` event handlers specify that the `soundtrackOn()` or `soundtrackOff()` method of the applet named `myApplet` is called whenever the corresponding radio button is clicked. As a slightly more complicated example (which illustrates passing arguments to Java methods), suppose the applet also has a method with a prototype of

```
public void changeText(String s);
```

which, when called, changes the text displayed by the applet to the value specified by string s. If the following elements were added to the form

```
<input type="text" name="newtext">
<input type="button" value="Change Text"
    onclick="document.myApplet.changeText(form.newtext.value)">
```

users could enter new strings into the text input field and have them reflected in the applet. When the Change Text button is clicked, the text field's value is extracted, converted to a Java String, and passed as the argument to the applet's `changeText()` method. This is a powerful paradigm. The ability to pass JavaScript objects to Java methods makes it possible to quickly and easily build attractive GUIs out of standard HTML forms augmented with JavaScript event handlers and to use them to control Java applets.

JavaScript Objects in Java

One of the most difficult and confusing aspects of calling Java methods from JavaScript can be getting the types of the arguments you pass to Java to match up with the types of the arguments the Java method is looking for. If the two sets of arguments don't match exactly, the attempted function call fails, and you get an error message saying that JavaScript couldn't find a Java method that was expecting the arguments you tried to pass.

Java is a strongly typed language (meaning that every variable has a specific, declared type), and all Java methods must declare, in advance, how many arguments they are expecting, of what type, and in what order. Within a Java program, any attempt to invoke a method with an argument sequence that doesn't exactly match, type for type, the method's declared argument sequence results in a compile-time error.

JavaScript, in contrast, has much more relaxed typing, and, as an interpreted language, must do all its checking at runtime anyway. JavaScript variables don't have a declared type; in fact, they don't have to be declared at all, because they can simply come into existence by being referenced. The same JavaScript variable can be assigned a string in one statement, an integer in the next statement, and an array in the next. How, then, are JavaScript objects converted into Java objects when they're passed to Java methods? How does Java know how to find a Java type that exactly matches the JavaScript object's structure? The short answer is that, in general, it doesn't. There probably is no such object. Unless the object happens to fall into one of the following exceptional cases, Java won't necessarily have a class that exactly mirrors the object's JavaScript type, so it simply assigns it a default type, `JSObject`, specifically designed to represent JavaScript objects in Java.

Fortunately, the aforementioned exceptional cases encompass some of the most common and useful data types, including JavaScript's three basic data types: strings, numbers, and Booleans. JavaScript strings (that is, string constants and variables that have most recently been assigned strings) appear in Java as instances of the Java `String` type. JavaScript numbers (numeric constants and variables most recently assigned integer or real numeric values) are converted to Java `Double` objects. JavaScript Boolean values (`true` and `false`) become Java `Boolean` objects. One other special case concerns JavaScript objects that are "wrappers" around Java objects. Such objects are simply "unwrapped" and converted to their original Java types.

Although this fact is currently undocumented, there is additional flexibility in passing JavaScript numbers directly to Java methods. An attempt to make a call such as

```
document.myApplet.setNumber(3.7);
```

would succeed if the `myApplet` applet had a method with a signature of

```
public void setNumber(type x);
```

where *type* is one of the following: `Double`, `double`, `float`, `long`, `int`, `short`, `char`, or `byte`, even though the documentation implies that only `Double` ought to be acceptable. Sources at Netscape say the documentation will be changed to reflect the actual behavior, and not the other way around. In cases where the applet has more than one overloaded method expecting one of these types, the first such method (the method closest to the top of the Java source file) is chosen. Tie-breaking by lexicographic location is probably not the best way to resolve conflicts between overloaded methods, and it is very likely that some other mechanism will be devised.

TIP

At the time this book was printed, the rules that govern the translation of JavaScript numbers into Java objects were being revised. Be sure to check current JavaScript documentation for the latest rules.

Working with JSObjects

Because complex JavaScript objects such as arrays and `window` objects are reflected in Java as objects of type `JSObject`, it's important to know how to manipulate these objects and extract information from them. When a `JSObject` represents a JavaScript array, it's useful to be able to examine the individual array elements, and when a `JSObject` represents a JavaScript `window`, `document`, `history`, or similar object, it's useful to be able to examine its properties.

It might at first seem tempting to avoid the whole issue by dissecting objects on the JavaScript side and breaking them into sets of simpler objects. Once broken apart, the elements could be sent to Java as sets of simple objects that would be translated into Java `String`, `Double`, and `Boolean` objects. The major drawback to that approach, other than being a lot of extra work, is that it leaves no way to handle objects of variable size. If it wasn't known, in advance, how many elements an array might have, there would be no way to pass each individual element to a Java method, because Java methods take a number of arguments that are fixed at compile-time. It's probably a better idea to simply pass complex JavaScript objects into Java "as is" and learn how to deal with them there.

NOTE

Be sure to include the `MAYSCRIPT` attribute in the applet tag of any applet you want to operate on `JSObject` objects. Without it, an applet doesn't have access to JavaScript objects and properties. This safeguard was designed to let HTML authors include untrusted Java applets on their pages without having to worry that those applets might have access to potentially sensitive information available only in JavaScript.

To make a concrete example out of such a situation, suppose that you wanted to use JavaScript as a GUI for a Java point-plotting applet. With the following variable and function declarations:

```
<script language="JavaScript">
var xvals = new Array();
var yvals = new Array();
function addPoint(x, y)
{
```

```
        xvals[xvals.length] = x;
        yvals[yvals.length] = y;
}
function plotPoints()
{
    document.myApplet.plotPoints(xvals, yvals);
}
</script>
```

and the following HTML form augmented with event handlers:

```
<form>
<input type=text name="xval">
<input type=text name="yval"><br>
<input type=button value="Add Point"
onclick="addPoint(form.xval.value, form.yval.value)"><br>
<input type=button value="Plot Points" onclick="plotPoints()">
</form>
```

you could collect (x,y) coordinate pairs using the two text input fields and the addPoint() function and then send them to the applet in one big batch using the plotPoints() function.

Doing things that way would allow you to send an arbitrary number of points to the applet to be plotted but would require dissection of the point arrays from within Java. This example's plotPoints() Java method is a good representation of things you can do with JSObjects. It might look something like this:

```
public void plotPoints(JSObject xvals, JSObject yvals)
{
    Double length = (Double) xvals.getMember("length");
    int n = Math.round(length.doubleValue());
    for (int i = 0; i < n; i++)
        try
        {
            String sx = (String) xvals.getSlot(i);
            String sy = (String) yvals.getSlot(i);
Double x = new Double(sx);
            Double y = new Double(sy);
            doPlot(x, y);
        }
        catch (NumberFormatException e)
            System.err.println("Illegal point specification");
}
```

Let's take a closer look at the relevant parts of that program, line by line.

```
public void plotPoints(JSObject xvals, JSObject yvals)
```

This method is expecting two JSObjects, an array of x-coordinates, and an array of y-coordinates. Note that the JavaScript arrays, even numeric ones, don't show up in Java as arrays of one of Java's built-in numeric types. If the function had instead been written with the signature

```
public void plotPoints(double[] xvals, double[] yvals)
```

or something similar, any attempt to call it from JavaScript would have failed. You're stuck with the JSObjects, then, instead of the numeric arrays you might have preferred.

```
Double length = (Double) xvals.getMember("length");
```

This call to getMember() is the first step in converting the arguments from the form in which they were passed into a more usable form. The getMember() method is used to obtain the length property of one of the array objects (the two arrays have the same length). getMember() returns a generic Java Object (the base class for all Java objects), so you need to cast it to a more appropriate and useful type. You know that the length property of JavaScript arrays is a numeric property, and you should recall that JavaScript numbers are reflected in Java as Doubles, so the object returned by getMember() is cast to a Double object. Note that there is no flexibility in the type chosen here; numbers obtained from JSObjects *must* be cast to Double. It is only when JavaScript numeric values are passed directly to Java as function arguments that they can initially appear as Java types other than Double.

```
int n = Math.round(length.doubleValue());
```

Although this statement doesn't directly involve any JSObjects, it does demonstrate a useful idiom for converting JavaScript numbers into useful Java numeric types. Programmers often find themselves in possession of Double objects when they're more interested in other types, so it can become necessary to convert them. In this case, the Double object's doubleValue() method is used to extract the actual numeric value, and the Math package's round() method to obtain the integer closest to that value.

```
String sx = (String) x.getSlot(i);
String sy = (String) y.getSlot(i);
```

Inside the loop, you need a way to obtain the numeric value of each element of the JSObject objects representing the xvals and yvals arrays. Here the getSlot() method is used to extract the individual element at a given array index. getSlot() takes an integer argument and returns the JavaScript object located at that index. getSlot(), like getMember(), returns a generic Java Object, so again it needs to be cast to a more useful type. You know that the xvals and yvals arrays are populated with JavaScript strings, so Java Strings are the correct type to use in this case. It may seem counterintuitive at first, because you've been thinking of the array elements as numbers, but String really is the correct cast to make. Remember that the values with which the arrays are populated were originally obtained from text input fields in an HTML form. In JavaScript, just because a string happens to look like a number (consisting entirely of digits) doesn't automatically mean that it is a number.

```
Double x = new Double(sx);
Double y = new Double(sy);
```

You need a way to convert strings that look like numbers into actual numbers, and this Double constructor fits the bill nicely. It takes a String as an argument, and returns a Double object corresponding to the double-precision floating-point value represented by the String. If the String doesn't represent a numeric value, a NumberFormatException is thrown, which is why these statements are wrapped in a try block. If an exception is thrown, the attempt to plot this point is aborted, and the next iteration of the loop begins.

```
doPlot(x, y);
```

This is where, having extracted the useful (x,y) coordinate values from the JSObjects, the call is made to the hypothetical low-level point-plotting method.

Although an exhaustive explanation of the JSObject class is beyond the scope of this book, one more example should help show off a few more of its methods. Suppose that you wanted to add a method to the applet that plots all the points the user had typed into the form so far, without waiting for the user to explicitly click the "Plot Points" button. A method like the following would allow the applet to venture out into the JavaScript world and inspect the relevant JavaScript objects whenever it wanted:

```
private void getPoints()
{
    // Get the window and the document.
    JSObject window = JSObject.getWindow(this);
    JSObject document = (JSObject) window.getMember("document");
    // Get the point arrays.
JSObject xvals = (JSObject) document.getMember("xvals");
    JSObject yvals = (JSObject) docuemnt.getMember("yvals");
    // Now, just call plotPoints()
    plotPoints(xvals, yvals);
}
```

Let's take a closer look at the lines in that program that introduce new methods or concepts not found in the preceding example.

```
private void getPoints()
```

Notice that this method is private—it isn't intended to be called from JavaScript. Notice also that it takes no arguments, because all the information necessary to complete its task is contained within JavaScript. The whole point of this exercise is that Java applets are free to seek objects and properties from JavaScript without waiting for some user action on the JavaScript side to start the ball rolling.

```
JSObject window = JSObject.getWindow(this);
```

The JSObject class has a static method called getWindow(), which can be used by an applet to obtain the JavaScript window object corresponding to the window that contains the applet. The object returned is simply the same object denoted by window in JavaScript. getWindow() is a particularly important and useful method, because it is the only way a Java applet can obtain a "new" JSObject (that is, a JSObject not derived from another, pre-existing JSObject) without being passed one explicitly from JavaScript; the JSObject class has no public constructors. The argument to getWindow() is the applet object itself.

```
JSObject document = (JSObject) window.getMember("document");
```

Once the window object is obtained, the `getMember()` method is used to extract a property by name. In this case, that property is the window's `document` object, the object denoted by `window.document` in JavaScript. The reason for this is that the variables `xvals` and `yvals`, like all variables defined at "top level" scope in a JavaScript script, are properties of the `document` object. Complex JavaScript objects like the `document` object are reflected in Java as `JSObjects`, so the `Object` returned by `getMember()` is cast to that type.

```
JSObject xvals = (JSObject) document.getMember("xvals");
JSObject yvals = (JSObject) document.getMember("yvals");
```

Once you have the `document` object, you can begin to extract the variables you're looking for. The `getMember()` method can once again be used for this purpose. The `xvals` and `yvals` objects are JavaScript arrays, which are reflected in Java as `JSObjects`, so the `Objects` returned by `getMember()` are again cast to that type.

```
plotPoints(xvals, yvals);
```

Now that you've obtained the `JSObjects` representing the `xvals` and `yvals` arrays, you can call the `plotPoints()` method from within Java, exactly as you would have called it from JavaScript.

Two other noteworthy methods of the `JSObject` class are `call()` and `eval()`, which have the following prototypes:

```
public Object call(String methodName, Object args[]);
public Object eval(String s);
```

`call()` calls its object's *methodName* method with arguments given by the `args` array. It is equivalent to calling

```
this.methodName(arg[0], arg[1], ...);
```

from within JavaScript. For example, the following within an applet

```
JSObject window = JSObject.getWindow(this);
Object args[] = { "Hello, world!" };
window.call("alert", args);
```

is equivalent to the following JavaScript:

```
alert("Hello, world! ");
```

An object's `eval()` method evaluates its argument string as a JavaScript expression. Evaluation occurs within the context of the object. Replacing the last line in the preceding example with

```
window.eval("alert('Hello, world! ')");
```

yields the same result. Note the use of single quotes inside the double quotes.

Setting Java Properties

Although it's usually not good programming style for Java classes to expose their data members (also called properties or fields) to direct outside access by declaring them `public`, occasionally situations arise when it can be useful to do so. When Java applets have public fields, JavaScript scripts have the power to directly modify them, just as they have the power to invoke public Java methods. For example, consider the following fragment of a Java applet:

```
public String theText;
public void setText(String s)
{
    theText = s;
}
```

It is probably better programming practice to set the text like the following:

```
document.myApplet.setText("Hello world!");
```

It would be equally possible to just write:

```
document.myApplet.theText = "Hello world!";
```

The same rules that govern translation of JavaScript objects into Java objects during function calls also apply here. This implies, by the way, that only the Java `String`, `Double`, `Boolean`, `JSObject`, and primitive numeric types can be directly set in this way, because all JavaScript variables are initially reflected in Java as one of those types.

Java Objects in JavaScript

Until now, this chapter has only discussed the problem of sending objects from JavaScript into Java. It is equally possible, however, to send objects the other way. Suppose you rewrote the `setText()` method to be a little more picky about acceptable values for `theText`, and you wanted a way to find out whether a given call to `setText()` had resulted in `theText` being successfully set. If you designed the new function to return a Boolean flag indicating success or failure, it might look something like this:

```
public boolean setText(String s)
{
    if (s.equals("Hello world!"))
{
        // I'm sick of that string; don't accept it.
        return false;
}
    else
{
        theText = s;
        return true;
}
}
```

If you wrote a JavaScript script that included this line:

```
var changed = document.myApplet.setText("Hello world!")
```

the value returned by `setText()` would be stored in `changed`. The question remains, though: Exactly how will the Java `boolean` value returned by `setText()` be converted into a JavaScript object? In this particular case, the answer is simple and intuitive: Java `boolean` values become

JavaScript Boolean values when they're returned to JavaScript. Passing Java objects to JavaScript isn't always quite so simple—a number of rules govern the exact translation for a given object—but the good news is that things often work out just the way you might hope. Java arrays become JavaScript arrays, Java numeric types become JavaScript numbers, Java `boolean` values become JavaScript Boolean values, and Java `Strings` become JavaScript strings. For completeness, here is the entire set of rules used to govern the conversion:

- Java numeric types (`byte`, `char`, `double`, `float`, `int`, `long`, `short`) become JavaScript numbers.

- Java `boolean` values become JavaScript Boolean values.

- Java `JSObjects` are converted back to their original JavaScript objects.

- Java arrays become JavaScript array objects.

- All other Java objects are converted to JavaScript "wrapper" objects that can be used to access the original Java members.

When an attempt is made to convert a JavaScript "wrapper" into a JavaScript string, number, or Boolean, the original Java object's `toString()`, `doubleValue()`, or `booleanValue()` method, if it exists, is called, and the value of the converted object is the value returned by the corresponding method. If the corresponding method doesn't exist, the conversion fails. Note that Java strings work as expected in JavaScript, even though they're technically passed to JavaScript as "wrapper" objects. Any attempt to use one in a context where a JavaScript string is expected causes the correct conversion to be applied.

Using Java Packages

JavaScript's ability to interact with Java isn't limited to applets. JavaScript scripts also have direct access to static methods and fields of core Java packages, and they may even construct new Java objects. Java packages are available in JavaScript within the containing document's `Packages` array. For example, Java's `java.lang.System` package, which can be used for console I/O, can be referenced in JavaScript as `Packages.java.lang.System`, and Java's `java.lang.Math` package can be referenced as `Packages.java.lang.Math`. As a result, to write the value of pi to the Java console, you could use the following:

```
var pi = Packages.java.lang.Math.PI;
Packages.java.lang.System.out.println("pi is: " + pi);
```

As a special shorthand, references to three of the most common packages—`java`, `sun`, and `netscape`—may safely omit the `Packages` keyword. That is, within a JavaScript document object, `java`, `sun`, and `netscape` are aliases for `Packages.java`, `Packages.sun`, and `Packages.netscape`, respectively. Using those aliases, it is possible to rewrite the pi-printing example as the following:

```
var pi = java.lang.Math.PI;
java.lang.System.out.println("pi is: " + pi);
```

It's also possible to dynamically construct new Java objects, using the new operator. This is a handy way to access some of Java's powerful built-in utility classes—hash tables, stacks, vectors, dates, and more—without having to write an entire Java applet. In the following JavaScript example, two Java Date objects are constructed, and they are compared using the after method of the Date class to see if the current date is after the deadline.

```
var theDate = new java.util.Date(); // the current date
var deadline = new java.util.Date(96, 6, 26); // July 26, 1996
if (theDate.after(deadline))
    alert("I missed my deadline!");
else
    alert("Made it!");
```

Using a Java Dialog Box

Many JavaScript developers have complained that the dialog windows offered by JavaScript are limited. There is no way to open the JavaScript prompt dialog without the title bar's saying "Netscape User Prompt." Furthermore, the caption always begins with "JavaScript Prompt:" followed by the text that you want to display. Preventing completely customized dialogs has been done for security reasons but results in terrible-looking dialogs. One alternative is to use a custom Java applet to display a dialog box and have it return data to your JavaScript program using LiveConnect. This allows you to display exactly what you want in the title bar and caption. The following sections show how to use LiveConnect and the DialogServer applet to display a custom dialog window.

> **RESOURCE**
>
> The DialogServer applet and its associated classes can be found on the CD-ROM that comes with this book. Further updates to the DialogServer applet can be found at Acadia Software's Web site at www.acadians.com.

Listing 26.1 shows how the DialogServer applet is embedded into the LiveDialog HTML page.

Listing 26.1. Adding the DialogServer applet to an HTML page.

```
<APPLET name="DialogServer"
    code=DialogServer.class
    id=DialogServer
    width=2
    height=2
    MAYSCRIPT>
    <param name=title value="User Info">
    <param name=labelOne value="Name">
    <param name=labelTwo value="E-mail">
    <param name=message value="Initializing...">
```

```
    <param name=insetX value=150>
    <param name=insetY value=150>
</APPLET>
```

Notice how the width and height are each set to 2 pixels. This essentially hides the applet on the page. Then, when needed, JavaScript is used to tell the applet to create a new dialog window and display it to the user. The only way the user knows that the applet was loaded is if he watches the applet status messages displayed at the bottom of the Navigator window.

> **WARNING**
>
> Don't specify applet width and height parameters to be less than 2 pixels. Doing so will disable the HTML buttons for that page in Netscape Navigator 3.0.

The parameters for the applet do the following:

`title`	The text to be displayed in the title bar of the dialog window.
`labelOne`	The caption to be placed next to the first data entry field.
`labelTwo`	The caption to be placed next to the second data entry field.
`message`	The caption to be displayed above the two data entry fields.
`insetX`	The x coordinate at which to place the upper-left corner of the dialog box.
`insetY`	The y coordinate at which to place the upper-left corner of the dialog box.

Figure 26.1 shows the `LiveDialog.htm` example after it has been loaded into Netscape. As you can see, there is no sign of a dialog window yet.

FIGURE 26.1.

`LiveDialog.htm` *loaded into Netscape Navigator.*

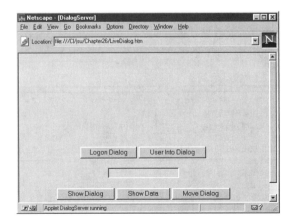

Each of the buttons in `LiveDialog.htm` accesses one or more of the DialogServer class's public methods. The following public Java methods are used by the LiveDialog HTML page:

`ShowDialog()`	Displays the dialog window.
`HideDialog()`	Closes the dialog window.
`MoveDialog(x,y)`	Moves the dialog window to a new location specified by *x* and *y*.
`GetDialogData()`	Returns a string containing the last data entered by the user, delimited by the pipe symbol (|).
`SetMessage(message)`	Displays the text specified by *message* inside the dialog window.
`SetLabels(title,labelOne,labelTwo)`	Sets the captions for the dialog window.

Opening the Dialog Window

After you click the Show Dialog button, the dialog window is shown for the first time. Its title is already set to User Info, its labels are set to Name and E-Mail, and its message is set to Initializing.... These attributes were specified by the applet's parameters. Once the dialog window has been opened, the JavaScript within `LiveDialog.htm` begins to change the message to present a "countdown" to the user. If the user doesn't finish entering the requested information before the allotted time is up, the script will close the dialog box. Listing 26.2 shows the global variables and functions used in `LiveDialog.htm` to open the applet's dialog window and alter the message.

Listing 26.2. The functions used to open the dialog window.

```
// Global variables
var gAppletData = ""
var gSecondsLeft = 10
var gTimerID = null
var gIsAppletReady = false
function initApplet() {
    if(!gIsAppletReady) {
        return
    }
    gSecondsLeft = 10
    document.forms[0].userInfo.value == ""
    document.applets[0].ShowDialog()
    gTimerID = setTimeout('countDown()',1000)
}
function countDown() {
    // Demonstrates how to update the applet.
    if(gSecondsLeft > 0) {
        gSecondsLeft--
        document.applets[0].SetMessage("You have "+
            gSecondsLeft+" seconds left.")
        gTimerID = setTimeout('countDown()',1500)
```

```
    }
    else {
        //Time's up!
        document.applets[0].HideDialog()
    }
}
```

When the user clicks the Show Dialog button, the `initApplet()` function is called. A check is then done to make sure the applet is ready for use by JavaScript. (It's important to do this preliminary check, as explained later in this chapter.) Once the number of seconds is set, the dialog is opened using the `ShowDialog()` method of the applet. The `countDown()` function is then called every second for the specified number of seconds. For each loop, the dialog window's message is updated with the remaining number of seconds. This is done using the applet's `SetMessage()` method. If `gTimerID` isn't cleared before `gSecondsLeft` reaches 0, the `HideDialog()` method is called, and the dialog window is hidden. Figure 26.2 shows the state of the dialog window after seven seconds have gone by.

FIGURE 26.2.

The dialog window after seven seconds of being open.

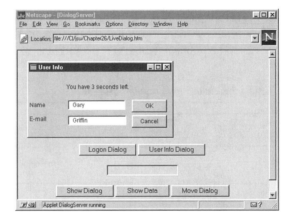

Looking only at Listing 26.2, there is no way for the countdown timer to be cleared before the time is up. Ideally, the timer should be cleared when the user clicked the OK or Cancel button on the dialog window. This is, in fact, what happens, and this is what is shown in Listing 26.3.

Listing 26.3. The `dialogOK` and `dialogCancel()` functions.

```
// Used by the DialogServer applet.
function dialogOK(field1, field2) {
    clearTimeout(gTimerID)
    alert(field1 + "," + field2)
}
function dialogCancel() {
    clearTimeout(gTimerID)
    alert("You pressed cancel")
}
```

The `dialogOK()` and `dialogCancel()` functions are included for use by the DialogServer applet. When the user clicks the OK button, the applet closes the dialog window. It then uses LiveConnect to pass the two values contained within its own data entry fields to the `dialogOK()` function. The countdown timer is cleared, and the two values are displayed in a JavaScript alert box. Figure 26.3 shows the results after some data has been entered into each data entry field and OK has been clicked. The `dialogCancel()` function is called if the user clicks Cancel. The contents of either function can be changed to react to the event in any way seen fit. However, the function names and number of arguments must remain the same.

FIGURE 26.3.

A JavaScript alert confirming a successful transfer of data.

Using DialogServer as a Logon Prompt

The LiveDialog HTML page also demonstrates how to change the title caption and field captions of the dialog window without reloading the document. The `logonLabels()` function shown in Listing 26.4 uses the public `SetLabels()` method of the applet to alter its appearance.

Listing 26.4. Setting the DialogServer captions using JavaScript.

```
function logonLabels() {
    // Change the ti
tle and field labels.
    if(!gIsAppletReady) {
        return
    }
    document.applets[0].SetLabels("Logon",
        "User Name", "Password")
}
```

> **WARNING**
>
> The DialogServer applet doesn't transmit data entered into the applet over the Internet and therefore doesn't pose any threat to security. However, if you use a script to extract the data from the applet, don't send the data over the Internet unless there is an appropriate level of security. For example, it's possible to extract the data from the applet and then fill the text fields of an HTML form. If the data can then be submitted, you might want to set up a secure session before allowing this to happen. For more information on setting up secure sessions, visit Netscape at `http://home.netscape.com`. For more information on using Java to create a secure session, visit Phaos Technology at `http://www.phaos.com/`.

The LiveDialog HTML page also allows the user to request the raw data held by the DialogServer applet. This can be done at any time by clicking the Show Data button, which calls the `getData()` function (shown in Listing 26.5). It uses the `GetDialogData()` method to extract the last data submitted by the user and assigns it to the `userInfo` text element. Figure 26.4 shows the results after the Show Data, Logon Dialog, and Show Dialog buttons have been clicked. Notice how the raw data uses the pipe symbol (|) to separate the two values.

Listing 26.5. The `getData()` function of `LiveDialog.htm`.

```
function getData() {
    // Manually extract data from the applet
    if(!gIsAppletReady) {
        return
    }
    gAppletData = document.applets[0].GetDialogData()
    document.forms[0].userInfo.value = gAppletData
}
```

FIGURE 26.4.

The dialog window after extracting the applet's data and altering its captions.

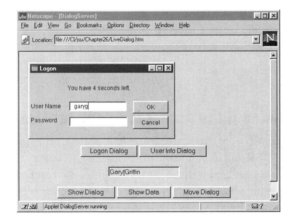

Moving the Dialog Window

The last feature of the DialogServer applet is its ability to be moved to a new location at any time using JavaScript. This can be done either before or after the dialog window has been displayed. Listing 26.6 shows the `moveDialog()` function, which is called when the Move Dialog button is clicked.

Listing 26.6. The `moveDialog()` function of `LiveDialog.htm`.

```
function moveDialog() {
    // Move dialog to specified coordinates.
    if(!gIsAppletReady) {
        return
    }
    document.applets[0].MoveDialog(250,150)
}
```

> **TIP**
>
> The coordinates are designed to be relative to the upper-left corner of the applet itself. However, be sure to test this, because you may get different results using different versions of Netscape Navigator. Figure 26.5 shows the results after moving the dialog box to the coordinates (250,150) from the location (150,150).

FIGURE 26.5.

The dialog window after being moved to (250,150).

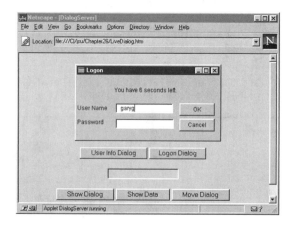

Determining if the Applet Is Ready for Use

It's important to note that the onLoad event of the document (that is, the <BODY> tag) triggers when the HTML document has finished loading, not when the applet has finished initializing. Therefore, it's possible for the user to click one of the LiveDialog buttons before the applet has been completely loaded. This can cause an error such as this:

```
Can't reflect applet "DialogServer": not loaded yet.
```

For this reason, a feature was added to the DialogServer applet that calls the predefined dialogReady() function once it's ready for use. By including this function in LiveDialog.htm (shown in Listing 26.7), you can set any variables that are needed to control access to the applet. Using the global variable gIsAppletReady, you now have an accurate way to determine if the applet is ready.

Listing 26.7. The dialogReady() function of LiveDialog.htm.

```
// Used by the DialogServer applet.
function dialogReady(isReady) {
    // Once the DialogServer applet is ready to receive
    // JavaScript calls, it calls this function, passing
    // the value true.
    gIsAppletReady = isReady
```

```
    window.status = "DialogServer is now ready."
    window.defaultStatus = "DialogServer is now ready."
}
```

Adding the DialogServer Applet to a Web Page

The DialogServer Applet can be added to any Web page by using the `<APPLET>` tag. All related Java classes must also be placed in the same directory as the HTML page. The DialogServer applet uses the following classes:

- `DialogServer.class`

- `AFrame.class`

- `DialogData.class`

- `DialogLayout.class`

- `DynLogin.class`

Then, depending on what the dialog is used for, a version of each of the following functions should be included in the head section of the HTML document. It's up to you what to do with the values that are passed back from the applet.

```
function dialogReady(isReady) {}
function dialogOK(field1, field2) {}
function dialogCancel() {}
```

By exposing a few methods and properties, an applet can become much more versatile and dynamic. In the future, you can expect to find more Java applets that can be manipulated using JavaScript. This will lead to Web sites that look and run smoother due to the tighter integration of objects offered by the site.

javascript: URLs

`javascript:` URLs provide a way for Java and JavaScript programmers to create dynamic Web content. Simple examples of `javascript:` URLs include

```
javascript:alert('hello world')
```

which causes an alert dialog to be displayed, and

```
javascript:"<h1>Hello World</h1> JavaScript is fun."
```

which interprets the string as HTML and displays it (properly formatted) in the browser window. `javascript:` URLs can be used in any context where a URL is allowed. They can be typed directly into a browser's location field, they can be the targets of HTML hyperlinks, and they can be used as arguments to JavaScript's `window.open()` method and Java's `AppletContext.showDocument()` method.

CAUTION

Microsoft Internet Explorer has only limited support for `javascript:` URLs. They are supported when used within HTML documents, but not when used within Java in conjunction with `ShowDocument()`.

A `javascript:` URL consists of the string `"javascript:"` followed by one or more JavaScript statements. Multiple statements are separated by semicolons. When the URL is executed, the statements are evaluated in sequence, and the "value" of the URL is the value of the last statement.

In JavaScript, any legal expression also can be a statement, so a string constant by itself is a perfectly good statement. This fact is of particular interest because it is precisely through the use of string constants (and string variables) that HTML-valued JavaScript is passed to the browser to be interpreted.

TIP

If the first character of a string constant or string-valued variable is a <, the browser interprets the contents of the string as HTML. If the string starts with any other character, it is interpreted as plain text.

To use a `javascript:` URL as the target of a hyperlink, simply include it within an HTML document anywhere you would use an HTTP or other URL. For example, clicking on

```
<a href="javascript:alert('You clicked me! ') ">Click me</a>
```

causes an alert box to appear, and

```
<a href="javascript: '<b>You clicked me at: </b>' + new Date()">Click me</a>
```

causes a new page displaying the current date to be loaded. Note the use of single quotes inside the double-quoted URL. Using single quotes, or escaped double quotes, is necessary to avoid prematurely ending the string containing the URL.

TIP

The HTML `&quot;` entity can be used to specify an escaped quote within a `javascript:` URL. Using `&quot;` is sometimes less confusing than using escaped quotes.

Integrating Java Applets with ActiveX Controls

Microsoft's ActiveX technology provides a means of embedding Microsoft OLE controls within HTML documents. An OLE control thus embedded is referred to as an ActiveX control. These controls are recognized by Microsoft Internet Explorer 3.0, or by Netscape Navigator equipped with an ActiveX plug-in, such as that provided by NCompass Labs. If such a browser loads an HTML document with an ActiveX control that isn't already present on the browser's host machine, the browser loads that control from the server as well. Naturally, because these controls are really OLE objects, they can execute only in a browser on an OLE-capable platform such as Microsoft Windows. This creates a portability issue for browser users who want to access such a document.

The following is an example of the HTML code for embedding an OLE control (in this case, an OLE `ButtonCtrl` object) in an HTML document:

```
<OBJECT ID="MyButton" WIDTH=83 HEIGHT=27
 CLASSID="CLSID:3472D900-5A27-11CF-8B11-00AA00C00903">
    <PARAM NAME="_ExtentX" VALUE="2196">
    <PARAM NAME="_ExtentY" VALUE="714">
</OBJECT>
```

The string given for the `CLASSID` attribute is the value of the `CLSID` entry of the `ButtonCtl` OLE control type as it appears in the Windows System Registry. Fortunately, it isn't necessary to generate this code manually. The code in this example was created by the ActiveX Control Pad application from Microsoft. The ActiveX Control Pad, in addition to enabling manual text-editing of HTML documents, provides semi-automated placement and scripting of ActiveX controls. When using the ActiveX Control Pad application to place an ActiveX control within an HTML document, a list of all OLE controls currently known to the System Registry can be summoned. All such OLE controls are available for use by HTML document authors.

An ActiveX control has a set of events, each of which can be associated with a piece of JavaScript code. For example, the `ButtonCtl` control has an `onClick` event similar to that of a button-type input in an HTML form. ActiveX controls can be arbitrarily complex, however; for example, the Calendar control has the following events that can be scripted: `AfterUpdate`, `BeforeUpdate`, `Click`, `DblClick`, `KeyDown`, `KeyPress`, `KeyUp`, `NewMonth`, and `NewYear`. The following is an example of the code for scripting an event for an ActiveX control:

```
<SCRIPT LANGUAGE="JavaScript" FOR="MyButton" EVENT="onClick()">
alert('hello universe')
</SCRIPT>
```

The ActiveX Control Pad application provides a point-and-click interface for associating actions with events for ActiveX controls, and assists in creating scripts such as the preceding one.

The JavaScript code for one ActiveX control can access event handlers and attributes of other ActiveX controls in the HTML document. For example, suppose the HTML document containing `MyButton` also contains the NCompass Labs Cube Control, which is a rotating cube that interacts with the user's mouse clicks and drags. The HTML to include this control, as generated by the ActiveX Control Pad application, looks something like this:

```
<OBJECT ID="MyCube" WIDTH=83 HEIGHT=83
 CLASSID="CLSID:A7048320-D56F-11CE-9046-00AA005CDAE1">
    <PARAM NAME="_Version" VALUE="65536">
    <PARAM NAME="_ExtentX" VALUE="2187">
    <PARAM NAME="_ExtentY" VALUE="2187">
    <PARAM NAME="_StockProps" VALUE="0">
    <PARAM NAME="Picture1" VALUE="">
    <PARAM NAME="Picture2" VALUE="">
    <PARAM NAME="Picture3" VALUE="">
    <PARAM NAME="Picture4" VALUE="">
    <PARAM NAME="Picture5" VALUE="">
    <PARAM NAME="Picture6" VALUE="">
    <PARAM NAME="BackgroundImage" VALUE="">
    <PARAM NAME="CubeStyle" VALUE="1">
    <PARAM NAME="PictureNo" VALUE="12488">
</OBJECT>
```

Suppose you include the following script in the HTML document:

```
<SCRIPT LANGUAGE="JavaScript" FOR="MyButton" EVENT="onClick()">
Cube1.AboutBox()
</SCRIPT>
```

When the HTML document is loaded, it displays a button and a rotating cube control. When the button is pressed, the `AboutBox()` method of the cube control is invoked, and the cube control's About Box appears.

If you consider the mechanisms discussed so far, you should see that if a document includes both Java applets and ActiveX controls, it's possible to script ActiveX control events so that they access Java applet members and methods. Suppose you have a Java applet called `myApplet` embedded in an HTML document with the following code:

```
<applet
 name="myApplet"
 width=20
 height=20
 code="testApplet.class"
 MAYSCRIPT>
</applet>
```

A member or method of this Java applet can be accessed from the script for an ActiveX control event in just the same manner as it would be from any other piece of JavaScript code. Suppose the Java code for `testApplet` looks like the following:

```
class testApplet extends java.applet.Applet
{
    private String itsString = "hello";
    public void myMethod()
    {
        itsString = "world";
    }
}
```

The code to invoke `myMethod()` by clicking the button `MyButton` looks like this:

```
<SCRIPT LANGUAGE="JavaScript" FOR="MyButton" EVENT="onClick()">
document.myApplet.myMethod()
</SCRIPT>
```

This section has shown how OLE controls can be embedded in HTML documents (assuming a suitable browser and browser platform) using the ActiveX technology, and how JavaScript interacts with these controls. It is a simple matter to integrate Java applets with ActiveX controls—you just access the Java applet members and methods from the scripts associated with the ActiveX control events.

Certainly the easiest way to author documents of the type described here is with the Microsoft ActiveX Control Pad application. Numerous books document the behavior of the huge variety of OLE controls. A discussion of those controls would be beyond the scope of this book.

Summary

This chapter described some of the ways JavaScript can communicate with Java. It enumerated the rules for translating JavaScript objects into Java and for translating Java objects into JavaScript. It also included a discussion of some of the most useful methods in the `JSObject` class.

JavaScript scripts can call methods in Java applets, access static members of core Java packages, and construct new Java objects. Java applets can obtain the JavaScript object associated with the window containing the applet and use it to access the rest of JavaScript.

`javascript:` URLs are useful for causing JavaScript scripts to be executed in situations where a URL would normally be loaded, such as when an HTML hyperlink is clicked, and for creating and displaying HTML on-the-fly.

JavaScript event handler scripts can also be used as the wiring for connecting ActiveX controls and Java applets.

ActiveX Scripting

IN THIS CHAPTER

CHAPTER 27

Given JavaScript's name and Silicon Valley roots, you may be much more likely to associate it with Java than with anything that comes from Microsoft. However, as you have seen in Internet Explorer 3.0, Microsoft has touted its version of JavaScript—called JScript—as a Web-based scripting language. As a result, Microsoft strongly supports the integration of JScript with its component technology, ActiveX. This chapter looks at ActiveX controls and how you can use JScript to trigger and respond to ActiveX events. It also looks closely at Microsoft's ActiveX Control Pad tool, which lets you embed ActiveX controls in your HTML file.

NOTE

You may find the varying terms *JavaScript* and *JScript* confusing. For the sake of accuracy, I refer to JScript primarily in this chapter because ActiveX controls run under Microsoft Internet Explorer. JScript isn't a completely different language, just a distinct dialect. JScript 1.0 is roughly the equivalent of JavaScript 1.0.

Understanding ActiveX Controls

If *ActiveX* is a new term for you, let me try to draw two comparisons. Depending on your background, one will probably be more applicable than the other. If you have a Web or Java background, ActiveX controls are Microsoft's answer to Java applets, the miniapplications that can run inside a browser window. Or, if you're from a Windows database development background, think of them as the Web equivalent to VBXs (Visual Basic controls), VCLs (Delphi components), or OCXs (OLE controls). As you will see, the actual tie with OCXs is far closer than a simple comparison.

NOTE

Microsoft Internet Explorer 3.0 comes with the following standard ActiveX controls:
- Animated Button
- Chart
- Gradient Control
- Label
- New Item
- Popup Menu
- Preloader
- Stock Ticker
- Timer

The term *ActiveX* is relatively new, but the technology behind ActiveX controls is not. Before Microsoft decided that ActiveX was a much better marketing term, essentially the same controls were called OCXs. ActiveX controls are built on top of OLE technology that has been available for several years. However, it should be noted that ActiveX controls have less overhead than a standard OLE control. Because an ActiveX control is never "linked" or "embedded" in the same way a Word document is, part of the OLE technology is removed from an ActiveX control. The result is a component that is quicker and has less of a footprint.

RESOURCE

An extensive array of information is available on the Microsoft Web site, along with a substantial number of downloads:

ActiveX Resource Area (`http://www.microsoft.com/activex/`) is the best online source of technical information about ActiveX controls.

ActiveX Gallery (`http://www.microsoft.com/activex/controls/`) displays hundreds of ActiveX controls and demos.

ActiveX Directory (`http://www.microsoft.com/internet/`) is a listing of available ActiveX controls.

Control Freaks (`http://www.microsoft.com/devonly/community/cbisv_6.htm`) showcases some third-party ActiveX controls.

Java's principal *raison d'être* is portability across all operating environments. In contrast, the primary selling point for ActiveX controls is compatibility with the dominant desktop operating system in the market—Windows 95 and Windows NT. This compatibility is demonstrated in that the same ActiveX controls that you use in a Web page can be used by any Windows application or development tool that can work with OCXs. The rationale is that because most Web users are already using Windows, ActiveX controls are a natural extension from their desktop on the Web. Having said that, it should also be noted that Microsoft has publicly stated that it is working on porting ActiveX to both UNIX and Macintosh environments.

RESOURCE

One of the best third-party Web sites with ActiveX information is hosted by Innovision at `http://www.active-x.com`.

Currently, Microsoft Internet Explorer 3.0 or higher is the only browser that provides direct support for ActiveX controls. NCompass does have an ActiveX Plug-In that lets Netscape Navigator 2.01 or higher run them. Because ActiveX controls are currently specific to the Windows platform, however, only the Win32 versions of Netscape Navigator support this plug-in.

As shown in Figure 27.1, ActiveX controls use a different distribution paradigm than Java. A Java applet downloads to your computer each time you access a page it's linked to. An ActiveX control is also downloaded to a client machine, where it's automatically installed in the WINDOWS\SYSTEM folder of the client and then run. Rather than downloading the ActiveX repeatedly (as you would with Java), each successive hit on the page simply activates the ActiveX that is local to the client.

Figure 27.1.
Working with an ActiveX control.

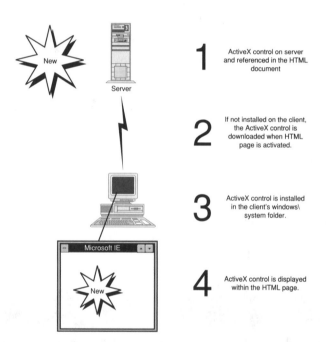

1   ActiveX control on server and referenced in the HTML document

2   If not installed on the client, the ActiveX control is downloaded when HTML page is activated.

3   ActiveX control is installed in the client's windows\system folder.

4   ActiveX control is displayed within the HTML page.

NOTE

Each ActiveX control has a Codebase property that lets you specify one or more URLs where the ActiveX control is located on the Web. Consequently, if a user accesses a page that contains an ActiveX control that is not on the client machine, the browser automatically gets it and installs it over the Web.

Both Java and ActiveX scenarios have advantages and disadvantages, and one will probably win over the other at some point. However, regardless of who will emerge as the "applet war" victor, you can be assured that JavaScript/JScript works with both of these technologies.

ActiveX Scripting is another term promoted by Microsoft. Essentially, it stands for Microsoft's implementation of a scripting language (either VBScript or JScript) within Microsoft Internet Explorer. When Microsoft talks about scripting, it often does so within the context of integration with ActiveX or Java applets—hence the ActiveX Scripting moniker.

ActiveX and Security

ActiveX has the concept of digital signing built into its components. A component developer can then "brand" a digital signature onto an ActiveX control to ensure users of the origin of the software itself. This digital signature is displayed by Internet Explorer as the control is downloaded. Users get the opportunity after seeing the signature to download or not download. For controls with no digital signature, users are informed that the control is from an unknown origin and are prompted to confirm or decline the download.

> **NOTE**
>
> You can set up an "auto-approval" process with a vendor you trust so that all components from that source are automatically approved.

Embedding ActiveX Controls into HTML Pages

Once you have some ActiveX controls to work with, you're ready to actually work with them in your HTML documents. ActiveX controls can be placed into HTML source files by using the `<OBJECT>` tag. If you're familiar with Java applets, you probably recognize that this is the same tag used to embed Java applets into a page.

> **RESOURCE**
>
> For more information about the `<OBJECT>` tag, you can see the World Wide Web Consortium (W3C) specification at `http://www.w3.org/pub/WWW/TR/WD-object.html`.

Just having the `<OBJECT>` tag in place is similar to having mountain-climbing boots at the foot of Mount Everest: Putting the boots on is essential to a successful climb, but the real task is the climb itself. Although equating manually embedding an ActiveX control into HTML with climbing Mount Everest is a slight exaggeration, both processes do require firm resolve, skill, and patience. The problem with trying to manually place ActiveX controls is the information that is required to do so. Take a look at the following HTML definition for the StockTicker ActiveX control:

```
<HTML>
<HEAD>
<TITLE>New Page</TITLE>
</HEAD>
<BODY>
</B
<OBJECT ID="iexrt1" WIDTH=213 HEIGHT=50
 CLASSID="CLSID:0CA4A620-8E3D-11CF-A3A9-00A0C9034920">
    <PARAM NAME="_ExtentX" VALUE="4509">
    <PARAM NAME="_ExtentY" VALUE="1058">
    <PARAM NAME="DataObjectName" VALUE="">
    <PARAM NAME="DataObjectNameProperty" VALUE="Name">
    <PARAM NAME="DataObjectValueProperty" VALUE="Value">
    <PARAM NAME="DataObjectRequest" VALUE="*">
    <PARAM NAME="ScrollSpeed" VALUE="220">
    <PARAM NAME="ReloadInterval" VALUE="10000">
    <PARAM NAME="ForeColor" VALUE="#9357FF">
    <PARAM NAME="BackColor" VALUE="#F70300">
    <PARAM NAME="BackColor" VALUE="-2147482633">
    <PARAM NAME="ScrollWidth" VALUE="2">
    <PARAM NAME="DataObjectActive" VALUE="2">
    <PARAM NAME="DataObjectVisible" VALUE="0">
    <PARAM NAME="OffsetValues" VALUE="10">
</OBJECT>
ODY>
</HTML>
```

Most of the definition isn't hard to interpret. The ID parameter is the object identifier, the WIDTH and HEIGHT parameters define its size, and the <PARAM> tag lists the properties of the object. What is less intuitive is the CLASSID parameter. CLASSID is used to represent the 128-bit unique identifier (CLSID) of an ActiveX control. The CLSID is stored in the registry when you install an ActiveX control.

Fortunately, Microsoft has provided a solution to this problem with its ActiveX Control Pad, which consists of several components to assist you in working with ActiveX controls in your Web pages:

- Several ActiveX user interface-oriented controls, as shown in Table 27.1.
- A "no-frills" text editor for basic HTML editing (see Figure 27.2).
- An Object Editor for visually embedding, sizing, and setting the properties of ActiveX controls.
- A Script Editor for writing JScript (or VBScript) code and attaching it to ActiveX control and JScript object events.
- A 2D (two-dimensional) visual layout editor for creating layout regions within an HTML page.

Table 27.1. ActiveX controls included with ActiveX Control Pad.

Control Name	Description
Microsoft Forms 2.0 Label	Standard text label
Microsoft Forms 2.0 TextBox	Standard edit box
Microsoft Forms 2.0 Combo Box	Standard combo or drop-down box
Microsoft Forms 2.0 List Box	Standard listbox
Microsoft Forms 2.0 Check Box	Standard checkbox
Microsoft Forms 2.0 Option Button	Standard radio option button
Microsoft Forms 2.0 Toggle Button	Button with on/off state
Microsoft Forms 2.0 Command Button	Standard pushbutton
Microsoft Forms 2.0 Tabstrip	Multipage control with tabs
Microsoft Forms 2.0 ScrollBar	Scrollbar, can be vertical or horizontal
Microsoft Forms 2.0 Spin Button	Up/Down arrow
Microsoft Image Control	Displays progressively rendered images
Microsoft Hotspot Control	Creates clickable regions on a page
Microsoft Web Browser Control	Displays ActiveX documents

27

ACTIVEX SCRIPTING

FIGURE 27.2.

The ActiveX Control Pad HTML Editor.

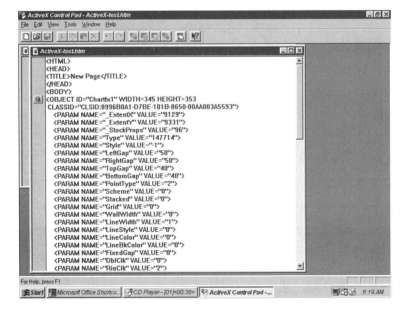

RESOURCE

The ActiveX Control Pad is available free on the Web at `http://www.microsoft.com/workshop/author/cpad/`.

To use the Control Pad to insert a control into a document, you first need to create a new HTML document or else open an existing one in the Control Pad text editor. Then select Edit | Insert ActiveX Control (or right-click the page itself) to display the Insert ActiveX Control dialog box, shown in Figure 27.3. It lists all the ActiveX controls that are installed on your computer.

FIGURE 27.3.

Insert ActiveX Control dialog box.

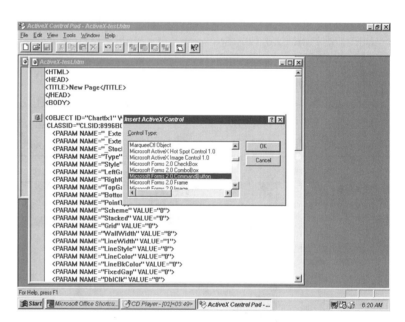

For this example, I use the Microsoft Forms 2.0 Command Button. After you select this control, the Object Editor Form is displayed, as shown in Figure 27.4. If you have used Visual Basic or a similar tool, this editor, while rudimentary, should seem familiar to you.

RESOURCE

You can read an online ActiveX Control Pad Tutorial at `http://www.microsoft.com/workshop/author/cpad/tutorial-f.htm`.

FIGURE 27.4.
The Object Editor Form.

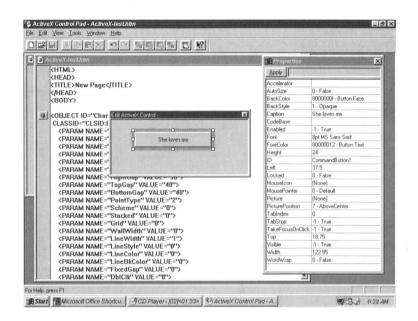

You can set the properties of the control using the properties table or resize it using the mouse. I made a single property change, changing the Caption property to She loves me. To exit the Object Editor Form, click the Close box on the form to return to the HTML text editor. The Control Pad automatically generates and inserts the <OBJECT> definition, as shown in the following code:

```
<HTML>
<HEAD>
<TITLE>New Page</TITLE>
</HEAD>
<BODY>

<OBJECT ID="CommandButton1" WIDTH=120 HEIGHT=40
 CLASSID="CLSID:D7053240-CE69-11CD-A777-00DD01143C57">
    <PARAM NAME="Caption" VALUE="Click Me">
    <PARAM NAME="Size" VALUE="2540;847">
    <PARAM NAME="FontCharSet" VALUE="0">
    <PARAM NAME="FontPitchAndFamily" VALUE="2">
    <PARAM NAME="ParagraphAlign" VALUE="3">
    <PARAM NAME="FontWeight" VALUE="0">
</OBJECT>
</BODY>
</HTML>
```

NOTE

At the time this book was written, ActiveX Control Pad provided no browser integration. Therefore, you need to save the HTML file and then open it from within Internet Explorer.

Before going further, you can test the ActiveX control in Microsoft Internet Explorer. When you access the HTML document, you see the customized command button, which is shown in Figure 27.5.

FIGURE 27.5.

*Customizing a
Command Button
control.*

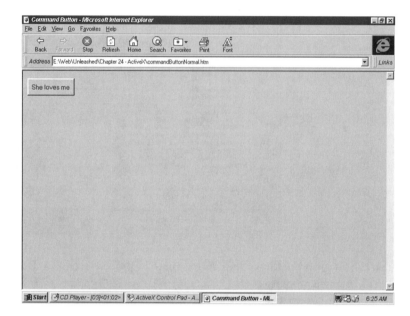

Integrating ActiveX Controls with JScript

Once the ActiveX control is embedded in your document, you can add JScript code and work with it like any other JScript object. You can set properties, respond to events, or call methods of an ActiveX control. This section looks at two ways to accomplish this. The first is through the ActiveX Control Pad's Script Wizard, and the second uses a standard editor.

Adding JScript Code with the Script Wizard

The Microsoft ActiveX Control Pad supports both JScript and VBScript to allow for easy integration of ActiveX controls with HTML. The interface to scripting is done through the Script Wizard, shown in Figure 27.6. You can access it by selecting Tools | Script Wizard or by right-clicking and selecting Script Wizard from the pull-down menu.

FIGURE 27.6.

The Script Wizard.

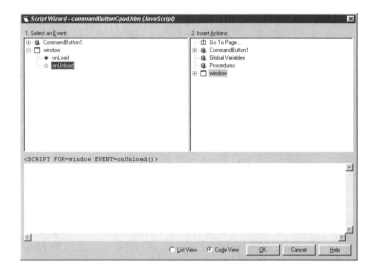

RESOURCE

Part Bank (http://www.partbank.com/activex) is a site devoted to ActiveX and other software components.

The purpose of the Script Wizard is to simplify the task of scripting as much as possible and to hide code from the script writer. Many developers may find the Script Wizard paradigm rather cumbersome, even confusing. Whether you use it or not is up to you (this book examines how to do it apart from the Script Wizard as well), but at a minimum, it's helpful to use when you're trying to determine methods or properties available for an ActiveX control.

TIP

Before using the Script Wizard, change the default language to JScript by choosing Tools | Options | Script and making the appropriate change in the Script Options dialog box.

The Script Wizard is divided into three parts:

■ Events: The Script Wizard is event-centric. Therefore, when you add code, you're adding it to an event handler. The top-left box is used to select an event you want to attach an event handler to. The box displays a Treeview list of the current objects and their associated events. By default, the window object always appears. If you have ActiveX controls inserted into the document, they are also in the list.

■ Actions: Once you have selected an event, the top-right box is used to locate an object method or property to use in the bottom code window. When you double-click a method (action) in the Treeview list, the method is placed, along with its associated object, in the code window. You can also define global variables or custom procedures by right-clicking and selecting the appropriate option from the pull-down menu.

■ Code: The bottom section is for displaying and editing JScript or VBScript code related to the event highlighted in the events box. You never see more than one method in this window at a time. There are two ways you can look at the script:

> Code View (see Figure 27.6) is the option that most experienced developers will be more comfortable with. It lets you deal with a single event handler in an editing environment apart from HTML itself. The Script Wizard is responsible for actually placing this method in the HTML document.

> Intended for nondevelopers or those new to scripting, List View, shown in Figure 27.7, provides a higher-level abstraction to ActiveX scripting. Rather than dealing with code per se, you deal with a list of objects and an associated action that is executed when an event is called. This view is limited to single-line commands, such as property assignments or method calls. For example, the Script Wizard can't display if...else or while logic in List View format.

FIGURE 27.7.

The Script Wizard's List View.

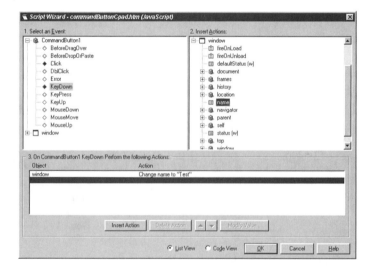

Using the Script Wizard, I can define the event handler for the command button's Click event. As an example, I use this event to change the defaultStatus property of the window object and the command button's caption. Figure 27.8 shows the code in the Script Wizard. After I add another example event handler—this time to the window's onLoad event—you can see how the JScript code is displayed in the HTML text editor (see Figure 27.9).

FIGURE 27.8.

Creating an event handler in the Script Wizard.

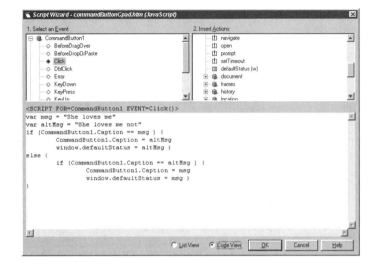

FIGURE 27.9.

Viewing the generated code.

You should immediately notice that the ActiveX Control Pad treats each event handling method as a separate script. (Whether you like that formatting style depends on your personal taste.) Beside each script is an icon. By clicking that icon, you can display the Script Wizard to modify the current event code.

You can run this code by saving the HTML text in the editor and running Internet Explorer. Figure 27.10 shows the result after the button has been clicked once.

FIGURE 27.10.

Custom code triggered when you click the command button.

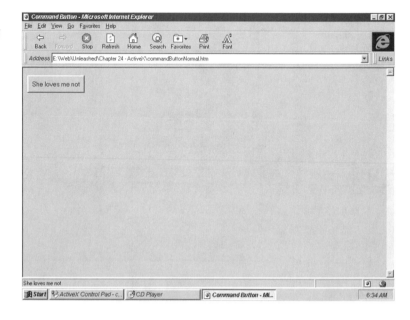

Adding JScript Code Using Your Normal Editor

Once you start working with ActiveX controls, you will see that there's nothing magical about attaching JScript code to them. As long as you know the properties and methods of the control, you can use your normal JScript editor instead of the Script Wizard if you like. Using the example shown in the preceding section, Listing 27.1 shows the JScript code for responding to the command button's Click method.

Listing 27.1. commandButtonNormal.htm.

```
<HTML>
<HEAD>
<TITLE>Command Button</TITLE>
<SCRIPT LANGUAGE="JavaScript">

    function loadBox() {
        alert("The Great Quesion")
    }

    function CommandButton1_Click() {

        var msg = "She loves me"
        var altMsg = "She loves me not"
        if (CommandButton1.Caption == msg ) {
            CommandButton1.Caption = altMsg
            window.defaultStatus = altMsg }
        else {
            if (CommandButton1.Caption == altMsg ) {
                CommandButton1.Caption = msg
                window.defaultStatus = msg }
```

```
            }
        }
</SCRIPT>
</HEAD>

<BODY onLoad="loadBox()">
    <OBJECT ID="CommandButton1" WIDTH=98 HEIGHT=32
     CLASSID="CLSID:D7053240-CE69-11CD-A777-00DD01143C57">
        <PARAM NAME="VariousPropertyBits" VALUE="268435483">
        <PARAM NAME="Caption" VALUE="She loves me">
        <PARAM NAME="Size" VALUE="2096;678">
        <PARAM NAME="FontCharSet" VALUE="0">
        <PARAM NAME="FontPitchAndFamily" VALUE="2">
        <PARAM NAME="ParagraphAlign" VALUE="3">
        <PARAM NAME="FontWeight" VALUE="0">
    </OBJECT>
</BODY>
</HTML>
```

Because the <OBJECT> tag doesn't allow you to add event handlers as parameters, you're forced to use an alternative event handling syntax of Microsoft's that states that an event handler for an object can be defined as ObjectName_EventName().

A second alternative would be to make use of Microsoft's expanded <SCRIPT> tag syntax to add the FOR and EVENT parameters. These tell JScript the object and event the code within the <SCRIPT> tags is designed for. The script would look like this:

```
<SCRIPT LANGUAGE="JavaScript" FOR="CommandButton1" EVENT="Click()">
    var msg = "She loves me"
    var altMsg = "She loves me not"
    if (CommandButton1.Caption == msg ) {
        CommandButton1.Caption = altMsg
        window.defaultStatus = altMsg }
    else {
        if (CommandButton1.Caption == altMsg ) {
            CommandButton1.Caption = msg
            window.defaultStatus = msg }
    }
</SCRIPT>
```

Adding 2D Style Layout to Your Pages

You may have noticed that you can place only a single ActiveX control at a time with the ActiveX Control Pad's Object Editor. This isn't a limitation of the tool, but of HTML itself. As currently implemented, the stream-based nature of HTML prevents you from being able to position multiple controls in exact X,Y coordinates on the page. The Microsoft ActiveX Control Pad is the first tool that solves this problem and allows you to utilize two-dimensional (2D) layout regions within your HTML page.

Using the Control Pad's layout editor, you can design a form filled with ActiveX controls in a manner similar to Visual Basic. In other words, you can place multiple controls on a form, positioning them precisely where you want. The layout editor saves this information in an .ALX file. This "2D region" is then displayed in your browser using an ActiveX control called the Microsoft HTML Layout Control, which uses the .ALX file as a parameter.

To embed a 2D region in an HTML document, open a file in the Control Pad's text editor. In the editor window, right-click and select the Insert HTML Layout option from the pull-down menu (or select Edit | Insert HTML Layout). Specify a location for the .ALX file and click OK. Or, if you want to create a new .ALX file and embed it later, choose File | New HTML Layout. Either way, the layout editor is displayed, as shown in Figure 27.11.

FIGURE 27.11.

Using the layout editor to create a 2D region.

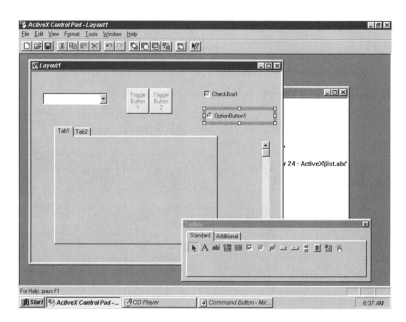

You can use the layout editor to place controls from the Toolbox onto the form, changing properties as you did earlier using the properties table. You can also use the Script Wizard to add JScript to one or more of the controls.

NOTE

Eventually, the World Wide Web Consortium (W3C) will probably have a final specification on 2D-style layout for HTML. At that time, Microsoft intends to provide a means to convert information stored in the .ALX file into HTML source.

To demonstrate the power of the layout editor, I built a sample `ListBuilder` form that contains a total of seven ActiveX controls. Figure 27.12 shows the form in the layout editor.

FIGURE 27.12.

A sample ListBuilder application that demonstrates ActiveX layout.

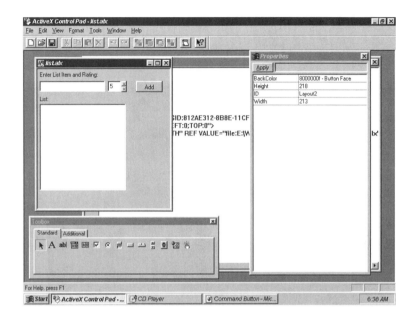

The purpose of the form is to fill the listbox with the contents of the Item and Rating edit boxes above. The Click method of the Add button is charged with performing this process. I also want the Rating to range from 1 to 10 and to be changeable only by clicking the SpinButton beside it. The SpinButton's SpinDown and SpinUp events will handle this task.

To define the handler for the Click event, select the command button from the Events Treeview list and navigate the tree until you find Click. In the Code View window, enter two lines of code to add a list entry for the current pair of entries in the Item and Rating edit boxes. These lines are shown in Figure 27.13.

FIGURE 27.13.

The Click event handler for the command button.

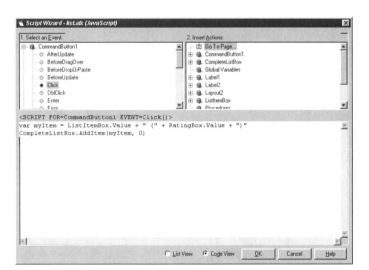

Next, define the event handlers for the SpinDown and SpinUp events of the SpinButton. Figure 27.14 shows the code for the SpinUp event handler. The SpinDown code is very similar, substituting a 1 for a –1 in the equation.

FIGURE 27.14.

SpinUp *event handler.*

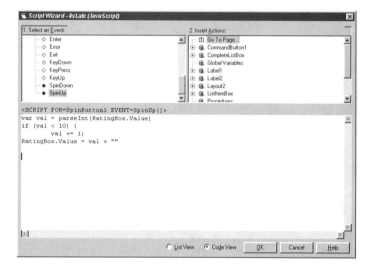

For this demonstration, stop coding here. Save the results into an .ALX file and then embed the layout into an HTML document. If you open the HTML document under Internet Explorer, you can see that the layout form comes across just as it was designed. Try entering data into the Item and Ratings fields; the listbox will grow for each entry, as shown in Figure 27.15.

FIGURE 27.15.

A JScript-enabled 2D region.

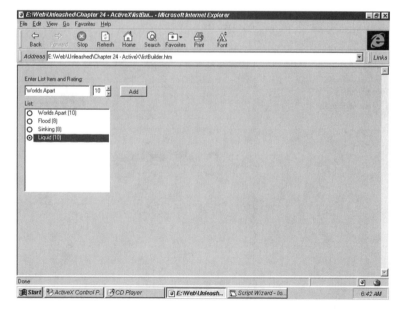

Listing 27.2 shows the code for the HTM form. The <OBJECT> tag uses the .ALX file as a parameter.

Listing 27.2. `ListBuilder.htm`.

```
<HTML>
<HEAD>
<TITLE></TITLE>
</HEAD>
<BODY>

<OBJECT CLASSID="CLSID:812AE312-8B8E-11CF-93C8-00AA00C08FDF"
ID="list_alx" STYLE="LEFT:0;TOP:0">
<PARAM NAME="ALXPATH" REF VALUE="file:E:\Web\Unleashed\Chapter 24 -
 ActiveX\list.alx">
 </OBJECT>

</BODY>
</HTML>
```

As you can see from the HTML file, there is no JScript code there. It is actually located in the .ALX file. The .ALX file is a text file that is essentially an extension to the associated HTML file. It uses the <DIV> HTML tag to group the ActiveX controls into a common division. As you can see in Listing 27.3, your JScript code keeps the same structure it would in an HTML file.

Listing 27.3. `List.alx`.

```
<SCRIPT LANGUAGE="JavaScript" FOR="SpinButton1" EVENT="SpinDown()">
<!--
var val = parseInt(RatingBox.Value)
if (val < 10) {
     val += -1}
RatingBox.Value = val + ""
-->
</SCRIPT>

<SCRIPT LANGUAGE="JavaScript" FOR="SpinButton1" EVENT="SpinUp()">
<!--
var val = parseInt(RatingBox.Value)
if (val < 10) {
     val += 1}
RatingBox.Value = val + ""
-->
</SCRIPT>

<SCRIPT LANGUAGE="JavaScript" FOR="CommandButton1" EVENT="Click()">
<!--
var myItem = ListItemBox.Value + " (" + RatingBox.Value + ")"
CompleteListBox.AddItem(myItem, 0)
-->
</SCRIPT>
```

continues

27

**ACTIVEX
SCRIPTING**

Listing 27.3. continued

```
<DIV ID="Layout2" STYLE="LAYOUT:FIXED;WIDTH:213pt;HEIGHT:218pt;">
    <OBJECT ID="ListItemBox"
     CLASSID="CLSID:8BD21D10-EC42-11CE-9E0D-00AA006002F3"
        STYLE="TOP:17pt;LEFT:4pt;WIDTH:105pt;HEIGHT:14pt;TABINDEX:1;ZINDEX:0;">
        <PARAM NAME="VariousPropertyBits" VALUE="679495707">
        <PARAM NAME="Size" VALUE="3704;508">
        <PARAM NAME="FontCharSet" VALUE="0">
        <PARAM NAME="FontPitchAndFamily" VALUE="2">
        <PARAM NAME="FontWeight" VALUE="0">
    </OBJECT>
    <OBJECT ID="Label1"
     CLASSID="CLSID:978C9E23-D4B0-11CE-BF2D-00AA003F40D0" STYLE="TOP:4pt;
        LEFT:4pt;WIDTH:109pt;HEIGHT:13pt;ZINDEX:1;">
        <PARAM NAME="Caption" VALUE="Enter List Item and Rating:">
        <PARAM NAME="Size" VALUE="3845;459">
        <PARAM NAME="FontCharSet" VALUE="0">
        <PARAM NAME="FontPitchAndFamily" VALUE="2">
        <PARAM NAME="FontWeight" VALUE="0">
    </OBJECT>
    <OBJECT ID="Label2"
     CLASSID="CLSID:978C9E23-D4B0-11CE-BF2D-00AA003F40D0" STYLE="TOP:42pt;LEFT:
        4pt;WIDTH:72pt;HEIGHT:14pt;ZINDEX:2;">
        <PARAM NAME="Caption" VALUE="List:">
        <PARAM NAME="Size" VALUE="2540;508">
        <PARAM NAME="FontCharSet" VALUE="0">
        <PARAM NAME="FontPitchAndFamily" VALUE="2">
        <PARAM NAME="FontWeight" VALUE="0">
    </OBJECT>
    <OBJECT ID="CommandButton1"
     CLASSID="CLSID:D7053240-CE69-11CD-A777-00DD01143C57"
        STYLE="TOP:13pt;LEFT:155pt;WIDTH:43pt;HEIGHT:17pt;TABINDEX:4;ZINDEX:3;">
        <PARAM NAME="Caption" VALUE="Add">
        <PARAM NAME="Size" VALUE="1517;600">
        <PARAM NAME="FontCharSet" VALUE="0">
        <PARAM NAME="FontPitchAndFamily" VALUE="2">
        <PARAM NAME="ParagraphAlign" VALUE="3">
        <PARAM NAME="FontWeight" VALUE="0">
    </OBJECT>
    <OBJECT ID="RatingBox"
     CLASSID="CLSID:8BD21D10-EC42-11CE-9E0D-00AA006002F3"
        STYLE="TOP:17pt;LEFT:113pt;WIDTH:21pt;HEIGHT:14pt;TABINDEX:5;ZINDEX:4;">
        <PARAM NAME="VariousPropertyBits" VALUE="679495707">
        <PARAM NAME="Size" VALUE="741;494">
        <PARAM NAME="Value" VALUE="5">
        <PARAM NAME="FontCharSet" VALUE="0">
        <PARAM NAME="FontPitchAndFamily" VALUE="2">
        <PARAM NAME="FontWeight" VALUE="0">
    </OBJECT>
    <OBJECT ID="SpinButton1"
     CLASSID="CLSID:79176FB0-B7F2-11CE-97EF-00AA006D2776"
        STYLE="TOP:17pt;LEFT:139pt;WIDTH:8pt;HEIGHT:13pt;TABINDEX:6;ZINDEX:5;">
        <PARAM NAME="Size" VALUE="282;459">
        <PARAM NAME="Max" VALUE="10">
    </OBJECT>
    <OBJECT ID="CompleteListBox"
     CLASSID="CLSID:8BD21D20-EC42-11CE-9E0D-00AA006002F3"
        STYLE="TOP:55pt;LEFT:4pt;WIDTH:138pt;HEIGHT:135pt;TABINDEX:0;ZINDEX:6;">
```

```
        <PARAM NAME="ScrollBars" VALUE="3">
        <PARAM NAME="DisplayStyle" VALUE="2">
        <PARAM NAME="Size" VALUE="4868;4771">
        <PARAM NAME="MatchEntry" VALUE="0">
        <PARAM NAME="ListStyle" VALUE="1">
        <PARAM NAME="FontCharSet" VALUE="0">
        <PARAM NAME="FontPitchAndFamily" VALUE="2">
        <PARAM NAME="FontWeight" VALUE="0">
    </OBJECT>
</DIV>
```

Don't let the simplicity of this example fool you. JScript integration with ActiveX controls offers a compelling alternative for application development on the Web. Trying to create a similar application using straight HTML tags would have been impossible. The notion of changing existing objects on an HTML document without a refresh from the server is revolutionary.

Summary

ActiveX controls can be tightly integrated with JScript. This chapter looked at what ActiveX technology is and how you can embed these controls into your HTML documents. It then looked at how you can add JScript code to set properties, respond to events, or trigger methods of an ActiveX control. Within this discussion, the principal tool available for working with ActiveX controls within your HTML, the Microsoft ActiveX Control Pad, was examined in detail.

Working with Netscape Plug-Ins

CHAPTER 28

Internet browsers, even Netscape Navigator and Microsoft Internet Explorer (MSIE), natively support content from only a few file formats (or file types), such as text and images. In order to do their work outside the Web browser, however, people regularly use many other file formats to perform different tasks. For instance, most word processing applications have their own native file format (such as Microsoft Word's .DOC file format), as do spreadsheet applications, presentation applications, multimedia applications, and so on. If the Web browser supports these various file formats, you can make a great deal of content readily available for communication on the Web, not to mention open up the Internet to new and exciting ways of presenting information. For Netscape (or any other company) to build native support into its browser for all the useful file formats, however, would be impractical because of the costs, time, and expertise that would be involved. Netscape does provide another solution: plug-ins. (Microsoft also provides a similar solution with ActiveX controls. See Chapter 27, "ActiveX Scripting.")

This chapter discusses in detail Netscape Navigator plug-ins and their interaction with JavaScript, as outlined in the following sections:

- Understanding plug-in technology
- Plug-ins and MIME types
- Available plug-ins
- Determining installed plug-ins with JavaScript
- Running plug-ins with JavaScript

Understanding Plug-In Technology

The concept of add-in programs for desktop applications is a good analogy for Netscape's plug-ins. With some applications, such as Microsoft Excel, Microsoft Access, or Adobe Photoshop, you can extend their functionality by installing an add-in program (often written by third-party vendors). For instance, an add-in program in Excel might help you perform more extensive statistical analysis than would otherwise be possible.

Similarly, Netscape has developed and made openly available an API (application programming interface) that helps third-party developers extend the functionality of the Navigator browser. Using the plug-in API, developers can develop plug-in (or mini-) applications that let the browser understand new file types and treat them as native browser elements (such as a QuickTime movie running directly in the browser window). The browser manages the interaction of plug-ins with the user, so additional plug-in functionality appears no different to the user than basic Navigator functionality.

> **NOTE**
>
> Plug-ins are also called inline plug-ins. As with inline images, the term *inline* refers to the fact that the plug-in data type can be seen in the browser window itself, without the need to run any other applications.

Some of the benefits of plug-ins include the ability to:

- Extend the capabilities of the Web browser to read more file types.

- Decrease time and effort involved in content creation by allowing Web authors to use already available content of various file formats.

- Increase the reach and functionality of the Internet by letting users view and manipulate content in a format specific to their needs (such as spreadsheets).

- Make Web content more dynamic and exciting (through the use of multimedia to enhance the message, for example, or by dynamically changing the layout of the screen).

- Reduce demand on the Web server. After the initial load of the Web page, many of the tasks now commonly done through the server (using CGI programming) can be done on the client through plug-ins and other client-side technologies.

- Reduce demand on bandwidth. Given that the plug-ins will perform some of the interactive work previously done by the server, less server activity should reduce demand on the bandwidth. This may result in more users (especially those who have slow dial-up links) being able to access and enjoy your Web pages.

Third-party developers develop plug-ins for Navigator with the help of Netscape's plug-in Software Development Kit (SDK). The SDK contains tools, documentation, samples, and header files to help develop plug-ins for all operating system platforms that Netscape supports.

Completed plug-ins are either bundled with Navigator (see the section "Plug-Ins with Netscape Navigator 3.0") or posted on the plug-in's developers' site.

28

WORKING WITH
NETSCAPE
PLUG-INS

> **RESOURCE**
>
> Netscape has a common page, `http://home.netscape.com/comprod/products/navigator/ version_2.0/plugins/index.html`, that categorizes, lists, describes, and provides a link to all currently available Navigator plug-ins. Once you have downloaded the plug-in, you must install and configure it properly before using it, which usually requires no more than choosing the right installation directory and following simple on-screen instructions.

Plug-Ins Versus Helper Applications

As opposed to plug-ins, which help Navigator run new file types inside its window, helper applications are external programs that Navigator can open if it comes across a file type that it can't open by itself. Also, helper applications normally open and control their own socket stream (with Winsock calls), as compared to plug-ins, which acquire their stream and data via Navigator.

A helper application is used, for instance, if there is no plug-in for AVI (Microsoft's video compression format) files, or the calling HTML file doesn't explicitly require the AVI file to be opened inside the browser. Here the browser opens a new application, such as MediaPlayer, to view the file. (Opening the AVI file inside the browser using an `<EMBED>` tag is explained in detail in the section "LiveVideo" later in this chapter.)

You can set up helper applications through the Navigator interface. For instance, if you're using Navigator 3.0, select Options | General Preferences... | Helpers. At this panel, shown in Figure 28.1, you define which local applications you want to use to open the various file types already registered with the browser. You can also add new file types to the registered list and associate them with available helper applications.

FIGURE 28.1.

Netscape Navigator 3.0's Helper Application setup window.

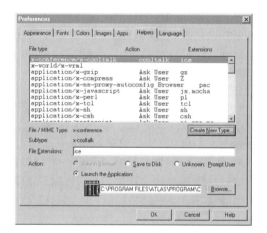

Helper applications have three attributes that describe them:

- File type: This attribute defines the MIME (Multipurpose Internet Mail Extensions) type supported. The MIME type helps the helper application understand the format of the file. MIME is explained in more detail in the section "Plug-Ins and MIME Types" later in this chapter.

- Action: This attribute identifies the action to perform when this data type (or MIME type) is encountered. This action commonly involves either opening a helper application to read the file or displaying a prompt that asks the user to choose the appropriate application to open the file.

■ File extensions: This attribute identifies the file extension that conforms to a particular data type.

Plug-ins are, for all intents and purposes, a replacement technology for helper applications, because helper applications provide a similar functionality. In comparison, however, helper applications have several problems that tend to deter people from using them, including the following:

■ Once a helper application is started, the browser loses control of the environment—in other words, the helper application becomes the foreground process. This can lead to user confusion (if the user "loses" the browser window). Plug-ins, however, are an integrated part of the browser environment, and they extend the number and type of files it can handle.

■ Helper applications stay resident in memory until the user manually exits the application (and sometimes even that doesn't totally clean up the memory). This can lead to possible browser lockups and inefficiencies. Plug-ins, however, are loaded into memory when the page calling the plug-in data type is called and are unloaded when the browser exits that page.

■ Helper applications need to be configured manually. This can often be confusing and require special knowledge. Most plug-ins have a very simple installation and require no further configuration.

■ Helper applications are sometimes big and expensive desktop applications. Plug-ins are commonly cheap (or free) and usually are smaller applications.

28

WORKING WITH NETSCAPE PLUG-INS

TIP

You can use Netscape's built-in URL to check what plug-ins are installed on your client. Go to Navigator's location box and enter about:plugins, or select Help | About Plug-ins.

To understand the practical difference between plug-ins and helper applications, follow these two examples:

Example 1: Read a Microsoft Word file called agenda.doc inside the browser, using the INSO Corporation's QuickView Plus plug-in. The HTML code to do this is shown in Listing 28.1, and the resulting browser window is shown in Figure 28.2.

NOTE

You can download INSO Corporation's QuickView Plus from http://www.inso.com/consumer/qvp/demo.htm.

Listing 28.1. `plugin.htm`.

```html
<html>
<head>
<title>Plugin Demo -- Word File Displayed with QuickView Plus</title>
</head>

<body>
<center><h1>Plugin Demo</h1></center>
<p><i>Show Word File below if Plug-in is installed</i></p>
<embed src="agenda.doc" height=500 width=640></embed>

</body>
</html>
```

FIGURE 28.2.

The Word document opened inside the browser window with the use of a plug-in.

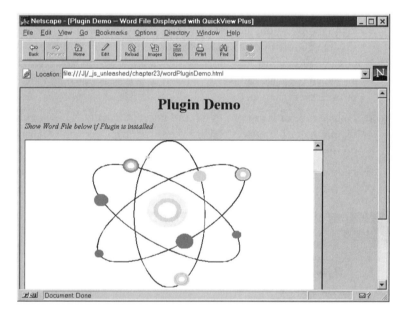

In this case, the QuickView Plus plug-in is already installed and registered to open .DOC files. So the browser (reading from the <EMBED> tag attributes) opens an inline window of size 500 × 640 and displays the .DOC file. This Microsoft Word file can now be viewed within the boundaries of the browser. The browser doesn't lose control.

Example 2: Read the same Microsoft Word file using a helper application. The code is shown in Listing 28.2, and the resulting helper application window—in this case, Microsoft Word itself—is shown in Figure 28.3.

Listing 28.2. `helper.htm`.

```
<html>
<head>
<title>Helper App Demo -- Word File opened with Word</title>
</head>

<body>
<center><h1>Plugin Demo</h1></center>
<p><i>Open the agenda file by clicking <A HREF="agenda.doc">here</a></i></p>

</body>
</html>
```

FIGURE 28.3.

The Word document opened with Microsoft Word as the helper application.

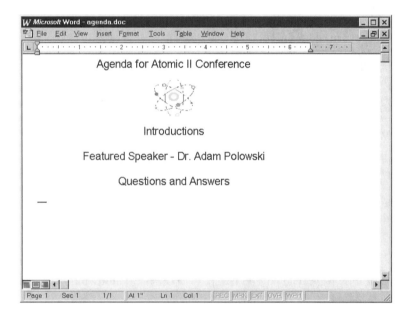

28

WORKING WITH NETSCAPE PLUG-INS

In this case, the browser no longer has control; once you're done reading the file in Word, you must manually go back to the browser to continue.

Plug-Ins and MIME Types

Plug-ins rely on MIME types to identify the data type being passed to them. By identifying the data type, the plug-in can figure out how to handle the data. MIME is an Internet standard that defines how file formats (except plain text) can be passed in Internet mail messages. (See Internet Request For Comment, RFCs 1521 and 1522, for complete details.) The impetus for this standard came from the fact that people wanted to exchange more than just plain text documents through e-mail. MIME now allows Internet e-mail applications to view formatted text, attachment files, and various other file types that can help enhance the message. The MIME standard can handle any file format created so far, including text, PostScript, image, sound, video, compressed files, and so on.

MIME types define the content type and the specific subtype of different file formats. This can be best explained with an example.

The MIME type for .WAV (Microsoft audio) files is defined as audio/x-wav. The first half of this definition, audio, describes the broader content type or category of files supported. x-wav describes the specific file type (or subtype) supported, as required by the browser to interpret .WAV files.

NOTE

An x before the subtype (as in audio/x-wav) indicates that this is a proposed MIME standard that is probably not yet widely accepted.

When Navigator is started, it scans its plug-ins directory and assigns a given MIME type to an appropriate plug-in that can read it. If multiple installed plug-ins support the MIME type, only the first plug-in that Navigator encounters is assigned to handle it. Once a MIME type is encountered, Navigator loads the assigned (or registered) plug-in into memory, and the MIME type is handled by the plug-in. The MIME type may be displayed in one of three ways:

- As an inline image: It displays on the page along with other content. The specific size of the plug-in is determined from values of the preset HEIGHT and WIDTH parameters.
- Full page: The plug-in covers all of the Navigator window, excluding the toolbars.
- Hidden: The plug-in is run in the background (as with some audio plug-ins).

NOTE

A plug-in might be able to handle one or more MIME types (such as INSO Corporation's QuickView Plus plug-in, which provides support for more than 200 file formats). However, two plug-ins can't be used to handle the same MIME type. Only the first compatible plug-in that the browser encounters will be assigned to that MIME type.

Available Plug-Ins

As plug-ins have become more widely accepted, the number of commercial and in-house plug-ins (primarily used on intranets) has skyrocketed. Currently, more than 130 commercial plug-ins, and thousands of in-house plug-ins, are available for Netscape Navigator, and more are being developed every week.

Third-party plug-ins designed to work with Netscape Navigator cover a wide range of functionality, from multimedia and graphics to business applications and utilities. These plug-ins can be roughly divided into five types (or categories). In the following sections, I'll discuss specific examples of each plug-in category, including details of their functionality and where you can download them from.

Types of Plug-Ins

Netscape plug-ins can be roughly divided into the following five categories:

- 3D and animation
- Video and audio
- Image viewers
- Presentations
- Business and utilities

You should check Netscape's plug-ins page at `http://home.netscape.com/comprod/products/navigator/version_2.0/plugins` for a complete and up-to-date listing. The following sections give some examples of each plug-in category.

28

WORKING WITH
NETSCAPE
PLUG-INS

3D and Animation

Cosmo Player by Silicon Graphics

Cosmo Player is a VRML 2.0 plug-in that lets you view 3D content. It includes sensors, scripts, and sound.

`http://www.sgi.com/cosmoplayer`

CyberHub Client by Black Sun Interactive

This plug-in lets you meet with other people on the Web by moving between 2D and 3D sites and interacting with them in 3D. You can also chat with other people, or even exchange business cards.

`http://ww3.blacksun.com`

mBED by mBED Software

This plug-in lets you build interactive multimedia Web content that can be scripted in simple text files.

```
http://www.mbed.com
```

Shockwave for Director by Macromedia

The Shockwave plug-in lets you interact with Macromedia Director presentations inside the Navigator window. Macromedia Director provides an integrated platform for developing sophisticated and interactive multimedia presentations and applications.

```
http://www.macromedia.com
```

Sizzler by Totally Hip

This plug-in lets you simultaneously view and interact with Web pages while streaming animation is delivered over the Web. You don't have to wait for the file to be completely downloaded before viewing it.

```
http://www.totallyhip.com
```

VR Scout VRML by Chaco Communications

This plug-in implements VRML 1.0 and lets you view 3D graphical scenes.

```
http://www.chaco.com
```

Audio and Video

CineWeb by Digigami

CineWeb brings real-time streaming audio and video to the Web using standard movie (MOV, AVI, and MPG), and audio (WAV, MIDI, and MP2) formats.

```
http://www.digigami.com/cineweb
```

Crescendo by Liveupdate

Crescendo is a music plug-in that delivers higher quality stereo MIDI music to the Web.

```
http://www.liveupdate.com
```

InterVU MPEG Player by InterVU

InterVU MPEG Player is an MPEG video plug-in that allows MPEG video to be played on a Web page, without specialized MPEG hardware or proprietary video servers.

```
http://www.intervu.com
```

RapidTransit by Fastman

This plug-in decompresses and plays music that has been compressed up to 40 times (a 40:1 ratio).

`http://www.monsterbit.com/rapidtransit/RTPlayer.html`

RealAudio by Progressive Networks

This plug-in delivers customizable, on-demand, and real-time audio over the Internet, and works effectively even on low-speed dial-up connections.

`http://www.realaudio.com`

ToolVox by Voxware

ToolVox lets you add speech audio to your Web pages and still keep the file sizes small through significant compression (as much as 53:1).

`http://www.voxware.com`

VDOLive by Vdonet

This plug-in delivers compressed video images to the Web page—without compromising quality on the receiving end—by determining the frames-per-second video delivery rate on the speed of the Internet connection.

`http://www.vdo.net`

Image Viewers

CMX Viewer by Corel

This graphic plug-in lets you view vector graphics online.

`http://www.corel.com/corelcmx`

DWG/DXF by Softsource

This plug-in lets you dynamically view AutoCAD (DWG) and DXF drawings over the Web. You can also pan and zoom a drawing, and hide and display layers.

`http://www.softsource.com`

Fractal Viewer by Iterated Systems

This plug-in lets you use inline fractal images (highly compressed digitized photographs and other bitmap images) on the Web.

`http://www.iterated.com/fracview`

Surround Video by Black Diamond

This plug-in adds seamless 360-degree panoramic images to applications and Web pages while maintaining real-time navigation and photo-realism.

`http://www.bdiamond.com`

WHIP by Autodesk

This plug-in lets you view, send, and share 2D vector data and design content over the Internet.

`http://www.autodesk.com`

Presentations

ASAP Webshow by Software Publishing Corporation

This plug-in is a presentation viewer for viewing, downloading, and printing graphically rich reports and presentations from the Web.

`http://www.spco.com`

Astound Web Player by Gold Disk

This plug-in lets you run Astound presentations (including sound, animation, graphics, video, and interactivity) online. Each slide is downloaded in the background while you view the current slide.

`http://www.golddisk.com/awp`

Powerpoint Animation Player and Publisher by Microsoft

This plug-in lets you view Powerpoint presentations online.

`http://www.microsoft.com/mspowerpoint/internet/player`

Business and Utilities

Acrobat Reader by Adobe

This plug-in lets you view, navigate, and print Portable Document Format (PDF) files from a Navigator window. PDF files are small, format-rich, print-ready documents that can be used for publishing format-sensitive material online.

`http://www.adobe.com/acrobat`

Carbon Copy/Net by Microcom

This plug-in lets you remotely control another PC over the Internet (including running applications, and viewing or editing documents).

`http://www.microcom.com`

Day-Timer Organizer by Day-Timer Technologies

This plug-in lets you view calendar and address information within the plug-in's interface. You also have the capability to perform searches and print.

`http://www.daytimer.com`

Formula One/Net by Visual Components

This is an Excel-compatible spreadsheet plug-in with built-in Internet functionality (including live charts, links to URLs, calculations, and clickable buttons).

`http://www.visualcomp.com`

Ichat Plug-In by Ichat

This plug-in integrates Internet chat capability directly into Netscape Navigator.

`http://www.ichat.com`

Isys HindSite by Isys/Odyssey Development

This plug-in remembers everywhere you have been and everything you have seen on the Internet. HindSite indexes and saves the text content of all Web pages visited during a (preset) timeframe, and lets you perform full-text searches on that content.

`http://www.isysdev.com`

Look@Me by Farallon

This plug-in lets you view, in real time, another Look@Me user's screen anywhere in the world.

`http://www.farallon.com`

NetZIP by Software Builders International

NetZIP integrates into Navigator for easy ZIP (compressed) file download and extraction. You can also view the contents of ZIP files from within Navigator.

`http://www.softwarebuilders.com`

Pointcast Network by Pointcast

This plug-in provides a free service that broadcasts customizable news (current events, weather, sports, stock quotes, and so on) to the computer screen; it can also be configured as a screen saver.

```
http://www.pointcast.com
```

Quick View Plus by Inso Corporation

This plug-in lets you view, copy, print, and manage—in original format—more than 200 file types (such as text files, images, word processor files, and so on) from the Navigator window.

```
http://www.inso.com
```

Plug-Ins with Netscape Navigator 3.0

Netscape Navigator 3.0 includes four new built-in plug-ins that let you embed rich content in Web documents and have them immediately and conveniently available to a large proportion of Internet users.

Navigator 3.0's built-in plug-ins consist of the following:

- LiveAudio: Plays audio files in WAV, AIFF, AU, and MIDI formats.
- LiveVideo: Plays AVI video files.
- QuickTime: Plug-in to play QuickTime movies.
- Live3D: Displays VRML (Virtual Reality Markup Language) content.

The source files for these plug-ins can be declared as inline objects in the browser window with an <EMBED> tag in the HTML file. Each plug-in has its own set of <EMBED> parameters (such as HEIGHT and WIDTH) that help define its specific characteristics. Some parameters are common among all four plug-ins, but many are different. These four plug-ins—including their control parameters, other unique characteristics, and some examples—are discussed in the next sections.

LiveAudio

LiveAudio plays audio files in WAV, AIFF, AU, and MIDI formats. Here is the HTML syntax you need to use an inline LiveAudio plug-in object:

```
<EMBED SRC= [URL] ...>
```

LiveAudio is discussed in detail in Chapter 29, "LiveAudio and Multimedia."

LiveVideo

LiveVideo plays video files in AVI (Video for Windows) format. Here is the HTML syntax you need to use an inline LiveVideo plug-in object:

```
<EMBED SRC= [URL] ...>
```

The <EMBED> attributes include the following:

- SRC=[*URL*]: The URL (location) of the source video file.

- AUTOSTART=[TRUE¦FALSE]: TRUE means the AVI file begins playing automatically when the Web page is loaded. The default is FALSE.

- LOOP=[TRUE¦FALSE]: TRUE means that the movie file plays continuously until the user clicks on the movie or goes to another page. FALSE means the movie will play only once.

- WIDTH=[# *PIXELS*]: Represents the width of the movie. Standard sizes include 120, 160, 240, 320, and 640 pixels. WIDTH usually has a 4:3 ratio to HEIGHT.

- HEIGHT=[# *PIXELS*]: Represents the height of the movie. Standard sizes include 90, 120, 180, 240, and 480 pixels. HEIGHT usually has a 3:4 ratio to WIDTH.

- ALIGN=[TOP¦BOTTOM¦CENTER¦BASELINE¦LEFT¦RIGHT¦TEXTTOP¦MIDDLE¦ABSMIDDLE¦ ABSBOTTOM]: Tells the browser how to align text around the plug-in object.

Listing 28.3 demonstrates some features of this plug-in, as you can see in Figure 28.4.

28

WORKING WITH NETSCAPE PLUG-INS

Listing 28.3. lvvideo.htm.

```
<HTML>
<HEAD>
<TITLE>LiveVideo Plug-in</TITLE>
</HEAD>

<BODY BGCOLOR="#ffffff">
<CENTER><H1>LiveVideo Plug-in Demo</H1></center>

<FONT SIZE=+1>Display my inline video</FONT>
<BR>
<BR>
<EMBED SRC="machines.avi" HEIGHT=240 WIDTH=320 AUTOSTART=TRUE
ALIGN=right LOOP=true>
This demonstrates how you can display an AVI movie right on the Browser
window itself. Click on the movie to stop it from playing.
Re-click on the movie to re-start it.
<BR>
</body>
</html>
```

FIGURE 28.4.

An inline LiveVideo object.

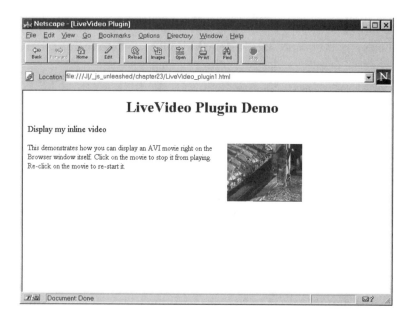

QuickTime

QuickTime plug-ins play QuickTime (MOV) files as inline objects in the browser. Here is the HTML syntax you need to use an inline QuickTime plug-in object:

```
<EMBED SRC= [URL] ...>
```

The <EMBED> attributes include the following:

- SRC=[*URL*]: The URL (location) of the source file.
- AUTOPLAY=[TRUE¦FALSE]: TRUE means that the QuickTime movie begins playing automatically when the Web page is loaded. The default is FALSE.
- LOOP=[TRUE¦FALSE¦PALINDROME]: TRUE means that the movie file plays continuously until the user clicks on the movie or goes to another page. FALSE means the movie will play only once. PALINDROME means the movie will play alternately forward and then backward. The default is FALSE.
- WIDTH=[# *PIXELS*]: Represents the width of the movie. Standard sizes include 120, 160, 240, 320, and 640 pixels. WIDTH usually has a 4:3 ratio to HEIGHT. Don't specify a WIDTH less than 2, because this causes problems for the browser.
- HEIGHT=[# *PIXELS*]: Represents the height of the movie. Standard sizes include 90, 120, 180, 240, and 480 pixels. HEIGHT usually has a 3:4 ratio to WIDTH. Don't specify a HEIGHT less than 2, because this causes problems for the browser.
- HIDDEN: This parameter has no other values and causes the movie to not be visible on the page. This may be useful for sound-only movies, where there are either no pictures or the pictures need not be shown.

■ CONTROLLER=[TRUE¦FALSE]: TRUE means that the movie controller is visible. Add an extra 24 to the HEIGHT parameter to display the controller. FALSE means that the movie controller isn't visible.

■ PLUGINSPAGE=[*URL*]: This optional parameter lets you specify a URL to obtain the plug-in from if it isn't installed. For QuickTime plug-ins, set the URL to http:// quicktime.apple.com.

■ PLAYEVERYFRAME=[TRUE¦FALSE]: TRUE means play every frame of the movie without any skips, even if it must be played at a slower rate. The default is FALSE. Note that this parameter shouldn't be set to TRUE if the movie has audio or MIDI tracks, because this will turn the sound off.

■ HREF=[*URL*]: Provides a link to another page if the movie is clicked on.

■ TARGET=[*FRAME*]: This parameter is used with HREF, and identifies the FRAME (in a <FRAMESET>) to link to.

■ PAN=[*FIXED NUMBER*]: This parameter lets you specify the initial pan angle, in degrees, for a QuickTime VR movie. The range of value is from 0 to 360. This parameter doesn't apply to a standard QuickTime movie.

■ TILT=[*FIXED NUMBER*]: This parameter lets you specify the initial field of view (FOV) angle, in degrees, for a QuickTime VR movie. The typical range of value is from 5 to 85. This parameter doesn't apply to a standard QuickTime movie.

■ FOV=[*FIXED NUMBER*]: This parameter lets you specify the initial tilt angle, in degrees, for a QuickTime VR movie. The typical range of value is from –42.5 to 42.5. This parameter doesn't apply to a standard QuickTime movie.

■ TILT=[*INTEGER*]: This parameter lets you specify the initial node for a multinode QuickTime VR movie. This parameter doesn't apply to a standard QuickTime movie.

■ CORRECTION=[NONE¦PARTIAL¦FULL]: This parameter applies only to a QuickTime VR movie.

28

WORKING WITH NETSCAPE PLUG-INS

Live3D

The Live3D plug-in displays VRML files as inline objects in the browser. The <EMBED> tag needs to be used to declare the VRML object and identify its location:

```
<EMBED SRC= [URL] ...>
```

RESOURCE

For more information on the Live3D plug-in, including technical documentation and examples, refer to Netscape's Live3D page:

http://home.netscape.com/eng/live3d

Plug-Ins with Netscape Communicator (Navigator 4.0)

Netscape Communicator is the upgrade to Netscape Navigator 3.0 and comes in two flavors: Standard and Professional Edition. Communicator is more than just the Navigator browser, however; it is a single product that tightly integrates several Netscape communication tools. These tools include the following:

■ Netscape Navigator: Strictly speaking, this is the upgrade to the Navigator 3.0 browser.

■ Netscape Messenger: This is the upgrade to the program previously called Netscape Mail (available through Navigator). This Communicator mail component adheres to open standards and support POP3, SMTP, and IMAP4 protocols.

■ Netscape Collabra: This component lets people in an organization share information and create a knowledge base similar to the way Internet newsgroups work.

■ Netscape Composer: Composer is essentially the new replacement for Netscape Gold, in terms of allowing users to easily edit and create HTML pages.

■ Netscape Conference: This component enables real-time audio and data collaboration, and it includes a chat tool and a shared whiteboard for exchanging text and graphics.

■ Netscape Calendar (Professional Edition only): This is a calendaring and scheduling component that lets you share your schedule online with others in the organization and maintain it offline.

■ Netscape AutoAdmin (Professional Edition only): This component helps an organization to centrally distribute, install, and manage Communicator.

■ Netscape IBM Host On-Demand (Professional Edition only): This is a Java-based component of Communicator, jointly developed with IBM, that lets users access legacy data (on any 3270 mainframe) easily through the browser.

Similar to Navigator 3.0, Navigator 4.0 (Communicator's browser component) does come with several built-in plug-ins. These consist of the following:

■ Netscape Media Player and Audio Streaming: Plays Streaming Audio Metafiles (which have a .LAM extension).

■ LiveAudio: Plays audio files in WAV, AIFF, AU, and MIDI formats.

■ LiveVideo: Plays AVI video files.

■ QuickTime: Plays QuickTime movies.

■ Live3D v2.0: Displays VRML (Virtual Reality Markup Language) content. This upgrade to Live3D (bundled with Navigator 3.0) is fully compliant with VRML 2.0 specification and has better performance and quality.

■ vCalendar v2.0 (available with Communicator Professional Edition): Complements Communicator's Calendar component and helps users track calendar events regardless of the page they resided on originally.

Source files for these plug-ins can be declared as inline objects in the browser window with an `<EMBED>` or an `<OBJECT>` tag in the HTML file. Navigator 4.0 supports the new `<OBJECT>` tag for plug-in declaration, unlike its predecessor. (You can read more about the `<EMBED>` and `<OBJECT>` tags later in this chapter.)

Downloading a Plug-In

You won't find many shrink-wrapped (in other words, "off the shelf") plug-ins. Most plug-ins are small applications that quickly become available on the Internet, usually in beta form to begin with for the public to test and give feedback. They can be downloaded from their developers' Web sites (or other complementary sites), often at no initial charge for an evaluation period, with a choice to purchase, at prices generally under $100.

CAUTION

Plug-ins aren't platform-independent. Be sure to download the plug-in that is compatible with your computer's operating system (that is, Windows 95, Windows 3.1, Macintosh, and so on). Many plug-ins are available for only one operating system and not another.

Because so many plug-ins are available and many more are being developed, sometimes it's difficult to know what plug-in to get and how to install it successfully. Use the checklist here as a rough guideline to help you:

28

1. Decide what type of extra browser functionality you need (such as business, utilities, presentation, multimedia, 3D, and so on).

2. Make sure you know the exact operating system on which you plan to install the plug-in (such as Windows 95, Windows NT, Macintosh, and so on). Plug-ins are platform-sensitive, so make sure you download the correct plug-in for your system.

3. Make sure you know the exact type and version of your browser (such as Navigator 2.02, Navigator 3.0, and so on). Certain plug-ins work only for specific versions of a browser.

4. Make sure you have a tool to decompress common formats of compressed files (such as zip or tar).

5. Go to Netscape's plug-in page at `http://home.netscape.com/comprod/products/navigator/version_2.0/plugins/index.html`. It contains links to all available Navigator plug-ins.

6. Use the plug-in categories (such as Presentation, Business and Utilities, and so on) and the descriptions noted for each plug-in to help you find the one that seems to best match your needs. Click the download hyperlink to go to the download site.

7. Choose the appropriate download file from the potential list of available files (such as the Shockwave for Director plug-in for Windows 95 and Netscape Navigator 2.0).

8. Make a note of any registration or licensing notes, including expiration date (if the plug-in is only an evaluation copy). Read the installation notes.

9. Download and save the file in a local directory.

10. Decompress the file if necessary.

11. Install the plug-in (usually from the plug-in's native setup file). Make sure the plug-in installation program identifies the correct Navigator directory. The plug-in must update Navigator's registry files to ensure that Navigator is aware of its presence and its capability to support certain MIME types. Plug-ins are commonly installed in the plugins subdirectory of the Netscape directory (where the application `netscape.exe` resides).

12. To verify installation, restart Navigator. In the location box, enter `about:plugins`. This lists all the plug-ins registered by Navigator.

CAUTION

If you have multiple copies of Navigator on your hard drive, make sure the plug-in installation program identifies the right browser installation to register the plug-in to. You can register a plug-in to only one browser at a time.

When to Avoid Plug-Ins

Even though plug-ins add a lot of extra functionality, there are times when you shouldn't use them in favor of a simpler technology that still gets your message across effectively. Some of these situations occur:

■ When the information can be displayed just as effectively using another (more basic) format. This probably means that the Web page is more widely supported—compatible with more browsers and more reliable (less chance of browser crash). Also, in the absence of typically larger plug-in file types, the performance (download time) for the Web page is generally better. For instance, if you just want to display your logo on-screen, you should probably use a small image rather than an elaborate Shockwave plug-in.

■ When the plug-in file types increase the download time such that the performance of the page becomes unbearably slow for a major group of users, such as those dialing in with slow modems. You should do a cost/benefit analysis to get a feel for whether it is worthwhile to persevere with the plug-ins. Do you add enough value to the content with the plug-ins to convince a user to put up with slow download times? For instance, could you replace some of the embedded audio files that describe the features of your site with a revolving (animated GIF) banner?

■ When the MIME type format isn't widely accepted. This is particularly relevant for newer or customized MIME types, and generally means that the user needs to freshly download the right plug-in to read your Web content. This is an inconvenience at best because it forces the user to leave your page. Many users may not come back.

■ When the majority of the anticipated users use a software platform (such as UNIX) that isn't supported by the plug-in. You need alternative techniques in this case, such as custom programming in Java, JavaScript, or (server-side) CGIs.

> **CAUTION**
>
> Don't use more than one plug-in data type per Web page; doing so in certain situations may cause various memory problems that may lead to a browser crash. If you want to use multiple plug-ins, put each on a different page.

Determining Installed Plug-Ins with JavaScript

Being able to determine what plug-ins are installed and which MIME types are supported on a client browser opens up a number of doors to a Web page developer in terms of controlling the content passed down to the user. For instance, one development scenario might be, "If the user does have the plug-in, show the page with all the relevant MIME types, or else show alternate (more basic) content." JavaScript can help you to do this programmatically, with a little help from Netscape Navigator.

Navigator (3.0 or later) has two built-in objects that reveal very useful information about the plug-ins and MIME types that a client browser supports:

■ `navigator.plugins`: This navigator object is an array of all the plug-ins currently installed on the client. This object has the following properties:

`name`: The name of the plug-in (for example, "shockwave").

`filename`: The name of the plug-in file.

`description`: A description of the plug-in (supplied by its vendor).

`length`: The number of elements in the array.

`[...]`: An array of `mimeTypes` objects that the plug-in can read.

■ `navigator.mimeTypes`: This navigator object is an array of all the MIME types supported on the client. This object has the following properties:

`type`: The name of the MIME type (such as audio/x-wav).

`description`: A description of the MIME type (supplied by its vendor).

`enabledPlugin`: Plug-ins that can be read by this MIME type.

`suffixes`: The filename extensions that the MIME type is identified by (such as WAV for MIME type audio/x-wav). Multiple suffixes are separated by commas.

Using these new Navigator objects with JavaScript, you can quickly determine whether a plug-in has been installed and how to proceed from there.

The next example checks to see if Macromedia's Shockwave plug-in has been installed, and follows this logic:

- If the required plug-in is installed, display the embedded plug-in data type.

- If not, display alternative information (just an JPEG image, for example, instead of a Shockwave object).

> **NOTE**
>
> If you have Netscape Communicator, you can take advantage of Navigator 4.0's new AutoInstall (and digital signing of plug-ins) feature to have required plug-ins automatically downloaded. With AutoInstall, if the browser encounters a MIME type that requires a plug-in that the browser doesn't have, the user will be prompted to download the plug-in and agree to a license. The user can then approve the installation of the plug-in based on whether there is a signature, or if the user trusts that signature.

Note that a variable is used to hold the value of the desired (or expected) plug-in:

```
var DesiredPlugin = navigator.plugins["shockwave"];
    // refers to NAME property of plug-ins object
if (DesiredPlugin) {
    document.write("<EMBED SRC="mymovie.dir" HEIGHT=240 WIDTH=320>");
} else {
    document.write("<IMG SRC="movietitle.jpg" HEIGHT=240 WIDTH=320>");
}
```

The navigator.plugins object also has a new method called refresh. This method causes Navigator to look for any newly installed plug-ins and update itself accordingly. If the argument true is used with the refresh method (such as navigator.plugin.refresh(true)), the presence of a new plug-in will be registered without the need to exit and restart the browser.

> **TIP**
>
> If navigator.plugins.refresh(true) is used, Navigator will only reload pages that might change as a result of a plug-in update. However, by default (if the refresh method isn't used), Navigator reloads all pages that contain any plug-in file types.

Using these new navigator.mimeTypes objects with JavaScript, you can also quickly determine whether a client supports a particular MIME type. The following example checks to see if the browser supports the application/x-director (for Macromedia Director movies) MIME type. It follows a logic similar to that of the previous example once the determination is made:

```
var DesiredMimetype = navigator.mimeType["application/x-director"];
if (DesiredMimetype) {
    document.write("<EMBED SRC="mymovie.dir"> HEIGHT=240 WIDTH=320>");
} else {
    document.write("<IMG SRC=" movietitle.jpg" HEIGHT=240 WIDTH=320>");
}
```

You can also use a simple JavaScript loop to display all MIME types supported on the client. Try this code:

```
for (i=0; i<navigator.mimeTypes.length; i++) {
    document.write(navigator.mimeTypes[i].type + "<br>");
}
```

Running Plug-Ins with JavaScript

JavaScript can be used in many creative ways to run (and otherwise manipulate) plug-ins, using the same HTML <EMBED> tag syntax discussed earlier. You saw an example of this in the preceding section, where a conditional JavaScript statement was used to perform either of two actions depending on whether a particular plug-in was installed. Other examples of JavaScript and plug-ins include the following:

- Plug-in source file manipulation: You can use JavaScript to set up and preload an array of plug-in objects to be used as source files (or URLs) for an embedded object. Then use a JavaScript loop (from 1 to the maximum size of the array) to step through the plug-in objects each time the page is loaded. This gives a dynamic feel to your page and encourages repeat visits.

- Plug-in source code hiding: You can hide the HTML and JavaScript source code by creating the HTML file, including the <EMBED> statements, through a JavaScript .js file. Thus, use JavaScript's document.write() object to define all the HTML tags and content, and from an HTML file, simply load the JavaScript file. This user can only view the HTML source code. Note, however, that not all browsers support the .js files.

28

> **NOTE**
>
> If you use JavaScript (.js) files in your code, try to limit each .js file to one narrowly defined function only. This is a good programming technique that will help you, in the long run, write reusable code (or JavaScript libraries).

The <EMBED> Tag

The HTML <EMBED> tag is used to insert plug-in objects into a browser window. Netscape Communicator also accepts the new <OBJECT> tag. The syntax for <EMBED> is slightly different for each plug-in; however, you will typically find something like this:

```
<EMBED SRC="URL" WIDTH=integer HEIGHT=integer ...>
```

The <EMBED> tag is extremely flexible in that it lets you define previously unspecified parameters to cater to the needs of a specific plug-in. For instance, you can define a parameter such as MYPARAM=""this is my parameter"". This parameter can be used by any plug-in that can identify it; others will simply ignore it. This unique coding flexibility means that any plug-in (current or future) can be inserted into a Web page as an inline object, with a set of <EMBED> parameters of its own. This situation poses several problems, however:

■ It's very difficult and time-consuming to find out all of the unique parameters of each plug-in.

■ This flexibility of the <EMBED> tag is inconsistent with the rest of the HTML specification. This means that for one plug-in you might have one set of attributes and, for another, a different set of attributes (or worse, the same attribute names but representing different things). This inconsistency means that the developer needs to constantly keep track of the attributes of each separate plug-in, as well as how those might change with upgrades. Also, JavaScript code that works perfectly with one version of a plug-in might not work at all with another version, and so on.

The <OBJECT> Tag

To resolve the problems with the <EMBED> tag (and other HTML inconsistencies across different browsers), the World Wide Web Consortium, or W3C (http://www.w3.org), has introduced a new HTML tag called <OBJECT>. The purpose of the <OBJECT> tag is to embody the role of the <IMG> tag, to provide a general solution for dealing with all types of new media (such as multimedia, virtual reality, Java applets, ActiveX controls, plug-ins, and the like), and to provide backward compatibility with existing browsers. Currently, only Netscape Communicator (Navigator 4.0) supports this tag.

> **NOTE**
>
> The World Wide Web Consortium is the group responsible for developing standards for the Web. Based at the Massachusetts Institute of Technology's Laboratory for Computer Science, W3C develops Web standards through the proposal of Internet Working Drafts. Working Drafts are then reviewed by W3C members and other interested groups; the drafts are modified and, if appropriate, declared as standards. W3C has developed the specification for every level of HTML up to the latest (HTML 3.2).

The syntax for the `<OBJECT>` tag is as follows:

```
<OBJECT attributes> ... </OBJECT>
```

The following attributes are used with `<OBJECT>`:

- ■ `DATA`: This parameter represents the URL of the object's data. (This is equivalent to the `SRC` attribute of `<EMBED>`.)

- ■ `TYPE`: This represents the MIME type of the object's data. (This is the same as the `TYPE` attribute of `<EMBED>`.)

- ■ `CODEBASE`: This represents the URL of the location of the object's implementation—if an additional URL is required. If nothing is specified, `CODEBASE` defaults to the main URL. (This attribute is the same as the `CODEBASE` attribute of `<EMBED>`.)

- ■ `CLASSID`: This represents the URL type of the specific object implementation data. This URL is used by the assisted installation process if a plug-in is registered on the user's computer. (This tag is similar to the `CODE` attribute of `<APPLET>`.)

- ■ `ID`: This represents the name of the object for scripting purposes. (This is equivalent to the `NAME` attribute of `<APPLET>` and `<EMBED>`.)

- ■ `HEIGHT`, `WEIGHT`, `ALIGN`: These are the same basic attributes that are used in tags like `<IMG>`, `<EMBED>`, or `<APPLET>`.

28

CAUTION

When using the `<OBJECT>` tag, be sure that you provide enough attributes and the attributes aren't in conflict with each other, or the plug-in can't be embedded. The communicator goes through the attributes of `<OBJECT>`, and parses or ignores them as appropriate, to identify the object type and then determine how to deal with it.

You should continue using the `<EMBED>` tag to declare plug-ins until the new `<OBJECT>` tag is widely implemented on different browsers. If you do choose to use it, be sure to inform your users about the browser level required, or, alternatively, write some code to determine the type of browser the user is using, and branch to one tag (`<OBJECT>` for Communicator) or the other (`<EMBED>` for other browsers) to declare your plug-in. If you know for certain that all users will have compliant browsers (for example, for an intranet environment), you can simply use the `<OBJECT>` code and not worry about checking for browser type.

RESOURCE

You can find more information about the `<OBJECT>` tag from the W3C site at

```
http://www.w3.org/pub/WWW/TR
```

Summary

This chapter introduced you to Netscape's plug-in technology and explained the distinctions between plug-ins, helper applications, and MIME types.

It also looked at the various types of available plug-ins (audio/video, 3D graphics, business, and so on) and discussed some examples of each. We progressed to Netscape Navigator 3.0's built-in plug-ins (LiveAudio, LiveVideo, QuickTime, and Live3D) and Netscape Communicator's plug-ins, and discussed the HTML syntax required to use them as embedded objects in your Web document. We continued by stepping through a checklist for downloading plug-ins, as well as discussing when to avoid plug-ins.

We progressed to JavaScript techniques for determining and activating installed plug-ins, and saw sample code to find specific plug-ins or activate a plug-in object, depending on the availability of a browser plug-in to support the underlying MIME type. We concluded by looking at the <EMBED> and <OBJECT> tags, as currently used for declaring and configuring plug-in objects.

LiveAudio and Multimedia

IN THIS CHAPTER

29

CHAPTER

LiveAudio is an integral part of the Netscape Navigator Web Browser—a built-in plug-in that allows Navigator to "natively" play sound files. LiveAudio, in essence, extends Navigator to accept a brand new type of content. This means that, if an audio-capable computer is used, a majority of Web users can painlessly receive (hear) audio files, because Netscape Navigator currently dominates the browser market. This, in turn, opens up a whole new world of opportunities for the Web developer—the ability to deliver information and entertain through audio.

LiveAudio is tightly integrated into the Navigator environment and can easily be manipulated with JavaScript and LiveConnect. These advantages, along with LiveAudio's wide availability, warrant a detailed discussion of LiveAudio. This chapter shows some examples of LiveAudio and discusses how you can use JavaScript to manipulate it.

> **NOTE**
>
> LiveConnect is a Netscape client technology framework that lets "live" objects—namely, plug-ins, Java applets, and JavaScript—communicate and interact. See Chapter 26, "LiveConnect: Integrating JavaScript and Java," for more information.

The term *multimedia* generally means the integration of audio, video, or animation into Web sites. In that sense, the creation and control of multimedia on a Web site is achieved through these common techniques:

- The deployment of plug-ins (and plug-in objects)
- Java applets
- ActiveX controls (specifically, with Microsoft Internet Explorer)

This chapter looks at how you can use JavaScript to control multimedia using the first two techniques (plug-ins and Java applets) and LiveConnect. (Refer to Chapter 27, "ActiveX Scripting," for more information on ActiveX controls.)

Using LiveAudio

LiveAudio was originally introduced as one of four built-in plug-ins (along with LiveVideo, Live3D, and QuickTime) that came with Netscape Navigator 3.0. It's also built into the new Netscape Communicator. You can use LiveAudio to play audio files in WAV, AIFF, AU, and MIDI formats.

You can utilize LiveAudio as a plug-in object in your HTML files by using either the <EMBED> or <OBJECT> HTML tag (only with Netscape Communicator) to declare and define the object. Here is the HTML syntax you need if you use the <EMBED> tag:

```
<EMBED SRC= [URL] ...>
```

NOTE

You can find more information about the <OBJECT> tag and its syntax in Chapter 28, "Working with Netscape Plug-Ins," in the section "Running Plug-Ins with JavaScript."

The <EMBED> attributes include the following:

- SRC=[*URL*]: The URL (location) of the source audio file.

- AUTOSTART=[TRUE¦FALSE]: TRUE means that the file begins playing automatically when the Web page is loaded. The default is FALSE.

- LOOP=[TRUE¦FALSE¦INTEGER]: TRUE means that the audio file plays continuously until the stop button is pressed on the console or the user goes to another page. FALSE means the sound will play only once. INTEGER indicates the number of times the sound repeats.

- CONTROLS=[CONSOLE¦SMALLCONSOLE¦PLAYBUTTON¦PAUSEBUTTON¦ STOPBUTTON¦VOLUMELEVER]: Defines which view (or control) to display for the plug-in. The default is CONSOLE.

    CONSOLE: Consists of Play, Pause, Stop, and Volume.

    SMALLCONSOLE: Consists of Play, Stop, and Volume. This view has smaller buttons than standard CONSOLE buttons, and the sound will "auto-start" by default.

    PLAYBUTTON: The Play button, which starts a sound.

    PAUSEBUTTON: The Pause button, which pauses a sound.

    STOPBUTTON: The Stop button, which stops and unloads a sound file.

    VOLUMELEVER: A lever to adjust the playback volume.

- STARTTIME=[*MINUTES:SECONDS*]: Gives you the option of identifying where in the audio file you would like to begin playback (implemented only on Windows 95, NT, and Macintosh).

- ENDTIME=[*MINUTES:SECONDS*]: Gives you the option of identifying where in the audio file you would like to end playback (implemented only on Windows 95, NT, and Macintosh).

- VOLUME=[0-100]: 0 represents no volume, and 100 represents maximum volume. If MASTERVOLUME (see the NAME attribute) is not used, this number sets the volume for the system. The default volume level is the client system's current volume level.

- WIDTH=[*# PIXELS*]: Represents the width of the inline object. Default is WIDTH=144 for a standard console.

- HEIGHT=[*# PIXELS*]: Represents the height of the inline object. Default is HEIGHT=60 for standard console.

29

LIVEAUDIO AND MULTIMEDIA

- `ALIGN=[TOP¦BOTTOM¦CENTER¦BASELINE¦LEFT¦RIGHT¦TEXTTOP¦MIDDLE¦ABSMIDDLE¦ABSBOTTOM]`: Tells the browser how to align text around the plug-in object.

- `HIDDEN=[TRUE]`: `TRUE` means that the control console will not be displayed, and the sound is played in the background.

- `NAME=[UNIQUE NAME TO GROUP CONTROLS TOGETHER SO THAT THEY CONTROL ONE SOUND]`: Sets a unique ID for a group of `CONTROLS` elements, so they all act on the same sound as it plays. For example, if you want to control one sound with two inline objects (say, `PLAYBUTTON` and `STOPBUTTON`), you must use `MASTERSOUND` to tell LiveAudio which of the two object tags (in `<EMBED>`) contains the sound file that you want to control. The `<EMBED>`s with no `MASTERSOUND` tag are ignored by LiveAudio.

- `MASTERSOUND`: Must be used when grouping sounds together in a `NAME` group. LiveAudio will not play a sound if a `NAME` attribute exists without a corresponding `MASTERSOUND` attribute. This attribute tells LiveAudio which file is the real sound file to play, and instructs it to ignore any stub file. Stub files are necessary to activate LiveAudio.

TIP

Stub files are commonly used when you design your own sound console with LiveAudio elements (such as VOLUME, PLAY, PAUSE, and so on) instead of using the default console. In such a case, you need to use multiple EMBED statements to declare all your controls. (You need one EMBED per control—that is, one EMBED to declare VOLUME, another for PLAY, and so on.)

However, you don't want to load the same audio file several times (as declared by the required SRC attribute of EMBED), because that significantly delays page download. To overcome this problem, LiveAudio lets you declare a stub (or dummy) file under SRC. Stub files are very small files that usually contain only one character. For instance, in Microsoft Notepad (or any other text editor), create a file with just a space character in it, and save it as stub1.wav. Be sure to save the file with an audio file type extension (such as .wav or .mid); otherwise, LiveAudio won't work. Typically, you will declare one legitimate sound file under SRC, and the rest will be stub files. So, if you've designed a console with three elements (or EMBEDs), you will need one real audio file and two stub files declared under the SRC attribute. The stub files should have unique names, such as stub1.wav and stub2.wav. Listing 29.1 shows an example of designing your own sound controls and also demonstrates the use of MASTERSOUND and stub files.

An Example of Using LiveAudio

Listing 29.1 demonstrates some features of LiveAudio (including the use of different LiveAudio consoles), shown in Figure 29.1. You'll see two techniques for controlling sound on a browser using LiveAudio. First I show the code for declaring a default LiveAudio sound console. Then I demonstrate how to design a customized sound console using elements of LiveAudio (such as PLAY, STOP, and VOLUME). The customized sound console code also shows the use of the MASTERSOUND and NAME attributes, as well as stub files.

Listing 29.1. lvaudio.htm.

```
<HTML>
<HEAD>
<TITLE>LiveAudio Plug-in</TITLE>
</HEAD>
<BODY BGCOLOR="#ffffff">
<CENTER><H1>LiveAudio Plug-in Demo</H1>
<FONT SIZE=+1>Show me a standard console at default size</FONT>
<BR>
<EMBED SRC="youmight.wav" CONTROLS=console HEIGHT=60 WIDTH=144>
<BR>
<BR>
<FONT SIZE=+1>Show me a small console at default size</FONT>
<BR>
<EMBED SRC="youmight.wav" CONTROLS=smallconsole HEIGHT=15 WIDTH=144>
<BR>
<BR>
<!-- Set up my own ControlPanel in a table, using a PLAYBUTTON, PAUSEBUTTON,
STOPBUTTON and VOLUMELEVER. Set these controls to their default sizes. -->
<FONT SIZE=+1>Show MY OWN CONTROL PANEL</FONT>
<BR>
<TABLE BORDER=5>
<TR>
<TD ALIGN=center><B>Play</B></TD>
<TD ALIGN=center><B>Pause</B></TD>
<TD ALIGN=center><B>Stop</B></TD>
<TD ALIGN=center><B>Volume</B></TD>
</TR>
<TR>
<TD><EMBED SRC="opendoor.wav" AUTOSTART=true volume=80 CONTROLS=playbutton
NAME="ControlPanel" MASTERSOUND HEIGHT=22 WIDTH=37></TD>
<TD><EMBED SRC="stub1.wav" CONTROLS=pausebutton NAME="ControlPanel"
HEIGHT=22 WIDTH=37></TD>
<TD><EMBED SRC="stub2.wav" CONTROLS=stopbutton NAME="ControlPanel"
HEIGHT=22 WIDTH=37></TD>
<TD><EMBED SRC="stub3.wav" CONTROLS=volumelever NAME="ControlPanel"
HEIGHT=20 WIDTH=74></TD>
</TR>
</TABLE>
</center>
</body>
</html>
```

FIGURE 29.1.

*Several inline
LiveAudio objects.*

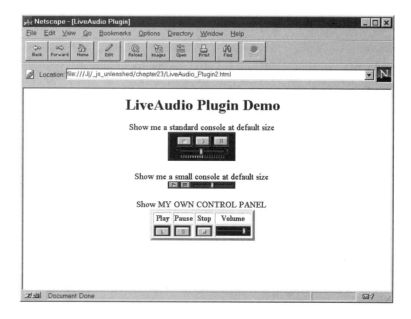

LiveAudio and LiveConnect

According to Netscape's Web site, "LiveAudio is LiveConnect-aware." This means that you can take advantage of the LiveConnect framework and JavaScript to control embedded (or inline) LiveAudio elements.

Using LiveConnect, LiveAudio, and JavaScript, you can programmatically accomplish the following:

- Create alternative sound control interfaces.
- Defer the loading of an audio file until a user interaction occurs (for example, clicking a "play" button).
- Create interface buttons that make "clicking" noises.
- Provide audio enhancement to user interaction. For instance, have an object say what it's doing when the user clicks it or moves the mouse cursor over it.

JavaScript Methods to Control LiveAudio

LiveAudio provides several JavaScript control methods to help a developer easily manipulate audio files embedded as in-line objects on a Web page. In order for these methods to be available to JavaScript, however, you must embed a LiveAudio console (any type of console is fine, even a hidden one) somewhere on your page. See Listing 29.1 for more details.

Here are the methods available to you to control LiveAudio through JavaScript:

- `play()`: Starts playing the sound. You can specify a loop value, similar to the LOOP attribute values, followed by an optional URL for the sound if the original URL isn't used.
- `stop()`: Stops the sound if it is currently playing.
- `pause()`: Pauses the sound at the current position. You can use the `play()` method, or the `pause()` method again, to continue the playback.
- `start_time()` and `end_time()`: Allow you to override the start and end times. Specify the value in seconds.
- `start_at_beginning()` and `stop_at_end()`: Reset the start and stop times to the beginning and end of the sound file.
- `setvol()`: Sets the sound's volume, from 0 to 100 percent.
- `fade_to()`: Sets the volume, but fades from the current value.
- `fade_from_to()`: Allows you to specify two values, and fades from one to the other. In addition, you can use the following methods, which return a value:

    `IsReady()`: Returns `true` if the sound is loaded and ready to play.

    `IsPlaying()`: Returns `true` if the sound is currently playing.

    `IsPaused()`: Returns `true` if the sound is currently paused.

    `GetVolume()`: Returns the current volume.

An Example of Using JavaScript, LiveAudio, and LiveConnect

The following example demonstrates the use of embedded sounds with LiveAudio and LiveConnect. The code shown in Listing 29.2 lets you load a sound and then control it using several buttons and JavaScript event handlers. Also, note the use of a hidden console to invoke LiveAudio initially. Figure 29.2 shows the resulting page in the browser.

Listing 29.2. Controlling embedded sounds with JavaScript.

```
<HTML>
<HEAD>
<TITLE>Embedded Sounds</TITLE>
</HEAD>
<BODY>
<H1>Embedded Sounds in JavaScript</H1>
<EMBED MASTERSOUND NAME="sound1" SRC="test.wav"
   VOLUME=100 HIDDEN=TRUE AUTOSTART=FALSE>
<HR>
<P>
This document includes a hidden embedded sound, which is loaded after the page
is loaded. You can use the JavaScript buttons below to control the sound.
<HR>
<FORM NAME="form1">
```

continues

29

LIVEAUDIO AND
MULTIMEDIA

Listing 29.2. continued

```
<INPUT TYPE="button" VALUE="Play"
    onClick="document.sound1.play(true);">
<INPUT TYPE="button" VALUE="Pause"
    onClick="document.sound1.pause();">
<INPUT TYPE="button" VALUE="Stop"
    onClick="document.sound1.stop();">
</FORM>
</BODY>
</HTML>
```

FIGURE 29.2.

Controlling embedded sounds in JavaScript.

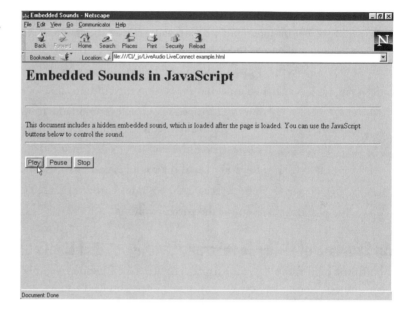

Using Sound in JavaScript

JavaScript doesn't provide any native functions for playing sounds. However, you can write your own function to do this by using the `window.location.href` property—similar to forcing a user to load another page. As such, when an audio file is requested (either through user interaction or JavaScript), the audio file will be downloaded to the browser. After the download is complete, the sound will be played by an audio player application.

You can play a sound file at any time during the execution of your JavaScript application. Commonly, audio files are used with event handlers (for example, `onClick` or `onLoad`) to enhance the user's experience. However, you may also use sound as an alternative to alert messages, and so on.

> **TIP**
>
> When using audio files to enhance your Web site, be sure to limit the size of these files. Large audio files—especially those that the user has no option to avoid (when used with onLoad events, for instance)—may significantly limit the performance of your page. Remember that many users (especially when dealing with Internet applications) have slow dialup connections, and downloading large audio files slows them down considerably.

Playing Sounds on JavaScript Events

As I mentioned earlier, you can use JavaScript to invoke sounds at any place within your site. Often, though, the most appropriate place to use sound to enhance a user's experience is with the "on" event handlers. The following example demonstrates this concept by showing you how to invoke several sounds on your page using the JavaScript event handlers onLoad, onUnLoad, and onClick.

The HTML code is shown in Listing 29.3. In this example, as the page is loaded, a keyboard-typing sound (type.wav) is played. To demonstrate the onClick event, when the user clicks the hyperlink, he hears the sound of a cash register, and clicking the button will result in the sound of a gunshot. Also, on the unloading of the page, the user hears glass shattering. The resulting browser window is shown in Figure 29.3.

Listing 29.3. soundevents.html.

```
<html>
<head>
<title>Sound on JS events</title>
<script language="javascript">
<!-- HIDE JAVASCRIPT from old browsers
function playSound(sfile) {
// load a sound and play it
    window.location.href=sfile;
}
// STOP HIDING -->
</script>
<body onLoad="playSound('Type.wav');"
onUnLoad="playSound('Glass.wav');">
<font size=+2>Sounds on JS Events</font>
<br>
<hr>
The following are example of JS event handlers used
to play sounds.
<hr>
<a href="#" onClick="playSound('Cashreg.wav');">
Click here for sound</a>
<br><br>
```

29

LIVEAUDIO AND
MULTIMEDIA

continues

Listing 29.3. continued

```
<form name="form1">
<input type="button" value="Press Button to play a sound"
onClick="playSound('Gunshot.wav');">
</form>
</body>
```

FIGURE 29.3.

Examples of invoking sounds on JavaScript events.

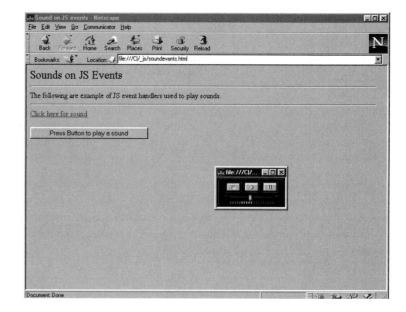

Configuring a Sound Player

Most of the recent versions of Netscape automatically install a helper application for sounds (.WAV and .AU files) called the Netscape Audio Player, or NAPLAYER.EXE. If you have your own audio player, you can designate it as the preferred application to launch to play audio files by configuring Netscape Navigator's Helper Application. (Refer to Chapter 28 for more information about this.) Otherwise, you can choose Netscape's NAPLAYER.EXE (usually located in the NETSCAPE\PROGRAMS directory) as your preferred choice.

Using Netscape's Audio player and JavaScript to open audio files in this way presents two potential problems:

■ Every time an audio file is played by the browser, a new window (or instance of NAPLAYER) is invoked. This occurs because one instance of NAPLAYER can play only one audio file. If you open several audio files and don't close their windows after the sound is played, you risk running low on system resources or crashing your browser.

■ The NAPLAYER window stays on top after it finishes playing the sound (that is, it becomes the active window on the desktop). Users may be inconvenienced by "losing" their active window like this—especially if they have several windows open at the same time.

To overcome the problems with NAPLAYER, you may want to recommend a sound player that exits after playing the sound (or can play multiple files from the same invocation). One program that does this is the shareware WPLANY.EXE, which can be downloaded from the Internet.

TIP

As you may have noticed, using helper applications to play sounds is not an ideal solution. If Netscape Navigator (version 3.0 or better) is your audience's browser of choice, you're better off using LiveAudio and embedding audio as inline objects. However, if you do need cross-browser functionality, you may also want to look at Java applets as a way of implementing audio.

Controlling Multimedia with JavaScript and LiveConnect

LiveConnect is a Netscape client-side technology that promises seamless manipulation of data between Navigator's three main client-side development environments—plug-ins, Java, and JavaScript. As I mentioned earlier, multimedia on the Web consists primarily of audio, video, and animation. This type of multimedia—especially when you're working with Netscape Navigator—is achieved through plug-ins or Java applets. The rest of this chapter discusses how you can use JavaScript to communicate between Java and plug-ins within the LiveConnect framework.

TIP

When you're developing for Internet Explorer, you can also use ActiveX controls to present multimedia on your Web page. Refer to Chapter 27 for more information on ActiveX.

> **NOTE**
>
> If you want to get started with LiveConnect development, you need to obtain the Live Connect/Plug-in Software Development Kit (SDK). It contains tools, documentation, sample code, and header files to get you started. You can download the SDK from Netscape's LiveConnect and Plug-in Developer's Guide page at
>
> `http://home.netscape.com/eng/mozilla/3.0/handbook/plugins/index.html`

JavaScript-to-Java Communication

LiveConnect allows JavaScript to communicate with Java in the following ways:

- Direct calls to Java methods
- Control over Java applets
- Control over Java plug-ins

These methods of communication are discussed in the following sections.

Direct Calls to Java Methods

If LiveConnect is enabled, you can use the following syntax to access a Java method:

`[Packages.]packageName.className.methodName`

where `packageName` and `className` are properties of the object `Packages`. The name `Packages` can optionally be omitted from the JavaScript call with Java, Sun, or Netscape packages. For instance, the Java class `java.class.System` can be referred to as either `java.lang.System` or `Packages.java.lang.System`.

For example, the following JavaScript code prints a message to the Java Console:

```
var System = java.lang.System     // assign the variable system to Java class
java.lang.System System.err.println("Greetings from JavaScript")
```

Control Over Java Applets

To take control of a Java applet using JavaScript, you don't need to know much about the construction of the applet. The applet's public variables, methods, and properties should be sufficient to let JavaScript take control of the applet.

You can reference the Java applet by name. Remember that the applet declared in the HTML page is regarded as a property of the JavaScript class `window.document`. For example, to call an applet named `myApplet`, you only need the following syntax:

`[window.]document.myApplet`

Declaring the top-level window class is optional.

You can also refer to myApplet with the following two techniques:

- document.applets[myApplet]
- document.applets[0]//

  myApplet is the first applet defined on the page, so its index number is 0 in the array of applets.

Control Over Java Plug-Ins

JavaScript regards each plug-in on a Web page as an item in an embeds array. For instance, document.embeds[0] represents the first EMBEDed object on the page.

If the plug-in is associated with the Java class netscape.plugin.Plugin, its static variables and methods can be accessed in the same way I showed you in the preceding section for accessing the Java applet's variables, methods, and properties.

Java-to-JavaScript Communication

To access JavaScript methods, properties, and data structures from a Java applet, you must first import the Netscape javascript package. This is done with the following syntax:

```
import netscape.javascript.*
```

netscape.javascript defines the JSObject class and the JSException exception object. You must allow an applet to access JavaScript by declaring the MAYSCRIPT attribute (with no arguments) for the APPLET tag. This prevents an applet from accessing JavaScript on a page without the developer's knowledge. An error occurs if the MAYSCRIPT attribute hasn't been declared.

TIP

Before you can access JavaScript, you must get a handle for the Navigator window. Use the getWindow method of the class netscape.javascript.JSObject to get a window handle. For example:

```
winHandle = JSObject.getWindow(this)
```

winHandle is a variable of the type JSObject.

To access JavaScript objects and properties, you need to use the getMember method of the class netscape.javascript.JSObject. This is done by calling getMember to access each contained JavaScript object in turn. You must be sure to get a handle for the JavaScript window first, however (use the getWindow method).

You can use the `call` and `eval` methods of the `netscape.javascript.JSObject` class to call JavaScript methods. Again, use `getWindow` to get a handle for the JavaScript window, and then use `call` or `eval` to access a JavaScript method. You can use the following syntax:

- `JSObject.getWindow().call("`*methodName*`", `*arguments*`)`

  methodName is the name of the called JavaScript method, and *arguments* is an array of arguments to pass to the method.

- `JSObject.getWindow().eval("`*expression*`")`

  expression is a JavaScript expression that evaluates to a JavaScript method.

Summary

This chapter discussed the Netscape LiveAudio plug-in in detail and showed you examples of how you can use LiveAudio to embed audio files (as inline objects) in your HTML pages.

We discussed how LiveAudio works within Netscape's LiveConnect client-side technology. We looked at the role of JavaScript within this environment, and we walked through available JavaScript methods to control and manipulate LiveAudio embedded objects.

We also talked about using JavaScript event handlers to invoke sounds within an HTML page, as well as how to set up external audio players as helper applications in order to hear the files.

We concluded by discussing how you can control multimedia (including audio) using the LiveConnect framework, with special emphasis on how JavaScript can be used to facilitate communication between multimedia plug-ins and Java applets.

PART

VIII

IN THIS PART

Server-Side JavaScript

Server-Side JavaScript Extensions Using LiveWire

IN THIS CHAPTER

Although JavaScript plays a key role on the client side, you can also use it to create server-based applications using Netscape LiveWire. LiveWire is a set of extensions that you can add to a Netscape server. It uses JavaScript as a server-based scripting language in place of CGI to perform server-specific tasks, such as creating dynamic HTML or accessing a server-based file. This chapter discusses Netscape LiveWire and its server-side extensions to the JavaScript language.

> **NOTE**
>
> With Netscape Enterprise Server 3.0, LiveWire's server-side JavaScript extensions are integrated into the server itself. Therefore, you no longer need to think of LiveWire as a separate product.

> **NOTE**
>
> LiveWire works only on Netscape servers, so you can't use server-side JavaScript with other Web servers at this time. Microsoft does support JScript in its Active Server platform, but these server-side language extensions are different than LiveWire extensions.

Developing a LiveWire Application

Before I get into the specifics of the server-side JavaScript language, I'll first look at the process of developing a LiveWire application. I find it easier to understand the language specifics if I know the context in which they are used. With that in mind, let's look at how to develop a LiveWire application. Figure 30.1 details the process.

> **RESOURCE**
>
> To download LiveWire, visit the Netscape home page at http://home.netscape.com/.

Creating Source Files for the Server Application

The first step in building a server-side JavaScript application is creating your source files, which can be one of two types:

- Source HTML documents: These documents can either be static pages or JavaScript-enabled pages. They have an .HTM or .HTML extension.

- JavaScript library files: These files, which have a .JS extension, serve as library files containing JavaScript functions. You don't need to use HTML tags in these files.

FIGURE 30.1.

*The LiveWire
development process.*

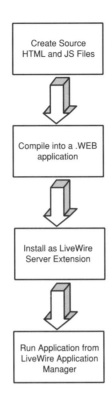

Source HTML Documents

In many cases, you will want to embed JavaScript code in your HTML documents, just as you do with client-side JavaScript. However, the way you embed server JavaScript in your HTML file can change the result. To embed JavaScript into your documents, you can use one of two options.

First, you can use the <SERVER> and </SERVER> tags to surround server JavaScript code. In many ways, the use of these tags is very similar to the <SCRIPT> and </SCRIPT> tags you use in client-side JavaScript. Suppose you wanted to generate a line of dynamic HTML. You could use the <SERVER> tags to do the following:

```
<SERVER>
    if (client.custid == null) {
        write("You have no customer ID") }
    else {
        write(Your customer ID is " + client.custid)
    }
</SERVER>
```

CAUTION

You can't place a <SERVER> tag within another HTML tag (that is, between the < and > of another tag).

Second, if you need to add a JavaScript expression inside another HTML tag, you can surround the code with backquotes (\Q). You will find that backquotes are useful when working with links, anchors, and form objects. For example, if you wanted to generate dynamic HTML with a link created on-the-fly based on the client's Web address, you could use the following:

```
<A HREF=\Qclient.WebAddress\Q>Your Home Page</A>
```

When you embed server JavaScript into your source HTML documents, the user sees only the result of the code, not the code itself. Server JavaScript thus contrasts with client-side JavaScript, which the user can see simply by viewing the source file in any Web browser. Listing 30.1 is a source HTML file with embedded JavaScript. When the application runs, however, the HTML source shown in Listing 30.2 is what the client can see if the source code is viewed in the browser. (Figure 30.2 shows the actual presentation of the HTML.) In case you're wondering about the meaning of the JavaScript expressions, I'll talk about the client object a little later in this chapter. At this point, think of these expressions as properties of an object that has already been created and defined elsewhere.

Listing 30.1. An embedded server script.

```
<html>
<head>
<title>Feedback</title>
</head>
<body>
<h1>"Superiffic" Feedback Confirmation</h1>
<p>Dear <SERVER>client.firstName</SERVER>,</p>
<p>Thank you for submitting feedback about our product. If you have asked us
to contact you, we will be using the following information:</p>
<blockquote>
<p><strong>E-mail:</strong> <SERVER>client.email</SERVER><br>
<strong>Telephone:</strong> <SERVER>client.phone</SERVER><br>
<strong>FAX:</strong> <SERVER>client.fax</SERVER></p>
</blockquote>
<p>If any of this information is incorrect, please go back to the feedback
form and change it. We thank you for taking the time to help us be a
"superiffic" company.</p>
<p>Sincerely,</p>
<p>Rupert Mydryl <br>
Manager, Customer Services</p>
</body>
</html>
```

Listing 30.2. The resulting document given to the client.

```
<head>
<title>Feedback</title>
</head>
<body>
<h1>"Superiffic" Feedback Confirmation</h1>
<p>Dear Charles:</p>
<p>Thank you for submitting feedback about our product. If you have asked us
to contact you, we will be using the following information:</p>
<blockquote>
<p><strong>E-mail: chappy@smiles.com</strong> <br>
<strong>Telephone: 808-555-1212</strong> <br>
<strong>FAX: 808-555-5050</strong> </p>
</blockquote>
<p>If any of this information is incorrect, please go back to the
feedback form and change it. We thank you for taking the time to help us be
a "superiffic" company.</p>
<p>Sincerely,</p>
<p>Rupert Mydryl <br>
Manager, Customer Services</p>
</body>
</html>
```

FIGURE 30.2.

The HTML document in the browser.

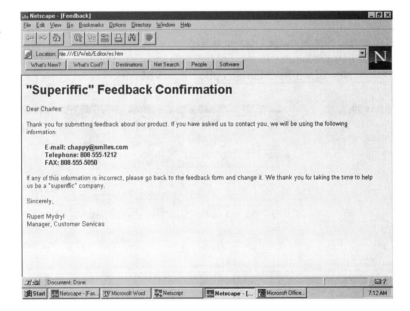

JavaScript Library Files

Any serious development environment needs a facility in which to place generic functions that can be called from a variety of sources. LiveWire provides this feature by allowing you to place JavaScript code in external text files denoted with a .JS extension. Inside the JavaScript library file, there should be functions, not HTML. You can then reference functions inside of these .JS files inside your HTML files. When your LiveWire application is compiled, the compiler resolves all the calls to external functions by looking at the .JS files in the LiveWire application directory.

Compiling LiveWire Applications

After you've finished creating the source files for your LiveWire application, you're ready to compile them. The LiveWire compiler creates a bytecode .WEB file from the .HTML documents and .JS library files. To compile an application, you can use either the LiveWire Site Manager or the command-line compiler.

> **NOTE**
>
> Acadia Infuse provides support for LiveWire, including LiveWire's server-side object model extensions as well as a means of compiling LiveWire applications within the editor itself. See Chapter 4, "Using Acadia Infuse to Create JavaScript Scripts," for more information on Infuse.

To use the Site Manager, shown in Figure 30.3, open it and find the directory in which your source files are located in the Folders section of the window. Next, select Site | Manage (or choose New Site if the Manage option is grayed out).

FIGURE 30.3.

LiveWire Site Manager.

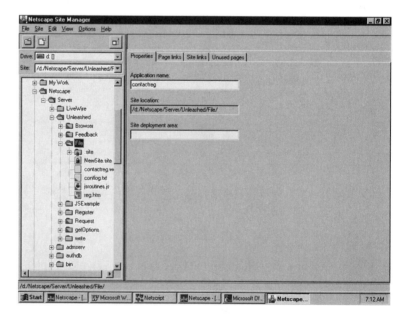

After the application is considered under Site Manager's supervision, you can compile it by choosing Site | Build Application. The Site Manager attempts to compile the application. If a syntax error occurs, a dialog box displays the error message, as shown in Figure 30.4.

FIGURE 30.4.

A compiler error.

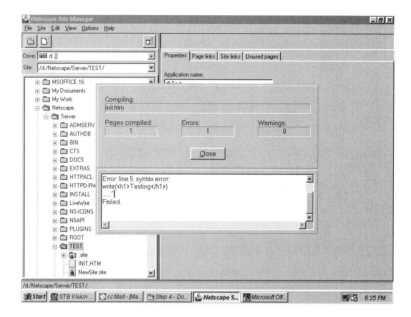

Otherwise, the Site Manager notifies you that the process finished successfully, as shown in Figure 30.5.

FIGURE 30.5.

A successful compile.

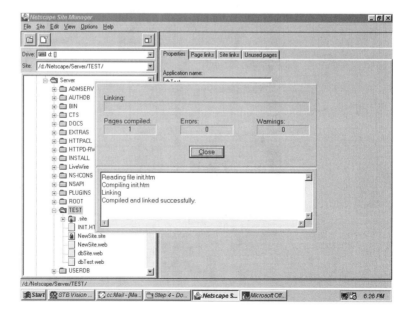

30

SERVER-SIDE
EXTENSIONS
USING LIVEWIRE

Alternatively, you can use the command-line compiler to compile the LiveWire application. Here is the syntax:

```
lwcomp [-c¦v¦d¦?] [-o outputfile.web] [doc1.htm...docn.htm] [lib1.js...libn.js]
```

The following list describes the options:

> -c checks the syntax only.
>
> -v compiles with verbose output.
>
> -d shows generated JavaScript contents.
>
> -? shows compiler syntax Help.
>
> -o creates a .WEB file using the specified name.

For example, the following command-line statement compiles (with verbose output) a LiveWire application into a file called `policy.web` using three HTML source files (`index.htm`, `toc.htm`, and `polpage.htm`) and two JavaScript library files (`jsroutine.js` and `jsdates.js`):

```
lwcomp -v -o policy.web index.htm toc.htm polpage.htm jsroutines.js jsdates.js
```

Installing LiveWire Applications on the Server

Before users can access your LiveWire application, you need to install it on the server using the LiveWire Application Manager. From the Application Manager, click the Add button to begin the installation process. After you click the Add button, the right frame of the window displays an HTML form for you to fill out, as shown in Figure 30.6.

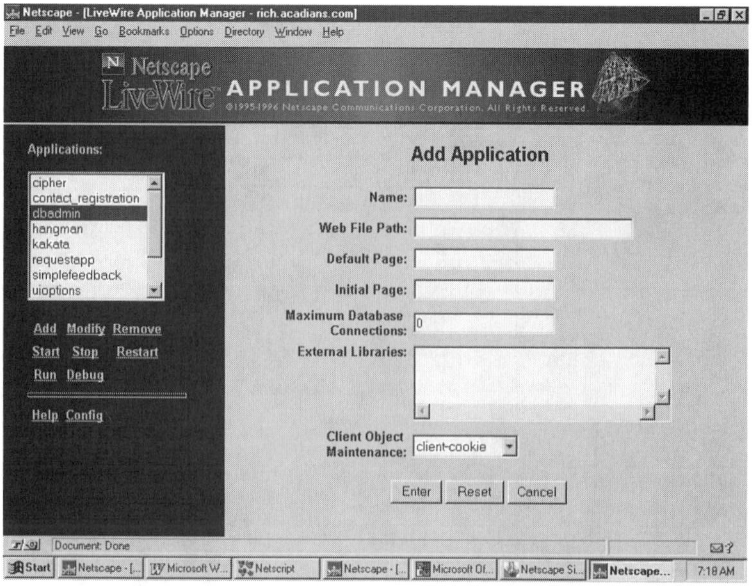

FIGURE 30.6.

LiveWire Application Manager.

Fill out the form based on the following information.

■ Name: Enter the name of the application. This name is used to access the application once it is installed. For example, if you name an application `fireball` on a server with a URL of `www.junebug.com`, you could access it with the following request:

```
http://www.junebug.com/fireball
```

> **CAUTION**
>
> Be sure you don't give an application the same name as an existing directory on the Web server. If you do, a client will be unable to access that directory on the server.

■ Web File Path: Enter the full path and filename of the .WEB application file.

■ Default Page: Optionally, enter an HTML filename to serve as the default page of an application. The default page is served when a client—who has already accessed the application—doesn't specify a file in the request.

■ Initial Page: Optionally, enter an HTML filename to serve as the opening page when the application is accessed by a client.

■ Maximum Database Connections: If you're accessing a SQL database and running off an NT server, enter the maximum number of concurrent connections your database server permits.

■ External Libraries: If your application uses external libraries (for example, dynamic link libraries), enter the full path in the space provided.

■ Client Object Maintenance: This field specifies the mode in which you're maintaining client object persistence. Available options are client cookie, client URL, server IP, server cookie, and server URL.

After you enter the application information, click the Enter button. LiveWire Application Manager checks your input values and installs the application on the server. Run the application by clicking Run.

> **NOTE**
>
> When you modify the source of an application and recompile, you must restart the application using the Application Manager before changes take effect.

Debugging Server-Side JavaScript Applications

If you work with both client-side and server-side JavaScript, you might get spoiled when you start working with the LiveWire JavaScript debugger; you will probably soon wish you could use the debugger for client-side JavaScript as well. LiveWire includes a debugger within the Application Manager. To run an application in debug mode, select the application from the list, and click Debug. This results in the opening of a new browser window with a trace frame (or window) displayed beside it, as shown in Figure 30.7. The trace window shows the current objects and their properties. You can also use the built-in `debug()` function to bring the result of a JavaScript expression to the trace window.

FIGURE 30.7.
LiveWire debugger.

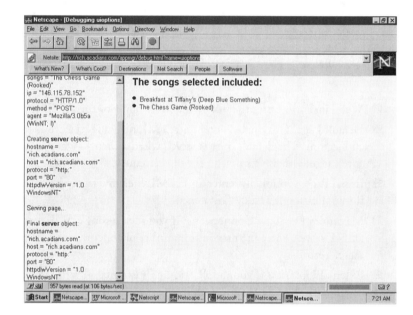

Generating Dynamic HTML

One of the most common uses of server JavaScript is creating dynamic HTML. You can use the built-in `write()` function to generate HTML based on the results of the JavaScript expression used as its parameter. You will probably notice the similarity of the `write()` function to the document object's `write()` method in client-side JavaScript. Although the context is entirely different, they both produce HTML in a similar fashion. However, note that the server-side `write()` function doesn't have an object associated with it. You never use dot notation to reference the function. For example, the following line produces HTML for the client:

```
write("Your IP address is " + request.ip)
```

NOTE

For another example of using `write()`, see Listing 30.3 later in this chapter.

Working with LiveWire Objects

Just as client-side JavaScript has a framework of built-in objects, so too does LiveWire. LiveWire contains four basic objects, called request, client, project, and server, as shown in Figure 30.8. The central purpose of these four server objects is to manage persistent data. Within the Web's stateless environment, these objects can store various types of data persistently across multiple requests per client, across multiple clients, and even across multiple LiveWire applications.

FIGURE 30.8.
The basic LiveWire object framework.

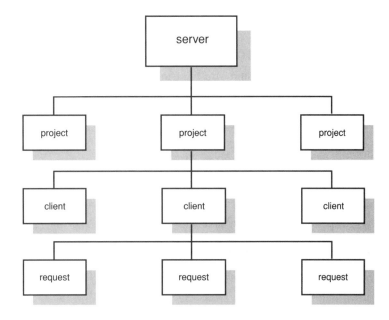

> **NOTE**
>
> LiveWire also has a `SendMail` object and several database-related objects. These will be discussed near the end of this chapter.

The meaning of persistence depends on the type of object you're dealing with. Table 30.1 lists the lifetime expectancy of the LiveWire objects.

Table 30.1. Life expectancy of basic LiveWire objects.

Object	Lifetime of Object
Request	Momentary, for a single request only.
Client	Ten minutes by default, although this can be changed using JavaScript.
Project	Open-ended (destroyed only when application is stopped).
Server	Open-ended (destroyed only when server is shut down).

LiveWire Object Properties

Some LiveWire objects come with built-in properties like what client-side built-in JavaScript objects have. You are also free to add new properties to these objects simply by declaring them. For example, if you wanted to add two properties called custID and custName to the client object, you could add these lines to your code:

```
client.custID = "120120"
client.custName = "Wagner, Richard"
```

LiveWire objects store all their property values as strings. You can assign a property a numeric or logical value, as shown in the following examples:

```
client.custid = 21020    // custid is stored internally as "21020"

client.premierMember = true // premierMember is stored internally as "true"
```

When you read from these object properties, you must first convert the data to its correct type. To use the properties in the previous examples, you need to do the following:

```
currentid = parseInt(client.custid)
if (client.premierMember == "true") {
    performAction() }
```

The Request Object

When a client makes an HTTP request for a specific URL, the request is sent to the appropriate Web server to handle. LiveWire assigns the request object to handle this incoming demand. A request object is instantiated for each new request received by the server. This newly created request object contains data from the current request of the client.

The request object has six built-in properties, which are listed in Table 30.2.

Table 30.2. Built-in properties of the request object.

Property	Description
agent	Client software information (such as name and version).
ip	IP address of the client.
method	HTTP method (typically GET or POST).
protocol	HTTP protocol level of client.
imageX	Horizontal location of the mouse pointer over an image map.
imageY	Vertical location of the mouse pointer over an image map.

Consider an example of how you can use this information in a LiveWire application. Suppose you wanted to display these properties in an HTML table when the user requested the application. To display the value of the agent property in a dynamically created HTML document, you would use the following code:

```
<server>write(request.agent)</server>
```

The write() function displays the result of the request.agent expression. Listing 30.3 shows the entire HTML document. When the application is run from the server, the page that the user sees looks like Figure 30.9.

Listing 30.3. request.htm.

```
<html>
<head>
<title>Request</title>

</head>
<body>
<h1>LiveWire Request Object Example</h1>
<table width=80%>
<tr><td width=50%>Browser Information</td><td width=50%><server>
     write(request.agent)</server></td></tr>
<tr><td width=50%>IP Address</td><td width=50%><server>
     write(request.ip)</server></td></tr>
<tr><td width=50%>HTTP Method</td><td width=50%><server>
     write(request.method)</server></td></tr>
<tr><td width=50%>HTTP Protocol</td><td width=50%><server>
     write(request.protocol)</server></td></tr>
</table>
</body>
</html>
```

FIGURE 30.9.
Request object properties.

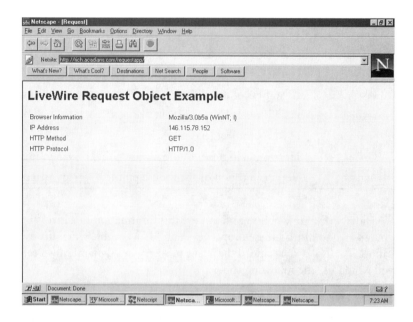

In addition to its predefined properties, the request object also has corresponding properties for each input element of a submitted HTML form. Suppose, for example, that a user submitted the form shown in Listing 30.4.

Listing 30.4. `regform_short.htm`.

```
<html>
<head>
<title>Online Registration</title>
</head>

<body>
<h1>Registration</h1>
<hr>
<form action="http://rich.acadians.com/lwobjects" method="POST">
<p>Please provide the following contact information:</p>
<blockquote>
<pre><em>            Name </em><input type=text size=35 maxlength=256
name="FullName">
<em>           Title </em><input type=text size=35 maxlength=256
name="Title">
<em>    Organization </em><input type=text size=35 maxlength=256
name="Organization">
<em>  Street address </em><input type=text size=35 maxlength=256
name="StreetAddress">
<em> Address (cont.) </em><input type=text size=35 maxlength=256
name="Address2">
<em>            City </em><input type=text size=35 maxlength=256
name="City">
<em>  State/Province </em><input type=text size=35 maxlength=256
name="State">
```

```
<em> Zip/Postal code </em><input type=text size=12 maxlength=12
name="ZipCode">
<em>          Country </em><input type=text size=25 maxlength=256
name="Country">
<em>       Work Phone </em><input type=text size=25 maxlength=25
name="WorkPhone">
<em>       Home Phone </em><input type=text size=25 maxlength=25
name="HomePhone">
<em>              FAX </em><input type=text size=25 maxlength=25 name="FAX">
<em>           E-mail </em><input type=text size=25 maxlength=256 name="Email">
<em>              URL </em><input type=text size=25 maxlength=25 name="WebSite">
</pre>
<p><input type=submit value="Submit"> <input type=reset value="Reset"> </p>
</form>
<p> </h5>
</body>
</html>
```

When a request object is created based on this form's submission, the following properties are associated with it:

```
request.FullName
request.Title
request.Organization
request.StreetAddress
request.Address2
request.City
request.State
request.ZipCode
request.Country
request.WorkPhone
request.HomePhone
request.FAX
request.Email
request.WebSite
```

> **NOTE**
>
> See Listing 30.9 later in this chapter for an example of how you can use these form properties.

The one form element that is a special case occurs when a select object is set to accept multiple values (that is, the MULTIPLE parameter is set in the <SELECT> definition). You can use the built-in getOptionValue() and getOptionValueCount() functions to iterate through multiple values of a select object. The getOptionValue() function is defined as

```
getOptionValue(name, index)
```

The *name* parameter is the select object name, and the *index* parameter is the index of the options array.

For example, look at the list of options in the select object defined in Listing 30.5 and shown in Figure 30.10. When the form is submitted to the server, topsongs.htm (shown in Listing 30.6) is requested. Using a familiar-looking for loop, you can iterate through each element that was selected. Figure 30.11 shows the resulting HTML form that the write() function creates dynamically.

Listing 30.5. songform.htm.

```
<HTML>
<HEAD>
<h2>Pick Your Favorite Songs From the List:</h2><p>
<FORM action="topsongs.htm" method="post" name="form1">
<select NAME="songs" SIZE=10 MULTIPLE>
<option>1979 (Smashing Pumpkins)</option>
<option>Breakfast at Tiffany's (Deep Blue Something)</option>
<option>The Chess Game (Rooked)</option>
<option>Don't Cry (Seal)</option>
<option>Flood (Jars of Clay)</option>
<option>Fortress Around Your Heart (Sting)</option>
<option>The Hounds of Winter (Sting)</option>
<option>Ironic (Alanis Morisette)</option>
<option>Kiss From a Rose (Seal)</option>
<option>Liquid (Jars of Clay)</option>
<option>Standing Outside a Broken Phone Booth (PRG)</option>
<option>Wake Up (Alanis Morisette)</option>
<option>Wonderwall (Oasis)</option>
<option>World's Apart (Jars of Clay)</option>
</SELECT><p>
<input type=submit value="Submit">
</FORM>
</BODY>
</HTML>
```

Listing 30.6. topsongs.htm.

```
<SERVER>
    write("<h2>The songs selected included:</h2><p>")
    var size = getOptionValueCount("songs")
    for (var i=0; i<size; i++) {
        write("<li>" + getOptionValue("songs", i) + "</li>")
    }
</SERVER>
```

The Client Object

As you have seen, request objects exist for a specific moment in time. When the request has been processed, the data no longer persists on the server. However, because a client's interaction with a server application often spans more than a single request, the client object is used to provide state throughout a series of stateless requests. LiveWire instantiates a new client object each time a new client accesses the application.

FIGURE 30.10.
A multiselection list.

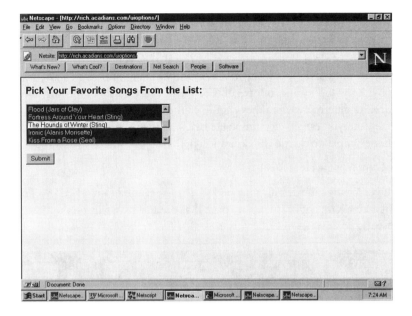

FIGURE 30.11.
A document generated on-the-fly.

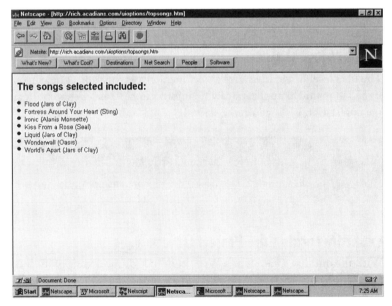

NOTE

Intended for application-specific uses, the client object contains no predefined properties.

Modifying the Life Span of a Client Object

As noted earlier in this chapter, the client object is designed to "self-destruct" after a specific duration of time. The reason behind this is that you want to maintain state across client requests, but you have no way to determine which request is a client's last request. Because you obviously don't want to leave unused client objects in memory any longer than possible, you need to determine when they should expire automatically. The default time period is 10 minutes, but you can change this value by using the client object's `expiration(`*seconds*`)` method. For example, to extend the expiration period to 20 minutes, you would use the following code:

```
client.expiration(1200)
```

If you change the default time period, the `expiration()` method must be defined in each page of a LiveWire application. Any page that doesn't have this method uses the default expiration setting.

> **NOTE**
>
> See Chapter 31, "Partitioning Client and Server Applications," to learn how to maintain client object persistence.

The Project Object

The next level in the LiveWire object hierarchy is the project object. The project object is designed to maintain application-wide information across clients and maintain persistence until the application is closed on the server.

> **NOTE**
>
> As with the client objects, the project object contains no predefined properties.

Explicitly Locking the Project Object

With the multiuser nature of a Web, hundreds or thousands of users could access a LiveWire application concurrently. As a result, it is not unusual for multiple persons to be either reading or writing to a project property at the same time. LiveWire automatically enforces implicit locking for the length of time it takes to read or set a property value.

You might sometimes need to explicitly lock a property. The best example of this is if you want to base the value of an autoincrementing number, such as an invoice number, on the existing value of a property. To pull this off, you need to read the old value, add a value to it, and then reassign the new value to the property. Implicit locking doesn't work in this context; however, you can use the project object's `lock()` method to perform this process. The `lock()` method places an explicit lock on the project object itself until an `unlock()` method is called. For example, to assign a new invoice number based on the existing one, you could use the following code:

```
project.lock()
project.invoiceNum += 1
project.unlock()
```

If another client tries to access the project object during this process, it is forced to wait until the process is finished.

> **NOTE**
>
> LiveWire ensures that a deadlock can't occur within a project by automatically releasing any locks after each client request.

The Server Object

When you're running a server-based application, certain pieces of information are specific to the server itself, apart from applications running on the server. The server object—which is the top level of the LiveWire object framework—is used to manage this global data. A server object is always present on a LiveWire server, because it's instantiated when the server is started. It is destroyed only when the server shuts down. The server object has four built-in properties, as shown in Table 30.3.

Table 30.3. Built-in properties of the server object.

Property	Description
hostname	Full name of the server (including port)
host	Server name
protocol	Internet protocol in use
port	Server port number used

As with the project object, the server object has `lock()` and `unlock()` methods that you can use to explicitly lock the server object when modifying server properties.

Redirecting Clients to an Alternative URL

You can redirect clients to a different URL by issuing a `redirect()` call. This built-in function uses a URL as a parameter. The following line diverts the client to the specified URL:

```
redirect("http://www.ouagodougou.com/burkina")
```

One possible use of `redirect()` is analyzing the client software when a request is made. If the agent property of the request object is recognized as a JavaScript-enabled browser, you can send the client to an enhanced page. Listing 30.7 shows an example of how you can do this. In this source file, the code examines the agent property and determines whether it supports JavaScript based on its value. If it does, the client is diverted to the `jsindex.htm` page, shown in Listing 30.8, which adds client-side JavaScript to the basic HTML.

Listing 30.7. `index.htm`.

```
<html>
<head>
<title>Kakata</title>
<SERVER>
    var browser = ""
    browser = request.agent
    if (browser.indexOf("Mozilla/") != -1) {
        ver = browser.substring(8,9)
        verNum = parseInt(ver)
        if (verNum >= 2) {
            redirect("http://rich.acadians.com/kakata/jsindex.htm")
        }
    }
</SERVER>
</head>
<body>
<h1>Welcome to the Kakata Home Page</h1>
<p>We are glad you found us!</p>
<p>Click here for the <a href="http://www.kakata.com/news">Latest News</a>
from the Land of Kakata.</p>
<p>Click here for more information on <a href="http://www.kakata.com/
legend.htm">The Legend of Kakaka</a></p>
</body>
</html>
```

Listing 30.8. `jsindex.htm`.

```html
<html>
<head>
<title>Kakata</title>
<SCRIPT LANGUAGE="JavaScript">
document.write("<h1>Welcome " + navigator.appName +
" user to the Kakata Home Page</h1><p>")
</SCRIPT>
</head>

<body>
<p>We are glad you found us!</p>
<p>Click here for the <a href="http://www.kakata.com/news">
Latest News</a> from the Land of Kakata.</p>
<p>Click here for more information on <a href="http://www.kakata.com/
legend.htm">The Legend of Kakaka</a></p>
</body>
</html>
```

Figures 30.12 and 30.13 show the varied results in versions 2.0 and 3.0 of Internet Explorer (IE). If you recall, Internet Explorer 3.0 supports JavaScript, but version 2.0 doesn't.

FIGURE 30.12.

The IE 3.0 client is routed to an enhanced page.

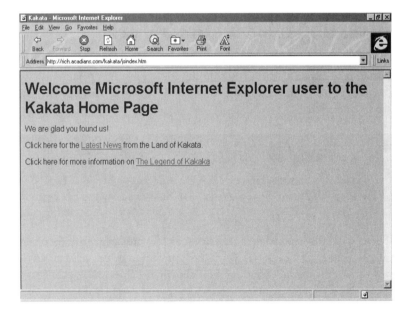

30

SERVER-SIDE
EXTENSIONS
USING LIVEWIRE

FIGURE 30.13.

The IE 2.0 client stays at the normal page.

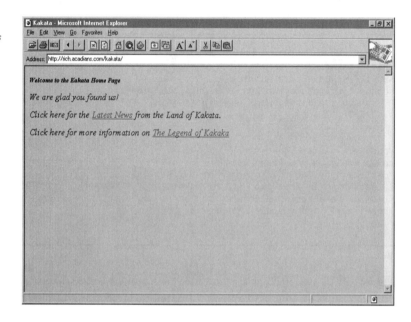

Accessing Files on the Server

LiveWire includes a file object to let you read and write data to a file on the server's file system. File storage can be a very useful solution for storing data persistently when you don't want to use a relational database. Additionally, anything you save to a disk is maintained even after the server shuts down.

> **CAUTION**
>
> For security concerns, be very careful in your use of the file object. You should ensure that a hacker can't access sensitive files on your server or write to the server disk.

The commands for reading and writing to files are largely standard across programming languages. Server JavaScript follows in this convention by providing many of the file-access methods you would expect, including those shown in Table 30.4. Table 30.5 shows some additional methods.

Table 30.4. Common file access methods.

Method	Description
open()	Opens the file for access.
close()	Closes a file.

Method	Description
read()	Reads data from the file into a string.
readln()	Reads current line of the file into a string.
write()	Writes data to a file.
writeln()	Writes data to a file and appends a carriage return.
flush()	Writes the content of the internal buffer to a file.
getLength()	Gets the length of the file.
getPosition()	Gets the current position in the file.
setPosition()	Sets the current position in the file.
eof()	Determines whether the file pointer is at the end of the file.
exists()	Determines whether the specified file exists.

Table 30.5. Additional file access methods.

Method	Description
byteToString()	Converts a number that represents a byte into a string.
stringToByte()	Converts the first number of a string into a number to represent a byte.
readByte()	Reads the next byte and returns its numeric value.
writeByte()	Writes a byte of data to a file.
error()	Returns the current error status.
clearError()	Clears the file error status.

You can create a file object using the new operator:

```
fileObject = new File("path")
```

Because the file object deals with the server's file system, the path parameter is a full path to the file, not a URL. For example, the following line creates a file object called policyInfo:

```
policyInfo = new File("e:/netscape/server/corp/policy.txt")
```

After a file object has been instantiated, you need to open it to prepare it for either reading or writing. Use the open() method for this task:

```
result = fileObject.open("mode")
```

result is a Boolean value: true if successful, false if unsuccessful. The mode parameter can be one of the options outlined in Table 30.6.

Table 30.6. File object open() method parameters.

Mode	Description
r[b]	Opens an existing file for reading. If the file does not exist, a false value is returned.
a[b]	Opens an existing file for appending new text. If the file does not exist, one is created.
w[b]	Opens a new file for writing. If the file exists, it is overwritten.
w+[b]	Opens a new file for reading and writing. If the file exists, it is overwritten.
r+[b]	Opens an existing file for reading and writing. If the file does not exist, false is returned. The position of the pointer is the start of the file.
a+[b]	Opens an existing file for reading and writing. If the file does not exist, false is returned. The position of the pointer is the end of the file.

On the Windows platform, you can use the optional b parameter to open a file as a binary file.

When you have finished working with an open file, issue a `close()` method to close access to it.

> **TIP**
>
> Although the file object doesn't have `lock()` and `unlock()` methods, you can still take advantage of the locking capabilities of the project and server objects to prevent multiple users from accessing the file simultaneously.

Listing 30.9 demonstrates the process of working with files. You can use this source HTML file to record a log of persons who submit the attached form. Each time a form is submitted, the server script opens the `contlog.txt` file and writes each field entry into the comma-delimited file.

Listing 30.9. reg.htm.

```
<html>
<head>
<title>Online Registration</title>
</head>
<body>
<SERVER>

    if (request.FullName != null) {
        cLog = new File("d:/netscape/server/unleashed/file/contlog.txt")
```

```
            project.lock()
            if (cLog.open("a") == true) {
                //isOpen = cLog.open("a")
                cLog.write(request.FullName + ",")
                cLog.write(request.Title + ",")
                cLog.write(request.Organization + ",")
                cLog.write(request.StreetAddress + ",")
                cLog.write(request.Address2 + ",")
                cLog.write(request.City + ",")
                cLog.write(request.State + ",")
                cLog.write(request.ZipCode + ",")
                cLog.write(request.Country + ",")
                cLog.write(request.WorkPhone + ",")
                cLog.write(request.HomePhone + ",")
                cLog.write(request.FAX + ",")
                cLog.write(request.Email + ",")
                cLog.writeln(request.WebSite)
                cLog.close()
            }
            project.unlock()
        }

</SERVER>
<h1>Registration</h1><hr>
<form method="post" action="reg.htm">
<p>Please provide the following contact information:</p>
<blockquote>
<pre><em>             Name </em><input type=text size=35 maxlength=256
name="FullName">
<em>            Title </em><input type=text size=35 maxlength=256
name="Title">
<em>     Organization </em><input type=text size=35 maxlength=256
name="Organization">
<em>  Street address </em><input type=text size=35 maxlength=256
name="StreetAddress">
<em> Address (cont.) </em><input type=text size=35 maxlength=256
name="Address2">
<em>             City </em><input type=text size=35 maxlength=256 name="City">
<em>   State/Province </em><input type=text size=35 maxlength=256 name="State">
<em> Zip/Postal code </em><input type=text size=12 maxlength=12 name="ZipCode">
<em>          Country </em><input type=text size=25 maxlength=256
name="Country">
<em>       Work Phone </em><input type=text size=25 maxlength=25
name="WorkPhone">
<em>       Home Phone </em><input type=text size=25 maxlength=25
name="HomePhone">
<em>              FAX </em><input type=text size=25 maxlength=25 name="FAX">
<em>           E-mail </em><input type=text size=25 maxlength=256 name="Email">
<em>              URL </em><input type=text size=25 maxlength=25 name="WebSite">
</pre>
<p><input type=submit value="Submit"> <input type=reset value="Reset"> </p>
</form>
<p> </h5>
</body>
</html>
```

Using the `SendMail` Object in Enterprise Server 3.0

The LiveWire included with Netscape Enterprise Server 3.0 contains a new object for sending SMTP mail. Using the `SendMail` object, you can send a message using server-side JavaScript. `SendMail` has the properties shown in Table 30.7.

Table 30.7. `SendMail` object properties.

Property	Description
To	A comma-delimited list of message recipients. Required.
From	Username of message sender. Required.
Cc	A comma-delimited list of additional recipients.
Bcc	A comma-delimited list of recipients whose names are hidden in the distribution list.
Organization	An organization name or other company information.
Replyto	A username to use instead of the From attribute as the address to which replies to the message should be sent. The default value is the From value.
Subject	The title of the message.
Body	The body text of the message.
Errorsto	The username to which to send errors concerning the message. The default value is the From value.
Smtpserver	The SMTP server name.

You can create a `SendMail` object using the familiar `new` operator:

```
smtpMessage = new SendMail()
```

To send a message, use the `send()` method as shown in the following example:

```
<server>

    smtpMessage = new SendMail();

    smtpMessage.To = request.EmailAddress;
    smtpMessage.From = client.SenderEmail;
    smtpMessage.Cc = client.MyBossEmail;
    smtpMessage.Subject = 'Registration of product';
    smtpMessage.Body = 'Thanks for registering your product. Your ' +
                       'registration number is ' + client.RegNum;
    smtpMessage.send();

</server>
```

Summary

In this chapter, you learned that JavaScript is not just for the client side anymore. Using Netscape LiveWire, you can employ the scripting language on the server side to produce server-side applications. The next chapter looks more closely at some of the issues surrounding client/server applications and how you can apply this architecture to the Web.

Partitioning Client and Server Applications

31

CHAPTER

The Web is, by default, a client/server environment. In the Web sense, clients are browsers, and servers are Web servers or database servers at some other (or possibly the same) location. The client and server are separate entities, completely independent of each other, until the client needs information from the server. The Web client/server concept has evolved beyond the server being a host for the HTML pages; the server side of the Web application now could be a true server that supports application processing and database storage—not just the static document storage facility it has been in the past.

Web-based client/server development is slightly different from traditional client/server development. Traditionally, the "server" in client/server is a database server used to store data and process data and calculation requests from the client. In the Web-based client/server, the server might not necessarily be a database; it can be just the Web server that is used for processing, administering, and performing calculations on HTML documents. The capability still exists to split processing between client and server, but the processing is usually centralized on the server.

Unlike traditional client/server development, when you consider Web application partitioning, you must be slightly more cautious in your design. Traditional client/server partitioning allows for many variations of the client/server relationship, ranging from the client being a presentation front only, to the client having all application control and the server being used only for data storage.

The client, in the case of the Web, could be just a Web browser terminal (dumb workstation). You don't have much control over the type of PC used for browsing the Web, nor do you have control of your application interface. Your front end to the server might be an older, slow PC that has few benefits other than viewing. Or your end-user might be using an older browser that can't handle extensive processing as the newer browsers can. In this case, you don't want much processing done on the client. Because you have no control over the client browser and you do have control over the server, as a developer you should place high-intensity processing and calculations on the server, because you can predict its speed and reliability.

TIP

Test processing speed on a generic client processor before deciding where to do the processing. Remember that not all users will have a browser client that's up to par with a developer's environment.

You can perform a minor amount of processing on the client side, because at some point it becomes more effective to move the processing to the client because the speed of the Internet and traffic concerns are also factors.

If processing is done on a client and the user considers it too slow, the usefulness of your Web page could be lost due to speed issues.

Fundamentals of Client/Server Architecture

In client/server application development, you will partition your application into two distinct pieces. In the traditional sense of client/server, the client or front end is a desktop workstation where the user can interact with the application. This workstation provides the user with an interface into the application (user interface), access to the back end, and some processing capabilities. Processing is spread between the client and the server depending on the necessary requirements.

In the typical client/server environment, it is reasonable to put processing on the client because you usually have some control over the client configuration and setup. You, the developer, can partition the application as you see fit, moving more or less processing to the client side depending on client capabilities, server processing load, and network traffic flow.

The server, or back end, is the processing engine for the application. Usually, the back end is a database server that stores and manages large amounts of data and performs the processor-intensive, large-scale calculations and system processing. The ability to segregate these two pieces of a system, making them largely independent of each other, has contributed to significant advances in the development of large-scale database systems. The capability to split these two pieces gives the developer more flexibility in application design. This is the two-tiered structure for client/server architecture.

The three-tiered methodology is used to overcome some of the limitations that are associated with the two-tiered methodology. Three-tiered architecture involves splitting user interface, processing, and data storage into three distinct pieces, or tiers, spreading the work load even further. The front end remains responsible for the user interface and minor processing, and the back end is still responsible for the data storage, but the processing and calculations (or business rules) have been moved to a middle layer. This allows changes to be made to the business rules without affecting the user interface or the database.

Unlike mainframes, whose "clients" were just dumb terminals with no processing capability whatsoever, today's PC-based desktop has given you, as the developer, the opportunity to create robust applications that can run processes on both the server and the client, splitting the workload and running the processing where it will be most effective.

This capability is also available in the Web world of client/server but with some cautions. You have far less control over the front-end PC (both Web browser and desktop workstation) in the Web environment than you do in the normal application environment. It is more difficult to judge how well processes run on the client side. This makes it more reasonable to run processes on the back end, because you do have control over that environment and can predict the outcome.

On the other hand, client/server issues in normal PC applications face some issues that a Web-based client/server don't. In a normal client/server database application, if the client-side module or front end is modified, you might need to redistribute the entire application. With a Web-based client/server, because the client or front end is a Web page, the new front end is just redistributed the next time the page is loaded. Any changes needed for cookies use (explained in the section "State Maintenance" later in this chapter) can be updated at this time also.

The browser client initiates the transaction by sending a request to the server to perform some operation, database request, calculation, processing request, or JavaScript function call. The client then waits for a response from the server before continuing.

Server-side processing allows code to remain on one centralized server for easier modification and also gives you the benefit of faster processing because the processing occurs on the server.

The client is responsible for handling all user-interface presentation; the server is responsible for handling all data storage and HTML document storage; and processing is split between the client and the server, depending on need or where it is most logical to put the processing. Intense data calculations are usually performed at the server level because a server is more robust than the clients.

JavaScript presents you with client/server architecture issues as well. JavaScript processing can be distributed between the client and the server, depending on your preferences. Processing speed on the client is completely dependent on the client's environment, memory, PC speed, and other internal factors; processing on the server is dependent on the amount of traffic on the Internet as well as traffic and processing on the server. Dividing processing over multiple entities is a good idea, keeping intense processing on the more known quantity—the server.

Thinking about architecture design early on in the development phase of a Web application helps you build a more stable application that gives you the most processing power available.

Client and Server Communication

The communication between client and server in a Web-based environment is an important component to consider—one that presents a new hurdle to be overcome. Unlike client/server environments on a normal network, the Web environment doesn't provide a constant connection to the server; instead, communication is through HTTP protocols using TCP/IP.

In a traditional client/server world, communication is done through a network protocol that allows the client to always maintain a connection to the server or to at least have the capability to reestablish a connection immediately. In the Web environment, the client doesn't maintain a connection to the server. The client sends a request to the server for information, the server responds to that client with the information, and then the connection is terminated. If the client session continues, the client sends another request, the connection is reestablished, and the cycle continues. This means that every time the client connects to the server, it is a new session to the server; the server has no knowledge of previous requests or former information regarding the client. Such one-time connections make it difficult to perform activities in the typical environment of client/server architecture.

Because of this nontraditional client/server behavior, there is a need for a methodology to maintain information about the client that can be sent to the server every time. When a client connects to the server, the server needs information sent to it regarding the previous state of the client and how it should treat the requests from this client during processing.

The methodology of sending information from client to server and vice versa can be described as taking place in a "transaction" set of events:

1. Connection between the client and server is established using TCP/IP.
2. Request is sent from the client to the server.
3. Response is sent from the server to the client.
4. Connection between the client and server is closed by either or both sides.

The communication between clients (browsers) and servers is a two-step process. The first step is the client request. This is the message sent by the browser requesting information from a server. The request could be as simple as a new static HTML page or could be as complex as posting data to a database and computing information using JavaScript/CGI.

The server answers this request with a server response. The server response message contains information returned from the server regarding the status of the request (among other values) and, most importantly, the returned HTML that was requested. Even if the client's request was just to perform a calculation, the server resends the original HTML document, which contains the updated information for the document as it occurred during processing.

The simple forms of HTML communication have evolved into the more complex processes of today, which include the use of JavaScript and CGI to enhance the HTML. The straightforward request and response metaphor had to become more complicated. Now, a request to the server is not simple. In interactive and data-related HTML applications, the server requires certain information pertaining to the client and its state information before it can properly process the requests that the client is sending—thus the need for state maintenance in HTML applications.

The methodologies for state maintenance involve storing information about the client in relation to a particular server and then sending that information back to the server when the request by the client requires it. Every request to a server may not require state information, and it may be required only for certain URLs on a particular server.

State Maintenance

One of the benefits of the Web and its design is also one of its biggest obstacles in applications that require client interaction with the server itself. Because a server is stateless, it can run faster, but it has to rely on the client to remind it who the client is when a client makes a request. The evolution of HTML out of static pages into interactive applications has made a formerly stateless environment look for ways to maintain state.

Because the client is not continuously connected to the Web server, there is the issue of knowing how to tell a Web server who the client is when the client "reconnects" to send a request back to the server. If Web applications remained continuously connected to the server, Web development would be as uncomplicated as generic client/server applications—but they aren't.

Web pages are sent to a client, but how does a server remember what state the client is in when the client sends a request back? State maintenance is required to help Web applications behave more like normal run-of-the-mill client/server applications.

State information about a client can be defined as information that the server needs to know about the client in order to correctly process the HTTP request that the client is sending. Required state information varies from server to server and even from URL to URL on the same server. A static URL on a server might not require any state information from the client before it responds to the client request; however, a shopping cart URL on the same server might require the client's name, last date to shop, and shopping list from last session before it can send back the requested response to the client.

State information can be so varied that some generic techniques for keeping or maintaining the state now exist.

There are several techniques for state maintenance, including the use of client cookies, client URL encoding, IP addresses on the server, short cookies, and short URL encoding. The first two techniques for state maintenance involve complete client-side state maintenance. IP addresses require the server to maintain the information. The last two techniques involve some of both server and client maintenance.

The benefit of using client cookies and client URL encoding is that there is less impact on the server, and the server is able to forget about the client after a request/response transaction is complete. If the client never returns to the site, the server is not holding any more extra information than before the client first accessed the server. This technique gives the added benefit of speed on the server because the server does not have to retrieve any information before processing the incoming URL. The URL or cookie contains all the data necessary to process the incoming request from the client.

Client Cookies

Cookies provide a Web server with a way of saving information about a client that can be used in future connections to the server. Cookies are client-based state maintenance methodology; the server saves all the relevant information that it needs about the client on the client itself and lets the client send the information back with every HTTP request. (For even more information on using cookies with JavaScript, see Chapter 25, "Cookies and State Maintenance.")

RESOURCE

More information on cookies can be found on the Web at http://www.netscape.com/ newsref/std/cookie_spec.html.

Cookies are stored in a text file on the client drive, and the server, as a means of keeping track of the client's state, writes to the cookie information that the server needs to know when the client sends a URL request to the server. Only one cookie file exists per browser, and all servers write cookie information to the same file, tagging sections in the cookie with the specific URL names as they are saved and updated.

CAUTION

Not all browsers support cookies. Be sure to use them at your own risk.

The size of this cookie file is limited, so only a certain amount of cookie information can be stored on any given client. This limits the number of Web servers that can store information on a specific client computer and the amount of information that each server can store.

With cookies, the possibility always exists that the user could delete the cookie file by mistake (after all, it is only a text file). Then every server would have lost whatever state information that it had been maintaining, and the client would need to start from scratch in establishing itself with the server.

Because cookie information is stored on the client side, it is not affected by server issues. It also allows the client to resend a request successfully, even if problems are encountered on the server side. Another benefit of cookies is that because the server isn't required to store any information about the client, the server can "forget" about the client after the initial request for information, and no storage of information is required on the server.

This is an important concept to keep in mind. The Web is growing at such a rapid pace that hundreds of thousands of clients might be accessing your Web site. Storing pieces of information about each of these clients (even those who never come back to your site) would be unreasonable. The storage required to keep this information could easily get out of hand as the access to your server increases.

Cookies do increase the amount of Internet traffic, because the server is sending and receiving extra information with every client URL request. Cookie information is transferred in the name/ value pair methodology, using the cookie protocol for transferring cookie information with requests. The following list outlines the advantages and disadvantages of using cookies for state maintenance:

Advantages

Cookies work in nondatabase applications, and no memory space is needed to store server information.

Cookies retain information with server restarts.

Disadvantages

Cookies increase Internet traffic, because more information needs to be passed from client to server.

There is a limited file size for the storage of cookies on the client machine.

Only certain browsers support cookies.

Client URL Encoding

The client URL encoding methodology for maintaining state information between client and server involves sending `name`/`value` pair information as part of the URL string at client HTTP request time. This method of storing state information has the same benefits for the server as cookies in that no information needs to be stored on the server.

Using this process to maintain client state requires that URLs be built dynamically each time a request is made. Because of the significant increase in size of the URL, there is a significant increase in the amount of Internet traffic using URL encoding.

Using client-side URL encoding allows for more flexibility when the need for state mainte-nance exists. Unlike cookies, client URL encoding isn't browser-specific, and because you don't know which type of browser is accessing your server, this is a more reliable method of main-taining state. The possibility always exists that a client's browser doesn't support cookies. In this case, the state of the client will be unknown at the time of its request to your server. The following list outlines the advantages and disadvantages of using client URL encoding to main-tain state:

Advantages

Client URL encoding works in nondatabase applications.

It isn't browser-specific.

It retains information with server restarts.

Disadvantages

Client URL encoding increases the amount of Internet traffic.

URLs must be dynamically generated for every request.

IP Address on the Server

The first two methods of maintaining state are client-side processes. The information is stored on the client and sent by the client at the time of a request. The server can update this information, but storage is on the client side.

The third method of maintaining state involves storing IP addresses and state information on the server. The server must have database access or shared memory in which to store the information. The state information of a client is stored based on the IP address of the client, and this information is held and usable only by this particular server.

Because of these drawbacks, this type of state maintenance is useful only if the following criteria apply:

- The clients are known to have fixed IP addresses.
- Only one server supports the application.

The practice of dynamically allocating IP addresses for a Web browser makes this type of state maintenance impossible to implement. Multiple Web servers can't be supported using this methodology either. The following list outlines the advantages and disadvantages of using the IP address on the server for state maintenance:

Advantages

The IP address isn't browser-specific.

It won't increase the amount of network traffic.

Disadvantages

It requires a database to store information.

It doesn't support multiuser systems or dynamic IP address providers.

Short Cookies

The short cookies technique uses a combination of cookies on the client and IP address maintenance on the server to maintain the state of the client.

Cookies are used to store only a name tag that has been generated by the server during the initial access to the server. The client sends the cookie information name tag to the server, and the server uses the name tag to retrieve the state information that it is maintaining. All state information is stored the same as it is in the "IP address on server" technique. The following list outlines the advantages and disadvantages of using short cookies for state maintenance:

Advantages

There's a small increase in the amount of network traffic.

Disadvantages

Short cookies require a database to store information.

A Netscape browser is required.

Short URL Encoding

The short URL encoding technique uses a combination of IP address maintenance on the server and client URL encoding.

The server generates a reference name for the client, and the client appends this reference name to every URL request. The server detects the name in the URL and refers to the state information that it is storing. The server maintains all state information, as it does in the IP address on server technique. The following list outlines the advantages and disadvantages of using short URL encoding for state maintenance:

Advantages

Short URL encoding isn't browser-specific.

There's a small increase in the amount of network traffic.

Disadvantages

Short URL encoding requires a database to store information.

URLs must be dynamically generated for every request.

Sending Information from Client to Server

The first substantial exchange of information between client (browser) and server is the client request.

Because of the nature of HTTP, it is necessary for browser clients to send requests to servers for all the information they want. Servers do not have a way of initiating an HTTP document transfer/connection. A request can have many forms and is used for various reasons. Request information can range from a request for a static page to a request to download a file or data from a database that is stored on the server.

The format for the HTTP request to the server can be a basic HTML page request, or it can be a request that contains content information or data (in the case of JavaScript and CGI-type processes) that needs to be processed or posted to the server. The second type of request has an additional piece of information included in the request message. This part of the request is termed the content or body of the request and contains data (content) to be used by the server, either from functions or data entry fields on the HTML document.

Servers should be tolerant of HTTP requests from bad clients. Not all clients conform completely to the specifications, and servers should be able to accommodate a bad request from a client. Servers should account for lines terminated incorrectly, as well as unrecognized or unimplemented HTTP header name values.

The HTTP request contains three basic groups of information:

- Request line: Method (GET, HEAD, POST), URL, and HTTP version
- Name/Value pairs for fields such as accept, referer, if-modified, user-agent, content-type, and content-length (defined in Table 31.2)
- Content: Information (data) being sent to the server for processing

The request line is the first line of the HTTP request calls that goes from client to server for information. It contains the following:

- A method to be applied to the requested document (see Table 31.1)
- The URL of the requested document
- The HTTP version requested

Table 31.1. Commonly used methods.

Method	Description
GET	This method, which is always supported, instructs the server to retrieve the information that is described by the URL (either a document or data information). If the URL is defined to run a process or a script, this action is performed, and the resulting information is returned.
POST	This is another frequently used method that creates another object subordinate to the original URL object. The POST method is used to add to existing documents (insert data), post files to a directory, and so on. The new URL is defined by the server and returned to client.
HEAD	This method returns the same information as the GET method but doesn't return the entire body of the document—only the HTTP HEAD.
TEXTSEARCH	This method is used to specify that the URL object can be searched with a text string. This is really a search form of the GET method. Use the ? operator to denote the search criteria.
SPACEJUMP	This is similar to TEXTSEARCH in that it implies a search and is a form of the GET method, but it searches for coordinates on a map and not text in the document.
SHOWMETHOD	This method is designed to give the client more information on object methods that are not fully defined in HTTP standards. The method name is defined by the previous HTTP response from the server, and the client can then request from the server more information on how to use the request method.

Name/pair values are sets of HTTP request fields that the client passes through to the server in reference to the request. These values include request headers and object metainformation. Table 31.2 lists the acceptable request headers.

Table 31.2. Request headers.

Header	Description
ACCEPT	A semicolon-delimited list of responses that are accepted in response to this request. Common ACCEPTs are text/plain, text/HTML, and image/gif.
USER-AGENT	Can be used to specify the type of software being used to generate this request. This parameter is useful for tracking and statistical purposes.
FROM	Used only in mail requests, this specifies the name of the user making the request. Usually used just for tracking purposes.
REFERER	This is an optional header that helps the server to maintain a list of links. This field specifies the URL from which the URL in the request was obtained.
IF-Modified-Since	This method is used in conjunction with the GET method, making the GET a conditional GET. The URL is only returned if it has been modified since the date specified in this header field.
ACCEPT-LANGUAGE	Used for the same principal reason as ACCEPT header but specifies the language that is preferable for the response.
ACCEPT-ENCODING	Used for the same principal reason as ACCEPT header but specifies the encoding types that are valid for the response.

Also acceptable in the request header section are certain object metainformation name/value pairs (these are defined in the next section). The Content-Type and Content-Length pairs are two of the valid pairs that can be used with the HTTP request as well as the HTTP response.

The name/value pair section (the combination of both request headers and object metainformation) of the request is terminated by a Carriage Return/Line Feed pair (a blank line).

Content follows the name/value pairs in the HTTP request. The content is the body of the request and contains information that is being sent to the server for processing.

A simple example of a request from client to server follows in Listing 31.1.

Listing 31.1. A sample HTTP client request.

```
POST /sampapp/sampform HTTP/1.0
Accept: text/plain
Accept: test/html
Accept: image/gif
Content-type: application/x-www-form-urlencoded
Content-length: 10

name=anderson
```

Sending Information from Server to Client

Once a client has sent a request to a server for information, that server will in turn send a message back to the client containing information that the client has requested. The server message packet is called the HTTP response to the client request. It contains the information that the client has requested, whether the client has rights to the information, and whether the server is able to send the response successfully.

HTTP responses take a similar format to HTTP requests, but they include at the end the returned HTML document (response).

Clients receiving a response from a server should be tolerant of the server when the response does not comply to the standards. Clients should be prepared to tolerate white space in a document as well as incorrectly terminated lines. Clients should accommodate servers using older versions of HTTP as well.

The HTTP response contains three basic groups of information:

- Response line
- Response headers
- Response data

Response line from the server has the syntax of HTTP version, status code (three-digit return code), and response line of text (not used by browser but can be used by humans for document interpretation).

The response line gives the browser some initial information about what it can expect to follow in the rest of the response. The version tells it how to begin interpreting the document response, and the status code tells it what to expect as far as the return. A response status code of 200 is "OK."

> **NOTE**
>
> There are a variety of response codes that relate to the state and content of the document being returned.

Name/pair values are sets of HTTP response fields that the server passes back to the client in reference to the original request and subsequent returned response.

Object metainformation (defined in Table 31.3) as commonly used is header fields used not in relation to the entire HTTP request document but only in relation to the specific HTTP object.

Table 31.3. Object metainformation.

Object	*Description*
CONTENT-TYPE	This pair specifies the format and encoding for data content being sent with the request and is necessary only if a body (or data) is included in the request packet of information.
CONTENT-LENGTH	As with content-type, this pair is not necessary if no data is associated with the request. If the body is included, this value specifies the exact binary length of the data field that has been included and tells the server to read the content directly as included with the request.
ALLOWED	These are request methods that the user is "allowed" to use when requesting from the URL. Default methods, if none are supplied, are GET and HEAD.
PUBLIC	Methods that anyone (not just this specific user) can use in relation to this response document. Default for this field is GET only.
DATE	Specifies the date that this URL was created.
TITLE	Defines the title of the URL document that is returned in this response.
EXPIRES	Specifies a date when this URL is no longer valid on the client side and must be re-requested from the server.
CONTENT-LANGUAGE	Defines the language in which the URL was written.
CONTENT-ENCODING	Specifies the encoding type to be used for the object.
MESSAGE-ID	Defines the unique identifier assigned for the HTTP object. A message ID must be unique at all times and never expire. No two documents can ever have the same message ID.

When defining the name/value pairs for the HTTP response, an important pair to include is the Content-Type pair.

Content-Type refers, as in client HTTP requests, to text/plain, text/HTML, image/GIF, and so on, but in this case, it is the content-type of response data that is to follow. The type used is usually the content-type that the client has said that it can or will accept as a response. Safe types are text/plain and text/HTML. It can be assumed that most browsers can handle these two types.

Again, the response name/value pairs are terminated by a blank line (Carriage Return/Line Feed).

The information that follows the Carriage Return/Line Feed is the body of the response or the response data. The response data is the final part of the HTTP response and is the format of a MIME message body. The significance of this data depends on the status code that is returned in the response header. The response data is usually in the form of an HTML document to be displayed in the client browser. This document is either a new document, a refresh of the current document (really a new document) containing updated data, or the confirmation that data to be posted to a server has been successfully posted.

Listing 31.2 is an example of a simple response from the server. It contains all parts of the response including the reference to the document being returned.

Listing 31.2. A sample HTTP server response.

```
HTTP/1.0 200 Ok
Date: Wed, 17 Jul 1996 9:30:35 GMT
Content-type: text/html
Content-length: 323
<returned HTML document>
```

Summary

Much thought needs to go into the architecture of the application before you can begin to build it for successful Internet use. Knowing your predicted audience and being able to anticipate access to your server helps when defining the methodologies and techniques that you choose to use to implement a client/server application. Adding JavaScript and database functionality brings on a whole new level of concerns and issues that must be accounted for.

Server-side versus client-side processing needs to be taken into account when deciding test speed and functionality of the JavaScript application. The methodologies of two-tier and three-tier need to be evaluated for the advantages and disadvantages on your particular application and its complexity and maintainability.

State maintenance methodology decisions become important based on the need in the particular application. You need to weigh all pros and cons before deciding on the route that you will take.

Finally, knowing the process by which client and servers send and request information from each other will help you to better develop your applications.

CHAPTER 32

Database Connectivity Using LiveWire

IN THIS CHAPTER

One of the compelling factors in companies moving to the Web as a development platform is the notion that this platform gives its users easier access to corporate data. Since the advent of the Web, CGI has been the typical means of connecting to databases and generating results in HTML format. Although client-side JavaScript doesn't have the capability to access data on a database server, you can use its server-based counterpart to perform this process.

This chapter looks at how you can use server-side JavaScript to connect to your back-end data. For this discussion, I'll highlight Netscape LiveWire, which provides built-in database access within its object framework. Recall from Chapter 30, "Server-Side JavaScript Extensions Using LiveWire," that LiveWire is Netscape's server-side application server technology for Netscape servers.

> **NOTE**
>
> LiveWire is a transitioning technology. Originally a separate product offering, LiveWire is now in the process of being tightly integrated into the Netscape Enterprise Server.

> **NOTE**
>
> If you haven't already done so, you will find it helpful to read Chapter 30 before working with databases and LiveWire. This chapter is intended to build on what you learned in Chapter 30.

LiveWire Database Connectivity

LiveWire provides the server extensions you need to access external data in a relational database. Figure 32.1 shows the architecture of a LiveWire database application. When a client submits a request that is associated with the database, that information is routed through the Web server to your LiveWire application. It accesses the database and returns a result to the client in HTML format.

> **NOTE**
>
> Before you can connect to a database through JavaScript, you need to have the necessary software installed and configured to provide access to the database server.

FIGURE 32.1.
The LiveWire database architecture.

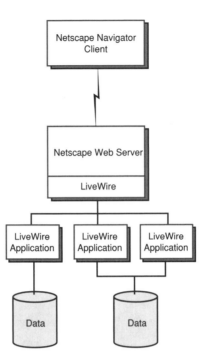

The LiveWire 1.x Database Object

In addition to LiveWire's state maintenance objects (request, client, project, and server), LiveWire 1.x also boasts a database object. The database object encapsulates all functionality related to interacting with a relational database. It contains no properties, so all its utility stems from its methods, which are shown in Table 32.1. If you have worked with databases using other programming languages, you can see that JavaScript has almost everything you would expect for interacting with SQL databases.

Table 32.1. Database object methods.

Method	*Description*
`connect("databaseType", "serverName", "username", "password", "databaseName")`	Connects LiveWire application to the specified database and creates the database object.
`connected()`	Returns true if the application is connected to a database.
`disconnect()`	Closes the database connection.

continues

Table 32.1. continued

Method	*Description*
cursor("*SQLSELECTStatement*", *updateable*)	Creates a database cursor for the specified SQL SELECT statement.
execute("*SQLStatement*")	Executes the specified SQL statement. Used for SQL statements that do not return a cursor.
SQLTable("*SQLSELECTStatement*")	Generates an HTML table to display the results of the SELECT query.
beginTransaction()	Starts a SQL transaction.
commitTransaction()	Commits the current SQL transaction.
rollbackTransaction()	Rolls back the current SQL transaction.
majorErrorCode()	Major error code returned by the database server or ODBC.
majorErrorMessage()	Major error message returned by database server or ODBC.
minorErrorCode()	Secondary error code returned by vendor library.
minorErrorMessage()	Secondary message returned by vendor library.

> **NOTE**
>
> The manner in which LiveWire objects are instantiated is anything but consistent. The set of request, client, project, and server objects are all created implicitly (when they are referenced), whereas the file object (discussed in Chapter 30) uses the conventional new operator.
>
> The database object is created in yet another way. When you connect to a database using the connect() method, a database object is implicitly created.

> **NOTE**
>
> LiveWire in Enterprise Server 3.0 divides the functionality of the database object into two separate objects: DbPool, which establishes a pool of database connections, and Connection, which enables an individual connection to the database. See the Netscape DevEdge Web site at http://developer.netscape.com for further details.

Connecting to a Database

The first step in working with a database is to connect to it using the connect() method. The parameters of connect() include all the pieces of information LiveWire needs to attach itself to an external database:

- Database type: LiveWire currently supports the following database types: INFORMIX, ODBC, ORACLE, and SYBASE.

- Server name: Use the server name on which the database resides. If you're using ODBC, use the ODBC service name defined in Control Panel's ODBC administration utility.

- Username: Use a valid username defined on the database server.

- Password: Use the password associated with the specified username.

- Database name: For SQL databases that allow multiple databases per server, use the name of the database.

> **TIP**
>
> Not all relational database management systems require or even support all the parameters specified in the connect() method. If your database software doesn't use one of the parameters, use an empty string ("") as the parameter.

For example, suppose you want to connect to a Microsoft SQL Server database named BEANS that is on a server called STARBUCK. Using the system administrator username (sa) with a password of "frap", the statement looks like the following:

```
database.connect("ODBC", "STARBUCK", "sa", "frap", "BEANS")
```

Before trying to perform an operation on the database, you should first check to see if connect() was successful by using the connected() method. For example, the following code attempts to connect to the BEANS database. If the process is not successful, a message is displayed to the user:

```
database.connect("ODBC", "STARBUCK", "sa", "frap", "BEANS")
if (!database.connected()) {
   write("Unable to connect to the database.") }
```

As you design your LiveWire application, you should give careful thought to the method by which the application connects to the database. Probably the most common approach is to open a connection in the application's initial startup page and keep it open. Other HTML pages within the application can then use this connection when the page needs access to the database. Using this method, multiple clients can access the database concurrently using this shared connection. You also have a performance benefit, because less overhead is involved with each database transaction.

A second approach is to explicitly connect to a server only when you're going to perform a database operation and then disconnect when you're finished. This is often called the *serial approach,* because only a single client can connect to the database at a time. You might also find it helpful to think of it as the "commando" approach, because the mission of the code is to get into the database, do business quickly, and leave as soon as you're finished.

Part of the serial methodology is to place an explicit lock on the database before attempting to connect to it. Just as a file object can call the project's (or server's) lock() method to prevent concurrent file access, the database object locks the project (or server) as well. Consider the following example:

```
project.lock()
database.connect("ODBC", "STARBUCK", "sa", "frap", "BEANS")
if (database.connected()) {
    database.execute('UPDATE coffee SET source = "Ethiopia" WHERE type =
    "Sidamo"')
    database.disconnect()
}
project.unlock()
```

Working with SQL SELECT Queries

One of the most common tasks of Web database applications is to perform a SQL SELECT query and return a result set to the user in HTML format. LiveWire gives you two approaches to performing this task: using the SQLTable() method, or using a database cursor.

> **NOTE**
>
> Your SQL statements should be ANSI 89-compliant SQL.

Using the SQLTable() Method

The easiest, but least flexible, approach is to use the database object's SQLTable() method. Using a SELECT statement as its parameter, SQLTable() submits a query to the database and transforms the result set into an HTML table. For example, to return a listing of all book records in a table, you could use the following code:

```
var queryString = "SELECT * FROM BOOKS"
database.SQLTable(queryString)
```

Working with Cursor Objects

The SQLTable() method provides a quick-and-dirty way to view result sets, but it doesn't have any mechanism to alter the presentation format of the HTML table. You can use a database cursor to get more control of the output of the result set. A database cursor is essentially a "virtual table" or a pointer to a result set of a query. A cursor maintains a current position (row) within it, allowing you to perform actions on the set of records associated with the cursor.

In LiveWire, a cursor object is contained by a database object and is instantiated when the `cursor()` method is called. The cursor object contains one property and several methods, as shown in Table 32.2.

Table 32.2. Properties and methods of the cursor object.

Property/Method	Description
`cursorColumn`	An array of objects corresponding to each column of the cursor.
`close()`	Closes the cursor.
`columns()`	Returns the number of columns in the cursor.
`columnName(columnIndex)`	Returns the name of the column specified by the `columnIndex` parameter.
`next()`	Moves the cursor to the next record in the table.
`insertRow("tableName")`	Inserts a record into the specified table after the current record.
`updateRow("tableName")`	Updates current record of the specified table.
`deleteRow("tableName")`	Deletes the current record of the specified table.

To create a cursor, use the database object's `cursor()` method based on the following:

```
cursorName = database.cursor("SELECTStatement", updateable)
```

The *updateable* parameter is a Boolean (true/false) value that specifies whether you want to allow updates within the cursor.

For example, the following code creates a read-only cursor named books:

```
books = database.cursor("SELECT * FROM BOOKS", false)
```

You can then use the cursor object's methods to navigate through the table. If you want to return the result set to the user as a series of records, you use the following code:

```
books = database.cursor("SELECT * FROM BOOKS", false)
while (books.next()) {
    write("<b>Author: </b>" + books.author + "<p>")
    write("<b>Title: </b><i>" + books.title + "</i><p>")
    write("<b>Edition: </b>" + books.edition + "<p>")
    write("<b>Year: </b>" + books.date + "<p>")
    write("<b>ISBN: </b>" + books.isbn + "<p>")
    write("<b>Publisher: </b>" + books.publisher + "<p>")
}
books.close()
```

The while loop uses the next() method to traverse through the entire cursor. The statements within the loop are performed on the current record within the cursor.

Notice that you can access the columns (also called *fields*) as a property of the cursor. When a cursor object is instantiated, an array of columns is created. You can access them by name, as shown in the preceding example, or by number (the column's position within the cursor).

> **NOTE**
>
> One of the few examples where JavaScript isn't case-sensitive is in referencing columns in a cursor.

For a second example, suppose you want to display the results of the same query in a tabular format. You could embed the HTML table definition tags within the code:

```
Books = database.cursor("SELECT * FROM BOOKS", false)
write("<TABLE>")
write("<TR>")
write("<TH>Author</TH>")
write("<TH>Title</TH>")
write("<TH>Edition</TH>")
write("<TH>Year</TH>")
write("<TH>ISBN</TH>")
write("<TH>Publisher</TH>")
write("</TR>")
while (books.next()) {
     write("<TR>")
     write("<TD>" + books.author + "</TD>")
     write("<TD>" + books.title + "</TD>")
     write("<TD>" + books.edition + "</TD>")
     write("<TD>" + books.year + "</TD>")
     write("<TD>" + books.isbn + "</TD>")
     write("<TD>" + books.publisher + "</TD>")
     write("</TR>")
}
write("</TABLE>")
books.close()
```

Alternatively, you could reference the columns by number rather than by name. Using the columnName() and columns() methods, you could build a more flexible piece of code:

```
books = database.cursor("SELECT * FROM BOOKS", false)
write("<TABLE>")
write("<TR>")
for (var i=0; i<books.columns(); i++) {
     write("<TH>" + books.columnName(i) + "</TH>")
}
write("</TR>")
while (books.next()) {
     write("<TR>")
     for (var i=0; i<books.columns(); i++) {
          write("<TD>" + books[i] + "</TD>")
```

```
    }
    write("</TR>")
}
write("</TABLE>")
books.close()
```

The first `for` loop iterates through each column of the table. Using `columnName()`, the name of the column is embedded within a `<TH>` and `</TH>` tag pair. The second `for` loop uses the `cursorColumn` array to return the value of the specified column and place it within the `<TD>` and `</TD>` tag pair.

> **NOTE**
>
> A cursor is limited in scope to the current HTML page of an application. As a result, you can't use it to span an entire multipage application.

Working with Updateable Cursors

You can create an updateable cursor to let your application modify the current record of the cursor. In order for a cursor to be updateable, the following conditions must be true for the query statement:

- The SELECT statement must be limited to a single table. You can't create an updateable cursor on a query containing table joins.

- You must include key values as part of the result set of the SELECT statement.

- Specialized queries such as GROUP BY queries are not updateable.

You can create an updateable cursor by using true as the second parameter of a `cursor()` method. For example, the following code creates an updateable cursor called students:

```
students = database.cursor("SELECT * FROM S_ROSTER", true)
```

Once you create an updateable cursor, you can make changes to the result set. For example, suppose you want to change all the records with an `Area_Code` column value of 402 to a new value of 949. You could use the following code:

```
var sqlStr = 'SELECT * FROM S_ROSTER WHERE Area_Code = "402"'
students = database.cursor(sqlStr, true)
while (students.next()) {
    students.Area_Code = "949"
    students.updateRow("S_ROSTER")
}
students.close()
```

The initial `next()` call puts the pointer on the first record of the cursor, so be sure you call `next()` before trying to update a table using `updateRow()`.

To add a record to a cursor, you need to follow a two-step process:

1. Assign values to the columns of the cursor.
2. Call the cursor's `insertRow()` method.

For example, suppose you want to add a new student to the student roster database based on information from an HTML form. You could use the following code:

```
students = database.cursor("SELECT * FROM S_ROSTER", true)
students.studentID = client.newID
students.lastName = request.lastName
students.firstName = request.firstName
students.address = request.address
students.city = request.city
students.state = request.state
students.zip = request.zip
students.homePhone = request.homePhone
students.email = request.email
students.insertRow("S_ROSTER")
students.close()
```

Sending Passthrough SQL Statements

In addition to using cursors, you can send passthrough SQL to the database using the database object's `execute()` method. *Passthrough SQL* is a SQL statement sent directly to the database server that does not return any data to your application. The primary advantage of using passthrough SQL is that it allows you to use a SQL database's native SQL dialect to perform data manipulation operations that otherwise might not be supported by other databases.

To perform passthrough SQL, use a valid SQL statement as the parameter for the `execute()` method:

```
var sqlStr = 'INSERT INTO CUSTOMER (FIRST_NAME, LAST_NAME, PHONE)
            VALUES ("' + client.firstName + '", "' + client.lastName
            + '", "' + client.phone + '")'
database.execute(sqlStr)
```

> **NOTE**
>
> Acadia Infuse, located on the CD, has several LiveWire scripts built in to give you a jump start to application development. Chapter 4, "Using Acadia Infuse to Create JavaScript Scripts," discusses Infuse in detail.

Performing Transactions

One of the central reasons that companies rely on SQL databases is their capability to maintain data integrity. Transaction control is a key reason for this database power. A *transaction* is a set of SQL commands that are executed together. When a transaction is *committed* to the database, the actions stick together as a team: Either they all succeed, or they all fail. Before a transaction is committed, you can choose to *roll back* (cancel) the changes that were made.

Unless you manage transactions explicitly, LiveWire treats each update to a database as a separate transaction. This functionality is called *autocommit* because transactions are committed automatically. However, you can use the database object's beginTransaction(), commitTransaction(), and rollbackTransaction() methods to bring transaction processing under your control in your application. For example, revisit the example earlier in this chapter that updated all 402 area codes to 949. To ensure data integrity of the S_ROSTER table, you want to treat the entire process as a single transaction. By providing explicit transaction control, you can ensure that all the records are updated or else none of them are updated. You can then place a beginTransaction() method at the start of the process and a commitTransaction() method at the end:

```
database.beginTransaction()
  var sqlStr = 'SELECT * FROM S_ROSTER WHERE Area_Code = "402"'
  students = database.cursor(sqlStr, true)
  while (students.next()) {
      students.Area_Code = "949"
      students.updateRow("S_ROSTER")
  }
  students.close()
database.commitTransaction()
```

Keep in mind the scope of transactions. A transaction is limited to the current HTML page of an application and can't be spread across an entire multipage application. Moreover, if a stray beginTransaction() method issued at the start of an HTML page is not accompanied by a rollbackTransaction() or commitTransaction(), LiveWire automatically commits the transaction when you leave the page.

NOTE

LiveWire doesn't support nested transactions. Sybase is the only major database vendor that does.

Working with Binary Data

LiveWire provides support for working with binary large objects (BLOBs) in your database. You can take one of two approaches to working with BLOBs:

- Store the filename of the binary file in the database and then reference the file when binary data is retrieved. When the file is requested, you can reference it using the value of the column name:

```
<SERVER>
write("<IMG SRC=" + employee.photoFile + ">")
</SERVER>
```

- Store the binary data within the database itself. If you do store the data within the database, you can use the cursorColumn methods blobImage() and blobLink() to retrieve the data or the blob() function to write binary data to the database.

Displaying Images

Using the following syntax, the blobImage() method displays an image stored in a database:

```
cursorObject.colName.blobImage("imageFormat" [, "text"] [, "align"],
[, "widthPixels"] [, "heightPixels"] [, "borderPixels"] [, isMap])
```

blobImage() creates an HTML image tag (<IMG>) based on these parameters, referencing a temporary file that is created in memory. The temporary file is deleted when the page is generated and sent to the client.

The only required parameter is "imageFormat", which is the type of image you are displaying. The most common formats are GIF and JPEG. For example, suppose you want to display an online catalog of apparel. Within an HTML table, you could display a GIF image of the piece of clothing using the following code:

```
sClothes = database.cursor("SELECT * FROM SPRING_APPAREL", false)
write("<TABLE>")
write("<TR>")
write("<TH>Item #</TH>")
write("<TH>Item</TH>")
write("<TH>Styles</TH>")
write("<TH>Sizes</TH>")
write("<TH>Colors </TH>")
write("<TH>Description</TH>")
write("<TH>Image</TH>")
write("</TR>")
while (sClothes.next()) {
    write("<TR>")
    write("<TD>" + sClothes.itemNum + "</TD>")
    write("<TD>" + sClothes.item + "</TD>")
    write("<TD>" + sClothes.styles + "</TD>")
    write("<TD>" + sClothes.sizes + "</TD>")
    write("<TD>" + sClothes.colors + "</TD>")
    write("<TD>" + sClothes.description + "</TD>")
    write("<TD>" + sClothes.image.blobImage("gif") + "</TD>")
```

```
      write("</TR>")
}
write("</TABLE>")
sClothes.close()
```

Creating Links to Binary Data

Because of the size of binary data, displaying BLOBs comes at a definite performance cost.
You might want to display images only when they are requested by the client. Also, there may
be times when you can't display the data anyway, such as if you're working with audio files.
You can use the blobLink() method to retrieve binary data from the database and create an
HTML link that references the temporary file. Here's the syntax for blobLink():

```
cursorObject.colName.blobLink("mimeType" , "linkText"]
```

The *mimeType* parameter is any valid MIME type, such as the following:

```
image/gif
```

```
image/jpeg
```

```
image/x-bitmap
```

```
audio/x-wav
```

To illustrate the use of blobLink(), modify the previous example so that the image is displayed
only if the user requests it. Using blobLink(), the following code creates a link using the name
of the clothing item (the value of sClothes.item):

```
sClothes = database.cursor("SELECT * FROM SPRING_APPAREL", false)
write("<TABLE>")
write("<TR>")
write("<TH>Item #</TH>")
write("<TH>Item</TH>")
write("<TH>Styles</TH>")
write("<TH>Sizes</TH>")
write("<TH>Colors </TH>")
write("<TH>Description</TH>")
write("<TH>Image</TH>")
write("</TR>")
while (sClothes.next()) {
      write("<TR>")
      write("<TD>" + sClothes.itemNum + "</TD>")
      write("<TD>" + sClothes.image.blobLink("image/gif", sClothes.item) + "</TD>")
      write("<TD>" + sClothes.styles + "</TD>")
      write("<TD>" + sClothes.sizes + "</TD>")
      write("<TD>" + sClothes.colors + "</TD>")
      write("<TD>" + sClothes.description + "</TD>")
      write("</TR>")
}
write("</TABLE>")
write("<i>Click the item name to view an image of the piece of clothing.</i>")
sClothes.close()
```

It's worth making note of the lifetime of a temporary binary file created by the blobLink()
method. When blobLink() is called, a temporary file is created in memory. It is removed either

when the client accesses the file by activating the link or 60 seconds after the request was processed—whichever comes first.

Inserting Binary Data into a Database

Another powerful feature of LiveWire is the capability to enter BLOBs into the database. You can use the built-in `blob()` function to assign binary data to a cursor column:

```
sClothes = database.cursor("SELECT * FROM SPRING_APPAREL", true)
sClothes.itemNum = project.newItemNum
sClothes.item = request.item
sClothes.styles = request.styles
sClothes.sizes = request.sizes
sClothes.colors = request.colors
sClothes.description = request.description
sClothes.image = blob(request.filename)
sClothes.insertRow("SPRING_APPAREL")
sClothes.close()
```

Handling Database Errors

When you're programming database applications, an important part of the coding effort should be accounting for database errors as you work with server data. When you send a SQL statement that fails, the database server responds by issuing an error message that specifies the reason for the failure. You can either access that information by its status code or request a more verbose description of the problem.

Most of the methods you use to interact with a database return a status code. A status code is an integer with a range of 0 to 27. A code of 0 indicates that the command completed successfully, whereas the other values, shown in Table 32.3, indicate specific errors from the server.

Table 32.3. LiveWire database status codes.

Status Code	Description
0	No error
1	Out of memory
2	Object not initialized
3	Type conversion error
4	Database not registered
5	Error reported by server
6	Message from server
7	Error from vendor library
8	Lost connection

Status Code	Description
9	End of fetch
10	Invalid use of object
11	Column does not exist
12	Invalid positioning within object (bounds error)
13	Unsupported feature
14	Null reference parameter
15	Database object not found
16	Required information is missing
17	Object cannot support multiple readers
18	Object cannot support deletions
19	Object cannot support insertions
20	Object cannot support updates
21	Object cannot support updates
22	Object cannot support indices
23	Object cannot be dropped
24	Incorrect connection supplied
25	Object cannot support privileges
26	Object cannot support cursors
27	Unable to open

The database object includes four error-handling methods that return error codes and messages from the database server. The values of what is returned depend greatly on the back-end database server. Tables 32.4 through 32.7 list the return values for each of the SQL databases supported by LiveWire.

Table 32.4. Informix database error methods for status code 7 (vendor library error).

Method	What It Returns
majorErrorMessage()	Vendor Library Error: *errorMsg* (*errorMsg* is text from Informix)
minorErrorMessage()	ISAM Error: *errorMsg* (*errorMsg* is text of the ISAM error code from Informix or an empty string (" ") if no ISAM error occurred)
majorErrorCode()	Informix error code
minorErrorCode()	ISAM error code (or zero if there is no ISAM error)

Table 32.5. Oracle database error methods for status code 5 (server error).

Method	What It Returns
majorErrorMessage()	Server Error: *errorMsg* (where *errorMsg* is translation of Oracle return code)
minorErrorMessage()	Oracle server name
majorErrorCode()	Return code as reported by Oracle Call-level Interface (OCI)
minorErrorCode()	Operating system error code as reported by OCI

Table 32.6. Sybase database error methods for status code 7 (vendor library error).

Method	What It Returns
majorErrorMessage()	Vendor Library Error: *errorMsg* (where *errorMsg* is error text from DB-Library)
minorErrorMessage()	Operating system error text (as specified by DB-Library)
majorErrorCode()	DB-Library error number
minorErrorCode()	Severity level (as specified by DB-Library)

Table 32.7. Sybase database error methods for status code 5 (server error).

Method	What It Returns
majorErrorMessage()	Server Error *errorMsg* (where *errorMsg* is text from SQL server.) If severity and message number are both zero, just the message text is returned.
minorErrorMessage()	SQL server name
majorErrorCode()	SQL server message number
minorErrorCode()	Severity level (as specified by SQL server)

To demonstrate the use of these error-handling methods, I'll return to an example shown earlier in this chapter. In the example shown in the section "Working with Updateable Cursors," I didn't add any code to handle possible errors that could arise during an insertRow() operation. You can make the code bulletproof with the following code:

```
students = database.cursor("SELECT * FROM S_ROSTER", true)
database.beginTransaction()
students.studentID = client.newID
students.lastName = request.lastName
```

```
students.firstName = request.firstName
students.address = request.address
students.city = request.city
students.state = request.state
students.zip = request.zip
students.homePhone = request.homePhone
students.email = request.email
status = students.insertRow("S_ROSTER")
if (status != 0) {
    database.rollbackTransaction()
    if (status == 5 || status == 7) {
       write("The following error was encountered when an attempt was made to
       insert the record into the table: <p>")
       write(database.MajorErrorMessage())
    else {
        handleError(status)
    }
else {
    database.commitTransaction()
    write(request.firstName + " " + request.lastName + " is now on record
         at Web University. <p>")
}
students.close()
```

Putting It All Together

To demonstrate many of the subjects covered in this chapter, I'll provide a more extended example of a database application. In this scenario, you are building a Web application for an imaginary school called Virtual University. The application has a threefold purpose:

- To allow people to enroll in the university.
- To allow students to register for classes.
- To allow students to get a schedule of classes.

Figure 32.2 shows the structure of the application.

FIGURE 32.2.
The structure of the Virtual University application.

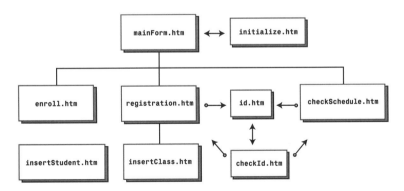

Initializing the Application

When users access the application, it requests `mainPage.htm`. The first responsibility of `mainPage.htm` is to check for a live connection to the database. If it has one, the home page is loaded, but if not, the client is sent to the `initialize.htm` file first:

```
if(!database.connected()) {
    redirect("initialize.htm")
}
```

If the user is accessing the page for the first time, it doesn't have a connection, so the `initialize.htm` file is requested. The first step of this page is to connect to the database:

```
if (!database.connected()) {
    database.connect("ODBC", "VSERVER", "guest", "lardgut", "SCHOOL")
}
```

If a connection is established, the first task to perform is getting a value for the `lastID` property for the project object. You use this property to determine a unique `StudentID` value (the key field of the VSTUDENTS table) for each new student entered in the database. To get this value, a cursor is opened on the VSTUDENTS table. Then, the code moves to the last record in the table and retrieves its `StudentID` value. (Because `StudentID` is the key, you can assume that the records are sorted by `StudentID`.) This code executes after a `lock()` is placed on the project to ensure that no one else can access the table at the same time. After this process, the client is directed back to the home page. This code is shown here:

```
if (database.connected()) {
    project.lock()
        project.lastID = 0
        vCursor = database.cursor("SELECT * FROM VSTUDENTS")
        while (cursor.next()) {
            project.lastID = vCursor.studentID
        }
        vCursor.close();
    project.unlock()
    redirect("mainpage.htm") }
else {
    write("We are vSorry, but we cannot serve you at this time.
    Please try at a later time.")
}
```

Figure 32.3 shows the home page.

Enrolling as a Student

The first option for a user is to enroll as a student. If the user clicks the Become a vStudent link, the client is sent to the `enroll.htm` page. This form, shown in Figure 32.4, is a standard HTML form that specifies `insertStudent.htm` as the ACTION= parameter.

FIGURE 32.3.
The Virtual University home page.

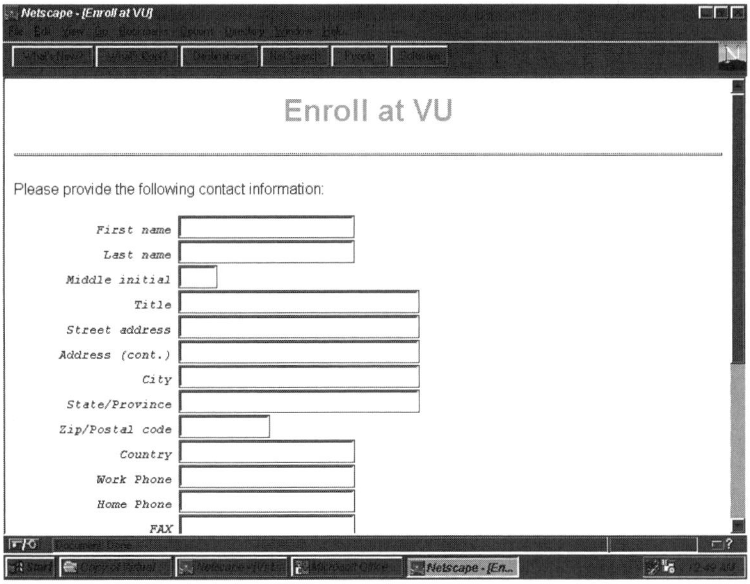

FIGURE 32.4.
The enrollment form.

When the user clicks the Submit button, insertStudent.htm is called. Its first task is to get the StudentID for this new student. To do so, it puts a lock() on the project, increments the project.lastID parameter by 1, and then assigns that value to the client object's studentID parameter:

```
project.lock()
project.lastID = parseInt(project.lastID) + 1
client.studentID = project.lastID
project.unlock()
```

Next, the form opens an updateable cursor on the VSTUDENTS table to assign the values from the enrollment form to the columns. After this is done for each column, the insertRow() method inserts the record into the table:

```
// Open up an updateable cursor on the VSTUDENTS table
// Assign form element values to the columns and
// insert the row into the table.
vStudent = database.cursor("SELECT * FROM VSTUDENTS", true)
vStudent.studentID = client.studentID
vStudent.lastName = request.LastName
vStudent.firstName = request.FirstName
vStudent.mi = request.MI
vStudent.address = request.StreetAddress
vStudent.address2 = request.Address2
vStudent.city = request.City
vStudent.state = request.State
vStudent.zip = request.ZipCode
vStudent.country = request.Country
vStudent.homePhone = request.HomePhone
vStudent.workPhone = request.WorkPhone
vStudent.fax = request.FAX
vStudent.email = request.Email
vStudent.url = request.URL
vStudent.dob = request.DateOfBirth
vStudent.sex = request.Personal_Sex
vStudent.major = request.major
status = vStudent.insertRow("VSTUDENTS")
vStudent.close()
if (status != 0) {
        write("Unable to add information at this time. <p>")}
else {
    write("<h1>We welcome you as a vStudent.</h1><p>")
    write("Keep this information for your records. Your StudentID number is " +
            client.studentID + ".<p><p>")
    write('You can now <A HREF="register.htm">click here</A>
to register for classes.')
}
```

Notice that the status code is checked on the insertRow() operation. If an error occurred, the user is notified of the problem. If the operation was successful, the user receives his StudentID number, as shown in Figure 32.5.

Registering for Classes

The second avenue for the application user is registering for classes. A user can get to the Class Registration form either from a link on the home page or after she has enrolled as a new student. Either way, the registration.htm page is called. This page first checks to ensure that the client has a StudentID. If it doesn't, the program redirects the client to an id.htm page after it assigns a value of "registration" to the gotoForm property of the client object:

```
if (client.studentID == null) {
    client.gotoForm = "registration"
    redirect("id.htm")
}
```

FIGURE 32.5.

A record successfully inserted into database.

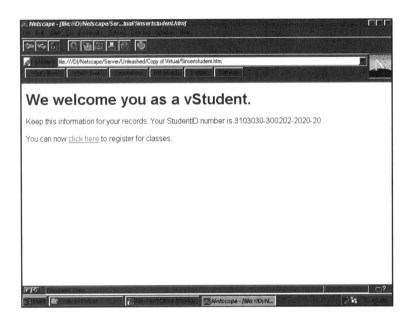

id.htm is a standard HTML form (see Figure 32.6) that prompts the user for her StudentID. When the user clicks the Submit button, the checkId.htm file is called by the form's ACTION= parameter.

The checkId.htm page is charged with validating the StudentID value entered by the user. Although a real-world application would surely use a password, this program will simply check for the existence of a record that has a StudentID equal to the value entered by the user. The cursor opened on the VSTUDENTS table returns a record if the StudentID number is valid. If nothing is returned, the user is asked to return to the id.htm form. If a value was returned, the StudentID is assumed to be valid. The studentID property of the client object is assigned the value of request.StudentID. Finally, the page determines who called the id.htm initially by checking the gotoForm property of the client. If it is the Class Registration page, the client is returned to that page. This code follows:

```
checkid = database.cursor('SELECT * FROM VSTUDENTS WHERE StudentID="' +
        request.StudentID + '"', false)
var i = 0
while (checkid.next()) {
    i++
}
checkid.close()
if (i == 0) {
    write('Invalid StudentID. <A HREF="id.htm">Please reenter</A>.')
```

```
else  {
    client.studentID = request.StudentID
    if (client.gotoForm == "registration") {
        client.gotoForm = null
        redirect("registration.htm") }
    else {
        client.gotoForm = null
        redirect("checkSchedule.htm")
    }
}
```

FIGURE 32.6.

The StudentID *prompt for the user.*

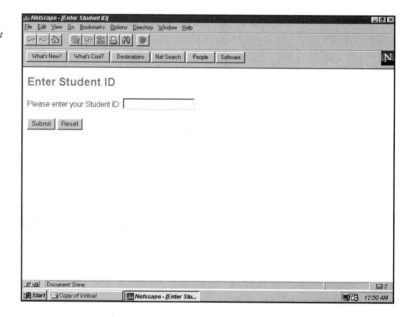

After the client has a valid StudentID, the Class Registration form is presented to the user, as shown in Figure 32.7. Obviously oversimplified for this example, this page allows the user to register for a single class by filling out the form and clicking Register.

When the Registration form is submitted, the insertClass.htm page is called. The process of inserting a class record into the VCLASSES table parallels the insertStudent.htm process shown earlier in this chapter:

```
vClass = database.cursor("SELECT * FROM VCLASSES", true)
vClass.studentID = client.studentID
vClass.className = request.ClassName
vClass.weekday = request.Weekday
vClass.time = request.Time
status = vClass.insertRow("VCLASSES")
if (status != 0) {
        write("Unable to add information at this time. <p>")}
```

```
else {
    write("You will receive email notification confirming
            your schedule.<p><p>")
    write('<A HREF="register.htm">Click here</A> to register
            for additional classes.')
write('<A HREF="mainpage.htm">Click here</A> to return to the home page.')
}
vClass.close()
```

FIGURE 32.7.

The class registration form.

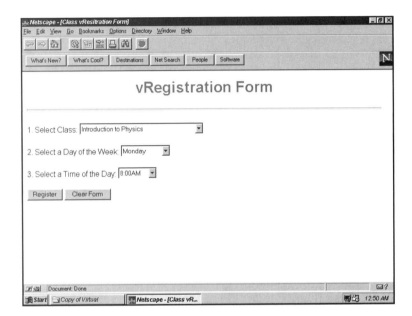

The user sees a page that confirms the class entry and lets the user register for more classes or return to the home page (see Figure 32.8).

Getting a Schedule of Classes

The final option for the user is receiving a list of the classes she chose. Clicking the Find Out Your Schedule link requests the checkSchedule.htm page. The checkSchedule.htm page first checks to see if the client has a studentID assigned. If not, the client is redirected to the id.htm page:

```
if (client.studentID == null) {
    client.gotoForm = "checkSchedule"
    redirect("id.htm")
}
```

The next step for the page is to perform a query to return the classes that the user scheduled. Because you already have the StudentID of the user at this point, you need no further information from the user to perform the query.

FIGURE 32.8.

This page appears after the user registers for a class.

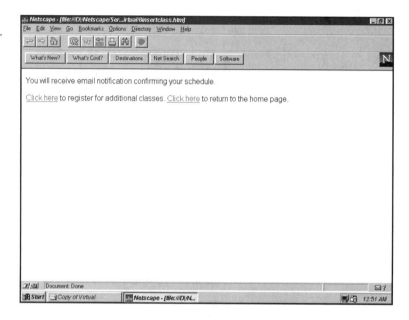

A cursor is opened on the VCLASSES table using a SELECT statement that returns all records with a StudentID value equal to the client.studentID value. The next step is to put the result set of the cursor into an HTML table. Using the same methodology used earlier in this chapter in building an HTML table on-the-fly, the class records are presented to the user:

```
vsched = database.cursor('SELECT * FROM VCLASSES WHERE StudentID = "' +
                         client.studentID + '" ORDER BY CLASSNAME', false)

write("<h1>Your Current Class Schedule</h1><p><p>")
write("<TABLE border=2 cellpadding=2 cellspacing=3 width=90%>")
write("<TR>")
for (var i=0; i<vsched.columns(); i++) {
    write("<TH>" + vsched.columnName(i) + "</TH>")
}
write("</TR>")
while (vsched.next()) {
    write("<TR>")
    for (var i=0; i<vsched.columns(); i++) {
        write("<TD>" + vsched[i] + "</TD>")
    }
    write("</TR>")
}
write("</TABLE>")
vsched.close()

write('<A HREF="mainpage.htm">Click here</A> to return to the home page.')
```

Figure 32.9 shows the results of a query.

FIGURE 32.9.

The Schedule of classes.

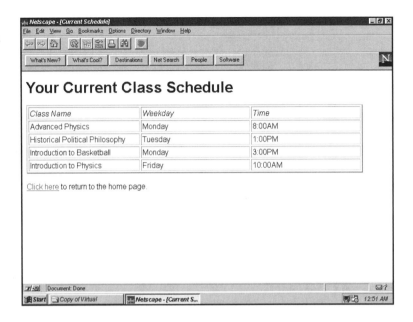

As you dissect this sample application, it is helpful to look at the entire source code for each of the pages of the application. Listings 32.1 through 32.9 provide this for you.

Listing 32.1. checkId.htm.

```
<HTML>
<BODY>
<SERVER>

// Check to see if the record exists in the table.
//
// If so, assign the value of the request.StudentID to the
// Client object parameter studentID. Then go to Registration form.
//
// If not, return to the ID form.
checkid = database.cursor('SELECT * FROM VSTUDENTS WHERE StudentID="' +
        request.StudentID + '"', false)
var i = 0
while (checkid.next()) {
    i++
}
checkid.close()
if (i == 0) {
    write('Invalid StudentID. <A HREF="id.htm">Please reenter</A>.')
else  {
    client.studentID = request.StudentID
    if (client.gotoForm == "registration") {
        client.gotoForm = null
        redirect("registration.htm") }
```

continues

Listing 32.1. continued

```
    else {
        client.gotoForm = null
        redirect("checkSchedule.htm")
    }
}
</SERVER>
</BODY>
</HTML>
```

Listing 32.2. checkSchedule.htm.

```
<HTML>
<HEAD>
<BODY>
<SERVER>

// Check to be sure that the user has a StudentID
// If not, redirect client to id.htm
if (client.studentID == null) {
    client.gotoForm = "checkSchedule"
    redirect("id.htm")
}

// Retrieve the classes of the current studentID
// and place them into a table.
vsched = database.cursor('SELECT * FROM VCLASSES WHERE StudentID = "' +
                    client.studentID + '" ORDER BY CLASSNAME', false)

write("<h1>Your Current Class Schedule</h1><p><p>")
write("<TABLE border=2 cellpadding=2 cellspacing=3 width=90%>")
write("<TR>")
for (var i=0; i<vsched.columns(); i++) {
    write("<TH>" + vsched.columnName(i) + "</TH>")
}
write("</TR>")
while (vsched.next()) {
    write("<TR>")
    for (var i=0; i<vsched.columns(); i++) {
        write("<TD>" + vsched[i] + "</TD>")
    }
    write("</TR>")
}
write("</TABLE>")
vsched.close()

write('<A HREF="mainpage.htm">Click here</A> to return to the home page.')
</SERVER>
</BODY>
</HTML>
```

Listing 32.3. enroll.htm.

```html
<html>
<head>
<title>Enroll at VU</title>
</head>

<body bgcolor="#FFFFFF">
<h1 align=center><font color="#FF0080">Enroll at VU</font></h1>
<hr>
<form action="insertstudent.htm" method="POST">
<p>Please provide the following contact information:</p>
<blockquote>
<pre><em>     First name </em><input type=text size=25 maxlength=256
name="FirstName">
<em>      Last name </em><input type=text size=25 maxlength=256
name="LastName">
<em>  Middle initial </em><input type=text size=4 maxlength=1 name="MI">
<em>           Title </em><input type=text size=35 maxlength=256
name="Title">
<em>  Street address </em><input type=text size=35 maxlength=256
name="StreetAddress">
<em> Address (cont.) </em><input type=text size=35 maxlength=256
name="Address2">
<em>            City </em><input type=text size=35 maxlength=256
name="City">
<em>  State/Province </em><input type=text size=35 maxlength=256
name="State">
<em> Zip/Postal code </em><input type=text size=12 maxlength=12
name="ZipCode">
<em>         Country </em><input type=text size=25 maxlength=256
name="Country">
<em>      Work Phone </em><input type=text size=25 maxlength=25
name="WorkPhone">
<em>      Home Phone </em><input type=text size=25 maxlength=25
name="HomePhone">
<em>             FAX </em><input type=text size=25 maxlength=25
name="FAX">
<em>          E-mail </em><input type=text size=25 maxlength=256
name="Email">
<em>             URL </em><input type=text size=25 maxlength=25
name="URL">
</pre>
<pre><em>   Date of birth </em><input type=text size=8 maxlength=256
name="DateOfBirth">
<em>             Sex </em><input type=radio checked name="Personal_Sex"
value="Male">Male <input type=radio name="Personal_Sex"
value="Female">Female</pre>
<pre><em>Expected major:</em> <select name="major" size=1>
<option selected>Software Development</option>
<option>Political Philosophy</option>
<option>Music</option>
<option>Art</option>
<option>Physics</option>
```

continues

Listing 32.3. continued

```
<option>Environmental Science</option>
<option>Writing</option>
<option>English Literature</option>
<option>French Studies</option>
<option>Sports and Physical Education</option>
<option>Biochemical Ergodynamics</option>
</select>
</pre>
</blockquote>
<p><input type=submit value="Submit Form"> <input type=reset
value="Reset Form"> </p>
</form>
<p> </h5>
</body>
</html>
```

Listing 32.4. id.htm.

```
<html>
<head>
<title>Enter Student ID</title>
</head>
<body bgcolor="#FFFFFF">
<h2><font color="#FF0080">Enter Student ID</font></h2>
<form action="checkid.htm" method="POST">
<p>Please enter your Student ID: <input type=text size=20
maxlength=256 name="StudentID"></p>
<p><input type=submit value="Submit"> <input type=reset value="Reset"></p>
</form>
</body>
</html>
```

Listing 32.5. initialize.htm.

```
<html>
<server>

// Attempt to connect to the database
if (!database.connected()) {
    database.connect("ODBC", "VSERVER", "guest", "lardgut", "SCHOOL")
}

// If connected, lock the project and get the last StudentID
// from the VSTUDENTS table. Assign it to the project property
// called lastID. You can then reference this property when
// the application is running instead of accessing the database
// directly.
//
// When this process is done, redirect client to mainpage
if (database.connected()) {
    project.lock()
```

```
            project.lastID = 0
            vCursor = database.cursor("SELECT * FROM VSTUDENTS")
            while (cursor.next()) {
                  project.lastID = vCursor.studentID
            }
            vCursor.close();
        project.unlock()
        redirect("mainpage.htm") }
else {
    write("We are vSorry, but we cannot serve you at this time.
Please try at a later time.")
}
</server>
<html>
```

Listing 32.6. insertClass.htm.

```
<html>
<body>
<server>

// Insert class record into the database by opening
// an updateable cursor.
vClass = database.cursor("SELECT * FROM VCLASSES", true)
vClass.studentID = client.studentID
vClass.className = request.ClassName
vClass.weekday = request.Weekday
vClass.time = request.Time
status = vClass.insertRow("VCLASSES")
if (status != 0) {
      write("Unable to add information at this time. <p>")}
else {
    write("You will receive email notification confirming your
          schedule.<p><p>")
    write('<A HREF="register.htm">Click here</A> to register for
          additional classes.')
    write('<A HREF="mainpage.htm">Click here</A> to return to
          the home page.')
}
vClass.close()
</server>
</body>
</html>
```

Listing 32.7. insertStudent.htm.

```
<html>
<body>
<server>

// Get a unique studentID from the project lastID property
```

continues

Listing 32.7. continued

```
project.lock()
project.lastID = parseInt(project.lastID) + 1
client.studentID = project.lastID
project.unlock()

// Open up an updateable cursor on the VSTUDENTS table
// Assign form element values to the columns and
// insert the row into the table.
vStudent = database.cursor("SELECT * FROM VSTUDENTS", true)
vStudent.studentID = client.studentID
vStudent.lastName = request.LastName
vStudent.firstName = request.FirstName
vStudent.mi = request.MI
vStudent.address = request.StreetAddress
vStudent.address2 = request.Address2
vStudent.city = request.City
vStudent.state = request.State
vStudent.zip = request.ZipCode
vStudent.country = request.Country
vStudent.homePhone = request.HomePhone
vStudent.workPhone = request.WorkPhone
vStudent.fax = request.FAX
vStudent.email = request.Email
vStudent.url = request.URL
vStudent.dob = request.DateOfBirth
vStudent.sex = request.Personal_Sex
vStudent.major = request.major
status = vStudent.insertRow("VSTUDENTS")
vStudent.close()
if (status != 0) {
        write("Unable to add information at this time. <p>")}
else {
      write("<h1>We welcome you as a vStudent.</h1><p>")
      write("Keep this information for your records.
            Your StudentID number is " + client.studentID + ".<p><p>")
      write('You can now <A HREF="register.htm">click here</A>
            to register for classes.')
}
</server>
</body>
</html>
```

Listing 32.8. mainPage.htm.

```
<html>
<head>
<title>Virtual University Home Page</title>
<server>
// If database is not connected, redirect client to the initialize page
if(!database.connected()) {
     redirect("initialize.htm")
}
</server>
```

```
</head>

<body bgcolor="#FFFFFF">
<h1 align=center><font color="#FF0080">Welcome to Virtual University
</font></h1>
<hr>
<p align=center><font size=2><em>&quot;Everyone deserves a chance at
an education, even if it has to be virtual.&quot;</em></font></p>
<p align=center><font size=2><em>-- Thomas Jeffson, Founder of VU </em>
</font></p>
<hr>
<p align=center><a href="enroll.htm">Become a vStudent</a></p>
<p align=center><a href="registration.htm">Register for vClasses</a></p>
<p align=center><a href="checkSchedule.htm">Find Out Your vSchedule</a></p>
<p> </p>
</body>
</html>
```

32

Listing 32.9. registration.htm.

```
<html>

<head>
<title>Class vResitration Form</title>
</head>

<body bgcolor="#FFFFFF">
<server>
// Check to be sure that the user has a StudentID
// If not, redirect client to id.htm
if (client.studentID == null) {
    client.gotoForm = "registration"
    redirect("id.htm")
}
</server>
<h1 align=center><font color="#FF0080">vRegistration Form</font></h1>
<hr>
<form action="insertclass.htm" method="POST">
<p>1. Select Class: <select name="ClassName" size=1>
<option selected>Introduction to Physics</option>
<option>Advanced Physics</option>
<option>Historical Political Philosophy</option>
<option>Object-Oriented Design Methodologies</option>
<option>Introduction to Basketball</option>
</select></p>
<p>2. Select a Day of the Week: <select name="Weekday" size=1>
<option>Monday</option>
<option>Tuesday</option>
<option>Wednesday</option>
<option>Thursday</option>
<option>Friday</option>
</select></p>
<p>3. Select a Time of the Day: <select name="Time" size=1>
<option>8:00AM</option>
```

continues

Listing 32.9. continued

```
<option>10:00AM</option>
<option>1:00PM</option>
<option>3:00PM</option>
<option>7:00PM</option>
</select></p>
<p><input type=submit value="Register"> <input type=reset
value="Clear Form"></p>
</form>
</body>
</html>
```

Summary

LiveWire helps bridge the gap between relational databases and the Web by providing tools to create data-enabled Web applications. This chapter discussed these capabilities by focusing on the LiveWire 1.x database and cursor objects. Using these techniques, you can create compelling database applications that any Web client can access.

IX
Part

IN THIS PART

Appendixes

JavaScript Language Summary

APPENDIX

A

While Sun was developing the much-lauded Java programming language, Netscape was busy developing a lightweight scripting language called LiveScript. This language was then redefined and renamed JavaScript. With JavaScript, you can provide almost limitless interactivity in your Web pages. The scripting language lets you access events such as startups, document loads, exits, and user mouse clicks. You can also use JavaScript to directly control objects, such as the browser status bar, frames, and even the browser display window. JavaScript also provides interactivity between plug-in modules and Java applets.

After providing a brief overview of creating dynamic documents with JavaScript, this appendix provides a reference section organized by object with properties and methods listed with the object to which they apply. A final reference section covers independent functions in JavaScript not connected with a particular object, as well as operators in JavaScript.

> **NOTE**
>
> JavaScript is supported by the Netscape Navigator version 2 and higher along with Microsoft Internet Explorer 3 and higher. For more information on JavaScript (including the entire script language documentation), visit the Netscape Web site (`http://home.netscape.com/`). The information provided here details how to include JavaScript scripts within HTML documents, not how to author actual scripts. Such information is well beyond the scope of this appendix.

Dynamic Documents with JavaScript

You can use JavaScript to control many parts of the browser (as defined in the JavaScript object model) and to respond to various user actions such as form input and page navigation. JavaScript is particularly valuable because all processing duties are written in the script (embedded into the HTML document), so the entire process defined by the script is carried out on the client side without referring back to a server.

You can write a JavaScript script, for example, to verify that the user entered numeric information in a form requesting a telephone number or ZIP code. Without any network transmission, an HTML script with embedded JavaScript can interpret the entered text and alert the user with an appropriate message dialog.

A script is embedded in HTML within a `<SCRIPT>` element as follows:

```
<SCRIPT>...</SCRIPT>
```

Attributes within the `<SCRIPT>` element are specified as follows:

```
<SCRIPT LANGUAGE="JavaScript">
  // JavaScript code is placed here
</SCRIPT>
```

Using the LANGUAGE attribute, you can also specify the version of JavaScript you want to use. The preceding example specifies the first version of JavaScript. For newer releases, you need to add the version number, as in the following example:

```
<SCRIPT LANGUAGE="JavaScript1.1">
  // JavaScript code is placed here
</SCRIPT>
```

Netscape Navigator 3.0 introduced version 1.1, and Netscape Navigator 4.0 introduced JavaScript 1.2. If a Web browser encounters a script using a JavaScript version newer than the one it can understand, the script is ignored completely.

The LANGUAGE attribute is required unless the SRC attribute is present to specify the scripting language. With some Web servers, you can use the SRC attribute to specify a URL to load a text file containing JavaScript into the browser's memory:

```
<SCRIPT LANGUAGE="JavaScript" SRC="separate.js">
```

When a JavaScript-enabled HTML document is retrieved by a browser that supports JavaScript, the script functions are evaluated and stored. The functions defined within the script are executed only upon certain events within the page (for example, when the user moves the mouse pointer over an object or enters text in a text box and so on).

So that non–JavaScript-capable browsers do not display the text of the script (browsers display anything they don't recognize as HTML as text on the page), you should enclose the script within comment elements, as in the following example:

```
<SCRIPT LANGUAGE="JavaScript">
<!-- Begin to hide script contents from old browsers.
  Script contents go here.
  End the hiding here.-->
</SCRIPT>
```

A

JavaScript Objects and Their Properties

This section describes JavaScript objects and their properties. Objects are presented in alphabetical order for easy reference. If an object, one of its methods, or one of its properties was not available in the first release of JavaScript, the version number that introduced the new feature is noted in parentheses. If an object's property or method was released in the same version of JavaScript as the object itself, the version for that property or method is not specified.

The Anchor Object

The Anchor object reflects an anchor element in an HTML document.

Properties

See the anchors property of the document object.

Methods

eval(*statement*) (v1.1)	Evaluates a string as a JavaScript expression or statement, in reference to the Anchor object.
toString() (v1.1)	Returns a string representation of the anchor object.
valueOf() (v1.1)	Converts the object to its primitive type (for example, number, Boolean, string, or function).

The Applet Object (v1.1)

The Applet object is a reflection of a Java applet embedded into an HTML document. See also the applets property of the document object.

Properties

All public properties made through the applet are available.

eval(*statement*) (v1.1)	Evaluates a string as a JavaScript expression or statement, in reference to the Applet object.
toString() (v1.1)	Returns a string representation of the Applet object.
valueOf() (v1.1)	Converts the object to its primitive type (for example, number, Boolean, string, or function).

Methods

All public properties made through the applet are available.

The Area Object (v1.1)

The Area object is a reflection of an area in an image map. Area objects are referenced through the links array.

Properties

target	A string value containing the name of the window or frame specified in the target attribute.
hash	A string value containing the anchor name in the URL.
host	A string value containing the hostname and port number from the URL.
hostname	A string value containing the domain name (or numerical IP address) from the URL.

href	A string value containing the entire URL.
pathname	A string value specifying the path portion of the URL.
port	A string value containing the port number from the URL.
protocol	A string value containing the protocol from the URL (including the colon but not the slashes).
search	A string value containing any information passed to a GET CGI-BIN call (that is, any information after the question mark).

Methods

eval(*statement*) (v1.1)	Evaluates a string as a JavaScript expression or statement, in reference to the Area object.
toString() (v1.1)	Returns a string representation of the Area object.
valueOf() (v1.1)	Converts the object to its primitive type (for example, number, Boolean, string, or function).

Event Handlers

onMouseOut	Specifies JavaScript code to execute when the mouse leaves the area.
onMouseOver	Specifies JavaScript code to execute when the mouse is over the area.

The Array Object (v1.1)

The Array object is a single-dimensional array. The length of a JavaScript array can be changed by simply creating a new element indexed with the new size.

Properties

length	Used to assign the number of elements in the array.
prototype	Used to assign a new property to the Array object.

Methods

join(separator)	Joins a string representation of each element in the array into one string, separated by the string specified with separator.
reverse	Reverses the order of all elements in the array.
sort	Sorts the elements of the array in lexicographic order or uses a user-defined sort function.

`eval(`*`statement`*`)` (v1.1)	Evaluates a string as a JavaScript expression or statement, in reference to the `Array` object.
`toString()` (v1.1)	Returns a string representation of the `Array` object.
`valueOf()` (v1.1)	Converts the object to its primitive type (for example, number, Boolean, string, or function).

The Boolean Object (v1.1)

The `Boolean` object allows you to work with Boolean values as objects.

Properties

| `prototype` | Used to assign a new property to the `Boolean` object. |

Methods

`eval(`*`statement`*`)` (v1.1)	Evaluates a string as a JavaScript expression or statement, in reference to the `Boolean` object.
`toString()` (v1.1)	Returns a string representation of the `Boolean` object.
`valueOf()` (v1.1)	Converts the object to its primitive type (for example, number, Boolean, string, or function).

The Button Object

The `Button` object reflects a pushbutton from an HTML form in JavaScript.

Properties

| `name` | A string value containing the name of the button element. |
| `value` | A string value containing the value of the button element. |

Methods

`click()`	Emulates the action of clicking the button.
`eval(`*`statement`*`)` (v1.1)	Evaluates a string as a JavaScript expression or statement, in reference to the `Button` object.
`toString()` (v1.1)	Returns a string representation of the `Button` object.
`valueOf()` (v1.1)	Converts the object to its primitive type (for example, number, Boolean, string, or function).

Event Handlers

onClick   Specifies JavaScript code to execute when the button is clicked. JavaScript version 1.1 allows you to return `false` to cancel the event.

The Checkbox Object

The `Checkbox` object makes a checkbox from an HTML form available in JavaScript.

Properties

checked   A Boolean value indicating whether the checkbox element is checked.

defaultChecked   A Boolean value indicating whether the checkbox element is checked by default (that is, it reflects the `checked` attribute).

name   A string value containing the name of the checkbox element.

value   A string value containing the value of the checkbox element.

Methods

click()   Emulates the action of clicking the checkbox.

eval(*statement*) (v1.1)   Evaluates a string as a JavaScript expression or statement, in reference to the `Checkbox` object.

toString() (v1.1)   Returns a string representation of the `Checkbox` object.

valueOf() (v1.1)   Converts the object to its primitive type (for example, number, Boolean, string, or function).

Event Handlers

onBlur (v1.1)   Specifies JavaScript code to execute when the checkbox loses focus.

onClick   Specifies JavaScript code to execute when the checkbox is clicked. JavaScript version 1.1 allows you to return `false` to cancel the event.

onFocus (v1.1)   Specifies JavaScript code to execute when the checkbox receives focus.

The event Object (v1.2)

JavaScript uses the `event` object to pass event information to an event handler when an event occurs.

Properties

type   The type of event.

x   The x location of the mouse pointer when the event occurs. Used only
              with mouse events.

y   The y location of the mouse pointer when the event occurs. Used only
              with mouse events.

The Date Object

The Date object provides mechanisms for working with dates and times in JavaScript. You can
create instances of the object with the following syntax:

```
newObjectName = new Date(dateInfo)
```

In this example, *dateInfo* is an optional specification of a particular date and can be one of the
following, where the latter two options represent integer values:

```
"month day, year hours:minutes:seconds"
year, month, day
year, month, day, hours, minutes, seconds
```

If no *dateInfo* is specified, the new object represents the current date and time.

Methods

eval(*statement*) (v1.1)   Evaluates a string as a JavaScript expression or statement,
                              in reference to the Date object.

getDate()   Returns the day of the month for the current Date object
                              as an integer from 1 to 31.

getDay()   Returns the day of the week for the current Date object
                              as an integer from 0 to 6 (where 0 is Sunday, 1 is
                              Monday, and so on).

getHours()   Returns the hour from the time in the current Date
                              object as an integer from 0 to 23.

getMinutes()   Returns the minutes from the time in the current Date
                              object as an integer from 0 to 59.

getMonth()   Returns the month for the current Date object as an
                              integer from 0 to 11 (where 0 is January, 1 is February,
                              and so on).

getSeconds()   Returns the seconds from the time in the current Date
                              object as an integer from 0 to 59.

`getTime()`	Returns the time of the current `Date` object as an integer representing the number of milliseconds since January 1, 1970 at 00:00:00.
`getTimezoneOffset()`	Returns the difference between the local time and GMT as an integer representing the number of minutes.
`getYear()`	Returns the year of the week for the current `Date` object as a two-digit integer representing the year less 1900.

`parse(dateString)`	Returns the number of milliseconds between January 1, 1970 at 00:00:00 and the date specified in *dateString*. *dateString* should take the following format:
	`Day, DD Mon YYYY HH:MM:SS TZN`
	`Mon DD, YYYY`

`setDate(dateValue)`	Sets the day of the month for the current `Date` object. *dateValue* is an integer from 1 to 31.
`setHours(hoursValue)`	Sets the hours for the time for the current `Date` object. *hoursValue* is an integer from 0 to 23.
`setMinutes(minutesValue)`	Sets the minutes for the time for the current `Date` object. *minutesValue* is an integer from 0 to 59.
`setMonth(monthValue)`	Sets the month for the current `Date` object. *monthValue* is an integer from 0 to 11 (where 0 is January, 1 is February, and so on).
`setSeconds(secondsValue)`	Sets the seconds for the time for the current `Date` object. *secondsValue* is an integer from 0 to 59.
`setTime(timeValue)`	Sets the value for the current `Date` object. *timeValue* is an integer representing the number of milliseconds since January 1, 1970 at 00:00:00.
`setYear(yearValue)`	Sets the year for the current `Date` object. *yearValue* is an integer greater than 1900.
`toGMTString()`	Returns the value of the current `Date` object in GMT as a string using Internet conventions in the following form: `Day, DD Mon YYYY HH:MM:SS GMT`
`toLocaleString()`	Returns the value of the current `Date` object in the local time using local conventions.
`toString() (v1.1)`	Returns a string representation of the `Date` object.

A

JAVASCRIPT
LANGUAGE
SUMMARY

`UTC(`*`yearValue, monthValue,`* *`dateValue, hoursValue,`* *`minutesValue, secondsValue`*`)`	Returns the number of milliseconds since January 1, 1970 at 00:00:00 GMT. *yearValue* is an integer greater than 1900. *monthValue* is an integer from 0 to 11. *dateValue* is an integer from 1 to 31. *hoursValue* is an integer from 0 to 23. *minutesValue* and *secondsValue* are integers from 0 to 59. *hoursValue*, *minutesValue*, and *secondsValue* are optional.
`valueOf()` (v1.1)	Converts the object to its primitive type (for example, number, Boolean, string, or function).

The document Object

The `document` object reflects attributes of an HTML document in JavaScript.

Properties

`alinkColor`	The color of active links as a string or a hexadecimal triplet.
`anchors`	An array of anchor objects in the order they appear in the HTML document. Use `anchors.length` to get the number of anchors in a document.
`applets` (v1.1)	An array of `Applet` objects in the order they appear in the HTML document. Use `applets.length` to get the number of applets in a document. (See `Applet` object.)
`bgColor`	The color of the document's background.
`cookie`	A string value containing cookie values for the current document.
`domain` (v1.1)	The domain name of the server that served the document. It is used to share documents across servers with the same suffix without using data tainting.
`embeds` (v1.1)	An array representing all `EMBED` elements in the order they appear in the HTML document. Use `embeds.length` to get the number of `EMBED` elements in a document.
`fgColor`	The color of the document's foreground.
`forms`	An array of form objects in the order the forms appear in the HTML file. Use `forms.length` to get the number of forms in a document.
`images` (v1.1)	An array of `Image` objects in the order the images appear in the HTML document. Use `images.length` to get the number of forms in a document.

`lastModified`	A string value containing the last date of modification of the document.
`linkColor`	The color of links as a string or a hexadecimal triplet.
`links`	An array of link objects in the order the hypertext links appear in the HTML document. Use `links.length` to get the number of links in a document.
`location`	A string containing the URL of the current document.
`referrer`	A string value containing the URL of the calling document when the user follows a link.
`title`	A string containing the title of the current document.
`vlinkColor`	The color of followed links as a string or a hexadecimal triplet.

Methods

`clear()`	Clears the document window.
`close()`	Closes the current output stream.
`eval(statement)` (v1.1)	Evaluates a string as a JavaScript expression or statement, in reference to the `document` object.
`open(mime)`	Opens a stream that allows `write()` and `writeln()` methods to write to the document window. `mime` is an optional string that specifies a document type supported by Navigator or a plug-in (for example, `text/html`, `image/gif`, and so on).
`open(mime,["replace"])` (v1.1)	Works the same as in version 1.0 of JavaScript but allows a second argument. If the string `"replace"` is passed as the second argument, the previous document's history is reused.
`toString()` (v1.1)	Returns a string representation of the `document` object.
`valueOf()` (v1.1)	Converts the object to its primitive type (for example, number, Boolean, string, or function).
`write()`	Writes text and HTML to the specified document.
`writeln()`	Writes text and HTML to the specified document followed by a newline character.

The FileUpload Object (v1.1)

The FileUpload object is a reflection of an HTML INPUT element of the type file. It is used to allow the client to upload a file.

Properties

form	A reference to the form that contains the file upload INPUT element.
name	The name of the INPUT element.
type	The type of the INPUT element (that is, "file").
value	The value of the data entry field for the INPUT element. Read-only.

Methods

blur()	Removes focus from the file upload element.
eval(*statement*) (v1.1)	Evaluates a string as a JavaScript expression or statement, in reference to the FileUpload object.
focus()	Sets focus to the file upload element.
toString() (v1.1)	Returns a string representation of the FileUpload object.
valueOf() (v1.1)	Converts the object to its primitive type (for example, number, Boolean, string, or function).

Event Handlers

onBlur	Specifies the JavaScript code to execute when the file upload element loses focus.
onChange	Specifies the JavaScript code to execute when the file upload element's value has changed and the element loses focus.
onFocus	Specifies the JavaScript code to execute when the file upload element gains focus.

The form Object

The form object reflects an HTML form in JavaScript. Each HTML form in a document is reflected by a distinct instance of the form object.

Properties

action	A string value specifying the URL where the form data is submitted.
elements	Array of objects for each form element in the order in which they appear in the form.
encoding	String containing the MIME encoding of the form as specified in the ENCTYPE attribute.
method	A string value containing the method of submission of form data to the server.
target	A string value containing the name of the window where responses to form submissions are directed.

Methods

eval(*statement*) (v1.1)	Evaluates a string as a JavaScript expression or statement, in reference to the form object.
reset() (v1.1)	Resets the form as if the user clicked on a reset button.
submit()	Submits the form.
toString() (v1.1)	Returns a string representation of the form object.
valueOf() (v1.1)	Converts the object to its primitive type (for example, number, Boolean, string, or function).

Event Handlers

onReset (v1.1)	Specifies the JavaScript code to execute when the form is reset.
onSubmit	Specifies the JavaScript code to execute when the form is submitted. The code should return a true value to let the form be submitted. A false value prevents the form from being submitted.

The frame Object

The frame object reflects a frame window in JavaScript.

Properties

frames	An array of objects for each frame in a window. Frames appear in the array in the order in which they appear in the HTML source code.
parent	A string indicating the name of the window containing the frameset.

`self`	An alternative for the name of the current window.
`top`	An alternative for the name of the topmost window.
`window`	An alternative for the name of the current window.

Methods

`alert(message)`	Displays *message* in a dialog box.
`blur()` (v1.1)	Emulates the action of removing focus from the frame.
`clearInterval(id)` (v1.2)	Clears the interval referenced by `id`.
`clearTimeout(name)`	Cancels the timeout specified by *name*.
`close()`	Closes the window.
`confirm(message)`	Displays *message* in a dialog box with OK and Cancel buttons. Returns `true` or `false` based on the button clicked by the user.
`eval(statement)` (v1.1)	Evaluates a string as a JavaScript expression or statement, in reference to the `frame` object.
`focus()` (v1.1)	Emulates moving focus to the frame.
`open(url,name,features)`	Opens *url* in a window named *name*. If *name* doesn't exist, a new window is created with that name. *features* is an optional string argument containing a list of features for the new window. The feature list contains any of the following name/value pairs separated by commas without additional spaces:

`toolbar=[yes,no,1,0]`	Indicates whether the window should have a toolbar.
`location=[yes,no,1,0]`	Indicates whether the window should have a location field.
`directories=[yes,no,1,0]`	Indicates whether the window should have directory buttons.
`status=[yes,no,1,0]`	Indicates whether the window should have a status bar.
`menubar=[yes,no,1,0]`	Indicates whether the window should have menus.

`scrollbars=[yes,no,1,0]`	Indicates whether the window should have scrollbars.
`resizable=[yes,no,1,0]`	Indicates whether the window should be resizable.
`width=pixels`	Indicates the width of the window in pixels.
`height=pixels`	Indicates the height of the window in pixels.
`prompt(message,response)`	Displays *message* in a dialog box with a text entry field with the default value of *response*. The user's response in the text entry field is returned as a string.
`scroll(x,y)` (v1.1)	Scrolls the frame to the coordinates specified by *x* and *y*.
`setInterval(expr,time)` (v1.2)	Evaluates the expression specified in *expr* after the number of milliseconds specified in *time* has elapsed. This method returns a value that can be used as the *id* for the method `clearInterval()`.
`setTimeout(expr,time)`	Evaluates the expression specified in *expr* after the number of milliseconds specified in *time* has elapsed. You can name the timeout with the following structure: `name = setTimeOut(expression,time)`
`toString()` (v1.1)	Returns a string representation of the `frame` object.
`valueOf()` (v1.1)	Converts the object to its primitive type (for example, number, Boolean, string, or function).

A

Event Handlers

`onBlur` (v1.1)	Specifies JavaScript code to execute when the frame loses focus.
`onError` (v1.1)	Specifies the JavaScript code to execute when an error occurs. This event handler applies only to JavaScript errors, not Navigator errors.
`onFocus` (v1.1)	Specifies JavaScript code to execute when focus is given to the frame.

The `Function` Object (v1.1)

The `Function` object provides a way to create functions during the execution of JavaScript code. You can create a new function with the following syntax:

```
newFunctionName = new Function(arg1, arg2, ... argn, functionBody)
```

In the following example, `statusHelp` is assigned a new function that takes one argument, `messageOne`:

```
var statusHelp = new Function("messageOne","window.defaultStatus = messageOne;
                window.status = messageOne")
```

The new `Function` object can then be used in the same way a typically declared function is used. Here it is used to reset the status bar message after an HTML document is loaded:

```
<BODY onLoad="statusHelp('Look here for help.')">
```

Properties

`arguments`	Used to assign an array holding each argument that was passed to the function.
`caller`	Used to assign the name of the function that called this function.
`prototype`	Used to assign a new property to the `Function` object.

Methods

`eval(statement)` (v1.1)	Evaluates a string as a JavaScript expression or statement, in reference to the `Function` object.
`toString()` (v1.1)	Returns a string representation of the `Function` object.
`valueOf()` (v1.1)	Converts the object to its primitive type (for example, number, Boolean, string, or function).

The Hidden Object

The `Hidden` object reflects a hidden field from an HTML form in JavaScript.

Properties

`name`	A string value containing the name of the hidden element.
`value`	A string value containing the value of a hidden text element.

Methods

`eval(statement)` (v1.1)	Evaluates a string as a JavaScript expression or statement, in reference to the `Hidden` object.
`toString()` (v1.1)	Returns a string representation of the `Hidden` object.
`valueOf()` (v1.1)	Converts the object to its primitive type (for example, number, Boolean, string, or function).

The `history` Object

The `history` object allows a script to work with the Navigator browser's history list in JavaScript. For security and privacy reasons, the actual content of the list is not reflected in JavaScript.

Properties

`current` (v1.1)	A string representing the complete URL of the current history entry.
`next` (v1.1)	A string representing the complete URL of the next history entry.
`length`	An integer representing the number of items on the history list.
`previous` (v1.1)	A string representing the complete URL of the previous history entry.

Methods

`back()`	Goes back to the previous document in the history list.
`eval(`*`statement`*`)` (v1.1)	Evaluates a string as a JavaScript expression or statement, in reference to the `history` object.
`forward()`	Goes forward to the next document in the history list.
`go(`*`location`*`)`	Goes to the document in the history list specified by *`location`*. *`location`* can be a string or integer value. If it is a string, it represents all or part of a URL in the history list. If it is an integer, *`location`* represents the relative position of the document on the history list. As an integer, *`location`* can be positive or negative.
`toString()` (v1.1)	Returns a string representation of the `history` object.
`valueOf()` (v1.1)	Converts the object to its primitive type (for example, number, Boolean, string, or function).

The `Image` Object (v1.1)

The `Image` object is a reflection of an HTML `IMG` element. It also allows the preloading of images if the client's cache has enough room to store the image. The following example creates a new `Image` object and loads it over the network:

```
myLogo = new Image()
myLogo.src = "logo.jpg"
```

To change an image on a web that has already been loaded, use the following code to pull the image from the cache:

```
document.images[0].src = myImage.src
```

Properties

border	Assigns the border attribute of the image.
complete	Assigns the Boolean value specifying if the image has completed downloading or the browser has given up trying to download the image.
height	Assigns the height attribute of the image.
hspace	Assigns the hspace attribute of the image.
lowsrc	Assigns the lowsrc attribute of the image.
name	Assigns the name attribute of the image.
prototype	Assigns a new property to the Image object.
src	Assigns the src attribute of the image.
vspace	Assigns the vspace attribute of the image.
width	Assigns the width attribute of the image.

NOTE

The border, hspace, name, and vspace properties are not used when creating a new image as in the previous example.

Methods

eval(*statement*) (v1.1)	Evaluates a string as a JavaScript expression or statement, in reference to the Image object.
toString() (v1.1)	Returns a string representation of the Image object.
valueOf() (v1.1)	Converts the object to its primitive type (for example, number, Boolean, string, or function).

Event Handlers

onAbort	Specifies the JavaScript code to execute when the client aborts the download of the image.
onError	Specifies the JavaScript code to execute when an error occurs during the attempt to download the image. This event handler applies only to JavaScript errors, not Navigator errors.
onLoad	Specifies the JavaScript code to execute when the image is displayed. Therefore, when an image is pre-loaded, the onLoad event handler is not called until the image is displayed.

The layer Object (v1.2)

The layer object reflects a layer element in an HTML document.

Properties

name	Assigns a reflection of the name attribute in a LAYER element. (Read-only)
width	Assigns a reflection of the width attribute in a LAYER element. (Read-only)
height	Assigns the height of the layer. (Read-only)
left	Assigns the horizontal position of the layer, in relation to its parent layer.
top	Assigns the vertical position of the layer, in relation to its parent layer.
zIndex	Assigns the z-order of the layer in relation to its siblings and parent.
visibility=[show,hide,inherit]	Specifies whether the layer is visible. If visibility is equal to inherit, its visibility is the same as its parent.
clip.top	Specifies the top of the clipping rectangle.
clip.left	Specifies the left of the clipping rectangle.
clip.right	Specifies the right of the clipping rectangle.
clip.bottom	Specifies the bottom of the clipping rectangle.
clip.width	Specifies the width of the clipping rectangle.
clip.height	Specifies the height of the clipping rectangle.
background	Assigns the Image object to use as the background for the layer. Optionally, you can set the background's src property directly.
bgColor	Assigns the string or RGB hexadecimal value of the background color for the layer.
siblingAbove	Assigns the layer object above this layer that shares the same parent layer. (Read-only)
siblingBelow	Assigns the layer object below this layer that shares the same parent layer. (Read-only)
above	Assigns the layer object above this layer in z-order without regard to its parent. (Read-only)

below	Assigns the `layer` object below this layer in z-order, without regard to its parent. (Read-only)
parentLayer	Assigns the `layer` object that contains this layer, if one exists. (Read-only)
layers	Assigns an array of all child layer objects if any exist. (Read-only)
src	Assigns the URL of the HTML document contained in the layer. (Read-only)

Methods

offset(*x,y*)	Changes the layer position by adding the *x* and *y* values to the current position's coordinates.
moveTo(*x,y*)	Changes the layer position to the coordinates specified by the *x* and *y* values.
resize(*width,height*)	Resizes the layer to the specified *width* and *height* values.
moveAbove(*layer*)	Moves this layer above the layer specified. It also reassigns the layer to share the same parent layer.
moveBelow(*layer*)	Moves this layer below the layer specified. It also reassigns the layer to share the same parent layer.

The Link Object

The `Link` object reflects a hypertext link in the body of a document.

Properties

target	A string value containing the name of the window or frame specified in the `target` attribute.
hash	A string value containing the anchor name in the URL.
host	A string value containing the hostname and port number from the URL.
hostname	A string value containing the domain name (or numerical IP address) from the URL.
href	A string value containing the entire URL.
pathname	A string value specifying the path portion of the URL.
port	A string value containing the port number from the URL.
protocol	A string value containing the protocol from the URL (including the colon but not the slashes).

search   A string value containing any information passed to a GET CGI-BIN call (that is, any information after the question mark).

Methods

eval(*statement*) (v1.1)   Evaluates a string as a JavaScript expression or statement, in reference to the Link object.

toString() (v1.1)   Returns a string representation of the Link object.

valueOf() (v1.1)   Converts the object to its primitive type (for example, number, Boolean, string, or function).

Event Handlers

onClick   Specifies JavaScript code to execute when the link is clicked.

onMouseOut (v1.1)   Specifies JavaScript code to execute when the mouse pointer moves off the link.

onMouseOver   Specifies JavaScript code to execute when the mouse pointer is over the hypertext link.

The location Object

The location object reflects information about the current URL.

Properties

hash   A string value containing the anchor name in the URL.

host   A string value containing the hostname and port number from the URL.

hostname   A string value containing the domain name (or numerical IP address) from the URL.

href   A string value containing the entire URL.

pathname   A string value specifying the path portion of the URL.

port   A string value containing the port number from the URL.

protocol   A string value containing the protocol from the URL (including the colon but not the slashes).

search   A string value containing any information passed to a GET CGI-BIN call (that is, any information after the question mark).

A

JAVASCRIPT LANGUAGE SUMMARY

Methods

eval(*statement*) (v1.1)	Evaluates a string as a JavaScript expression or statement, in reference to the location object.
reload([true]) (v1.1)	Reloads the URL specified in the href property of the location being reloaded. Passing true as the parameter results in an unconditional HTTP GET from the server.
replace(*urlStr*) (v1.1)	Replaces the current history entry while loading the URL specified in *urlStr*.
toString() (v1.1)	Returns a string representation of the location object.
valueOf() (v1.1)	Converts the object to its primitive type (for example, number, Boolean, string, or function).

The Math Object

The Math object provides properties and methods for advanced mathematical calculations.

Properties

E	The value of Euler's constant (roughly 2.718), used as the base for natural logarithms.
LN10	The value of the natural logarithm of 10 (roughly 2.302).
LN2	The value of the natural logarithm of 2 (roughly 0.693).
PI	The value of pi, used in calculating the circumference and area of circles (roughly 3.1415).
SQRT1_2	The value of the square root of one half (roughly 0.707).
SQRT2	The value of the square root of two (roughly 1.414).

Methods

abs(*number*)	Returns the absolute value of *number*. The absolute value is the value of a number with its sign ignored, so abs(4) and abs(-4) both return 4.
acos(*number*)	Returns the arccosine of *number* in radians.
asin(*number*)	Returns the arcsine of *number* in radians.
atan(*number*)	Returns the arctangent of *number* in radians.
ceil(*number*)	Returns the next integer greater than *number*—in other words, rounds up to the next integer.

`cos(number)`	Returns the cosine of *number*, where *number* represents an angle in radians.
`eval(statement)` (v1.1)	Evaluates a string as a JavaScript expression or statement, in reference to the `Math` object.
`exp(number)`	Returns the value of E to the power of *number*.
`floor(number)`	Returns the next integer less than *number*—in other words, rounds down to the nearest integer.
`log(number)`	Returns the natural logarithm of *number*.
`max(number1,number2)`	Returns the greater of *number1* and *number2*.
`min(number1,number2)`	Returns the smaller of *number1* and *number2*.
`pow(number1,number2)`	Returns the value of *number1* to the power of *number2*.
`random()`	Returns a random number between zero and one. (Currently, this method is available only on UNIX versions of Navigator 2.0.)
`round(number)`	Returns the closest integer to *number*—in other words, rounds to the closest integer.
`sin(number)`	Returns the sine of *number*, where *number* represents an angle in radians.
`sqrt(number)`	Returns the square root of *number*.
`tan(number)`	Returns the tangent of *number*, where *number* represents an angle in radians.
`toString()` (v1.1)	Returns a string representation of the `Math` object.
`valueOf()` (v1.1)	Converts the object to its primitive type (for example, number, Boolean, string, or function).

A

JAVASCRIPT
LANGUAGE
SUMMARY

The `MimeType` Object (v1.1)

The `MimeType` object represents one of the MIME (Multipurpose Internet Mail Extension) types supported by the browser.

Properties

`description`	The description of the MIME type.
`enabledPlugin`	A reference to the `Plugin` object configured for the MIME type. If no plug-in is configured for the MIME type, then `enabledPlugin` is null.
`type`	The name of the MIME type.
`suffixes`	The file extensions associated with the MIME type.

Methods

eval(*statement*) (v1.1)   Evaluates a string as a JavaScript expression or statement, in reference to the MimeType object.

toString() (v1.1)   Returns a string representation of the MimeType object.

valueOf() (v1.1)   Converts the object to its primitive type (for example, number, Boolean, string, or function).

The navigator Object

The navigator object reflects information about the version of Navigator being used.

Properties

appCodeName   A string value containing the code name of the client (for example, "Mozilla" for Netscape Navigator).

appName   A string value containing the name of the client (for example, "Netscape" for Netscape Navigator).

appVersion   A string value containing the version information for the client in the following form:

versionNumber (*platform*; *country*)

For example, Navigator 2.0, beta 6 for Windows 95 (international version) has an appVersion property with the value 2.0b6 (Win32; I).

mimeTypes (v1.1)   An array representing all the MIME types supported by the client. Use mimeTypes.length to get the number of MIME types available. (See the MimeType object.)

plugins (v1.1)   An array representing all the plug-ins supported by the client. Use plugins.length to get the number of plug-ins available. (navigator.plugins.refresh([true|false])) (See the Plugin object.) The plugins array has its own method:

refresh(reload)   Calling refresh reloads all plug-in information including any newly installed plug-ins. The parameter reload can be either true or false. If true, the refresh also reloads any documents containing the EMBED element. If false, no documents are reloaded.

userAgent   A string containing the complete value of the user-agent header sent in the HTTP request. It contains all the information in appCodeName and appVersion:

Mozilla/2.0b6 (Win32; I)

Methods

eval(*statement*) (v1.1)	Evaluates a string as a JavaScript expression or statement, in reference to the navigator object.
javaEnabled() (v1.1)	Returns true if Java is enabled by the client; otherwise, it returns false.
taintEnabled() (v1.1)	Returns true if data tainting is enabled; otherwise, it returns false.
toString() (v1.1)	Returns a string representation of the navigator object.
valueOf() (v1.1)	Converts the object to its primitive type (for example, number, Boolean, string, or function).

The Number Object (v1.1)

The Number object allows you to work with number values as objects.

Properties

MAX_VALUE	Used to assign the largest number you can represent with the Number object.
MIN_VALUE	Used to assign the smallest number you can represent with the Number object.
NaN	Used to assign a constant representing a value that is not a number.
NEGATIVE_INFINITY	Used to assign a constant representing negative infinity.
POSITIVE_INFINITY	Used to assign a constant representing positive infinity.
prototype	Used to assign a new property to the Number object.

Methods

eval(*statement*) (v1.1)	Evaluates a string as a JavaScript expression or statement, in reference to the Number object.
toString() (v1.1)	Returns a string representation of the Number object.
valueOf() (v1.1)	Converts the object to its primitive type (for example, number, Boolean, string, or function).

The Option Object (v1.1)

The Option object reflects one of the items in a SELECT element. To add an option to an existing SELECT element, use the following syntax:

```
var optionName = new Option(text, value, defaultSelected, selected)
selectName.options[index] = optionName
```

text is the string to be displayed in the SELECT list.

value is the string to be submitted with the form.

defaultSelected specifies whether the option is initially selected.

selected is set to true when the option is selected; otherwise, it is set to false.

To remove an option from an existing SELECT element, assign null to the option.

Properties

defaultSelected	Used to assign the initial selection state of the option.
index	Used to assign the index of the option in the SELECT element.
prototype	Used to assign a new property to the Option object.
selected	Used to assign the current selection state of the Option object.
text	Used to assign the text displayed for the Option object.
value	Used to assign the value submitted with the form for the Option object.

Methods

eval(*statement*) (v1.1)	Evaluates a string as a JavaScript expression or statement, in reference to the Option object.
toString() (v1.1)	Returns a string representation of the Option object.
valueOf() (v1.1)	Converts the object to its primitive type (for example, number, Boolean, string, or function).

The Password Object

The Password object reflects a password text field from an HTML form in JavaScript.

Properties

defaultValue	A string value containing the default value of the password element (that is, the value of the value attribute).

| name | A string value containing the name of the password element. |
| value | A string value containing the value of the password element. |

Methods

blur()	Emulates the action of removing focus from the password field.
eval(*statement*) (v1.1)	Evaluates a string as a JavaScript expression or statement, in reference to the Password object.
focus()	Emulates the action of focusing in the password field.
select()	Emulates the action of selecting the text in the password field.
toString() (v1.1)	Returns a string representation of the Password object.
valueOf() (v1.1)	Converts the object to its primitive type (for example, number, Boolean, string, or function).

The Plugin Object (v1.1)

The Plugin object reflects a plug-in (or helper application) that is installed on the client's computer. The Plugin object is also an array of MimeType objects. (See the MimeType object.)

Properties

description	A description of the plug-in, if one is supplied by the plug-in software.
filename	The filename of the plug-in software.
length	The number of elements in the Plugin object's array of MimeType objects. (See the MimeType object.)
name	The name of the Plugin object.

Methods

eval(*statement*) (v1.1)	Evaluates a string as a JavaScript expression or statement, in reference to the Plugin object.
toString() (v1.1)	Returns a string representation of the Plugin object.
valueOf() (v1.1)	Converts the object to its primitive type (for example, number, Boolean, string, or function).

The Radio Object

The Radio object reflects a set of radio buttons from an HTML form in JavaScript. To access individual radio buttons, use numeric indexes starting at zero. For example, individual buttons in a set of radio buttons named testRadio could be referenced by testRadio[0], testRadio[1], and so on.

Properties

checked	A Boolean value indicating whether a specific button is checked. It can be used to select or deselect a button.
defaultChecked	A Boolean value indicating whether a specific button is checked by default (that is, reflects the checked attribute).
length	An integer value indicating the number of radio buttons in the set.
name	A string value containing the name of the set of radio buttons.
value	A string value containing the value of a specific radio button in a set.

Methods

click()	Emulates the action of clicking a radio button.
eval(*statement*) (v1.1)	Evaluates a string as a JavaScript expression or statement, in reference to the Radio object.
toString() (v1.1)	Returns a string representation of the Radio object.
valueOf() (v1.1)	Converts the object to its primitive type (for example, number, Boolean, string, or function).

Event Handlers

onBlur (v1.1)	Specifies JavaScript code to execute when the radio button loses focus.
onClick	Specifies JavaScript code to execute when a radio button is clicked. JavaScript version 1.1 allows you to return false to cancel the event.
onFocus (v1.1)	Specifies JavaScript code to execute when the radio button receives focus.

The Reset Object

The Reset object reflects a reset button from an HTML form in JavaScript.

Properties

name	A string value containing the name of the reset element.
value	A string value containing the value of the reset element.

Methods

click()	Emulates the action of clicking the reset button.
eval(*statement*) (v1.1)	Evaluates a string as a JavaScript expression or statement, in reference to the Reset object.
toString() (v1.1)	Returns a string representation of the Reset object.
valueOf() (v1.1)	Converts the object to its primitive type (for example, number, Boolean, string, or function).

Event Handlers

onBlur (v1.1)	Specifies JavaScript code to execute when the reset button loses focus.
onClick	Specifies JavaScript code to execute when the reset button is clicked. JavaScript version 1.1 allows you to return false to cancel the event.
onFocus (v1.1)	Specifies JavaScript code to execute when the reset button receives focus.

The Select Object

The Select object reflects a selection list from an HTML form in JavaScript.

Properties

length	An integer value containing the number of options in the selection list.
name	A string value containing the name of the selection list.

options	An array reflecting each of the options in the selection list in the order they appear. The options property has its own properties:

	defaultSelected	A Boolean value indicating whether an option was selected by default (that is, reflects the selected attribute).
	index	An integer value reflecting the index of an option.
	length	An integer value reflecting the number of options in the selection list.
	name	A string value containing the name of the selection list.
	options	A string value containing the full HTML code for the selection list.
	selected	A Boolean value indicating whether the option is selected. It can be used to select or deselect an option.
	selectedIndex	An integer value containing the index of the currently selected option.
	text	A string value containing the text displayed in the selection list for a particular option.
	value	A string value indicating the value for the specified option.

selectedIndex	Reflects the index of the currently selected option in the selection list.

Methods

eval(*statement*) (v1.1)	Evaluates a string as a JavaScript expression or statement, in reference to the Select object.
toString() (v1.1)	Returns a string representation of the Select object.
valueOf() (v1.1)	Converts the object to its primitive type (for example, number, Boolean, string, or function).

Event Handlers

onBlur   Specifies JavaScript code to execute when the selection list loses focus.

onFocus   Specifies JavaScript code to execute when focus is given to the selection list.

onChange   Specifies JavaScript code to execute when the selected option in the list changes.

The String Object

The String object provides properties and methods for working with string literals and variables.

Properties

length   An integer value containing the length of the string expressed as the number of characters in the string.

Methods

anchor(*name*)   Returns a string containing the value of the string object surrounded by an A container tag with the name attribute set to *name*.

big()   Returns a string containing the value of the string object surrounded by a BIG container tag.

blink()   Returns a string containing the value of the string object surrounded by a BLINK container tag.

bold()   Returns a string containing the value of the string object surrounded by a B container tag.

charAt(*index*)   Returns the character at the location specified by *index*.

eval(*statement*) (v1.1)   Evaluates a string as a JavaScript expression or statement, in reference to the String object.

fixed()   Returns a string containing the value of the string object surrounded by a FIXED container tag.

`fontColor(color)`	Returns a string containing the value of the string object surrounded by a FONT container tag with the COLOR attribute set to *color*, where *color* is a color name or an RGB triplet.
`fontSize(size)`	Returns a string containing the value of the string object surrounded by a FONTSIZE container tag with the size set to *size*.
`indexOf(findString,startingIndex)`	Returns the index of the first occurrence of *findString*, starting the search at *startingIndex*, where *startingIndex* is optional. If *startingIndex* is not provided, the search starts at the beginning of the string.
`italics()`	Returns a string containing the value of the string object surrounded by an I container tag.
`lastIndexOf(findString,startingIndex)`	Returns the index of the last occurrence of *findString*. This is done by searching backward from *startingIndex*. *startingIndex* is optional, so the search begins at the last character in the string if no value is provided.
`link(href)`	Returns a string containing the value of the string object surrounded by an A container tag with the HREF attribute set to *href*.
`small()`	Returns a string containing the value of the string object surrounded by a SMALL container tag.
`split(separator)` (v1.1)	Splits the string returning an array of strings. If the separator string is not found, the array returned contains one element containing the original string.
`strike()`	Returns a string containing the value of the string object surrounded by a STRIKE container tag.
`sub()`	Returns a string containing the value of the string object surrounded by a SUB container tag.
`substring(firstIndex,lastIndex)`	Returns a string equivalent to the substring starting at *firstIndex* and ending at the character before *lastIndex*. If *firstIndex* is greater than *lastIndex*, the string starts at *lastIndex* and ends at the character before *firstIndex*.

`sup()`	Returns a string containing the value of the string object surrounded by a SUP container tag.
`toLowerCase()`	Returns a string containing the value of the string object with all characters converted to lowercase.
`toString()` (v1.1)	Returns a string representation of the String object.
`toUpperCase()`	Returns a string containing the value of the string object with all characters converted to uppercase.
`valueOf()` (v1.1)	Converts the object to its primitive type (for example, number, Boolean, string, or function).

The Submit Object

The Submit object reflects a submit button from an HTML form in JavaScript.

Properties

`name`	A string value containing the name of the submit button element.
`value`	A string value containing the value of the submit button element.

Methods

`click()`	Emulates the action of clicking the submit button.
`eval(statement)` (v1.1)	Evaluates a string as a JavaScript expression or statement, in reference to the Submit object.
`toString()` (v1.1)	Returns a string representation of the Submit object.
`valueOf()` (v1.1)	Converts the object to its primitive type (for example, number, Boolean, string, or function).

Event Handlers

`onBlur` (v1.1)	Specifies JavaScript code to execute when the submit button loses focus.

| onClick | Specifies JavaScript code to execute when the submit button is clicked. JavaScript version 1.1 allows you to return `false` to cancel the event. |
| onFocus (v1.1) | Specifies JavaScript code to execute when the submit button receives focus. |

The Text Object

The `Text` object reflects a text field from an HTML form in JavaScript.

Properties

defaultValue	A string value containing the default value of the text element (that is, the value of the `value` attribute).
name	A string value containing the name of the text element.
value	A string value containing the value of the text element.

Methods

blur()	Emulates the action of removing focus from the text field.
eval(*statement*) (v1.1)	Evaluates a string as a JavaScript expression or statement, in reference to the `Text` object.
focus()	Emulates the action of focusing in the text field.
select()	Emulates the action of selecting the text in the text field.
toString() (v1.1)	Returns a string representation of the `Text` object.
valueOf() (v1.1)	Converts the object to its primitive type (for example, number, Boolean, string, or function).

Event Handlers

onBlur	Specifies JavaScript code to execute when focus is removed from the field.
onChange	Specifies JavaScript code to execute when the content of the field is changed.
onFocus	Specifies JavaScript code to execute when focus is given to the field.
onSelect	Specifies JavaScript code to execute when the user selects some or all of the text in the field.

The Textarea Object

The Textarea object reflects a multiline text field from an HTML form in JavaScript.

Properties

defaultValue	A string value containing the default value of the textarea element (that is, the value of the value attribute).
name	A string value containing the name of the textarea element.
value	A string value containing the value of the textarea element.

Methods

blur()	Emulates the action of removing focus from the textarea field.
eval(*statement*) (v1.1)	Evaluates a string as a JavaScript expression or statement, in reference to the Textarea object.
focus()	Emulates the action of focusing in the textarea field.
select()	Emulates the action of selecting the text in the textarea field.
toString() (v1.1)	Returns a string representation of the Textarea object.
valueOf() (v1.1)	Converts the object to its primitive type (for example, number, Boolean, string, or function).

Event Handlers

onBlur	Specifies JavaScript code to execute when focus is removed from the field.
onChange	Specifies JavaScript code to execute when the content of the field is changed.
onFocus	Specifies JavaScript code to execute when focus is given to the field.
onSelect	Specifies JavaScript code to execute when the user selects some or all of the text in the field.

A

JAVASCRIPT
LANGUAGE
SUMMARY

The window Object

The window object is the top-level object for each window or frame and the parent object for the document, location, and history objects.

Properties

closed(v1.1)	Used to display a Boolean value that specifies whether a window is closed.
defaultStatus	Used to display a string value containing the default value displayed in the status bar.
frames	Used to display an array of objects for each frame in a window. Frames appear in the array in the order in which they appear in the HTML source code.
history(v1.1)	Used to display an array of strings representing the URLs stored in the history of the window.
length	Used to display an integer value indicating the number of frames in a parent window.
name	Used to display a string value containing the name of the window or frame.
opener(v1.1)	Used to display a reference to the window that opened this window (if this window was opened with the open() method).
parent	Used to display a string indicating the name of the window containing the frameset.
self	Used to display an alternative for the name of the current window.
status	Used to display a message in the status bar by assigning values to this property.
top	Used to display an alternative for the name of the topmost window.
window	Used to display an alternative for the name of the current window.

Methods

alert(*message*)	Displays *message* in a dialog box.
blur() (v1.1)	Emulates the action of removing focus from the window.
clearInterval(id) (v1.2)	Clears the interval referenced by id.
clearTimeout(*name*)	Cancels the timeout specified by *name*.
close()	Closes the window.
confirm(*message*)	Displays *message* in a dialog box with OK and Cancel buttons. Returns true or false based on the button clicked by the user.
eval(*statement*) (v1.1)	Evaluates a string as a JavaScript expression or statement, in reference to the window object.
focus() (v1.1)	Emulates moving focus to the window.

`moveBy(x,y)` (v1.2)	Moves the window by the number of pixels specified by *x* and *y*.
`moveTo(x,y)`	Moves the window to the coordinates specified by *x* and *y*.
`open(url,name,features)`	Opens *url* in a window named *name*. If *name* doesn't exist, a new window is created with that name. *features* is an optional string argument containing a list of features for the new window. The feature list contains any of the following name/value pairs separated by commas without additional spaces:

`toolbar=[yes,no,1,0]`	Indicates whether the window should have a toolbar.
`location=[yes,no,1,0]`	Indicates whether the window should have a location field.
`directories=[yes,no,1,0]`	Indicates whether the window should have directory buttons.
`status=[yes,no,1,0]`	Indicates whether the window should have a status bar.
`menubar=[yes,no,1,0]`	Indicates whether the window should have menus.
`scrollbars=[yes,no,1,0]`	Indicates whether the window should have scrollbars.
`resizable=[yes,no,1,0]`	Indicates whether the window should be resizable.
`width=pixels`	Indicates the width of the client window in pixels.
`height=pixels`	Indicates the height of the client window in pixels.
`outerWidth=pixels` (v1.2)	Indicates the width of the window in pixels.
`outerHeight=pixels` (v1.2)	Indicates the height of the window in pixels.
`left=pixels` (v1.2)	Indicates the distance from the left side of the screen to place the window.
`top=pixels` (v1.2)	Indicates the distance from the top of the screen to place the window.

`alwaysRaised=[yes,no,1,0]` (v1.2)	Indicates whether the window will always be in front of the others.
`z-lock=[yes,no,1,0]` (v1.2)	Indicates whether to lock the window in its current z-order.
`prompt(message,response)`	Displays *message* in a dialog box with a text entry field with the default value of *response*. The user's response in the text entry field is returned as a string.
`resizeBy(x,y)` (v1.2)	Resizes the window by moving the bottom-right corner the number of pixels specified by *x* and *y*.
`resizeTo(width,height)` (v1.2)	Resizes the window by changing the outer width and outer height properties of the window to the values specified in *width* and *height*.
`scroll(x,y)` (v1.1)	Scrolls the window to the coordinates specified by *x* and *y*.
`scrollBy(x,y)` (v1.2)	Scrolls the window by the number of pixels specified by *x* and *y*.
`scrollTo(x,y)` (v1.2)	Scrolls the window to the coordinates specified by *x* and *y*.
`setInterval(expr,time)` (v1.2)	Evaluates the expression specified in *expr* after the number of milliseconds specified in *time* has elapsed. This method returns a value that can be used as the *id* for the method `clearInterval()`.
`setTimeout(expr,time)`	Evaluates the expression specified in *expr* after the number of milliseconds specified in *time* has elapsed. You can name the timeout with the following structure: `name = setTimeOut(expression,time)`
`toString()` (v1.1)	Returns a string representation of the `window` object.
`valueOf()` (v1.1)	Converts the object to its primitive type (for example, number, Boolean, string, or function).

Event Handlers

`onBlur` (v1.1)	Specifies JavaScript code to execute when the window loses focus.
`onError` (v1.1)	Specifies the JavaScript code to execute when an error occurs. This event handler applies only to JavaScript errors, not Navigator errors.
`onFocus` (v1.1)	Specifies JavaScript code to execute when the window receives focus.
`onLoad`	Specifies JavaScript code to execute when the window or frame finishes loading.
`onUnload`	Specifies JavaScript code to execute when the document in the window or frame is exited.

Independent Functions, Operators, Variables, and Literals

This section describes JavaScript's independent functions, operators, variables, and literals.

Independent Functions

escape(*character*)	Returns a string containing the ASCII encoding of *character* in the form %*xx*, where *xx* is the numeric encoding of the character.
eval(*expression*)	Returns the result of evaluating *expression*, where *expression* is an arithmetic expression.
isNaN(*value*)	Evaluates *value* to see if it is NaN. Returns a Boolean value. This function is available only on UNIX platforms where certain functions return NaN if their argument is not a number.
parseFloat(*string*)	Converts *string* to a floating-point number and returns the value. It continues to convert until it hits a non-numeric character and then returns the result. If the first character cannot be converted to a number, the function returns NaN (zero on Windows platforms).
parseInt(*string,base*)	Converts *string* to an integer of base *base* and returns the value. It continues to convert until it hits a non-numeric character and then returns the result. If the first character cannot be converted to a number, the function returns NaN (zero on Windows platforms).
unescape(*string*)	Returns a character based on the ASCII encoding contained in *string*. The ASCII encoding should take the form "%integer" or "hexadecimalValue".

Operators

JavaScript provides the following categories of operators:

- Assignment operators
- Arithmetic operators
- Bitwise operators
- Logical operators

- Comparison operators
- Conditional operators
- String operators

After you read about each type of operator in the following sections, the section "Operator Precedence" outlines the operator precedence in JavaScript.

Assignment Operators

=	Assigns the value of the right operand to the left operand.
+=	Adds the left and right operands and assigns the result to the left operand.
-=	Subtracts the right operand from the left operand and assigns the result to the left operand.
*=	Multiplies the two operands and assigns the result to the left operand.
/=	Divides the left operand by the right operand and assigns the value to the left operand.
%=	Divides the left operand by the right operand and assigns the remainder to the left operand.

Arithmetic Operators

+	Adds the left and right operands.
-	Subtracts the right operand from the left operand.
*	Multiplies the two operands.
/	Divides the left operand by the right operand.
%	Divides the left operand by the right operand and evaluates to the remainder.
++	Increments the operand by one (can be used before or after the operand).
- -	Decreases the operand by one (can be used before or after the operand).
-	Changes the sign of the operand.

Bitwise Operators

Bitwise operators deal with their operands as binary numbers but return JavaScript numerical values.

AND (or &)	Converts operands to integers with 32 bits, pairs the corresponding bits, and returns one for each pair of ones. Returns zero for any other combination.
OR (or ¦)	Converts operands to integers with 32 bits, pairs the corresponding bits, and returns one for each pair in which one of the two bits is one. Returns zero if both bits are zero.

XOR (or ^)   Converts operands to integers with 32 bits, pairs the corresponding bits, and returns one for each pair in which only one bit is one. Returns zero for any other combination.

<<   Converts the left operand to an integer with 32 bits and shifts bits to the left the number of bits indicated by the right operand. Bits shifted off to the left are discarded, and zeros are shifted in from the right.

>>>   Converts the left operand to an integer with 32 bits and shifts bits to the right the number of bits indicated by the right operand. Bits shifted off to the right are discarded and zeros are shifted in from the left.

>>   Converts the left operand to an integer with 32 bits and shifts bits to the right the number of bits indicated by the right operand. Bits shifted off to the right are discarded and copies of the leftmost bit are shifted in from the left.

Logical Operators

&&   Logical "and." Returns `true` when both operands are true; otherwise, it returns `false`.

|| Logical "or." Returns `true` if either operand is true. It returns `false` only when both operands are false.

!   Logical "not." Returns `true` if the operand is false and `false` if the operand is true. This unary operator precedes the operand.

Comparison Operators

==   Returns `true` if the operands are equal.

!=   Returns `true` if the operands are not equal.

>   Returns `true` if the left operand is greater than the right operand.

<   Returns `true` if the left operand is less than the right operand.

>=   Returns `true` if the left operand is greater than or equal to the right operand.

<=   Returns `true` if the left operand is less than or equal to the right operand.

Conditional Operators

Conditional expressions take one form:

`(condition) ? val1 : val2`

If `condition` is true, the expression evaluates to `val1`; otherwise, it evaluates to `val2`.

String Operators

JavaScript provides two string-concatenation operators:

+	This operator evaluates to a string combining the left and right operands.
+=	This operator is a shortcut for combining two strings.

Operator Precedence

JavaScript applies the rules of operator precedence as follows (from lowest to highest precedence):

Comma	,
Assignment operators	= += -= *= /= %=
Conditional	? :
Logical or	¦¦
Logical and	&&
Bitwise or	¦
Bitwise xor	^
Bitwise and	&
Equality	== !=
Relational	< <= > >=
Shift	<< >> >>>
Addition/subtraction	+ -
Multiply/divide/modulus	* / %
Negation/increment	! - ++ --
Call, member	() []

Fundamentals of HTML

IN THIS APPENDIX

By developing a solid base of HTML knowledge, the developer can more fully implement Java-Script and other interactive and high-level HTML functionality. The fundamental design of HTML documents and the tags used are seemingly basic and harmless.

Although developing simple HTML documents, simple tags, and basic form design is easy, the advantage of using HTML is that you also can create more complex documents by building on the simple ones. If you use the more complex tags and the attributes associated with them, your documents will grow in complexity and usability with only minor research and trial and error.

Remember that the standards of HTML are changing constantly. The current standards document under development is for HTML 3.2. This document is still evolving with new elements as well as new and refined attributes for these elements.

NOTE

Netscape and Internet Explorer also are continually improving their browsers and HTML capabilities. Remember that tags available for use in these browsers might not have been defined in the standards document. You also might find tags and capabilities that are implemented in one of these browsers but not the other.

By keeping up-to-date on the latest version releases of the most popular browsers, you, as an HTML designer, can keep abreast of the enhancements and implement them as they become available for use to the general public. Luckily, for the most part, enhancements included in HTML 3.2 and the newest browser releases aren't dangerous when displayed in HTML 2.0 browsers. You should always test your document in older browsers to ensure that the new tags and custom tags you design with don't negatively affect users of older browsers.

An example of a tag that doesn't work correctly in multiple browsers is the <MARQUEE> tag available for the Microsoft Internet Explorer. In older browsers and in Netscape, it displays as straight document text.

This example provides an important reason for you to write a well-defined and segmented document and to account for multiple browsers as you design.

RESOURCE

Sites to watch for information about HTML changes for Netscape, Internet Explorer, and the overall HTML 3.2 standards include the following:

Netscape: http://www.netscape.com

Internet Explorer: http://www.microsoft.com

HTML standards: http://www.w3.org

HTML Basics

Because JavaScript works so closely with HTML, before you write JavaScript scripts, you must first know the basics of HTML document structure and document tags. Writing Web pages is fairly straightforward if you know the HTML basics. A Web page is made up of page text, tags, and sometimes comments.

Text is easy to comprehend. You write text, and it appears on the Web page. The part of Web page design that needs more description is the use of tags to surround and enhance the text. Tags tell your page how to behave, tell your text how to display, and let you write complex documents for a Web browser.

An HTML tag always begins with the < and ends with the >.

Tags can be just a single marker, as in <P> for a new paragraph. Single markers are either defined as empty tags, or they are nonempty tags that can be terminated other than with their normal termination tag.

<BASE>, for example, is an empty tag. It doesn't apply formatting to text surrounding it. It just defines the document.

The <TD> tag, on the other hand, isn't an empty tag. You use it to specify that the text following that tag is text to display in a table cell. The </TD> tag isn't required in this case because the <TD> elements are terminated by subsequent <TD> tags and also by the </TR>.

Some tags require an end tag to tell them where to terminate. These tags are called *container tags* because they always contain information (normally text) between the start and end tags. In the following example, note that the end tags always have a / before the tag name:

```
<B>Make this text bold</B>
```

Terminator tags are identical to the begin tags except that they contain the additional character.

More complex tags also can have attributes to tell the tag how to behave. If a tag has attributes associated with it, some (or maybe none) of the attributes might be required for the tag to perform as requested. <TABLE WIDTH=3>, for example, defines a table with a width of 3.

Tag location within a document is sometimes very important. Certain tags must be placed inside other tags. (The <INPUT> tag must be inside the <FORM> tags.) Some tags may or may not contain other tags (<HEAD> tags, for example).

B

FUNDAMENTALS
OF HTML

Basic HTML Document Structure

Structure is sometimes very important. Incorrect placement of tags can cause unwanted and unexpected effects. In the basic HTML document shown in Listing B.1, you can see, in Figure B.1, that the document always starts and ends with <HTML></HTML>. The two main tags inside these tags are <HEAD> and <BODY>. You also can include tags inside each of these two container tags.

Listing B.1. Basic HTML page.

```
<!DOCTYPE HTML PUBLIC "-//W3C//DTD HTML 3.2//EN">
<HTML>
<HEAD>
<TITLE>Basic HTML document</TITLE>
<SCRIPT LANGUAGE="JavaScript">
</SCRIPT>
</HEAD>
<BODY >
<FRAMESET>
<FRAME></FRAME>
<NOFRAMES></NOFRAMES>
</FRAMESET>
<H1>Heading of Basic Document</H1>
<FORM>
<INPUT NAME="EnterBtn" TYPE="SUBMIT">
</FORM>
<OL TYPE=1>
<LI>One
<LI>Two
<LI>Three
<LI>Four
</OL>
<A HREF="HTTP://www.acadians.com"></A>
<BR><BR>
<TABLE WIDTH=3 HEIGHT=3 BORDER>
<TH>Table</TH>
<TR>
<TD>cell1<TD>cell2<TD>cell3
</TR>
<TR>
<TD>cell4<TD>cell5<TD>cell6
</TR>
</TABLE>
<P>
This is a Basic HTML document structure.
</BODY>
</HTML>
```

FIGURE B.1.

Basic HTML document generated from Listing B.1.

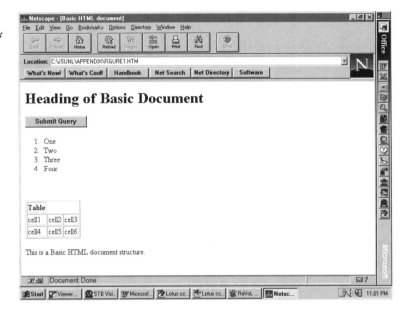

Attribute Generalizations

The following attributes are referenced in the numerous HTML tags that follow. These three attributes have the same functionality for each HTML tag that uses them:

class = specifies the class to which the HTML tag belongs.

id = defines a unique value for this element in reference to the entire document.

style = specifies the style information.

HTML Tags

<!-- -->

The HTML comment tags are <!-- and -->. Comment tags normally begin with <!-- and end with -->. Anything between these two tags is interpreted by the browsers as a comment. Comments can span multiple lines in your document. Any text enclosed in the comment tags isn't displayed by the browser.

Comment tags also are used to hide <SCRIPT> element information from older browsers. The JavaScript interpreter ignores the <!-- --> markings as it reads your document, so you can, in a sense, comment out the <SCRIPT> information from the browser and let the browser choose to interpret it, if it can.

Attributes: none

<!DOCTYPE>

<!DOCTYPE> is the first tag in your document, and it specifies the version of the HTML language supported by this document. The standard string that follows the tag is the public text identifier.

```
<!DOCTYPE HTML PUBLIC "-//W3C//DTD HTML 3.2//EN">
```

Attribute:

The only attribute is the public text identifier string.

<A> (End Tag Required)

<A> (or anchor) defines a hypertext link in the document. The information between the <A> and </A> may be text or an image. The anchor has one required attribute. You must have either the href attribute, which points to a hypertext link (URL), or the name attribute, which points to a location for use as a target for hypertext links within the same document.

```
<A HREF="http://www.w3.org" >Get newest HTML standards</A>
```

The block of text within the anchor is displayed differently by the browser than normal text or images. The browser normally highlights or underlines the text.

Most browsers also track links that you explored previously and display those links differently, normally by changing the color of the text.

<A> elements can contain the usual text formatting tags but can't contain another <A> element.

Attributes:

class

href = specifies the location target of the hypertext link.

id

name = defines the destination of a hypertext link within a document.

rel = defines the relationship of the link to the current HTML document. (Valid values are SAME, NEXT, PARENT, and PREVIOUS.)

rev = defines the reverse link to this link.

style

target = (Netscape Navigator only) defines the target frame or window in which to load the selected URL. Without this attribute, the browser loads the link into the current active browser.

title = defines the assumed title of the linked document. The actual title of the document can't be guaranteed until the link is actually accessed, but this attribute does let you title and untitle the document.

<ADDRESS> (End Tag Required)

<ADDRESS> defines the author information for the document, It includes electronic signatures, lists of authors, and other address information. As such, this tag is usually included near the end of document for reference information.

<ADDRESS> can contain the normal text formatting tags as well as <A>.

Attributes: none

<APPLET> (End Tag Required)

<APPLET> specifies the applet (currently JAVA is the only supported applet) to be loaded and run from this location in the document. The parameters for an applet must be defined by the <PARAM> tag, which can be included inside the <APPLET> tags.

<APPLET> run and load parameters aren't defined in the <APPLET> tag itself because these elements can vary widely depending on the <APPLET>. As a result, the ability to define independent name/value parameter statements is implemented using the <PARAM> element.

Listing B.2 shows the definition of the StrangeMarquee applet that requires the ScrollValue parameter to run.

Listing B.2. Basic applet.

```
<HTML>
<HEAD></HEAD>
<BODY>
<APPLET CODE="StrangeMarquee.class" HEIGHT="100" WIDTH="100">
<PARAM NAME="ScrollValue" VALUE="25">
</APPLET>
</BODY>
</HTML>
```

<APPLET> is a container element, so it can contain text and the normal text formatting tags.

Attributes:

align = defines the <APPLET> alignment on the page.

alt = specifies the alternative text that displays in text-only and non-Java–supported browsers.

code = is the required element that specifies the relative URL where the applet is located.

codebase = references the base URL for the code URL. If the attribute isn't used, the document URL is the base.

download = specifies the order in which the image will be downloaded.

height = is a required element to specify the height needed by the element in the document.

B

FUNDAMENTALS OF HTML

hspace = specifies the horizontal distance between the applet and surrounding text.

name = defines a name for this <APPLET> to be used in reference to other applets in the document.

title = defines the advisory title used when activating the applet.

vspace = specifies vertical distance between the applet and surrounding text.

width = is the required element to specify the width needed by the element in the document.

<AREA>

<AREA> elements must be contained in <MAP> tags. <AREA> defines the specific area in a map region that the user can select. Multiple areas can be specified on a specific map. The selection of the area accesses the URL defined by the href attribute. (See Listing B.4 for an example of the use of <AREA> with the <MAP> element.)

Attributes:

alt = specifies the alternative text for use with text-only browsers.

class

coords = (Internet Explorer only) defines the coordinates of the shape. Rectangles have four coordinates to specify the corners, circles have three (horizontal and vertical coordinates of the center and radius), and polygons can have many coordinate points.

href = (Internet Explorer only) specifies a hypertext link (URL) to be accessed when the area of the map is selected.

id

nohref = (Internet Explorer only) specifies that the browser should "do nothing" if the area is selected. If no <AREA> is supplied for a map, the default value is nohref.

shape = (Internet Explorer only) specifies the shape of the area. The default shape is rectangle (rect), but circle (circ) and polygon (poly) are also valid.

style

tabindex = defines the position of this area within the tab order of the HTML document.

target = defines the window into which to load the link. (Valid values for *window* are window, _blank, _parent, _self, and _top.)

title = defines the title for balloon help.

`<B>` (End Tag Required)

The `<B>` element encloses document text to be displayed in bold.

Attributes: none

`<BASE>`

`<BASE>` specifies the base address for all URL references relative to this document. The attribute for `<BASE>` is required.

Attributes:

`href` = specifies the URL that is the base URL for all others in the document.

`target` = (Netscape Navigator only) specifies to load all links on the current document into the targeted window. (Valid values for *window* are `window`, `_blank`, `_parent`, `_self`, and `_top`.)

`<BASEFONT>`

`<BASEFONT>` defines the base font to use in a document. The font is used to override the default font of the browser. You should use this tag before any text in the `<BODY>` to ensure that all text is displayed in the same font.

Attributes:

`color` = (Netscape Navigator only) defines the color in the base font.

`name` = (Netscape Navigator only) defines the name of the base font.

`size` = (Netscape Navigator only) specifies the font size to be used (valid numbers are 1 to 7).

`<BGSOUND>` (Internet Explorer Only)

`<BGSOUND>` defines the background sound to be used when your document is displayed in the browser.

Attributes:

`loop` = specifies the number of times a sound clip is played. (The default is 1.)

`src` = specifies the location of the file (audio) to be played.

`<BIG>` (End Tag Required)

`<BIG>` encloses text that is displayed in a bigger font than the normal font of text.

Attributes: none

<BLINK> (End Tag Required)

The <BLINK> element does exactly as you would expect, making any text enclosed in it blink.

Attributes: none

<BLOCKQUOTE> (End Tag Required)

<BLOCKQUOTE> defines the contained text as a quotation and directs the browser to display it as such. Browsers render <BLOCKQUOTES> differently.

Attributes: none

<BODY> (End Tag Required)

The <BODY> tag defines the body or the visible section of the HTML document. The <BODY> element and <HEAD> element compose the document and are contained inside the HTML element. The majority of the HTML text and tags are contained in these tags.

Attributes:

alink = specifies the color of the current active hyperlink.

background = defines the location of an image file to be displayed as the background for the document.

bgcolor = (Netscape Navigator only) specifies the color for the background.

bgproperties = (Internet Explorer only) the only allowed value is fixed. This attribute specifies that the background is fixed, not scrolling.

class

id

leftmargin = (Internet Explorer only) defines the left margin for the entire page. This setting overrides the default margin that is currently set.

link = (Netscape Navigator only) specifies the color of unvisited links.

style

text = (Netscape Navigator only) specifies the color of document text.

topmargin = (Internet Explorer only) defines the top margin for the entire page. This setting overrides the default margin that is currently set.

vlink = specifies the color of visited links.

\<BR\>

The \<BR\> tag is an empty element used to force a line break in the document.

Attributes:

`class`

`clear` = informs the browser of how far down to go before displaying any more information. `Clear` can take values of `left`, `right`, and `all`.

\<CAPTION\>

The \<CAPTION\> tag defines the caption to give the table object in the document. The \<CAPTION\> tag is contained in the table tags and can contain the normal text formatting tags.

Attributes:

`align` = specifies to the browser how to align the text in relation to the table.

`valign` = defines the vertical alignment of the table caption.

\<CENTER\> (End Tag Required)

\<CENTER\> horizontally centers the enclosed text on the document page.

Attributes: none

\<CITE\> (End Tag Required)

The \<CITE\> element specifies that the enclosed text is a citation and should be displayed as such by the browser.

Attributes: none

\<CODE\>

The \<CODE\> element specifies that the enclosed text is code (such as in computer code) and should be displayed as such by the browser.

Most browsers display the \<CODE\> element in a fixed-width (monospace) font.

Attributes: none

\<COL\>

The \<COL\> element specifies the properties associated with one or more columns in a document, and properties set in \<COL\> always override previously set properties in \<COLGROUP\>.

This element is used only within a table.

Attributes:

`align` = specifies the alignment of the text within the column.

`span` = specifies the number of columns (consecutive) that the properties affect.

<COLGROUP>

<COLGROUP> is used to set the properties of multiple <COL> tags within a table.

Attributes:

`halign` = specifies the horizontal alignment of the text within the cells.

`span` = specifies the number of columns (consecutive) that the properties affect.

`valign` = specifies the vertical alignment of the text within the cells.

`width` = specifies the width of each column within the group.

<CREDIT> (End Tag Required)

<CREDIT> is used to define the credits or acknowledgments for a <BLOCKQUOTE> or <FIG>, and thus is applicable for use only with these elements.

Browsers that can't use this tag display enclosed text as normal document text.

Attributes: none

<DD>

<DD> specifies a corresponding definition description for a <DT> tag in a list. <DT> and <DD> elements normally occur in pairs in a <DL> list.

Attributes:

`class`

`id`

`style`

<DFN>

The <DFN> tags are used to enclose text that is a definition (or term) used in a document.

Attributes: none

<DIR>

<DIR> defines a list of short items, such as a directory. Elements of the list are defined by <LI> elements.

Attribute:

`compact` = takes no values but specifies to the browser to display the list in a compact format.

<DIV> (End Tag Required)

<DIV> defines a logical division of information in an HTML document. This element doesn't have significant formatting capability but does help define sections of the document. The <DIV> tag terminates the previous <P>.

Attributes:

`align` = (Netscape Navigator only) specifies how to align the block of text within the document.

`class`

`id`

`lang` = (Netscape Navigator only) specifies the ISO standard language used in the section. Accepted values are the standard language abbreviations.

`nowrap` = (Netscape Navigator only) specifies that lines of text aren't automatically wrapped by the browser.

<DL> (End Tag Required)

<DL> defines a list of definitions. The definition terms and description are defined by the <DT> and <DD> elements enclosed in the <DL> tags.

Attribute:

`compact` = takes no values but specifies to the browser to display the list in a compact format.

<DT>

<DT> specifies a definition term to be displayed in the <DL> list. <DT> is normally paired with <DD> elements, but not always. A list may be defined to have many <DT> elements correspond to one <DD> element.

Attributes: none

<EM>

<EM> specifies that the enclosed tag should be marked emphatically. Most browsers display this text in an italicized font.

Attributes: none

<EMBED>

<EMBED> defines an embedded object within the document. <OBJECT> is the currently accepted format for defining objects, but <EMBED> is still acceptable.

Attributes:

height = specifies the height of the object in the document.

name = defines the name of this object when used in reference to other objects in the document.

palette = defines the color palette for the foreground and background colors of the object.

src = defines source data that might be needed for input to the object.

width = specifies the width of the object in the document.

<FIG> (HTML 3.0 Only)

The <FIG> elements better define the use of figures or images in HTML 3.x documents. <FIG> defines a formal figure in a document. Figures are defined as floating objects anchored in the document by the align attribute. Text flows around the figures unless specified by the noflow attribute.

Attributes:

align = specifies how to align the figure in the document.

imagemap = specifies the active figure for use with this element.

noflow = tells the browser to not let text flow around the figure.

<FN> (HTML 3.0 Only)

<FN> defines a footnote for a document. Footnotes are normally presented as hidden elements and displayed only when requested and referenced through the id tag.

Attribute:

id = specifies the reference name to be used to link to the footnote from elsewhere in the document.

<FONT> (End Tag Required)

<FONT> defines the font size to be used for the enclosed text. The tag can either be used as a relative or absolute font size.

Attributes:

`color` = (Internet Explorer only) specifies the color for normal text enclosed in these tags.

`face` = (Internet Explorer only) defines a list of fonts that should be used. The font names are listed in a comma-delimited list. The first font is used if it is available; if not, the second is used if available, and so on.

`size` = (Netscape only) defines font size to use. Absolute fonts are specified by a number. Relative fonts use the + or - and a number to specify the increase or decrease amount from the <BASEFONT>.

<FORM> (End Tag Required)

<FORM> tags enclose the <INPUT> tags of the document that accept user input for use by either CGI, JavaScript, or other interactive processing. <FORM> can't include other <FORM> tags and must include one of the following user input elements: <INPUT>, <SELECT>, or <TEXTAREA>.

Attributes:

`action` = defines the URL to which all form content is sent. Action is normally directed to a program to run but also can be a `mailto:` address.

`enctype` = specifies the MIME type of data to be sent.

`method` = specifies the manner, `get` (default) or `post`, in which the data is sent to the server.

`script` = defines the script to run from the <FORM>.

`target` = (Netscape Navigator only) specifies the window into which to load the form submission. (Valid values for *window* are `window`, `_blank`, `_parent`, `_self`, and `_top`.)

<FRAME>

<FRAME> defines the properties of a frame to be displayed in your frameset. A frame is basically a subset or divided portion of your browser. The important attribute of <FRAME> is `src`. `src` defines the URL to be displayed as the frame document. Without this attribute, the frame is empty or blank.

Attributes:

`align` = (Netscape Navigator only) specifies the alignment of the frame with respect to the surrounding text.

`frameborder` = (Internet Explorer only) defines a 3D border on the frame. (A 1 displays the border; 0 displays no border.)

marginheight = (Netscape Navigator only) defines the height of the top and bottom margins of the <FRAME>. The margin height can't be 0 (to ensure that the margin has some space). If this attribute is left blank, the browser determines the appropriate spacing.

marginwidth = (Netscape Navigator only) defines the width of the left and right margins of the <FRAME>. The margin width can't be 0 (to ensure that the margin has some space). If this attribute is left blank, the browser determines the appropriate spacing.

name = (Netscape Navigator only) specifies the name to be given to this frame. By naming your frame, you give your browser a reference, and the frame can be referenced from the <TARGET> of some other tag.

noresize = (Netscape Navigator only) specifies to the browser that the user can't resize this frame. By default, this means that bordering frames also can't be resized. The default is to allow resizing.

scrolling = (Netscape Navigator only) specifies to the browser how scrollbars should be used in the frame. The default is auto, which lets the browser decide whether the scrollbars are necessary. Yes always displays scrollbars, and no never displays scrollbars.

src = (Netscape Navigator only) specifies the URL for the document to be loaded into this frame. If src isn't specified, the frame is empty by default.

<FRAMESET> (End Tag Required)

<FRAMESET> encloses the set of frame definitions for the document. This tag defines the setup of how the frames are displayed in the document (as demonstrated in Listing B.3). The two allowable attributes of the <FRAMESET> are cols and rows. You must include one of these two, but not both, attributes.

Listing B.3. <FRAMESET> and <FRAME> definition example.

```
<FRAMESET ROWS="10%,80%,10%">
<FRAME NAME="IntroFrame" SCROLLING="NO" NORESIZE>
<FRAME NAME="BodyFrame" SCROLLING="AUTO">
<FRAME NAME="FOOTFrame" SCROLLING="NO" NORESIZE>
<NOFRAMES>
<BODY>
You are viewing a document that's best suited for a frames capable browser.
You may continue on from here or download Netscape for a more complete document
</BODY>
</NOFRAMES>
</FRAMESET>
```

Attributes:

`cols and rows` = (Netscape Navigator only) specify a comma-separated list of widths or heights of the frames. The number of values in the attribute corresponds to the number of `<FRAME>` definitions within the `<FRAMESET>`. Values can be defined in three formats: a number representing a fixed pixel width or height, a percentage (number and percent sign) to represent the percentage of the document that each `<FRAME>` will occupy, or a relative value. The relative values are assigned in relation to other fixed numbers or percentages and are allocated until the document has been 100 percent completed.

`frameborder` = (Internet Explorer only) defines a 3D border on the frame. (A 1 displays the border; 0 displays no border.)

`framespacing` = (Internet Explorer only) defines the amount of additional space, in pixels, between frames.

<Hx> (End Tag Required)

`<Hx>` are heading tags, where *x* represents a number from 1 to 6. Headings grow progressively smaller as the numbers decrease. `<H1>` is a main document heading; `<H6>` is a much smaller subheading.

You can use either the `src` or `dingbat` attribute, but not both.

Attributes:

`align` = specifies the horizontal alignment of the heading.

`dingbat` = defines the entity name of a symbol file to be used with the heading. The symbol is placed in front of the heading test.

`Seqnum` = defines a sequence number of the heading relative to other headings in the browser and allows reference to these headings if a style sheet is used.

`skip` = defines the number to skip in the sequence numbering scheme. Setting this attribute lets you keep a consistent number scheme while still being able to skip numbers if required.

`src` = specifies the URL of an image file to be used as a symbol to go before the heading.

<HEAD> (End Tag Required)

`<HEAD>` specifies the definition section of your document. Because information included in the `<HEAD>` section isn't displayed in the browser, only certain information is appropriate to include in the `<HEAD>` section. Normally, these tags contain the `<TITLE>`, `<BASE>`, `<ISINDEX>`, `<LINK>`, `<META>`, `<NEXTID>`, `<RANGE>`, `<STYLE>`, and `<SCRIPT>`. Other elements are located in the `<BODY>` section.

Attributes: none

<HR>

The <HR> tag displays a horizontal rule (or line) across the document page.

Attributes:

`align` = specifies the alignment of the line on the page.

`class`

`color` = (Internet Explorer only) defines the color of the line.

`id`

`noshade` = (Netscape Navigator only) overrides the default display (shaded bar/chiseled look) to show a solid black line.

`size` = (Netscape Navigator only) specifies the thickness of the line.

`style`

`width` = (Netscape Navigator only) specifies the width (or length) of the line. This value can be reflected as the number of pixels or as a percentage relative to the width of the document page itself.

<HTML> (End Tag Required)

<HTML> encloses your entire document. These tags tell the browser that everything included inside these tags is an <HTML> document. The <HEAD> and <BODY> sections are contained within the <HTML> tags, and normally one or both of these tags are included.

Attributes:

`class` = defines the <HTML> class for the entire document.

`version` = is used in the same manner as the version definition in the <!DOCTYPE> element, so this element isn't needed if <!DOCTYPE> tags have been included.

<I> (End Tag Required)

<I> defines the enclosed text so that it is displayed in an italicized font.

Attributes: none

<IFRAME> (Internet Explorer Only)

<IFRAME> defines a floating frame within the document.

Attributes:

`align` = (Internet Explorer only) specifies the alignment of the frame in relation to the surrounding text. (Valid values are LEFT, CENTER, RIGHT, TOP, and BOTTOM.)

frameborder = (Internet Explorer only) defines a 3D border on the frame. (A 1 displays the border; 0 displays no border.)

height = (Internet Explorer only) defines the height, in pixels, of the floating frame.

marginheight = (Internet Explorer only) defines the height of the top and bottom margins of the <IFRAME>. The margin height can't be 0 (to ensure that the margin has some space. If this attribute is left blank, the browser determines the appropriate spacing.

marginwidth = (Internet Explorer only) defines the width of the left and right margins of the <IFRAME>. The margin width can't be 0 (to ensure that the margin has some space). If this attribute is left blank, the browser determines the appropriate spacing.

name = (Internet Explorer only) specifies the name to be given to this frame. By naming your frame, you give your browser a reference, and the frame can be referenced from the <TARGET> of some other tag.

noresize = (Internet Explorer only) specifies to the browser that the user can't resize this frame. By default, this means that bordering frames also can't be resized. The default is to allow resizing.

scrolling = (Internet Explorer only) specifies to the browser how scrollbars should be used in the frame. The default is auto, which lets the browser decide whether the scrollbars are necessary. Yes always displays scrollbars, and no never displays scrollbars.

src = (Internet Explorer only) specifies the URL for the document to be loaded into this frame. If src isn't specified, the frame is empty by default.

width = (Internet Explorer only) defines the width of the floating frame, in pixels.

<ILAYER> (End Tag Required)

<ILAYER> defines layers that appear where they are naturally placed within the document. These inflow layers don't appear on a separate line unless they are prefaced within a break or within <DIV> tags. These types of layers occupy space within the document, and they also share space with other elements in the document.

Attributes:

above = defines the stacking order of this layer with other layers. This attribute is mutually exclusive with the below and z-index attributes.

background = specifies the image to be used as the background for the layer.

below = defines the stacking order of this layer with other layers. This attribute is mutually exclusive with the above and z-index attributes.

bgcolor = defines the background color of the layer.

clip = defines the area of the layer that can be viewed within the document. This value can be less than the defined width and height of the layer.

left = specifies the relative left horizontal position of the layer within the document.

name = specifies the name of the layer within the document. This setting allows other layers and JavaScript scripts to access the layer.

src = specifies the file that contains the layer information for this particular layer.

top = specifies the relative left vertical position of the layer within the document.

visibility = defines whether the layer is currently visible.

width = specifies the width of the layer (and thus the right margin).

z-index = defines the stacking order of this layer with other layers. This attribute is mutually exclusive with the above and below attributes.

<IMG>

<IMG> defines an inline image to be displayed in the document text. Currently, the .GIF format of images is the only universally understood image format. Other commonly used formats are X-bitmaps (.xbm), X-Pixelmaps (.xpm) and JPEG (.jpeg or .jpg) formats. Use these formats with caution because all browsers may not be capable of displaying them correctly. Listing B.4 shows the use of a balloon image and also the alternative text if the image isn't supported.

Images can be placed anywhere in your document, and in this respect, they are just as easy to place inline as text is.

The image can be defined as an image map, allowing the image in clickable areas on the document.

Listing B.4. Image with mapped areas example.

```
<A HREF="/anchor/testmap">
<IMG SRC="ballon.gif" ALT="Balloon Picture" HSPACE=10 VSPACE=10 USEMAP="#TestMap"
ISMAP>
</A>
<MAP NAME="TestMap">
<AREA  SHAPE="circ" COORD="5,10,30,35" HREF="TestArea.html">
</MAP>
```

Attributes:

align = specifies the alignment for the image on the page.

alt = specifies alternative text for the browser to display instead of the image. The information is important in text-only browsers and very useful overall, enabling a smooth-flowing document if the user chooses not to load images.

border = (Netscape Navigator only) specifies the width of the border to be rendered surrounding the image.

class

controls = (Internet Explorer only) specifies that viewer controls should be displayed for the AVI clip.

dynsrc = (Internet Explorer only) defines the URL of an AVI-formatted video clip. With this control, the `control`, `loop`, `loopdelay`, and `start` are also applicable.

height = specifies the actual height of the image to be displayed.

hspace = (Netscape Navigator only) defines the horizontal space, in pixels, to be left between floating images and the surrounding text.

id

ismap = specifies that the image is a server-side image map and the server decides, based on the `<A>` given, the URL to access upon selection of the image in the browser.

loop = (Internet Explorer only) specifies how many times a video clip is played. The default is 1, and the value of `"infinite"` is a valid loop parameter. `Infinite` causes the clip to play continuously while the document is loaded.

loopdelay = (Internet Explorer only) specifies the delay between replays of the video clip. The value is expressed in milliseconds.

lowsrc = (Netscape Navigator only) specifies the low-resolution image to be displayed when the main `src` image is loading.

src = specifies the URL to locate the source file for the image. This attribute is required.

start = (Internet Explorer only) defines when the video clip should begin playing. Valid values are `start` and `mouseover`. Both can be used in a comma-delimited format.

start = specifies when the URL defined in the `dynsrc` attribute starts playing. The two options for this attribute are `FILEOPEN` and `MOUSEOVER`.

style

units = defines the types of units to be used for height and width. The default is pixels. Also available as a unit of measure is en, which indicates to the browser that this text should be displayed in one half the point size of normal text in the document.

usemap = specifies that the image is a client-side image map by including `<MAP>` and `<AREA>` tag references inside the `<IMG>` definition.

vspace = (Netscape Navigator only) defines the vertical space, in pixels, to be left between floating images and the surrounding text.

width = specifies the actual width of the image to be displayed. If the image itself is a different size, the browser scales the image to fit the height and width that have been defined.

<INPUT>

<INPUT> tags define fields on your document where users can enter input. <INPUT> elements, by definition, must be contained inside <FORM> elements . The user input gathered from <INPUT> tags can be used in CGI applications as well as JavaScript and other methods of HTML processing. The important mandatory attributes for <INPUT> are name and type.

Attributes:

align = defines the alignment for the <INPUT> element on the page.

checked = specifies the checked state of radio buttons and checkboxes.

class

id

max = defines the upper limit of the range slider.

maxlength = specifies the maximum length of text to be accepted in text and password inputs.

min = defines the lower limit of the range slider.

name = defines the name of the field. Multiple radio buttons with the same name are mutually exclusive.

notab = specifies that this element doesn't appear in the tab order of the document.

size = defines the physical size of the field. When used in association with text and password <INPUTS>, size defines the number of characters to be accepted before the text begins to scroll.

src = specifies the URL of the image to be used.

style

tabindex = specifies the tab order that this element has within the document.

title = defines the advisory title for this element.

type = specifies the type of input field to display in the document. Valid types are as follows:

Text accepts a single line of text input from the user.

Password behaves the same as Text, except that the text entered isn't displayed to the user.

CheckBox displays a single checkbox (Boolean on/off). Results are sent to the server only when the box is checked.

Radio fields are similar to the CheckBox in that they are either selected or not selected. Unlike a CheckBox, you can define multiple mutually exclusive radio fields by giving them the same names.

Image fields display a clickable image for the user. The results sent to the server are the coordinates of the selection on the image.

Hidden fields are input fields that are never displayed to the user. Hidden fields are always sent back to the server and are generally used for hard-coded data.

Submit fields are displayed as buttons and are used to send all information in the contained <FORM> back to the server. Action (JavaScript action) can be taken upon the click of the submit button. If an image is specified in the src attribute, the button is displayed as an image with the same functionality.

Reset fields are also buttons but have different actions than submit. The reset buttons reset all input fields contained within the form. If an image is specified in the src attribute, the button is displayed as an image with the same functionality.

Range fields are displayed as a slider bar. They let the user select a number to be sent to the server. The left and right values of the range are specified by the min and max attributes.

File fields automatically associate a browse button. They let the user select a file (local) to send to the server.

Scribble fields are defined as graphical images (defined in the src attribute) onto which the user can scribble or draw.

value = specifies different things depending on the <INPUT> type. For buttons (submit and reset), it's the label on the button itself; for text, password, and hidden input, it's the default value; for checkboxes and radio buttons, it's the value returned to the server.

<ISINDEX>

<ISINDEX> defines this document as searchable. This means that the document can be queried using a keyword search, and the browser should prompt the user for a search string. The search string is gathered on the client side and sent back to the server using keywords appended to the URL. The search is performed on the server.

Attributes:

action = (Netscape Navigator only) defines the program to which the string should be passed for searching.

href = defines a URL to direct the query if the URL is different from the URL of the document itself.

prompt = defines the prompt string that the user sees when a search is requested.

B

FUNDAMENTALS
OF HTML

<KBD> (End Tag Required)

<KBD> encloses text that should be displayed as keyboard input to the user. The browser typically displays this text in a fixed-width (monospace) font.

Attributes: none

<LAYER>

<LAYER> defines a layer that you can explicitly place within your document. By manipulating the top and left attributes, you can place the layer anywhere in the document, overlaying any elements that currently exist in that position.

Attributes:

above = defines the stacking order of this layer with other layers. This attribute is mutually exclusive with the below and z-index attributes.

background = specifies the image to be used as the background for the layer.

below = defines the stacking order of this layer with other layers. This attribute is mutually exclusive with the above and z-index attributes.

bgcolor = defines the background color of the layer.

clip = defines the area of the layer that can be viewed within the document. This value can be less than the defined width and height of the layer.

left = specifies the absolute left horizontal position of the layer within the document.

name = specifies the name of the layer within the document. This setting allows other layers and JavaScript to access the layer.

src = specifies the file that contains the layer information for this particular layer.

top = specifies the absolute left vertical position of the layer within the document.

visibility = defines whether the layer is currently visible.

width = specifies the width of the layer (and thus the right margin).

z-index = defines the stacking order of this layer with other layers. This attribute is mutually exclusive with the above and below attributes.

<LH> (End Tag Required)

<LH> defines a header for a list. This tag is contained inside any of the list tags (<DL>, <OL>, <UL>) and should be the first tag immediately following the first list tag.

Browsers that can't interpret this tag display the text at the beginning of the list with no special formatting applied. All normal text tags can be used inside this tag.

Attributes: none

<LI> (End Tag Required)

<LI> defines items that make up a list. <LI> tags are contained in a list type of either <UL>, <OL>, <MENU>, or <DIR> and enclose the lines of text for these lists.

<LI> tags can contain text and any of the text markup tags.

Attributes:

class

id

style

type = defines the type of bullet display to be used for the list. <UL> acceptable values are disc (solid circle), circle (open circle), and square (square). <OL> acceptable values are I (uppercase Roman numerals), i (lowercase Roman numerals), A (uppercase alphabetized), a (lowercase alphabetized), and 1 (numeric).

value = defines the start of a numeric counting sequence for a list. List numbering starts at value and continues sequentially for remaining items in the list.

<LINK>

<LINK> defines this document's association or relationship with another document. It is used similarly to and has attributes like the <ANCHOR> tag. <LINK> can be used to maintain a chain of documents or to preload documents with a page.

Attributes:

href = specifies the URL of the document to link to.

rel= (or rev) defines what the actual relationship of this document is to another (that is, next, previous).

rev = indicates that the document to which this document has links also has the reverse links back to this document.

title = defines the title for this document link in the current document.

type = specifies the media type and parameters used in conjunction with linked style sheets.

<LISTING>

<LISTING> defines the enclosed text as displayed in a fixed-width (monospace) font.

Attributes: none

<MAP> (End Tag Required)

<MAP> specifies the set of areas (it must contain <AREA> tags) to be used on client-side image maps. (See Listing B.4 for an example of the use of <AREA> with the <MAP> element.) The <MAP> element is used as a container to hold the information on all areas (coordinate-defined regions) that are grouped together to form the mapping plan for an element.

Many <MAP> tags can be used in a document. A <MAP> tag doesn't necessarily have to be in the current document. You can define a <MAP> in a document and use the <MAP> (that is, the usemap attribute of an <IMG>) in another document. In this case, you need to include the entire URL path in the usemap statement instead of just the map name.

Attribute:

name = (Internet Explorer only) specifies the distinct name for this map area in this document.

<MARQUEE> (Internet Explorer Only; End Tag Required)

<MARQUEE> is a container tag that behaves exactly as you would expect from its name. It displays a scrolling text string in the document like an advertisement marquee. The text contained between the <MARQUEE> tags is used to scroll.

<MARQUEE> displays as normal text in browsers not capable of supporting this element.

Attributes:

align = specifies how to align the surrounding text with the marquee.

behavior = defines the behavior of the text in the marquee box. The default is scroll, whereby the text starts at one side of the box and scrolls completely off the screen on the other side. Slide slides the text across the screen and stops it at the margin on the other side. Alternate bounces the text back and forth across the screen.

bgcolor = specifies the color of the marquee box behind the text.

direction = specifies the direction for the text to scroll.

height = specifies height of the marquee. This value can be in two formats: pixels or percentage of the document screen.

hspace = defines the margin that is left on the left and right sides of the marquee.

loop = specifies the number of times the marquee processes before it stops.

scrollamount = specifies the space (number of pixels) to allow between redisplaying of the marquee.

scrolldelay = specifies the amount of time to delay the next start of the marquee scroll.

vspace = specifies the width of the marquee. The narrower the marquee, the more difficult the text is to read.

<MATH> (End Tag Required)

<MATH> tags are container tags used to enclose mathematical expressions in a document. These additional tags are needed to account for some of the symbols that are difficult to display, as well as letters that are associated with mathematical and scientific expressions.

Attributes:

box = specifies that the mathematical expression should be framed by a box (or outlines) when it is displayed in the browser.

class = defines the class of the mathematical expression, giving the browser further definition on the correct display formats.

<MENU> (End Tag Required)

<MENU> defines a list of menu items. It is another list-definition element designed to include short "menu-like" items. The items in this list are displayed in a compact manner.

This element has the same basic functionality as an unordered list <UL> element.

Attribute:

compact = specifies that the list should be displayed in a more compact format than the default.

<META>

<META> specifies information about this document that isn't included in other tags. <META> is basically a place to store very detailed specification information regarding the document and its setup and composition.

Attributes:

charset = specifies the character set to be used with the document. It isn't the preferable attribute for specifying this value; the http-equiv is preferred.

content = (required) specifies the content associated with the http-equiv or name.

http-equiv = (Netscape Navigator only) defines information to be used in the response header that is generated in association with the content information and the <META> information.

name = Specifies the name for the META information file. It is assumed that the browser can understand and interpret this name.

url = indicates this document's URL.

<NEXTID>

<NEXTID> is used in the document to assign a unique identifier to the document. This identifier is used by browsers to determine the identity of the document. <NEXTID> has a required attribute of n.

Attribute:

n = specifies the sequence number to assign to the document.

<NOBR> (Netscape Navigator Only)

<NOBR> (no line break) gives you, the HTML designer, more direct control over text formatting in a browser by specifying to the browser where it can't break a line of text when displaying in the browser.

You use this element to override the browser's default assumptions of how to break lines of text when displaying them in the browsers.

Attributes: none

<NOFRAMES> (End Tag Required)

<NOFRAMES> is a container tag. Between the tags is text that is displayed if the browser doesn't support frames. <NOFRAMES> is important to use so the document isn't unreadable if a browser isn't frame capable.

The text that is enclosed in the <NOFRAMES> tag doesn't display in a browser if frames are enabled.

Because this information is displayed as the entire body of a document in non-frame–enabled browsers, the <NONFRAMES> container should include a fairly complete <BODY> document to display in the browser. All text formatting tags as well as tags normally used in the <BODY> section of the document can be used inside the <NOFRAMES> container.

```
<NOFRAMES>
<BODY>
You are viewing a document that's best suited for a frames capable browser.
You may continue on from here or download Netscape for a more complete document
</BODY>
</NOFRAMES>
```

Attributes: none

<NOTE> (End Tag Required)

<NOTE> specifies that the contained text is a comment block for the document. There are three main types, or classes, of notes: note, caution, and warning.

Browsers capable of supporting notes display the note along with a graphic related to the defined class.

Because not all browsers support <NOTE>, you should include formatting (such as <P> tags) inside the <NOTE> container to distinguish the note from other text in the unsupporting browsers.

Attributes:

class = specifies the type of note. Warning, caution, and note are the three most common classes, but others can be defined.

src = defines a graphic that the browser should use as the icon associated with the <NOTE>.

<OBJECT>

<OBJECT> defines an object with the HTML document. An object can be an image, applet, control, or document. The object itself can contain any ordinarily used HTML elements to define itself.

Nested objects are thus allowed within the <OBJECT> element.

Attributes:

align = specifies the alignment for the object in relation to the surrounding text. (Valid values are LEFT, TEXTTOP, MIDDLE, TEXTMIDDLE, BASELINE, TEXTBOTTOM, CENTER, and RIGHT.)

border = defines the width of the border to be used for the element.

classid = defines the implementation of the object. The valid values for the right side of the equation depend on the left side of the equation. CLSID is used as the left side value for ActiveX controls.

codebase = defines the code-base used to create the object.

codetype = defines the Internet media type to be used for the object.

data = specifies the data to used in relation to this object.

declare = declares the object to be used in cross-referencing but doesn't instantiate the object in the document.

height = specifies the height of the object.

hspace = specifies the horizontal space to the left between the object and any object or text to the left and right sides of the object.

name = defines the name of the object, for reference purposes within the document.

B

FUNDAMENTALS OF HTML

notab = specifies that the object isn't to be included in the tab order of the document.

shapes = specifies that this object contains shaped hyperlinks.

standby = defines the message to display when the object is loading into the browser.

tabindex = specifies the tab order of this object within the document.

title = defines the advisory title for the element.

type = defines the Internet media type to be used with the element.

usemap = defines any image map to be used with the element.

vspace = specifies the vertical space to be left between this object and any objects or text above or below it.

width = defines the width of the object.

`<OL>` (End Tag Required)

`<OL>` defines an ordered list. An ordered list means that the browser displays the list with alphabetic or sequentially numbered marking preceding the actual list items.

`<LI>` tags are enclosed in this container tag to define the list items. `<LI>` tags are the only tags allowed inside the `<OL>` container, and they are ordered according to the browser's numbering scheme.

```
<OL COMPACT TYPE=A START=C>
<LH>Ordered List Sample
<LI>Internet
<LI>Browser
<LI>HTML
<LI>JavaScript
</OL>
```

As with `<UL>` (unordered lists), `<LI>` items should always be kept brief and concise. The purpose of a list is to create short, meaningful statements that stand out in the browser. If the information in list items becomes too involved, the list isn't as meaningful.

Attributes:

class

compact = specifies to the browser to display the list in a more compact manner than it would with the normal-sized font.

continue = specifies to the browser not to start numbering at the beginning, and to instead begin numbering where the ordered list stopped.

id

start = specifies the value to use to begin numbering the first item in the list.

style

type = defines the type of numbering scheme that the browser should use when displaying the list. Acceptable types are A, a, I, i, and 1. The default for lists without a TYPE attribute is 1. The other types follow the alphabetic or Roman numeral scheme as specified.

<OPTION>

<OPTION> defines the text string choices that are available in the <SELECT> statement. Multiple <OPTION> tags are allowed for a <SELECT> container element and must be contained within the <SELECT> tags.

Because <OPTION> may be a container element or may be terminated by other means, the normal set of text formatting tags aren't allowable with the option element. <OPTION> can be terminated by </OPTION>, the beginning of another <OPTION>, or by the </SELECT> (end of the <SELECT> container).

Attributes:

disabled = specifies to the browser to display this <OPTION> as disabled (or grayed out) in <SELECT> group. The <OPTION> isn't hidden in the document, but it displays in a grayed or dimmed font color.

selected = tells the browser to display this <OPTION> as selected. Selected <OPTION>s aren't mutually exclusive, and therefore more than one <OPTION> in a <SELECT> container can be selected. Using <SELECT> is a good way to define the default selection for the <SELECT> group.

shape = defines the <OPTION> as a geographic shape within the <SELECT>, if the <SELECT> has been defined as an image. As with the <AREA> element, this attribute is defined using coordinates on the document to map out the region of the <OPTION> within the <SELECT> image.

value = specifies what the value (or text string) of the <OPTION> is. The value is optional and the actual content of the <OPTION> string is used as the value if the value attribute isn't explicitly set.

<OVERLAY>

The <OVERLAY> element is used only in conjunction with the <FIG> element and is contained in the <FIG> container to define the image to load as an overlay for the <FIG> image.

Attributes:

imagemap = defines the URL link where the click is sent on the server.

src = defines the URL for the location of the <OVERLAY> image.

units = defines the size (height and width) of the <OVERLAY> image.

x = defines the x coordinate on the <FIG> image where the overlay starts. This coordinate starts from the left side of the <FIG>.

y = along with the x coordinate, further defines the relation of the <OVERLAY> image on the <FIG> image. This coordinate starts from the top of the <FIG>.

<P>

<P> is used to define logical paragraphs or groups of text in a document. The actual outcome is similar to the <BR> tag, but <P> is used to better define blocks of text. Depending on the browser, you also can see first line indentation.

The end </P> isn't necessary because a <P> is automatically terminated by the next <P>; but for consistency, using <P> as a container tag is appropriate, thus explicitly marking the end of one paragraph before beginning another.

Unlike <BR>, multiple <P> doesn't produce multiple breaks in the document. <P> isn't an empty element, and thus successive <P> tags aren't allowed.

Attributes:

align = specifies the alignment of the <P> relative to the margins of the document.

class

id

style

<PARAM>

<PARAM> defines a parameter attribute for the <APPLET> in which the <PARAM> tag is contained. The <PARAM> tag is the method by which <APPLET>-specific parameters are defined for the browser. This element is needed because attributes of an <APPLET> are completely dependent on the nature and type of the APPLET. PARAM has two attributes that are used in a distinct pair relationship.

Attributes:

name = defines the name of the Parameter attribute.

type = defines the Internet media type used by this element.

value = defines the value for that attribute.

valuetype = specifies how to interpret the value of this element. (Valid values for valuetype are DATA, REF, and OBJECT.)

<PLAINTEXT> (End Tag Required)

<PLAINTEXT> defines the text within the tags as fixed-width type, and all processing tags and HTML parsing are disabled until the end tag is encountered. All text following the </PLAINTEXT> tag is returned to normal formatting.

Attributes: none

<PRE> (End Tag Required)

<PRE> tells the browser to display the contained text in the browser exactly as written. This container of information is extremely useful when the text has been preformatted outside the browser.

<PRE> maintains all tabs, line returns, and other text markings and displays the information in a fixed-width (monospace) font, with no line spacing adjustments.

Because <PRE> is used to display already-formatted text, using HTML text formatting tags within the <PRE> container isn't recommended.

Attribute:

width = defines the maximum width of the text line for display.

<RANGE>

<RANGE> defines sections of a document as a logical group of information. The purpose of <RANGE> is to define markings that can be used for developers or for other events to distinguish groups of information.

<RANGE> has two mandatory attributes: from and to. These attributes hold the information for id tags in the document that mark the beginning and end of this specified range.

These document flags, or markings, are denoted by using the spot tag in the <BODY> of a document or the name attribute of the <A> element.

Attributes:

class = defines the class to which this range belongs. This attribute helps to distinguish the reason for marking this section of a document as a specific range.

from = defines the beginning <ID> tag for this range in the document.

id = defines the <ID> tag (or location name) of this particular range element. This allows the range to become a part of another range in the document.

to = defines the ending <ID> tag for this range in the document.

<S> (End Tag Required)

<S> encloses text that's displayed in the document using the normal text format and the addition of a strikethrough line running the length of the text in the container.

Attributes: none

<SAMP> (End Tag Required)

<SAMP> displays this text as sample output from another source. A browser normally displays this text in a fixed-width (monospace) font.

<SCRIPT> (End Tag Required)

The <SCRIPT> tag is used to enclose all scripting language statements. <SCRIPT> statements are normally used in the <HEAD> section of the document, but they also can be placed in the <BODY> section.

Multiple <SCRIPT> containers are allowed in a document to enable flexibility in defining interactive documents.

Normally, <SCRIPT> containers in the <HEAD> section are composed of JavaScript functions that are called from methods within the <BODY>. <SCRIPT> containers in the <BODY> can be placed directly into the document flow and used in place of method function calls.

Attributes:

language = defines the type of scripting language (that is, JavaScript) in which the statements are written. Currently, if no language attribute is assigned, JavaScript is assumed to be the language.

```
<HEAD>
<SCRIPT LANGUAGE="JavaScript">
<!--
function displayinformation()
{
alert("You have written JavaScript code")
}
//-->
</SCRIPT>
</HEAD>
```

src = specifies the name of the file to locate the script statements. If script statements aren't written inline, src informs the browser where the script file is located. The correct file extension for JavaScript files is .js.

```
<HEAD>
<SCRIPT SRC="separate.js">
</SCRIPT>
```

```
</HEAD>
```

<SELECT> (End Tag Required)

The <SELECT> container tag encloses a set of <OPTION> tags (a set may, in fact, be only one <OPTION>) that the document displays to select from. <SELECT> itself has no other purpose than to tell the browser that the enclosed lines (defined by <OPTION> tags) should be displayed as options for the user to select from. An example of SELECT with OPTIONs is shown in Figure B.2; the code for this figure is shown in Listing B.5.

You must include <SELECT> inside a <FORM> container. You can't place it inside the <TEXTAREA> container or another <SELECT> container.

Listing B.5. SELECT example with multiple and single selection options.

```
<HTML>
<HEAD></HEAD>
<BODY><FORM>
<SELECT NAME="Select Box" SIZE=5 MULTIPLE>
<OPTION>First Option
<OPTION>Second Option
<OPTION SELECTED>Default Option
<OPTION>Third Option
<OPTION DISABLED>Disabled Option
<OPTION>Last Option
</SELECT>

<SELECT NAME="Select Box" SIZE=1 >
<OPTION>First Option
<OPTION>Second Option
<OPTION SELECTED>Default Option
<OPTION>Third Option
<OPTION DISABLED>Disabled Option
<OPTION>Last Option
</SELECT>
```

FIGURE B.2.
Use of SELECT *and* OPTION *with multiple and single selection options.*

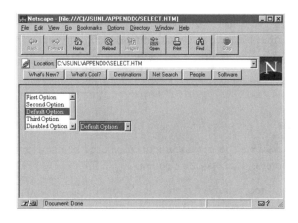

B

FUNDAMENTALS
OF HTML

```
</FORM></BODY>
</HTML>
```

If the `<IMG>` attribute for `<SELECT>` is defined, the `<SELECT>` container no longer displays as a list of elements (as defined in the `<OPTION>` tags) within the document. Instead, it displays the image and regions (or areas) of the image that can be selected. These regions are defined by the `shape` attribute of the `<OPTION>` elements that make up the `<SELECT>` container.

Browsers that can't display the `<SELECT>` as an image (and thus the `<OPTION>`s within that image) will display the `<SELECT>` container in its default state.

Attributes:

`align` = specifies how to align the `<SELECT>` element in relation to surrounding document text.

`img` = defines the URL for the image to be displayed as the `<SELECT>` element.

`multiple` = specifies to the browser that the user can select multiple options from the list. If `multiple` isn't used, the list is mutually exclusive.

`name` = defines the name of this object.

`size` = specifies that number of options (items) that are displayed at any one time. The normal display type is a drop-down type list or multiselect box. If `multiple` is used, the browser defines the `size` attribute internally.

<SMALL> (End Tag Required)

The `<SMALL>` container tags are used to enclose text that should be displayed in a smaller font than the normal font of text in the document.

Attributes: none

<SPAN> (End Tag Required)

`<SPAN>` specifies the style information that should be applied within the document.

Attribute:

`style`

<SPOT>

`<SPOT>` marks a spot in the document to be used as a label reference, such as with the `to` and `from` attributes of the `<RANGE>` element.

`<SPOT>` is ignored by browsers that don't support location marking in documents.

Attribute:

`id` = is a mandatory element that specifies the name value to be assigned with this marking.

<STRIKE> (End Tag Required)

See the definition of the `<S>` element.

Attributes: none

<STRONG> (End Tag Required)

`<STRONG>` tells the browser to give a strong emphasis to this text. Normally, this text is displayed in a bold font, but in some browsers it may be underlined and is sometimes displayed identically to the `<EM>` marking. This container also can contain other text formatting tags.

Attributes: none

<STYLE>

`<STYLE>` defines the inline style sheet of the document to be used by the browser when displaying the document. Style sheets are used to apply default font and marking styles to certain specified tags used by the document.

Defining style sheets within the `<STYLE>` container has the same result as loading a separate style sheet file using the `<LINK>` tag.

The `<STYLE>` element is handy for maintaining consistency in the document as well as simplifying the markup in a document. Text formatting tags can be applied in the `<STYLE>` container to define the style of the document.

Attributes:

`title` = defines the advisory title.

`type` = defines the style information file type.

<SUB> (End Tag Required)

The `<SUB>` container encloses text that is displayed in subscript. Subscript text is displayed in a small font and is slightly below center of the mid-line of normal text.

Attributes: none

<SUP> (End Tag Required)

The `<SUP>` container encloses text that will be displayed in a superscript to text surrounding it. Superscript text is displayed in a small font and is above center of the mid-line of normal text.

Attributes: none

<TABLE> (End Tag Required)

<TABLE> container tags are used to enclose the definition tags that constitute a table object in the document.

The <TABLE> element itself is basically just the holding container for the other table definition tags. No actual document can be contained within the TABLE element unless it's contained by the other <TABLE> definition tags, which include <CAPTION>, and <TR> (which contains the <TH> and <TD> tags). An example is shown in Figure B.3. (Listing B.6 defines the HTML for Figure B.3.) Optional elements that can be contained within the <TABLE> container are <THEAD>, <TBODY>, and <TFOOT>. These optional elements give the table further structuring capability for the elements, resulting in better document display options.

Listing B.6. Defining a table.

```
<HTML>
<HEAD></HEAD>
<BODY>
<TABLE WIDTH=50% HEIGHT=25% BORDER=2>
<CAPTION>Time Table</CAPTION>
<THEAD>
<TR>
<TH>Train time and prices</TH>
</TR>
</THEAD>
<TBODY>
<TR ALIGN=CENTER VALIGN=MIDDLE>
<TD>10:00</TD>
<TD>20</TD>
<TD>40</TD>
<TD>60</TD>
</TR>
<TR ALIGN=CENTER VALIGN=MIDDLE>
<TD>12:00</TD>
<TD>10</TD>
<TD>30</TD>
<TD>50</TD>
</TR>
<TRALIGN=RIGHT VALIGN=MIDDLE>
<TD>2:00</TD>
<TD>5</TD>
<TD>10</TD>
<TD>15</TD>
</TR>
</TBODY>
</TABLE>
</BODY>
</HTML>
```

FIGURE B.3.

Table frame with variable alignments.

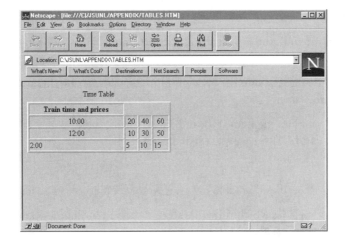

Attributes:

align = specifies the table alignment in the document. (Valid values are LEFT, CENTER, RIGHT, BLEEDLEFT, BLEEDRIGHT, and JUSTIFY.)

background = (Internet Explorer only) defines a background picture for the table.

bgcolor = (Internet Explorer only) defines the background color for the element.

border = (Internet Explorer only) specifies the thickness of the border displayed around the table frame. A table frame border defaults to the thinnest border of 1.

bordercolor = (Internet Explorer only) defines the border color and is valid only if used with the border attribute.

bordercolordark = (Internet Explorer only) defines the independent control over the color of one of two colors used in 3D borders. This attribute is valid only if used with the border attribute.

bordercolorlight = (Internet Explorer only) defines the independent control over the color of one of two colors used in 3D borders. This attribute is valid only if used with the border attribute.

cellpadding = specifies the space that should be left between the walls of the table cell and the contents of that cell.

cellspacing = specifies the spacing between cells in the table grid and thus the thickness of the grid lines.

`class`

`clear` = defines the formatting of the text immediately following the table. (Valid values are NO, LEFT, RIGHT, and ALL.)

`cols` = defines the number of columns in the table. Using this attribute can speed up processing of the table.

`frame` = defines the frame type to be used for the table. (Valid values are BORDER, VOID, ABOVE, BELOW, HSIDES, LHS, RHS, VSIDES, and BOX.)

`id`

`nowrap` = specifies that table rows not wrap if text exceeds line length.

`rules` = specifies which rules (lines) are displayed for interior borders. (Valid values are NONE, GROUPS, ROWS, COLS, and ALL.)

`style`

`valign` = specifies the vertical alignment of the table within the document.

`width` = defines the width of the table within the document. This value can be pixels or percentage of the current document window.

<TBODY>

<TBODY> defines the body section of the table element, specifically, <TR> and <TD>. This tag is unnecessary in the absence of <THEAD> and <TFOOT> tags but provides better continuity in table definition.

Attributes:

`class`

`id`

`style`

<TD>

The <TD>, or table data element, defines the information to be displayed in the table cell in the table frame. <TD> tags are contained with <TR> (table row) tags. Termination of a <TD> element is assumed by the start of another <TD> element or by the </TR>. As a result, </TD> tags aren't required. Multiple <TD> elements can be defined with the <TR> container to display multiple rows in a table.

<TD> can contain any data type, but you must first enclose string or text information in a <P> container.

Attributes:

`align` = defines the alignment of the `<TD>` element within the table cell.

`background` =

`bgcolor` = (Internet Explorer only) defines the color of the document background behind this particular cell element in the table.

`bordercolor` = (Internet Explorer only) defines the border color and is valid only if used with the border attribute.

`bordercolordark` = (Internet Explorer only) defines the independent control over the color of one of two colors used in 3D borders. This attribute is valid only if used with the `border` attribute.

`bordercolorlight` = (Internet Explorer only) defines the independent control over the color of one of two colors used in 3D borders. This attribute is valid only if used with the `border` attribute.

`class`

`colspan` = specifies the number of table cells in the current column that this cell should span. Setting `Colspan="0"` sets the cell to span the entire length of the table column.

`height` = defines the height of the table cell.

`id`

`nowrap` = specifies that the word isn't allowed in the table cell.

`rowspan` = specifies the number of table cells in the current row that this cell should span. Setting `rowspan="0"` sets the cell to span the entire length of the table row.

`style`

`valign` = (Internet Explorer only) defines the vertical placement the `<TD>` element within the cell.

`width` = defines the width of the table cell.

`<TEXTAREA>` (End Tag Required)

The `<TEXTAREA>` element is always contained in the `<FORM>` element of the `<BODY>`. A `<TEXTAREA>` element defines an area (or blob-type input field) where multiple lines of input can be accepted in the document. Listing B.7 shows an example of a `<TEXTAREA>`.

Like `<INPUT>` and `<SELECT>` elements, `<TEXTAREA>` is a `<FORM>`-level element used to collect information from the user for processing.

B

Listing B.7. TEXTAREA example.

```
<FORM>
<TEXTAREA NAME="BlobInfo" WRAP=VIRTUAL ROWS=10 COLS=30></TEXTAREA>
</FORM>
```

Attributes:

align = defines the alignment of the text area in relation to surrounding text. This attribute is available for use in this environment because browsers treat the <TEXTAREA> element as an <IMG>-type element, thus allowing alignment to surrounding text.

cols = specifies the number of document columns that the field spans in the document.

name = defines the name of the <TEXTAREA> to be used when referencing the TEXTAREA in from other places in the HTML document.

rows = specifies the number of document rows that the field spans in the document.

wrap = specifies that word-wrap is allowed in the <TEXTAREA>.

<TFOOT> (End Tag Required)

<TFOOT> defines a footer section to a table frame, similar to the <THEAD> element. The <TFOOT> text is displayed as the last row in a table frame and continues to display even if table data rows scroll out of the area that can be viewed.

<TFOOT> must always be defined as the final element in the <TABLE> container.

Attributes:

align = specifies the horizontal alignment of the footer text within the cell.

class

id

style

valign = specifies the vertical alignment of the footer text within the cell.

<TH> (End Tag Required)

The <TH> element defines the header content for the table element. The content of this tag can be any acceptable HTML content, but straight text must first be enclosed in a text formatting tag container.

Attributes:

`align` = defines the alignment of the `<TD>` element within the table cell.

`background` = (Internet Explorer only) defines a background picture for the table.

`bgcolor` = (Internet Explorer only) defines the background color for the element.

`bordercolor` = (Internet Explorer only) defines the border color and is valid only if used with the `border` attribute.

`bordercolordark` = (Internet Explorer only) defines the independent control over the color of one of two colors used in 3D borders. This attribute is valid only if used with the `border` attribute.

`bordercolorlight` = (Internet Explorer only) defines the independent control over the color of one of two colors used in 3D borders. This attribute is valid only if used with the `border` attribute.

`class`

`colspan` = specifies the number of table cells in the current column that this cell should span. Setting `Colspan="0"` defines the cell to span the entire length of the table column.

`id`

`nowrap` = specifies that the word isn't allowed in the table cell.

`rowspan` = specifies the number of table cells in the current row that this cell should span. Setting `rowspan="0"` defines the cell to span the entire length of the table row.

`style`

`valign` = defines the vertical placement of the `<TD>` element within the cell.

`width` = defines the width of the table heading.

`<THEAD>`

The `<THEAD>` element is used to provide more flexibility to the `<TH>` tag, by allowing you to enclose multiple `<TH>` tags in it.

`<THEAD>` also lets you keep the table header consistent if the table scrolls.

`<THEAD>` elements (if implemented) are required to be the initial element of the `<TABLE>` container. `<THEAD>` must always precede the `<TFOOT>` element.

Attributes:

`align` = specifies the horizontal alignment of the footer text within the cell.

`class`

`id`

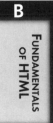

`style`

`valign` = specifies the vertical alignment of the footer text within the cell.

<TITLE>

<TITLE> is a container tag in the <HEAD> section. It defines the text of the title for the document that displays in the title bar of the browser. Every document must have only one title element.

Because <TITLE> isn't displayed in the document itself, it can't include any other HTML formatting or reference tags.

Defining <TITLE> elements correctly is important because they aren't solely used to display as document titles in the browser title bar. The <TITLE> text also is the link name saved when a user creates an HTML bookmark to your page. Additionally, <TITLE> is used as search criteria when your document is indexed. So, as a rule of thumb, title your documents accurately—it's important!

Attributes: none

<TR>

<TR> elements are used to contain the row attributes for tables. <TR> doesn't contain any content itself, containing instead the <TH> and <TR> elements that define the table cells.

Attributes:

`align` = specifies the horizontal alignment of the footer text within the cell.

`bgcolor` = (Internet Explorer only) defines the background color for the element.

`bordercolor` = (Internet Explorer only) defines the border color and is valid only if used with the `border` attribute.

`bordercolordark` = (Internet Explorer only) defines the independent control over the color of one of two colors used in 3D borders. This attribute is valid only if used with the `border` attribute.

`bordercolorlight` = (Internet Explorer only) defines the independent control over the color of one of two colors used in 3D borders. This attribute is valid only if used with the `border` attribute.

`class`

`id`

`nowrap` = specifies that the table rows don't wrap if the text exceeds the cell length.

`style`

`valign` = specifies the vertical alignment of the footer text within the cell.

<TT> (End Tag Required)

The <TT> container element encloses text that's displayed in teletype—a fixed-width (monospace) font.

Attributes: none

<U> (End Tag Required)

The <U> element encloses text that is displayed underlined by the browser.

Attributes: none

<UL> (End Tag Required)

The <UL> container element is used to define an unordered list. Listing B.8 shows an example of this element. Unordered lists aren't marked by numbers or sequenced letters; they are marked instead with bullets or, depending on your browser, another small symbol.

Listing B.8. Unordered list example.

```
<UL TYPE=CIRCLE>
<LI>Circle
<LI>Square
<LI>Rectangle
<LI>Polygon
<LI>Triangle
</UL>
```

Items of the <UL> are defined by the <LI> tags enclosed in this container. Again, you should probably keep the list text concise so that you don't lose the purpose of HTML lists.

Attributes:

`class`

`compact` = tells the browser to display the list in a more compact manner than it would with normal-sized font.

`dingbat` = defines an alternative entity to be used as the symbol preceding the list.

`id`

plain = specifies that the list should be displayed plain and that no bullet should be used.

src = specifies the URL file to be used as the image for the bullet.

style

type = defines the type of bullet to use as a symbol preceding the list items. Type options are square (displays a small square), circle (displays a small open circle), and disc (displays a small, closed circle).

wrap = defines a list that can wrap either vertically or horizontally, allowing you to define multicolumn lists.

<VAR> (End Tag Required)

The <VAR> element container defines the enclosed text as being a variable name (as in code); thus, the browser should display in the font that the browser normally uses for variable references. The default is italicized text.

Attributes: none

<WBR>

The <WBR> element, or word break, specifies to the browser that a word break is allowable if one is needed.

<WBR> is used in conjunction with the <NBR> element to define for the browser how to break up text in a document when no line breaks are called for.

Attributes: none

<XMP> (End Tag Required)

<XMP> defines that the text within the tags is example text and should be displayed in a fixed-width (monospace) font.

Attributes: none

Comparing JavaScript with VBScript

IN THIS APPENDIX

JavaScript is not the only Web scripting language available. The server side has languages such as Perl that have been around for many years. However, scripting on the client side is a new phenomenon. This arena has two players at the moment—JavaScript/JScript and VBScript—that are contending to become the scripting language standard for the Web. Although that battle will rage for some time, it is helpful to look at VBScript and compare its strengths and weaknesses with JavaScript. In this appendix, I discuss what VBScript is, contrast it with JavaScript, and provide a sample VBScript application for you to examine.

> **NOTE**
>
> Current research reveals that the actual use of VBScript on the Web is a small fraction of the total sites supporting JavaScript.

What Is VBScript?

VBScript, a Web scripting language developed by Microsoft, directly parallels JavaScript. VBScript's legacy is much different from that of JavaScript. Whereas JavaScript was essentially created from scratch loosely based on C++ and Java, VBScript is a part of the Visual Basic family of languages, as shown in Figure C.1. Other family members include Visual Basic—the ubiquitous Windows programming language—and Visual Basic for Applications—a macro language for Microsoft Office and other applications. If you've ever developed software using Visual Basic, you'll be able to pick up VBScript much more quickly than you would otherwise.

Figure C.1.

The Visual Basic family of languages.

Visual Basic	Visual Basic for Applications	VBScript Script
General Windows programs. Client/server database applications.	Scripting language for Microsoft Office and other Windows applications.	Scripting language for the World Wide Web.

If you have digested this book and have a solid understanding of JavaScript, you can think of VBScript as JavaScript in a Visual Basic wrapper. In other words, you can apply what you've already learned about the JavaScript object model and coding techniques and begin to develop VBScript code rather quickly.

NOTE

Look for the latest VBScript information online on Microsoft's site at http://www.microsoft.com /vbscript/.

Comparing and Contrasting JavaScript and VBScript

Although JavaScript and VBScript have many similarities, they also have several differences. In this section, I outline these similarities and differences.

Both Are Embedded HTML Languages

Like JavaScript, VBScript is a scripting language embedded in an HTML file. VBScript uses the <SCRIPT> tag in the same way as JavaScript, using "VBScript" or simply "VBS" as the language parameter. For example, the following script shows an alert dialog box when the page is loaded:

```
<HTML>
<HEAD>
<SCRIPT LANGUAGE = "VBS">

    alert("Is this JavaScript or VBScript?")

</SCRIPT>
</HEAD>
</HTML>
```

Interestingly, for an example as basic as an alert dialog box, the syntax of the two languages is the same. If you change the LANGUAGE parameter to "JavaScript", the same process is performed.

Both Have Similar Object Models

Perhaps the single most important factor when comparing JavaScript and VBScript is that they use the same basic object hierarchy, although various versions of JavaScript and/or VBScript may reveal minor differences. To a Web developer who might need to use both languages on occasion, this is a major coup; dealing with language syntax differences is much easier than working with two completely different programming paradigms. If you ever need to convert JavaScript code to VBScript, or vice versa, your conversion typically will be a line-by-line process.

C

COMPARING
JAVASCRIPT WITH
VBSCRIPT

> **NOTE**
>
> You can find an excellent resource on the Microsoft Internet Explorer scripting object model on Microsoft's site at http://www.microsoft.com/intdev/sdk/docs/scriptom/ local000.htm. This object model is essentially the same (but not necessarily) as the JavaScript/JScript object model.

Not only is the language object model identical for both scripting languages, but the way in which you work with HTML objects is the same as well. Just as JavaScript can react to events triggered by an event handler of an HTML object, so can VBScript. For example, in the following JavaScript code sample, the text entered in the myText field is converted to uppercase when the user clicks the Convert button:

```
<HTML>
<HEAD>
<SCRIPT LANGUAGE = "JavaScript">
<!--
    function convertText() {
        document.SampleForm.myText.value = document.
        SampleForm.myText.value.toUpperCase()
    }
-->
</SCRIPT>
</HEAD>

<BODY>
<FORM Name="SampleForm">
<INPUT Type=text Name="myText" </INPUT>
<INPUT Type="button" Value="Convert" OnClick="convertText()"</INPUT>
</FORM>
</BODY>
</HTML>
```

If you perform the same process using VBScript, the code resembles the following:

```
<HTML>
<HEAD>
<SCRIPT LANGUAGE = "VBS">
<!--
    Sub convertText()
        document.SampleForm.myText.value =
        UCase(document.SampleForm.myText.value)
    End Sub
-->
</SCRIPT>
</HEAD>

<BODY>
<H1></H1>
<FORM Name="SampleForm">
<INPUT Type=text Name="myText" </INPUT>
<INPUT Type="button" Value="Convert" OnClick="convertText()"</INPUT>
</FORM>
</BODY>
</HTML>
```

JavaScript Has Wider Industry Support

VBScript's principal asset is its Visual Basic legacy. VBScript gives the millions of Visual Basic programmers an easy segue to Web scripting. However, its biggest liability is that it is currently supported in a single Web browser—Microsoft Internet Explorer 3.0—and in two operating environments—Windows and Macintosh. Microsoft is working with third-party vendors to provide UNIX support, but currently this effort has not resulted in a release. And in case you're wondering, don't expect Netscape Navigator to support VBScript anytime soon.

JavaScript, on the other hand, is supported in both Netscape Navigator and Microsoft Internet Explorer and is compatible with any operating environment under which those browsers run. Additionally, JavaScript has been selected by many vendors—such as Borland and PowerSoft—as their scripting language in Web products. As a result, JavaScript currently has the edge in industry support, but with the muscle of Microsoft behind it, don't necessarily count out VBScript.

VBScript Has More Complex Data Types

On the surface, VBScript appears to be very limited in its capability to work with data types. VBScript has this appearance because it has only one data type, `variant`. However, on closer inspection, you will notice that VBScript actually has more power in handling data types than JavaScript does. The `variant` type contains information about the value it's working with at the time and can determine the data type it's being asked to handle in a variety of situations. In other words, if you're using a `variant` variable in the context of a string, as in the following example, VBScript treats `myVar` as a string value:

```
myVar = "String1" + "String2"
```

In the same way, if you're working with numbers, as in the following example, VBScript treats the variable as a numeric value:

```
myVar = 1 + 2
```

Strings and numbers are treated as subtypes within the `variant` type. Table C.1 shows VBScript's numerous subtypes.

Table C.1. Subtypes of VBScript's `variant` type.

Subtype	Description
String	A variable-length string (a maximum length of some 2 billion characters).
Byte	An integer between 0 and 255.
Integer	An integer between –32,768 and 32,767.

continues

C

COMPARING
JAVASCRIPT WITH
VBSCRIPT

Table C.1. continued

Subtype	*Description*
Long	An integer between –2,147,483,648 and 2,147,483,647.
Single	A single-precision, floating-point number between –3.402823E38 and –1.401298E-45 for negative values and between 1.401298E-45 and 3.402823E38 for positive values.
Double	A double-precision, floating-point number between –1.79769313486232E308 and –4.94065645841247E-324 for negative values and between 4.94065645841247E-324 and 1.79769313486232E308 for positive values.
Date (Time)	A number that represents a date between 1/1/100 and 12/31/9999.
Boolean	A logical value (True or False).
Empty	An uninitialized variable. The value is 0 for numeric variables or an empty string ("") for string variables.
Null	The variant contains no valid data (different from Empty).
Object	An ActiveX object.
Error	A VBScript error number.

VBScript has a set of conversion functions that go beyond JavaScript's parseFloat and parseInt built-in methods.

NOTE

VBScript is a loosely typed language like JavaScript.

VBScript and JavaScript Offer Varied Strengths

In addition to the data type issue, both VBScript and JavaScript have different strengths and weaknesses from a programming language standpoint.

VBScript is stronger than early versions of JavaScript in the following areas:

■ Error handling: VBScript has greater error-handling capabilities than JavaScript 1.0. It has an Err object to capture information about runtime errors, as well as an OnError control structure to maintain error-handling routines in your code. However, Java-Script 1.1 now supports the onError event.

■ Looping: Both VBScript and JavaScript 1.0 have a while looping capability, which repeats a code block while a condition is true. However, VBScript adds an additional capability with its Do...Loop, which repeats a code block while or until a condition is true. For example, the following loop executes until the i variable is equal to 100:

```
<SCRIPT LANGUAGE = "VBS">

    Dim i
    i = 0
    Do Until i = 100
        document.write("I will not chew gum.<p>")
        i = i + 1
    Loop

</SCRIPT>
```

However, JavaScript 1.2 negates this advantage because it has a Do While loop.

■ Message boxes: VBScript's MsgBox, shown in Figure C.2, and InputBox, shown in Figure C.3, are similar to alert() and prompt(), respectively, but they provide greater

FIGURE C.2.

MsgBox *message box.*

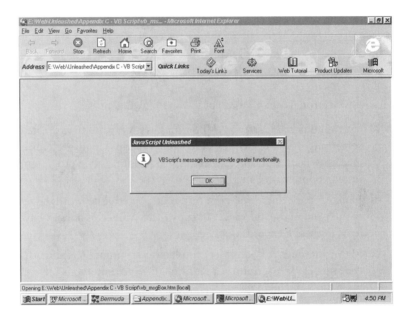

customization capabilities, such as title and icon settings, and they don't have the same annoying "JavaScript Alert" or "JavaScript Prompt" flags appearing in them.

■ Enhanced <SCRIPT> tag: VBScript expands the <SCRIPT> tag to allow you to define a script to be directed to a specific object using the FOR parameter or to handle a specific event from this object using the EVENT parameter. For example, the following code defines the event handler for the OkButton object:

```
<form name="TestForm">
    <input type="button" name="OkButton" value="OK">
    <SCRIPT FOR="OkButton" EVENT="onClick" LANGUAGE="VBS">
        msgBox("Thanks for your input.")
    </SCRIPT>
```

FIGURE C.3.

InputBox.

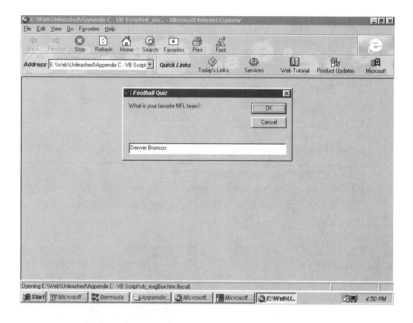

JavaScript is stronger than VBScript in the following areas:

- Custom objects: Currently, VBScript has no capability to create custom objects, something that is fundamental to the JavaScript language. This is perhaps VBScript's greatest weakness; it forces you to use procedural-style programming methodologies instead of object-oriented ones.

- Object referencing: JavaScript has some powerful keywords to reference objects, such as the this, with, and for...in constructs. VBScript doesn't have functional equivalents to these keywords.

- Math: Although VBScript lets you handle commonly used math functions, such as Tan and Cos, JavaScript has a set of math-related methods for even more complex mathematical equations.

VBScript Has Different Procedure Types

VBScript has two different types of procedures: subroutines and functions. A subroutine—denoted using Sub...End Sub—is a procedure that doesn't return a value, whereas a function—denoted by Function...End Function—is a procedure that does return a value. For example, the following subroutine, when called, assigns the string literal "See Spot Run" to the TextField text object but doesn't return a value to the calling procedure:

```
<SCRIPT LANGUAGE = "VBS">
    Sub convertText()
        document.MyForm.TextField.value = "See Spot Run."
    End Sub
</SCRIPT>
```

For an example of a VBScript function, look at the following code. The showText() subroutine calls the getText() function, which returns the value of the TextField text object:

```
<SCRIPT LANGUAGE = "VBS">

    Function getText()
        getText = document.MyForm.TextField.value
    End Function

    Sub showText()
        alert(getText())
    EndSub

</SCRIPT>
```

In contrast, JavaScript has a single procedure type—method (also called function)—that uses the function keyword regardless of whether a value is returned to the calling procedure.

Programming in VBScript

To give you a glimpse of programming in VBScript, I will show you a rudimentary example. In the following code, VBScript multiplies two values entered by the user and displays the result in an alert message box:

```
<html>
<head>
<title>Wizard</title>
<SCRIPT LANGUAGE="VBS">
    Sub calculateValues()
        Dim num1, num2, greaterNum, totalVal
        num1 = document.form1.Number1.value
        num2 = document.form1.Number2.value

        totalVal = num1*num2
        alert(totalVal)
    End Sub
</SCRIPT>
</head>


<h1>Stump the Wizard</font></h1>
<p>Without connecting to a backend server or using a Java applet,
   the Browser Wizard will multiply the two numbers...</p>

<form name="form1" method="POST">
<pre>First Number:  <input type=text size=5 maxlength=5 name="Number1"></pre>
<pre>Second Number: <input type=text size=5 maxlength=5 name="Number2"></pre>
<p><input type=button name="WizButton" value="Multiply"
   onClick="calculateValues()"></p>
</form>
</body>
</html>
```

Figure C.4 shows the result.

FIGURE C.4.

The Result message box.

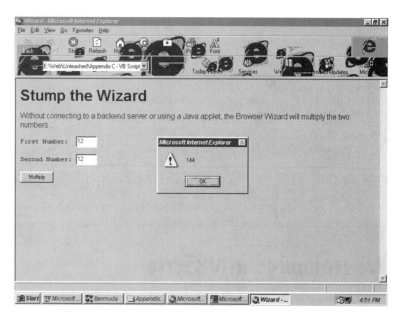

The equivalent JavaScript code is shown here to provide a source of comparison:

```
<html>
<head>
<title>Wizard</title>
<SCRIPT LANGUAGE="JavaScript">

    function calculateValues() {
        num1 = parseFloat(document.forms[0].Number1.value)
        num2 = parseFloat(document.forms[0].Number2.value)
        result = num1 * num2
        alert(result);
    }

</SCRIPT>
</head>

<body>
<h1>Stump the Wizard</h1>
<p>Without connecting to a backend server or using a Java applet, the Browser
   Wizard will multiply the two numbers..</p>

<form name="form1" method="POST">

<pre>First Number:  <input type=text size=5 maxlength=5 name="Number1"></pre>
<pre>Second Number: <input type=text size=5 maxlength=5 name="Number2"></pre>
<p><input type=button name="WizButton" value="Multiply"
   onClick="calculateValues()"></p>
</form>
</body>
</html>
```

Summary

In this appendix, you looked at VBScript and saw how it's similar to and different from JavaScript. You also looked at the basics of developing client-side scripts using VBScript.

Microsoft provides a scripting alternative to JavaScript in VBScript. If you're accustomed to programming in Visual Basic and your users will exclusively be using Microsoft Internet Explorer, VBScript may be your best choice for a Web scripting language. However, until VBScript gains greater support throughout the industry, it will remain a language that is limited to narrow contexts.

C

COMPARING
JAVASCRIPT WITH
VBSCRIPT

JavaScript Resources on the Internet

APPENDIX D

Because JavaScript is a Web-based technology, you probably won't be surprised at the wealth of information about JavaScript available on the Internet. In this appendix, you'll look at resources you might find helpful as you develop JavaScript applications. This appendix includes information on the Web, Usenet newsgroups, CompuServe, and Listserv mailing lists.

The World Wide Web

The Web offers a plethora of JavaScript sites. Sifting through the maze, I've included some of the best JavaScript pages here.

NOTE

Due to the nature of the Web, links change often. Because some of these sites contain maintained JavaScript indexes, however, going to these locations should get you headed in the right direction for JavaScript application development.

Netscape

URL: `http://www.netscape.com/`

Best of Site: Information on future releases of JavaScript, official JavaScript Authoring Guide.

Because Netscape is the developer of the JavaScript language, you would expect its home page to be filled with JavaScript information. The Netscape site is an excellent resource for JavaScript language documentation and other basic JavaScript information. It's also the best place to turn for obtaining information on future versions of JavaScript. Currently, its weak point is that actually finding the JavaScript information on the site is difficult, even when you know what you're looking for.

For the JavaScript Authoring Guide, go to `http://home.netscape.com/eng/mozilla/3.0/handbook/javascript/index.html`.

For the latest on JavaScript 1.2, go to `http://developer.netscape.com/library/documentation/communicator/index.html`.

For JavaScript developer information, go to `http://developer.netscape.com/`.

To download the official JavaScript language specification, go to `ftp.netscape.com/pub/review/jsspec.ps.gz`.

> **TIP**
>
> As future betas of Netscape Navigator become available, be sure to check the developer information related to those betas. You can often find information on the latest JavaScript features covered there.

Microsoft

URL: `http://www.microsoft.com/`

Best of Site: ActiveX controls, JScript information, Script Debugger, ActiveX Control Pad.

Microsoft has a great deal of JScript information available on its Web site for developers. You can find details about Microsoft Internet Explorer's scripting object model, VBScript, ActiveX controls, and much more. You also can find the ActiveX Control Pad on this site. Using this Control Pad, you can work with ActiveX controls and JScript.

To download the latest version of JScript, go to `http://www.microsoft.com/msdownload/scripting.htm`.

> **TIP**
>
> Watch the Microsoft site for free Web tools to download. Because Microsoft is committed to gaining marketshare in the Web industry, it's giving away much of its Internet software. Look for the ActiveX Control Pad and other Web developer tools.

ECMA Scripting Language Specification

URL: `http://www.ecma.ch/TC39.htm`

Best of Site: Get the latest information on the standardization of JavaScript.

Acadia Infuse Home Page

URL: `http://www.acadians.com/infuse`

Best of Site: Acadia Infuse home page, JavaScript news.

Acadia Software is the developer of Acadia Infuse, the Web's first visual JavaScript editor. In addition to product information, you can read about the latest news from the world of JavaScript.

> **TIP**
>
> Several of the authors of this book are employed at Acadia Software. We invite you to visit us on our Web site and hope you find the JavaScript page useful.

JavaScript Tip of the Week

URL: `http://www.webreference.com/javascript/`

Best of Site: Best site on the Web demonstrating practical examples of JavaScript. If you work with JavaScript, be sure to check out this site.

Ask the JavaScript Pro

URL: `http://206.2.216.11:8080/techtips/js_pro/`

Best of Site: Another excellent site with a number of practical scripts.

The JavaScript Planet

URL: `http://www.geocities.com/SiliconValley/7116/`

Best of Site: JavaScript examples and much more. Good resource.

Gamelan

URL: `http://www.gamelan.com/`

Best of Site: JavaScript samples, links.

Known as one of the best sites for Java resources, Gamelan also has a vast library of JavaScript information, samples, and tools.

hIdaho Design

URL: `http://www.hidaho.com`

Best of Site: ColorCenter (a JavaScript application), hIdaho Frameset.

hIdaho Design is the home of two well-known resources in the JavaScript community. First, the ColorCenter is one of the best examples of the power of JavaScript as an application development programming language. Second, the hIdaho Frameset is a library of JavaScript functions that simplify the development of multiframe applications.

Live Software's JavaScript Resource Center

URL: `http://jrc.livesoftware.com/`

Best of Site: JavaScript applet samples.

This site contains some good JavaScript examples from Sams.net's *Java Unleashed,* as well as links to other JavaScript sites.

Danny Goodman's JavaScript Pages

URL: `http://www.dannyg.com/javascript`

Best of Site: Good JavaScript learning resource.

Presented by author Danny Goodman, this site provides an excellent JavaScript resource for beginning JavaScript developers, particularly if you come from an HTML background. The site contains advanced examples and techniques as well.

Gordon McComb's JavaScript Pages

URL: `http://gmccomb.com/javascript/`

Best of Site: JavaScript experiments.

Another good JavaScript resource presented by author Gordon McComb. This site provides JavaScript sample code and experiments.

JavaScript Voodoo Page

URL: `http://rummelplatz.uni-mannheim.de/~skoch/js/script.htm`

Best of Site: Introduction to JavaScript.

This site provides a good tutorial for learning JavaScript.

JavaScript FAQ

URL: `http://www.freqgrafx.com/411/jsfaq.html`

Best of Site: "Just the facts."

This site provides frequently Asked Questions on JavaScript.

Yahoo!'s JavaScript Page

URL: `http://www.yahoo.com/Computers_and_Internet/Languages/JavaScript/`

Best of Site: Hey, it's Yahoo!.

Yahoo!, one of the best known catalogued indexes on the Web, has a section on JavaScript links. It's well worth a visit.

Netscape World

URL: `http://www.netscapeworld.com/`

Best of Site: Good example of JavaScript-enabled frames.

Netscape World is an online electronic magazine (e-zine) that focuses on the Netscape software product line. The site effectively uses JavaScript as a presentation tool.

Web Informant

URL: `http://www.informant.com/`

Best of Site: Articles and downloads from *Web Informant* magazine.

Web Informant is a new periodical devoted to Web developers. You can find information on JavaScript, Java, ActiveX, and other Web technologies covered in its pages. *Web Informant* is published by Informant Communications Group, which also publishes *Delphi Informant, Oracle Informant,* and *Web Publisher.*

JavaWorld

URL: `http://www.javaworld.com/`

Best of Site: Online articles on JavaScript.

JavaWorld is a periodical devoted to Java programming issues. It also includes a regular technical column on JavaScript. You can read past issues on this site. *JavaWorld* is published by IDG Communications, which publishes *PC World* and *ComputerWorld.*

Borland International

URL: `http://www.borland.com`

Best of Site: Intra and Latte Support and Documentation.

Borland is the developer of Intra, a Web database development tool that uses JavaScript as its native programming language. This company also is the developer of Latte, a state-of-the-art visual Java development environment.

Macmillan Computer Publishing Home Page

URL: `http://www.mcp.com/`

Best of Site: Information on JavaScript books, sample chapters.

The Macmillan Computer Publishing (MCP) site is the home of Sams.net Publishing and other MCP imprints, such as Que and New Riders. It is a good resource to find out about upcoming JavaScript and related books. The site often has sample chapters from JavaScript books for you to peruse.

Sun Microsystems

URL: `http://java.sun.com`

Best of Site: Home of Java.

For the latest news and betas available of Java, visit Java's home at Sun Microsystems.

Usenet Newsgroups

A growing number of Usenet newsgroups are devoted to JavaScript and related technologies. These groups are included here.

comp.lang.javascript

This newsgroup is focused on JavaScript development.

news.livesoftware.com/ livesoftware.javascript.developer

This newsgroup also focuses on JavaScript development. It is presented by Live Software.

news.livesoftware.com/ livesoftware.javascript.examples

This JavaScript newsgroup is intended to highlight JavaScript sample applications, applets, and code.

comp.lang.java

This newsgroup is devoted to Java programming techniques.

CompuServe

CompuServe, although one of the best resources for standard programming languages, has only a minimal amount of information available on JavaScript. The Java Forum has a section devoted to JavaScript. From my experience, the traffic has been relatively light.

Listserv Mailing Lists

If you want to join a listserv mailing list concerning JavaScript and related information, you can choose from the lists presented here.

javascript-list@inquiry.com

The `javascript-list@inquiry.com` mailing list features a wide range of JavaScript issues—some beginner, some advanced. To subscribe, send a message to

```
listmaster@inquiry.com
```

In the text body of your message, enter the following:

```
subscribe javascript firstname lastname
```

java@borland.com

The `java@borland.com` mailing list features general information on Java as well as Borland's Java product Latte. To subscribe, send a message to

```
listserv@borland.com
```

In the text body of your message, enter the following:

```
subscribe java firstname lastname
```

Miscellaneous JavaScript-Related Articles on the Web

The following are additional JavaScript-related articles you should check out:

"ActiveX vs. Java: Scripting," *Windows Sources.*

```
http://www.zdnet.com/wsources/content/0197/sub3.html
```

"Jeff's Internet Adventures: JavaScript usage charts dramatic growth," *PC Week.*

```
http://www.pcweek.com:80/ir/0819/19jia.html#story
```

"Windows 97: The Web-Centric Desktop," *PC Magazine.*

```
http://www.pcmag.com/news/trends/t970115a.htm
```

APPENDIX

E

Java from a JavaScripter's Perspective

IN THIS APPENDIX

JavaScript is a unique scripting language that empowers the developer with the tools necessary to create cross-platform, networked applications quickly. The capability to layer event handlers on top of basic HTML form objects allows the developer to perform client-side validation and custom presentation of data. After the programmer has mastered the structure and syntax of JavaScript, it becomes apparent that using the scripting language to build large, complex application frameworks quickly becomes unwieldy. The loosely typed conventions free the programmer from having to understand variable conversion techniques but result in code that must be tested extensively by a runtime validation suite to find type-matching errors. The capability to create and control access to multitiered data classes is contrived rather than an integral part of the language. JavaScript is most effective when it's used as its designers envisioned—as the program glue that binds application objects into an event-driven system. If a programmer wants to create discrete, reusable data structures and objects, he should use the Java language. JavaScript code can readily access multiple Java objects in a script file, preserving the investment in the scripting language.

This appendix provides an overview of the development tools necessary to create Java modules and describes the structure and syntax of the Java language. Particular attention is given to the divergence of the Java language from JavaScript conventions and new concepts and techniques that are unique to Java.

Comparing JavaScript with Java

Understanding a new programming language is never a trivial task, but the similarities between Java and JavaScript decrease the learning curve necessary to switch languages. The structure and syntax of the Java language are closely correlated to the implementation of JavaScript. Reserved words, operators, and flow control statements are almost identical. Because Java is a compiled language, a more strict definition of the code tokens is required. As a result, in two main areas, Java diverges from JavaScript protocol: in variable type rules and in class encapsulation methodologies. Table E.1 summarizes the attributes of JavaScript compared with Java.

Table E.1. Comparison of attributes in the JavaScript and Java languages.

JavaScript	*Java*
Scripting language	Programming language
Loose variable type checking	Strong variable type checking
Rudimentary access control	Tiered-access control definitions
No ability-derived types	Full object-oriented capabilities or inherited attributes
No array checking	Strict array access checks
Instance hierarchy	Object hierarchy
JavaScript objects	Java class

In JavaScript, variables and functions are declared as either local or global in scope. Java enforces a flexible tiered-access convention for variables and methods (functions), whereby elements are visible according to their access modifier: `private`, `protected`, or `public`. The modifiers allow the programmer to hide object attributes and implementation details from the public interface of the object, giving her more latitude in modifying the underlying code supporting a published interface while still maintaining backward compatibility. Java instance variables are declared in a rigorous manner, and every variable specified must be assigned a primary or derived component type. In contrast, JavaScript code doesn't require a specification. Java has specialized, built-in data types that optimize the behavior and size of the variable. Another distinction to note is that JavaScript has a more general classification schema (number or string) than Java (`int`, `long`, `float`, and `char`). Although JavaScript objects don't scale effectively into more complex object types, you can create Java classes that group the variables into object components.

You can consider JavaScript an object-oriented language because it supports an instance hierarchy. Objects are defined with specific variables and methods capable of being referenced using the dot convention but not extended through derivation of subclasses. Although the Java language syntax is similar to the JavaScript scripting language in relation to referencing and creating component objects, Java is a true programming language that bears a more striking resemblance to C++. Using Java code, object definitions can be reused to serve as the framework for a more complex architecture. Object classes are the building blocks of Java code. Unlike JavaScript, every Java function and variable must be defined inside the class structure. Furthermore, Java lets you aggregate the classes into packages of related objects or define abstract interface conventions for categories of objects.

Another difference is that Java source code is compiled into bytecode by the developer, creating binary components that can be used by other programmers. You can use the created components, class objects, to build derived classes that inherit the functionality of the base class and extend the base class attributes. The ability to extend the base class is the basis for code reuse in large-scale application systems and improved programmer efficiency. Strong type checking is performed by the Java compiler, requiring the programmer to explicitly declare and cast instance variables as either built-in or derived types. JavaScript code allows the programmer to switch the type identifier of a variable transparently without regard to its original type definition.

The high level of integration between the two languages allows the developer to embed JavaScript calls in Java code and access Java class methods in JavaScript. The capability enhances the value of JavaScript programmers who have knowledge of the Java framework. Both languages are built for creating cross-platform networked applications and contain network navigation features. Java extends the network capabilities by providing access to communication sockets between the client and host server.

Programmers familiar with JavaScript will have a minimal learning curve switching to Java when compared to the cost necessary to learn other languages. Java is a more powerful language and allows the developer to model complex systems in an efficient manner. The transition from JavaScript to Java requires understanding a more rigorous language and object hierarchy. Furthermore, you must also understand new development tools and procedures.

The Java Language

The Java language was created by a team of programmers at Sun Microsystems who were influenced by their knowledge of C++ and object-oriented programming techniques. The goal was to create a network-centric third-generation language whose binary execution objects could run on a disparate collection of computer systems. They chose to develop a system that discarded the system-dependent roots of C++ (memory pointers, data allocation, and system-dependent variable size). The language wouldn't require the developer to target multiple hardware platforms; instead, he could target a single virtual machine. Source code would be compiled into machine-independent bytecode and executed inside a Java virtual machine available on every supported platform. The language would shield programmers from system-crashing memory code errors and the underlying hardware that the module eventually executes over.

Java is an object-oriented programming language in which every object is defined as a class. A *class* is a collection of methods and instance variables. All objects can trace their lineage back through parent superclasses to a common root class, Object. A Java class is analogous to a JavaScript object, which is made up of functions and properties. The class methodology promotes the creation of discrete code modules because the class exposes a distinct interface through which other objects access and manipulate the instance variables contained in the class. The internal operation of the class is hidden from the calling object. The object hierarchy is created by the programmer when new class objects are derived from existing base classes. The following code shows a simple Java class object definition:

```
class  tag
{
// definition of class variables
private String tagname;
// definition of class methods
tag(String uname)         // class constructor
{
 tagname = new String(uname);
}
void finalize()
{
tagname = null;    // remove reference to tagname
}

private String Get_tag()
{
return(tagname.toString() );
}
}    // end of class block
```

This definition is an example of a simple Java class that represents HTML editing tags.

The class is implicitly derived from the superclass `Object` and is called `tag`. The code provides the capability to set the HTML tag string when declaring the class constructor. Also, the `Get_tag()` method provides the capability to return the tag name after the object has been created. Creating a class object is dependent on knowledge of the Java language primitives.

The Java source code is a collection of language tokens that are individually defined as keywords, variable operands, literal operands, operators, or separators. In the following sections, I explain the Java language syntax used to define these elements.

Keywords

The keywords in Java closely match those declared in JavaScript. In fact, identifiers and reserved words in JavaScript aren't always implemented by the JavaScript language, but you can safely use them in Java code. Java reserved keywords closely correlate to their counterparts in the C++ language. The following list outlines the keywords that are reserved in the Java language:

abstract	finally	private
boolean	float	protected
break	for	public
byte	generic	reset
byvalue	goto	return
case	it	short
cast	implements	static
catch	import	super
char	inner	switch
class	instanceof	synchronized
const	int	this
continue	interface	threadsafe
default	long	throw
do	native	transient
double	new	true
else	null	try
extends	operator	var
false	outer	void
final	package	while

The purpose and use of the keywords are described later in this appendix, but a detailed treatment is outside the scope of this book.

Types

JavaScript doesn't have explicit built-in primary variable types, but the Java language defines four: character, integer, floating point, and Boolean (see Table E.2). These basic types are used to create more complex data representations. The programmer should select the data type based on the range of values that the instance variable is expected to represent. Proper matching of a data type with the variable's value can result in a significant reduction in memory usage by a program.

Table E.2. Java built-in data types.

Type	*Keyword*	*Variable Size*	*Example*
Character	`char`	16-bit Unicode	`char cbin = 'a';`
Integer	`byte`	8 bits	`byte bbin = 127;`
	`short`	16 bits	`short ibin = 32767;`
	`int`	32 bits	`int = 2147483648;`
	`long`	64 bits	`long = 200;`
Floating point	`float`	32-bit single	`float fbin = 1.15;` (15-digit) precision
	`double`	64-bit double	`double dbin =5.1222;` (19-digit) precision
Boolean	`boolean`	Logical true/false	`boolean bvalue = true;`

CAUTION

The keyword unsigned doesn't exist in the Java language. All variables are signed instances and return error messages if literal values are assigned out of range without a cast statement. The code fragment `byte bbin = 128;` returns an error message because the literal value, 128, is out of the range of a variable of type byte (-127 to 127). Assigning the literal value 128 to byte bbin with a cast (`byte bbin = (byte)128;`) results in bbin being set to -1.

The character type is commonly used for storing information in human-readable format. The `String` object is available as a higher-level interface for character representations and is more commonly used in Java. `Strings` allow the programmer to use the addition operator (+) to concatenate text fragments. Integers are used to represent numeric amounts that don't require decimal values, and floating-point types are used when decimals are required. The Boolean type is used to store the result of logical expressions or the binary state of an object (on/off). Note that Boolean instances aren't implicitly converted (casted) to numbers in logical expressions. This code quirk means that the third comparison in the following example (if (bvalue == 0)) doesn't compile, yet the first and fourth print statements execute if this method is called.

```java
public void bool_check()
{
boolean bvalue = false;
if (!bvalue)    // compiles without error
    System.out.println(" is zero");     // will print out when bvalue is false!!
if (bvalue)
    System.out.println(" is true");     // will not print out in this example!!
if (bvalue == 0)    // generates an error when compiling
    System.out.println(" is would be zero");
if (bvalue == false)
    System.out.println(" is false");    // will print out!!
}
```

> **CAUTION**
>
> Assigning a variable operand to another operand of smaller size can result in loss of numeric value. Assigning a floating point-type operand to an integer-type operand results in loss of precision. The decimal portion of the amount is truncated. You should avoid these two cases.

JavaScript is a loosely typed language in which the programmer doesn't have to define the variable type explicitly. For example, declaring a string using the code fragment str = "jscript"; is valid code. Data types are converted between objects during the execution of the program. A programmer can assign an integer number to the str variable that was previously declared as a string type, and a runtime error doesn't occur. In Java, a variable type must be explicitly declared for example variables; otherwise, the compiler returns the error Undefined variable: str. Also, assigning elements to variables that are a different type isn't allowed unless a cast operator is used. The following code example presents a proof of Java type behavior:

```java
public void check_type()
{
short i = 1;
char cbin = 'a';
long b = 100;
b = i;        // cast is not needed when going from
//smaller to larger variable bit size
i = (byte)b;    // explicit cast necessary,
//variable is being assigned to type of smaller bit size
i = (short)32768;    // explicit cast necessary,
//literal is out of range. i = -1

cbin = (char)i;    // explicit cast is necessary,
//changing from numeric to character type
}
```

Type Wrappers

Type wrappers should be familiar elements to JavaScript programmers. They allow object-oriented behavior to be displayed by basic objects because object-oriented code is wrapped around the base implementation. For example, the character type wrapper retains the basic elements of a character variable but also allows the programmer to perform methods on characters such as isUpperCase, isDigit, and toLowerCase. Type wrappers are differentiated from their fundamental base type by the use of a capital letter as the first character in the type (Boolean, Character, Long, Float, and so on).

The requirement of declaring variable types and casting operand assignments is beneficial because strongly typed languages can check for syntax errors at the compiler level and optimize the program for memory use and speed. Type wrappers are useful for adding object-oriented behavior to basic Java types and are also present in the JavaScript language. The basic variable types can be aggregated into classes and arrays. The array is the most basic method used to combine instance variables into a common structure.

Arrays

In JavaScript, a custom function is used to create arrays. Also, array record elements can have differing (mixed) types. Array elements slots can always be accessed, even if they are outside the boundaries declared for the array. If an array element hasn't been explicitly assigned by the programmer, it can still be accessed, but the resultant value is null. In contrast, Java enforces array bounds and generates a compiler error message or runtime exception window if the code tries to access array elements that haven't been explicitly created.

> **CAUTION**
>
> Specifying array dimensions in the declaration statement without the new operator isn't allowed. For example, char c[5]; is invalid. Similar error-message behavior is found in JavaScript.

The declaration of arrays in Java is straightforward. The variable instance is declared as an array without dimensions and initialized via the new operator:

```
char c_array[];
c_array = new char[5];
```

The size of the array and the variable type are defined as modifiers for the new operator. In the preceding example, the array variable c_array is created with five elements of type char. You can also create arrays with more than one dimension by appending brackets. For example, c_array[][] defines a two-dimensional array.

> **TIP**
>
> Variable arrays in Java are zero based, and the maximum array reference is one less than the number of elements (*n*-1). In Java, the references for a 10-element array range would be defined as c_array[0] to c_array[9]. This is different from standard JavaScript conventions in which arrays are defined using a one-based system. JavaScript arrays are referenced from c_array[1] to c_array[*n*], where *n* is the number of elements.

Literals

Literals are language token elements that are used to enter hard-coded values into the code. Table E.3 summarizes the declaration conventions used for assigning literal amounts to different variable types. For example, the following statement assigns an explicit value of 1.1 to the variable fvar of type float:

```
fvar = 1.1f;
```

Table E.3. Declaring types for literals.

Variable Type	Literal Declaration
boolean	true, false
character	'c'
integer	1
float	1.1f
double	1.1d
String	"print string"

Operators

Operators are used to perform an action on a class or variable. The following list displays the operators used in Java. Operators are executed according to their level of execution precedence. Placing parentheses around operator-operand pairs is a good code technique; with parentheses, the execution order is explicitly declared in the code.

.	[ ]	( )	++
- -	!	~	*
/	%	+	-
<<	>>	>>>	<

>	<=	>=	==
!=	&	^	&&
||	?:	=	,
|	+=	-=	*=
/=	%=	^=	&=
!=	>>=	>>>=	<<=

These operators can be further classified according to four categories: unary, binary math, relational and equality, and logical.

A separator is used to identify blocks of code and define code tokens. The concepts of block scope and block statements are important in Java. The curly braces ({}) define execution levels in the code. The semicolon is used to terminate a Java command line. An example is `iValue = 1;cValue = 'a';`. Java separators include {}, ;, and . (period).

Unary Operators

Unary operators are used when the operation is performed on only one operand. Table E.4 lists Java's unary operators.

Table E.4. Java unary operators.

Token	Operation
-	Unary negation
~	Bitwise complement
++	Increment
--	Decrement

Execution of the unary negation operator changes the sign of the operand. The bitwise complement operator reverses each bit of the variable. If the variable bit was 1, it is changed to 0, and if the variable bit was 0, it is changed to 1. To quickly increment or decrement an operand by one, you use the unary increment or unary decrement operators. These operators are commonly used to optimize the code because they execute faster than their binary counterparts. For example, the increment operator performed on the variable `iValue` is faster than specifying `iValue = iValue + 1;`.

Binary Math Operators

A binary math operator executes an operation on two operands and returns a result based on the operator implementation. The execution of binary math operators in Java mimics their JavaScript counterparts. Table E.5 lists the binary math operators available in Java.

Table E.5. Java math operators.

Token	Operation
+	Addition
-	Subtraction
*	Multiplication
/	Division
%	Modulus
&	Bitwise AND
¦	Bitwise OR
^	Bitwise XOR
<<	Left shift
>>	Right shift
>>>	Zero fill right shift

The modulus operator (%) returns the remainder of a division operation. The result of 10 modulus 3 is 1. The bitwise mask operators (&, ¦, and ^) are commonly used on variables that may have mutually exclusive subvalues. You use the shift operators to rotate values to lower or higher byte or nibble boundaries.

Relational and Equality Operators

The relational and equality operators in Java also correlate to their JavaScript equivalents. The list of available relational and equality operators for Java is provided in Table E.6.

Table E.6. Java relational and equality operators.

Token	Operation
<	Less than
>	Greater than
<=	Less than or equal to
>=	Greater than or equal to
==	Equal to
!=	Not equal to

Logical Operators

Logical operators are useful for aggregating logical expressions. For example, if you want to execute *statement1* if both *variable1* and *variable2* are equal to 1, you code the following:

```
if ( (variable1 == 1) && (variable2 == 1) )
    statement1;
```

The logical operators available in Java are given in Table E.7.

Table E.7. Java logical operators.

Token	Operation
&&	Logical AND
¦¦	Logical OR

You use logical operators to condense code that would otherwise be represented by multiple if...else conditions.

Flow Control Statements

Flow control statements are the core of any computer program. The list of valid Java statement types and keywords is defined in Table E.8. They define the execution sequence of the code based on expression results.

Table E.8. Java statements.

Statement Type	Keyword
Selection statements	if...else
	switch
Label statement	case
Iteration statements	while
	do...while
	for
Jump statements	goto
	continue
	break
	return

The Java statements are similar to those available in JavaScript and should present no difficulty for the JavaScript programmer to learn. The following are some short fragments of code examples and the rationale behind their use.

The `if...else` statement is used to select execution between two statement blocks based on the result of an expression. If the expression is true, the first statement block executes. Otherwise, if the expression is false, the second statement block executes. The syntax follows:

```
if (expression1)
{
statement block1
}
else
{
statement block2
}
```

The existence of the `else` keyword and *statement block2* is optional. Another type of selection statement is the `switch` statement.

The `switch` statement lets the programmer select a code block for execution based on a match between *expression1*, a matching expression listed after the `case` statement. In the following example, if *expression1* is equal to *expression3*, *statement2 block* executes until a `break` statement is reached. The code execution is then transferred from the break line to the statement immediately following the end of the `switch` statement block.

```
switch(expression1)
{
case expression2: statement1 block;
            break;
case expression3: statement2 block;
            break;
. . . .
case expressionX: statementX block;
            break;
} // end of switch statement block
// code execution begins here after break statement is executed
```

NOTE

The `switch` statement isn't available in JavaScript. Also, you should avoid the `goto` statement because it leads to convoluted program execution.

The `for...loop` statement is used to enumerate over a variable range while executing *statement2* until *expression1* is false. Here is the basic `for...loop` syntax:

```
for(statement1;expression1;statement3)
    statement2;
```

A `while` statement performs a task until the expression is evaluated as false. These loops are commonly used for iterating over lists. The `break` statement can be used in both `for...loops` and `do...while` loops to exit the code block. The syntax of the `do...while` loop is shown here:

```
do
statement1;
while(expression1)
```

Object Scope

The most difficult paradigm shift for JavaScript programmers when writing Java code is understanding the different rules related to object existence scope and object access scope. Object access scope can be defined as the ability for code objects to be referenced from other code fragments. The object's existence scope is the life span of a code object. In JavaScript, all objects exist from the time they were first referenced to the time that all references to the object are deleted. Every object has a well-defined creation, life span, and destruction. The following code is necessary to create a simple array object:

```
// JavaScript Code Describing Array Construction
function makearray(n)
{
//this.length = n;    // assigning this.length is done for convenience
//for(i=1;i<=n;i++)    // zeroing out the array
//is also not necessary, but good code
//    this[i] = 0;
return(this);        // function must return 'this' reference to create object
}

function test_scope_create()
{
str = new makearray(2);
str[1] = 1;
}

function test_scope_valid()
{
alert(str[1]);
}
function test_array()
{
test_scope_create();
test_scope_valid();
}
```

You can declare global variables inside or outside functions but preferably at the top of the script. When you're writing JavaScript, the physical order of variable declarations in the script is irrelevant when you're deciding object access scope.

Variable access scope in Java is based on the block scope, not declaration order. A block is defined by curly braces ({}) and can represent a method or a group of Java statements. A Java variable instance has a scope that exists in the current code block and any code blocks that are defined inside the block where the declaration occurred.

The following code listing demonstrates the concept of block scope use in Java:

```
public void VarScope()
{        // LineRef_1
int ivar = 1;
if (ivar == 1)
    {    // LineRef_4
    int loopvar = 0;  // The scope of ivar is from LineRef4to Line x-1
```

```
while(loopvar < 10)
    {
ivar++;  // ivar is still in scope
loopvar++;
}
}     // LineRefX-1
}         // LineRef_X
```

The scope of ivar is from LineRef_1 to LineRef_X, and the scope of loopvar is from LineRef_4 to LineRef_X-1. Referencing the variables outside their implied scope generates a compiler error.

Access scope modifiers are used in Java to further restrict the scope of methods and instance variables.

In Java, the access modifiers, in conjunction with block scope, define the access scope of an object. Table E.9 lists the access scope modifiers and their effect on accessing an object.

Table E.9. Access scope modifiers.

Keyword	Definition
Public	The object is available to all
Protected	The object is available only to derived classes and classes in the same package
Private	The object is accessible only to the class that declared the method or member variable

Java methods and variables are automatically declared to be protected if no access identifier is specified. Declaring methods as public in scope and variables as private in scope is good code practice.

The static keyword modifier indicates that a variable or method will be shared for all classes. It is the equivalent of declaring a global variable or method in JavaScript.

In JavaScript, the keywords private, protected, public, and static are reserved words but have no implementation in the language. Currently, their use generates an error.

TIP

Use the var keyword in JavaScript to declare local variables and explicit types when possible. It helps identify variables and aids in porting the code to Java. You can't currently declare variables in JavaScript using the Java simple types (char, int, float, and boolean).

Exceptions

Exceptions are generated as a result of an error condition. A code block throws an exception in an attempt to find an error handler that can clear the cause of the exception. If the code throwing the exception was bound by a try block, the Java machine calls the corresponding catch block, which attempts to solve the error. The following code segment illustrates this concept:

```
class MyException extends Exception
{
}

public void test_exception()
{
try
    { // code between these braces will
//call error handler1 for exceptions of type MyException
// some code
    }
catch( MyException e)
    {     // error handler1
    }
}
```

Java has exception classes that define the most common types of errors. Examples of exception classes are NullPointerException and ArrayStoreException. A corollary to the try/catch block is the try/finally block. The try/finally combination results in a body of code being executed no matter how the code in the try block tries to exit. For example, the following code listing always executes statementblock1:

```
try
{
//some code
}
finally
{
// perform housekeeping functions to ensure proper termination
}
```

Currently, no true correlation exists to exceptions built into the JavaScript language. In JavaScript, the window.onerror property can be set to a custom error handler. This handler traps all error window messages if the handler returns true. If the handler returns false, the JavaScript interpreter assumes that the handler didn't trap the message and displays the standard error window. To disable all error windows, set window.onerror to null.

TIP

You can nest exceptions. Nested exceptions result in code that can exhaust all methods available to clear an error by repeatedly throwing the exception to alternative error-recovery routines.

Java Objects

An *object* is a discrete component that has a predefined set of states and behaviors. An object can exist as a simple type (character, integer, floating point, or boolean) or as a composite type (arrays, classes, interfaces, or packages). Reducing real-world entities to a collection of objects forces the programmer to focus on the individual elements of a system. In Java programs, every variable and function must be part of a class object.

Class

The Java class is the building block for all Java components. Object-oriented programming is an exercise in modeling concepts as a collection of state variables and methods. Methods are equivalent to functions in JavaScript and are defined with explicit return types and parameters. Member variables, which are referred to as instance variables, correlate to the JavaScript `properties`. Every object in Java is defined as a class object, which has been derived from a base class. If no base class is specified, the Java `Object` base class is used by default.

The use of the object-oriented paradigm has been widely accepted because it allows a building block approach to programming. Classes can be built to define common functionality. For example, you can create a generic HTML tag object. You can extend this base class by creating a new derived class that contains all the functionality of the base class and defines new specialized behavior. In the HTML language, the `TITLE` tag is an object that has specialized functionality. The ability to wrap a new class object around an existing class while maintaining transparent access to the base class procedures is called *inheritance*. The following code example presents the definition for the `Title_tag` class, which is built on the base class `HTML_tag`. Note the use of the `super` keyword, which allows the `HTML_tag` constructor to be executed properly:

```
class  Title_tag extends HTML_tag
{
public void draw() { System.out.println(Get_tag() ); }
Title_tag(String uname)
{
super(uname);
}
}// end of class block
```

In Java, every class must be derived from a subclass. The only exception to this rule is the superclass `Object`, which is built into the Java language implementation.

Methods

A class object displays unique behavior and functionality through the existence of methods (functions). In Java, methods must have a return type specified. If no information is to be returned by the method, a return type of `void` is defined. Furthermore, method definitions are placed inside the class definition. This coding rule diverges from the JavaScript language, which defines an object method through the assignment of a function to a JavaScript property variable. For example, to define a method function in JavaScript, you use the following code:

```
function MyClass()
{
this.membervariable = 1;
this.MyClassMethod = MyClassMethod;
return(this);
}
function MyClassMethod()
{
// function body of method which operates on MyClass
return(this.membervariable);
}
```

Similar Java code has the following syntax:

```
public class MyClass
{
int membervariable = 1;
int MyClassMethod
{
return(membervariable);
}
}
```

Constructors and Destructors

The ability to model complex entities requires that objects be implicitly initialized when created. Also, objects should perform housekeeping functions when destroyed (close files, deallocate memory, and close windows). Java language, like JavaScript, allows for the initialization of an object when it's created by a function called the class constructor. The method name for the class constructor is the name of the class itself.

You use the new operator to create an instance of a class and execute the creation method (constructor) for the class. The constructor method should initialize all variable members. For example, the class Body_tag has a constructor defined as follows:

```
public class Body_tag extends Object
{
protected int width,height;
public Body_tag(int ux, int uy)     // object constructor
{
width = ux;
height = uy;
}
public finalize()     // object destructor
{
}

}
```

> **TIP**
>
> Creation methods in Java don't have to return the member this, as is commonly performed in JavaScript. In fact, the constructor is the only method that isn't required to have an explicit return type defined.

The destruction method of an object is invoked after all references to the object go out of scope. Before an object is destroyed, the finalize() method is called for the class. The execution of this method doesn't occur immediately after the object goes out of scope, because the method is called by the garbage collection algorithm that scans the object space for freed object instances. Destruction methods should be used to release resources allocated by the class.

> **NOTE**
>
> The Java Applet class uses the init() and destroy() methods to perform creation and destruction operations.

Overloaded Methods

In some instances, creating different versions of the same function is advantageous. This capability makes the code more maintainable because developers don't have to remember cryptic names that perform the same operations. For example, the Body_tag(int,int) method is called to initialize the class when the object is declared. When allocated as an array, the Body_tag() method is called. Another useful example of *overloading* is a situation in which arguments are added onto existing methods. A developer can choose to overload the method and support two versions with the same name. This way, existing code can run without modification. The following code example shows how you would overload the constructor method for the class Body_ tag:

```
public Body_tag(int ux, int uy)    // object constructor
{
width = ux;
height = uy;
}
public Body_tag()
{
width = 0;
height = 0;
}
```

Casting Class Objects

Another difficult concept for programmers learning to code in an object-oriented language is the relationship between classes and casting objects to different class types. A superclass can safely be casted to its derived subclass. In fact, Java doesn't require explicit cast operators to be specified when assigning a superclass to a subclass variable. In contrast, an explicit cast is necessary when assigning a subclass to a superclass. Because superclasses usually add variables and functionality to a subclass, a subclass isn't equal to a superclass. Conversions from subclass objects to superclass objects are potentially dangerous.

> **TIP**
>
> The super keyword serves as a reference to the superclass in the subclass object.

Abstract Methods

Abstract methods are definitions of suggested methods for a derived class and don't contain any code that implements the method. To use a defined abstract method, the subclass must contain code that performs the method. The following example creates a class that has the abstract method draw(). If a superclass uses this class as its base, it should create an implementation of the function draw(), but it isn't required to do so.

```
abstract ClassName
{
private char VarInstance;
abstract void draw();
public initialize()
{
VarInstance = null;
}
}
```

> **CAUTION**
>
> If any method in the class is declared abstract, the class must be declared abstract also.

Interfaces

An *interface* is an entirely abstract class that is used as a suggested template for future derived classes. The interface defines common methods that the derived class should implement; the methods are useful when a developer wants to create a group of classes that should behave in the same manner. For example, you might want to create an interface named Tag that specifies

the elements all language tags should represent. To define an interface class, the keyword
`interface` is used instead of `class`:

```
public interface Interface_name
{
// interface definition
String Get_tag();        // get the object identifier
void Set_Name(String a);    // instance name
String Get_Name();
void Set_Value(String a); // instance value
String Get_Value();
}
```

NOTE

All methods in an interface shouldn't contain a method definition. A method definition is the actual implementation of the function (the part between the braces).

Interface definitions must initialize all instance variables defined and can't define constructor methods.

Classes that implement interfaces are declared in the following manner:

```
public class Classname extends Superclass
implements Interface_name [ , Other_interface]
{
}
```

You could define the HTML tag class as an extension of the existing interface `Tag` and allow the subclasses to implement expected behavior, as follows:

```
class  HTML_tag extends Object implements Tag
{                  // definition of class variables
private String tagname;
private String Name;
private String Value;
              // definition of class methods
HTML_tag(String uname)     // class constructor
{
 tagname = new String(uname);
}
public void finalize()        // class destructor
{
tagname = null;    // remove reference to variable objects
Name = null;
Value = null;
}
public String Get_tag()
{
return(tagname.toString() );
}
public String Get_Name()
{
```

```
return(Name.toString() );
}
public String Get_Value()
{
return(Value.toString() );
}
public void Set_Name(String uname)          // class constructor
{
 Name = new String(uname);
}
public void Set_Value(String uname)          // class constructor
{
 Value = new String(uname);
}
}     // end of class block
```

Packages

Packages are used to bundle a collection of related classes. The HTML tag classes in the preceding examples could be bundled into a document type definition (DTD) package. Packages allow the programmer to reference code modules quickly; for example, a Java coder could import the entire `netscape.javascript` package in one line: `import netscape.javascript.*`.

The basic Java virtual machine is extended by the standard packages in the same way the computer is extended by the operating system. The standard Java packages are responsible for the basic functionality listed in Table E.10.

Table E.10. Java packages from Sun Microsystems.

Package Name	Definition
`java.lang`	Contains essential Java classes for system operation
`java.io`	Input and output streams for files, strings, and other sources
`java.util`	Miscellaneous utility classes
`java.net`	Provides network support
`java.awt`	The Abstract Window Toolkit presents classes to manage user interface
`java.awt.image`	Manages image data
`java.awt.peer`	Connects AWT components to platform-specific implementations
`java.applet`	Base class that enables the creation of Java modules

To create a class to be included in a Java package, place the following declaration in the `.java` file:

```
package package_name;
```

This declaration creates a subdirectory called `package_name` and places the class file in the subdirectory. The file can now be referenced as a member of the package. Understanding the nuances of Java package referencing will take beginners a fair amount of time.

To use a Java package, you specify the `import` keyword with the package name. For example, `import netscape.javascript*` includes the entire JavaScript package, whereas `netscape.javascript.JSObject` imports only the JavaScript wrapper class.

CAUTION

The `CLASSPATH` environment variable should point to the directory containing the package root and the standard library package. For example:

`CLASSPATH=c:/java/lib;c:/javacode/package_root;`

All packages should be created off the *package_root*. For example, the path to the sample package package_name would be `c:/javacode/package_root/package_name;`.

Built-In JavaScript Objects

In the Netscape framework, JavaScript objects are available in Java and are of class type `JSObject`. Their methods and members are imported from the `netscape.javascript` package. The ability to access JavaScript objects from Java code results in a sophisticated environment that allows the programmer wide latitude in mixing and matching objects. See Chapter 26, "LiveConnect: Integrating JavaScript and Java," for more information on calling JavaScript objects from Java.

Java Development Tools

When you create JavaScript code, the only tools you need are a JavaScript-enabled browser and a text editor. Developing Java modules requires Java library modules and a Java compiler, which you can obtain for free from Sun Microsystems. Numerous software developers are committed to supporting the Java language and have released development tools or libraries targeting Java. However, currently, tools for Java development aren't mature offerings like their C++ counterparts, which are capable of developing large-scale, mission-critical applications. In this section, I don't attempt to describe or compare individual development tool offerings (look for back articles in the industry trade magazines or visit the sites listed in the following Resource) but rather explain the tool categories that aid the developer in creating Java applications: code generators, GUI visual tools, integrated development environments, Java libraries, and Java compilers.

RESOURCE

Developers can find Java information from Netscape at `http://developer.netscape.com/`. The Java directory is at `http://www.gamelan.com`. The official Java site from Sun Microsystems is at `http://java.sun.com/`.

Libraries

The basic Java class library from Sun is contained in the `classes.zip` file. This file is in standard zip format, but file compression has been disabled. If you want to review or replace the standard Java classes, just unzip the file using your standard utility program. You can modify the functionality of significant Java components (`SecurityManager`, `Thread`, `ClassLoader`, and `FileOutputStream`) by replacing the original modules with your own renditions.

Netscape provides its version of the class library that resides in the `java/classes` subdirectory. The Netscape implementation includes special packages. One such package, `Netscape.javascript`, contains the `JSObject` used for Java-to-JavaScript communication. Also, the standard library classes are included in the Netscape library file.

Compilers

The Sun JDK contains the standard compiler that most developers use. Many vendors have established licensing agreements with Sun Microsystems and developed Java compilers. These compilers typically are marketed as being faster than the original Java Development Kit (JDK) version. However, the accuracy of the generated bytecode by the clone compilers is questionable. A Java code validation suite is currently not publicly distributed by Sun, so no structured methodology exists for outside parties to evaluate different compilers.

Installing the Sun JDK

Read documentation from the Sun site and follow the directions to download and install the JDK. On Windows platforms, you should unzip the JDK executable from the current directory where you want the Java Development Kit to be appended. (The toolkit creates a Java subdirectory off the base directory.)

Proper use of the toolkit requires that you initialize the following environment variables:

- `PATH=execution directory of Java tools`; Example: `PATH=\Java\bin\;`
- `CLASSPATH=directory` containing file(s) to reference for import statements. Example: `CLASSPATH=\Java\lib\classes.zip;`
- `HOME= directory` used by Applet Viewer to find the `.hotjava` directory. Example: `HOME=\users\Default\;`

IDEs

Integrated development environments (IDEs) allow a programmer to manage the steps necessary to edit, compile, and debug a Java module from one central location. The leading software companies for programming tools (Symantec, Microsoft, and Borland) are committed to releasing IDE packages for the Java language. Future releases should include the ability to generate Java application skeleton frameworks and design a graphical user interface.

GUI Visual Tools

Development applications that allow the developer to create the front-end interface of the application using visual tools are called *visual application builders.* They have existed in development environments for desktop applications for some years and are recently being created for HTML, JavaScript, and Java languages. They provide the developer with drawing tools or selection palettes capable of visually creating a graphical user interface.

E
JAVA FROM A
JAVASCRIPTER'S
PERSPECTIVE

Code Generators

Code generators create Java skeleton frameworks based on developer response to a set of wizard dialog boxes. They are useful for quickly creating prototypes in rapid application development environments. The prototypes are presented to the client for validation of design specifications and discarded after feedback has been received. Code generators are commonly limited in their flexibility and have the ability to hinder the programmer during complex development cycles. If you use them for a production system, you should have access to the underlying library base source code so that all aspects of the application can be modified. For example, Microsoft makes the MFC library source code available for programmer review and modification.

A Window into the Java Library: The Java Console

The Java Console is a window in Netscape Navigator that is used to display system messages. The developer uses it to gain feedback on code execution and uncaught Java exceptions. Instead of using the alert dialog to display debug messages, the Java console is sent messages via the `System.out.println(String);` method. To open the console while in Netscape Navigator, choose Options | Show Java Console.

Summary

This appendix demonstrated that the Java language is extremely similar to JavaScript but includes many desirable aspects that JavaScript programmers will want to access. The development of large production systems requires that system specifications be distilled into discrete components. The investment in time necessary to learn the Java language will be rewarded through the ability to extend the JavaScript language by creating custom Java objects that seamlessly integrate with the JavaScript code.

I

INDEX

A V I A C O M   S E R V I C E

The Information SuperLibrary™

Bookstore	Search	What's New	Reference	Software	Newsletter	Company Overviews
Yellow Pages	Internet Starter Kit	HTML Workshop	Win a Free T-Shirt!	Macmillan Computer Publishing	Site Map	Talk to Us

CHECK OUT THE BOOKS IN THIS LIBRARY.

You'll find thousands of shareware files and over 1600 computer books designed for both technowizards and technophobes. You can browse through 700 sample chapters, get the latest news on the Net, and find just about anything using our massive search directories.

All Macmillan Computer Publishing books are available at your local bookstore.

We're open 24-hours a day, 365 days a year.

You don't need a card.

We don't charge fines.

And you can be as LOUD as you want.

The Information SuperLibrary

http://www.mcp.com/mcp/   ftp.mcp.com

MACMILLAN COMPUTER PUBLISHING USA
A VIACOM COMPANY

Technical Support:

If you need assistance with the information in this book or with a CD/Disk accompanying the book, please access the Knowledge Base on our Web site at **http://www.superlibrary.com/general/support**. Our most Frequently Asked Questions are answered there. If you do not find the answer to your questions on our Web site, you may contact Macmillan Technical Support **(317) 581-3833** or e-mail us at **support@mcp.com**.

Teach Yourself Java 1.1 in 21 Days, Second Edition

Laura Lemay and Charles Perkins

This updated bestseller is the definitive guide to learning Java 1.1. This book carefully steps you through the fundamental concepts of the Java language, as well as the basics of applet design and integration with Web presentations. You'll learn the basics of object-oriented programming and Java development, create stand-alone cross-platform applications, and add interactivity and animation to your Web sites with Java applets. The CD-ROM includes Sun's Java Development Kit 1.1, Sun's Java Development Kit 1.02 for Macintosh, and Sun's Bean Development Kit for Windows 95, Windows NT, and Solaris.

$39.99 USA/$56.95 CAN   1-57521-142-4   Sams.net
Internet/Programming   *New - Casual - Advanced - Expert*

Java 1.1 Unleashed, Third Edition

Michael Morrison, et al.

Completely revised, updated, and expanded, this comprehensive reference gives users all the information they need to master Java 1.1 programming, program advanced Java applets, and successfully integrate Java with other technologies. This book has extensive coverage of Java 1.1, the Java extension APIs, JavaBeans, JavaOS, and more, and it has a 200-page reference section that covers Java APIs. The CD-ROM contains Sun's JDK and other Java development tools, sample applets and applications, and the book's entire reference section in HTML format, as well as a selection of related books in electronic format.

$59.99 USA/$84.95 CAN   1-57521-298-6   Sams.net
Internet/Programming   *Accomplished - Expert*   *1,400 pages*

Maximum Java 1.1

Glenn Vanderburg, et al.

This fast-paced, expert-level programming guide is the ultimate book for programmers who want to take Java to the next level. Written by Java experts, this must-have resource explores the Java 1.1 language, tools, and core Java API, without reviewing fundamentals or basic techniques. It's loaded with in-depth coverage of the most advanced topics. It explores advanced applet programming, animation, writing 2D games, JavaBeans, security, VRML applets, GridBagLayout, and Advanced Event Handling in detail. You'll see how new Java class libraries and frameworks make Java work with client/server systems, relational databases, and persistent object databases. The CD-ROM is packed with source code from the book, Sun's JDK, and a collection of the best Java development tools.

$49.99 USA/$70.95 CAN   1-57521-290-0   Sams.net
Internet/Programming   *Expert*   *900 pages*

Laura Lemay's Web Workshop: JavaScript

Laura Lemay and Michael Moncur

This book provides a clear, hands-on guide to creating sophisticated Web pages. You will explore various aspects of Web publishing—whether JavaScripting and interactivity or graphics design or Netscape Navigator Gold—in greater depth than with the *Teach Yourself* books. The CD-ROM includes the complete book in HTML format, publishing tools, templates, graphics, backgrounds, and more.

$39.99 USA/$56.95 CDN   1-57521-141-6   Sams.net
Communications/Online/Internet   *Casual - Accomplished*   *400 pages*

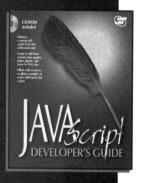

JavaScript 1.1 Developer's Guide

Wes Tatters

This book is the professional reference for enhancing commercial-grade Web sites with JavaScript. Packed with real-world JavaScript examples, this book shows the developer how to use JavaScript to combine Java applets, multimedia programs, plugins, and more on a Web site. You'll also discover ways to add interactivity and Java applets to Web pages.

| $49.99 USA/$70.95 CDN | 1-57521-084-3 | Sams.net |
| Internet/Programming | Accomplished - Expert | 600 pages |

Laura Lemay's Web Workshop: ActiveX and VBScript

Paul Lomax and Rogers Cadenhead

ActiveX is an umbrella term for a series of Microsoft products and technologies that add activity to Web pages. Visual Basic Script is an essential element of the ActiveX family. With it, you can add animation, multimedia, sound, graphics, and interactivity to a Web site. This book is a compilation of individual workshops that show you how to use VBScript and other ActiveX technologies within your Web site. The CD-ROM contains the entire book in HTML format, a selection of the best ActiveX development tools, scripts, templates, backgrounds, borders, and graphics.

| $39.99 USA/$56.95 CDN | 1-57521-207-2 | Sams.net |
| Internet/Programming | Casual - Accomplished | 450 pages |

VBScript Unleashed

Brian Johnson

This book presents Web programming techniques in a logical and easy-to-follow sequence that helps you understand the principles involved in developing programs. You'll learn the basics of writing programs, and then you'll add interactivity, multimedia, and more to Web page designs. You'll also learn about communication across the Internet, safety, security, CGI, and more.

| $39.99 USA/$56.95 CDN | 1-57521-124-6 | Sams.net |
| Internet/Programming | Casual - Accomplished - Expert | 650 pages |

ActiveX Programming Unleashed

Weiying Chen, et al.

ActiveX is Microsoft's core Internet communication technology. This book details that technology, giving you the knowledge you need to create powerful ActiveX programs for the Web and beyond. This book covers ActiveX controls—the full-featured components of the Internet. It also teaches you how to use ActiveX documents, server framework, ISAPI, security, and more.

| $39.99 USA/$56.95 CDN | 1-57521-154-8 | Sams.net |
| Internet/Programming | Accomplished - Expert | 700 pages |

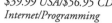

Add to Your Sams.net Library Today with the Best Books for Programming, Operating Systems, and New Technologies

The easiest way to order is to pick up the phone and call
1-800-428-5331
between 9:00 a.m. and 5:00 p.m. EST.
For faster service please have your credit card available.

ISBN	Quantity	Description of Item	Unit Cost	Total Cost
1-57521-142-4		Teach Yourself Java 1.1 in 21 Days, Second Edition (book/CD-ROM)	$39.99	
1-57521-298-6		Java 1.1 Unleashed, Third Edition (book/CD-ROM)	$59.99	
1-57521-290-0		Maximum Java 1.1 (book/CD-ROM)	$49.99	
1-57521-141-6		Laura Lemay's Web Workshop: JavaScript (book/CD-ROM)	$39.99	
1-57521-084-3		JavaScript 1.1 Developer's Guide (book/CD-ROM)	$49.99	
1-57521-207-2		Laura Lemay's Web Workshop: ActiveX and VBScript (book/CD-ROM)	$39.99	
1-57521-124-6		VBScript Unleashed (book/CD-ROM)	$39.99	
1-57521-154-8		ActiveX Programming Unleashed (book/CD-ROM)	$39.99	
		Shipping and Handling: See information below.		
		TOTAL		

❏ 3 ½" Disk

❏ 5 ¼" Disk

Shipping and Handling: $4.00 for the first book, and $1.75 for each additional book. Floppy disk: add $1.75 for shipping and handling. If you need to have it NOW, we can ship product to you in 24 hours for an additional charge of approximately $18.00, and you will receive your item overnight or in two days. Overseas shipping and handling adds $2.00 per book and $8.00 for up to three disks. Prices subject to change. Call for availability and pricing information on latest editions.

201 W. 103rd Street, Indianapolis, Indiana 46290

1-800-428-5331 — Orders   1-800-835-3202 — Fax   1-800-858-7674 — Customer Service

Book ISBN 1-57521-306-0

What's on the CD-ROM

The companion CD-ROM contains many useful third-party tools and utilities, plus the source code and JavaScript samples from the book.

Macintosh Installation Instructions

1. Insert the CD into the CD-ROM drive.
2. When an icon for the CD appears on your desktop, open the CD by double-clicking its icon.
3. Double-click the icon named Guide to the CD-ROM, and follow the directions that appear.

Technical Support from Macmillan

We can't help you with Windows or Macintosh problems or software from third parties, but we can assist you if a problem arises with the CD-ROM itself.

E-mail support: Send e-mail to support@mcp.com.

CompuServe: Type GO SAMS to reach the Macmillan Computer Publishing forum. Leave us a message addressed to SYSOP. If you want the message to be private, address it to *SYSOP.

Telephone: (317) 581-3833
Fax: (317) 581-4773
Mail: Macmillan Computer Publishing
Attention: Support Department
201 West 103rd Street
Indianapolis, IN 46290-1093

Here's how to reach us on the Internet:

World Wide Web (The Macmillan Information SuperLibrary)
http://www.mcp.com/sams

Windows 95 Installation Instructions

1. Insert the CD into the CD-ROM drive.
2. From the Windows 95 desktop, double-click the My Computer icon.
3. Double-click the icon representing your CD-ROM drive.
4. Double-click the icon called SETUP.EXE to run the installation program.
5. Installation creates a program group named JavaScript Unleashed 2. This group will contain icons you can use to browse the CD-ROM.

NOTE

If Windows 95 is installed on your computer, and you have the AutoPlay feature enabled, the SETUP.EXE program starts automatically whenever you insert the CD into the CD-ROM drive.

Windows NT Installation Instructions

1. Insert the CD into the CD-ROM drive.
2. From File Manager or Program Manager, choose File | Run.
3. Type *drive*\SETUP.EXE and press Enter, where *drive* corresponds to the drive letter of your CD-ROM. For example, if your CD-ROM is drive D:, type D:\SETUP.EXE and press Enter.
4. Installation creates a program group named JavaScript Unleashed 2. This group will contain icons you can use to browse the CD-ROM.